Warfare, State and Society in South Asia
500 BCE–2005 CE

edited by
Kaushik Roy

New Delhi | Mumbai | Chennai | Kolkata | Bangalore | Hyderabad | Kochi | Guwahati

First Published 2010

Viva Books Private Limited

4737/23, Ansari Road, Daryaganj, New Delhi 110 002
Tel. 42242200, 23258325, 23283121, Email: vivadelhi@vivagroupindia.net

76, Service Industries, Shirvane, Sector 1, Nerul, Navi Mumbai 400 706
Tel. 27721273, 27721274, Email: vivamumbai@vivagroupindia.net

Jamals Fazal Chambers, 26 Greams Road, Chennai 600 006
Tel. 28294241, 28290304, Email: vivachennai@vivagroupindia.net

B-103, Jindal Towers, 21/1A/3 Darga Road, Kolkata 700 017
Tel. 22816713, Email: vivakolkata@vivagroupindia.net

7, GF, Sovereign Park Aptts., 56-58, K. R. Road, Basavanagudi, Bangalore 560 004
Tel. 26607409, Email: vivabangalore@vivagroupindia.net

101-102, Moghal Marc Apartments, 3-4-637 to 641, Narayanguda, Hyderabad 500 029
Tel. 27564481, Email: vivahyderabad@vivagroupindia.net

First Floor, Beevi Towers, SRM Road, Kaloor, Kochi 682 018
Tel. 0484-2403055, 2403056, Email: vivakochi@vivagroupindia.net

232, GNB Road, Beside UCO Bank, Silpukhuri, Guwahati 781 003
Tel. 0361-2666386, Email: vivaguwahati@vivagroupindia.net

www.vivagroupindia.com

ISBN: 978-81-309-1015-4

Published by Vinod Vasishtha for Viva Books Private Limited
4737/23 Ansari Road, Daryaganj, New Delhi 110 002

Printed & bound by Swan Press, New Delhi

Warfare, State and Society in South Asia
500 BCE–2005 CE

Dedicated to
Prof. Indivar Kamtekar, my Ph.D. guide,
who always encouraged me to pursue military history

Contents

Preface

The aim of this reader is to focus on the interrelationship between war, state and society in Indian history from ancient to modern times by reprinting scholarly articles and chapters from important works. In order to retain originality of the pieces by the various authors, no attempt is made to establish consistency in spellings and terms used throughout the volume. Most of the reprints are from old journals and books which are not easily accessible to the scholars. These reprint pieces throw light not only on social and cultural aspects of warfare but also include analytical studies of operations, battles, doctrines and command. By bringing together the hitherto scattered pieces written by the Indian officers who participated in the campaigns, as well as essays by modern researchers, the volume under consideration attempts to chart the linkages between military hardware and the changing nature of warfare. Besides warfare in land, this volume also brings into focus warfare in the sea and air. In terms of spatial and temporal scope, this volume is the only one of its kind. Another strength of this volume is that it also covers war conducted by the stateless marginal groups. In total 26 essays (which have not been reprinted previously) have been included and they are organized under five sections. The introduction by the editor attempts to provide a background by putting the reprint pieces in a historical context. Also, the introduction portrays the changing contours of military historiography. Another attraction of this reader is the bibliography which will be of great help in guiding researchers and those interested in further studies. This volume will cater to the scholars and students of South Asian History, Indian Ocean Studies, International Relations and Political Science. The military officers as well as the strategic community will be interested due to the present implications of some of the trends discussed in the essays of this volume. In addition to the specialists, the objective is also to attract the section of literate public with general interest in military affairs.

Kolkata, 2009 KAUSHIK ROY

Acknowledgements

The editor and publisher wish to thank the following for permission to use copyright materials.

Pradeep Mittal, Low Price Publications for the chapter from P.C. Chakravarti's, *The Art of War in Ancient India* (1941, reprint, Delhi: Low Price Publications, 1989), pp. 22-31.

Firma KLM for the essay: Bimal Kanti Majumdar, 'Military Pursuits and National Defence of the Hindus from the Fall of the Mauryas to the End of the Second Magadhan Empire (c. 185 BC-AD 550) from Majumdar's book titled *The Military System in Ancient India* (Calcutta: Firma KLM, 1960), pp. 75-93.

Chairman, Centre for Studies in Civilizations, Project of History of Indian Science, Philosophy and Culture, New Delhi for the essay: U.P. Thapliyal, 'Weapons, Fortification and Military Training in Ancient India', pp. 104-135, in S.N. Prasad (ed.), *Historical Perspectives of Warfare in India: Some Morale and Material Determinants*, in History of Science, Philosophy and Culture in Indian Civilization, General Editor D.P. Chattopadhyaya, PHISPC, Centre for Studies in Civilizations (New Delhi, Distributed by Motilal Banarasidas, 2002).

Dr. B. Sobhanan, Professor and Head, Department of History, University of Kerala for the article: K.S. Lal, 'The Striking Power of the Army of the Sultanate', *Journal of Indian History*, vol. LV (Aug. 1977), pp. 85-110.

Dr. Sukumar Bhattacharya, Director, Institute of Historical Studies for the article: Jagadish Narayan Sarkar, 'Guerrilla Warfare in Medieval India', *The Quarterly Review of Historical Studies*, vol. 13, no. 1 (1973-4), pp. 29-36.

Prof. Ramakanta Chakrabarty, General Secretary, The Asiatic Society for the article: J.N. Sarkar, 'A Phase in Mughal-Assam Relations: Raja Ram Singh's Futile Expedition (1668-71)', *Journal of the Asiatic Society*, vol. 29, no. 1 (1987), pp. 29-71.

Prof. Sabyasachi Bhattacharya and Dr. Anup Taneja for the article: Iqtidar Alam Khan, 'Origin and Development of Gunpowder Technology in India: AD 1250-1500', *Indian Historical Review*, vol. 4, no. 1 (July 1977), pp. 20-29.

Prof. Iqtidar Alam Khan and Mr. Rajen of Social Scientist for the article: Iqtidar Alam Khan, 'Gunpowder and Empire: Indian Case', *Social Scientist*, vol. 33, nos. 3-4 (March-April 2005), pp. 54-65.

Dr. A.K. Bag, Editor of *Indian Journal of the History of Science* for the article: Jean Deloche, 'Gunpowder Artillery and Military Architecture in South India (15th-18th Century)', *Indian Journal of History of Science*, vol. 40, no. 4 (2005), pp. 573-95.

Mr. Ashok Jain, Director, Munshiram Manoharlal Publishers Pvt. Ltd. for the article: Vitor Luis Gaspar Rodrigues, 'Military Structure of the Portuguese Navy in the Indian Ocean—The First Half of the 16th Century', in K.S. Mathew (ed.), *Ship-building and Navigation in the Indian Ocean Region, AD 1400-1800* (New Delhi: Munshiram Manoharlal Publishers, 1997), pp. 140-46.

Asian Educational Services for the essay: Surendranath Sen, 'Hyder Ali's Fleet', in Sen, *Studies in Indian History: Historical Records at Goa* (1930, reprint, New Delhi: Asian Educational Services, 1993), pp. 146-54.

Dr. Anirudh Deshpande and Mr. Ram Reddy, Editor *Economic and Political Weekly* for the article: Anirudh Deshpande, 'Limitations of Military Technology: Naval Warfare on the West Coast, 1650-1800', *Economic and Political Weekly*, vol. 27, no. 17 (April 1992), pp. 900-904.

Dr. Bruce Vandervort, Editor *Journal of Military History* for the article: Kaushik Roy, 'Military Synthesis in South Asia: Armies, Warfare, and Indian Society, c. 1740-1849', *Journal of Military History*, vol. 69 (July 2005), pp. 651-90.

Mr. G.T. Verghese, Executive Director, Indo-British Historical Society for the article: James W. Hoover, 'The Recruitment of the Bengal Army: beyond the Myth of the Zamindar's Son', *Indo-British Review*, vol. 21, no. 2 (1996), pp. 144-56.

Prof. Ranjan Chakraborty, Department of History, Jadavpur University for the article: Kaushik Roy, 'Company Bahadur against the Pandies: The Military Dimension of 1857 Mutiny Revisited', *Journal of History*, vol. 19 (2001-2), pp. 25-47.

Permanent Black and Dr. Razit K. Mazumder for the chapter from Rajit K. Mazumder's, *The Indian Army and the Making of Punjab* (Delhi: Permanent Black, 2003), pp. 47-92.

Ms. Payal Kumar, Vice President, Editorial and Production of Sage Publications India, Pvt. Ltd., and Anirudh Deshpande for the article: Anirudh Deshpande, 'Sailors and the crowd: popular protest in Karachi, 1946', *Indian Economic and Social History Review*, vol. 26, no. 1 (1989), pp. 1-27.

Director, United Service Institution of India for the article: Daljit Singh and Katherine Singh, 'Decentralization and Diffusion of Power in the Army Structures of India and Pakistan', *Journal of the United Service Institution of India*, vol. CI, no. 425 (Oct.-Dec. 1971), pp. 306-318.

Dr. Ajai Sahni, Executive Editor, *FAULTLINES: Writings on Conflict & Resolution* for the article: Kanchan L., 'Negotiating Insurgencies: The Naga Imbroglio', *Faultlines: Writings on Conflict and Resolution*, vol. 11 (April 2002), pp. 127-152.

Mr. Bharat Verma, Lancer Publishers for the article: Squadron Leader P.M. Sinha, 'Air Power in the Information Age', *Indian Defence Review*, vol. 16, no. 3 (July-Sept. 2001), pp. 44-49.

Dr. Fahmida Ashraf, Director (South Asia) and Associate Editor Institute of Strategic Studies, Islamabad for the article: Fahmida Ashraf, 'Maoist Uprising in Nepal', *Strategic Studies*, vol. 22, no. 2 (Summer 2002), pp. 62-80.

Lieutenant-General Depinder Singh and the Natraj Publishers for the chapter from: Lieutenant-General Depinder Singh's, *Indian*

Peacekeeping Force in Sri Lanka: 1987-89 (DehraDun: Natraj, 2001), pp. 107-28.

Prof. Mridula Mukherjee, Director Nehru Memorial Museum and Library for the article: Matin Zuberi, 'The Proposed Indian Nuclear Doctrine', *Contemporary India*, vol. 1, no. 1 (2002), pp. 53-64.

Major-General (retired) Afsir Karim, Editor *Aakrosh* for the article: Bhasyam Kasturi, 'The Role of Special Forces in the War in Afghanistan', *Aakrosh*, vol. 5, no. 15 (April 2002), pp. 53-77.

Every effort has been made to trace all the copyright editors, but if any have been advertently overlooked the editor and the publisher wish to apologize.

Notes on Contributors

SINHA, B.P., is the author of an article on ancient Indian military history.

MAJUMDAR, BIMAL KANTI, used to teach at Jadavpur University and is the author of *The Military System in Ancient India* published in 1955.

CHAKRAVARTI, P.C., is the author of *The Art of War in Ancient India,* originally published in 1941.

THAPLIYAL, U.P., was previously the Director of the History Division, Ministry of Defence. He has published widely on various aspects of ancient India's military history.

LAI, K.S., is a medievalist and has published on the Khaljis.

SARKAR, JAGADISH NARAYAN, used to teach at Jadavpur University. His focus of research was warfare in medieval India and has published several monographs on the theory and practice of warfare under the Delhi Sultanate and the Mughals.

KHAN, IQTIDAR ALAM, has retired as professor from Aligarh Muslim University. He specializes on the use of gunpowder in medieval India and is the author of *Gunpowder and Firearms: Warfare in Medieval India* (2004).

DELOCHE, JEAN, is a senior member of the Ecole francaise d' Extreme-Orient and the French Institute of Pondicherry. He specializes on the evolution of cavalry warfare and fortress architecture and is the author of *Studies on Fortification in India.*

Rodrigues, Vitor Luis Gaspar, is an expert on Portuguese maritime technology during the early modern era.

Sen, Surendranath, is the doyen of Indian history who has published widely on early modern India's maritime affairs, Marathas and the 1857 Uprising.

Deshpande, Anirudh, teaches in a college at Delhi and specializes on the social aspects of warfare in British-India. He is the author of *British Military Policy in India: 1900-45* (2005).

Roy, Kaushik, is an Associate Researcher at the Centre for the Study of Civil War at International Peace Research Institute, Oslo. He specializes on modern India's military history and is the author of *The Oxford Companion to Modern Warfare in India* (2009).

Hoover, James W., is Assistant Professor of South Asian and World History at Salem State College in Salem, Masachusetts. He is the author of *Men Without Hats: Dialogue, Discipline and Discontent in the Madras Army, 1806-07* (2007).

Mazumder, Rajit K., is the author of *The Indian Army and the Making of Punjab* (2003). He is now an Assistant Professor in the Department of History at DePaul University, USA.

Reddy, K.N., has done a Ph.D. titled 'The Growth of Public Expenditure in India: 1872-1966' and used to teach at the M.S. University of Baroda.

Singh, Daljit, and Singh, Katherine, are the joint authors of an article on the post-colonial South Asian armies, which was published in the *Journal of the United Service Institution of India.*

Kanchan, L., is a Research Associate at the Institute for Conflict Management and Assistant Editor of the *Faultlines.*

SINHA, SQUADRON LEADER P.M., a serving officer of the Indian Air Force writes on various issues of air power.

ASHRAF, FAHMIDA, is a Senior Research Fellow at the Institute of Strategic Studies, Islamabad and is one of the Associate Editors of Strategic Studies published from the above mentioned institute.

SINGH, LIEUTENANT-GENERAL DEPINDER, retired as General Officer Commanding Southern Command on 29 February 1988. Before retirement, he also functioned as the commander of the Indian Peace Keeping Force in Sri Lanka. His memoir of the Sri Lanka episode has been published as *Indian Peacekeeping Force in Sri Lanka* (2001).

ZUBERI, MATIN, retired as Professor, School of International Studies, Jawaharlal Nehru University and was also a Member of the Nuclear Doctrine Group of the National Security Advisory Board.

KASTURI, BHASHYAM, has written on terrorism, intelligence systems and special forces operations in various journals and newspapers.

Introduction

Warfare, State and Society in South Asia: 500 BCE–2005 CE

Warfare has always been a part and parcel of Indian heritage from time immemorial. Both literature and archaeological remains speak of the importance of warfare. The royal *prashasti*s in a hyperbolic tone describe the expansionist activities of the *chakravartin*s. The Gupta coins represent the emperors armed with bows on horseback. The vedic literature in spite of its metaphysical content, speaks of warfare between the Aryans and conflict between the Aryans and the non-Aryans. The two epics—*Ramayana* and *Mahabharata*—speak of Aryan penetration into peninsular India and the great inter-Aryan warfare in north India. The *niti* literature which evolved from the third century BCE especially focuses on the relationship between statecraft and warfare. Kautilya's *Arthasastra* introduces the term *yuddha* for warfare. And Kamandaka, in his *Nitisara*, describes warfare as *vigraha*. It is to be noted that *yuddha* and *vigraha* not only comprise war between polities but also civil war and strife. The ancient Indian *acharya*s like the ancient Chinese military theoretician Sun Tzu, considered warfare as a mixed bag comprising diplomatic coercion, economic blockade, as well as confrontation between the armies of hostile states. In contrast, the nineteenth century Prussian military philosopher Carl Von Clausewitz's concept of warfare is narrow. Clausewitz conceptualizes warfare as clashes occurring among the regular soldiers of the different states. In this volume, under the rubric war, we will analyse both conventional warfare (war between the regulars of the enemy states) as well as unconventional warfare (civil war, etc., the modern jargon for such conflicts is sub-conventional warfare or low-intensity campaigns).

The medieval Islamic scholars wrote mostly about the campaign history of the sultans in highly ornate and flowery language. The glorious saga of Islamic conquest was occasionally portrayed as *jihad* by them. In the colonial period, one of the favourite pastimes of the colonial officials was to write about how the numerically superior 'natives' were repeatedly defeated by the small number of racially superior Britons. In the post-independence era, one witnesses the flowering of literature on 'glorious regimental traditions' of independent India's army. Graves and war memorials in the various cities and small towns are reminders of the importance of warfare in the subcontinent's history.

Nevertheless, military history has never been the 'in thing' in independent India's historical landscape due to both ideological factors and problems related with sources. It is almost difficult, if not impossible, to date the ancient Hindu texts. This is because these texts were originally composed orally and written down quite a while later. Hence, it is difficult to disentangle fact from myth and also to identify the later interpolations. Further, ancient India did not generate historical texts. Thus, ancient India cannot boast of any work comparable to Herodotus' *Histories* and Thucydides' *History of the Peloponnesian War*, not to speak of purely military texts like Josephus' *Jewish War*, etc. Ancient India's bureaucrats, generals, and emperors did not write military biographies and autobiographies like Tacitus' *Agricola*, Xenophon's *Anabasis* and Julius Caesar's *The Civil War*.

The availability of sources for military affairs as regards the medieval Indian period is a definite improvement over the ancient era. We are lucky to have *Babur Nama*, and voluminous court chronicles like *Akbar Nama*, which give adequate attention to battles and campaigns. However, postcolonial India's medieval historians are uncomfortable in dealing with the issue of Islamic military supremacy over Hindu India. Modern writings on medieval Indian military history started with the British officers who were tinged with the ideology of Social Darwinism. William Irvine, in his history of the Mughal Army, asserts that the racial decline of the Mughals resulted in the conquest of post-Mughal India by the British.[1] The next man to take up the banner of Mughal military history is Jadunath Sarkar. Sarkar deserves praise for his mastery over Persian sources and his battle-centric approach[2] (which in turn was influenced by Edward Creasy and Colonel G. B. Malleson[3]), but his paradigm suffers from Hindu communal bias. Aurangzeb's anti-Hindu policy, claims Sarkar, resulted in the disintegration of the Mughal Empire.[4]

The dominance of Marxist historians in India marginalized military history within the discipline of history. From the 1960s, Mughal history, at least in India, has been dominated by the 'Aligarh School' personnel who are mostly Muslims settled in India. Following Classical Marxist methodology, they link the rise and fall of the Mughal Empire with economic overexploitation of the small peasants. Again, to avoid providing grist to the mills of the 'Hindu rightists', the issue of Hindu military collapse against the Islamic warriors from Afghanistan between ninth to twelfth centuries is also avoided. To be politically correct is another issue which prevented the liberals and the Marxist historians of ancient India from giving attention to the issue of Aryan invasion of India. Studying military history, assume the liberal and Marxist historians, will open up further faultlines between the Aryans and the Dravidians, between high castes and low castes, and also between the Hindus and the Muslims in an already fissiparous Indian society.

The 1990s witnessed the rise of culture studies in the Indian universities. The best brains in the social sciences concerned themselves with tribals, women, Dalits, and the nameless, faceless common mass. Female researchers whose numbers are increasing (history is commonly perceived as a 'soft' discipline suited for females while 'hard' subjects like engineering and mathematics are for males), ask themselves, why study military which is an all-male domain and is an economic burden in a poverty ridden society? Another factor which resulted in the sidelining of military history is the dominance of the Bengali Hindu intelligentsia (who has no martial tradition) in the discipline of history. A cultural studies expert might say that this statement is akin to the argument of the Martial Race theorists of British India. But, where is the evidence of large-scale military recruitment of Bengali Hindus in history?

Some of grand debates in global military history also touch upon the military history of South Asia. The relationship between war and state is still debated. While one group of scholars argue that war made state, the other group of scholars emphasize that state made war. Probably, the relationship between warfare and state formation as well as disintegration is a dialectical one. This issue, in turn, is linked with the weak state versus strong state debate. The interrelationship between warfare and the social structure is also a lively area of debate. Another issue which touches on Indian history is the rise of the West vis-à-vis the rest. And the debate regarding colonial and postcolonial continuities is also interlinked with the question of rise of modernity in Europe in particular and Afro-Asia in general. Finally, after 9/11, non-conventional warfare is emerging as a market-friendly topic both in the West and in India. Rather than providing merely a summary of the articles reprinted in this volume, the Introduction attempts to introduce these debates in the Indian context, especially in relation to the articles reprinted in this volume. Moreover, these pieces will be contextualized within the evolving historiographical matrix. We will analyse how different methodologies shaped and continue to shape the writing of military history.

Periodization of history is problematic. The traditional periodization of Indian history is into four parts: ancient Hindu India, medieval Muslim India, the British or colonial period, and finally, the postcolonial era. The tripolar division of Indian history into ancient, medieval and modern is advanced by R. C. Majumdar, H. C. Raychaudhuri and Kalikinkar Datta in a textbook.[5] The three authors conclude that ancient India stretched up to the reign of the Rashtrakutas and the medieval era started with the advent of the Arabs in Sind in the eighth century AD. In contrast, D. N. Jha, in *Ancient India* published in 1977, brings the ancient Indian era to a close with the collapse of the Gupta Empire in the sixth century CE.[6] But, in *Early India* published in 2004, Jha replaces the term 'ancient India' with the term 'early India' and covers the period till the collapse of the Rashtrakuta power in early ninth century CE and the beginning of Arab penetration in Sind.[7] Here, we are back to the three author schema. Though Romila Thapar in a textbook uses the term early India, unlike Jha, she concludes that early India ended around 1300 CE.[8] Each of these periods are further subdivided into various parts by different scholars. However, the boundaries of each period and sub-periods are fluid and vary with different historians. The ancient period is subdivided into the early Vedic age (Rig Vedic era), later Vedic age, and the post Vedic age. Some historians divide the medieval era into the early medieval era and late medieval era. The late medieval era, at times, stretches up to the eighteenth century and is thus parallel with the early modern era. To give an example, for M. Athar Ali, the distinguished historian of Aligarh School, the medieval period extended from *c.*1000 to *c.*1750.[9]

Despite problems, a historian cannot escape from periodization of history. From the perspective of South Asian military history (including contemporary history, to use Geoffrey Barraclough's term), this volume is divided into five parts on the basis of important debates which straddle the field of global military history. The military historians of Indian antiquity are not concerned with the issue whether warfare is the product of nature or nurture. Due to paucity of works on military history of prehistoric India, we have to leave the Indus Valley Civilization outside our scope of study. The ancient Indian period, for our purpose starts from the Vedic age and continues till the collapse of the Rashtrakutas. The dominant debate for this period was whether ancient Indian warfare was a ritualized combat or did ancient Indians engage in lethal battles. The next period is depicted as the age of horses which started in the ninth century CE and ended only in *c.*1700 with the advent of efficient gunpowder weapons. The third period covers the eighteenth and early nineteenth centuries and the principal debate as regards this period is whether early modern India experienced a Military Revolution (hereafter MR) or not. And can we explain Western dominance of India in particular and Afro-Asia in general with the aid of the MR model? The fourth period covers the second half of the nineteenth century and the first half of the twentieth century. As regards this period, we have to balance the contradictory claims about whether British imperialism in India was the product of military confrontation or military collaboration or both. And finally, the last period which starts with decolonization and the partition, dabbles in the issue of how far the postcolonial age reflects continuity as well as discontinuity with the colonial era. The Revolution in Military Affairs (henceforth RMA) concept also throws light on the above concern.

This volume comprises 26 articles which cover the period from 600 BCE till 2002 CE and deal with various aspects of warfare in South Asia. South Asia as a geographical expression (deliberately, this volume avoids national boundaries) covers the following countries: Bangladesh, India, Bhutan, Nepal, Pakistan, Afghanistan, and Sri Lanka. Till 1947, Pakistan had no existence and Bangladesh came into existence only in 1971. There has been very little study of military history of Nepal and Bhutan. For these reasons, most of the essays deal with India. In this collection, one article deals specifically with Afghanistan and one with Sri Lanka. Since the lion's share of research has been done on military history of the last 300 years (due to availability of sources especially in English), the organization of this volume reflects this imbalance. While four articles cover ancient India, six articles deal with medieval India, another four deal with early modern India, and four deal with British India of the late nineteenth and early twentieth centuries. Finally, there are eight essays which cover postcolonial South Asia. As far as military history is concerned, most of the researches till this date deal with the army and comparatively fewer researches have been done on naval and air power. So, in this collection there is only one article that deals with air power and three articles with naval power. Not only most of the military historians are landlubbers, but most of them follow the north India-centric approach. This is because in history, those powers which controlled the Kabul–Kandahar–Lahore–Delhi axis dominated the subcontinent politically and militarily, if not economically. Armies from Kabul and Delhi invaded south and east India and not vice versa. So, we have only two articles focusing on the north-eastern part of South Asia and two essays dealing with peninsular India. India and Pakistan became nuclear powers only a few years ago. Hence, only one article refers to the nuclear question. Six essays come under the paradigm of unconventional war. Now, let us look at the various debates and different approaches used for studying military history of the world in general and South Asia in particular.

War, Armed Forces and Society

The war and society approach attempts to study the impact of armies and warfare on society and also how the social structures shape the evolution of the armed forces and influence the dynamics of warfare. The assumption is that inherent characteristics and group interest of a particular social community shape the behaviour of the members of that community. The rise of so-called New Military History focuses on the sociological aspects of the militaries rather than on political or strictly military aspects. Instead of command and campaigns, the war and society approach is more interested in assessing the effect of demography on warfare and the relationship between social mobility and military service. The spirit of the New Military Historians is aptly reflected in the Indian historian Anirudh Deshpande's statement: 'a military history which is comprehensive in scope and removed from the banalities of the battlefield.'[10] Deshpande further states: 'military questions, like other histories in general, are essentially *contextual, social* and *political*.'[11]

Stephen Peter Rosen, an American political scientist, assumes that the combat effectiveness of an army is shaped by the structure of the host society. In an article published in 1995, Rosen, while taking a *longue duree* approach, makes a comparative analysis of various societies generating differential military power. And in a book published a year later, Rosen links India's weak military from the Vedic age to the nuclear age with *varna* divisions in the Indian society. A divisive social structure gives rise to a divisive army. Such an army containing the strains of social faultlines is ineffective in the battlefield. In contrast, a homogeneous society generates a socially united army which is capable of power projection outside the national boundaries. The Indian and Italian societies were divisive. Hence, the Indian armies historically and the Italian Army during the two World Wars proved to be a bad joke. Is there any way out for the rulers of a divisive society to create a strong military power? Rosen claims that the ruling elite could create a strong army by separating the military from the divisive host society. The Roman legions recruited from the Italian society was such an example. But, such an army completely separated from the society proved to be a double-edged sword. Though combat effective, such armies, like mercenary forces, proved to be disloyal to their political masters. In contrast, the Indian rulers from the Vedic age till the Mughal era never tried to separate their armies from the society which was divided along caste, religious and linguistic lines. The net result was that the army never became a political threat in ancient and medieval India. But, such armies remained weak combat institutions and repeatedly failed against the external invaders. The British, in their ignorance, tried to separate the colonial army from Indian society. The result was the 1857 Mutiny. In the aftermath of 1857, the British cleverly followed the age-old Indian policy of integrating the army with society; the postcolonial government of India also followed this policy. As a result, both in the colonial and postcolonial eras, the army reflected societal divisions. Though it remains a weak instrument for power projection, India has escaped a military coup till this date.[12] A very pessimistic model indeed. There seems to be no way out for India's political managers who are still caught between the devil and the deep blue sea.

Rosen's model is influenced by Stanislav Andreski, who claims that a military organization is the mirror effect of the host social structure. Andreski, in turn, is influenced by the German sociologist Max Weber. Andreski hints at group solidarity and writes that the notion that people fight better if they are well-off economically is erroneous. In fact, those who led miserable lives fight better than those who live in comfort. He continues that the rude rustics make the best soldiers (an idea which was accepted by the Martial Race theory which dominated the British Indian Army during the late nineteenth century). Andreski states that every society is stratified and the social organization is more or less based on violence. Challenging sociologist Herbert Spencer, Andreski writes that the more a society is geared towards warfare, the less are the chances of inequality. The ratio of men under arms compared to the total population of a society is known as the Military Participation Ratio (MRP). Andreski says that the MRP is determined by the political relation between the conquered and the conqueror. A small band of invading elite will always try to disarm the vast defeated host society. Following Andreski, Rosen has written in his book, *Societies and Military Power*, that the Ottoman Empire and Mughal India represented the supremacy of small conquering elite over a host society. Despite India's demographic resources, the MRP remained quite low. Andreski asserts that generally professional armies and not conscripts or militia intrude into politics. And ethnic homogeneity gives rise to socially homogeneous armies which are more likely to intervene in politics.[13]

In contrast to Rosen, Tarak Barkawi, in a recent article, makes a case study of the Indian Army in Burma during 1944–5 and claims that the *jawans* fought well. Barkawi rightly dismisses the ideology of nationalism functioning as a motivating force in case of colonial armies like the British Indian Army. Ethnic identities were definitely an important factor which shaped the soldiers' morale. The British Indian Army incorporated, shaped and conditioned ethnic differences. The articulation of community honour with warrior masculinity triumphed. However, adds Barkawi, ethnic identities are shaped and conditioned by the military organization and war time experiences. For the combat troops, the identity constructions are generated within the military and in the context of the campaigns rather than being pre-given by civilian society,[14] as Rosen and Andreski assume. To an extent, Barkawi is trying to fuse social history with battlefield history.

The role of ethnicity has somewhat influenced the social historians of the British Indian Army. The British historian David Omissi, influenced by Cynthia H. Enloe, Terrence Ranger, and E. J. Hobsbawm's argument about the state shaping ethnicity of different communities for security purpose, writes that the British selected certain groups in South Asia and created ethnic communities and then incorporated them into the colonial army. These selected communities became British India's martial races. Recruitment based on absorbing the 'martial' ethnic communities became important, especially after the 1857 Mutiny which discredited the Bengal Army's reliance on the high castes of Bihar and Awadh.[15]

The British had to depend on South Asian military personnel for several factors. Indigenous troops were cheaper compared to the British soldiers and in South Asia's climate and terrain, the brown troops performed better than the white troops who frequently succumbed to drink and disease. Third, Britain lacked the demographic resource to maintain a big all white army in South Asia.[16] It is now well-established that British rule in India was based on collaboration (in some cases collaboration under duress) with several communities of the indigenous society rather than on naked organized violence. And the British Indian Army (aka the

Sepoy Army or the colonial Indian Army) provided the platform for collaboration between the traditional illiterate martial clans/ tribes from the countryside and the British 'gentlemen' officers.

In the 1850s, the Bengal Army mustered around 110,000 men. The Bengal Army in the pre-1857 era was mostly dependent on men recruited from south-west Awadh. James W. Hoover, in his piece reprinted in this volume, writes that the Bengal Army relied on the Bains and Chauhan clans among the Rajputs and the Bhumihar Brahmins. Most of the soldiers came from small peasant families and lesser landlords to avoid poverty. Besides pay and pension, the recruits joining the Bengal Army while serving also demanded freedom of worship from the sahibs.

Hoover develops this line of argument in the published version of his doctoral thesis. He argues that the Madras Army remained loyal in 1857 but it exhibited disloyalty in 1806. The Vellore Mutiny of 1806 affected one-fourth of the Madras Army's personnel. Hoover asserts that the 'native' officers of the Madras Army were not politically inert as the British officers tinged with Victorian liberalism believed (the civil servant turned historian Philip Mason also believed)[17] but were politically conscious. The Vellore Mutiny was a case of the Madrasi soldiers challenging the erroneous policy of the East India Company (hereafter EIC) but not the Company itself. Inflation, rise of the European officers' power at the cost of the Indian officers, etc., alienated the Indian personnel. Hoover claims that previously the sepoys were allowed to negotiate with the British officers over the service conditions (both material and non-material aspects). However, due to rise of bureaucratic techniques, the dialogic process was stifled. To cap it all, the order that the Madras sepoys had to wear European type leather *topis* added salt to the wound. Besides declining economic incentives, the sepoys were faced with loss of caste in their society. The sepoys' disaffection and the subsequent protest resulted in the Vellore Mutiny. The Company authorities learnt from this mistake. From 1807 onwards, the sahibs took care of the sepoys' religious and cultural sensibilities.[18] In return, the Madras Army's sepoys gave loyalty to their white masters even during the disturbances of 1857 which ripped apart the Bengal Army.

Before Hoover, Seema Alavi, in her monograph published in 1995, argued that between 1770 and 1830, the Bengal Army's infantry regiments functioned as a channel for the upward mobility of the Bhumihars of west Bihar and Awadh. Pay and pension allowed the Bhumihar soldiers to buy land in their ancestral villages which in turn raised their status in the local society. Further, the British officers of the Bengal Army, by sponsoring caste rituals (like *Ramlila*, etc.) as part of the regimental tradition encouraged in the construction of martial identity of high caste Hindu sepoys who were also known as *Purbiyas*. On a *longue duree*, a shift occurred from the urban *ashraf* class Muslim cavalry soldiers to Hindu high caste peasant infantry. However, towards the end of the first half of the nineteenth century, the group interest of the *Purbiyas* was adversely affected due to the penny pinching policies of Lord Bentinck. This was an important factor behind the outbreak of large-scale mutiny during 1857 in the Bengal Army.[19] This argument is more or less in tune with Amiya Barat's view. However, Barat focuses more on the decreasing economic incentives for the sepoys and administrative mismanagement by the British officers to explain the 1857 Mutiny.[20] To a great extent, Hoover and Alavi accept Eric Stokes' formulation that the sepoys were merely peasants in uniform.

Though the 1857 Mutiny/Uprising is well-known, very few historians have studied the mutiny of the British soldiers of the Bengal Army in 1859–60. The Australian historian Peter Stanley turns his attention to the White Mutiny. He establishes a linkage between the social background of the Bengal European personnel and their behaviour. Since, most of the British personnel of the Bengal Army's European units came from the literate lower middle class (artisans and clerks), they were aware of the rights of the British citizens. Unlike the rank and file of the British Army, they were not the 'scum of the earth' (Duke of Wellington's phrase) and did not join the military service out of sheer desperation. Rather, the educated British personnel joined the EIC's European regiments in an attempt to better themselves. The literate white soldiers, egged on by the lawyers in uniform, considered London's decision to amalgamate the EIC's European regiments with the British Army's regiments as unjust. Hence, they protested against the British policy which went against their corporate and individual interests.[21]

Influenced by the modernization theory, DeWitt Ellinwood claims that military participation in the Great War (First World War), especially when they were deployed in France, transformed the mentality of the Indian soldiers. The sepoys, after seeing the world, brought back the ideas about female emancipation, modern methods of agriculture, and the Western concept of time into their atavistic villages. As a result, not only the sepoys but also the village communities from where they hailed were transformed. The net result was that the very nature of British rule in India was transformed.[22]

Razit K. Mazumder's piece included in this volume analyses the impact of the First World War on Punjab's society. He especially focuses on the changes in the agrarian structure. Mazumder rightly says that within the colonial context, Punjab was economically overdeveloped compared to the other provinces in British India. The economic overdevelopment of Punjab was due to the military demands of the Raj. Since most of the combatants of the Sepoy Army came from Punjab's villages as a result of the Martial Race theory, the Raj tried to keep the peasants in good humour by extending irrigation facilities. Punjab had the largest amount of irrigation facilities in the subcontinent. This resulted in expansion of agriculture. The canal colonies resulted in bumper crops, especially cotton and wheat. The rich farmers had surplus crops to sell. Punjab had the largest length of road and railways compared to the other provinces of British India. The Raj constructed roads and railways in Punjab for troop transportation to the volatile north-west frontier. The highly developed transportation system aided in the emergence of a market and also boosted trade and commerce. The net result was increasing economic prosperity of Punjab which in turn kept the Punjabis loyal to the Raj.[23] The positive multiplier effect of military expenditure on colonial society was put forward by Clive Dewey in a long article quite a few years before Mazumder.[24] Dewey and Mazumder, unlike the traditional Marxist historians, did not automatically assume that military expenditure is always negative.

All hell broke loose for the British in India in the immediate aftermath of World War II. In a recent article, Barkawi asserts that at least the Indian commissioned officers, whose numbers rapidly rose during World War II, were tinged with nationalist aspirations.[25] There was discontent in the million strong Indian Army. Chandar Sundaram, in his numerous articles, notes that the level of political consciousness among the Indian soldiers was increasing from late 1941 onwards.[26] Also, there were instances of mutinies in the Royal Indian Air Force (February 1946) and the Royal Indian Navy (henceforth RIN).

Deshpande's article included in this volume focuses on the intricacies of revolt of the ratings of the RIN at Karachi and Mumbai in 1946. Most of the ratings, unlike the 'martial races' in the Indian Army, came from Bengal and south India. The wave of sympathy for the Indian National Army (hereafter INA) swept over Karachi. The anti-British wave had a populist element and reflected Hindu–Muslim unity. At times, the uprising was spontaneous but in general the anti-colonial wave had Congress support. At Mumbai, the police and CPI also joined the rebellious ratings. The Muslim League was also tilting towards the Muslim personnel of the INA. The Indian Army's loyalty towards its white masters was on the razor's edge. Besides soaring inflation, famine-like conditions, bad rations, and racial discrimination of the British officers, the growing national consciousness was also a key factor behind the amalgamation of the uprising of the ratings and the 'have nots'.

The issue of disloyalty in the Indian armed forces after 1945 has been elaborated by Deshpande in his PhD turned monograph. He asserts that due to the demands of Total War, mass recruitment in the Indian Army was necessary between 1939 and 1945. The pressure of mass mobilization swept away the Martial Race theory and brought new types of recruits with new expectations into the armed forces. These recruits' new aspirations proved difficult for the British to satisfy after 1945. Racial discriminations and the British failure to provide jobs for the demobilized soldiers due to the financial strain under which the British Empire was operating sounded the death knell of the Raj. Here, one finds an echo of Correlli Barnett's work on economic decline and British military collapse on the global plane. The Raj also raised a large volunteer army during the First World War. Then why the Raj did not collapse in 1919? Deshpande claims that mostly illiterate peasants joined the Indian Army between 1914 and 1918. After the war, they were satisfied with the *jagir*s which were granted to them, especially in the Punjab canal colonies. But during World War II, especially in the technical branches, skilled educated personnel joined. To cap it all, the Raj in 1946, unlike in 1919, did not have adequate land for distribution among the demobilized personnel.[27]

Tan Tai Yong, by focusing on the interrelationship between agrarian society and the Raj, notes that the dislocation of the loyalty of the Punjabis had started towards the end of World War II. During World War I, when the prices of food grains were skyrocketing, the Punjabi peasants of the canal colonies made a huge profit by selling their surplus crops. Further, their sons served in the army. Infusion of military pay and pension into the canal colonies aided capital intensive agriculture. For the inter-war era, the Raj instituted the mechanism of District Soldiers' Boards (hereafter DSB) which functioned as a link between agrarian society of Punjab and the government. The DSB took care of the soldiers and their families and introduced the measure of tax remission when the ex-soldiers and their families tilling land faced any economic upheavals. But, in 1943, when the horrendous Bengal famine hit the Raj, the British policy makers had to fix the price of grain and took the surplus grain from Punjab to the famine affected areas. This alienated the Punjabi peasants who could not make high profit and also angered their sons in the army.[28]

Deshpande, Yong, and Sanjoy Bhattacharya accept that the loyalty of the Indian soldiers was weakening towards the end of World War II. However, unlike Deshpande, but like Yong, Bhattacharya harps more on the economic incentives of military service rather than on rising nationalism which shaped the *jawan*s' behaviour till 1945. Bhattacharya notes the very surveillance mechanism which the British constructed in wartime to keep a tab on the mentality of the soldiers created a picture of gloom and doom in the minds of the strategic managers of the British Empire. In 1946, the surveillance mechanism noted that while on one hand the *jawan*s were wavering on their loyalty, the British soldiers were also unwilling to serve on in the subcontinent.[29]

Despite the voluminous production of works on agrarian history, trade history, etc., not much work has been done on the economic aspects of warfare. The only monograph dealing with economic affairs of warfare in ancient India is Ranabir Chakravarti's *Warfare for Wealth* published in 1986. This book does not deal with warfare *per se*, but with the causes of war. Chakravarti's methodology is influenced by Classical Indian Marxist historians like D. D. Kosambi[30] and B. N. Mukherjee, who emphasize the material bases of ancient Indian history. Chakravarti assumes that human beings are especially *homo economicus*. Between the Vedic age and twelfth century CE, the reasons for interstate warfare and the regions where war occurred were dominated by economic factors. In the Vedic age, warfare occurred against the pastoral background and the Aryans fought for cattle. The transition to agrarian economy occurred around 600 BCE and the subsequent big powers like the Nandas and the Mauryas went to war with the objective of economic (agrarian wealth) exploitation of the vulnerable powers. In fact, Mukherjee shows that the expansion and subsequent contraction of the Kushanas in the Indus Valley were shaped by economic forces.[31] Most of the wars, writes Chakravarti, were fought in and for the highly productive zones like the Ganga Valley and Indus Valley. To sum up, the objective behind imperialism was the prospect of making financial gains out of existing economic potentialities.[32]

The political economy of the EIC before the 1857 Uprising has been the focus of Douglas M. Peers' work. Peers, partly influenced by historian John Brewer's study of early modern British government as a fiscal military sponge[33] and the political scientist Harold Lasswell's concept of the Garrison State, writes that the EIC state was a fiscal military organization. The army enjoyed a disproportionate share of the revenue and influence in the Company state. The ruling elite of this polity was characterized by militarism (Alfred Vagt's concept), as they believed that the state came into existence for the army and will survive due to the army. To an extent, this polity approached something of being a militocracy because the military officers at times occupied the civilian posts also.[34]

The economic impact of defence expenditure on society from colonial to postcolonial times is the subject of K. N. Reddy's article included in this compilation. Reddy goes for a statistical analysis. Between 1872 and 1880, defence expenditure as a percentage of national income was 2.87. It is to be noted that the Raj fought the

Second Afghan War between 1878–80. For the period between 1911 and 1920 (including the First World War), the figure remained 2.87. The figures jumped to 4.68 between 1938–47 (due to the impact of World War II). Between 1961–7 (including the India–China War and the Second India–Pakistan War), defence expenditure as percentage of national income was 3.38 per cent. Between 1872 and 1947, defence expenditure accounted for 30 per cent of the total government expenditure. Between 1951–60, defence expenditure fell to 16 per cent of the total government expenditure and for the period between 1961–7, the figure was 15.74 per cent. The overall conclusion is that for the whole pre-Independence period, with the exception of 1915–20 and 1937–47, defence expenditure as a proportion of national income spent was 2.5 per cent. Between 1950 and 1967 (excluding the years after 1962), the proportion of defence expenditure in national income remained 2 per cent. One can conclude that the Nehruvian government tried to reduce the defence burden but post-Independence India failed to drastically reduce defence expenditure.

In recent times, ecology/geography has emerged as a crucial integer in explaining South Asia's social history. The Dutch historian Dirk Kolff writes that one of the characteristics of the subcontinent from time immemorial is the vast demographic resources. The rural populace was armed because they had descended from militarized pastoral nomadic formations who later turned to sedentary cultivation. The marginal peasants hired themselves as war bands to the prospective political entrepreneurs during drought and flood. The loot which they obtained in waging successful military campaigns enabled them to buy land in their villages. This cyclical model continued to function till *c.*1800 CE. The free-floating armed militia constituted a military labour market which limited the centralizing effect of the polities. No polities before the British Indian Empire were able to absorb or demilitarize the armed rural mob.[35] John F. Richards, in one of his articles, notes that many other non-European pre-modern polities (like Tokugawa Japan) were able to demilitarize the armed peasantry. Why no pre-modern Indian government was able to do that is a question worth looking into by the future historians.[36] The military labour market concept is emerging as a heuristic device to explain the contours of South Asian history.

Jos Gommans, influenced by this concept, in one of his recent articles argues, that the pre-modern Indian political economy was somewhat similar to the Central Asian and Middle Eastern political economies which were in turn distinct from the West European political economy. The South Asian political economy was characterized by the presence of frontiers both inside and outside the subcontinent. The outer frontier was represented by the jutting of the Central Asian arid zone into Punjab, and the inner frontiers were characterized by the presence of semi-pastoral groups within the subcontinent. Constant tension and tussle between the sedentary societies and the semi-nomadic pastoral groups (which provided personnel to the military labour market) had been the ongoing feature of South Asian history.[37] One detects here the influence of Rudi Paul Lindner's linkages between grasslands, nomadism, and cavalry.[38]

The British somehow were able to demilitarize the military labour market. The argument that the EIC state till the first half of the nineteenth century had a strong fiscal–military base and its positive interaction with the South Asian military labour market also finds resonance in Randolf G. S. Cooper's monograph. He asserts that the Maratha collapse was because the British bought off the European mercenary officers of the Marathas and also by offering higher bids controlled the dynamics of the military labour market. By providing economic incentives and proper managerial measures, the EIC also co-opted key elements of the Indian civil society. This, in turn, enhanced the logistical reach plus military effectiveness of the British Indian Army.[39] Overall, the War, Armed Forces and Society School, taking a structuralist stance focuses on material factors. The role of non-tangibles in shaping the course of history is the focus of the next approach discussed below.

Postmodernism and Military History

Gender, culture and memory are the defining characteristics of this new genre of military history writing. While in the 1960s and 1970s, applying Marxist theoretical concepts (primitive accumulation, mode of production, etc.) was considered as the fashion in Indian history writing, from the 1990s the postmodernists/culture studies experts have started introducing Michel Foucault's power theory (different from the power politics paradigm of the realist and the neo-realist theorists of international relation studies) and theories of literary criticism. They argue that the reality can never be known because there is no single reality. Further, the historians construct an artificial reality based on the sources which are also not a reflection of reality but as good as fiction. One author even claims that Thucydides' work is not a piece of history but a historical fiction.[40] Since texts are considered as constructed (following Hayden White) and not transparent, archival studies lost importance in their paradigm. For the postmodernists, the voluminous colonial archival materials are merely a constructed 'Oriental' knowledge system (influence of Edward Said) generated by the 'bad, biased and ignorant' British.

The French historian Georges Duby's *The Legend of Bouvines,* which was published in French in 1973 and translated into English in 1990, is a typical example of postmodern military history. Duby asserts: 'The outlook of positivist history . . . viewed the Battle of Bouvines as specifically pertaining to the dynamics of the history of power.'[41] Duby accuses the positivist historians for focusing unduly on the political actions, on its motivations and consequences.[42] Hence, Duby's corrective is to look at the memory of the battle from the perspective of an anthropologist. His heavy prose continues: 'to attempt to perceive both the battle and the memory as wrapped up in a cultural whole different from the one which at present molds our own relationship with the world.'[43] Duby writes that 'I will also attempt to observe the impact that the imaginary and oblivion have on information, the insidious penetration of the marvellous, of the legendary, and, in the course of a sequence of commemorations, the fate of a memory in the midst of a changing set of mental representations.'[44]

Duby does not tell us how and why Otto I, the German Emperor, despite possessing quantitative and qualitative superiority in military assets, failed against the French at Bouvines. He suggests that battle was a spectacle and not mere killing, at least for the knights. In the battlefield, the knights in shining armour displayed the joust of the tournaments which they practiced for acquiring women and money in peacetime. One historian at least has marshalled adequate facts which show that even in the late Middle Age, the knightly tournaments were serious military exercises aimed at generating team spirit and acquiring proficiency in handling various types of arms.[45]

About the limitations of military historians whom Duby considers as obsolete positivists (he has J. F. Verbruggen in mind), he asserts: 'they had to locate the exact position of the "true fact" at the very spot, at once resultant and causal, lying at the juncture of the facts' ins and outs. Yet these goals are unreachable. This is so because we all know that the field of vision of all the participants in a battle... is limited; they can only see a confused melee. No one has or ever will perceive in its total reality the whirl of a thousand tangled actions which on that day, in the plain of Bouvines between noon and five in the afternoon, came to be inextricably interwined.'[46] Such an approach among the postmodern historians is known as dispersive narrativism, which argues that no historical phenomenon can be fully represented and any such representation by a historian is false because then the singularity of the individual phenomenon is reduced in favour of artificial grand illustration.[47] The assertion of Duby that reconstruction of the past and 'dialogue with the dead' can at best be fragmentary and imaginary is somewhat similar to the argument pushed by the noted British military historian John Keegan in his most famous work, *The Face of Battle*, which came out in 1976.

While writing about the British Army in Somme on 1 July 1916, Keegan notes: 'Even sixty years later, it is very difficult to discover much that is precise, detailed and human about the fate of a great number of the battalions of the Fourth Army on 1 July.'[48] Keegan asserts: 'I do not intend to write about generals or generalship . . . I do not intend to say anything of logistics or strategy and very little of tactics in the formal sense.'[49] Keegan claims that the study of generals and generalship is useless as most of these studies are merely hagiographies. And the rhetoric of battle history is merely 'myth history'.[50] Here, Keegan comes close to Duby who also asserts that battle is a spectacle and the writing of battle history is actually myth making by the chroniclers with vested interests who had their own axes to grind. Keegan's objective comes clear in the following assertion: 'to suggest how and why the men who have had (and do have) to face these weapons control their fears, staunch their wounds, go to their deaths. It is a personal attempt to catch a glimpse of the face of battles'.[51] Keegan tries to recreate how the common soldiers controlled their chief emotions (i.e. fear) in the battlefield and how they perceived the firefight. In Keegan's view, none of the common soldiers either perceived the total reality in the battlefield nor were they interested in it. They were merely interested to somehow survive the dusty, smelly, danger-filled environment by hovering in one corner of the battlefield.

Just as some scholars under the influence of postmodernism claim that the past cannot be known, some international relations experts influenced by postmodern science (chaos theory as part of the post-Newtonian science) claim that warfare cannot be studied with any certainty. Following chaos theory, they argue that warfare is a complex phenomenon dealing with several non-linear systems. Such unstable systems are characterized by small inputs resulting in high outputs. This is known as the 'butterfly effect', i.e. a butterfly flapping its small wings somewhere in China might cause a dangerous storm in New York. Hence, causality is out and unpredictability is in.[52]

Influenced by postmodernism, military historians are now considering culture as one of the crucial integers for explaining military changes. However, unlike the strategic culture approach of the political scientists, the historians influenced by postmodernism do not study the high culture of the elites shaping strategic behaviour of the nations.[53] Rather, these historians' *forte* are day-to-day cultural activities of the common mass. However, culture is like a black box or *terra incognita* of Tacitus. Culture for these new military historians is somewhat similar to what race was to the colonial historians.

For instance, the American military historian John A. Lynn, whose specialization is France's *ancien* regime's army, writes that the British supremacy in South Asia was due to the unique culture of the British. The Western battle culture of forbearance enabled the British soldiers to engage in close quarter combat successfully. This unique battle culture was partly the product of drill. It was fused with the regimental culture of the all male community. Later, the British inducted sepoys into the regiments but modified the western regimental/military culture by absorbing the indigenous cultural codes of *izzat* and *rasuq* (community honour).[54]

To an extent, Lynn seems to be influenced by Victor Davis Hanson, the American military historian of ancient Greece, who claims that decisive set-piece battles which involve face-to-face encounter was invented by the Classical Greeks. This cultural invention was the product of agrarian ethos of the small landholders who dominated the *polis*. This tradition of decisive battles was inherited and elaborated upon by the Romans and later by the West Europeans.[55]

An ex-American army officer turned historian, Jeffrey Greenhut, deals with the problematic of the sahib–sepoy relationship. The sepoys fought for the sahibs because both interpreted the relationship in terms of their own cultures. While the British officers perceived themselves as country squires leading their retainers, the sepoys considered fighting as their *dharma*, i.e. caste duties. The sepoys considered the sahibs as their *mai–bap*. The sepoys, while doing their duties, demanded that the white officers should take care of their needs. The glue between the sahibs and the sepoys was not bureaucratic as in the professional Western armies but personalized and paternalistic.[56] One is reminded of Andre Wink's assertion that Indian history is dominated by the twin concepts of *dharma* and *fitna*.[57] And when, young British officers with no conception of the sepoys' culture were appointed to lead the sepoy battalions in France during 1914–5, the result was chaos.[58]

One example of postmodern understanding of the Martial Race theory is the British anthropologist Lionel Caplan's monograph on the Gurkhas published in 1995. Caplan argues that the image of the heroic, valiant and simple Gurkhas which we have is the production of the British officers between late nineteenth and early twentieth centuries. They imagined the Gurkhas as possessing the above-mentioned characteristics. Such writings, claims Caplan, is a sort of Orientalist discourse (Said's influence) shaped by the configurations of power of the colonizers over the colonized. The British generated a knowledge system which is monolithic, timeless and relying heavily on stereotypes is a sort of rhetoric and a mechanism for subordinating that colonial community to the power structure of colonialism. Through the exercise of power and use of animal imagery, the inferiors (Nepalis) in British eyes were transformed into cherished pets (Gurkhas).[59]

Heather Streets' comparative analysis of Scottish Highlander, Sikh and Gurkha identities in *Martial Races* published in 2004, is a classic example of the postmodern intervention in the sphere of British imperial and colonial military history. In her paradigm, British imperialism in Scotland and in South Asia was a cultural project. Streets claims that: 'the savage representations of masculinity that lay at the heart of Martial Race ideology were a crucial imaginative site upon which the Anglo-Indian military elites responded to and attempted to manipulate, historically specific global-imperial politics after 1850'.[60] The popular British media aided to bring the racial and gendered constructs before a wide public. In contrast to the formulations of the military historians (like Stephen Cohen,[61] T. A. Heathcote, Apurba Kundu, Pradeep Barua, Jeffrey Greenhut, and Lieutenant-General S. L. Menezes), Streets claims that the British Army in India was neither apolitical nor marginal to the British culture. In fact, the representatives of the army tried their best to shape the values of Victorian culture. Their racial and gendered constructions profoundly affected the identities of the so-called 'martial race' populations in both Britain and India, who embraced and manipulated their own representations as martial heroes. The newspapers, periodicals, music halls and literature of Victorian England, thanks to the efforts of the army and influence of colonial warfare, reflected an increasingly jingoistic, militaristic and imperially minded popular culture. The study of martial races, continues Streets, require transcending both the European 'self' and foreign 'other'. Rather than depending on dry and dusty official files and private papers of the imperial elites, Streets asserts that her work depends on a variety of sources like art, music, advertisements, popular journalism and school textbooks.[62]

Following the dicta of gender studies, construction of masculinity is a favourite topic of several historians influenced by the postmodernism. Rosalind O'Hanlon, in a long article, shows the shift from Mughal military masculinity to British masculinity during the eighteenth and nineteenth centuries. Mughal masculinity was the product of the Persian *javanmardi* concept (incorporating the *adab* culture) partly influenced by Sufi cults. Sufi devotionalism influenced by Brahmanical tradition of *brahmacharya* emphasized male spiritual power and bodily comportment. The goals of such masculinity were the sexual conquest of beautiful women and to excel in imperial service. In contrast, the British code of manliness during the first half of the nineteenth century was shaped by the morality of the Evangelicals. Towards the end of the nineteenth century, moral courage, sexual purity and civic virtue constituted the muscular imperial masculinity.[63]

Given the postmodernists' penchant for studying mentality, some scholars have turned their lens of enquiry to evaluate the minds of the Indian soldiery and the warlords of pre-modern South Asia. It seems that the secularization of mind and warfare which occurred in post-Enlightenment West Europe did not occur in pre-British South Asia. Simon Digby (by no means a postmodernist) claims that the Mughal soldiers during Aurangzeb's Deccan campaigns were motivated by the Sufi doctrine. The Sufi leaders played an important role in strengthening the morale of the Muslim soldiers.[64] In 1965, before postmodernism became current in the academic circuit of social science, Digby, in two articles, reconstructed the mental world of a seventeenth century Afghan soldier named Dattu Sarvani settled in India. Digby shows that Sarvani's mental cosmos was partly tinged by Sufi thoughts.[65]

Besides the rank and file, the political managers of the subcontinent were not only religious but were also willing to use troops maintained by several religious leaders. William R. Pinch asserts that the British demilitarized all the bands of religious warriors because the sahibs had a different conception of religion.[66] The basic assumption of these authors seem to be that it's all in the mind. Different mentality of the sahibs, write Jos Gommans[67] and Dirk Kolff, also enabled them to establish a monopoly of violence by the state. This brings us to the weak state–strong state debate.

Weak State, Segmented Armies, Flower War versus Strong State, Regular Armies, Decisive Battles

One group of scholars argues that all the pre-British polities in South Asia were weak political entities. And these fragile political organisms maintained part-time peasant militia which engaged in indecisive skirmishes. This model was frozen in time. For explaining the multi-layered state in Indian history, Burton Stein introduced the theory of the segmentary state. Stein, in turn, has been influenced by the anthropologist Aidan Southall who has found evidence for segmentary states in African and Asian history. The segmentary state was characterized by ritual sovereignty of the ruler co-existing with political decentralization. The ruler of such polities might have some modicum of power at the core but at the periphery, it was almost a theatre state.[68] The intrusion of the Turks, at least for some scholars within this camp, resulted in patrimonial bureaucratic empires (Stephen Blake's term). In such entities, loyalty is to the ruler. Complete centralization which enabled harnessing of the military assets in an efficient manner occurred only with the entry of the British in South Asia.[69] Gommans writes that the Mughals in the traditional Indian way used the army (a loose conglomerate of war bands) not for destruction of the enemy in the battlefield, but for constructing a favourable political settlement with the enemy who were absorbed as subordinated warlords.[70] The implication is that Indian warfare should not be understood in the Clausewitzian concept of *Ausgeschaltet* (complete liquidation) of the enemy in the battlefield. In fact, Indian battles were more political rather than *schlacht* (butchering) of the soldiers in the battlefield. In contrast, another group of historians (who are mostly Indians) assert that the pre-British Indian polities like the Mauryas, Guptas, the Suri Sultanate, and the Mughal Empire were strong political entities that maintained standing armies which waged decisive set-piece battles and sieges for annexing hostile territories.[71]

Torkel Brekke, a Norwegian scholar who specializes in classical Hindu religious philosophy, argues that the ancient Hindu philosophers were never concerned with *jus ad bellum* (the right resort to war) or the justice in going to war which involves just cause for war, right authority for initiating war, right intention for starting war, proportionality of ends and war as a last resort. While the medieval European religious philosophers like Thomas Aquinas differentiated between external and internal violence, the Hindu philosophers failed to differentiate between private and public violence. The *Mahabharata* conceptualized war as a private enterprise for the heroes. The two epics portray warfare as a duel between the heroes of opposing sides. Even Kautilya does not distinguish between internal repression by the state and power projection by the state in the international arena. This is because the pre-modern Indian state is an amorphous entity with fuzzy territorial borders.[72] Here, we find Brekke influenced by Stein's thesis of segmentary states.

It would be an overstatement to argue that all the pre-British political entities in South Asia were segmented polities with fragmented armies. This is not to suggest that all the empires in India were centralized entities. For instance, the Rashtrakuta Empire in central India comprised several feudatory states. The Vijaynagar Empire, during the sixteenth century, was a decentralized structure with the semi-autonomous *nayaka*s at different localities maintaining their own armed retainers.[73] The Rajput principalities were based on the *bhai-bant* system in which the nobles considered themselves as co-sharers in the state and the ruler was first among the peers. In the seventeenth century, the *bhai-bant* system was replaced with the *pattadari* system. The latter was somewhat a decentralized feudal system, with the Rajput chiefs enjoying land grants for maintaining military retainers. The *pattadari* system was in many ways similar to the Mughal *jagir* system.[74] My take is that recent historiography has overemphasized the decentralized nature of polities and armies in Indian history whereas new researches are showing that armies and the states in Europe till the Enlightenment era were not that centralized and bureaucratic.

B. P. Sinha, Bimal Kanti Majumdar, P. C. Chakravarti, and U. P. Thapliyal claim that the ancient Indians waged decisive battles and conducted lethal sieges. Sinha's essay, reprinted in this volume, claims that from the Rig Vedic era onwards, encounter battles emerged in India. And the instrument for waging warfare was the *chaturanga bala* (four-limbed army) which comprised chariots, elephants, infantry and cavalry. The elephants were used as battering rams against the enemy's forts and also functioned as heavy weights in land battles. Each war elephant carried three archers and a *mahout* (driver) equipped with *ankush* (goad for controlling the beast) on its back. Elephants proved to be so effective that both Seleucus (305 BCE) and Antiochus III (206 BCE) took war elephants from India and used them in the Near East against their opponents. Besides swords and spears, the Indian infantry was armed with slings and had shields. The cavalry was not as effective as the steppe nomadic mounted archers. Though the Indians used bits and saddles, they failed to master the use of stirrups. The *Rig Veda* mentions clashes among opposing groups of chariots. The armoured chariot warriors equipped with spears, bows and arrows dominated the Vedic battlefield.

P. C. Chakravarti's chapter in this collection elucidates on the use of war chariots. They were used as battlefield taxis as well as elevated mobile platforms in the battle zone, which gave an advantage to the charioteer over the foot soldiers. In the Vedic and Epic age, the army mainly comprised chariots and foot soldiers. Chariots were the monopoly of the noble warriors. One finds traces of gradual evolution of the chariots. Initially, the wheels were made of solid wood and later wheels with spokes were used. Larger four-wheeled chariots became common in the post-Vedic age. The *chaturanga bala* of the Mauryas included chariots which were deployed in Tinnevelly district far in the south. In fact, the Maurya Army used to make roads for the chariots.

A global history approach enables us to look at the uniqueness of a particular region's history as well as to find the commonalities in historical developments sprawling across the vast mass of Eurasia over a long period. Historians working on South Asia (some exceptions are Sanjay Subrahmanyam and Jos Gommans) shy away from applying the global history/world history approach. The global history approach opens up new vistas as regards military history. To give an example, war chariots were not unique in ancient India. Sargon II's Assyrian Army dominated the Near East in the late eighth century BCE with a chariot-based force.[75]

Bimal Kanti Majumdar and Thapliyal vehemently put forward the view that the armies of ancient India were not stagnant but evolved with time, especially due to interaction with the invaders across north-west India. Majumdar's chapter from his book included in this collection shows the transition in the Hindu military organization during the post-Maurya era. Chariots gradually became obsolete. The Andhras had a tripolar military comprising 1,00,000 infantry, 2,000 cavalry and 1,000 elephants. The Greek, Scythian and Parthian invaders introduced chain armour for the cavaliers equipped with long lances. The Guptas had a hierarchical officer corps and imitated horse archery from the nomads.

Thapliyal, in his essay reprinted here, writes that the principal weapon of the horse archers was the composite bows. The Guptas used such bows and they adopted this from the Parthians, Sakas and the Kushanas who were using such bows from the beginning of the Common Era. Even before the Guptas, during the third century CE, armoured mounted archers galloped into battle. Siege warfare was also evolving with time. Initially, the Aryans constructed forts which had ramparts of hardened earth with palisades and ditches. The Maurya period witnessed the addition of gates and towers for enhancing the defensive value of the forts. For sieges, the epics tell us that the ancient Indians used *yantras* (stone throwing machines). For conducting decisive battles and sieges, ancient India did not depend on an undisciplined rabble. The epics and Kautilya's *Arthasastra* emphasize the importance of a small, well-trained army compared to a large indisciplined militia. There were several institutions for military training. The kshatriya boys learnt about *dhanurveda* (science of archery) in the *asramas* (military gymnasiums) under the supervision of brahmin teachers. In the *asramas*, the young kshatriya boys led a regimented life. One is reminded of the young Spartiates' harsh preliminary training for becoming hoplites.

In another essay, Thapliyal notes the various types of troops recruited in the armies of ancient India. There were hereditary soldiers, mercenaries, allied troops, soldiers furnished by the forest chieftains (who were sustained by loot), and finally soldiers maintained by the *srenis* (guilds). In addition, deserters from the enemy army as well as soldiers of a defeated enemy army were also often pressed into service. Regional specialization emerged with time. While the soldiers of Magadha were good in fighting from the elephant back, men recruited from north-west India made good cavalry soldiers and the troops enlisted from south India were excellent swordsmen. Kamandaka's *Nitisara* emphasizes the linkages between logistics and military effectiveness. The *Manusmriti* speaks of *sastrasalas* (arms factories) maintained by the state. The *Sukraniti* reflects on the necessity of regular payment to the soldiers. For gathering strategic and tactical intelligence, the ancient Indian political treatises focused on the importance of maintaining a spy establishment. Further, the ancient Hindus had a definite system for organizing the army. The *Rig Veda* speaks about the decimal system for organizing troops.[76]

While Thapliyal speaks mostly about north India, J. Sundaram turns the limelight onto Deccan and peninsular India. Sundaram writes that during seventh century CE, chariots became obsolete in south India. By the twelfth century, horsemen armed with sword supported by a frontal charge of elephants became the dominant technique for conducting warfare. Sundaram claims that the Cholas maintained a standing army. The general opinion among the military historians is that South Asia, till the advent of the British failed to evolve disciplined heavy infantry organized in permanent units. The Macedonian *phalangites* were to a great extent responsible for destroying Paurava's force. And no Indian empires could boast of anything like the Roman legions. The rise of Spanish *tercios* during the sixteenth century and then British and French infantry organized in regiments gave the West a decisive superiority over non-Western forces in land battles. However, Sundaram makes a revolutionary statement by saying that the Chola infantry was organized in permanent units akin to the regiments. There were regiments of archers under Rajaraja. While a regiment was commanded by the *nayakan*, the commandant in charge of training was known as the *valavan*. Each regiment with its own regimental centre (which was occasionally a temple) was granted land for its own maintenance. The rulers maintained special *bazaar*s and merchants for supplying provisions to the army.[77] The Chola Army, continues Sundaram, was capable of conducting decisive battles. The Chola King Rajadhiraja I fought the Battle of Kopppam (1054 CE) against the Chalukya ruler Ahavamalla. The Chola reserve, under Rajendra II, was responsible for gaining victory. Again, at the Battle of Kudalasangamam (1062 CE), the Chola advance guard attacked first with elephants and then the reserve advanced to deliver the *coup de grace*.[78]

As regards siege warfare conducted by the rulers in medieval India, R. K. Saxena writes that the Turks maintained specialized units for siege operations. The *mufrid*s (military engineers) manned and repaired the siege weapons. One mechanical siege engine was the *kharak* which was a large beam (that revolved on a socket) with an iron point. It was used for creating holes in the wall. The traditional siege engines from early medieval India were *manjaniq*s (catapults) and *arrada*s (stone throwing machines). *Turrah* was a movable wooden screen mounted on wheels which was brought close to the wall and from the shelter of the *turrah* the besiegers attacked the besieged garrison. *Pasheb* was a high structure constructed for attacking the tower of the fort as well as for putting the siege engines on a higher ground. Gradual evolution in siege weapons and techniques occurred with time. Mining for breaching the walls of a fort was resorted to by Alauddin Khalji during the Siege of Ranthambhor (1299–1300 CE). For scaling the walls, Muhammad Tughlaq used leather ladders. The Mughals, under Akbar, used *sabat*s which were covered passages for protecting the sappers and miners and for bringing the storming party close to the walls of the enemy fort. Since siege operations were time-consuming, the Mughals had a logistical apparatus for sustaining the troops engaged in besieging a fort. The troops acquired food grains from the imperial kitchens, *langarkhanas* (charitable kitchens) set up by the nobles, and the *banjara*s. In addition, the besieging army also established *thanah*s and *golah*s which functioned as supply depots.[79]

If we turn the limelight on the western part of Eurasia, we observe many instances of the so-called segmentary states with fragile armies. Bernard S. Bachrach, the American historian of early medieval Europe, says that in the later Roman Empire, personal armed followings of the magnates rather than the legions became dominant. The Merovingian Empire during the sixth and seventh centuries was a loose confederacy, like Harsha of Kanauj's empire. The Merovingian Army comprised the personal following of the landed magnates which engaged both in policing as well as in military operations. At times, despite the king's order, the local magnates refused to mobilize their levies.[80] In the mid-eleventh century CE, the Byzantine central government disintegrated and the local semi-autonomous landlords maintained their own armed retainers. R. J. Barendse writes that feudalism was a social formation in world history and spatially it stretched from India in the East up to France in the West. The characteristic of feudalism was the domination of the peasants by the aristocracy of mounted warriors who were more powerful than any central government's institution. The European fief like the Ottoman *timar* and the Mughal *jagir* was a loose bundle of contradictory claims on land by the mounted warrior aristocracy.[81]

Technology and Military History

There is no denying that technology is one of the crucial drivers of world history. But how far technology affected the historical processes of different regions at different times is worth pondering. So, the basic dilemma is whether we can speak of agency in technology or only behind it. How far do certain communities or individuals at different moments of time create situations that provide technology with adequate power to drive history? Again, scholars are divided between hard and soft determinism. Ulrich Wengenroth emphasizes the role of societal and cultural values which enable a society to grasp the importance of a particular piece of technology in a particular time period. The presence of a particular piece of technology is also a question of power enjoyed by a certain group over others in a society. Wengenroth concludes that after all, technological determinism is historical and local.[82] To be precise, military technology has two parts: hardware (the artifacts) and software (which comprises doctrine, tactics and organization of the militaries). An important issue is why some technological devices were considered more handy in some societies but marginalized in other societies. Here, social, cultural and managerial aspects come into play. Nevertheless, technological devices had their own intrinsic worth which a community could only disregard at its own cost. The presence of a particular piece of technology might lead to restructuring of the values of a society in a certain time period. Further, the pace of diffusion of military technology along different geographical axes shaped the contours of Eurasian history. The pace of diffusion and innovation is a contingent process shaped by local historical contexts. Here, culture, institutions and personalities play an important role. The rate of diffusion and innovation are also dependent on the transfer of information as well as the availability of economic resources. External pressure also at times accelerated the process of diffusion and innovation.

Cavalry became dominant in the battlefields of medieval Eurasia. In 1885, C. W. C. Oman launched the first salvo. In his words: 'Feudalism, in its origin and development, had a military as well as a social side, and its decline is by no means unaffected by military considerations. There is a point of view from which its history could be described as "the rise, supremacy, and decline of heavy cavalry as the chief power in war.". . . Between Adrianopole, the first, and Marignano, the last, of the triumphs of the medieval horsemen.'[83] In Oman's view, at Adrianopole in 378 CE, the destruction of 40,000 Roman legionaries by the heavy (armoured) Gothic cavalry marked the replacement of infantry armed with swords and *pilums* (throwing spears) by the cavalry equipped with lance and bows. After this defeat, the Roman Empire reacted by increasing the number of cavalry. The Roman Army used horse archery and lancers to check the Huns at the Battle of Chalons. One can draw a striking parallel with the Gupta Emperor Skandagupta who also checked the Huns at the Indus river with the aid of horse archery. In the eleventh century, Oman asserts, the mail-clad feudal cavaliers had established superiority over all the types of troops pitted against them: from the Magyar horse archers in the East to the Anglo-Danish axe wielding infantry in the West. The Battle of Hastings marked the culmination of feudal cavalry superiority over the axe-wielding infantry. The military balance shifted against the feudal cavalry with rise of Swiss pike wielding infantry in the fourteenth century.[84] Two years after Oman, Heinrich Brunner supported the linkage between heavy cavalry and fief holdings. The Feudal Revolution gave rise to the Heavy Cavalry Revolution in the Carolingian realm.[85] The use of stirrup and increasing effectiveness of heavy cavalry is established by Lynn White Jr in 1962.

The dominance of knightly cavalry in the medieval European battlefields is challenged by Bachrach. After studying the later Roman, Merovingian and Carolingian military operations, he writes that rather than battles, raids, skirmishes, and siege operations were more numerous. In such operations, infantry armed with bows and battering rams rather than armoured cavalry played the important role. During the eighth and ninth centuries, stirrups were little appreciated by the Carolingian horsemen.[86] Bachrach's assertion is yet not accepted by the vast majority of military historians dealing with West Europe.

The 'Age of Horse' in the South Asian military landscape started with the attack of the Arabs and the Turks around 900 CE. K. S. Lal's article in this volume shows that the 'slave soldiers' (*ghulams*) mounted on the horses imported from Central Asia and West Asia enabled the Delhi Sultans to dominate the battlespace. Ghiyasuddin Balban captured boys aged 8 to 9 who later grew up as slave soldiers of the sultan. Alauddin Khalji maintained 50,000 slave boys. The slave soldiers functioned as shock troops. The mounted troops were constantly trained in the use of crossbows (which had a greater range than the bows of the Rajputs) and lances. In fact, a slave soldier was trained for seven long years before he became a mature *ghulam*. The Hindu powers down south imported horses from West Asia. In order to impair the military efficiency of the Hindu polities as well as to replenish their own supplies, the defeated Hindu rulers were obliged to hand over their war mounts to the victorious army of the Delhi Sultanate. The Ghaznavids first introduced the use of bronze stirrups in India. The use of metal stirrups by the heavy cavalry (richly caparisoned and equipped with lances and bows) established the battlefield supremacy of the Ghaznavids and the Ghorids. The Rajputs failed to master these new technologies. In contrast, the Delhi Sultanate created a bureaucratic apparatus for recruiting, equipping and maintaining the mounted forces with the latest technologies in a high state of readiness. Overall, the conclusion of Lal is supported by Ali Athar's recent study of the Delhi Sultanate's army.[87]

Jean Deloche, a French historian, in a path-breaking work based on sculptures of the Hindu temples down south asserts that the Hoysalas of Mysore during the twelfth and thirteenth centuries used stirrups which underwent gradual evolution. The principal arm of the Hoysala Army was cavalry equipped with lances. One is reminded of the feudal knights of contemporary West Europe. Further, the Hoysalas mastered the technique of shoeing the horses. This goes against A. Jan Qaisar's argument that the Turks first introduced in India the practice of shoeing horses.[88] Rather than technological inferiority, the south Indian polities collapsed against the Sultanate Army because of the latter's superiority in mounted archers. Not only Deloche's view is original but his methodology of using iconography for understanding pre-modern India's military technology is an innovative one.[89]

The shift from horse to guns occurred in early modern Europe and the model used for explaining this change is known as the MR. This concept was first popularized by a historian of early modern Spain, Geoffrey Parker, in the Lees Knowles Lecture of 1984. Parker argues that between 1500 and 1750, warfare on land and sea was transformed. This radical transformation enabled the West to overwhelm the rest. The revolution in land warfare involved the rise of disciplined standing armies equipped with artillery and hand-held firearms. Such armies were sustained by centralized bureaucratic states. In response to firepower of the siege artillery, the fortress architecture was revolutionized. The new style of fort architecture is known as *trace italienne* or *alla moderna.* Parker emphasizes on both military hardware and management techniques to explain radical military changes. Parker derived the MR model from Michael Roberts, the specialist of early modern Sweden. Roberts' approach was narrow. He focused on the tactical revolution in the Swedish Army of Gustavus Adolphus during the Thirty Years' War. Parker expands the geographical ambit of the MR thesis by bringing under scrutiny the operations of the Spanish Army in Italy and Flanders. Further, he focuses on the Revolution in Naval Warfare, i.e. RNA (rise of sea-going battle fleets equipped with broadsides) and links it with the expansion of the maritime powers into Afro-Asia.[90] Parker's model is much more sophisticated and nuanced than Daniel R. Headrick's *The Tools of Empire* which emphasizes on raw technology (telegraph, quinine and the breechloader revolution) in order to explain the West gobbling up China and Africa from the second half of the nineteenth century.[91]

Parker's model of paradigm shift (influenced by Thomas Kuhn who used the idea of paradigmatic shifting in order to explain the Scientific Revolution) in early modern European warfare is still debated by the scholars. While one group argues that MRs also occurred under Napoleon and during the late nineteenth century, another group claims that the indices of MR are also present in medieval West European warfare. In response, a group of political scientists and historians have come up with the idea of successive MRs occurring in West Europe between 1300 CE and 2000 CE.[92] Clifford J. Rogers borrows the punctuated equilibrium concept from biology to explain slow innovations (evolutions) and sudden radical changes (MRs) to explain West Europe experiencing successive MRs from the Hundred Years War.[93] Now, most of the historians like Kelly DeVries,[94] Jeremy Black,[95] etc., are arguing for slow incremental changes in warfare from medieval to late modern times. Hence, the term, Military Evolution, is used to explain the gradual transformation of warfare in West Europe between 1000 CE and 2000 CE.

With time, the MR model became attractive for historians focusing on regions outside West Europe. In an article published in 1994, Pradeep Barua writes that the post-Mughal states failed to integrate the MR because the polities were proto-feudal in nature. Though these polities modernized their military machines, they failed to upgrade their political system. Hence, they fell prey to the onslaught of the EIC.[96] A similar argument was advanced by Gordon in an article published in 2002, where he writes that the steppe nomadic nobility obstructed total adoption and complete adaptation to Western technologies. This, in turn, prevented the MR from becoming successful among the Indian powers in the eighteenth century.[97] G. J. Bryant, in an article dated 2004, notes that due to an artificial symmetry between the indigenous powers, the South Asian militaries remained cavalry-centric. Such medieval armies folded easily when faced with the British Army, which was the product of MR of West Europe.[98] Gommans, in an article published in 2007, influenced by the MR model, and by also trying to integrate ecology for explaining military changes asserts that Asia (especially the arid zone) between 1000 CE and 1800 CE experienced a horse warrior revolution which in turn was shaped by the agrarian revolution. Horse economies dominated India and China and the horse traders established post-nomadic frontier states rather than gunpowder empires in these regions.[99]

Let us look at the development of artillery in West Europe. From late fourteenth century onwards, West Europe started manufacturing very large cannons made from both bronze and iron, known as bombards. Generally, the bore diameter of a bombard was greater than 30 cm. The barrel of a bombard was made from several longitudinal staves of iron bound together with a series of iron hoops which were heat shrunk over the staves. In the bombard, the barrel and the powder chamber were permanently joined together and the powder charge and the ball were loaded from the muzzle. The bombards fired stone shots and were used mainly as siege artillery. By the fifteenth century, the bombards, writes Robert Douglas Smith, were replaced by cast iron breech loaders.[100] Cast iron technology gave the West a decisive superiority over the Asian agrarian bureaucratic states.

The path-breaking work on Mughal gunpowder technology is done by Iqtidar Alam Khan, an exception among the Aligarh

School. Rather than the revenue system, his passion is military technology. Khan's piece in the *Social Scientist*, included in this compilation, notes the linkages between diffusion of gunpowder technology and formation of empires. Gunpowder reached India through several directions. The Bengal sultans during the sixteenth century got gunpowder technology from south China through Assam. Khan, in an article published in *Indian Historical Review* which is included in this volume, notes that the Mongols learnt the use of gunpowder from the Chinese during mid-thirteenth century and then the Mongol invaders introduced its use in north-west India in the same century. Under the Delhi Sultanate, gunpowder was used in pyrotechnic devices, i.e. *ban*s (rockets) rather than in artillery and firearms. Zahiruddin Babur (1526–30) refers to the use of *ban*s packed with sharpnel and a range of 1,000 yards by the Afghans in the Battle of Ghagra.

Khan develops his arguments in his monograph *Gunpowder and Firearms*[101] where he writes that during the fifteenth century, the artillery pieces were made of brass or bronze which being very costly could only be manufactured by the big states and not by the zamindars. The sixteenth century witnessed enormous advances especially as regards design and casting in the manufacture of heavy mortars. This was due to the expertise brought by Babur and contact with the Portuguese. The use of manual bellows was a constraint as regards improving the quality of casting. The *shutarnal* (light cannon fitted to a swivel on the back of a camel) which was also known as *zamburaks* came to India from West Asia at the beginning of the seventeenth century. The *shutarnal* was an instance of adoption of gunpowder technology within the paradigm of mounted combat. And mounted combat remained the core doctrine of Mughal warfare. However, it would be erroneous to believe that the Mughal *Padshah*s were oblivious of the rising importance of firearms in warfare. Between 1526 and 1595, the strength of the foot-musketeers in the Mughal service rose. Overall, there was one musketeer for every eight horsemen and in 1689, the ratio changed to one musketeer for five horsemen. Moreover, the musketeers, unlike the *mansabdar*s' cavalry force, were under direct control of the Mughal central government. Many musketeers were also mounted. In 1696, the Mughals had flintlock muskets but the problems of using such muskets from horseback prevented the flintlocks from becoming popular in the Mughal military establishment.

Some metallurgists argue for the continuous evolution of cannon technology in India from the medieval to the early modern era. In the sixteenth century, in eastern India, wrought iron cannons were made through the forge welding system. In addition, bronze and brass cannons were also manufactured.[102] Sher Shah Suri in the sixteenth century manufactured small mobile wrought iron cannons which were about 4–5 feet in length and with a muzzle diameter of 1–2 inches. R. Balasubramaniam claims that while Indians adopted the bronze casting technology from the Ottoman Turks, forge welded cannon technology was developed through contact with the West European powers. For casting large bronze cannons, Babur followed the practice of casting the powder chambers and the stone chambers separately. Then, these two chambers were joined together with the help of iron rings. Under Akbar, the Mughals mastered the practice of casting of fully complete bronze cannons. The European practice of casting a solid gun barrel and then boring out the central portion by drilling was adopted by the Indian powers during the eighteenth century. Tipu Sultan's military engineers used European type water powered boring machines.[103]

How far the evolution of gunpowder weapons shaped the military architecture in south India during the late medieval and early modern era is the subject of Deloche's article reprinted in this volume. By undertaking painstaking research of the architectural ruins of the old forts, Deloche extends and elaborates the argument of his article in a monograph on fortifications in India.[104] Forts like Bijapur had a curtain wall protected by long towers. A rectangular or circular solid isolated tower which was accessible by staircases was another characteristic feature of the Deccani forts. An important innovation in fortress architecture in response to the threat posed by the siege guns was the emergence of the cavaliers (platforms used as a support for the cannons) which were either circular, rectangular, or square, or polygonal in shape. On the cavalier, a large paved stone platform was constructed and in its centre was a circular socket for holding the pivot of the gun. Towards the back of the gun, a recoil wall was constructed for absorbing the recoil of the gun and to prevent strain on the pivot while firing. The cavaliers came into existence between sixteenth and eighteenth centuries and provided flanking fire. For the period mentioned above, the besiegers used only spherical stone balls and not the more lethal iron balls against the forts. Stone cannon balls bounced over the wall without making any substantial damage. Moreover, the siege guns were so heavy that they were virtually immovable. Since gunpowder artillery was not that efficient in India, the Indian military engineers did not go for the *trace italienne* sort of architecture. Rather than artillery, bribery and treachery, claims Deloche were the principal instruments in Indian siege warfare. Here, we are back to Irvine's conclusion.[105]

Let us have a flashback to Europe. Siena, the premier Italian state, modified the forts according to the new architectural principles which emerged in Renaissance Europe. However, the forts of the Sienese state fell to the Spanish Army of Charles V during the first half of the sixteenth century. Rather than storming, the Spanish, in pre-colonial Indian style blockaded the forts, and the garrisons, facing starvation, surrendered.[106] Further, *trace italienne* sort of fortification was also absent in East Europe.[107]

As far as South Asian land warfare during the eighteenth century and the first half of the nineteenth century was concerned, there was no MR. Cavalry, which became unimportant in early modern Europe, remained important in the Indian battlefields.[108] However, we cannot speak of Military Evolution either because between *c.*1740 and 1849, warfare in South Asia was radically transformed. Rather, as Kaushik Roy in his article reprinted here argues, the EIC emerged supreme because it was able to integrate both Western techniques of warfare with traditional elements of warmaking in South Asia. This balanced synthesis of Indian and Western elements of warfare is termed as Military Synthesis. This formula of balancing Western military techniques with indigenous elements of warfare enabled the EIC, I argue (in another of my article reprinted in this volume) to overwhelm the rebel personnel of the Bengal Army during 1857–8.

The case for an RNA in the Indian Ocean during the late medieval and early modern era is more sustainable. Let us look at the evolution of navies in West Europe. At the beginning of the

Hundred Years War (1337–1453), the sea-going vessels of West Europe were clinker-built. The hulls were formed from shells of overlapping plan, built up from the keel and fastened at the edges. The nails which secured the planks were driven in from the outside and on the inner face of each plank they were hammered flat or riveted. The forecastle at the bow and the after castle at the stern had originated during the twelfth century. The Mediterranean shipbuilders used the skeleton construction. It involved constructing a skeleton of heavy frames on which the planks were fastened with iron nails. The skeleton construction was adopted by West European shipbuilders during the late fifteenth century. During the Hundred Years War, the English crews on the ships fought with longbows and the French naval crews depended on crossbows. The medieval naval battles were decided by boarding actions of the crews as the ships (each weighing generally between 200 to 250 tonnes) grappled with each other. Guns became dominant in West European naval battles from the mid-fifteenth century.[109] From 1500 onwards, naval artillery was used for bombarding coastal fortifications as well as an anti-personnel device rather than for sinking ships. The trend from the mid-fifteenth century was the naval gun becoming larger. These guns were loaded with ball and powder from the rear and these guns had removable chambers which were interchangeable between all similarly sized guns. Initially, a swivel was added to the base of the gun and then it was mounted on the side of the hull or castle and in the case of a galley, on the bow or the stern. This gunpowder weapon, known as a port piece, remained the standard till the early seventeenth century. The advent of the gunports resulted in changes in the construction of ships. Clinker-built ships could not take the strain of added gundecks and it also resulted in the replacement of galley with its limited capability of housing guns. The gunport finally led to the broadside revolution.[110]

Anirudh Deshpande, in an article reprinted in this volume, asserts that as far as naval warfare between 1650 and 1800 in the west coast of India was concerned, rather than the naval technologies associated with the MR, geography, local politics, forts and finance determined the naval outcome. He writes that the Arab *dhows* were successful in the coastal areas. The Maratha Navy under Angria was destroyed in the second half of the eighteenth century due to the British divide and rule policy which pitted the Maratha central government against Angria.

At present, US aircraft carriers and submarines with nuclear power plants and equipped with nuclear missiles cannot operate properly in shallow water like the Palk Strait or the Red Sea. But, no strategist would argue that US Navy does not enjoy global maritime supremacy. After all, naval supremacy means power projection over long distances. It was the Portuguese and the British who were fighting in the coastal waters of South Asia and not the Marathas, Mysore and King Zamorin fighting in the Atlantic against the British and French men of war. From the sixteenth century onwards, the high sea fleet has never been suited for coastal control. For establishing control in the coastal regions, low technology crafts and specialized tactics were necessary. Deshpande rightly says that Angria had better intelligence. Even in the era of satellite imagery, the US Navy requests the Indian Navy to pass on data regarding hydrographic affairs when the former's craft operate in the central region of the Indian Ocean. However, no sane person would argue that the Indian Navy is stronger against the US Navy or in a naval encounter the Indian Navy would emerge victorious. Similarly, it would be erroneous even to imply that the Maratha Navy had any chance of holding its own against the might of the Royal Navy. Deshpande could at best argue that the British had trouble in establishing coastal supremacy but that does not dent the fact that the Asian states had lost control over the maritime highways of the world's oceans long ago. In the naval encounters, the South Asian grabs, gallivats and the ketches, though some of them weighed 300 tons, were no matches against the firepower of the frigates and the West European battleships. The Indian navies stuck to the medieval doctrine of boarding actions rather than exchange of gunfire in the high ocean. Lastly, historians often suggest that the British divide and rule policy accelerated the destruction of the Indian powers. The divide and rule policy was also followed by the Indian powers against the Western powers. Nana Phadnis, Haidar Ali and Tipu Sultan continuously played off the French against the British. But, the point to be remembered is that the British divide and rule policy was successful because it was backed by robust military power which in turn was sustained by a strong state with a stable political economy. The British divide and rule policy definitely aided the emergence of *Pax Brittannica* in Afro-Asia.

The rise of Portuguese naval power east of Africa resulted in the trade in the Indian Ocean passing from Arab to Portuguese hands. The Mughal Empire had no ocean-going navy. However, the Portuguese faced a sort of maritime challenge from some of the minor states of south India. Before analysing the navies of those south Indian powers, let us have a glance at the structure of the Portuguese Navy. Vitor Luis Gaspar Rodrigues' essay, reprinted in this volume, argues that better ships and naval artillery enabled the Portuguese to defeat the Mamluks and the Ottomans and dominate the Red Sea route. The Portuguese ships were able to sail even in winter. The Portuguese craft had an edge in building techniques as well as in the materials used. From the mid-sixteenth century, the Portuguese Navy in India underwent a process of demodernization. Rather than depending on battleships equipped with artillery, the Portuguese started to depend more on the Mediterranean galleys. This was partly because at that time there was no hostile navy threatening the Portuguese and also for the fact that Portugal was facing political and financial crisis. As a result, the Portuguese Navy became a easy prey to the Dutch and then the British navies.

Though the Portuguese Navy was inferior to the British and French navies, still it proved superior to the navies of the South Asian powers. The ships of the Kunhali Marakkars which fought the Portuguese were constructed without iron nails.[111] During the engagement with the Indian ships off the coast of Calicut in 1501, Vasco Da Gama deliberately aimed his gunpowder weapons below the waterlines of the opposing ships, sinking three of them in the first 10 salvos he fired.[112]

Among the post-Mughal polities, three powers—Mysore, the Maratha Confederacy, and the Khalsa Kingdom offered stiff resistance to British imperialism. Of these three powers, the first and second one attempted to maintain navies. But these navies were brown or green water navies and hence no match for the blue water navy of the British. The piece on Haidar Ali's fleet in this volume by Surendranath Sen shows that the Mysore strongman wanted to build a navy to challenge the British naval dominance but failed. After the conquest of the Malabar coast, Haidar started thinking of constructing a navy. For constructing the fleet, Haidar was dependent on foreign personnel. In 1764, Haidar hired an Englishman for constructing grabs and gallivats. However, Haidar did not trust him and he put a Muslim cavalry officer in charge of the fleet. This alienated the English mercenary. In 1768, the Bombay Government sent an amphibious expedition to destroy Haidar's fleet at Onore. Then, the English mercenary in charge of Haidar's fleet deserted. In 1778, Haidar employed Joze Azelars, a shipwright in the service of Dutch East India Company, for strengthening the harbour of Bhatkal. Haidar had eight three-masted ships and each of them carried between 28 to 40 guns. In December 1780, Edward Hughes destroyed the grabs and ketches of Haidar at Mangalore.

Sen asserts that the Gaikwads of Baroda maintained a fleet which cruised around Surat and levied contributions from merchant vessels belonging to all the nationalities. In 1749, Appaji Pandit, the Gaikwad admiral, with several ketches, pals, grabs, and gallivats boarded British vessels. In December 1751, while attacking a Portuguese convoy near Surat, Appaji died. Sen writes that though the European sources portray Appaji as a pirate, he was actually trying to establish Gaikwads' sovereignty over the coastal regions of Gujarat. Like the European companies, Appaji also forced the foreign vessels to buy permits issued by him. Those ships which lacked such permits were boarded.[113] This concept of establishing a ruler's sovereignty over the coastal waters was a new development which occurred in early modern India but was absent in medieval India. The crucial integer in this development was close encounters between the European navies and the Indian potentates' ships from Vasco Da Gama's time onwards.

Whether one accepts the concept of MR or not, in general the historians and the political scientists are unanimous that modern warfare was introduced in South Asia by the British during the eighteenth century. The chief feature of modern warfare is that such warfare is conducted by a standing army administered by a centralized bureaucracy and commanded by a professional hierarchical officer corps. The postcolonial armies of India and

Pakistan are in many ways products of the colonial legacy.[114] Though the Indian Army remains apolitical, several scholars opine that frequent deployments in aid to civil power and dependence on a narrow ethnic segment for recruitment might spell trouble for the Indian Army in the near future.[115] The degeneration of the British-induced professionalism in the Pakistan Army, we are told, resulted in the intrusion of military into politics.

Daljit and Katherine Singh's joint article in this collection throws light on this issue. In 1947, the military force of the Raj was divided on a 3:1 ratio between India and Pakistan. Due to a dearth of commissioned officers, 500 British officers were offered service in the Pakistan Army. Only in 1951, the post of commander-in-chief was occupied by a Pakistani named Ayub Khan. The 1,50,000 strong Pakistan Army continued to recruit from the traditional recruiting grounds in Punjab and the North-West Frontier Province. In 1956, a 2 per cent quota was fixed for the East Pakistanis. This was because like the British officers, the Pakistani military officers believed that the Bengalis were not martial. The failure of the Pakistan Army to integrate the East Pakistanis was one of the principal causes behind the rise of secessionist movement in East Pakistan. Pakistan continued the colonial system of making the commander-in-chief of the army the defence minister with a berth in the cabinet. Thus, the army was allowed to intrude into the political system. While the Pakistan Army's political power continued to increase, the Indian Army came under the jackboots of the *babu*s due to administrative reorganization. Thus, we see both tradition and transition in the armed forces in the postcolonial era.

The recent RMA concept put forward the view that rapid advance in precision weapons, surveillance satellites, and computer-based information processing has revolutionized warfare. The presence of precision guided munitions has transformed C3 (command, control, and communications) into C4I (command, control, communication, computers, and information). The speed, memory capacity, and networking capability of the computer are the crucial components of RMA. Hence, many dub the new system as the IT-RMA. The role of information superhighways, sensor technology, automated control systems and weapons based on particle beams and lasers in directing battles has also transformed RSTA (reconnaissance, surveillance, targeting and acquisition).

The weapons platforms are now operating within the time cycle of nanoseconds. This revolution is well-represented, claim the proponents of the RMA, in the use of high technology weapons by the US during the 1991 Gulf War.[116] While the proponents of the MR thesis (for example, John Lynn,[117] John Stone,[118] and others who are mostly historians) emphasize on the broader social and economic aspects, the doctrinaires of the RMA (who are mostly political scientists and serving as well as retired military officers) follow a more narrow approach and overemphasize the role of raw technology.

The Indian Air Force officers are especially enamoured with the US-led concept of a RMA centred round information technology. Squadron Leader P. M. Sinha's short essay included in this collection asserts that a transition has occurred from the Industrial Age to the Information Age. One finds here the influence of the Tofflers' 'wave theory'.[119] Warfare has been revolutionized in the Information Age and the new war would be dominated by the use of air power. The term 'aerospace war' is becoming current in the military jargons. Information superiority would depend on the use of the latest communication technologies and the new form of airpower would be represented not by fighters, fighter bombers, and bombers manned by humans, but by unmanned combat aerial vehicles controlled by robots with the aid of high speed fibre optic and satellite communication links. One is reminded of George Lucas' Star War trilogy here.

India's acquisition of nuclear power towards the end of the twentieth century might be construed as a complete break with the colonial past, at least in terms of technology. However, in certain non-technological matters related with nuclearization, one finds traces of continuity. Matin Zuberi's article in this volume traces the contours of India's nuclear doctrine which is still evolving and touches upon the above-mentioned issues. First, a country acquires nuclear weapons and then it initiates a nuclear doctrine. Occasionally, inter-service rivalries shape the evolution of doctrine. Zuberi asserts that nuclear weapons are political tools for averting nuclear blackmail and coercion and not war fighting tools for waging and winning nuclear wars. Tactical nuclear weapons, which the NATO (North Atlantic Treaty Organization) maintains, are not part of India's nuclear arsenal and doctrine. India's nuclear doctrine emphasizes 'no first use'. This posture facilitates tight civilian control. Civilian supremacy of the politicians over the military is a fact which India inherited from the Raj. No first use doctrine in turn requires a robust C3I system which will be able to absorb a first strike by a nuclear power and then launch a devastating counter-blow. However, the counter-blow by India need not be as devastating as the MAD (Mutually Assured Destruction) doctrine of USA during the height of the Cold War. What India needs is a credible minimum nuclear deterrent-retaliatory capacity based on a triad (land, sea, and airpower) supported by space-based communications and intelligence systems.

Elements of discontinuity are also present in other aspects of the nuclear programme. The National Security Advisory Board has been set up to provide the government with advice regarding grand strategy. However, instead of the experts dominating the body, the ex-bureaucrats dominate this body. D. Shyam Babu writes that civilian supremacy in post-1947 India has degenerated into civil servants' supremacy.[120]

Most political scientists like Shyam Babu, Zuberi and others attempt to interpret the nuclear programmes of India and Pakistan in realist terms. However, Stephen P. Cohen claims that Pakistan's nuclear doctrine is shaped by Islamic ideology. The clergy and the politicians of Pakistan have repeatedly claimed that Pakistan possesses an Islamic bomb. Moreover, the officer corps are no more secular. From Zia-ul-Haq's time onwards, the Pakistan Army's officers are imbued with a high dose of Islamic theology. Cohen claims that Pakistan's concept of massive nuclear retaliation to inspire fear among its opponents is not based on Western deterrence theories but on the Islamic precept of inspiring fear and awe in the heart of the *kafirs*.[121] An attempt to interpret India's nuclear programme through the lens of aggressive Classical Hinduism is attempted by Bharat Karnad.[122]

Unconventional War: New War or Old Wine in New Bottle

A group of scholars like Martin Van Creveld, Mary Kaldor, Rupert Smith, Herfried Munkler, etc., are arguing that the post-Cold War era is witnessing a new generation of warfare. Instead of interstate war, the global military landscape will be dominated by intrastate warfare. Smith introduces the term 'war amongst the people'. In case of such intrastate warfare (also termed asymmetric warfare) characterized by de-territorialized and non-state forms of violence, the nuclear forces and the conventional armies will be sitting ducks. Instead of great power rivalry, the New War is the product of breakdown of the USSR and subsequent globalization and is characterized by the degeneration of states and the rise of privatized violence. Weak states have resulted in the government forces losing monopoly of violence and the rise of private gangs and warlords. The targets of such irregulars are the civilian population and the non-military infrastructure.[123]

In contrast, two British military historians, Hew Strachan and Ian F. W. Beckett, rightly argue that there is nothing much new in the post-1990 New War. Strachan writes: 'Today's wars are being fought for very traditional reasons—for religious faith, political ideology, nationalism, and ethnic identity. Moreover they are being waged in parts of the world where armed conflict and political instability have been endemic for decades.'[124] Let us have a flashback on the evolution of theory and praxis of unconventional warfare from a global perspective.

Modern revolutionary guerrilla warfare, writes Beckett, might be termed as insurgency.[125] Unlike the guerrillas, the terrorists, writes Beckett, are not interested or capable of taking over the state apparatus but use violence in an indiscriminate manner.[126] Guerrilla warfare is conducted by small bands of irregulars equipped with light weapons. Rather than set-piece battles, guerrillas focused on hit-and-run expeditions and ambushes. Instead of the enemy army, their lines of communication are the obvious choice of the guerrillas. During the first half of the nineteenth century, the French theoretician Baron Jomini advocated national/popular uprising supported by a nucleus of professional troops against the invading/occupying power. The Italian radical Carlo Bianco in 1828–9 established a linkage between guerrilla warfare and radical politics. Sustained guerrilla warfare, he argued, would develop over time into a true people's war involving all sections of the society. In the later stages of the war, flying columns and then a regular army would be formed when guerrilla warfare would be transformed into regular warfare. T. E. Lawrence, the British Army officer of the First World War who raised a Arab guerrilla force against the Ottoman Turks, stressed the political aspects of guerrilla warfare and considered that only one-third of guerrilla warfare comprises the military dimension. The Chinese theoretician Mao-Tse Tung noted that without the people's support, guerrilla warfare would fail. However, for Mao, guerrilla forces have to transform themselves into a regular army for capturing the state structure. The transition from guerrilla warfare into regular warfare is known as the stage of mobile warfare.[127] Che Guevera theorized that an insurrection in itself could create the necessary conditions for a revolution without the necessity of a prolonged ground work by the guerrillas. Such an insurrection could be organized by a small group of dedicated guerrillas who would constitute the *foco* (focus). Unlike Mao, Guevera is oblivious of the decade long political work among the rural mass before launching the guerrilla struggle against the government. The assumption is that the governmental force's inability to crush the mobile elusive guerrillas would force it into overreaction against the population and in the long run it would alienate the populace from the government. The *foco* would thus function as a catalyst for the wider popular insurrection.[128]

Most of the guerrillas, being from the urban educated middle class, could not integrate themselves properly with the ruralites. Then, increasing urbanization resulted in the theory of the countryside encircling the cities which emerged in rural China between the 1920s and the 1940s, as becoming outdated. Rather, the cities being centres of political, economic, and military power are assaulted by the guerrillas. Further, urban attacks generate greater media publicity for the guerillas and expose government imbecility. Hence, urban guerrilla operations emerged as an option among the Latin American theorists (like Carlos Marighela) in the 1960s.[129]

In 1811, the occupying French forces faced guerrilla warfare in Calabria in the Kingdom of Naples. Religious fanaticism rather than nationalism fuelled resistance against the French. The Catholic clergy provided ideological support to the guerrillas and the monasteries gave refuge to the guerrillas. In Spain, it was the depredations of the French Army which turned the local populace against the French and provided support to the guerrillas. Further, the Spanish guerrillas could not have survived without the logistical support provided by Britain and operations of the British Army under Wellington, which distracted the French Army from focusing on the counter-insurgency operation.[130]

Jagadish Narayan Sarkar, in his piece on guerrilla warfare in medieval India which is reprinted in this volume, provides conceptual and empirical details as regards unconventional warfare in pre-modern India. He claims that guerrilla war/irregular war/small war differs from conventional or regular war in concept, organization, armament, logistics, strategy, tactics and command. Guerrilla war did not start with the communist revolutionary warfare during the 1940s. Following Mao, J. N. Sarkar asserts that guerrilla warfare is a weapon of the weak. And to be successful, guerrillas require popular support. J. N. Sarkar continues that the guerrilla warfare under Shivaji during the second half of the seventeenth century and the irregular war conducted by the Sikhs during the first half of the eighteenth century were successful because the peasants of Maharashtra and Punjab supported the guerrillas against the Mughals. In fact, the theoretical principles of small war could be traced back to *Sukranitisara* which says that the guerrillas should cut the provisions of the occupying power and such wars are going to be attritional. Unlike Clausewitz's concentration of forces for eliminating the enemy's *schwerpunkt* (centre of gravity which happened to be its army), the effectiveness of guerrilla warfare depends not on the concentration of forces but rather on the dispersal of forces. Effective guerrilla warfare has to be mobile and gradually develop into regular warfare for the final destruction of the enemy. Shivaji's light cavalry avoided pitched battles and was able to cover 50 miles every day. Their primary objective was to cut the Mughal's supply lines. After the end of the campaigning season, the Maratha cavalry bands dispersed to their homes and again concentrated during emergencies. Under Baji Rao I, the Marathas made a transition from guerrilla warfare to regular warfare.

The Ahom guerrillas, during 1661–3, raided the enemy camps during night but never met the Mughals head on under Mir Jumla. After Mir Jumla's failure in Assam, the Mughals launched another expedition. J. N. Sarkar in an article included in this collection, shows that the Ahoms defeated the amphibious Mughal expedition between 1668–71 through a combination of regular and irregular warfare. In 1667, Aurangzeb ordered Ram Singh to advance into Assam and capture Kamrup and Gauhati. In 1668, with about 20,000 cavalry, 15,000 archers, 500 artillerymen and 40 ships, Ram Singh advanced. The Ahoms realized that their *paik*s (infantry) would be defeated in a land battle with the heavy Mughal cavalry. Hence, under the supervision of their general, Lachit Barphukan, the Ahoms initiated the policy of strategic retreat and lured the Mughals deep into Assam. The Mughal camps and communication lines were subjected to sudden night attacks and ambushes. The Ahom term for such small war was *daga yuddha*. The Ahoms conducted hit-and-run tactics against the scattered Mughal detachments by issuing out from the large number of small forts constructed at the top of the mountains. These mountains were so narrow that the Mughal guns could not be dragged at the top of these hills for breaching the walls of these forts. Continuous attrition plus heavy rainfall weakened and demoralized the Mughal Army by the time they reached the outskirts of Gauhati in the beginning of 1671. Then, the Ahoms passed from strategic defence to strategic offence and guerrilla warfare strategy was replaced by regular war strategy. In March 1671, the Ahoms made a sudden naval attack and destroyed the Mughal *nawarra* (river flotilla). The Mughals had no option but to retreat. Till they reached the border of Bengal, the retreating Mughals were subjected to continuous depredation, by the victorious Ahoms.

From the very beginning of the British rule in India, the British Indian Army was repeatedly deployed in pacification duties. Lorenzo M. Crowell in an article narrates the Madras Army's pacification duties in the Madras Presidency.[131] British India conducted continuous 'Butcher and Bolt' expeditions against the Indus tribes. Alan Warren, an Australian historian and T. R. Moreman, a British historian note the failure of the British Indian Army to pacify the trans-Indus region between 1860 and 1947. Equipped with low technology weapons, the *lashkar*s (tribal war bands) proved more than equal against the capital intensive army of the Raj. Armoured cars, artillery and heavy machine guns did not provide victory to the soldiers of the Raj. The rugged terrain and the tribal network sustained the insurgency. Islam and the *mullahs* were crucial players in motivating the insurgents to fight the *kafirs*.[132]

From the Raj, the Indian Republic inherited insurgencies both in the north-east and north-west parts of the subcontinent. L. Kanchan's piece in this volume turns the spotlight on Nagaland. The objective of the National Socialist Council of Nagaland-Isak Muviah (NSCN-IM) is the establishment of a *Nagalim* (Greater Nagaland) comprising all the Naga inhabited areas of the neighbouring states like Assam, Manipur, Arunachal Pradesh and some parts of Myanmar. In Shillong, many of the NSCN-IM's sympathizers are enrolled and for training they move into Bangladesh. Even guerrillas require money for functioning. Besides the NSCN-IM, the National Socialist Council of Nagaland-Khaplang collect taxes from the government employees and the trading community. The guerrilla outfits also derive money from the narcotics trade in the Golden Triangle, which comprises the rainforest area in Laos, Thailand and Myanmar. The money obtained from the narcotics trade is used for buying arms and paying the cadres.

India also had to tackle the insurgents in Sri Lanka when the Indian Peace Keeping Force (IPKF) in 1987 was sent to fight the Liberation Tigers of Tamil *Ealam* (hereafter LTTE). The IPKF was withdrawn in 1990. Lieutenant-General Depinder Singh, who was the General Officer in charge of south India and Overall Force Commander IPKF, in his memoir describes the Indian Army's confrontation with the LTTE. One chapter from his memoir is included in this compilation to give the readers an idea about how the senior echelon of the Indian Army perceived combat with the guerrillas in Sri Lanka. Singh is candid that an insurgency cannot be tackled only by military means. It requires a political solution. Military pressure should be applied for pushing the insurgents towards the negotiating table. Simultaneously, the hearts and minds of the populace in the disturbed areas have to be won to cut off popular support to the guerrillas. He emphasizes the role of public relations and psychological warfare. And this sort of warfare involves launching of TV and radio programmes. He also argues for a more positive interaction with the press for winning the support of the domestic society against the insurgents. It is a long-term policy and hence counter-insurgency is going to be an attritional campaign. The LTTE cadres were highly motivated and used cyanide capsules to avoid capture. The LTTE acquired arms from Singapore and received financial aid from Tamil Nadu. The LTTE had trained scuba drivers who could damage ships in the harbour. In fact, the Indian Navy had taught the LTTE cadres this skill earlier. As regards the military aspects of the counter-insurgency operation, Singh tells us that the Indian Army's experience of fighting the Naga guerrillas since 1956 confirmed that small unit patrol under junior leadership was most effective.

The retired Colonel Gautam Das and M. K. Gupta Ray in their monograph dealing with the IPKF put the onus on the civilian intelligence agencies of the India government for misinforming India's strategic managers as regards the strength and objective of the LTTE. Close cooperation between the Indian Navy, Indian Air Force and the Indian Army was absent. Needless to say, no joint task force commander was ever appointed. Further, the infantry units of the IPFK were not only under strength but also lacked adequate amount of communication equipment. Despite all these shortcomings, the Indian Army performed quite well. During the Jaffna Operation of October 1987, the Indian Army used minimum force to reduce collateral damage to the Tamil civilians. In accordance with this philosophy, airpower, artillery and tanks for fire support were not used. It is to be noticed that one of the features of a successful counter-insurgency operation is the minimum force philosophy to prevent the populace of the disturbed zone from joining the guerrillas. Following Smith, for the war against LTTE, one could apply the term of war amongst people. The LTTE cadres dressed in *lungi* like the Tamil civilians fought amongst them, using the civilians as a human shield. Though Jaffna fell, the war did not cease and the IPKF was hamstrung by the LTTE's hit and run attacks and sudden ambushes. The two authors note: 'But fighting against militancy is like fighting against an unseen ghost.'[133]

From the dawn of history, Afghanistan has been characterized by fighting between various tribal factions. In case of any great power intervention, whether it was Alexander's Greeks, the Mughals, the British in the nineteenth century, USSR towards the end of the twentieth century, and finally USA in the beginning of the new millennium, the Afghan tribes had proved to be a hard nut to crack. Bhashyam Kasturi's article included in this collection throws light on the US-led counter-insurgency operation against the Taliban. To a great extent, writes Kasturi, the Gulf War and Bosnian War shaped Operation Enduring Freedom. The US started the war against terrorism in Afghanistan with air and cruise missile strikes. Use of joint direct attack munitions supplemented by Tomahawk land attack cruise missiles gave the war the characteristic of being a techno-savvy operation. Use of air power was the dominant feature of American military operation. Pinpoint air strikes first destroyed the military infrastructure of Taliban and then aided the ground actions of the special operation teams which hunted for the higher echelons of the *Al-Qaida* leadership. Due to continuous air-to-ground strikes, the forces of the Northern Alliance were able to rout the retreating Taliban. However, warns Kasturi, air power is not the panacea for all problems related with counter-insurgency operations. Large-scale deployment of ground troops is required and the US is eager to avoid it. Obviously, US domestic society would not accept large number of body bags returning as was the case in Vietnam in the late 1960s. Hence, not only the top leaders of Taliban are still roaming around but also the Taliban forces are still alive and kicking.

Unlike Afghanistan and Kashmir, Nepal in recent times experienced an armed communist insurrection. The Maoists, under the Communist Party of Nepal (CPN-M), have been waging an insurgency since 1996. Fahmida Ashraf's article analyses the roots behind the Maoists insurgency. The CPN-M's objective is to establish a people's government through, people's war. The failure of the political parties to give good governance and initiate economic upliftment of the poor gave rise to the insurgency. Nepal is the second poorest country in the world with 71 per cent of the population below the absolute poverty level. The landless peasants and the women are supporting the Maoists because they are advocating distribution of the landed estates of the landlords among the landless and equal rights for women in property, etc. Due to the insurgency between 1996 and 2001, about 4,000 people have died. For waging a people's war, the Maoists acquired arms by looting from the police and through the black market in Bihar. After an attack on the camp of the Royal Nepal Army on 26 November 2001, the army was deployed against the Maoists.

The latest theory in the field of unconventional warfare is the concept of Fourth Generation (hereafter 4G) Warfare, first propounded in 1989. This theory is built on the thought of late American officer John Boyd. 4G Warfare is USA's response to the rise of insurgencies after the collapse of the USSR. Interestingly, the 4G Warfare concept, instead of focusing only on technology (as is the case with the RMA theorists), also takes into account social, cultural and political factors. The 4G War depends on the small mobile teams with decentralized command system and rudimentary logistics conducting manoeuvre operations. The principal aim is not the physical destruction of the insurgents (who are bound to be scattered and decentralized) but psychological destruction of such groupings. The key to victory is the OODA loop (observe, orient, decide and act faster than the enemy). The counter-insurgent forces have to take into account the local fluctuating political situation and cultural factors to isolate the insurgents who then like a closed system will face a system collapse.[134] In history writing, all the concepts first emerge in the West and then it takes some time to diffuse in the academic circuits of the non-Western regions. Such developments could be explained with the time lag theory. The 4G Warfare concept is yet to make its mark in the South Asian military landscape.

The Future of South Asia's Military History

The literate public of India outside the discipline of history are interested in semi-academic military literature dealing with European affairs rather than with Indian military history. In general, Erwin Rommel's *panzer blitzkrieg* in North Africa is well-known compared to General Zorawar Singh's expedition to Tibet. Normandy and Stalingrad attract the Indian reading public more than the activities of Indian soldiers in Arakan during 1943–4 or the clash of Indian and Pakistani armour at Khem Karan in 1965. Hence, Indian publishers are not much interested in publishing semi-academic military history.

Overall, military history does not touch the emotional chords of ordinary Indian people because in comparison to Europe, USA and China, very few people have actually died due to warfare in India in the last 300 years. During World War I, the casualties of the one million strong Indian Army were only 1,21,600. Much more people died due to the influenza epidemic during 1918–9.[135] In contrast, Britain experienced the phenomenon of 'lost generation' due to the casualties of trench warfare in the Western front. Two examples will suffice. On 1 July 1916, on the first day of the Battle of Somme, the British Expeditionary Force suffered 57,470 casualties.[136] During the autumn of 1917, the wastage rate of the British Army in north France and Flanders numbered to 76,000 men per month.[137] While only 30,000 Indian soldiers died (total casualties including missing, prisoners of war, etc., numbered to 1,65,000 men) during World War II, about 3 million people died due to the Bengal famine.[138] Britain, with a much smaller population compared to India, lost some 4,85,000 soldiers during World War II.[139]

Towards the end of the twentieth century, several policy institutes came into existence in Delhi. However, the thrust of research in these institutes are on terrorism, insurgencies and counter-insurgencies rather than on military history. The research programmes of these institutes are understandable. Given the fact that these institutes are heavily dependent on government funding, the strategic managers of the Indian Republic are more interested in the origins of Kashmiri and Naga terrorism and probable policy implications about how to handle these insurgencies, rather than in the tactics and strategies of Aurangzeb's campaigns in the Deccan. A strategic institute like IDSA (Institute for Defence Studies and Analysis), following the ahistorical approach, favours international relations experts working on current militaries rather than on the dynamics of military power five centuries ago. The topics on which research grants are given are whether the Indian Army could advance 10 miles into Pakistani territory in case of a large-scale insurgent action in Kashmir sponsored by the Inter-Services Intelligence of Pakistan or whether the Indian Air Force is capable of delivering nukes, etc., rather than the evolution of siege technology under the Delhi Sultanate or the logistics of the British Indian Army in the north-west frontier during the late nineteenth century.

The future scenario of academic military history in India is bleak. None of the famous universities of India has any chair on military history. One is reminded of Oxford University's chair on war history. Again, there is no war studies department in any of the top universities of South Asia like the War Studies Department of University of London. There is no particular centre in India which would keep fellows specializing in military history. Worse, if any postgraduate student shows interest in military history, he (for most of the cases) or she is bound to get rejected especially before the boards providing foreign scholarships for pursuing PhDs. The hot topics with an interdisciplinary stance which are favourites of the history 'bosses' are certainly no more agrarian history but exotic ones. Topics like sexual harassment of women by men in the workplace, the dietary and sexual activities of some half naked tribes on a particular new moon, theorizing the structure of language and power relations inherent in discourse of marginal groups, etc., are favoured by both students and the top academicians. Neither at the undergraduate level nor at the postgraduate level is there a single course on military history. This further discourages publishers from publishing works on military history. There is no prestigious publisher in India (excluding Lancer, Natraj, etc.) which specializes in military history. Nor any prestigious Indian publishing house, like Ashgate and Routledge, has any series on military history. Recently, Routledge India has started a series on modern warfare. Excluding the journals published by the retired military officers and military institutions, civilian historians of South Asia have shown no interest in running military history journals like the *Journal of Military History* (USA), *War in History* (UK) and *War and Society* (Australia).

It is interesting to note that none of the famous historians (Indian as well as foreign) working on South Asia are military historians. On exception is Stephen P. Cohen. However, he is known more among the strategic studies community rather than in the South Asian history academic circuit. To give some examples, C. Bayly is an economic and social historian. Partha Chatterjee has made his mark in social and cultural history. R. Thapar (for ancient India) and B. D. Chattopadhyay (for early modern India), Sumit Sarkar and Rajat Kanta Ray (for modern India) are famous as social historians. The fashionable Subaltern School has undergone a transition from studying economic history to social history and then cultural history in accordance with the shifts in the broad parameters of history writing. In the 1960s, the famous historians were more or less Marxist in orientation or studied economic history. The names which come to mind are D. D. Kosambi, B. N. Mukherjee, Irfan Habib, S. Nurul Hasan, Eric Stokes, etc. Bipan Chandra, Asin Dasgupta and Sabyasachi Bhattacharya continued the tradition of focusing on economic history in the 1970s and early 1980s. Before the 1940s, the political historians ruled the roost. Some of the big names are H. C. Raychaudhuri, Ramesh Chandra Majumdar, etc.

Under the encouragement of the Indian National Science Academy (hereafter INSA) located at New Delhi, several metallurgists are now analysing the technical aspects of pre-modern Indian cannons. Our knowledge about the metallic content of the barrel of such cannons, their bore diameter, charge required to fire the balls, etc., are bound to increase in the near future. However, such studies need to be integrated within the social, cultural and economic aspects of late medieval and early modern Indian history. Otherwise the valuable work of these scholars working under INSA's auspices would suffer the same neglect as the path-breaking work on ancient and medieval arms and armoury done by the late G. N. Pant.

Western domination is still shaping the writing and publishing of history in general and military history in particular. An individual (for mostly a European or an American) in a Western university or in a research organization would get funds for writing a world history of warfare, where India and China will get a cursory treatment.[140] The focus of such world histories remain Greece and Rome during the ancient period, France, Germany and Britain, for the Middle Age and the early modern age. The focus of such world military histories for the period starting from the mid-nineteenth century onwards is on USA, in addition to West Europe. Such world histories of warfare give a lot of space to the American Civil War but not to the Taipeng Rebellion of China, though the Taipeng Rebellion resulted in larger number of casualties. Western publishers readily accept such work. A Western publisher will never commission a Chinese, Japanese, or Bangladeshi for such a work. At best, such regional scholars/specialists will be asked to contribute particular chapters dealing with their regions in edited volumes. If an Indian or Pakistani historian attempts to write a world history in general or global military history in particular, such an attempt would raise a hollow laugh in the Western academic circuit. Even if such a work is written, no South Asian publisher will accept it, claiming that their distribution system is limited within the subcontinent.

Again, most of the theories circulating in the military history circuit are products of the European and American scholars who made case studies of some regions of Europe and then applied these theories globally. This is the case in general history writing also. Take, for instance, Parker's MR theory. After taking early modern West Europe as an ideal case, this model is applied to explain the *stasis* in military developments of other parts of the world from *c.*1700 onwards. Again, Mary Kaldor's New War concept is based on the case study of the breakdown of Yugoslavia in the 1990s. Now, we are told that the concept of New War can be applied to the broad spectrum of conflicts occurring from Afghanistan in the East up to Bosnia in the West. Non-western historians focusing on different regions of Afro-Asia have to engage with these theories to prove that they are also updating themselves with the latest theories in circulation. In the near future, the writing of world history will remain dominated by Westerners.

As regards military history, ancient India's military history is really in a bad shape. The last monograph to come out on ancient India's military history by a professional historian was in the 1960s. In recent times, some scholars like Brekke and the editor of this volume[141] are working on ancient Hindu military philosophy. For medieval history, to an extent, Ali Athar and Raziuddin Aquil with some modifications will continue the tradition of Iqtidar Alam Khan. From the 1990s, there have been some studies on the social histories of the British Indian Army. This trend will probably continue. To sum up, rather than the term class conflict, terms like phenomenology, homology, discourse, etc., have become more common in the histories generated by the top level of Indian academicia. This is because Marxism is down and out and postmodernism is in. However, postmodernism has only marginal influence in military history and only some historians dealing with modern South Asian military history are influenced by this ideology. With the decline of Marxism, along with economic history, studies dealing with economic impact of armies and warfare are on a downslide. Due to continuing insurgencies in Kashmir, north-east

India, and the rise of the Maoist threat, writings on state building and counter-insurgencies by retired military officers and political scientists will continue to increase in the near future. However, military history remains in limbo. This is despite the fact that till 1947, the army in the subcontinent was the largest government employer and consumed the biggest amount of the state's income.

NOTES

1. William Irvine, *The Army of the Indian Moghuls: Its Organization and Administration*, 1903; reprint, Delhi: Low Price Publications, 1994.
2. Jadunath Sarkar, *Military History of India*, 1960; reprint, Bombay: Orient Longman, 1970.
3. Edward Creasy, *The Fifteen Decisive Battles of the World*, n.d; reprint, London: Everyman's Library, 1963; Colonel G. B. Malleson, *The Decisive Battles of India from 1746 to 1849*, n.d; reprint, Jaipur: Aavishkar Publishers, 1986.
4. Jadunath Sarkar, *A Short History of Aurangzeb: 1618–1707*, 1930; reprint, New Delhi: Orient Longman, 1979.
5. R. C. Majumdar, H. C. Raychaudhuri and Kalikinkar Datta, *An Advanced History of India*, 1946; reprint, Madras: Macmillan, 1991.
6. D. N. Jha, *Ancient India in Historical Outline*, 1977; reprint, New Delhi: Manohar, 2003.
7. D. N. Jha, *Early India: A Concise History*, New Delhi: Manohar, 2004.
8. Romila Thapar, *The Penguin History of Early India from the Origins to AD 1300*, 2002; reprint, New Delhi: Penguin, 2003.
9. M. Athar Ali, 'The Islamic Background to Indian History: An Interpretation of the Islamic Past', in Ali, *Mughal India: Studies in Polity, Ideas, Society, and Culture*, New Delhi: Oxford University Press, 2006, p. 3.
10. Anirudh Deshpande, *British Military Policy in India, 1900-45: Colonial Constraints and Declining Power*, New Delhi: Manohar, 2005, pp. 21–2.
11. Emphasis in original. Deshpande, *British Military Policy in India*, p. 145.
12. Stephen Peter Rosen, 'Military Effectiveness: Why Society Matters', *International Security*, vol. 19, no. 4, 1995, pp. 5–31; Rosen, *Societies and Military Power: India and its Armies*, Delhi: Oxford University Press, 1996.
13. Stanislav Andreski, *Military Organization and Society*, 1954; reprint, Berkeley/Los Angeles: University of California Press, 1968.
14. Tarak Barkawi, 'Peoples, Homelands, and Wars? Ethnicity, the Military, and Battle among British Imperial Forces in the War against Japan', *Comparative Studies in Society and History* (hereafter *CSSH*), vol. 46, no. 1 (2004), pp. 134-63.

15. David Omissi, '"Martial Races": Ethnicity and Security in Colonial India, 1858-1939', *War & Society*, vol. 9, no. 1, 1991, pp. 1–27; Omissi, *The Sepoy and the Raj: The Indian Army, 1860–1940*, Houndmills, Basingstoke: Macmillan, 1994.
16. Arthur N. Gilbert, 'Recruitment and Reform in the East India Company Army, 1760–1800', *Journal of British Studies*, vol. 15, 1975, pp. 89–111.
17. Philip Mason, *A Matter of Honour: An Account of the Indian Army, Its Officers and Men*, n.d.; reprint, Dehradun: EBD Educational Pvt. Ltd, 1988.
18. James W. Hoover, *Men without Hats: Dialogue, Discipline and Discontent in the Madras Army, 1806-1807*, New Delhi: Manohar, 2007.
19. Seema Alavi, *The Sepoys and the Company: Tradition and Transition in Northern India, 1770–1830*, New Delhi: Oxford University Press, 1995.
20. Amiya Barat, *The Bengal Native Infantry: Its Organization and Discipline, 1796–1852*, Calcutta: Firma KLM, 1962.
21. Peter Stanley, '"Dear Comrades": Barrack Room Culture and the "White Mutiny" of 1859–60', *Indo-British Review*, vol. 21, no. 2, 1996, pp. 165–75; Stanley, *White Mutiny: British Military Culture in India, 1825-75*, London: C. Hurst, 1998.
22. DeWitt C. Ellinwood, 'The Indian Soldier, the Indian Army, and Change, 1914-18', in Ellinwood and S. D. Pradhan (eds), *India and World War I*, New Delhi: Manohar, 1978, pp. 177–211.
23. See also Razit Mazumder's 'Military Imperatives and the Expansion of Agriculture in Colonial Punjab', *International Journal of Punjab Studies*, vol. 8, no. 2, 2001, pp. 157–85.
24. Clive Dewey, 'Some Consequences of Military Expenditure in British India: The Case of the Upper Sind Sagar Doab, 1849–1947', in Dewey (ed.), *Arrested Development in India: The Historical Dimension*, New Delhi: Manohar, 1988, pp. 93–159.
25. Tarak Barkawi, 'Culture and Combat in the Colonies: The Indian Army in the Second World War', *Journal of Contemporary History*, vol. 4, no. 2, 2006, pp. 325–55.
26. Chandar S. Sundaram, 'Soldier Disaffection and the Creation of the Indian National Army', *Indo-British Review*, vol. 18, no. 1, 1990, pp. 155–62.
27. Deshpande, *British Military Policy in India*, pp. 33–4, 200–1.
28. Tan Tai Yong, 'Maintaining the Military Districts: Civil-Military Integration and District Soldiers' Boards in the Punjab, 1919-39', *Modern Asian Studies* (hereafter *MAS*), vol. 28, no. 4, 1994, pp. 833–74; Yong, *The Garrison State: The Military, Government and Society in Colonial Punjab, 1849–1947*, New Delhi: Sage Publications, 2005.
29. Sanjoy Bhattacharya, 'British Military Information Management Techniques and the South Asian Soldier: Eastern India during the Second World War', *MAS*, vol. 34, no. 2, 2000, pp. 483–510; Bhattacharya,

Propaganda and Information in Eastern India, 1939-45: A Necessary Weapon of War, Richmond, Surrey: Curzon, 2001.

30. D. D. Kosambi, *The Culture and Civilization of Ancient India in Historical Outline*, n.d.; reprint, New Delhi: Vikas, 2001.
31. B. N. Mukherjee, The *Economic Factors in Kushana History*, 1970; reprint, Kolkata: Progressive Publishers, 2002.
32. Ranabir Chakravarti, *Warfare for Wealth: Early Indian Perspective*, Calcutta: Firma KLM Pvt. Ltd., 1986.
33. John Brewer, *The Sinews of Power: War, Money and the English State, 1688-1783*, London: Unwin Hyman, 1989.
34. Douglas M. Peers, 'War and Public Finance in Early Nineteenth-Century British India: The First Burma War', *International History Review*, vol. 11, no. 4, 1989, pp. 628–47; Peers, 'Between Mars and Mammon; The East India Company and Efforts to Reform its Army, 1796–1832', *Historical Journal*, vol. 33, no. 2, 1990, pp. 385–401; Peers, *Between Mars and Mammon: Colonial Armies and the Garrison State in India, 1819-1835*, London: I. B. Tauris, 1995.
35. Dirk H. A. Kolff, *Naukar, Rajput & Sepoy: The Ethnohistory of the Military Labour Market in Hindustan, 1450–1850*, Cambridge: Cambridge University Press, 1990.
36. John F. Richards, 'Warriors and the State in Early Modern India', *Journal of the Economic and Social History of the Orient* (henceforth *JESHO*), vol. 47, no. 3, 2004, pp. 390–400.
37. Jos Gommans, 'The Silent Frontier of South Asia, c.AD 1100–1800', *Journal of World History* (hereafter *JWH*), vol. 9, no. 1, 1998, pp. 1–23.
38. Rudi Paul Lindner, 'Nomadism, Horses and Huns', *Past and Present*, no. 42, August 1981, pp. 3–19.
39. Randolf G. S. Cooper, 'Beyond Beasts and Bullion: Economic Considerations in Bombay's Military Logistics, 1803', *MAS*, vol. 33, no. 1, 1999, pp. 159–83; Cooper, *The Anglo-Maratha Campaigns and the Contest for India: The Struggle for Control of the South Asian Military Economy*, Cambridge: Cambridge University Press, 2005.
40. Richard H. Moye, 'Thucydides' "Great War": The Fiction in Scientific History', *CLIO*, vol. 19, no. 2, 1990, pp. 161–80.
41. Georges Duby, *The Legend of Bouvines: War, Religion and Culture in the Middle Ages*, 1973, English translation by Catherine Tihanyi, Cambridge: Polity Press, 1990, p. 5.
42. Duby, *Bouvines*, p. 5.
43. Duby, *Bouvines*, p. 6.
44. Duby, *Bouvines*, p. 6.
45. Helen Watanabe-O'Kelly, 'Tournaments and their Relevance for Warfare in the Early Modern Period', *European History Quarterly*, vol. 20, no. 4, 1990, pp. 451–63.
46. Duby, *Bouvines*, p. 5.

47. Jurgen Pieters, 'New Historicism: Postmodern Historiography between Narrativism and Heterology', *History and Theory*, vol. 39, no. 1, 2000, p. 30.
48. John Keegan, *The Face of Battle: A Study of Agincourt, Waterloo and the Somme*, 1976; reprint, Middlesex: Penguin, 1978, p. 261.
49. Keegan, *Face of Battle*, pp. 76–7.
50. Keegan, *Face of Battle*, pp. 25, 35.
51. Keegan, *Face of Battle*, p. 77.
52. Alan Beyerchen, 'Clausewitz, Nonlinearity, and the Unpredictability of War', *International Security*, vol. 17, no. 3, 1992–3, pp. 62–5.
53. Alastair Iain Johnston, 'Thinking about Strategic Culture', *International Security*, vol. 19, no. 4, 1995, pp. 32–64.
54. John A. Lynn, 'Heart of the Sepoy: The Adoption and Adaptation of European Military Practice in South Asia, 1740–1805', in Emily Goldman and Leslie C. Eliason (eds), *The Diffusion of Military Technology and Ideas*, Stanford: Stanford University Press, 2003, pp. 33–62.
55. Victor Davis Hanson, *Warfare and Agriculture in Classical Greece*, Berkeley: University of California Press, 1998.
56. Jeffrey Greenhut, 'Sahib and Sepoy: An Inquiry into the Relationship between the British Officers and Native Soldiers of the British Indian Army', *Military Affairs*, vol. XLVIII, no. 1, 1984, pp. 15–8.
57. Andre Wink, 'Sovereignty and Universal Dominion in South Asia', in Jos J. L. Gommans and Dirk H. A. Kolff (eds), *Warfare and Weaponry in South Asia: 1000–1800*, New Delhi: Oxford University Press, 2001, pp. 99–130.
58. Jeffrey Greenhut, 'The Imperial Reserve: The Indian Corps on the Western Front, 1914-15', *Journal of Imperial and Commonwealth History*, vol. 12, no. 1, 1983, pp. 54–73.
59. Lionel Caplan, *Warrior Gentleman: 'Gurkhas' in the Western Imagination*, Providence/Oxford: Berghahn Books, 1995.
60. Heather Streets, *Martial races: The Military, Race and Masculinity in British Imperial Culture, 1857–1914*, Manchester/New York: Manchester University Press, 2004, p. 1.
61. Stephen P. Cohen, *The Indian Army: Its Contribution to the Development of a Nation*, 1990; reprint, Delhi: Oxford University Press, 1991.
62. Streets, *Martial Races*, pp. 2–5.
63. Rosalind O'Hanlon, 'Manliness and Imperial Service in Mughal North India', *JESHO*, vol. 42, no. 1, 1999, pp. 47–93.
64. Simon Digby, *Sufis and Soldiers in Aurangzeb's Deccan*, New Delhi: Oxford University Press, 2001.
65. Simon Digby, 'Dreams and Reminiscences of Dattu Sarvani, A Sixteenth Century Indo-Afghan Soldier', *Indian Economic and Social History Review*, vol. 2, no. 1, 1965, pp. 52–80; no. 2, 1965, pp. 178–94.

66. William R. Pinch, *Warrior Ascetics and Indian Empires*, Cambridge: Cambridge University Press, 2006.
67. Jos Gommans, 'Indian Warfare and Afghan Innovation during the Eighteenth Century', *Studies in History*, vol. 11, no. 2, 1995, pp. 261–80. See especially pp. 279–80.
68. Aidan Southall, 'The Segmentary State in Africa and Asia', *CSSH*, vol. 30, no. 1, 1988, pp. 52–82; Burton Stein, *A History of India*, 1998; reprint, New Delhi: Oxford University Press, 2004.
69. Pradeep P. Barua says that though the battles of ancient India were bloody, the military techniques remained stagnant from 1500 BCE till AD 1000 because of the geographical isolation of the subcontinent and decentralized multilayered state systems (Barua, *The State at War in South Asia*, Lincoln/London: University of Nebraska Press, 2005, pp. 3–85).
70. Jos Gommans, *Mughal Warfare: Indian Frontier and High Roads to Empire, 1500-1700*, London/New York: Routledge, 2002.
71. Jha, *Early India*; R. K. Mookerji, *Chandragupta Maurya and his Times*, Delhi: Motilal Banarasidas, 1960.
72. Torkel Brekke, 'The Ethics of War and the Concept of War in India and Europe', *NUMEN*, vol. 52, 2005, pp. 59–83.
73. J. Sundaram, 'Warfare in South India—The Background', in S. N. Prasad (ed.), *Historical Perspectives of Warfare in India: Some Morale and Material Determinants*, New Delhi: Motilal Banarasidas in association with the Centre for Studies in Civilizations, 2002, p. 170.
74. R. K. Saxena, 'The Mughal and Rajput Armies', in Prasad (ed.), *Historical Perspectives of Warfare in India*, pp. 301–13.
75. Kelly DeVries, 'Catapults are not Atomic Bombs: Towards a Redefinition of "Effectiveness" in Premodern Military Technology', in DeVries, *Guns and Men in Medieval Europe: 1200–1500: Studies in Military History and Technology*, Aldershot: Ashgate, 2002, p. 458.
76. U. P. Thapliyal, 'Military Organization in the Ancient Period', in Prasad (ed.), *Historical Perspectives of Warfare in India*, pp. 68–103.
77. J. Sundaram, 'Chola and other Armies—Organization', in Prasad (ed.), *Historical Perspectives of Warfare in India*, p. 184–208.
78. J. Sundaram, 'Chola and other Armies—Deployment', in Prasad (ed.), *Historical Perspectives of Warfare in India*, pp. 209–34.
79. R. K. Saxena, 'Medieval Forts, Logistics and Heraldry', in Prasad (ed.), *Historical Perspectives of Warfare in India*, pp. 336–56.
80. Bernard S. Bachrach, 'Military Organization in Aquitaine under the Early Carolingians', in Bachrach, *Armies and Politics in the Early Medieval West*, Brookfield: Variorum, 1993, pp. 1–33.
81. J. Barendse, 'The Feudal Mutation: Military and Economic Transformations of the Ethnosphere in the Tenth to Thirteenth Centuries', *JWH*, vol. 14. no. 4, 2003, pp. 509, 513–28.

82. Ulrich Wengenroth, 'Does Technology Drive History? The Dilemma of Technological Determinism', *Technology and Culture*, vol. 39, no. 4, 1998, pp. 755–58.
83. C. W. C. Oman, *The Art of War in the Middle Ages: AD 375-1515*, Oxford: Oxford University Press, 1885, p. 2.
84. Oman, *Art of War*, pp. 4, 11, 16, 62–5.
85. John France, 'Recent Writings on Medieval Warfare: From the Fall of Rome to c.1300', *Journal of Military History* (hereafter *JMH*), vol. 65, no. 2, 2001, pp. 445–6.
86. Bernard S. Bachrach, 'Charles Martel, Mounted Shock Combat, the Stirrup, and Feudalism', in Bachrach, *Armies and Politics in the Early Medieval West*, pp. 49–75.
87. Ali Athar, *Military Technology and Warfare in the Sultanate of Delhi: 1206–1398 CE*, New Delhi: Icon Publications Pvt. Ltd, 2006.
88. A. Jan Qaisar, 'Horseshoeing in Mughal India', *Indian Journal of History of Science*, (henceforth *IJHS*), vol. 27, no. 2, 1992, pp. 133–44.
89. Jean Deloche, *Military Technology in Hoysala Sculpture (Twelfth and Thirteenth Century)*, New Delhi: Sitaram Bhartia Institute of Scientific Research, 1989.
90. Geoffrey Parker, *The Military Revolution: Military Innovation and the Rise of the West, 1500-1800*, Cambridge: Cambridge University Press, 1988.
91. Daniel R. Headrick, *The Tools of Empire: Technology and European Imperialism in the Nineteenth Century*, New York/Oxford: Oxford University Press, 1981.
92. MacGregor Knox and Williamson Murray (eds), *The Dynamics of Military Revolution: 1300–2050*, 2001; reprint, Cambridge: Cambridge University Press, 2003.
93. Clifford J. Rogers, 'The Military Revolutions of the Hundred Years War', in Rogers (ed.), *The Military Revolution Debate: Readings on the Military Transformation of Early Modern Europe*, Boulder: Westview, 1995, pp. 55–93.
94. Kelly DeVries, 'Catapults are not Atomic Bombs', in DeVries, *Guns and Men in Medieval Europe*, pp. 467, 469.
95. Jeremy Black, 'A Military Revolution? A 1660-1792 Perspective', in Rogers (ed.), *The Military Revolution Debate*, pp. 95–114.
96. Pradeep Barua, 'Military Developments in India, 1750–1850', *JMH*, vol. 58, no. 4, 1994, pp. 599–616.
97. Stewart N. Gordon, 'Symbolic and Structural Constraints on the Adoption of European-Style Military Technologies in the Eighteenth Century', in Richard B. Barnett (ed.), *Rethinking Early Modern India*, New Delhi: Manohar, 2002, pp. 155–78.
98. G. J. Bryant, 'Asymmetric Warfare: The British Experience in Eighteenth-Century India', *JMH*, vol. 68, 2004, pp. 431–69.

99. Jos Gommans, 'Warhorse and post-nomadic empire in Asia, *c.*1000-1800', *Journal of Global History*, vol. 2, 2007, pp. 1–21.
100. Robert Douglas Smith, 'Monster Cannons: Wrought Iron Bombards of Europe', *IJHS*, vol. 40, no. 4, 2005, pp. 451–64.
101. Iqtidar Alam Khan, *Gunpowder and Firearms: Warfare in Medieval India*, New Delhi: Oxford University Press, 2004.
102. Pranab Kumar Chattopadhyay, 'Cannons of Eastern India', *IJHS*, vol. 40, no. 4, 2005, pp. 465–85.
103. R. Balasubramaniam, 'Development of Cannon Technology in India', *IJHS*, vol. 40, no. 4, 2005, pp. 503–38.
104. Jean Deloche, *Studies on Fortification in India*, Pondichery: Pondichery Centre of the EFEO, 2007.
105. Irvine, *Army of the Indian Moghuls*, pp. 270, 272.
106. Judith Hook, 'Fortifications and the End of the Sienese State', *History*, vol. 62, no. 206, 1977, p. 387.
107. Mahinder S. Kingra, 'The *Trace Italienne* and the Military Revolution during the Eighty Years' War, 1567–1648', *JMH*, vol. 57, 1993, p. 445.
108. G. J. Bryant, 'The Cavalry Problem in the Early British Indian Army, 1750-1785', *War in History*, vol. 2, no. 1, 1995, pp. 1–21.
109. Ian Friel, 'Winds of Change? Ships and the Hundred Years War', in Anne Curry and Michael Hughes (eds), *Arms, Armies and Fortifications in the Hundred Years War*, 1994, reprint, Woodbridge, Boydell, 1999, pp. 183–6, 189.
110. Kelly DeVries, 'The Effectiveness of Fifteenth-Century Shipboard Artillery', in DeVries, *Guns and Men in Medieval Europe*, pp. 389, 394–6.
111. K. K. N. Kurup, 'Indigenous Navigation and Ship-building on the Malabar Coast', in K. S. Mathew (ed.), *Ship-building and Navigation in the Indian Ocean region: AD 1400–1800*, New Delhi: Munshiram Manoharlal, 1997, pp. 22–3.
112. Kelly DeVries, 'Effectiveness of Fifteenth Century Shipboard Artillery', in DeVries, *Guns and Men in Medieval Europe*, p. 393.
113. Surendranath Sen, *Studies in India History: Historical Records at Goa*, 1930; reprint, New Delhi: Asian Educational Services, 1993, pp. 180–84.
114. Raymond Callahan, *The East India Company and Army Reform, 1783–98*, Cambridge, Massachusetts: Harvard University Press, 1972; Lorenzo M. Crowell, 'Military Professionalism in a Colonial Context: The Madras Army, *c.*1832', *MAS*, vol. 24, 1990, pp. 249–73.
115. Margaret MacMillan, 'The Indian Army since Independence', *South Asian Review*, vol. 3, no. 1, 1969, pp. 45–58; Apurba Kundu, 'The Indian Armed Forces' Sikh and Non-Sikh Officers' Opinion of Operation Blue Star', *Pacific Affairs*, vol. 67, no. 1, 1994, pp. 46–69.

116. Leslie C. Eliason and Emily Goldman, 'Introduction: Theoretical and Comparative Perspectives on Innovation and Diffusion', in Goldman and Eliason (eds), *Diffusion of Military Technology and Ideas*, pp. 1, 3.
117. John A. Lynn, 'The *trace italienne* and the Growth of Armies: The French Case', in Rogers (ed.), *The Military Revolution Debate*, pp. 169–99.
118. John Stone, 'Technology, Society, and the Infantry Revolution of the Fourteenth Century', *JMH*, vol. 68, no. 2, 2004, pp. 370–6.
119. Alvin and Heidi Toffler, *War and Anti-War: Survival at the Dawn of the 21st Century*, 1993; reprint, London: Warner Books, 1994.
120. D. Shyam Babu, 'India's National Security Council: Stuck in the Cradle?', *Security Dialogue*, vol. 34, no. 2, 2003, pp. 215–30.
121. Stephen P. Cohen, *The Pakistan Army*, 1984; reprint, Karachi: Oxford University Press, 1993, pp. 86–104.
122. Bharat Karnad, *Nuclear Weapons & Indian Security: The Realist Foundations of Strategy*, Delhi: Macmillan, 2002.
123. Martin van Creveld, 'Technology and War II: Postmodern War?', in Charles Townshend (ed.), *The Oxford Illustrated History of Modern War*, Oxford: Oxford University Press, 1997, pp. 298–314; Herfried Munkler, 'What is Really New about the New Wars?—A Reply to the Critics', in John Andreas Olsen (ed.), *On New Wars*, Oslo: Norwegian Institute for Defence Studies, 2007, pp. 67–82; Rupert Smith, *The Utility of Force: The Art of War in the Modern World*, 2005; reprint, London: Penguin, 2006; Mary Kaldor, *New & Old Wars: Organized Violence in a Global Era*, 1999, reprint, Dehradun: Natraj, 2005.
124. Hew Strachan, 'War and Strategy', in Olsen (ed.), *On New Wars*, p. 24.
125. Ian. F. W. Beckett, *Modern Insurgencies and Counter-Insurgencies: Guerrillas and their Opponents since 1750*, 2001; reprint, London/New York: Routledge, 2005, p. vii.
126. Beckett, *Modern Insurgencies and Counter-Insurgencies*, pp. vii–viii.
127. Beckett, *Modern Insurgencies and Counter-Insurgencies*, p. 4.
128. Azeem Ibrahim, 'Conceptualisation of Guerrilla Warfare', *Small Wars & Insurgencies*, vol. 15, no. 3, 2004, pp. 112–20.
129. Ibrahim, 'Conceptualisation of Guerrilla Warfare', pp. 120–1.
130. Beckett, *Modern Insurgencies and Counter-Insurgencies*, pp. 6, 8–9.
131. Lorenzo M. Crowell, 'Logistics in the Madras Army circa 1830', *War & Society*, vol. 10, no. 2, 1992, pp. 1–33.
132. Alan Warren, '"Bullocks treading down Wasps?": The British Indian Army in Waziristan in the 1930s', *South Asia*, vol. 19, no. 2, 1996, pp. 35–56; Warren, *Waziristan: The Faqir of Ipi and the Indian Army, The North West Frontier Revolt of 1936–7*, Karachi: Oxford University Press, 2000; T. R. Moreman, *The Army in India and the Development of Frontier Warfare, 1849–1947*, Houndmills, Basingstoke: Macmillan, 1998.

133. Gautam Das and M. K. Gupta Ray, *SriLanka Misadventure: India's Military Peace-Keeping Campaign, 1987–90*, New Delhi: Har-Anand, 2008. The quotation is from p. 122.
134. Frans Osinga, 'On Boyd, Bin Laden, and Fourth Generation Warfare as String Theory', in Olsen (ed.), *On New Wars*, pp. 168–97.
135. DeWitt Ellinwood, 'Indian Soldier, the Indian Army, and Change', in Ellinwood and Pradhan (eds), *India and World War I*, p. 184.
136. Tim Travers, 'The Army and the Challenge of War 1914–18', in David Chandler (General Editor) and Ian Beckett (Associate Editor), *The Oxford Illustrated History of the British Army*, Oxford: Oxford University Press, 1994, p. 227.
137. Peter Simkins, 'The Four Armies', in Chandler and Beckett (eds), *Oxford Illustrated History of the British Army*, p. 261.
138. Indivar Kamtekar, 'A Different War Dance: State and Class in India, 1939–45', *Past & Present*, no. 176, August 2002, p. 212.
139. Alex Danchev, 'The Army and the Home Front 1939–45', in Chandler and Beckett (eds), *Oxford Illustrated History of the British Army*, p. 328.
140. Some exceptions are Jeremy Black, Hew Strachan, and Dennis E. Showalter, who are critical of the Eurocentric perspective.
141. Kaushik Roy, 'Just and Unjust War in Hindu Philosophy', *Journal of Military Ethics*, vol. 6, no. 3, 2007, pp. 232–45.

SECTION I

Ancient Indian Warfare from 300 BCE–600 CE: Ritual Combat or Lethal Battle

CHAPTER 1

Art of War in Ancient India (600 BC–AD 300)

B. P. Sinha

I

War is one of the oldest aspects of human existence. According to ancient Hindu literature, political organization—the State and Kingship—grew out of the necessities of war. The Devas in their struggle against the Asuras were defeated because they lacked a king and, having chosen one, thereafter vanquished the Asuras.[1] Even in the Paleolithic age, man was turning out stone weapons and tools to attack his enemies—human or animal—and to gather food. With the evolution of agriculture and the consequent institution of landed property, fights for land between different clans became more frequent and ferocious, and resulted in the improvement of weapons of war, as a matter of fact, the progress of civilization from one stage to another may be seen in the progressive advance in the nature of warlike weapons. As success or failure of a tribe or people depended on victory or defeat in the battlefield, it was natural that much attention should be paid to war. Thus an art of war evolved from the earliest times, with attention paid to both offensive and defensive weapons.

Indian archaeology has brought to light weapons from Palaeolithic and Neolithic ages. The ancient sites of Mohenjodaro and Harappā have yielded weapons of bronze and also the remains of strong fortifications which are believed to be pre-Vedic. In the earliest Vedic literature, i.e. the Rgveda, we have references to many wars including the 'Battle of the Ten Kings'.[2] The great epics of the *Rāmāyana* and the *Mahābhārata* have war as their main themes. The Buddhist age dawns with the rise of monarchies and their military conflicts with one another and with the non-monarchical states, culminating in the growth of Magadhan imperialism under the 'Ekrāt' Mahāpadmananda. The empire of the Mauryas, which embraced practically the whole of India except the southernmost part of the peninsula, was won by the sword. The Bactrian Greeks, the Parthians, the Śakas, and the Kusānas, one after another, plunged India into war. Thus it is obvious that from the earliest times down to AD 300 and even after, war continued to be one of the most dominant and persistent features of Indian history.

Wars in ancient India were fought for many reasons. Seizure of cattle, one of the most important elements of wealth in an agricultural country such as India, occasioned war between the Trigarttas and the Matsyas in the *Mahābhārata.*[3] A dispute about the share in a mine of precious stones was one of the reasons for war between Ajātaśatru, king of Magadha, and the Lichchhavis of Vaiśālī.[4] Ambition to become the sole monarch of the whole country explains the wars of Mahāpadmananda and Chandragupta Maurya. According to Kauṭilya, the domination of the universal emperor (Chakravartin) extended from the Himalayas to the ocean. Every Indian king was therefore anxious to increase his territory and impose his overlordship at the expense of the rest. Kauṭilya certainly advocated a policy of annexation, since, according to him, among the acquisition of a friend, of gold, and of territory, the last one was most desirable.[5]

Indian social organization also encouraged wars. Hindu society was divided into four castes or varnas, of which the Kṣatriya was one. Their duty was to protect the social order by force of arms and to rule righteously. To die in battle was the duty of Kṣatriyas. 'Death on the battlefield was highly commended as bestowing the greatest religious merit on the warrior.' The state, attained by stages after long and tedious penance, is immediately reached by warriors who meet death in warfare. In the *Mahābhārata* in the Udyog Parva there is a sacrifice (*Śastrayajna*) from which the virtues of all religious sacrifices are said to result.[6] War was thus not an undesirable thing to be shunned, but was welcomed by the leading caste, the Kṣatriyas, since it gave them an opportunity to enjoy material life more fully or to ascend to the heaven of bliss in case of death on the battlefield. Thus religion did not discourage war, and, since the Vedic times, kings, in order to gain the merits of performing *Aśvamedha Yajna* or horse sacrifice, carried on wars of conquests, 'going round the earth completely, conquering on every side and offering the horse in sacrifice'.[7] A large number of kings are mentioned in the *Śatapatha Brāhmaṇa* as having performed the horse sacrifice. Samudragupta, the second Gupta emperor, also performed *Aśvamedha* sacrifices as is known from the inscriptions of his descendants and from his coins bearing the epithet '*Aśvamedhaparākramah*'. Wars were also waged for failure to pay tribute or refusal to give maidens, or to exterminate rivals and refractory vassals.[8] It was one of the first principles of the code for the Kşatriyas that when challenged, one must fight.

Naturally, when war was so eulogized, especially for a particular class, the Kşatriyas, and when it was so persistent, regular, and necessary, the army was logically given much importance. According to Kauṭilya, 'army' is one of the seven elements of sovereignty. The possession of a powerful army makes even an enemy friendly. A later authority, Śukra, observes that 'without the army there is neither kingdom, nor wealth, nor prowess'. Bhīşma observes that 'the king's roots are his treasury and army'.[9]

Traditionally the ancient Indian army was composed of four elements—the chariot troops, elephant troops, cavalry, and infantry. *Vālodaka Jātaka* refers to any army complete in its four parts—elephant, horse, chariot, and infantry. Brahmadatta, king of Vārānasi, marched to Takşaśilā and arranged his army thus: 'Here be the elephants, here the horse, the chariots here and here the foot-soldiers'. The Jātakas refer to a period before the Mauryas, presumably to 600 BC or near about. In the *Mahābhārata* and the *Rāmāyana* also we have references to the fourfold army. In the Virāṭ Parva we learn of chariots, foot-soldiers, horsemen, and elephants meeting each other in battle. The army of Yuyudhāna consisted of infantry, cavalry, chariots, and elephants. The army of Rāvaṇa was similarly composed.[10] Ajātaśatru in his question to Buddha refers to elephant-riders, cavalry, charioteers, and archers (foot-soldiers).[11] Kauṭilya in his *Arthaśāstra* speaks of the fourfold army in many places. He says, 'elephants, cavalry, chariots and infantry shall each be officered with many chiefs'. Again, he advises that 'Foot-soldiers, horsemen, charioteers, elephant-riders shall be given necessary training'. Later the Hathigumphā inscription of Khāravela, belonging to the first or second century BC, refers to Khāravela's army as composed of horse, elephant, foot, and chariot corps. The army of Śaka chief Mahākṣatrapa Rudradāman (second century AD) had the same four elements[12] and *Kāmandīkiya Nītisāra*, a work which is ascribed to the Gupta period, 'proves beyond doubt that the fourfold division of the chariots, infantry, cavalry and elephant corps continued to be the chief sections of the army of the Guptas.' According to Dikshitar, the army of ancient Tamils, as known from Kural, consisted of the fourfold forces.[13] Much later Yuan Chwang, who visited India in the first half of the seventh century AD, in the time of Harṣavardhana, found that the army was composed of foot, horse, chariot, and elephant soldiers.[14]

Thus it is clear that the traditional complexion of the ancient Indian army as *Chaturangabala* or *Chaturanginī Senā* persisted from about the sixth century BC to the seventh century AD, and even later, as is clear from the references in the Jātakas, the *Epics,* the early inscriptions, and literature on polity. A much later work, *Sukranitī,* which is attributed to the thirteenth or fourteenth century AD, refers to the fourfold army. Dikshitar[15] thinks that the organization of the Indian army as *Chaturanga* was based on the ancient game of chess; but a likelier explanation is that the game of chess (*Chaturanga-Śataranja*) was based on the military organization.

The ancient Indian army did not, however, confine itself to the four elements. The army of Chandragupta Maurya, according to Megasthenes, included a navy and commissariat besides the four traditional elements. References to provisions and wagons during the march of the army and its encampment are met with in the *Mahābhārata,* but the introduction of the war-fleet as a unit of the army appears to have been a innovation of Chandragupta Maurya. *Kāmandikīya Nītisāra*[16] regards the army as consisting of six units—*Ṣadangabala*—and adds *Koṣa* (treasury) and *Mantra* (diplomacy). Kālidāsa also refers to six kinds of armed forces. The so-called spurious Nālandā and Gaya copper-plate inscriptions of Samundragupta refer to great ships, elephants, and horses. Camel corps and navy are both included in the army of Jīvitagupta II. Śukra also includes the camel corps as a unit of the army.[17] It is clear, therefore, that the Indian army, at one time or another, included in its fold chariots, elephants, infantry, cavalry, camelry, a navy, and a commissariat.

All the units of the army were not equally important at all times, and as a matter of fact, in course of time, one or the other became more important or fell into disuse. Moreover, all four or six parts were not uniformly useful in all kinds of battlefields; their respective uses depended on the nature of the ground on which they had to play their part. Naturally, too, their equipment differed from one another. Each was expected to play its allotted part on the basis of its nature and qualities. It would, therefore, be desirable to study separately the use and equipment of the different parts of the army in the period under review.

II

From the Ṛgvedic period the chariot appears to have enjoyed pre-eminence in war. No evidence of horsedrawn chariots being used in warfare is available from the pre-Vedic sites of Mohenjodaro and Harappā. It is, therefore, very likely that the Vedic Indo-Āryans introduced these. The word '*Rathin*' or '*Rathistha*' occurs frequently in the early Vedic literature, showing the charioteer to have been a common type of warrior. On one occasion he is designated as *a-sthatr*, i.e. warrior standing in the chariot. The phrase *ratha-saniga* occurring in the Rgveda denotes the hostile encounter of chariots.[18] Chariots were used by Brahmadatta in his war against the City of Takṣaśilā. In the *Bhanddasāla Jātaka* we find that the commander-in-chief of Kośala set forth in a chariot with his wife and defeated the 500 Lichchhavi chiefs on chariots at Vaiśālī.[19] The great 'Mahābhārata War' was principally a war between charioteers. The king of Trigarttas was mounted on a golden chariot in his encounter against the Matsyas. Arjuna, seated on a chariot, defeated the entire Kaurava army. Drona rode on a chariot, Bhīṣma fought from one. Bhīma, enumerating the great warriors of the Kauravas and Pāṇdava army, refers only to charioteers—Rathīs and Atirathīs. Among the Rathīs were Duryodhana and others; Kripa was an Atrirathī, probably Salya also. Aśvatthāmā was a Mahārathī, so was Drona. Yudhisthira, Nakula, and Sahadeva were Rathīs, Dhṛstadyumna was an Atirathī and Arjuna was the greatest of chariot warriors.[20] In the Great War we find that battles were virtually fought between the charioteer—Arjuna versus Bhīṣma, Drona versus Dhrstadyumna, Karna versus Arjuna, and that soldiers on either side depended on their charioteers for protection from the enemy chariot troops.

The famous heroes never fought on horseback, and rarely on elephants, their place being on a chariot. In his war against Rāma, the demon chief of Janasthāna, Khara had used chariots, Rāma fighting from the ground. Hence Indra, the king of gods, sent his own car to Rāma.[21] The importance of chariots as an indispensable branch of the army persisted in the Buddhist and the Mauryan ages. In the War of Relics fought between the army of Kuşinagara and the seven other chiefs we find that the besieging allied army included chariots, and one of the chiefs appeared on a chariot. In the war against Alexander, Porus used 300 chariots as one of the divisions of his vast army. In the army of the Sudracae (Kşudrakas) and the Malloi (Mālavas), who resisted Alexander, there were 900 war-chariots. In the army of the Nanda king, Xandrames, there were 2,000, according to Diodorus, while, according to Plutarch, their strength was 8,000. From Megasthenes, we learn that Chandragupta's army included chariots. Kauṭilya refers to the battle-chariot (Sangramika), and the superintendent of chariots was to see to its proper construction and equipment. Chariots were one of the four constitutent parts of the army, and the army of Khāravela, the king of Kalinga, also included them. The Saka ruler Rudradāman's army used them as well as elephants and cavalry.[22] Thus, it is evident that from the Vedic period down to the middle of the second century AD, chariots constituted an important element of the ancient Indian army.

The Vedic chariot was of 'simple construction'.[23] Generally it had two wheels on a wooden axle, and as a rule two horses were attached on either side of a pole, though chariots with three, four, or five horses were also known. The extra horse was attached to the front or side.[24] In the *Mahābhārata* also the chariots are said to have two wheels as there were a pair of wheel-guards to guard the chariot in war; but four-wheeled and eight-wheeled chariots are also referred to. Chariots were drawn by two or four horses.[25] Four horses were yoked in the chariots stationed in the war-camp of Duryodhana.[26] Chariots drawn by two and four horses are shown in one of the Sanchi reliefs. In one scene is seen a two-wheeled chariot drawn by two horses, while on the Northern Gateway of

Sanchi a four-horse chariot is depicted, and a two-horse chariot guards the City or Kapilavastu. Another Sanchi relief represents a king on royal chariots drawn by two horses. The *Visvantara Jātaka* story is represented on another panel in Sanchi, and it shows the prince in exile on a four-horse chariot. The chariots of the army of Porus were drawn by four horses.[27]

The chariot in the early period contained the warrior and the driver (charioteer), but later on it was enlarged in size. In the Vedic period the driver stood on the right while the warrior was on the left, and he could stand or sit as he liked, as chariots had seats. In the Great Epic also we generally have the knight and the charioteer, the knight sometimes standing to the left and sometimes in the rear of the car driver. In the chariot of the great warrior Arjuna or Karna, there were only the knight and the charioteer—Kṛṣṇa or Salya. In the Sanchi reliefs depicting life in pre-Buddhist and Buddhist times we find the knight and the charioteer, but later on the size of the chariot was much enlarged and, according to Curtius, every chariot of the army of Porus accommodated six men, of whom two were shield-bearers, two archers posted on each side of the chariots and the other two charioteers as well as men-at-arms, for when the fighting was at close quarters they dropped the reins and hurled darts against the enemy. Wilson doubts that the chariot of Porus contained as many as six men. According to Megasthenes, the chariot of the Maurya army contained two warriors besides the charioteer.[28] At one place in the *Mahābhārata* it is observed that in cars drawn by four horses, there were two charioteers.[29]

From the Ṛgvedic period onwards, chariots were the most important unit of the army. The king who led the hosts fought on chariots, and so did the nobles and leaders of the army. Naturally, therefore, when the fate of a war depended on the victory or defeat of the charioteer, much attention was paid to the construction and equipment of the chariot and the warrior, and training in driving chariots and managing the horses was indispensable for a Vedic or epic hero. The charioteer therefore enjoyed great prestige and honour, and the noblest princes could be chariot-drivers. Kṛṣṇa of the Vṛṣṇi race was the sārathi of Arjuna, and Salya, the King of the Madras, agreed to be the charioteer of Karna. Sumanta, charioteer of Dasaratha was highly respected.

Chariots were made of wood but could also be of iron in certain parts. Golden or gold-plated chariots are referred to in many places in the *Mahābhārata,* e.g. the gold-embroidered cars of Drupada's sons. Various weapons and things which the warrior might need in course of the battle, such as quivers, javelins, missiles, spears, bows, flagstaffs and banners, and even timber and planks for repairing the damages sustained by the car in the battlefield were kept in the chariot which even contained drugs for first aid. Care was taken to make the car and driver safe from enemy attacks. Cars are said to have been cased in armour, their sides covered with skins of tigers, elephants and leopards, and with sharp-edged circular planks of wood.[30] The car-warrior was provided with helmet, breastplate, and finger protectors made of leather, sometimes embossed with iron or gold plates. On the horse were spread colourful fabrics and on his head was a wreath of flowers, as is clear from ancient Indian art reliefs. Every chariot carried a distinctive banner flying on a long pole at the rear and providing a symbol for rallying and inspiring the troops. The standard bearing a monkey device belonged to Arjuna, while the palm-tree standard was the distinctive feature of Bhīṣma's car.[31]

Chariots were used as an important section of the army not only in ancient India but also in other parts of the ancient world. As a matter of fact, the history of their use in warfare by various ancient peoples suggests that they were introduced first by the Aryans in about 2000 BC. The Kassites, who conquered Babylonia *c.*1800 BC, made the use of chariots by kings and nobles popular. In a stele at the Louvre, King Idingiranagin is standing on a chariot attended by the charioteer; the chariot has a rimmed balcony.[32]

Later on the Hyksos from Asia introduced war-chariots in Egypt. According to Professor G. Maspero, 'it is probable that the Hyksos owed their rapid victory to the presence in their arms of a factor hitherto unknown to the Africans—the war-chariots.' After the explusion of the Hyksos from Egypt by Ahmose, the founder of the eighteenth dynasty in the sixteenth century BC, the 'Egyptian army possessed chariotry as a result of the contact with the Hyksos.' Thutmose III led his campaign into Asia and fought the battle of Megiddo in a shinning chariot. Ramses II also had chariots in his army against Asia. The Hittites used chariots in warfare, and a Hittite prince with a round, high cap on his head is seen stretching his bow as he stands on a two-wheeled chariot drawn by two horses. The Cretans also employed chariots in war, and in the Homeric period, the Greek nobles fought with them.[33]

The Assyrians made extensive use of chariots in numerous wars throughout their long history. Sargon is seen on his war-chariot of two wheels, each of eight spokes, and drawn by two horses. The king was accompanied by an attendant with a parasol over his head, besides the driver. These chariots were small, were mounted from behind, and sometimes contained four men, the king with two attendants bearing circular shields besides the driver. Horses were driven with bits. Often chariot-horse was covered from the ears to the tail with rich cloths, and below the collar was a breast plate. Egyptian chariots were lighter than the Assyrian and were swifter. The Assyrian car-warrior, like the Egyptian counterpart, wore a coat of mail covered with small plates or scales of metal reaching down to his knees. He had short sleeves covering the shoulders and upper arms but the elbow and forearm were quite undefended. The main weapons of the charioteer in Assyria or Egypt were bow and arrow. Though there were no quivers attached to the chariot, a projection at one or both corners may have served as an arrow case. The Egyptians knew the use of quivers, as did the Indians, and had borrowed them from the Hyksos. Besides the bow and arrow, the warrior in the car had a short sword suspended at his left side by a strap, and a spear was within his reach. Chariots were the main source of Assyrian strength and the despair of their enemies. The Israel prophet Nahum said that God would burn the Assyrian chariots in smoke. The Medes and the Persians also used chariots, and King Darius III, in the battle of Arbela against Alexander, was riding one.[34]

Thus, chariots were a favourite branch of the army in the ancient world, mostly because of their mobility and rapidity, but they could be useful only on such grounds as are 'splendidly firm, free from mounds and pits, not wet, free from thorns, trees and plants', and in the war against Alexander, the chariots of Porus on rain-soaked ground proved absolutely helpless, and all those which were sent to stop the landing of Alexander's forces on the left side of the Jhelum were captured as a result.[35]

Experience showed the weakness of the chariot as an arm: the Medes and Persians relied more on cavalry, and in India also, chariotry gradually gave way to the elephantry and cavalry. Porus fought Alexander not from a chariot, but from the back of an elephant. In the Gupta period chariotry was practically insignificant. On no gold coin of the imperial Guptas is the king depicted seated on a chariot, though he is found on elephant or horseback. In the army of Harşavardhana there is no mention of chariots by Bāṇa, although Hiuen Tsang mentions them.[36]

III

Chariotry was superseded by elephantry in the period immediately following Alexander's invasion. It is significant that though elephants must have been known to the Ṛgvedic Indians and were known to the earlier people of Harappā and Mohenjodaro as is seen in the seals, they are not known to have been used in warfare in the Vedic period. In the Epic period also, their use in war was secondary to the chariots, on which much reliance was placed. There are references to elephant divisions in the armies of the contending parties and to elephants of both sides joining the encounter. Duryodhana arranged his men, elephants, cars, and steeds into three classes, namely, superior, medium, and inferior. Before the battle began, Duryodhana was seen riding on an elephant. Elephants used in warfare were disciplined by training. Bhānumat, king of Kalinga, fought seated on elephant, as did the king of Magadha in the Great War. The elephant division of Magadha was exterminated by the son of Subhadrā. Bhagadatta, king of Kamarupa, fought on elephants against Daşarna, similarly mounted. Droṇa was killed while grieving over the death of Aśvatthāmā, an elephant. Even the second Pāṇdava, Bhīma, once fought mounted on an elephant cased in iron armour. Salya, the ruler of the Mlechchhas, mounted on an elephant, fought the Pāṇdavas furiously, and his elephant charged the Pāṇdava host dangerously,[37] showing that the animals were trained to fight. Thus, it is obvious that in the Mahabharata war the elephantry was coming into prominence, though still second in importance to chariotry.

The use of elephants in war appears to be a distinction of the Indian art of war. The Assyrians, the Egyptians, and the early Greeks had no elephant corps in their army. Alexander met elephants in battle for the first time in the battle of Arbela against Darius III, and it is very possible that the Persians borrowed these from India. In the period before Alexander's invasion, elephants were used in warfare in India. In the *Bhīmasena Jātaka* we are told that Bhīmasena rode on a war-elephant sheathed in complete armour. Elephants were used assailing the gates and ramparts of the enemy's fortress, as Bodhisattva stormed the City of Vārāṇasi with the help of the war-elephant which he had trained.[38] On one of the architraves of Sanchi's western gate a triumphal procession of charioteers, elephant riders, horsemen, and foot-soldiers is depicted. The *Visvantara Jātaka* refers to the costly jewelled trappings of the elephant of Visvantara, and this is shown in the Ajanta frescoes. In the scene depicting the triumph of Buddha over Māra and his host beneath the Bodhi tree, the panic-stricken elephants and horses are trampling one another down in their headlong flight. In the scene depicting the 'War of Relics', one of the chiefs among the claimants is seated on an elephant, and the same scene is depicted on the western gateway showing four of the seven chiefs on elephants.[39]

By the time Alexander invaded India, the elephantry had become the vanguard of the Indian army. Porus had pinned his faith in this arm and had put the war-elephants in front at a small distance between one another interspersed with infantry. The army looked like a walled city with the elephants as the high towers. Even Alexander became aware of the danger that faced him. He said, 'I see at last a danger that matches my courage. It is at once with wild beasts and men of uncommon mettle that the contest now lies.' It is no doubt true that, the slow-moving elephant force proved of no avail against mounted archers and phalanxes of pikemen, but Alexander's troops were impressed by war-qualities of the trained elephants. When his troops refused to move east of the Beas, Alexander enquired whether they dreaded the monstrous size of the elephants of the army of the Gangaridae and Prasii. According to Diodorus, Alexander did not undertake the expedition against the Gandaridae (Gangaridai) defended by the multitude of their elephants. According to Curtius, the king of Gangaridai and Prasii had 3,000 elephants, while Plutarch says 6,000.[40] According to Tarn,[41] Alexander had won the battle of Hydaspes but at a price; it was the beginning of that change of feeling in the army which, aggravated by the rain and other causes, showed itself in the mutiny on the Beas. According to Pliny and

Plutarch, the army of Chandragupta Maurya included 9,000 war-elephants. The reliance placed on them in war during this period is confirmed by the statement of Kauṭilya that 'it is on elephants that the destruction of an enemy's army depends.'[42] Seleukos, the king of Syria, who accompanied Alexander, was so much impressed by the qualities of war-elephants that he ceded four provinces to Chandragupta Maurya in return for the present of 500 elephants. He then included elephantry in his army and the elephant became the symbol of his dynasty. His victory over Antigonos in the battle of Ipsos is attributed to the use of elephants. In the war against Rome, the Syrian army of Antiochus III included elephants, and Antiochus who crossed the Indian border in 206 BC, went back after receiving presents, including 150 elephants from King Subhagasena (Sophagasenus).[43] The Bactrian King Demetrius I had an elephant head on his coins, which shows that he mastered elephants and must have included them in his army. On the coins of Heliokles also the elephant is depicted, and on the coins of Menander is an elephant's head, as well as bulls. Not only did the Indians and Bactrian Greeks use elephants but even in the war against Rome, Pyrrhus, King of Epirus, used them to the terror of the Romans. Hannibal began his attack on the Roman army at the battle of Trebbia by a charge of elephants.[44]

Thus we find that the use of elephants in war was also being tried outside India in western Asia, Europe and North Africa. Their usefulness was apparent in a number of respects. According to Kauṭilya, they were useful for 'marching in front, preparing the roads and camping grounds, protecting the sides, standing firm, forcing an entrance into impregnable forces, breaking a compact army, destroying the walls, gates and towers (of the enemy's fortress), and for carrying treasure.'[45] They could also be useful in crossing water. Naturally, therefore, their capture was carefully planned, elephant forests were a royal monopoly, and possession of an elephant privately was prohibited.[46]

Elephants obtained for purposes of war were given seven kinds of military training, such as assailing forts or cities, trampling and killing enemies, and waging havoc in the enemy's rank by wielding weapons. Aolian observes that elephants were caught when young and reared like children, great care, attention, and a long course of training being given them. Kauṭilya observes that the victory of kings in battle depends mainly upon elephants. Naturally, therefore, war-elephants were provided with armour, ornaments, and weapons such as clubs and quivers. Strabo remarks that the elephants become so tame and docile that they can learn to throw a stone at a mark, to use weapons of war, and to swim most admirably. When Porus was wounded in battle, the elephant on which he rode, though itself suffering from many wounds, nevertheless gently and carefully drew out with its trunk the darts with which the body of Porus was pierced and continued to do so until it observed that its master was becoming weak due to excessive loss of blood. Then it slowly knelt down so that the body of Porus might not fall violently to the ground.[47]

According to Megasthenes, the war-elephant carried three archers and the driver with his goad. According to Agni Purāṇa, six warriors could ride on the back, two with maces, two archers, and two swordsmen, but in Sanchi reliefs and Ajanta paintings we find only three riders. In addition to arrows, we find missiles, knives, stones, daggers, and pots of oil showered on enemies in the Mahābhārata War by riders on elephants. War-elephants were covered with armour and with ornaments, including pearl necklaces, and seven footmen guarded each animal. Later on, e.g. in the Gupta period, we find elephants generally carrying archers. The king went hunting with bow and arrow on an elephant. On the coins of Satakarni we have elephants with raised trunks, showing the importance of elephants in the growth of Satavahana power.[48]

But the elephant corps was slow-moving and proved ineffective against the very mobile horse-mounted archery. Moreover, when wounded, the elephants went out of control and injured friends and foes indiscriminately. Their failure against cavalry as demonstrated in the battle of Hydaspes between Alexander and Porus, and elephants wounded by the showers of arrows from horsemen and spears from the Greek phalanx proved a terror to the army of Porus. But it is strange that the Indian military experts learned nothing from the experience, and the pathetic reliance on elephants proved dangerously harmful to the Indians against Scythians and later, the Muslims.

IV

Cavalry, although used from early days, did not receive the prominence it deserved until the conquest of north-western and western India by the Scythians in the early centuries of the Christian era. Though horses were known in the Vedic period, the use of cavalry in battle was unknown. In the Mahābhārata War between the Kauravas and Pāṇḍavas, some horsemen took part, but we do not find any distinguished warrior fighting on horseback. Horsemen appear as guards of the cars or war-elephants.[49] It seems that the value of cavalry in war was then not realized.

With the beginning of the Buddhist period, cavalry or horse-riding became more respectable and important. From the *Bhojajāniya Jātaka* we learn that the Bodhisattva was born as a horse, and mounted on it, the king of Brahmadatta broke the enemy's camps. Kings of Assaka and Kalinga fought on horseback with spears in hand.[50] In the siege of Kuṣinagara, depicted in the scene of the War of Relics, cavalry also takes part,[51] besides the elephantry and chariotry. On the western gateway of Sanchi, Prince Siddhartha is on horseback attended by a chhatra-bearer. In another architrave of the same gate, we find horsemen leading a procession.[52]

It is reasonable to presume that the growing importance of cavalry in India during that period was due to contact with the Medes and the Persians, who relied more on cavalry and infantry than chariotry in war. In the time of the younger Cyrus, the horsemen were fully protected with helmets, coats of mail, and greaves. Their chief weapons were two javelins, a knife and a short sword, and they bore no shields. The horse was also protected with armour—the head by a frontlet, the breast by a breastplate, while sides and flanks had special coverings.[53] In the battle of Gaugamela, the Persians relied on cavalry against Alexander.[54] According to Toynbee, the Achaemenians had made a start in armouring the war-horse as well as the rider.[55] In Assyria also, cavalry became important later on in the eighth century BC. Earlier, Tigleth Pileser I speaks of his chariots not cavalry, but by the time of Sargon and Sennacherib, chariots were confined to kings alone and horsemen were the main arms of the army.

The cavalry soldiers of the period rode without saddle, and their legs and feet were bare. Instead of riding with legs hanging, they drew them up until their knees were on a level with the chargers' backs. The cavalryman carried bow and sword and a shield was also carried, although there is no instance of its being used. An attendant accompanied the horse-archer. In the later period the attendant disappeared and the cavalryman's main weapons were bows and arrows and spears; as a matter of fact, the horsemen were divided into archers and spearmen. The cavalry soldier in this period was completely protected by armour, with the exception of his two arms. He wore a close-fitting tunic, his legs were encased in close-fitting trousers, and laced boots or greaves reached up to the knees. Thus the Assyrian cavalry was heavily armed. The first representation of the cataphract or heavy lance-carrying horseman is found in one of the Assyrian reliefs of the seventh century BC, and it may be due to contact with the Scythian horse-archers that the Assyrians combined the Scythian horse-archer with the Assyrian infantryman's defensive armour and perhaps invented heavy-armed cavalry. The heavy-armed cavalry of the Goths defeated the Roman legionaries.[56]

Mounted archers of Central Asia were a source of great strength to Alexander in his Indian campaigns.[57] The Greek cavalry was, from the very beginning, in personal relation to the king. Philip, king of Macedon, assigned the offensive to the cavalry, a practice which was followed by Alexander to great advantage in the battle of Hydaspes against Porus. On the authority of Arrian, Greek cavalry fought with a thrusting lance which proved superior to the Persian throwing spears in cavalry engagement.[58] The horseman was armed with helmet and corselet. The chief strength of the Carthaginian leader, Hannibal, lay in his cavalry,[59] and, in the battle of Cannae, Hannibal's superior strategy and cavalry triumphed over Roman legions. The Scythian horsemen were most terrible. They rode on horses and shot arrows while riding fast. They had compound double curved bows 2'6' long, and gold-plated quivers. Their arrows of reed of wood were also 2'6' long with points of stone, iron, bronze, or bone. They also had daggers not more than 2' long and carried an oval or round shield, but wore no armour.[60]

It is therefore not strange that from about the sixth century BC, cavalry became a recognized and important unit of the Indian army, and various kings had a large contingent of cavalry in their armies facing Alexander. According to Arrian, the Assakenians had 20,000 horsemen. Porus had put 4,000 horsemen in the field. From information received in Alexander's camp, it was learned that the king of Gangaridai and Prasii had 20,000 horsemen in his army. The united army of the Ksudrakas and the Mālavas which faced Alexander included a cavalry contingent of 10,000, and when defeated, they gave to Alexander a present of 300 horses. Even the small republican State of the Sabarcae had 6,000 horsemen in its army.[61] According to Megasthenes the army of Chandragupta had 30,000 horses,[62] while the strength of cavalry in the Andhra army was 2,000. One of the six boards which looked after army administration of Chandragupta had charge of the cavalry. Horse and elephant were so indispensable for the strength of the king that a private person was not allowed to keep either.[63] Persons were trained from boyhood to control horses. Kauṭilya speaks of a Superintendent of Horses to take care of royal horses. Horses were regularly trained for war purposes and employed in the destruction of the enemy's commissariat, for supervision of the army, for protection of the flanks of the army, for seizing treasury, for attacking in the rear, and for pursuing the defeated enemy.[64]

Cavalry became all the more important with the coming of the Scythians in the first century AD, and in the Junagarh inscription of Rudradāman, cavalry tops the list of the four constituent parts of the army. In the Gupta period, it became one of the most distinguished units of the army. Chandragupta II introduced the horsemen type of coins, which show that he was a great cavalry leader, like the Indo-Parthian and Scythian rulers, with whom this type of coin was quite common. Cavalry was an important unit in the army of Harṣavardhana.[65]

So far as the equipment of horse and rider are concerned, Arrian, speaking of the Mauryan period, says: 'The horsemen are equipped with two lances and with a smaller buckler than that carried by foot-soldiers. They do not saddle the horses nor do they curb them with bits like the bits used among the Greeks and Celts, but fit round the horse's mouth a circular piece of stretched raw ox-hide studded with iron or brass points directed inwards. In the horse's mouth is put an iron prong like a skewer to which the reins are attached.'[66] This is partly confirmed by the representation of horses on bas-reliefs at Sanchi and Bharhut. From a drawing of two horses of a chariot on a Sanchi gateway, we learn that there is no bit in the mouth of the horses. They have crests on the head, manes are plaited, and two rows of ropes are tied round the mouth and carried over the neck attached to the reins.[67] So far as saddle is concerned there are references to *pīthaka, pīthamaṇda, aśvastara* in the *Mahābārata.* These should mean saddles, but Hopkins thinks that they were blankets. However, the saddle, complete with stirrups, is clearly perceptible on some of the horses at Sanchi, and according to Sir John Marshall, 'this is the earliest example by some five centuries of the use of stirrups in any part of the world.'[68] The saddle is represented on the Aśvamedha type of coins. On several specimens of the horsemen type of coins of Chandragupta II, leather straps on the neck and a strap passing under the tail can be seen. In Class II of the horsemen type of Kumaragupta, the horse is fully accoutred.[69] While the shield of the infantry soldier is 3½ feet long and 1½ feet broad, the shield of the horseman is always 2 feet long and of a peculiar form, being shaped like a belt with a very wide mouth and much rounded at the bottom. A cavalry shield on the western gate bears only a crescent and two stars.[70] Horses were driven by whips tied to the wrist of the horseman, who wore a breastplate and carried a spear, lance, or sword. In one of the sculptured reliefs on the Rani Gumpha in Orissa, belonging to pre-Christian times, may be seen a caparisoned horse on which a prince carrying an unsheathed sword is taking away the princess.[71] On some coins, Azes is on horseback holding a spear, and Śoter Megas is also represented on horseback. On some types of coins, the Gupta kings are on horseback, holding bow and arrow,[72] showing imitation of the Scythian mounted archers, and on others the king carries a sword. In the Ajanta frescoes, horsemen are equipped with spears. Greek cavalry carried spears. It appears that horse-archery never became popular with the Indians, and with the end of the Gupta rule it disappeared from military practice. This was another defect in the Indian art of war, and caused the Indians to meet defeats by Alexander, the Scythians and later the Turks, who were past masters in this art.

V

Infantry constituted by far the largest single unit in the army but was certainly not the most important. From the native informant, Bhagalar or Bagela, whose statements were later confirmed by Porus, Alexander learned that the king of the Gangaridai and Prasii nations maintained a large army which consisted of 200,000 foot-soldiers. Chandragupta Maurya maintained a still larger army of 600,000 foot. The allied army of Malloi-Oxydrakai included 80,000 or 90,000 foot, while the Agalassoi had resisted Alexander with 40,000 foot. According to Arrian, the Assakenians pitted against Alexander a large force including 300,000 infantry, while Porus had 30,000 infantry. The tradition of maintaining a large infantry force was continued down to much later periods. In the army of Harṣa at the beginning of his campaign, the foot-soldiers numbered 50,000. According to Nunez, in the army of Kṛṣṇadev Ray of Vijayanagara (in the sixteenth century) against Raichur there were 703,000 foot-soldiers.[73]

In the beginning the foot-soldiers were respected and considered very useful. One of the epithets of the great God Rudra is 'Lord of foot-men' (*Pattināmpati*) in the Śatarudriya liturgy of the *Vajasaneyī Samhitā*. The *Atharva Veda* refers to the charioteer's powerful opponents—the men fighting on foot.[74] It appears that, with the growing popularity of chariotry in war, the foot-soldiers were gradually reduced to secondary importance, the base of a knightly pyramid; but the increasing number of infantry in the army was considered to be a source of strength. Prthu, who sprang from the right arm of Vena, was in the form of a foot-soldier clad in mail and armed with seimitars. Bhīsma was of the opinion that 'any army which has a large infantry forces is (regarded as) very strong.' Kauṭilya thinks that even effete persons could be recruited in the army to terrify the enemy by numbers. He assigns a separate department of infantry manned by many chiefs to look after this unit of the army. Śukra is also in favour of an army which has a predominance of foot-soldiers.[75] This may explain the large infantry force maintained by ancient Indian states. It was 'the sheer weight of numbers (in the army) which brought predominance for a century to the Achaemenian dynasty of Persia.'[76] But the large infantry force in India was assigned the subsidiary role of carrying weapons. In the Mahābhārata War also, the foot-soldiers are referred to as fighting confused battles and making much noise, but always as mere camp-followers of the charioteers and protectors of the charioteers and elephant-mounted warriors. Ten foot-soldiers were assigned to each horse. Bhīṣma promised to kill 10,000 warriors daily,[77] which shows that the foot-soldiers were easy targets for the charioteers.

Infantry was, however, assigned a very valuable role in the armies of some of the ancient nations. The first sculptured relief showing the regular infantry massed in rows is to be seen the Louvre Museum in Paris, and is known as the Stele of Vulture. It shows soldiers marching in close ranks with peaked helmets covering the head down to the ears. They are wearing long robes extending down to their feet, curved under the right shoulder and over the left arm. They are carrying lifted spears and shields with embossed circles. The stele illustrates the march of the phalanx of Eannatum, the king of Lagash, against the state of Umma. Ennatum is leading the phalanx. He is wearing a long cloak of woollen material, possibly quilted, and carrying a spear and a throwing stick. The front rank soldiers are carrying battle-axes and huge bucklers covering them from head to foot; behind these march the spearmen carrying in both hands long pikes which project beyond the bucklers of the first rank. This arrangement of the infantry soldiers anticipates the phalanx of the Macedonians. 'It is a regular Macedonia phalanx and one can imagine that its impact must have been hard to resist.'[78] Breasted rightly observes that 'this is the earliest example of grouping men together in a compact mass, forming a single fighting unit, called a phalanx.'[79]

The phalanx was essentially a Greek evolution and was perfected by Philip and his son, Alexander the Great. The Greek army in the earlier period was essentially an army of nobility bound to serve their prince or king as horsemen. It was only in the fourth century BC that the infantry was organized in the same way as the cavalry, recruited and arranged according to districts. Philip or his brother gave the title of *Pezhetairoi* to the infantry, as the cavalry was called *Hetairoi*. Philip was the creator of the famous Macedonian phalanx.[80] The phalangite was armed with a long spear, a small round shield, a sword and pelta carried by a ring on the arm, and he wore a helmet, greaves and a leather jerkin strengthened with metal. These soldiers were arranged in deep formation, and the phalanx moved slowly and maintained the order of the line even in thickest battle. Its thrust was enormously heavy, and it was aided by lightly-armed infantry, *Hypaspists*, who moved quickly and made connection between the cavalry and the phalanx. In the war against Persia, the Macedonian phalanx proved superior to the Persian infantry. A phalanx—the heavy infantry line—consisted of 1,500 men under one commander. Roman Consul Lucius, who defeated a Macedonia phalanx in the war with Perseus, was forced to admit that the Macedonian phalanx was the most formidable, and terrifying sight that had ever met his eyes![81]

But the Macedonian phalanx suffered from a serious defect in being an inflexible massive unit. The Romans realized this in the course of their long and varied military experiences, especially against the swift Carthaginian military movements under Hannibal. So they improved the Macedonian phalanx by introducing the manipular system. The Roman legion was divided into thirty maniples, each consisting of 120 men. The phalanx was divided into three divisions, front, middle, and rear. Each division was six men deep, and there was a narrow space between the divisions. The army was thus divided horizontally into three lines and vertically into maniples. Young and vigorous men formed the front division, and as soon as a gap was found the troops of the second division advanced and filled up the gap. Thus, the division was cut up crosswise into short sections so that a section could advance without carrying the whole division forward. Such a section or maniple of a division had a front about 20 men wide and 6 men deep. As Breasted observes, each maniple in advancing to fill a gap in the forward division was 'like a football back'. But the three divisions were invariably kept together; they were inseparable.

Rome's defeat in the battle of Cannae at the hands of Hannibal led Scipio to introduce another reform designed to make Roman infantry still more flexible. The divisions were to act independently. The Roman phalangite was armed with a spear *(pilum)* in his right hand with the point upwards, and he wore a heavy short sword girdled high on his right side. He carried a shield, had a helmet on his head and a leather corselet from the waist to just above the knees. The Macedonian phalangite relied more on his long spears when fighting, but the Romans used spears only when the battle began, hurling them into the enemy ranks at short range. After this the battle was fought with short swords easily handled at close quarters. The inflexible Macedonia phalanx had to submit to the Roman legions with their deadly short sword and their puzzling divisions behind the lines shifting into unexpected positions.[82]

Though it is true that Indian infantry was not so scientifically and consciously arranged as the Sumerian, Macedonian, and Roman, the Indian foot-soldier was not sparsely equipped. Infantry was very useful on uneven ground and in forest regions or stony tracts.[83] Naturally, the foot-soldier was adequately equipped with offensive and defensive weapons. In Vedic literature the soldier is referred to as equipped with bow and arrow.[84] He had a quiver hung on his back, and lances, spears, swords, axes and sling-stones were also used. The warrior's body was protected by a coat of mail and helmet. His arm was also protected from the friction of the bow-string by an arm-guard, and his fingers had finger-protectors. In the Great Epic also we find the foot-soldiers armed with bows and arrows (with quivers on their backs), and swords.[85] From Herodotus we learn that the Indian soldiers in Xerxes' army 'were clad in garments of cotton and carried bows of cane and arrows of cane, the latter tripped with iron.'[86] According to Arrian, the foot-soldier carried a bow equal to the length of the bearer and to shoot an arrow rested one end of the bow on the ground, pressed against it with his left foot and then drew the string backward. The arrow was little less than three yards long, and there was nothing which could resist the Indian archer's shot. In his left hand the archer carried a large shield of undressed ox-hide. There is no doubt that in the battle of the Hydaspes the muddy and slippery ground made the use of the long bow very difficult. Those foot-soldiers carried a broad and heavy two-handed sword. Another class of foot-soldiers carried a similar sword and shield and also a javelin in place of a bow.

The bas-reliefs and painting of ancient India largely confirm this description of the equipment of foot-soldiers. In the scene depicting the War of Relics sculptured on Sanchi's western gateway, the foot-soldiers are using bow and arrow, and lances. Their bows are long.[87] The quiver is fastened to the right shoulder and the leather straps fastening it are passed over both shoulders, crossed in front and carried to the back, where they are probably passed through a ring in the end of the quiver. The soldier is wearing a kilt, but there was also a tight-fitting jacket of some kind to cover the body. The swords are short, scarcely exceeding three cubits in length, but are broad, and in actual close fight were grasped in both hands. The foot-soldiers besieging the city are invariably carrying a bow which is shorter than the bearer and so different from the long bow described by Arrian. Some of the foot-soldiers in the sculptured relief appear to be using darts rather than arrows shot by bows. One is probably wearing something resembling peltae, made of raw-hides.

The Indian use of slings to throw stones at the enemy is referred to by classical historians of Alexander's invasion. Stein found on the top of a ruined fort in Swat valley water-worn stones of different sizes brought there to be used in slings. The shield borne by the infantry is long and narrow and round at the top, covering the bearer from head to knee, but it is smaller than that described by Megasthenes.[88] While according to Megasthenes, all foot-soldiers including archers have shields in their hands, in the Sanchi reliefs the archers have no shields although the swordsmen or lance-bearers invariable do. A bas relief belonging to about the time of Kaniska (first century AD) depicts a procession of men in masks and soldiers. They are carrying round shields, spears, swords and daggers. They are wearing leather armour down to the knee. The hands below the arm are free from any armour. The equipment resembles Greek or Roman though the men evidently belong to the Himalaya region, and the kilt resembles the Highlander's dress. In the Śaka–Kusāṇa period, the soldier wore close-fitting trousers or breeches and laced boots up to the knee. The Gupta kings on the archer type of coins are wearing such a dress.[89]

It may be of some interest to refer to the equipment of the foot-soldiers in other parts of the ancient world. In the sculptures of the earliest period, Assyrian foot-soldiers wear a short tunic, and the arms, legs, neck and feet are bare. Swordsmen used short swords and a convex metal shield or an oblong shield of wickerwork.

Spearmen carried a similar shield, and in their right hand they had a javelin or pike (5 feet long), and a short sword. The Assyrian archers used bows not more than 4 feet long with arrows not more than 3 feet long. The quiver was hung at the back and a sword was suspended at the left side by a cross belt. Some of the foot-soldiers also carried maces of bronze or iron. Archers are depicted in pairs, one guarding with the shield while the other shoots. Later on the Assyrian soldiers are divided into two classes—archers and spearmen—and archers were light-armed or heavy-armed. The light armed had no shield or helmet—only a ribbon on the forehead—and their dress was scanty. But the heavy archer was clothed in a coat of mail from the neck to the waist, arms were partly covered, below the waist was a fringed tunic, sandals and a pointed helmet were worn. While shooting an arrow, he was protected by a spearman carrying a heavy shield, the height of a man and of oblong shape. Spearmen generally had no coat of mail, their tunic barely reaching the knee; the helmet was surmounted by a crest of one kind or other. They had a circular shield, and the spear was 4 or 6 feet long. Sennacherib used singers also, who were completely armed with helmet, coat of mail, tunic, close-fitting trousers, and short boots, while in Egypt the slingers were very lightly clad. Among the foot-soldiers of Sennacherib were those who wielded a double-headed axe to prepare the path for the army.[90]

The Egyptian foot-archers were world famous for their aim. Heavy infantry was armed with huge metal-tipped lances, slings, swords, clubs and axes. The soldier protected his head by a padded cap, and carried an oblong shield which was not long but of great width. A short loin cloth was wrapped round the hips and a triangular apron of leather covered the stomach and the upper thighs. While the Egyptian soldier was very lightly clad or armoured the Assyrian was practically cased in metal. Alexander's phalangite wore helment, breast-plate and greaves and carried a long shield and a spear 24 feet long.[91]

VI

The history of the navy as a unit of the army in ancient India is not well-known. In a famous hymn of the Ṛgveda is an account of Bhujya sailing on a hundred-oared galley against some of his enemies. In the *Mahābhārata* the Pāṇdavas escaped in a ship provided with all necessary machinery and weapons of warfare. In the *Ayodhyā kaṇda* of the *Rāmāyana*, the Kaivarta young men are asked to wait in five hundred ships to resist the enemy's passage. Megasthenes is the first to refer to a full-fledged war fleet belonging to the time of Chandragupta Maurya. Kauṭilya also refers to a naval unit under a superintendent and also pirate ships. That the Indians knew how to construct ships for the passage of the army is proved by the fact that Alexander crossed the Indus on boats supplied by the Indians. According to Arrian the huge fleet in retreat under Nearchus included thirty ships of war. After the Mauryas, the Indian power which presumably maintained a war-fleet was the Andhras, because on some of the coins of Andhra rulers like Pulumayi there is a representation of a ship with two masts. From the fact that on some coins of Maues, Posidon with trident and thunderbolt is represented, it is suggested that Maues won some naval victories in India.[92]

Megasthenes includes transport and commissariat as one of the six elements of the Mauryan army. This department was administered by a committee of five members. It was responsible for the supplies to the army, bullock-carts for carrying engines of war, food for soldiers, provender for cattle and other military needs. The Persians made commissariat arrangement on a large scale, and a baggage-train sufficient to supply the host for a few months accompanied the army. 'The Persian army was rarely in any difficulty with respect to its subsistence.'[93]

The ancient Indian army was largely a standing and professional army. It received regular pay and its only duty was to fight. According to Megasthenes, 'the entire force—men-at-arms, war-horses, war-elephants and all are maintained at the king's expenses'; the pay that they received from the state was so liberal that 'they can with ease maintain themselves and others besides.'[94] Kauṭilya also regards an unpaid army as a source of trouble. The commander of the army received the highest salary, equal to the minister and the *purohita*. The trained soldier received the salary of 500 *panas*.[95] It is significant to note that in the history of Rome, systematic payment to the yeomanry began during Rome's war with Veii (406–396 BCE), thus making 'the first stage of the transformation of a citizen militia into a professional army.'[96]

Such an Indian army was composed not only of hereditary and directly paid troops, known as *maula*, but also of mercenary troops (*bhṛta*), corporations of soldiers (*śreṇībala*), allied troops (*mitrabala*) deserters from the enemy (*amitrabala*), and forest tribes (*ātavi* troops). Kauṭilya prefers the hereditary army to other kinds of troops, as the former depends on its master and is constantly drilled.[97] Mercenary troops numbering 7,000 took part in the defence of Massaga against Alexander. We know from the Mandasore inscription of Kumaragupta II that some of the members of the silk-weavers' guild were proficient in the use of bows and other weapons.[98] It is also possible that there were corporations of warriors who peddled their services. Kauṭilya refers to Kṣatriya śreṇīs who lived by the profession of arms as well as by agriculture, trade and cattle-breeding.[99] Both the Kaurava and the Pāṇdava armies in the Mahābhārata War had allied troops in their midst. So far as enemy troops are concerned, Kauṭilya advises the conqueror to try to win them over and to use such deserters for his own purpose. Wild troops may have been recruited in the same manner as the Red Indians used by the French and the English in North America.[100]

The Indian army was efficiently administered. Megasthenes says that the military administration was under a board of thirty members divided into six committees of five members each, entrusted with the management of the six units of the army, respectively. Kauṭilya also informs us that 'Elephants, cavalry, chariots and infantry shall each be officered with many chiefs.'[101] A commander-in-chief was considered indispensable for the army to be successful in its objective. Duryodhana told Bhīṣma, 'Without a commander even a mighty army is routed in battle like a swarm of ants.' The commander was to be 'well versed in military sciences, in various kinds of battle formations', was 'to know how to make regular soldiers and volunteers act their parts', and he was to be expert 'in the matter of marching the troops, disposing them in battle and in withdrawing them'. Karna, in recommending the name of Drona for the office of the commander-in-chief of the Kaurava army, observed, 'There is not a single warrior who will not follow Drona when the latter goes to battle. This Drona is the foremost of military leaders, the foremost of all wielders of weapons, and the foremost of all intelligent persons.' 'Nobility of birth, learning, years, intelligence, powers, skill, and knowledge of worldly affairs'[102] appear to be additional qualification for a commander. According to Kauṭilya, the leader of the army should know about the favourable time for acting about the suitability of the battle ground for his army, about the method of sowing dissension in the enemy ranks, and about when and how to advance or attack the enemy fortress. He should also be responsible for the discipline of forces on the march, in the camp, and in the battlefield.[103] Discipline was well-maintained in the Greek army, as even in the thick of the battle the phalanx was not disturbed. The Macedonian soldiers were well drilled and exercised for fighting, matching, and manoeuvering in all seasons, day and night.[104] According to Breasted, 'in military discipline the Romans surpassed all other nations in the ancient world.'[105] But the Indian battles were confused and 'there was no order whatsoever after the first plunge into the fight....'[106]

The best time for march of the army was December or March; though for special reasons the army could march in May–June (*Jyeṣṭha*). Astrologers, soothsayers, physicians, etc., followed in the train of the army on the march. Foodstuffs and other provisions were carried in double the quantity estimated to be necessary. The rate of march was two *yojanas* daily and the nature of the arrangement of the army on the march depended on the nature of the ground traversed. Water-channels on the way were crossed by bridges, boats, timber-planks, elephants, and baskets covered with skins.[107]

The army on the march encamped on one of several sites. According to Kauṭilya, the site was to be selected on the basis of *Vāstuvīdya* (the science of architecture) and was to be properly set out (square, rectangular or circular) by the carpenter in consultation with the astrologer and military leader (*nāyaka*). The camp was to be protected by ditches, ramparts and towers. There were to be four gates and six roads, and proper places were to be allotted to the king, the harem, the arsenal, the chariots, the cavalry and others. The approaches to the camp were to be made still more difficult by placing thorns, mounds and wells near it. It was to be guarded by spies and sentinels. Bhīṣma advises that in pitching the camp, places near woods should be preferred. The camp of the Pāṇdavas was near the river Hiraṇyavati.[108] The Persians also preferred an open space, and water nearby was a necessity for their encampment. They also surrounded the camp by a ditch, and the earth so dug up was thrown inside to make a rampart round the camp; when in sandy regions, the camp was protected by sand bags. Soldiers armed with spears and large shields guarded the approaches. The Egyptian war camp was not much different from this. Their camp was always rectangular in plan, surrounded by a ditch. The earth thrown up inside formed the enclosing rampart, the outside of which was covered with shields. The camp had only one entrance, guarded by two detachments of mounted men armed with clubs and naked swords. The Assyrian war camp was oval or circular, surrounded by a wall of dried brick provided with towers. The interior was divided into four equal parts by two roads.[109]

Before battle, the king won the loyalty of the soldiers by declaring himself to be just like them, a wage-earner. The priest encouraged the army by invoking the *Vedas*. The astrologers declared the invincibility of the king and the impenetrability of battle formations. Awards were offered to the brave, and a share in the spoils was promised. Sacrifices were offered to the gods and the king fasted the day before the battle started and lay down in his chariot with the weapons. Before the actual encounter began, the army was arranged in a particular way. Kauṭilya speaks of many battle arrays such as *Bhoga, Daṇda, Maṇdala Kākapadī, Vajra, Ardhachandrika* and others.[110] In the *Mahābhārata* it is said that when an army was pitted against a larger force, the former should be arranged in Needle Formation (*Śuchī-vyuha*). In the *Māhabhārata* we are told of *Vajra, Krauncharuna, Gārudī, Makara, Chakra,* and *Ardhachandra* arrays or *vyuhas*.[111] All this suggests that in ancient India the art of war developed so much that many kinds of battle formations were devised. Porus had arranged the army against Alexander in an almost copybook fashion.

It is important to observe that in the camp and on the battlefield a regular medical corps of physicians and surgeons together with nurses was present to treat and cheer the wounded. Kauṭilya says, 'Physicians with surgical instruments, remedial oils, and cloth (for bandages), and women (nurses) with prepared food and beverages should stand behind giving encouragement of the men.' When Bhīṣma was pierced with countless arrows in the Māhabhārata

War, surgeons came to pick out the arrows from his body. When the eldest Pāṇḍava, Yudhiṣṭhira, was injured in battle, he was treated by the foremost surgeons in the camp.[112]

VII

Battles were not only fought in the open field as in the Māhabhārata War or the battle of the Hydaspes, but also round the forts. The siege of forts constituted the main feature of war in ancient India. A fort was considered a source of strength, and according to Pāraśara, quoted by Kauṭilya, difficulties due to bad fortification were more serious than those due to the enemy. Kauṭilya goes so far as to say that 'for those who have forts there seems to be no destruction'. Of the island in the midst of water (*audaka*), or fort in the forest (*vanadurga*), or fort in the desert (*dhānvana*), he takes the mountainous fort (*parvata*) to be the most useful.[113] Manu also prefers a hill-fort to others and to emphasize the indispensability of forts he says that it is prescribed in the *śāstras* that the king must possess a fortress.[114] The existence of fortification at Harappā proves that forts were maintained even in the pre-Vedic period. The Vedic literature refers to the '*purs*' of the enemies of the Vedic Aryans, some of which were autumnal forts *(śārah)*. Some of these had a 'hundred walls' (*saradi*). Some are said to have been provided with *śataghni* (literally, 'hundred-killers') for defence against the attack of the enemy. Harappā excavations have cast doubt on the theory that the forts mentioned in the Vedic literature were temporary earth structures.[115] The Jātakas which refer to the early Buddhist period mention many strongholds protected by one or three ditches and surrounded by strong walls with towers and battlements. Vārānasi and Mithilā were such strongly fortified cities. Lankā, the capital of the demon king, Rāvana, was surrounded by encircling ramparts with stately domes and tall turrets, and beyond it lay a deep moat.[116]

Alexander, during his campaign on the north-west frontier of India, came up against many forts. His wars in the region show that Kauṭilya was right in holding that the mountain fort was the best for defence. In the assault against Massaga, Alexander had much difficulty because of the deep moat surrounding and the precipitous slope of the hill on which the fort was situated.[117] In order to provide the strongest possible defence for the fort, Kauṭilya recommends that it be surrounded by three parallel ditches, one full of water, one full of mud and one empty. Round the nearest ditch should be a high and broad rampart provided with parapets and towers and with *Indrakośa*s in between to enable archers to shoot their arrows against the besiegers. Outside the rampart numerous obstructions such as thorns, pits, mounds, waterpools, etc., were to be provided to make the enemy's approach more hazardous.[118] According to Megasthenes the city of Pātaliputra was encompassed by a ditch which was 600 feet in breadth and 30 cubits in depth and by a wall containing 570 towers and 64 gates. From the sculptures on the gateways of Sanchi and Bharhut we learn that Kuşinagara and Kapilavastu were fortified cities, each surrounded by a ditch and a wall provided with battlements and towers.[119]

The importance of forts was equally obvious to other nations of the ancient world. The remains of the fortification of Abydos, belonging to the Sixth Dynasty of Egypt, show that the rectangular rampart must have been at least 40 feet high and that the walk round the rampart was protected by a low parapet with rounded battlements reached by narrow staircases. At various points posterns were provided for archers defending the garrison.[120] According to Herodotus, Babylon was surrounded by a deep and wide moat, then by a rampart 50 royal cubits in breadth and 200 in height; the city had 100 gates of brass and also an inner wall with towers. Within the inner wall ran the broad procession street. High defensive walls, from which missiles could be thrown on the invaders, rose by sides of the street. The Assyrian capital, Nineveh, was also surrounded by a moat and then by a rampart, 100 feet high and 50 feet thick.[121]

'In an age when war was looked upon as the only liberal profession, the fenced city must have been the primary concern.'[122] According to Kauṭilya, 'the haven of the king and his army is strong fort.' He further says that 'He [the king] should entrench himself in a fort inhabited by men and provided with stores and supplies.' 'It is in the fortified towns that the treasury and the army are secured; they are a secure place for the people and a powerful defensive instrument in times of danger for the king.' According to Manu, the fort should be well-provided with weapons, money, grain and beasts of burden with Brāhmaṇas, artisans, engines, fodder and water. Bhīṣma advises the king to flood the ditch round the front with water and fill it with crocodiles and sharks, and to place *śataghnis* and other weapons on the ramparts and destructive engines on the gate.[123]

Naturally, therefore, the enemy had to besiege the fort in order to overtake it. According to the authors of the Vedic Index, the siege of forts is mentioned in the *Samhitās* and the *Brāhmaṇas.*[124] In the *Jātakas* there are numerous references to sieges of cities. Defenders of the city of Vārāṇasī threw boiling mud, stones and other missiles on the besiegers. Ultimately the trainer of the royal elephants (Bodhisattva in a previous incarnation) broke through the iron bars of the gate riding an elephant and breaking the pillars. Brahmadatta of Vārāṇasī laid siege to Takṣaśilā but retired on seeing the rampart and the towers of the city. Brahmadatta during his siege of Mithilā tried to fill up the deep moat which lay between him and the fort, ordered the walls of the fort to be mined, and finally attempted to starve the inmates into surrender by cutting off the water supply of the city and the supply of food coming to the garrison.[125] The defenders fought by hurling javelins, spears, and arrows on the besiegers, Kauṭilya refers to many machines used by defenders. *Bāhumukha* was a tower situated on the top of the fort and protected with a leather cover. It faced in all directions to enable the archers to shoot at their enemies all round. *Pārjanyaka* was a machine 50 yards long placed outside the fort wall to throw missiles at the enemy. *Ardhavāhu* and *Urdhwavāhu* were large pillars made to fall down in or be thrown at the approaching enemy. *Devadaṇda* was a long pole with iron nails attached to it. It was placed on the top wall of the fort and was hurled down on the besieging enemy. *Śataghni*, or hundred-killer, had a large number of iron nails attached to it and was placed on the walls of the fortress and pushed down on the enemy hammering at the gate of the stronghold. The fort could also be protected against enemy missiles by covering the towers and the parapets with *Sūkarikā*, a kind of leather covering. An instrument called *Hastivarka*, 'a long rod with two or three points' was used against attacking elephants.

We have seen that the Jātakas and the *Arthaśāstra* refer to the direct part played by elephants in breaking open the gates of the fortified cities. Defenders also threw stones by hand or by a machine called *Yantrapāṣāna* or by a rod known as *Ghoṣpanapāṣāna*. But it is significant that in representations of sieges on Bharhut and Sanchi gateways we do not find the defenders using any machine. They are seen hurling stones and shooting arrows from the ramparts. However, that the defenders used slings and showered stones on the attackers from above is proved by the existence of such stones on the top of a fort in Swat valley.[126]

If the besieged found it difficult to hold back the enemy, they came out to fight, 'running against the enemy like a moth against a flame as death or victory is certain for one who is reckless of life'. The besiegers also developed methods of storming a stronghold. Before they began the siege they had to collect an abundance of corn, raw materials, machines, weapons, and labourers in the camp. They also made adequate arrangements for the defence of the camp and assured the safety of supply lines. The siege might begin by contaminating the waters of the ditch or by emptying it. The ramparts and the parapets might be assailed by making use of underground tunnels (*suranga*) and iron rods. Elephants and horse-riders would make direct assault on the gates. Archers would shoot arrows against the defenders on the walls. By means of ropes the walls of the fort might be scaled, and a blockade of the besieged, might also be attempted. According to Kauṭilya, 'grains, oil, jaggery and salt' reaching the fort should be seized. Grass and wood should be set on fire, the underground tunnels of the stronghold widened and the stored provisions secretly removed. Manu also observes: 'When he has shut up his enemy in a town, let him sit encamped, harass his [enemy's] kingdom, and continually spoil his grass, food, fuel and water.'[127] Kauṭilya says that if all these methods fail to capture the fort, the enemy should try to set fire to it by tying inflammable powder (*agniyoga*) to the tails of birds like pigeons which have nests in the walls, and letting them fly back to the fort; or spies masquerading as the watchmen of the fortress should tie inflammable powder to the tails of domesticated animals such as monkeys, cats and dogs and let them go over the roofs of the thatched houses in the fort. Archers from elevated posts in the camp might throw fire-balls (*agnidhāraṇa*) on the fortress as well as fire-arrows called *viśvāsghāti*.[128] It is important to note that there is no reference to battering rams or catapults. As a matter of fact, in the sculptures depicting besieged cities, neither side is shown using any of the above-mentioned machines. In the siege of Kuśinagara, we find the city with its high ramparts, battlements and towers being besieged by an army of seven chiefs, composed of elephants, horses, chariots and infantry. The attackers are using bows and arrows, though they carry swords also. The defenders are hurling arrows and stones, and one is carrying a mace in his hand. Besiegers are forcing their way though the gates and two of them appear to have succeeded, while others are trying to scale the walls (presumably with a rope). There is no sign of a ladder being used.[129]

Siege warfare was prevalent in other parts of the ancient world. The Egyptians used to break down the gates of the fortress by axes or set fire to the doors. The archers aimed their arrows at the defenders, and the lancers with metal-tipped spears tried to penetrate the walls. If nothing else succeeded, a prolonged blockade causing the starvation of the defenders was resorted to, and treachery was practised. The famous fortress of Megiddo in Asia surrendered because the Egyptians had invested the fortress, and the Asiatics were starving.[130] The Assyrians were great experts in siege warfare. They assailed the strongholds by scaling with long ladders placed against different portions of the wall. These brave soldiers were armed with long spears and shields or with bows and arrow. Assyrian archers also shot arrows from below against the defenders on the ramparts. For protection against missiles thrown from above, the archers were attended by a shield-bearer who carried a long shield with a handle in the middle, resembling the Persian *gerrohn*. Sometimes this shield was placed against the wall of the fort, and the archer shot arrows against enemies on top of the wall without fear of being hit by them. Some warriors under the protection of such a shield mined the walls at the foot of ramparts, unhurt by missiles hurled from above, by swords, spears or pick-axes. Gates were attacked by axes or were set on fire. The Assyrians used battering rams and moveable towers against the besieged. The battering ram moved on wheels and was protected by skin or felt against the missiles from above. Some of the rams had a head shaped like a spearpoint and were driven against the walls. Defenders would try to set fire to the battering ram, made of wood, by throwing inflammable material or burning torches on it from above; therefore the soldiers on the ram were provided with water which they could direct through leather or metal pipes. Defenders would also try to put the ram out of action by lowering chains to catch the point of the ram and pull it upward, and the ram was therefore provided with hoods underneath to entangle the chain. As the besieged were on a higher level, the ram was also often put on artificially raised mounds. In the moving towers, soldiers in heavy armour and armed with bows and arrows, swords, long spears and lances attacked the besiegers on level ground. Some think that the Assyrians also used catapults or ballista, which were of great height and well-protected with hides. These were worked from a mound or inclined plane to throw missiles to the top of the ramparts, and the defenders attacked them with fire.[131]

Alexander's army was equally well provided with engines of siege warfare. In the siege of the forts of the Aspasians, Alexander used ladders to scale the walls and archers to attack the defenders. Alexander used a battering ram against the walls of Massaga and a moving tower placed on an inclined mound from which archers threw arrows against the defenders on top of the wall. He also constructed a high mound near the ditch and raised towers over it from where the engines threw missiles at the defenders on the ramparts. Against the stronghold of Sangala, Alexander used battering rams and ladders for scaling the walls, and undermined the wall. It was in scaling the walls of the citadel of the capital of the Malloi that Alexander was severly injured.[132]

VIII

Ancient Indians used many kinds of weapons which were classified as *mukta* (thrown), *amukta* (not thrown), *muktamukta* and *yantramukta* (thrown by machines)[133] and so on. We have already referred to many of these weapons in our study of the equipment of the fourfold army. The primary weapon was the bow and arrow, and military science in India was known as *Dhanurveda*, or the science of archery. The bow was made of bamboo, horn or metal, and arrows of reed and iron are known. *Nārācha*s were iron shafts. Even reed arrows were tipped with metal heads, and in the Indus Valley arrow-heads of bronze and copper have been found. The Indian bow was very long, like the Egyptians's, though the Greek bow was smaller. Śukra refers to arrows two cubits long. Barbed and poisoned arrows are met with in the ancient literature.

*Nalikā*s are mentioned in the *Mahābhārata*, where they were used as blow-pipes to fire small pieces of iron.[134] Later they stand for guns and cannons. Swords *(asi),* battle-axes (*paraśu*), spears (*śakti*), javelin (*śūla*), clubs (*gada*), and maces were used by warriors. Slings to throw stones were used by Indian, Egyptians, Greeks, and other ancient peoples.

Various kinds of engines were used, and the earliest references to these concern *Ajātaśatru* in his war against Vaiśāli. From Uvāsayadasao we learn that Ajātaśatru invented two engines; one was *Mahasīlakaṇtaga,* which threw big stones in succession and was worked by some mechanical device; the other was *Rathamuśala* a chariot to which a mace was attached. Kauṭilya refers to many machines which were used in siege warfare by both sides, such as *śataghani, jāmadagnya, sanghāti* (a long pole to set fire to the towers of the fort), *audhghātima* (an instrument to put down towers), *sarvatabhadra* (a cart with wheels which could be rapidly turned and which could throw stones in all directions) and many others. There is no reference to the use of gunpowder in the period under review. The *Nalikās* referred to in the *Mahābhārata* cannot be guns because there is no mention of smoke in the battlefield as a result of their use. *Śukranīti* refers to gunpowder (*agnichūrna)* and guns and cannons; but the work is taken to be of a much later period, not earlier than the thirteenth or fourteenth century. In the *Mahābhārata* there are references to many divine weapons, mostly arrows, such as *Pāśupata, Aindra, Vāyavya, Brahma Nārāyaṇa, Sammohana,* etc., which were used after invoking *mantras*. Therefore 'they are regarded as weapons of magic used after meditation.'[135]

Besides wielding offensive weapons, the Indian warrior was well protected with defensive armour. The authors of the Vedic Index refer to corselet (*kavacha*), a coat of metal (*varman*), and a left-arm-guard (*hastagna*). The helmet (*śipri*) was also known. It is very possible that this defensive equipment was made of some stiffer material and strengthened with metal plates.[136] In the *Mahābhārata* the warrior was fully armoured. 'The coat of mail of Śatānika, brother of Virāt, was of adamantine steel, burnished with gold.' His younger brother's coat of mail was 'plated with gold and capable of resisting every weapon.' The coat of mail of the Matsya king was decorated with a hundred suns, a hundred circles, and a hundred eyes.[137] The Epic car-warriors were protected by breast-plates, cuirasses, finger-guards, helmets, neck-protectors, and other limb guards (*gātravaraṇi*). Bhīṣma, the second Pāṇdava,* was so heavily accoutred as to be scarcely recognizable by his own followers. In the *Bhojājaniya Jātaka* there is a reference to a noble heavily armed from head to foot.[138] Porus was wholly protected by armour. 'Only his right shoulder was unprotected, the rest of his body was rendered shot-proof by his coat of mail, which was remarkable for its strength and the closeness with which it fitted his person.'[139] According to Hopkins, the Epic hero was covered with netted armour or wire.[140] Kauṭilya's *lohajālika,* a coat of mail to cover the whole body, refers to something similar. He also mentions *paffa* (a coat of mail without cover for arms), *kavacha* (a coat of iron made of different pieces and joined together to cover the head, trunk and arms), *śūtarka* (to cover the hips and the waist), *śirastrāṇa* (cover for the head), *kanthatrāna* (cover for the neck), *kūrpasu* (cover for the trunk), *kanchuka* (a coat extending as far as the knee-joints); *varavana* (a coat extending as far as the heels), and *nāgaodarikā* (gloves). Coats of mail were not only made of metal but also of cotton. Kauṭilya mentions *varmas* (coats) made under the orders of the Superintendent of Weaving who was closely associated with those who manufactured ropes and mail armour.[141] Cotton armour worn by Indian warriors in the Persian army is mentioned by Herodotus; it was so strong that no weapon could pierce it.[142]

Not only men but even animals wore armour. Bhīṣma rode on an elephant in armour of iron. In the equipment of the war-elephant, Kauṭilya included mail armour. Horses were also provided with armour. In the Jātakas there is a reference to a war-elephant 'sheathed in complete armour'! The *Bhojājaniya Jātaka* refers to a war-horse (which was Bodhisattva in a previous incarnation) 'sheathed in mail.'[143] The warrior was not only protected by armour, but he also carried a shield, larger in the case of the foot-soldier than in the case of horseman. The scene depicting the siege of Kuşinagara corroborates this. The shield was made of some such

* Editor's Note: Bhima was the second Pandava. Bhīṣma was *pitamaha* of both the Pandavas and the Kauravas.

metal as iron, or if made of wood, was often strengthened by metal bosses to blunt the point of the enemy's weapon. The Assyrian warrior was as heavily armed as the Indian. In Persia the war-horse was fully clothed with armour. His head was covered with a frontlet, neck and breast with a breastlet, and the sides and flanks also had special coverings. According to Toynbee, in Persia in the Achaemenian age a start was made in armouring the rider and the horses. The Massagitae are described by Herodotus as armouring their horses in the fashion that is ascribed by Xenophon to the Achaemenian cavalry.[144] It is possible to imagine some connection between the Indian equipment of horse and rider and that of the Persian cavalry. It is important to note that cavalry in ancient India appears to have come into vogue not long after contact was made between the Achaemenians and Indians.

All weapons and armour of men and animals were manufactured in government factories. Kauṭilya assigns this job to the Superintendent of Armoury, who employed skilled artisans for the purpose, who were full-time government servants. All the manufactured weapons were to be marked with the king's seal and entered in the armoury. Private persons were not permitted to import weapons nor were they allowed to bear arms without licence. Megasthenes informs us that 'There are royal stables for horses and elephants and also a royal magazine, for the arms, because a soldier has to return his arms to the magazine, and his horse and the elephant to the stables.' Bhīṣma also favoured kings' manufacturing weapons and armour. He says that kings desirous of victory should manufacture a variety of arms and armour both for animals like elephants and bulls, and for soldiers.[145]

Military authorities did not rely only on weapons for success in battle. In ancient India, military espionage was well-understood and organized. In the *Māhabhārata, chara,* meaning spies, were included in the list of eight elements of an army. In Kauṭilya's *Arthaśāstra,* military espionage is dealt with at great length. Spies were used to win over dissatisfied, frightened, ambitious and haughty enemies. They were used to break the morals of the enemy or to delude him in many ways, or to tempt him by offers of elephants, women and wealth. According to Śukra, there is no other means of subjugating the foe except by causing disaffection among his soldiers.[146]

It was believed that war was not only won by weapons or diplomacy but that the favour of the gods was essential to victory. In the Vedic literature, there are clear references to priests praying and sacrificing for the victory of their patrons. Kauṭilya's *Arthaśāstra* also refers to sacrifices before and after the battle. The authority of the Vedas was cited to infuse spirit among the warriors. Oblations were made and prayers were offered for the victors and for those who died in the battle. According to Curtius, an image of Hercules was kept in front of the infantry of Porus. The Assyrians also enlisted the support of their gods in their wars, and their standard in front of the chariot had figures of a bull's head and of Assur shooting arrows.[147] The Egyptian army carried figures of deities.

War was certainly a cause of much cruelty and destruction, but the Indian authorities tried to make war as humane as possible. There was a code of conduct agreed upon between both parties. When the Mahābhārata War was about to begin, the Kauravas and the Pāṇdavas entered into a covenant for conducting the war. Persons equally matched were to encounter one another, i.e. a car-warrior would fight a car-warrior, a horseman a horseman, and so on; those who left the field were not to be slain; no one was to attack a man already engaged in fighting another, nor one bereft of weapons or unarmoured; charioteers, standard-bearers and trumpeters were not to be attacked. Brave warriors were not to shoot weapons at one who had given up or whose supply of arrows were exhausted. Bhīṣma prohibited the use of barbed and poisoned arrows and advised against attacking wounded and weak enemy.[148] Knights were not to use their weapons against non-combatants. Notice was to be given to person before striking him. Women, children and old men, priests and cows were not to be attacked. Even a person bearing a female name was not to be attacked by worthy warriors.[149] According to Baudhāyana, poisoned or barbed arrows should not be used. Manu also advised against the use of weapons concealed in wood, barbed or poisoned weapons, or weapons whose points were blazing with fire. The eunuch, or one who climbed an eminence, or joined the palms of his hands in supplication, or was in sorrow or in fear, was not to be attacked. Megasthenes informs us that the non-combatants were not injured and that the farmers went on with their work as usual. Battle was fought in the day and was suspended at dusk.[150] It is pleasant to be able to record that in India at such an early period a chivalrous code was framed to guide the warriors in their encounters, when in other parts of the ancient world such a thing was hardly known.

In actual battle all these laws may not have been rigorously followed. In the Mahābhārata War itself, which is considered as a war between good and evil, we find the agreed covenant being violated by both the just Pāṇdavas and the unjust Kauravas. The careless and weaponless Abhimanyu was attacked by six car-warriors with showers of arrows. Drona was killed by the Pāṇdava commander, Dhṛṣṭadyumna, when the former was in *prāya* (meditation). Arjuna, the third Pāṇdava, killed Karna while the latter was on the ground trying to extricate the wheel of his car from the mire. Poisoned and barbed arrows were gathered in the camp, and Abhimanyu pierced Karna with a barbed arrow. Kṛṣṇa did not regret the use of unfair means by the Pāṇdavas against the Kauravas and observed, 'If I had not adopted such deceitful ways in the battle, victory could never have been yours, nor kingdom nor wealth.' Even the general rule that only equally matched men should fight one another was not followed, and we find car-warriors fighting elephant-riders, elephant-riders fighting horsemen and car-warriors fighting foot-soldiers. Kauṭilya suggests many deceitful measures to be taken against the enemy and refers to, besides open battles, silent battles when the enemy is killed by spies, and treacherous battle. 'The enemy was to be struck when tired, careless and confused.' Various kinds of missiles or balls that held fire or poison were thrown into the enemy camp, causing blindness or death; even water, grass and fields could be poisoned or made desolate.[151] But this should not prevent us from giving due credit to the framers of rules to make war more humane.

Contrasted with this was the situation in Assyria where utmost cruelty on the battlefield was the general rule. The Assyrians, unlike the ancient Egyptians, were not satisfied with wreaking their wrath on enemy kings and the principal instigators of the war, but made the entire enemy population their victims. Persons falling into their hands in time of siege were cruelly tortured, cut to pieces, and impaled alive on stakes. When the city fell, it was razed to the ground. The king was proud of these activities. Instead of leaving the fleeing enemy as the Indians did, the Assyrians pursued the enemy to the end. The Assyrians have been rightly characterized in the scriptures as 'a fierce people'. They impaled the rebels, flayed the captives with knives, announced rewards for heads, and deported large populations from their native countries. 'Desolation followed upon the track of the Assyrian army. In order to make the country of the enemy uninhabitable and unfertile the Assyrians even had salt strewn upon the ruined cities.' As against this, we have the testimony of Megasthenes that the Indian armies 'neither ravage an enemy's land with fire, nor cut down its trees.' Even Kauṭilya wants the victor to cover the vices of his enemy by his virtue.[152] The treatment of the conquered in ancient India left nothing to be desired.

NOTES

1. K. P. Jayasval, *Hindu Polity*, Calcutta; Butterworth & Co., 1924, II, pp. 4–5.
2. M. Mackay, *Early Indus Civilization*, London, Lucas & Co., 1948, pp. 95–101; Stuart Piggott, *Prehistoric India to 1000 BC*, Harmondsworth, Middlesex, Penguin Books, 1950, Ch. VI; E. J. Rapson, *The Cambridge History of India* Part I, Cambridge University Press, 1935, p. 81.
3. *Mahābharata*, 'Virāṭ Parva', tr. P. C. Ray, Calcutta, 1890, p. 77.
4. Hemachandra Raychaudhuri, *Political History of Ancient India*, 6th edn, University of Calcutta, 1953, pp. 211–2.
5. Kauṭilya, *Arthaśāstra* Part III, tr. Mahāmahopādhyāya T. Ganapathi Śastri, Trivandrum Sanskrit Series, Trivandrum 1925, p. 45; Idem, tr. Shamasastry; Government Oriental Library Series, *Biblioteca Sanskrita* no. 37, Part II, Bangalore, 1915, Book VII. Ch. IX, p. 358.
6. Mahāmahopādhyāya P. V. Kane, *History of Dharmasāstra* Part III, Poona: Bhandarkar Oriental Research Institute, 1946, 211; *Śukranīti*, vol. III, tr. Binoy Kumar Sarkar (*The Sacred Books of the Hindus*), Allahabad, 1914, vs. 624-5, p. 248; quoted by H. C. Ray, *Journal of Department of Letters*, vol. XIV, Calcutta University, 1927, no. 7, pp. 2*ff.*
7. Quoted from *Attireye Brahmaṇa* by R. C. Raychaudhuri, *Political History of Ancient India*, 6th edn, University of Calcutta, p. 170.
8. D. G. Sircar, *Select Inscriptions*, Part I, University of Calcutta, p. 412: Anant Sadhasiva Alterkar, *Catalogue of Gupta Gold Coins*, Bombay: Numismatic Society of India, p. 40, pl. IV; V. R. R. Dikshitar, *Annals of Bhandarkar Oriental Research Institute*, vol. VIII, 1926-7, pp. 381-2.
9. Kauṭilya, (Shamasastry), pp. 319, 394: *Śukranīti*, op. cit., Sec. VII. vs. 7–8, p. 217; *Mahābhārata*, 'Sānti Parva', p. 419.

10. *The Jātakas*, tr. E. B. Cowell, vol. II, no. 183, p. 66, 1; op. cit., *Patāyi-Jātaka*, no. 229, p. 152; *Mahābhārata*, 'Virāṭ Parva', p. 79 and 'Udyog Parva', p. 42; *Vālmiki Rāmāyana*, tr. Griffith, Canto VII, p. 517.
11. T. W. Rhys Davids, *Buddhist India*, 1903, first Indian edn, September 1950, p. 57.
12. Kauṭilya, Book. 2, Ch. III, p. 62; Book 5, Ch. III, p. 309; Sirkar, op. cit., vol. I, pp. 173, 207-8.
13. V. R .R. Dikshitar, *Gupta Polity*, University of Madras, 1952, p. 212; idem, *The Art of War as Practised in South India*, vol. VIII, *Annals of Bhandarkar Oriental Research Institute*, Poona, 1926–7, p. 182.
14. Thomas Waters, *On Yuan Chwang's Travels in India*, vol. I, London: Royal Asiatic Society, 1904–5, p. 171.
15. Kane, op. cit., vol. III, pp. 212–3; *Śukranīti*, Sec. VII, vs. 5–6, p. 215; Dikshitar, *War in Ancient India*, Macmillan & Co. Ltd., 1948, pp. 254–5.
16. J. W. M'Crindle, *Ancient India as Described by Megasthenes and Arrian*, Calcutta, 1926, Fragments XXXIV, p. 88; Dikshitar, *Gupta Polity*, p. 212.
17. *Raghuvamsa*, Canto IV, p. 26; Śircar, op. cit., pp. 263, 265; Fleet, *Gupta Inscriptions*, p. 214*ff*; Śukranīti, Sec. VII, v. 41, p. 218.
18. A. A. Macdonnell and A. B. Keith, *Vedic Index, of Names and Subject*, Part I, London, 1912, p. 64; II, p. 206.
19. *Jātakas*, vol. I. no. 229, p. 152; vol. IV. no. 465.
20. *Mahābhārata*, 'Virāṭ Parva', pp. 79–80; 'Bhīṣma Parva', p. 429, 'Udyoga Parva', pp. 466–99, 486-91.
21. N. K. Siddhanta, *Heroic Age of India*, London: Routledge and Kegan Paul, 1929, p. 139; Vālmīki, *Rāmāyaṇa*, Book III, Canto XXV, p. 309; Book VI, pp. 561, 586.
22. J. Marshall, *Monuments of Sanchi*, vol. I, Plate 15.3; V. A. Smith, *Early History of India*, 3rd edn, p. 66; J. W. M'Crindle, *The Invasion of India by Alexander the Great*, new edn, Westminister; Archibald Constable and Company, 1916, pp. 102, 234, 281–2, 310; J. W. M'Crindle, *Ancient India*, Fragments XXXIV, p. 88; Kauṭilya, Book 2, Ch. XXXIII, p. 175; Sircar, op. cit., vol. I, pp. 173, 207–8.
23. Rapson, op. cit., vol. I, p. 98.
24. Macdonnel and Keith, op. cit., vol. II, pp. 201–2.
25. E. W. Hopkins, 'The Social and Military Position of the Ruling Caste in Ancient India', *Journal of American Oriental Society*, vol. VIII, pp. 205, 235, 237.
26. *Mahābhārata*, 'Udyoga Parva', p. 451.
27. J. Fergusson, *Tree and Serpent Worship*, London: India Museum, 1868, Plate III, Fig. 6; pls VI and XXXIII; Marshall, op. cit., vol. II, pls XI, and XXII; J. W. M'Crindle, *Invasion of India*, Curtius, p. 207.
28. Macdonnell and Keith, op. cit., vol. II. p. 203; Hopkins, op. cit., p. 286;

J. W. M'Crindle, *Invasion of India*, p. 207; idem, *Ancient India as Described by Megasthenes and Arrian*, p. 88.

29. *Mahābhārata*, 'Udyoga Parva', p. 451.
30. Śukranīti, Sec. VII, v. p. 60: *Mahābhārata*, 'Udyoga Parva', pp. 202, 450–1. (Provided with sharp-edged circular planks of wood, such chariots may suggest the scythe chariots of the Persians.)
31. Hopkins, op. cit., p. 205.
32. *Cambridge Ancient History*, vol. II, p. 227: G. Maspero, *The Dawn of Civilization*, ed. Prof. Sayoe, 5th edn, London, 1910, p. 606.
33. G. Maspero, *The Struggle of the Nations*, 2nd edn, London, 1910, p. 51; *Cambridge Ancient History*, vol. II, Cambridge, 1940, pp. 43, 69–70, 142; J. H. Breasted, *The Conquest of Civilization*, Harper & Bros., 1926, p. 259, Fig. 130, pp. 245*ff*, 290: N. K. Siddhanta, *Heroic Age of India*, p. 140 points out that the distinguished heroes in the *Iliad*, like Indians, used the chariot in fighting.
34. G. Rawilson, *The Five Great Monarchies of the Ancient Eastern World*, vol. I, London, 1862, p. 368; vol. II, p. 1*ff*. According to Curtius, Indians did not know the use of bits on horses. Bits are not found on the horses of the sculptured reliefs in Sanchi (*Bhilsa Topes*, pl. 3; pp. 19–20); Ulrich Wilcken, *Alexander the Great*, tr. G. C. Richards, Chatto & Windus, London, 1932, p. 132.
35. Quoted from Kauṭilya, Book 10, Ch. IV, p. 445; J. W. M'Crindle, *Invasion of India*, p. 208; All the 120 chariots were captured running headlong in mud (Rapson, op. cit., vol. I, pp. 364–5).
36. R. N. Saletore, *Life in the Gupta Age*, Bombay, 1943, p. 137.
37. *Mahābhārata*, 'Virāṭ Parva', p. 78; 'Udyoga Parva', p. 450; 'Bhīṣma Parva', pp. 65, 161, 199, 236, 239; 'Drona Parva', p. 88; 'Karna Parva', p. 36; 'Salya Parva', p. 75.
38. J. W. M'Crindle, *Invasion of India*, p. 94, note 2; *Jātakas*, vol. I. no. 80, p. 205; vol. II. no. 182; *Samgāmavachara Jātaka*, p. 64.
39. *Bhilsa Topes*, tr. Cunningham, p. 229; Lady Herringham, *Ajanta Frescoes*, Oxford University Press, 1915, p. 13; G. S. Hodgson Marshall, op. cit., vol. I, p. 114, pl. 613; p. 214, pl. 15.3.
40. J. W. M'Crindle, *Invasion of India*, pp. 209, 222, 224, 310: idem, *Ancient India as Described by Megasthenes and Arrian*, p. 201.
41. W. W. Tarn, *Alexander the Great*, vol. II, p. 168.
42. Dikshitar, *The Mauryan Polity*, p. 190; Kauṭilya, Book 6, Ch. XI, p. 363.
43. Raychaudhuri, op. cit., pp. 272, 362: *Cambridge Ancient History*, vol. VI, pp. 408–9; P. C. Chakravarty, *Art of War in Ancient India*, University of Dacca, 1941, p. 49; Howard H. Scullard, *A History of the Roman World*, London, 1935, p. 282.
44. R. B. Whitehead, *Catalogue of Coins in the Punjab Museum—Lahore* Indo-Greek Coins, Oxford, 1914, p. 13, pl. I, no. 21, p. 62 pl. III, no. 148, no. 507; Scullard, op. cit., pp. 130–1, 245.

45. Kauṭilya, Book 10, Ch. IV, p. 446.
46. J. W. M'Crindle, *Ancient India as Described in Classical Literature*, Strabo, pp. 48–9: Kauṭilya, Book 2, Ch. II, p. 55.
47. Kauṭilya, Book 2, Ch. II, p. 56; Ch. XXXII, p. 137, 172; J.W. M'Crindle, op. cit., Strabo, p. 50, p. 137; Aolian, p. 139.
48. J.W. M'Crindle, *Ancient India as Described by Megathenes and Arrian*, Fragment XXXIV, p. 89; Dikshitar, *War in Ancient India*, p. 170; Chakravarty, op. cit., p. 52; Hopkins, op. cit., p. 267; Altekar, op. cit., p. cvi, p. cix; Rapson, *Catalogue of the Indian Coins in the British Museum, Andhras and W. Kṣatrapas*, British Museum, London, 1908, p. 3, pl. 1, no. 5.
49. Chakravarty, op. cit., p. 33.
50. *Jatãkas*, vol. I, no. 23, pp. 61–2; represented in Bharhut relief—B. M. Barua, *Bharhut*, vol. II, p. 89, pl. XLVI, scene 90.
51. Marshall, op. cit, vol. II, pl. 61.
52. *Bhilsa Topes*, op. cit., pp. 218–27.
53. Rawilson, op. cit., vol. IV, pp. 113, 119*ff.*
54. Tarn, op. cit., vol. II., p. 183.
55. A. J. Toynbee, *A Study of History*, Oxford University Press, 1945, vol. IV, p. 440.
56. Rawilson, op. cit., vol. II, p. 22*ff*: Toynbee, op. cit., vol. IV, p. 439*ff*, note 4.
57. Tarn, op. cit., vol. II, p. 194; Rapson, op. cit., vol. I. p. 351.
58. Wilcken, op. cit., pp. 31, 87.
59. Scullard, op. cit., p. 207.
60. *Cambridge Ancient History*, vol. III, p. 198.
61. J. W. M'Crindle, *Invasion of India*, pp. 66, 101, according to Diodorus, 3,000 horsemen (p. 274); p. 22, according to Plutarch, 80,000 horsemen (p. 310); pp. 234, 252.
62. Davids, op. cit., p. 177.
63. J. W. M'Crindle, *Ancient India, as Described by Megasthenes and Arrian*, Fragment LVI, pp. 140–1: Fragment XXXIV, p. 88; Fragment XXXVI, p. 90.
64. Kauṭilya, pp. 164*ff*, 445-6.
65. H. C. Ray, 'Notes of War in Ancient India', *Journal of Department of Letters*, vol. XIV, no. 7, University of Calcutta, 1927, p. 41; Sircar, op. cit., vol. I, p. 173; Altekar, *Catalogue of the Gold Coins in the Bayana Hoard*, pp. lxxvii, lxvxi, note 3; idem, *Epigraphia India*, vol. VII, no. 22, p. 150.
66. Arrian, quoted in *Mauryan Polity*, p. 191.
67. Fergusson, op. cit., pl. III, Fig. 6. Chakravarty, *Art of War*, pp. 38–9 adds that the Indians used bits, and sculptured reliefs prove this.
68. *Guide to Sanchi*, p. 138, no. 3.
69. Altekar, op. cit., pp. lxxii, xcix.
70. *Bhilsa Topes*, op. cit., pp. 217–8, pl. xxiii, 3, 4, 5.
71. Dikshitar, *War in Ancient India*, p. 137.

72. Whitehead, op. cit., vol. I. p. 114, pl. XI; p. 160, pl. XVI; Altekar, op. cit., pp. xcviii, pl. XXII, 7.
73. A. V. Smith, *Early History of India*, 3rd edn, pp. 93, 125–6, J.W. M'Crindle, *Invasion of India*, p. 234, Curtius, pp. 66, 101.
74. Chakravarty, op. cit., p. 15.
75. *Mahābhārata*, 'Sānti Parva', pp. 117, 321; Kauṭilya, Book 6, Ch. XII, p. 367; Book 2, Ch. IV, p. 62; *Śukranīti*, p. 219, Sec. VII, vs. 45–6.
76. *Cambridge Ancient History*, vol. III. p. 99.
77. Kauṭilya, Book 10, Ch. IV, p. 446; *Mahābhārata*, 'Udyog Parva', pp. 452, 454.
78. Rev. James Baikei, *Life of the Ancient East*, London, 1923, pl. XVIII, p. 204.
79. Maspero, *Conquest of Civilization*, p. 137.
80. Tarn, *Alexander the Great*, pp. 31–2.
81. Toynbee. op. cit., vol. IV, p. 434.
82. Maspero, op. cit., p. 542.
83. *Mahābhārata*, 'Sānti Parva', pp. 100–123: Kauṭilya, Book 10. Ch. IV, p. 445.
84. Keith and Macdonnell, op. cit., pp. 388–9.
85. *Mahābhārata*, 'Udyog Parva', pp. 450-2.
86. Rapson, op. cit., vol. I. p. 340.
87. Marshall, op. cit., vol. II, pl. XV.
88. A. Stein, *On Alexander's Track to the Indus*, Macmillan, 1929, p. 38; *Bhilsa Topes*, pp. 216–8.
89. Chakravarty, op. cit., p. 19; V. A. Smith, *History of Fine Art in India and Ceylon*, Oxford, 1930, 2nd edn., pl. 37, p. 62; Altekar, op. cit., pls I, II, V.
90. Rawilson, op. cit., vol. II. pp. 28–36, 41.
91. Maspero, *Struggle of the Nation*, p. 627; J.W. M'Crindle, op. cit., p. 19.
92. J. W. M'Crindle, *Ancient India as Described by Megasthenes and Arrian*, p. 88; Kauṭilya, Book 2, Ch. XXVIII, pp. 156–7; J.W. M'Crindle, *Invasion of India*, p. 83; V. A. Smith, *Commerce of the Ancient*, vol. I, p. 12; quoted in R. K. Mookerji, *A History of Indian Shipping*, p. 101; Rapson, *Catalogue of the Indian Coins in the British Museum, Andhras and Westerm Ksatrapas*, p. 22, pl.V, nos. 95 and 96; Whitehead, op. cit., p. 98, pl. X; Tarn, *The Greeks in Bactria and India*, p. 102.
93. J. W. M'Crindle, *Ancient India as Described by Megasthenes and Arrian*, p. 88; Rawilson, op. cit., vol. IV, p. 140.
94. J. W. M'Crindle, op. cit., pp. 40, 217.
95. Kauṭilya, Book 8. Ch. V. p. 405; Book 5, Ch. III. pp. 307–38.
96. Scullard, op. cit., pp. 130–1.
97. Kauṭilya, Book 2, Ch. XXXIII, p. 175; Bk. 9, Chap. 11, p. 417.
98. J. W. M'Crindle, *Invasion of India*, pp. 68–9; Sircar, op. cit., vol. 1, p. 292.
99. Kauṭilya, Book II, Ch. 1, p. 455.
100. Rapson, op. cit., vol. 1, p. 490.

101. J. W. M'Crindle, *Ancient India as Described by Megasthenes and Arrian*, p. 88; Kauṭilya, Book. 2, Ch. IV, p. 62.
102. *Mahābhārata,*, 'Udyoga Parva', pp. 453, 486; 'Drona Parva', p. 14.
103. Kauṭilya, Book 2, Ch. XXXIII, p. 176.
104. Wilcken, op. cit., p. 33.
105. Breasted, op. cit., p. 527.
106. Hopkins, op. cit., p. 223.
107. Kauṭilya, Book 9, Ch. I, p. 413; *Laws of Manu,* sec. VII, V, pp. 182, 245; *Mahābhārata,* 'Sānti Parva', p. 319; Kauṭilya, Book 10 Ch. II, pp. 483–9.
108. Kauṭilya, Book 10, Ch. 1, p. 437; *Mahābhārata,* 'Santi Parva', p. 320; Dikshitar, *War in Ancient India*, p. 106.
109. Rawilson, op. cit., vol. IV, p. 137; Maspero, op. cit., pp. 221–2, 32–3.
110. Kauṭilya, Book 10, Ch. III, pp. 442, 450–2.
111. *Mahābhārata,* 'Bhīṣma Parva', pp. 60–1, 185, 209, 259, 293, and 'Drona Parva', p. 112.
112. Kauṭilya, Book 10, Ch. III, p. 443; *Mahābhārata,* 'Bhīṣma Parva', p. 450; 'Karna Parva', p. 347.
113. Kauṭilya, Book 8, Ch. I, pp. 392–3; Book 2, Ch. I, p. 56; Book 7, Ch. 10, pp. 361–2.
114. *Laws of Manu,* tr. Marx Muller, *Sacred Books of the East,* vol. XXV, p. 57–9.
115. Keith and Macdonnel, op. cit., vol. 1, pp. 538–9; Rapson, op. cit., vol. V. pl. I, p. 86.
116. *Jātakās,* vol. II, no. 182, p. 64: vol. VI, no. 546, p. 197; *Valmiki Rāmāyana* tr. Griffith, Book IV, Lanka Canto II, pp. 477–8.
117. J. W. M'Crindle, *Invasion of India,* p. 195.
118. Kauṭilya, Book 2, Ch. III. pp. 57–8.
119. J. W. M'Crindle, *Ancient India as Described by Megasthenes and Arrian,* p. 67: Marshall, op. cit., vol. II, pl. XV.
120. Breasted, op. cit., pp. 450–51.
121. Baikei, op. cit., pp. 233–6, 296.
122. Baikei, op. cit., p. 328 (quoted).
123. Kauṭilya, Book. 7, Ch. XIV, p. 374; Ch. XV, p. 376; Book 8, Ch. 1, p. 392; *Laws of Manu,* p. 288; *Mahābhārata,* 'Sānti Parva', p. 226.
124. Keith and Macdonnell, op. cit., vol. I, p. 539.
125. *Jatākās,* vol. III, no. 182, p. 64; no. 229, p. 152; vol. VI, p. 201.
126. Kauṭilya, Book 2, Ch. XVIII, p. 124; G. S. Hodgson Marshall, op. cit., vol. I, pl. 61, 1. p. 118; Stein, op. cit., p. 38.
127. Kauṭilya, Book 7, Ch. XV, p. 377; Book 13, Ch. IV, pp. 486–7; Book 12, Ch. V, pp. 412–3; *Laws of Manu,* vol. VII, v, pp. 195, 247.
128. Kauṭilya, Book 13, Ch. IV, pp. 471–2.
129. G. S. Marshall, op. cit., vol. II. pl. 15; p. 214; *Bhilsa Topes,* op. cit., p. 215; Fergusson, op. cit., p. 141.
130. *Cambridge Ancient History,* vol. II, p. 71.

131. Rawilson, op. cit., vol. II, pp. 77, 82: Maspero, *Struggle of the Nations*, p. 637. According to Toynbee (*Study of History*, vol. IV. p. 474), the Assyrians did not use catapults, but only battering rams and rolling towers.
132. J. W. M'Crindle, *Invasion of India*, pp. 62, 66, 117–20, 146–7.
133. Dikshitar, *War in Ancient India*, p. 92.
134. Keith and Macdonnell, op. cit, vol. I, p. 81: *Mahābhārata*, 'Udyoga Parva', p. 143.
135. Raychaudhuri, op. cit., p. 213; Kauṭilya, Book 2, Ch. XVII. pp. 124–5; *Sukra*, p. 389*ff*; P. V. Kane, op. cit., vol. III, p. 213; Hopkins, op. cit., p. 297 (*JAOS*, XVII).
136. Keith and Macdonnell, op. cit., vol. I, pp. 60–1.
137. *Mahābhārata*, 'Virāṭ Parva', pp. 77–8.
138. Hopkins, op. cit., pp. 304–6; *Mahābhārata*, 'Udyog Parva', p. 168; *Jātakas*, Cowell, vol. I, no. 23, pp. 61–2.
139. J. W. M'Crindle, op. cit., p. 108.
140. Hopkins, op. cit., p. 305.
141. Kauṭilya, Book 2, Ch. XVIII. p. 126; Ch. XVIII. p. 126: Ch. XXIII, pp. 140–42.
142. Rapson, op. cit., Vol. I, p. 340.
143. *Mahābhārata*, 'Karna Parva', p. 36: Kauṭilya, Book 2, Ch. XXXII, p. 173; *Jatakas*, vol. 1, no. 80. p. 205; no. 23, pp. 61–2.
144. Marshall, op. cit., vol. I, pl. 61; I, Toynbee, op. cit., vol. IV, pp. 440–41.
145. Kauṭilya, Book 2, Ch. XVIII. p. 123; Book 5. Ch. III, p. 310; J. W. M'Crindle, *Ancient India as Described by Megasthenes and Arrian*, p. 88; Dikshitar, op. cit., p. 218.
146. P. V. Kane, op. cit., vol. III, p. 203; Kauṭilya, Book 1, Ch. XIV, p. 29; Book 9, Ch. IV and V; Book 13, Ch. II, pp. 479–80; *Śukranīti*, Sec. VII, p. v, p. 375, p. 235.
147. Kauṭilya, Book 10, Ch. III, p. 442; J. W. M'Crindle, *Invasion of India*, p. 208; Maspero, op. cit., pp. 629–30.
148. *Mahābhārata*, 'Bhīṣma Parva', pp. 3–4; 'Karna Parva', p. 361; 'Sānti Parva', p. 306.
149. Hopkins, op. cit., pp. 227–8.
150. Kane, op. cit., vol. III, p. 210: *Laws of Manu*, vol. VII, vs 90–93, pp. 230–1; J. W. M'Crindle, *Ancient India as Described by Megasthenes and Arrian*, p. 32; *Mahābhārata*, 'Bhīṣma Parva', p. 317.
151. *Mahābhārata*, 'Drona Parva', pp. 143, 145, 645; 'Karna Parva', p. 361*ff*: 'Udyoga Parva', p. 413; 'Salya Parva', p. 239; 'Bhīṣma Parva', p. 276; Kauṭilya, Book 10, Ch. III, p. 441; Book 14, p. 495*ff*.
152. Maspero, op. cit., p. 637 Breasted, op. cit., p. 172; Rawilson, op. cit., vol. I, pp. 302–4: J.W. M'Crindle, op. cit., p. 32; Kauṭilya, Book 13, Ch. V, pp. 491–2.

CHAPTER 2

Military Pursuits and National Defence of the Hindus from the Fall of the Mauryas to the End of the Second Magadhan Empire (*c*.185 BC–AD 550)

Bimal Kanti Majumdar

Foreign Invasions and Military Achievements

A few words are needed by way of introduction to explain briefly at the outset the nature of defence that Hindu kingdoms organized and of military endeavours made in the north and south after the collapse of the mighty empire of the Mauryas, before we consider the military system of the second Magadhan empire, i.e. the Gupta Empire. As soon as the strong arm of Aṣoka was withdrawn the forces of disruption set in[1] and the Maurya Empire rapidly declined. In central and eastern India the Mauryas were succeeded by the Śungas (*c*.185–*c*.112 BC) and the Kāṇvas (*c*.112–*c*.78 BC). In the western and north-western part the Maurya princes first asserted their independence and then fell a victim to foreign aggression.[2] A fairly big empire sprang into existence in the Deccan. It was the Sātavāhana Empire founded by one Simuka in the first century before Christ.[3] From the fall of the Maurya power to the rise of the Kūṣāṇas, northwest India became the battleground for foreign powers. The Bactrians, the Parthians and the Śakas played their part as conquerors and rulers. These foreigners established their strong rule in Afghanistan, the Punjab and western India generally. Northern India was a bundle of petty independent or semi-independent states. There was no central authority—no organized defence. But individual kings were not militarily weak. If some of the Buddhist *Jātaka*s are to be assigned to this period of confusion and weakness, it is possible to get some information about the composition of the army of Indian kings. The *Vessantara Jātaka*[4] says that king Sanjaya had an army of 60,000 warriors. It consisted of horses, chariots, soldiers and elephants, the number of elephants being 14,000, a surprisingly huge number not to be met with in the writings of classical authors. The *Mahāunmagga Jātaka*[5] refers to an army of 60,000 soldiers. The same work tells us that the army was composed of thirty and nine thousand warriors.[6] The Buddhist writer Aśvaghosa, who flourished in the first century AD and was a contemporary of Kaṇiṣka, prescribes in his *Saundarānanda Kāvya* an elaborate curriculum of study for the prince which includes, among other things, the use of the lances, archery, rules of battle array and strategy.

Spirit of Resistance in the North

The foreign tribes which had settled in the north-west and west in post-Maurya times made many unsuccessful attempts to push their conquests far into the country. It was one long chapter of fierce warfare between the foreigners stationed in India and the Indian princes—the Śungas fighting with the Bactrian Greeks and the Sātavāhanas exchanging their blows with the Śaka satraps of western India. It was really a period of invasion and forcible intrusions from without and of general insurrection within, a clear indication of India's setback from the political and military points of view. Nevertheless, in the history of ancient India, the four hundred years that elapsed between the decline of the Maurya power and the reappearance of Hindu imperialism under the Guptas were scarcely a period which might be counted as absolutely ineffective and inglorious. A revival of her military power was in sight. A question may be asked here—Was the Śunga-Kāṇva military system completely out of gear? The military records of the Śungas, however, tell a different tale. From our point of view the most important political event of Pusyamitra's reign was the Greek or Yavana invasion from the north-west referred to by Pataṇjali in his *Mahābhāṣya* and Kālidāsa in his *Mālavikāgnimitram.* The Yavanas, it is stated, came as far down as Madhyamikā (Nagari in Chittor) and Sāketa (Ajodhyā) and these two cities were virtually in a state of siege.[7] The Greek invasion led by the Bactrian King Demetrios, son of Euthydemos, was successfully repulsed by Vasumitra, a

Śunga prince. The battle was fought on the southern bank of the river Sindhu (in central India). The hurling back of the Yavana attack was no mean achievement on the part of the Śunga prince. Unfortunately, we have no knowledge of the respective strength of the armies and of the tactics that decided the issue, but the defeat itself shows that the military renown of the Maurya times was not a past memory. The territories of the Śungas were less extensive, their defence problem was, therefore, not as difficult as that of the Mauryas. They probably took care to guard their frontier fortresses by placing them under able officers. One Vīrasena was placed, as Kālidāsa[8] says, in charge of a frontier fortress on the bank of the Narmada. Demetrios' invasion was the last of the series of Greek invasions which had begun with Alexander. Antiochus III of Syria invaded India in about 206 BC.[9] Polybius refers to a king called Sophagasenus (Subhagasena), probably a successor of Vīrasena, an independent ruler of Kāsmīra after Aṣoka's death. The passage quoted below will explain the nature and result of Antiochus III's invasion of India's borderland and renewal of his friendship with an Indian king:

> He (Antiochus the Great) crossed the Caucasus and descended into India, renewed friendship with Sophagasenus, the King of the Indians, received more elephants until he had 150 altogether, and having once more provisioned his troops, set out again personally with his army, leaving to Androsthenes of Cyzicus, the duty of taking home the treasure which the King had agreed to hand over to him.

The going back of the Syrian king after the renewal of friendship with the Indian ruler suggests that the wishes of the Seleucids were not fulfilled. The Kingdom of Kāsmīra might have cried a halt to the march to the Syrian monarch. Although the Maurya Empire had already begun to break up, the Indian defences were not completely broken through until the days of Demetrios and Menander who exercised control over Indian territories for some time.[10]

Trans-Vindhyas Defence

Turning now to the trans-Vindhyan India we find the Sātavāhana Empire (*c.* 1st century BC to 2nd century AD) rise to the position of a strong military power in the Deccan. The greatest king of the dynasty was Śātakarṇi I. He married Nāganikā, the daughter of Mārațhi chief, conquered eastern Malwa and styled himself '*Daksinṭpathapati*'.[11] The celebration of Aśvamedha sacrifice by him indicates his position as the paramount sovereign of south India[12]—a position attained later on by Samudragupta and Chandragupta II Vikramāditya in the north. Surrounded as the Sātavāhanas were by hostile peoples, they had to maintain considerable forces to retain their supremacy. They are believed to have introduced the system of military governors (*Strategos*), a system apparently borrowed from the Śakas. They also appointed district officers bearing the title of Senāpati.[13] They were 'reputed to possess military force second only to that at the command of the King of the *Prasii*, Chandragupta Maurya. The Andhra territory included thirty walled towns, besides numerous villages, and the army consisted of 100,000 infantry, 2,000 cavalry and 1,000 elephants.'[14] There were occasional conflicts between the Sātavāhana kings and the foreign tribes that had formed settlements in western and southwestern India, and it is no exaggeration to say that the period between the second century BC and the second century AD was really the time of chronic rivalry between the indigenous and foreign governments for supremacy over the Deccan and the western region. The result was an alternate swing of success and failure. Twice in this period—once towards the end of the first century BC and again in the beginning of the second century AD, the Sātavāhana power seems to have been eclipsed by a dynasty called the Kṣaharata or Kṣatrapa. After Śātakarṇi I they had to yield important possessions to the Scythians.[15] Nahapāna, who ruled over a considerable portion of Mahārāṣtra was the most notable ruler of the Kṣaharāta family. Epigraphic record would have us believe that in about AD 124 the dynasty was overthrown by Gautamīputra Śatakarṇi, who has been described as the '*Śaka-Yavana-Palhava-nisūdana*' and as the 'restorer of the glory of Sātavāhana family'.[16] The successors of Gautamīputra carried on warfare with those who came to wield power after Nahapāna in the western Deccan. Rudradāmana I of the line of Chashṭana of Ujjainī twice defeated, as the Junagadh inscription[17] says, Śatakarṇi, the lord of the Deccan, although there was no incorporation of his territories. According to R. G. Bhandarkar,[18] the lord of Daksināpatha worsted by Rudradāmana was Yajṇaśrī Śātakarṇi. From the political events narrated above we may draw the conclusion that it was due to the fighting capacity, heroism, love of country of the Sātavāhana rulers and their unflagging zeal to rid the land of foreigners that the Deccan was saved from being completely Scythianized in the first stage of the Sātavāhana empire-building. The fall of the Sātavāhana Empire after three hundred years of existence may in all probability be attributed rather to internal aggression and the rise of number of a new dynasties in the upper Deccan and in the far south than to any inherent weakness in its military system. Their political achievements which are so varied and glorious, may have been the outcome of their excellent military system.

War Matters in Indian Sculptures and Coins

We pass on now to the consideration of the military pursuits of the Indians in the period under review by a brief examination of their sculptures and coins. We find in the obverse of the Persian and Macedonian types of coins a mounted horseman with lance at rest and in the reverse a tall figure holding a spear and thunderbolt. Apollodotus I wears a trident in the right hand, a shield hanging from the left.[19] In the coins of the Greek, Scythian and Parthian invaders, the king wears coat of mail in chain armour. Helmets with straight swords and lances are found. Some of the kings stand on horses or elephants. Spears, clubs and other weapons also find place.[20]

Indian sculptures of the second and first centuries BC are also helpful to some extent. In the Bhārhut (Nogrod State, Madhya Pradesh) stūpa are found boats, chariots drawn by horses, carriages drawn by bullocks, many musical instruments, the old Indian sword and also the representation of a procession of soldiers. In Stūpa No. I, for example, are seen soldiers attacking the enemy down with armours and stones—a representation of 'War of relics.'[21] In the south gateway (back) and the west gate (back) we find the 'War of the Relics' beautifully sculptured.[22] As already noted, ancient cities were provided with lofty gates, towers and ramparts.[23]

In a bas-relief of the Sānchi stūpa we have a representation of city walls,[24] and as Rhys Davids points out, 'it is very probable that in earlier times the fortifications were often similar in kind.'[25] A relief on the south gate of Sānchi Stūpa shows the siege of the fort of Kusinārā with what is technically called *Indrakośa* (i.e. shooting posts for arrows and bows built into the wall). This fits in with Kauṭilya's description of fortification.

Gupta Military System

The political history of a country is inseparable from its military chronicle. For nearly three centuries preceding the foundation of the second Magadhan Empire (*c.*AD 320), northern India was practically dominated by the Kuṣāṇas, a warlike central Asian tribe that had set up an extensive empire extending from Afghanistan to as far east as Mathurā, and possibly Bihar, Gangetic delta and Orissa.[26] The establishment of an empire by aliens in northern India which was, in a sense, more stable and widespread than that of the Yonas (Greeks) was an indication of the silent revolution in the military system through which the country had been passing since the age of the Mauryas. The Scythian rulers of north-western and western India became thoroughly acquainted with Indian system of administration and evolved an administrative framework, civil and military, on the lines of the Mauryas and of their own institutions. We hear of a number of military officers of the Śakas and Kuṣāṇas bearing the titles of Mahāsenāpati,[27] Daṇḍanāyaka[28] and subordinate officers like Senāgopas, Gaulmikas[29] (Captains), Āraksādhikrtas[30] (guards), Asvavarakas[31] (troopers), Bhaṭamanuṣyas,[32] (mercenaries) etc. H. C. Raychaudhuri[33] finds close correspondence between the first two military officials of the Scythian period and the Senāpati and Nāyaka of Kauṭilya's *Arthaśāstra.*[34] The Moṇikiyala inscription of Kaṇiṣka refers to Lala, the Daṇḍanāyaka of the family of Guṣaṇa.[35] Military officers bearing the Indian title of Mahāsenāpati existed along with *Strategos* (general or governor). As in the time of Kauṭilya and the *Mahābhārata,* the employment of spies specially Samcharamtakas (wandering emissaries) in the Scythian period was probably a common feature.[36]

Chandragupta I, the first independent ruler of the Gupta dynasty of Magadha, assumed the title of Mahārājādhirāja.[37] The kingdom he brought into existence was destined to grow in all directions. The conquests made by his successors like Samudragupta and Chandragupta II Vikramāditya enlarged and consolidated it. The empire, when at the height of its glory, roughly extended from the eastern to the western sea,[38] from the Himalayas in the north to the Narmadā in the south. How this vast empire was defended is the next question that we must try to answer. The military system of the Guptas was substantially the same as that of the Mauryas; but there was possibly a certain looseness in the organization. Samudragupta, being a typical Dharmavijayī, granted some amount of autonomy to conquered territories subject to payment of tribute and allegiance to the Gupta sovereign as their overlord. He thus created a band of feudatories. The trend of Hindu politics in the third and fourth centuries was such that it favoured distinct feudal tendencies and provincial separatism.

The centralization of the Mauryas was conspicuous by its absence and the empire built in the fourth century contained within itself a number of Sāmanta princes paying tribute and supplying contingents to the imperial forces. With regard to the administration of Bengal, for example, Majumdar[39] observes, 'The Gupta emperors did not directly administer the whole territory which was formally included within the empire. They were feudal chiefs, referred to as Mahāsāmanta who assumed the title of "Maharaja".' The same process might have been extended to other units of the empire. Mātṛviṣṇu of the Eran Stone pillar inscription of Budhagupta (CII, p. 89) is looked upon as a Gupta feudatory. A seal matrix cut in the rock of Rohtasgarh (CII, p. 284), refers to Śrī-mahāsāmanta Śaśāṅka. His identification with Śaśāṅka, King of Gauda, is not altogether impossible.[40]

Samudragupta was the ablest member of the Gupta ruling house. He seriously attempted to bring the whole of India under his political control but as already stated, the Hindu polity was then running a different course and Samudragupta, in spite of his wide conquests, was unable, it may be presumed, to bring all India under one uniform system, and had to follow a middle course between a strict imperial control and full local autonomy. Such a system has always been a source of weakness and often a hindrance to the formulation of a durable policy of national defence. All the Gupta emperors, from Chandragupta I to Skandagupta, were skilled warriors imbued with imperial ambition. The empire under their direct control was well defended. For two centuries there was nothing to disturb the peace till troubles came from the

Puṣyamitras and the Hūṇas during Skanda's rule (*c*.455–AD 467). Chandragupta II (*c*.380–AD 413) augmented the empire by annexing Malwa, Gujarat and Kathiawar. A believer in Aryan institutions and Kṣatriya glory, he was determined to free the country from the hated Scythians and proclaimed a 'holy war' against the Śaka Satrap of western India. Rudrasimha III was defeated and slain and eastern and western Malwa and Kathiawar were in Gupta hands.[41] If these conquests added valuable financial resources to the empire, they at the same time involved greater military responsibilities which Skandagupta had to be careful about. Troubles developed thick and fast with the incoming of the Hūṇas. The Gupta territories, when the conquests of Chandragupta II were over, looked very much like a pan-Indian empire. If the identification of Chandra of Meharauli inscription with Chandragupta II is deemed acceptable, the Punjab had come within his sphere of influence. The imperial Guptas had, however, failed to exercise an effective control over the Punjab and the Khyber pass. In this respect the Gupta military organization was distinctly inferior to that of the Mauryas. Had they successfully guarded the north-western frontier, 'the critical battle with the Hūṇas would have been fought beyond the Indus'.[42]

From inscriptions[43] we know that Skanda had to contend with two formidable foes—the Puṣyamitras—a local power in the Narmada valley according to Majumdar, and the Hūṇas. The Gupta empire, already threatened with ruin by their depredation, was given a brief lease of life by Skanda as crown prince, who by subduing the Puṣyamitras and the Hūṇas, saved the empire. In his endeavour to beat back the invasion of the nomads, Skanda left no stone unturned and spent 'a whole night on a couch that was the bare earth' to save his own realm and defeat the enemy. His anxiety as the ruler to guard the land of the Saurāṣṭras and his appointment of Parṇadatta[44] as governor may be taken as his well thought out precautionary measure and the emperor was at particular pains to appoint a series of Wardens of Marches to protect his dominion from future invasion.[45] The Hūṇas, who had already gained a foot hold in Gandhāra and the Punjab came again and again and despite Skanda's successful defence the empire was to collapse as the result of a second invasion after Skanda.[46] In the military annals of ancient India, Skanda's heroic resistance against the Hūṇas reminds us of

Puru's bold stand against Alexander. Regarding Skanda's war K. P. Jayaswal[47] appends an account from *Candragarbhapariprchcha* cited by Buston in his *History of Buddhist Doctrines.* It runs thus:

King Mahendrasena[48] who was born in the country of Kausāmbi, had a son with arms of irresistible might. After he had passed the age of 12, Mahendra's Kingdom was invaded upon by three foreign powers in concert—Yavanas, Palhikas and Sakunas who first fought amongst themselves. They took possession of Gandhāra and countries to the north of the Ganges. The young son of Mahendrasena of weighty hands and other congenital military marks distinguishing his person, asked for permission to lead his father's army. The enemy was numbered three hundred thousand men under the commands of the foreign kings, the chief of whom was the Yavana (or Yauna). The son of Mahendra put his army of two hundred thousand men divided into five hundred commanders, son of ministers and other orthodox Hindus. With extraordinary quickness and a terrible drive he charged the enemy. In fury his veins on the forehead appeared like a visible mark (*tilaka*) and his body became steeled. The prince broke the enemy army and won the battle. On his return his father crowned him King, saying, 'henceforth rule the Kingdom' and himself retired to religious life. For twelve years after this the new king fought these foreign enemies and ultimately captured and executed the three kings. After that he ruled peacefully as the emperor of Jambudwīpa.'

'It seems' writes Jayaswal,[49] 'that this account is based on fact. The foreign army composed of three elements had penetrated up to the Ganges. It was the indomitable will and skill of Skanda which won the battle. He led the flower of orthodox Hindu India, i.e. excluding Buddhists, younger sons of ministers and noblemen, and played, like his grandfather Chandragupta II under Rāmagupta, a game of sheer courage, in making an impetuous charge against the enemy, numerically stronger. The battle was won, its fame spread in Hunnic Asia, in the Mlechha countries, as Chakrapālita puts it.'

Feudal Element in the Gupta Army

Samudragupta's 'digvijaya,' as described by Harisena,[50] shows that the Gupta emperor possessed an invincible army. The military departments being the vital part of the Gupta administration, enabled Samudragupta, Chandragupta II and the later imperial Guptas to launch upon a career of conquest to win fresh laurels and give shape to the policy of imperial expansion. As in the past, their army consisted of infantry, cavalry, chariots, elephants and ships.[51] If the existence of a number of Sāmanta princes or feudal chiefs bearing the titles of mahārāja, mahāsenāpati, mahāsāmanta, etc., mentioned in various Gupta epigraphs[52] is accepted, then it is reasonable to conclude that the Guptas in their wars and conquests and in their task of guarding the frontiers, requisitioned the services of feudal militia. The days of standing armies were drawing to a close.

Horse Archery

Both in the early and later Vedic period it was the usual practice with warriors to shoot arrows from their chariots, and even in the age of Magadhan greatness we find men showering arrows riding on chariots and elephants. There is not a single reference before the Scythian period to horse archers. The great epic throws out no hint about it and Alexander's historians make no mention of horsemen provided with bows. But in their coins kings Azas I, Azisiles, Azes II and Satrap Zeionises appear as horsemen provided with bows.[53] From certain types of coins of the Gupta times it is possible to conclude that horse archery was in use in the Gupta period. Chandragupta II, Kumārgupta I and Prakasaditya are represented in coins as horse archers.[54] It might have been introduced by the Parthians but its history is short-lived. On this point, one recent writer[55] on ancient Indian art of warfare observes, 'The art of mounted archery did not strike roots in the Indian soil. Introduced by the Parthians and continuing for a time as a sickly exotic, it withered away shortly after the Gupta period. This is the impression that one gathers from a study of the records of post-Gupta India.' But it goes without saying that the continued existence of mounted archers would have added a stimulating chapter to India's military annals and given a new turn to India's struggle against foreign foes in the early medieval period.

Military Officials

Inscriptions seem to point out clearly that in the Gupta period each office—civil and military—had probably two grades—the higher being distinguished by the addition of prefix 'Maha'. The following are some of the higher military officials next to the emperor mentioned in the inscriptions:

1. Mahādandanāyaka (the great general)[56]
2. Mahāsandhi-vigrahika (the great minister of war and peace)[57]
3. Mahāsenāpati (the great general)[58]
4. Mahābalādhikṛta (the great commander—Field Marshal)[59]
5. Mahāpilūpati (the head of the elephant force)[60]
6. Mahābalādhyakṣa (the great general)[61]
7. Mahāsāmanta (a feudatory title—the same as Mahāsenāpati)[62]
8. Bhaṭāśvapati (Lord of the army and cavalry)[63]
9. Balādhikaraṇa (chief of the military forces or it may simply mean war office)[64]
10. Raṇabhāṇḍāgārādhikaraṇa (office of the Chief Treasurer of the war department)[65]

Apart from a host of military officials mentioned above, inscriptions contain names of various Gupta civil officials, such as the Amātya, the Rājasthāniya, the Mahāpratīhāra, the Mahākumāramātya, the Uparika, etc., but Raychaudhuri[66] seems to hold the view that 'as in the case of most of the Pradhanas of Shivaji there was no clear-cut division between civil and military officials. The same person could be Sāndhi-vigrahika, *Kumārāmatya* (cadet minister) and Mahādaṇdanāyaka, great commandant of the army, and a mantrin could become a Mahābalādhikṛta, chief commander of forces. 'While the civil officials could hold military ranks and there was usually no separation between the two branches of the State Service (Pṛthvisena was at first a minister of Kumāragupta I and subsequently became a Mahābalādhikṛta),[67] the Gupta military department appears to be a strong and separate organization and the Sāndhivigrahika, as Majumdar and Altekar[68] say, served as the hyphen that joined the king and the military department. All three worked in close cooperation. A department of military finance was distinguished from the civil side is suggested by the Basarh seals when they mention a Raṇabhāṇḍāgara.[69]

Maritime Activities and Military Enterprise

From the second to the fifth centuries AD the Hindus, belonging particularly to south India, showed signs of maritime activities which culminated in the establishment of their political power beyond the seas. The fascinating account of Hindu colonial and cultural expansion beyond India proper—the plantation of Hindu colonies in Sumatra, Java, Malay peninsula, Champa and Kambuja and the establishment of the Kingdom of Śrīvijaya (modern Palembang) under the Śailendra Kings—should ever remain a glorious episode in ancient Indian History.[70] The Hindu expansionist movement began in the third century and was completed in the seventh century AD. The spirit of adventure—the spirit that led Indians in later ages to go abroad, to found kingdoms, to maintain and spread their own civilization—was in them ever since the Rgvedic times. This cultural expansionist movement was born primarily of military enterprise, love of adventure and commercial gain. Although a military adventurer sometimes seized political power as the story of Abhirāja of the Sākya clan of Kapilavastu and his occupation of upper Burma seem to give the impression, the cultural domination over various races in different parts of the Indo-Chinese peninsula and Indonesia was not secured by military aggrandizement. The theory of Hindu colonization as a result of military or political conquest cannot be dismissed as altogether impossible, but the evidence is lacking. Indian literature bears no record of a prolonged and intimate political contact and of detailed geographical knowledge between the mother country and the colonies (vide R. C. Majumdar, *Baroda Lecturers*, 1953–54, pp. 6–7). The maintenance of kingdoms and political authority far away from homeland no doubt requires stout hearts and efficient military organization to quell from time to time internal troubles and external aggression. Things, however, changed in the tenth century and military zeal got the upper hand under the Cholas of Tanjore. The naval organization of this Tamil power reached its high watermark of efficiency under Rajendra Chola I (1014–44), surnamed Gongaikonda. He made extensive overseas expeditions and conquered a number of islands in the Eastern Archipelago or modern Indonesia.[71] 'Gongaikonda', it has been rightly stated, 'came into possession of one of the great strategic keys of the world. The Bay of Bengal was converted into a Chola lake and the old movement of Colonization was given a new impetus.'[72] The strategic importance of the S. E. Pacific with reference to India's defence, so dangerously threatened in modern times, especially during World War II, was unthinkable. Japan was in the lap of feudalism, America was yet to be discovered, European powers were in medieval trammels and the birth of the Far Eastern Question was distant still.

It will not be out of place to note here that the military organization of Hinduized states that grew up following the Hindu colonization in South-East Asia, namely, Funan, Champā, Kambujadeśa, Srivijaya, and Java during the early centuries of the Christian era was evidently of the Indian pattern so far as the composition of the army methods of warfare and art of diplomacy are concerned. Hindu civilization was absorbed in all its essentials in South-East Asian lands. Referring to the Kingdom of Champā R. C. Majumdar[73] writes:

> The art of diplomacy as practised in India, was fairly understood. The neighbouring states were classified as friends (*Mitra*), enemies (*Ari*) and neutrals (*Udāsīna*), and the relation with these powers was guided by the four political expedients of *Sāma* (conciliation), *Dāna* (gift), *Bheda* (discord) and *Daṇda* (chastisement). Sometimes *Daṇda* (punishment) is replaced by Upapradhāna (*bribery*). What is more important still is the reference to the '*Sādgunys*' which is undoubtedly identical with '*Sadgunya*' of Kauṭilya meaning the six measures of royal policy.

In one of the bas-reliefs in the world-famous Angkor Vat Viṣṇu temple built by Sūryavarman II, there appears the grand review of the *Khmer* army. There can be seen a long procession of warriors on the march. These warriors hold spears and shields. There are foot soldiers, horses, elephants and chariots representing the fourfold ancient Indian army. There are also Thai mercenaries armed with bows, arrows and spears.

R. C. Majumdar quotes the Chinese accounts of the New Ming Dynasty in respect of Ka-la to show that Indian system of warfare existed in the Hindu colonial kingdoms in the Far East.[74]

Division of the Army

About the divisions, composition of the Gupta army and the equipment of soldiers, literary notices, epigraphs and coins furnish us with a few facts which enable us to say that the Gupta land forces were generally composed of three elements—infantry, cavalry and elephants. One or two inscriptions of the period omit chariot.[75] The use of camels as part of the army became frequent among the states of Rājaputānā in the seventh and eighth centuries AD. The Gupta fighting forces consisted really of hereditary troops (maula), local levies and feudal militia.[76] Recruits were drawn not from any particular class, i.e. exclusively from the Ksaṭriyas. Puṣyamitra Śunga, Prithvīsena, and others were Brāhmanas who were, as we know, elevated to the position of Commander-in-Chief (Mahābalādhikṛta). Some seals found in different places within the Gupta Empire seem to indicate that the army had different quarter-masters in different localities.[77] Kālidāsa[78] mentions such weapons as bows, arrows, swords, battle-axes, spears, javelins, barbed darts, lances and iron arrows, etc. The poet also says that soldiers were supplied with armour and helmets. This is corroborated by epigraphic evidence (vide Fleet CII, III, p. 6).

Navy

We have already seen that the Mauryas had created a naval department. The naval tradition of the first Magadhan empire continued in the second. The Gupta Empire reached the sea both in the east and west[79] and there are reasons to believe that they fought a number of naval battles too. The Allahabad Pillar Inscription[80] states that Samudragupta's sway extended over the dwellers of islands, Simhala included. Such a position is imaginable only if the possession of a navy by the Gupta sovereign is thought of.[81] There is a reference to the 'victorious camp' of Jīvita Gupta II in the Deobaranak inscription. The camp was 'invincible through (its) equipment of great ships and elephants, horses and foot soldiers.'[82] The Apṣad inscription of Ādityasena which refers to a naval victory over Susthitavarma, King of Kāmrūp, runs thus: 'The mighty fame of Mahāsenagupta marked with honour of victory in war over the illustrious Susthitavarman . . . is still constantly sung on the banks of river Lohitya.'[83] In the Gunaighar Copper Plate inscription of

Vainyagupta[84] (Gupta year AD 188–507), there is a reference to ship but not to chariot as part of the army. The addition of the former and the omission of the latter shows that the navy was a factor in the army of Indian princes in the sixth century and that the chariot, the earliest instrument of warfare was growing less useful.

Gupta Military Strategy

In one complete sense, the Gupta period was the turning point in the history of ancient Indian military strategy in respect of the methods of positional and mobile warfare in particular and pitched battles in general. It is necessary at this stage to recall the military strategy adopted in previous periods and its consequences. The pre-Maurya and Maurya strategy centred round huge elephant forces which were especially useful in positional warfares in jungle areas, but the Indian elephant corps had to give in before the mobile Macedonian cavalry. Likewise, in the Scythian period, cavalry, equipped with lances and long bows shooting at long range and protected by heavy armour, was unquestionably a formidable factor in all operations, whether offensive or defensive. The lessons of the Maurya and post-Maurya periods were not totally lost upon Indian princes in the period under review, and as a result we find a new orientation of the Gupta methods of warfare.

It is quite likely that immediately after the overthrow of the Kusāna power and with the growth of Magadhan imperialism under the Guptas, there was a reorganization on the Scythian model of the Gupta army. More and more reliance came to be placed on heavy-armed horsemen. We learn from *Raghuvamsa,* Canto IV (Raghu's conquest in Aparānta and the western region as depicted by Kālidāsa) that each horseman was equipped with a coat of mail going down to knees, a long lance, a powerful bow and a quiver of arrows. The cavalrymen marched in well-ordered lines and in close formations. Chariot formations of earlier days were conspicuous by their absence, having lost their effectiveness in Indian warfare even from the fourth century AD. 'The whole conception of warfare as developed in the fourth canto of the *Raghuvamśa*', writes Agrawala,[85] 'is based on movement. The idea of entrenched forces, however well-defended, does not seem to have played an important part in Gupta strategy. The entire strategy of the Hūṇa war, which swayed from the north-western region right up to Ajodhyā and Allahabad was developed on mobile fighting columns and garrisons. It seems that after the decline of the Gupta power when the lessons of Hūṇa warfare had been forgotten there was a reversal to the old strategy of static defences.'

With the fall of the Guptas in about AD 550, a brilliant period of ancient India, a period of political excellence, military glory and cultural progress ended. In the post-Gupta period the centre of political gravity was shifted from Magadha in the east to Kanauj in the north. The traditional fourfold army, so long the bulwark of national and territorial defence, was undergoing a change. The disappearance of chariot or its partial subordination to elephant corps seemed to be a new feature. The abandonment of mobile warfare with more reliance on static defences and pitched battles, appeared to be the characteristics of the period that followed, although in matters of recruitment, encampment, fortification, battle array, espionage, and general strategical plans, there was no appreciable departure.

NOTES

1. The adoption of the policy of Dharmavijaya in place of Digvijava (cf. Rock Edict No. IV) must have impaired the military efficiency of the Maurya empire under Asoka's successors allowing dependent states to throw off the yoke and foreigners to pour in.
2. Vide PHAI 5th ed., Subhagasena and Maurya disruption, pp. 361–2.
3. The chronology adopted by H. C. Raychaudhuri (PHAI 5th edn, p. 408) has been accepted here. While discussing the chronology of the Sātavāhana Kings, Purushottam Lal Bhargava places Simuka between 46 and 23 BC, vide IHQ, December 1950.
4. *Jat.* tr., vol. VI, p. 298.
5. *Jat.* tr., vol. VI, pp. 223–4.
6. *Jat.* tr., vol. VI, p. 231.
7. I. A. 1872, p. 300. (Shri R. G. Bhandar's article on the date of Patanjali). For the identification of the Greek (Yavana) invader see Dr Smith, EHI, p. 211; Dr H. C. Raychaudhuri, PHAI, p. 267, and the *Journal of the Ganganatha Jha Research Institute*, vol. IV, pt. I, November 1940.
8. *Mālanikāgnimitram*, Act I.
9. Polybius, XI, p. 34. Vide Dr B. C. Sen's article in the *Proceedings of the Indian History Congress*, 1949, p. 62.
10. For the extent of their Indian conquests as described by Appollodoros of Artemita and as determined by the diffusion of Menander's coins, see PHAI, 5th edn, pp. 380–1.
11. Luder's List no. 1112.

12. Ibid., no. 1112 (Nānāghāt Cave Inscription).
13. A. H., p. 131.
14. EHI, 4th edn, pp. 217–8. Some writers are inclined to believe that the Sātavāhanas maintained a fleet of their own. The coins belonging to the reign of Pulamāyī and Yajñaśrī bear the figure of a two-masted sailing ship (Rapson, *Catalogue of Indian Coins*, p. 22.)
15. The cave inscription of Nahāpana's son-in-law Ushavadatta proves the inclusion of some territories in many places within Nahapāna's political influence (see *Ep. Ind.*, vol. VIII).
16. *Ep. Ind.*, vol. VIII, p. 60*ff.*
17. *Ep. Ind.*, vol. VIII, p. 42*ff.*
18. *Early History of the Dekkan*, p. 50.
19. EHI, vol. I, pt. 11, p. 389. 'In one bas-relief King Pasenadi of Kośala is represented as issuing forth on his chariot drawn by horses.
20. Ibid., pt. VII.
21. Sir Alexander Cunningham, *The Stupa of Bhārhut,* pl. XXXII.
22. Sir John Marshall, *A Guide to Sanchi*, pl. nos IV & V.
23. Ibid., pls XXVI and XXVII.
24. *Buddhist India* (Indian edn), p. 47.
25. Adris Banerjee, *Eastern Expansion of the Kusana Empire*, IHQ, December 1951.
26. *Maha Janaka Jātaka*, 539.
27. Lüder's Inscription, nos. 1124 and 1146.
28. Ibid., no. 1328.
29. Ibid., no. 1200.
30. Ibid., no. 1200.
31. Ibid., nos. 381, and 728.
32. Ibid., no. 1200.
33. PHAI, p. 520.
34. *Arthaśāstra,* Book X, and Chs 1, 2 and 5.
35. N. G. Majumdar, *List of Kharosthi Inscriptions*, no. 36.
36. PHAI, p. 526.
37. CII, vol. III, p. 6*ff.*
38. Chandragupta II's territories included Sauráśhtra (Kathiawar) after the fall of the Śaka power. North Bengal (Puṇdravardhanabhukti) formed part of the Gupta Empire. A recently discovered epigraph proves the inclusion of Kalinga being ruled in AD 569 by Prithivīvigraha, the Gupta Viceroy. D. C. Sircar, however, holds a contrary view (IHQ, March 1950).
39. HB, vol. I, p. 264.
40. Ibid., vol. I, p. 59.
41. Silver coins of the Garuda type and some coins bearing the date 90 (= AD 409) (Allan, p. xciv). Udayagiri inscription of Sābhā, CII, 35 Bāṇa's *Harşacarita* refers to the fall of the Saka power.

42. *A New History of the Indian People*, vol. VI, p. 3.
43. Bhitari and Junāgadh inscriptions, CII, pp. 55–6.
44. CII, vol. II, p. 63.
45. PHAI, p. 390.
46. According to MMK (sec. 25), this Hūṇa raid is to be dated 50 years later and the Gupta empire broke up not under Skanda but in the reign of Budhagupta (AD 496 coins) after AD 500. (Jayaswal, *Imperial History*, p. 37).
47. *Imperial History*, p. 46.
48. Identified with Kumāragupta I.
49. *Imperial History*, p. 37. Vide Bhitari pillar inscription of Skanda.
50. CII. 6*ff.*
51. Dco Baranak inscription of Jivitagupta II, CII, p. 217.
52. CII, p. 289.
53. Smith, *Catalogue of the Coins in the Indian Museum*, Calcutta, pp. 43–44; and Percy Gardiner, *The Coins of the Greek and Scythic Kings of Baciria and India in the British Museum*, pls XX 3 and XIX 4.
54. Allan, *Gupta Coins*, pl. VIII, pp. 11–19; pl. XXII.
55. P. C. Chakravarty, AWAI, p. 42.
56. *Mahādandanāyakas* probably occupied a position inferior to that of *Mahāsenāpatis* (ASI, 1911–2, p. 52).
57. CII, III, p. 6.
58. CII, III, p. 289.
59. *Ep. Ind.*, p. 134, CII, no. 43.
60. *Ep. Ind.*, XXV, 52*ff.*
61. CII, III. 179.
62. CII, III. 286*ff.*
63. Basarh seals.
64. Basarh seals.
65. Basarh seals.
66. PHAI, 5th edn, p. 560.
67. *Ep. Ind.*, X, p. 71.
68. *A New History of Indian People*, vol. VI, p. 279.
69. PHAI, 5th edn, p. 563*fn.*
70. R. C. Majumdar, *Hindu Colonies in the Far East*, Ch. II, p. 13.
71. SII, vol. II, part I, 'For struggle between the Colas and the Sailendras of Srīvijaya', vide *Hindu Colonies in the Far East*, pp. 34–5.
72. AWAI, p. 65.
73. *Ancient Indian Colonies in the Far East*, Champā, p. 154.
74. *Suvarnadvipa*, Part I, pp. 76, 147.
75. Gunaighar Ins., IHQ, VI, p. 53*ff.*
76. AHI, p. 194.
77. ASI(R), 1903–4, p. lo8.
78. *Raghuvamsa*, VII, pp. 48–9.

79. *Damodarpur* plates of the time of Kumāra Gupta I, Allahabad Pillar Inscription. Udayagiri Cave Inscription CII, III. Bāna's *Harşacarita* also refers to the fall of the Śaka power in western India (Allan, *Gupta Coins*, p. XCIV).
80. CII, III, 6*f.*
81. Samudragupta is compared with Varuna (the Indian sea god). It probably refers to his suzerainty over the sea. The Malayan epigraph speakers of the *mahānāvika* (the great sailor), Budhagupta hailing from *rakta mittika*, i.e. red clay, i.e. *Rangāmāti*, 12 miles south of Murshidabad in West Bengal. Vide CII, no. I and PHAI, p. 547. Some scholars, however, locate *rakta mittika* on the gulf of Siam (Coedes Etats, p. 89).
82. CII, III, p. 217.
83. Hoernle, JRAS, 1903, p. 561.
84. IHQ, VI, p. 53*ff.*
85. *Proceedings of the Indian History Congress*, 1949, p. 33. 'Narasimha Bālāditya is sometimes identified with Bhanugupta, the hero of "a very famous battle" fought near Eran in the Central Province' (vide AHI, p. 151).

CHAPTER 3

The War Chariots

P. C. Chakravarti

Historical Outline

The use of chariots in warfare marks an important stage in the evolution of the world's military system. Man was, as stated before, originally a foot-soldier. But when tribes were fused into states and distant marches became a necessity, it must have been found that a foot-soldier who, encumbered with arms and armour had a long distance to march before coming to close quarters with his adversary, was at the disadvantage of being partly out of breath at the commencement of the conflict. It was then realized that the soldier who could be carried without fatigue and placed fresh upon the spot where he would be obliged to exert every energy in deadly conflict, would have a great advantage in a hand-to-hand struggle over one who had been obliged to march heavily laden for a long distance. This is probably one of the most important reasons which led to the use of chariots in ancient warfare. But there was possibly another equally important reason. The chariot-warrior could carry with him a larger number of weapons than an ordinary foot-soldier could do. Moreover, being elevated over his opponent, and partly protected from his weapons by the chariot-screen, he enjoyed the same advantage over a foot-soldier as the mail-clad feudal chivalry of medieval Europe enjoyed against the combatants of foot.

The use of war-chariots was not an isolated phenomenon in the history of India. They are known to have been in use throughout almost all the ancient world—China, Egypt, Assyria, Babylon, Greece and Persia. In India they were employed as early as the Vedic age. There are numerous references to war-chariots in the Rgveda (i. 20, 3; iii. 15, 5; iv. 4, 10; 16, 20; x. 103, 10, etc.).[1] In the epics they constitute the most important arm. The car-warrior is the main strength of the epic army, the stay and hope of contending hosts. So completely does he dominate in the battle-scenes, so controlling is the role that he fills, that the period represented by the epics may well be designated as the veritable chariot-age of Indian history.

Both Vedic and epic evidence, however, prove that chariots were more or less a monopoly of warriors belonging to the noble classes. The rank and file fought on foot. Just as the knight in medieval Europe was followed by his squires or the Optimati attended by one or two personal retainers, the epic car-warrior in India was followed by two 'wheel-guards' *(cakra-raksau),* attended by a retinue of foot-men. These 'wheel-guards' were often younger members of the noble classes, who were thus 'winning the name of hero by useful service under some renowned knight'.[2] In the course of a brilliant analysis of the position of epic car-warrior, Hopkins writes:

> The knight's adversaries are generally of his own class. If he becomes *apratirathah,* or has no foeman worthy of his steel, he rushes about the field till he meets one. Incidentally as it were, he may shoot a few hundred common soldiers. He never makes a premeditated attack upon the foot-soldiers alone, but when their chief is killed, of whom they are, like the horses, an appendage, they ought to disperse; and if they do not they are shot as nuisances, not as antagonists. Especially is this the case with the 'heel-catchers' or soldiers deputed to annoy the rear. These are legitimately shot as cowardly villains, though they never appear to do much harm.
>
> The knight in his chariot is equal to an army. Frequently we find thousands running from one mounted hero. In the case of a national hero, of course, no bounds are set in description. Through fear of Arjuna, everybody, even the knights ran away; the horse-riders abandoned their horses, the elephant-riders their elephants—falling from war-cars, elephants and horses.[3]

In dealing with the epics, we must, of course, make due allowance for poetic effusions. But there is always a grain of truth behind a mass of husks. And that grain of truth, in this case, seems to be that the car-warriors enjoyed unchallenged supremacy in the military organization of post-Vedic India.

When we come down to age of Alexander, we are, however, struck by a profound change in the Indian military situation. The chariots were still in use, but no longer as the most important arm.

Unlike the average epic knight, king Porus came to the field of battle riding, not a chariot, but an elephant. Though not perhaps wholly accurate, it shows the direction in which the wind was blowing. After his enumeration of the military forces maintained by various Indian states, Megasthenes makes the pregnant remark: 'In fact, no one invested with kingly power ever keeps on foot a military force without a very great number of elephants and foot and cavalry.'[4] The omission of war-chariots is noteworthy. The tables seem to have turned.

It is worthwhile recounting here the story of the part played by the Paurava chariot corps in the battle of the Hydaspes. We learn from the classical authors that in the preliminary encounter of the advanced guard, which Porus had sent under his son to oppose the landing of Alexander on his side of the river, the chariots 'proved to be of scarcely any service, for the storm of rain (which had raged during the night) had made the ground slippery and unfit for horses to ride over, while the chariots kept sticking in the muddy sloughs formed by the rain and proved almost immovable from their great weight. Yet ignoring this strategic difficulty, the drivers rode at full speed into the midst of the battle, 'thinking they could thus most effectively succour their friends.' The idea probably was to use the momentum of the weight and speed of the horse and chariot as an offensive weapon. But it was not to be. The Macedonian foot-soldiers, who were exposed to the first shock of the onset, were no doubt trampled down; but the Paurava car-men themselves 'were hurled from their seats, when the chariots in rushing into action, jolted over broken and slippery ground. Again some of the horses took fright and precipitated the carriages not only into the sloughs and pools of water, but even into the river itself.'[5]

Even after this disaster, however, Porus had some 300 chariots left to his army.[6] When he found a place where he saw there was not clay, but that the ground from its sandy nature was all flat and firm, and suited for the movements of cavalry whether charging or falling back, he drew up his army in order of battle and placed the chariots in front of the cavalry on the two wings.[7] But in the final action the chariots fared hardly better than in the preliminary skirmish. The first onset of Macedonian cavalry threw them into confusion. Arrian says that the drivers of the chariots were all slain, and the chariots were broken into pieces.[8] Diodorus mentioned that 'the Macedonian cavalry began the action, and destroyed all the chariots of the Indians'.[9] It may be added that the Greeks, even before they came down to India, had learnt the art of fighting chariots to the best advantage. In the battle of Arbela they had boldly faced the dreadful scythed chariots of the Persians, and crushed them by means of their superior cavalry.

The disastrous experience must have served as an eye-opener to contemporary military leaders; but it did not lead to the immediate rejection of chariots as an instrument of war. The evidence of Megasthenes, on the contrary, proves that they were maintained at considerable strength in the Mauryan empire, and one of the six boards in Chandragupta's war-office was entrusted with the special duty of supervising this branch of the service. Krishnaswami Aiyangar has pointed out that ancient Tamil literature contains references to Mauryan war-chariots going out on expedition to the distant south. Thus Māmulnār, an old Tamil author, speaks of the war-cars of the Mauryas as having penetrated as far as the Podiyil Hill on Tinnevelly District. 'The newly-installed Mauryas, whose army contained a very large number of elephants, marched down to attack them; and their beautifully decorated cars wore down hill sides, making dark passages through which clear water flowed in torrents,' Elsewhere the poet refers to the same hill 'worn by the bright rolling-wheels of the cars of the Mauryas, who marched towards the south'. Another ancient Tamil poet, called Paranar or Param Korranār, mentions the 'cutting down of the hill to make a roadway for the war-chariots of the Mauryas.'[10]

We do not know much about the history of war-chariots in the post-Mauryan epoch. It is reasonable to assume that they continued to be used in Indian warfare for several centuries yet. They are not only mentioned in the Junāgadh Inscription of Rudradāman (AD 151 or 152)[11] but occasionally, too, in the records of a much later period. In his preliminary description of the Indian army, Hiuen Tsang says that it was composed of Foot, Horse, Chariot and Elephant soldiers. The chariot was occupied by an officer, was drawn by four horses, and was guarded on both sides by the infantry.[12] In the Daulatpur Plate of Bhojadeva I (AD 706), the camp (*skandhāvāra*) of this king is said to the been 'furnished with many boats, elephants, chariots and foot soldiers'.[13] The

Sāmnad copper-plate grant of Dantidurga or Dantivarma II (also called Khadgāvolaka), dated AD 753–4 (Śaka 675), tell us that this monarch 'overcame the countless army of Karnātaka,' with a force 'of chariots and horses which were not to be conquered.'[14]

Yet the decline of chariots must have commenced many centuries earlier. Though they lingered on here and there, they appear to have been rejected as an arm by the more powerful states of post-kushan period. There is not an iota of evidence to prove that they were employed by the Guptas and it is certain that they were not used in the empire of Harsa. In the famous Madhuban copper-plate, there is no mention of chariots, though the other arms have been specifically referred to.[15] Bāna and Hiuen Tsang describe, with an extraordinary wealth of detail, the military resources of their patron king. They speak of his foot soldiers, cavalry and elephant corps, but are significantly silent about chariots.[16] The Chinese pilgrim also supplies us with a description of the military organization of Pulakeśin II, whose court he had visited in the year AD 641, and here again he makes no mention of war-chariots.[17] Similarly the Gaudavaho of Vakpati, though it gives interesting details regarding the military organization of Yaśovarman, is characteristically silent about war-chariots. Finally, Muhammad bin Kasim, who invaded and conquered Sindh early in the eighth century AD, did not encounter war-chariots in any of the numerous armies with which he had to fight.

The final disappearance of chariots from India's military system probably came about in the eight century AD. The reasons which led to it are not difficult to guess. The doom of war-chariots had already been signalled many centuries earlier in the fateful field on the Hydaspes. Ancient military thinkers recognized that chariots needed a dry and plain soil for their use, that they could not be employed in hilly tracts or morasses, nor in the rainy season.[18] Such restricted employment must have reacted fatally upon their utility as instruments of war. With growing complexities in the texture of Indian political and military life, a premeditated selection of soil and season became more and more difficult, and consequently war-chariots fell more and more into disuse.

Another important reason which conspired to bring about the same result appears to have been, as stated by Wilson, the infusion of Scythic tribes and manners about the commencement of the Christian era.[19] It is reasonable to believe that the influx of these foreign tribes with their traditions of superior horsemanship must have led to a reorientation of military outlook, and to a recognition of the fact that the functions which a chariot corps was expected to perform in war could be discharged more efficiently by a trained and well-equipped cavalry.[20] Indeed, there are good reasons to think that as with the Greek, so with the Hindus, the horse came to supersede the chariot.

Equipment, Size, etc.

In the Vedic period the chariot was usually a small-sized two-wheeled vehicle.[21] It was drawn by two horses, occasionally by three or even four.[22] The body of the car appears to have been exceedingly light, consisting of a wooden framework fixed on an axle-tree (*akṣa*), fastened by cow-hide thongs. The framework consisted of a floor (*garta*) to stand on, and a guard of some sort round it. It was also provided with a seat (*vandhura*) where the warrior could sit when he wanted. The pole (*īṣā, praüga*) of the car was probably attached to the middle of the axle; and at the end of the pole was the yoke (*yuga*).

'Normally there was, it seems, one pole, on either side of which the horses were harnessed, a yoke (*yuga*) being laid across their necks; the pole was passed through the hole in the yoke (called *kha* or *tardman*), the yoke and the pole being then tied together.'[23]

'The horses were tied by the neck (*grīvā)* where the yoke was placed, and also at the shoulder, presumably by traces fastened to a bar of wood at right angles to the pole, or fastened to the ends of the pole, if that is to be regarded as it probably should be, as of triangular shape, wide at the foot and coming to a point at the tip. The traces seem to be denoted by *raśmi* and *raśanā.* These words also denote the reins, which were fastened to the bit (perhaps *śiprd*) in the horse's mouth. The driver controlled the horses by the reins, and urged them on with a whip (*kaśā*). The girths of the horse were called *kakṣyā*.[24]

The wheels, like the body of the chariot, were of wood. It is probable that originally solid wheels were used, but gradually these were replaced by those with spokes (*ara*).[25] Besides the spokes, a wheel consisted of a rim (*pavi*), a felly (*pradhi*), and a nave (*nabhya*). The rim and the felly together constituted the tire (*nemi*).'[26]

The dimensions of a Vedic chariot may be inferred from the following passage in the Sulba Sūtra of Āpastamba (VI. 75): 'The masters of the cartwright profession say that the *īṣā* (the pole of the chariot, which lies in the middle lengthwise—this has been compared with the centre line, the *pṛṣṭhya* or backbone of a *vedī)* measures 188 *(angulis),*[27] perpendicular *(tiryak)* to which *(īṣā)* are *akṣa* (hind part of the car) equal to 164 (*angulis*) and *yuga* (the forepart) equal to 80 (*angulis*); such is the chariot (constructed according to the rules of the gild). These are the measures of the car.' This quotation has been given by Āpastamba as an authority for certain measures he proposes for the *nirūdhapaśubandha-vedī*. It is evident, however, that the pole of a standard chariot measured 188 *anguli*s (finger-breadths), the axle 104 *anguli*s, and the yoke 86 *angulis*. The Baudhāyana and Kātyāyana Sulba Sūtras (Baudh, 1, 10-12: Kāt, II, pp. 1–4) mention the same dimensions for a chariot.

Passing over to the epics, we notice two types of chariots being employed in contemporary warfare. The first of these was a vehicle of small size, two-wheeled and two-horsed, very much like its Vedic forerunner. The second variety, however, was of comparatively larger and thicker build, occasionally resting on fourwheels, and generally drawn by four horses. C. V. Vaidya's assertion that the epic war-chariot was 'always a four-wheeled construction'[28] is not justified by evidence. Epic testimony, on the contrary, tends to show that in spite of the development of four-wheelers, the two-wheelers still continued to hold their ground. Thus in the Drona Parva (83, 15), Kṛṣna's chariot is expressly said to have had 'two wheels like the sun and the moon.' Elsewhere (ibid., 188, 54), it is stated that a wheel came off a car, and then 'the horses dragged the car with one wheel only.' In another passage were read: 'the one yoke, the one pole, the two wheels and the one axle we broken, cut to pieces by arrows.'[29] Instances like these may be multiplied; but it is clear that the epic war-chariot was not always a four-wheeled construction. The bas-reliefs at Sānchi prove beyond doubt that two-wheeled, small-sized chariots were still in vogue as late as the first century BC.[30]

And yet it is true that in the post-Vedic period, chariots with increasing size and weight and provided with four wheels were coming more and more into fashion. In both the Rāmāyaṇa and the Mahābhārata, there are occasional references to four-wheeled and even eight-wheeled cars.[31] There are references, too, to chariots being drawn by four horses. In the opening scene of battle in the Udyoga Parva (155, 13 *ff.*), we are told that 'all the cars were drawn by four horses (*caturyuj*), and equipped with arrows and spears, and a hundred bows apiece; for each car were two pole-horses, directed by one driver (*dhuryayor hayayor ekah . . . rathī*), and two outside horses fastened to the axle-end (*pārṣṇi*), and driven by one driver apiece (*pārṣnisārathi*).[32] It must be remembered, however, that four horses do not necessarily imply four wheels; the one has no connection with the other. Kṛṣṇa's two-wheeled chariot, to which reference has been made, is expressly stated to have been drawn by four horses.[33]

The number of charioteers, however, depended on the number of horses. When two horses are sufficient, one *sārathi* or charioteer is sufficient. In the case of four horses, (two fastened to the pole, two by straps outside, not tandem: *dhur* and *pārṣṇi*), we have one charioteer in the middle, who guides the pole-horses, and on each side of him the two drivers of the outer steeds, *pārsṇisārathi*.'[34]

The Vedic car-warrior usually stood on the left hand of the charioteer, on whose skill he so largely depended.[35] In the epics, however, the charioteer is generally represented as standing in front of the chariot, and never in a line with the knight. It is probable that the floor of the chariot was a little elongated so as to consist of two parts, viz., the *upastha* ('the chariot lap'), where the knight usually took his stand and the *nīda* ('the chariot nest'), 'the little shelf in front where the charioteers stood.[36] The use of such terms as *vandhura* and *ativandhura* suggests that the charioteer was provided with a seat.[37] Whether the knight was similarly provided with a seat is not quite clear, although it is not impossible that he had one, called *talpa*.[38]

The epic war-car, like its Vedic fore runner, appears to have been provided with a sort of 'guard' or fence-rim (*varūtha*) to prevent the warrior from falling down while engaged in action. One verse in the Udyoga Parva (155, 8) suggests that the rim of the fence was made of tiger skins and other stiff leather.[39]

A few additional details with regard to the construction of the epic chariot are also available. For instance, it was provided with a pole (*ratha- īṣā)*, which was 'fastened to the box of the car (*kāṣṭha*) and to the double yoke (*yuga*) that crosses it, and rests in turn on the necks of the steeds.'[40] It was, moreover, embellished with standards and flags with the distinctive devices of each knight.[41] Another noteworthy part of the car's furniture was the *chattra* (umbrella). Whether it served merely the purpose of sun-screen or approached anything in the nature of a real protector cannot, however, be ascertained. Hopkins says: 'In spite of its frequent occurrence in the descriptions of spoils, it does not seem to play any part in the action, and I fancy it does not really come into the poem until a later age, but properly is to be associated with the mass of effeminate luxuries depicted long after the original.'[42] Still another apparatus of the war-car was *anukarṣ* ('drag'), which has been explained by the commentator as a 'piece of additional wood fastened beneath the car for the purpose of quickly repairing damages done in battle.'[43]

On the size and construction of war-chariots in the age of Alexander and the Mauryas, the classical authors supply us with a few hints. Megasthenes, perhaps referring to Magadhan practice, says that each war-car carried two men, who sat beside the charioteer.[44] We learn from Curtius Rufus that after their subjugation, the Malloi and the Sudracae sent some presents to Alexander, which included, *inter alia,* one thousand and thirty chariots, 'each drawn by four horses.'[45] Describing the chariotry of king Porus, the same writer observes that each car 'was drawn by four horses and carried six men, of whom two were shield-bearers, two archers posted on each of the sides of the chariot, and the other two, charioteers as well as men-at-arms, for when the fighting was at close quarters they dropped the reins and hurled dart after dart against the enemy.'[46]

Both Wilson and Hopkins maintain that Curtius' account of the Paurava war-chariot 'does not seem to be correct,' on the ground that it is so radically different from the 'native account.' A reference to the *Arthaśāstra* (Bk. II. Ch. 33) will, however, show that the Indian account is not so divergent as it might appear at first sight. Kauṭilya is here describing the different kinds of chariots, used both for peaceful and warlike purposes. Of the latter, he especially specifies three, namely, the *sāmgrāmika* (battle chariots), the *parapurābhiyānika* (chariots used in assaulting the enemy's strongholds), and *vainayika* (training chariots). Regarding the size of chariots, he says: 'The best chariots should accommodate ten persons, and in extreme cases twelve. After this there should be six more varieties of chariots with gradually decreasing weight and size till we come down to one which might contain four persons ordinarily, and six in exceptional cases.'[47]

There is no discrepancy between the above statement and the account given by Curtius. It may be inferred, therefore, that with the passage of time, the old, light, two-horsed chariots were gradually superseded by bulkier prototypes.[48]

NOTES

1. The *Atharva-veda* (vol. VI, p. 125) contains a beautiful hymn to the war chariot, 'compact with thongs of leather'. It is described as the 'bolt of Indra, vanguard of the Maruts, close knit to Varnua, and Child of Mitra'.
2. *JAOS*, vol. XIII, p. 205.
3. Ibid., vol. XIII, pp. 261–8.
4. J. W. McCrindle, *The Indika of Megasthenes*, p. 135.
5. J. W. McCrindle, *India and its Invasion by Alexander*, pp. 207–8.
6. Ibid., p. 108.
7. Ibid., p. 108.
8. Ibid., p. 107.
9. Ibid., p. 275.
10. Proceedings and Transactions of the Second Oriental Conference, pp. 319–22. It may be contended, however, that the Mauryas referred to in Tamil literature were the Mauryas of Konkan, not of Magadha.
11. *Ep. Ind.*, vol. VIII, p. 48.
12. Watters, vol. I, p. 171.
13. *Ep. Ind.*, vol. V. p. 211.
14. *Ind. Ant.*, vol. XI, p. 108; vol. XII, p. 140.
15. *Ep. Ind.*, vol. I, p. 72.
16. Beal, Records, vol. I, p. 213; *Harsacarita*, tr. Cowell and Thomas, 1897, Ch. VII.
17. Walters, vol. II, p. 239.
18. Kauṭilya, Book X, Ch. 4; Śānti parva, 100, 22; Ag. P., 242, pp. 29–30; Yakti, *Kalpataru*, p. 7, v, p. 45.
19. Wilson, *Works*, vol. IV, p. 297.
20. These functions are enumerated in many ancient texts. Ct. Kauṭilya

Book X, Chs 4 and 5; Kām., vol. XX, p. 4; Ag. P., 242, p. 23*ff.*, etc.

21. Chāndogya Upanisad, vol. IV, 16, 5; *Jalminya Upanisad Brāhmana*, vol. III (16), p. 7; *Kausitaki Upanisad*, I, p. 4.
22. Three horses in *Rv.*, vol. X, p. 33, 5; four in ibid., vol. II, (81), p. 1; *Kāthaka Samhitā*, vol. XV (2) refers to even five stallions as yoked to a chariot; *ratha-pancavāhi.*
23. *Vedic Index*, vol. II, p. 208.
24. Ibid.
25. Ibid., vol. II, p. 201.
26. Ibid.
27. Karavindaswāmī says in his commentary: '*munibhirangulisamkhyoktam rathaparimānam*'.
28. *Epic India*, p. 257.
29. *JAOS*, vol. XIII, p. 230.
30. Maisey, *Sanchi and its Remains*, Pl. XX, Two-wheeled chariots are also implied as the regular form in the Sūtra period. Comp., e.g., ASV. *Grhyasūta*, vol. III, 12, p. 1*ff*; *Pār Gyhyasutra*, vol. III (14), p. 2.
31. Cf. *Rām Lankā*, p. 44, p. 27; *aṣatacakrasamayukta maharathi*; Dronaparva, 165, p. 38; ibid., 173, p. 13., etc.
32. *JAOS*, vol. XIII, p. 231.
33. Op. cit., in *Rām Lankā*, 90, 39 (also ibid. 48, 49), Indrajit's car is described as drawn by four black horses with gilded trapping.
34. *JAOS*, vol. XIII, p. 237.
35. *Cambridge History of India*, vol. I, p. 98.
36. *JAOS*, vol. XXX, p. 236.
37. Comp. Vanaparva, 240, 31; Drona Parva 35, 31.
38. Comp. Drona Parva, 191, 68.
39. *Vyāghra-carma-parlvārā, dvipi-carmāvrtāśca te.*
40. JAOS, vol. XIII, p. 240.
41. Ibid., vol. XIII, pp. 243–4.
42. Ibid., vol. XIII, p. 246.
43. Udyoga Parva, 15, 3: Bhīṣma Parva, 89, 38.
44. *Indika*, Fragment XXXIV.
45. J. W. McCrindle, *India and its Invasion by Alexander*, p. 251.
46. Ibid., p. 207.
47. The original runs thus: *Daśapurāna dvadaśantara rathan. Tasma dekantardvara asadantardditi sapta rath.* Scholars differ in their interpretation of this passage. Shām and Gaṇ. have taken *puruan* in the sense of measurement. See Shām's tr., p. 170; Gaṇ, vol. I, p. 337. Meyer has, however, shown that Kauṭilya always uses the term *paurusa* and not *puruṣa* in the sense of measurement. *Das Altindische Buch Vom Welt-Und Staatsleben*, 1926, pp. 223–4. I have accepted Meyer's interpretation.

48. The *Purānas* often mention chariots and their ornaments. 'But their descriptions,' says Rajendralal Mitra, 'lead me to suppose that their idea of the car was the ratha of the modern times, a tower-like structure of many storeys, a cumbrous apparatus altogether,' and 'utterly unfit for warlike purposes' (*The Antiquities of Orissa,* vol. I, Calcutta, 1875, p. 131).

CHAPTER 4

Weapons, Fortifications and Military Training in Ancient India

U. P. Thapliyal

Man's association with weapons is traceable to Paleolithic times, a period when Indians had started using hand axes and copper tools. In the Neolithic age, arrow-heads made of crescent shaped or triangular stone pieces made their appearance. Subsequently, horns and bones were used for making weapons. The people of the Indus Valley Civilization (2500–1500 BC) used bronze and copper for making weapons such as the bow, spear, axe, mace, etc. It is likely that the use of armour, sword and shield was unknown to them.

The inhabitants of the Indus Valley were conquered by the Aryans, who introduced a new system of weapons and warfare in India. It is believed that the swords, spears and axes associated with the Copper Hoard Culture of India (1200–1000 BC) were of Aryan origin. In the *Ṛgveda* there are references to weapons like axes (*svadhiti*), shining spears (*riṣṭih*) and arrows (*iṣuh*) made of copper or brass. It is likely that arrow-heads were also made of copper. With the advancement in mineralogy, some refinement must have occurred in the production of weapons as well.[1]

The bow was the most popular weapon of the Âryans and hymns were composed in its honour.[2] The arrow was made about three feet long and its hind part was provided with feathers to balance the flight. Arrows were carried in a quiver (*iṣudhi*). The spear was widely used and the terms *rambhiṇi* and *śakti* were applied to it. Aryans also used the sword. The other weapons of the Vedic age included the axe and mace. Use of armour (*varma*), head-gear (*śirastrāṇa*), and hand-guard (*hastandha*) was common as well.

In the later Vedic age, about 1000 BC, the science of metals made great progress with the knowledge of lead, brass and tin. The manufacture of weapons was now entrusted to professionals such as the bow-maker (*dhanuṣkāra*), arrow-maker (*isukāra*), and string-maker (*jyākāra*),[3] which was a new development. The discovery of iron called black metal (*śyāma-ayas*)[4] sometimes between 1000 BC and 600 BC further added to the science of weaponry. The *Aṣṭādhyāyī*, refers to weapons like the sword, bow, spear, axe, and javelin.[5] In the Epic age, the bow continued to dominate the battlefield. The other notable weapons of the age included the sword (*asi* or *khaṅga*), axe (*paraśu*), mace (*gadā*), and quoit (*cakra*). Some machine (*yantra*) -driven weapons were also in use.

Classification of Weapons

In the Epic age the growing number of weapons led to different kinds of classifications in the literature of the period. The *Mahābhārata* refers to four types of weapons, but does not describe them.[6] Most probably these were the *mukta* (hurled), *amukta* (unhurled), *mantramukta* (hurled with the power of *mantras),* and *mukta-amuka* (hurled and held type) as mentioned in the *Nītiprakāśikā.*[7] Another classification in the *Agni Purāṇa* divides weapons into five categories, namely, the *yantramukta, pāṇimukta, muktasanghārita, amukta,* and *bāhuāyudha.*[8]

The *Arthaśāstra*[9] classifies weapons into eight categories namely, fixed machines, mobile machines, weapons with piercing points, arrows, swords, razor type weapons, stone weapons, and defensive weapons.

The first category which included weapons such as *sarvato-bhadra, jāmadagnya,* etc., were operated from fixed positions. The second category, i.e. mobile machines which included fifteen types, such as *pañcālika, devadaṇḍa, śataghni, cakra,* etc., were intended to be hurled down from the ramparts. Weapons with piercing points included more than eleven types such as *śakti, prāsa, kunta, śula,* etc., and were all of the javelin type with minor variations. Arrows performed the triple function of cutting, piercing, and striking. Their tips were made of iron, bone, or wood. The swords were used for slashing and cutting. The razor type weapons included the *paraśu, kuṭhāra, paṭṭasa,* etc. Stones were also used as weapons and were hurled with the help of machines, slings, and even hands.

The defensive weapons included coats of mail, armour of fabrics, helmet, shield, etc. The manufacture of weapons was carried out under the supervision of the *Āyudhāgādhyakṣa*.[10]

P. C. Chakravarty has classified weapons of this period in two categories, i.e. offensive and defensive.[11] In ancient India the category of offensive weapons included the bow, sword, and spear. The category of defensive weapons included the shield, armour, and helmet. Other weapons could be included in either of the two categories. A few important weapons of ancient India are described below.

Bow

The bow was used by the inhabitants of the Indus Valley as early as 2500 BC.[12] Its dominance in the Indian battlefield was to the extent that Indians applied the term *Dhanurveda* not only to their science of weapons but also to their art of warfare.[13] According to the *Śukranīti*, *Dhanurveda* was a subsidiary of *Yajurveda* and its knowledge enabled a person to battle, to wield weapons, and to form battle arrays.[14]

In the Vedic age, it was,

> . . . composed of a stout staff bent into curved shape (*vakra*) and of a bow string (*jyā*) made of a strip of cow-hide . . . which joined the ends. The tips of the bow, when the string was fastened were called *ārtnī.* Relaxed when not in actual use, the bow was strung up when needed for shooting.[15]

No warrior ever went out without his bow and parted with it only when dead. In fact, the funeral rites of an Aryan ended with the removal of the bow from the right hand of the dead man.[16]

In the *Arthaśāstra* bows made of *cāpa* (bamboo), *daru* (wood), *tala* (wood of tāla tree) and *śṛnga* (horn) are called *kodaṇḍa, druṇa, kārmuka* and *dhanu* respectively.[17] Of these the bows made of bamboo and horn were more widely used.

There is little information about the shape and size of the bow, used by the Harappans and the Vedic Aryans but, in fourth century BC, Indian soldiers carried a bow made equal to the length of the bearer.

> This they rest upon the ground, and pressing against it their left foot thus discharge the arrow, having drawn the string far backwards; for the shaft

they use is little short of being three yards long, and there is nothing which can resist an Indian archer's shot—neither shield, nor breast plate nor any stronger defence if such there be.[18]

It seems that after the battle of the Jhelum, Indians discarded this big bow in favour of a convenient smaller bow. The Śaka Kuṣāna invaders with their dependence on the mounted archer also found no use for it. This is also evident from the frequent representation of smaller bows in the art of Sāñcī,[19] though the big bows were not altogether discarded. The *Agni Purāṇa* says that the bow could be made of bamboo, metal, horn, or wood and its string of bamboo, hemp, or skin.[20] However, a bow made of bamboo, which grows in autumn, was considered the best of all.

The use of horn for making bows became current in India before the beginning of the Christian era. Indians either learnt its use from the nomadic invaders or else the changing mode of warfare led to its invention. Probably the bow of pure horn was the link between the wooden bow and the composite bow of a later age.[21] The composite bow which was made by joining two curved pieces of wood by a central piece, perhaps an iron plate, may have served the mounted archer exceedingly well. Such bows are commonly depicted in the Gupta gold coins. This curved bow was indeed a contribution to Indian weaponry by the Śaka Kuṣāṇas who learnt its use from the Sarmatians and the Hūṇas, their former neighbours in Central Asia.

Arrow

The arrow comprised a shaft, a pointed head, and feathers. The shaft was generally made of reed though occasionally metal, wood, and bamboo were also used. The feathers which balanced the arrow during the flight, were gathered from birds such as the goose, peacock, osprey, vulture, wild cock, etc.[22] The arrow-head was generally made of wood, bone, or metal so as to pierce, rend, or cut.[23] In the Epic and the *Dhanurveda*, many types of arrow-heads are mentioned.[24] Poisoned arrows were also used.[25]

A change in the shape and size of the bow around the beginning of the Christian era entailed a change in the design of arrows as well.

Without exception all the arrow-heads found at Taxilā were intended for shafts made of reeds. Since the reed arrow was in general use among the Iranians and Central Asians as well as Indian people it is reasonable to infer that these 'double tanged' heads, as we may call them, were an adoption of western socketed type rather than an eastern one and this being so, it seems not improbable that they were introduced at Taxilā by the Bactrian Greeks.[26]

Simultaneously, two new types—conical and three-bladed—made an appearance. The latter seems to have been favoured by the Śakas as it has been found along with a four-bladed type at many sites in Taxilā.

The excavations at Kauśāmbī have yielded double-tanged and three-bladed arrow-head types. As these are different from other types discovered at the site, their foreign association appears more than probable. Incidentally, prior to this, no such arrow-heads have been discovered from any site in the Gangetic Valley. Further, special make and resemblance with the types met at Taxilā suggests that these were brought to Kauśāmbī by foreign invaders from the north-west. It is notable that the Greeks, Śakas, Pahlavas, and Hūṇas, who have been associated by Marshall with the three arrow-head types discovered at Taxilā, were also connected with Kauśāmbī.[27]

About the size and length of the arrows, there was no specified standard. Perhaps these were made in accordance with the needs of warfare in various periods of history. In the fourth century BC, the arrows were made about three cubits (4'6") long.[28] Regarding the capability of the weapon in terms of range, speed and strength, little information is available in the early literature. *Vaśiṣṭha-Dhanurveda*, however, furnishes some information on the range, albeit indirectly. It says that 'the target placed at a distance of 60 *dhanus* (240 cubits) from the bow-man is the best, that placed at a distance of 40 *dhanus* (160 cubits) is medium, while that located at a distance of 20 *dhanus* (80 cubits) is inferior.'[29] This implies that bow shot could be effective up to a distance of 120 yards (240 cubits).

A quiver variously called *iṣudhi* or *niṣaṅga* was slung by a bow-man on his back to carry the arrows.[30] In the Epic age it appears that warriors carried two large quivers fastened together on the right back.[31] In the considered opinion of Hopkins, a quiver carried ten to twenty arrows.[32] Quivers are widely represented in the art of Sāñcī and Ajaṇṭā.

The Mounted Archer

A variation in the use of the bow and arrow was presented by the mounted archer who fought from horseback. Though the cavalry arm as such was known to Indians since the Vedic times, the earliest literary evidence on the mounted bowman is present in the *Mahābhārata*.[33] But this evidence is somewhat doubtful because it had been inserted at a time when Indians had established contact with the Scythians or Śakas, who invaded India about 150–140 BC.[34]

That the Scytho-Kuṣāṇas introduced mounted archery in the Indian battlefield is further confirmed by the art evidence discovered at Harwan in Kashmir. Some brick tiles dated prior to the third century AD depict horsemen in armour riding an accoutred horse at full gallop, drawing his bow. On the right side hangs the quiver attached to the saddle.[35] The weapons and accoutrement of the archers suggest definite Central Asian connections. The earliest evidence of a mounted archer in India is traceable to the coins of Pahlava rulers of north-west India.[36]

In the Śaka-Kuṣāṇa system of warfare the mounted archer played a decisive role, while the Gupta rulers emulated the Śaka-Kuṣāṇas and patronized this arm, as is evident from their coins.[37] The wall paintings of Ajaṇṭā represent many warriors as mounted archers.[38] Chakravarty says that

> . . . the art of mounted archery did not strike deep roots in Indian soil. Introduced by the Parthians and continuing for some time as a sickly exotic, it withered away shortly after the Gupta period. This is the impression that one gathers from a study of the records of post Gupta India.[39]

Indians had to pay dearly for neglecting this agile mode of warfare during the Turk invasion.

Along with the mounted archer some accoutrements such as the stirrup, saddle, and bit were also introduced. An early evidence of the stirrup in India is present in the art of Sāñcī.[40] Marshall maintains that this is the earliest example by some five centuries of the use of stirrups in any part of the world.[41] It perhaps reached India through the north-west of India, with the Scytho-Kuṣāṇa invaders. The fact that *padādhāra* and *ārohiṇi,* two words used for stirrup, are not of Sanskrit origin also suggests that the contrivance was adopted by the Indians from foreigners.[42]

The domestication of the horse implies the use of some kind of bridle and indeed the bit. In the Vedic literature, the word *raśmi* and *rasanā* signify the reins fastened to the bit (*śipra*) in the horse's mouth.[43] In the fourth century BC the Indians knew of the bit but not the curb-bit as they directed the horse by a spike outside, i.e. behind the jaw.[44] In the *Mahābhārata* also there are no clear references to the bit.[45] In the Sāñcī art, horses both with and without bits are represented.[46] In this connection, the reference to a *kharkhalīna* (thorny bit) in the *Harṣacarita* is significant. It is stated to have been incorporated into Sanskrit from the Greek language.[47] If this is true, then the thorny bit may have been introduced into India by the Greeks around the beginning of the Christian era.

Indians did not use a proper saddle in the fourth century BC.[48] The Epics refer to some kind of covering like the *pīṭhaka, khalīna, paristoma,* or *rāṅkava,* etc., but these perhaps consisted of only *kaṁbala* (blankets).[49] Perhaps the saddle as such was introduced in India by the foreign invaders, who patronized cavalry as their principal arm and this seems to explain its appearance in the art of Bhārhut and Sāñcī.[50] The finest specimens of the saddle are depicted in the *Aśvamedha* type of coins of Kumāragupta[51] and later in the art of the Ajaṇṭā.

Sword

The sword perhaps came into vogue after the bow. The excavations at Mohenjodaro have yielded a number of arrow-heads but, surprisingly not a single sword.[52] The Vedic Aryans knew of the sword,[53] but as an effective weapon it came into vogue only in the Epic age.[54] It is significant that Indian swords were exported to Western Asia as early as the sixth century BC and two such swords were seen by Ktesias in the court of the Achaemenid emperor of Iran.

In the fourth century BC, the Greeks had seen Indians wielding a heavy sword. According to Arrian 'all (soldiers) bear a sword, which is broad in the blade, but no longer than three cubits; and this when they engage in close fight (which they do with reluctance) they wield with both hands, to fetch down a lustier blow.'[55] It seems that the sword represented in the art of Bhārhut was similar to these swords.[56]

The *Arthaśāstra* refers to three types of swords—*Nistrimśa* (with curved point), *Asiyaṣṭi* (with rod shape), and *Maṇḍalagra* (with rounded point).[57] This suggests the growing popularity of the weapon. Meanwhile, the Śaka Kuṣāṇa invaders introduced some new types. On the coins of Scythian kings both straight and curved swords are represented. The Kuṣāṇas introduced a new type of sword, which was big and long.[58]

The hilt was an integral part of sword. It could be made of the horn of buffalo or rhinoceros or the tusk of an elephant or wood or bamboo root.[59] With the passage of time it became fashionable to decorate the hilt. The sword was carried in a sheath (*kośa*), made of the skin of cow, tiger, or goat.[60] But a wooden sheath was also popular. Before the Christian era, the sword was carried hanging down from the shoulder with the help of a belt.[61] This was perhaps necessary because these swords were heavy.

The Kuṣāṇas carried their sword in a sheath tied to the waist belt.[62] Strabo says that the swords of the steppe people were of an 'enormous size which they wield with both hands.' Bows and arrows then played a secondary role.[63] Rosenfield suggests that scabbard slide originated among the nomads of Central Asia and the model was popularized in all directions by the Yueh-chi.[64] In India it came with the Kuṣāṇas, a scion of the Yuehchi tribe. That the Guptas patronized the Kuṣāṇa sword is evident from the sword represented on the coins of Kumāragupta I.[65]

As stated earlier, Indians had started producing some fine swords as early as the fifth century BC. In the *Mahābhārata*, the kingdoms of Niṣāda and Aparānta are admired as the producers of excellent swords.[66] The *Agni Purāṇa* is, however, very discerning and states that:

> Swords manufactured in Khāṭa or Khāṭṭava country are known to be worthy of being seen. Those in the region called Ṛṣi were noted for their cutting capacity, those in Sūrpāraka for their strength, those in Aṅga for their sharpness, while swords manufactured in Vaṅga are sharp and capable of cutting.[67]

The *Agni Purāṇa* also refers to thirty-two manoeuvres (*maṇḍalāni*) related to the use of the sword.[68]

Spear

The spear was known both to the Harappans[69] and Vedic Âryans.[70] It was widely used in the Epic war.[71] In the fourth century BC, the Greeks had witnessed Indians fighting with spears, five to seven cubits in length.[72] The *Arthaśāstra* refers to many kinds of spears.[73] The Sāñcī sculptures indicate the popularity of the spear around the beginning of the Christian era,[74] and the Śaka Kuṣāṇas used it widely.[75] It seems that the heavy spear discovered at Taxilā was either introduced by the Bactrian Greeks, or the Śakas, or the Pahlavas.[76] Rosenfield says that 'a giant spear as a war implement was a prominent part of the armament and symbolism of the Indo-Śakas. This in itself involves basic issues of military tactics and larger cultural orientation.'[77] It gained further popularity during the Gupta age.[78]

Mace

The antiquity of mace is traceable to the Indus civilization.[79] In the Epic war warriors like Bhīma, Duryodhana, and Śalya excelled in its use. The *Arthaśāstra* applies the terms *mausala, yaṣṭi,* and *gadā* to mace.[80] In the fourth century BC, Indian soldiers went to war with maces. Alexander suffered a blow from a mace on his neck while fighting the people of Malloi.[81] The mace was made of iron or wood, some four cubits in length and shaped hexagonal or octagonal. The famous Kaṇiṣka statue at Mathurā museum represents a mace.

Yantras

The term *yantra* is variously used in the Epics. Though in battle scenes it is described as a contrivance of almost any kind, generally it denotes a defence appliance in a fort or at the gates of towns.[82] The *Arthaśāstra* gives a detailed description of *yantras* and classifies them into two categories—the immobile (*sthita*) and mobile (*cala*). The immobile category comprised the following engines of war: *sarvatobhadra, jāmdagnya, bahumukha, viśvāsaghāti, saṁghāti, yānaka, parjanyaka, bāhū, ūrdhvahāhu,* and *ardhabāhū.*[83] Among the mobile machines, the *Arthaśāstra* includes the *Pāñcālika, devadaṇḍa, sūkarikā, musalayaṣṭi, hastivāraka tālavṛnta, mudgara, gadā, kuddāla, spṛktalā, asphāṭima, utpāṭima, uddhāṭima, śataghni, triśūla*, and *cakra*.[84]

Not much is known about the functional capabilities of these machines. But *Śataghni*, literally meaning killer of hundred people, is frequently mentioned in the Epics in relation to the defence of forts. The gates of the fort of Lankā were defended by hundreds of *śātaghnis*, made of iron.[85] The description of this *yantra* in the Epic suggests that it was wheeled and manually handled to discharge with force round balls of stones in it.[86] Kane says that in *śataghni*, resinous powder was used in some cylindrical contrivance (or rockets) mounted on wheels and it was capable of throwing stones.[87] In this connection, the observations made by Basham are significant:

> Indians possessed the ancient world's equipment of artillery—ballistas (not known before Mauryan times), battering ram, and other siege engines. The inspiration for the wonderful weapons of the poets may have come from the incendiary missiles, fireballs, fire-arrows, and the like, which were a special feature of Indian military equipment, though disapproved of as unfair by the Smrti writers. . . . It gives brief formulae for the composition of inflammable material which are clear enough to show that this was not gunpowder.[88]

Besides these weapons, some other means were also adopted to scare away or beat back the enemy. In the *Agni Purāṇa*, it is advised that incense should be burnt to stupefy the enemy.[89] This was perhaps the precursor of modern poisonous gases used in war.

Shield

The shield was the ancient weapon of defence. In the fourth century BC, Indian foot-soldiers used bucklers of undressed ox-hide, while those used by cavalry being somewhat shorter.[90] The most detailed reference to shields occurs in the *Arthaśāstra*. It mentions as many as eight varieties of shields, namely, the *carma, hastikarna, tālamūla, dhamanikā, kapāṭa, kiṭikā, apratihatā*, and *balāhakānta*.[91]

The earliest representation of the shield in India exists in the art of Sāñcī, where it is depicted as embossed with geometrical patterns or moon and star symbols.[92] Some of these types indicate a foreign influence in their origin and might have been introduced by the Śaka Kuṣāṇas. The round shields represented in the Gandhāra art of the first and second centuries AD, are invariably found in association with the people of foreign origin.

Codrington has classified the shields represented at Ajaṇṭā into three types—parrying, round, and curved oblong. According to her, the first was made of metal, the second of hide and the third of black and white bamboo basket work.[93] It seems that after the beginning of the Christian era, small shields came to be widely used because of the popularity of cavalry arm in the battlefield.

Body Armour

The wide use of the terms, *varman* and *drapi* in the *Ṛgveda* suggests that body armour was known in the Vedic age.[94] Even some hymns were composed in the honour of *varman.*[95] In the later Vedic period, the word *kavaca* also came into vogue for corselet.[96]

In the fourth century BC, Porus went to fight Alexander protected by body armour. It was shot-proof and remarkable for its strength and the closeness with which it fitted his person. He was wounded in the right shoulder, where he was unprotected by mail.[97] It is notable that his armour was ornamented with gold and silver and looked very majestic.[98] Probably the use of armour was then restricted to the rulers and nobles while soldiers in general did not don any armour.

The Epics frequently refer to *kavaca* or *varman*, which it was necessary for the soldiers to wear before joining the war.[99] A helmet (*śirastrāna*) made of metal and adorned with gems protected the head.[100] The neck-guard (*kanṭhatrāna*) protected the neck, but it provided only limited protection, as there are many references to swords digging in to the neck, in the Epics.[101]The hand-guards (*hastavāpa*) which protected the hands, made a resounding noise in the battlefield when struck by the bow-string.[102] Finger-guards *(aṅgulitrāṇa)* gave protection to the fingers against the rubbing of the bow-string.[103]

The *Arthaśāstra* refers to many types of armour, namely, the *lohajālikā, paṭṭa, kavaca, sūtrakankaṭa, carmakhūra, kañcuka, varavāṇa,* and *nāgodarikā.*[104] Commentators have explained *lohajāla* as the helmet for the head, *jālikā* as headless armour, *paṭṭa* as armour, and *kavaca* as armour with many flaps or folds. *Sūtrakankaṭa* was perhaps made of cotton cloth with stuffing inside and *carmakhūra* was the entire skin with hooves, horns, etc. *Kūrpāsa* was a half-sleeved garment, *kañcuka* came down to the knees, *varavāṇa* ended at the ankles and the *paṭṭa* was without arms. *Nāgodarikā* was a thigh-guard.[105] The *Arthaśāstra* states that armour was either made of metal rings or metal plates, fabrics, or skins.[106] In the course of time, armour made of cotton and tree bark also came into vogue.[107]

The late appearance of armour in the art of Bhārhut and Sāñcī gives support to the view that the use of armour was introduced in the Indian battlefield by the foreign invaders. Robinson says that the Indians did not use any defence armour other than the shield and that for centuries it was the only defensive armour depicted in the Indian sculptures.[108] It is also significant that the use of armour in early Indian art is generally presented in association with soldiers who were certainly not Indian.[109] Marshall maintains that the practice of equipping soldiers, horses, and elephants with armour was introduced by foreigners.[110] It is said that the Sarmatians, a people inhabiting Central Asia, were famous for their heavy armour. The Śakas and Kuṣāṇas who had lived in their proximity for a long time perhaps learnt the use of heavy armour from them[111] and subsequently introduced it in India. In this context, it is remarkable that in the Epics, armour is specially related to foreigners like the Śakas and the Kambojas.[112] However, the literary evidence takes the antiquity of armour in India further back to Vedic times.

A general review of the weapons leads to the conclusion that Indians were fairly advanced in this sphere. They had invented a large variety of weapons for use in different situations of war. The bow, sword, javelin and mace were the principal weapons and each was produced in a number of shapes and sizes. The defensive weapons (*yantras*) meant to protect the forts received special attention. The mobile types could be carried to any part of the fort, whereas the immobile types were placed over the ramparts and gates to inhibit any scaling effort.

Fire Power

The *Arthaśāstra* furnishes some details of how fires inside enemy forts or cities could be started. Kauṭilya describes three recipes of fire powder, namely *agni-dhāraṇa, agni yoga,* and *viśvāsaghātī.*[113] Different ingredients went into the making of each of them. Balls of *sarala, devadāru,* stinking grass, bedellium, pine-resin, *sāla* resin, lac, and the dung of donkeys, camels, goats, and sheep were considered good retainers of fire (*agni-dhāraṇa*). The powder of *priyāla,* the soot of *avalguja,* wax, and the dung of horses, donkeys, camels, and bullocks made a fire mixture which could be hurled *(kṣepyoagniyogah).* The powder of all metals of the colour of fire, or the powder of *kumbhī,* lead or tin, mixed with the flowers of *pāribhadraka,* and *palāśa,* the soot of *keśa,* oil, wax, and pine resin made a fire mixture, one that kills the trusting (*agniyoga viśvāsaghātī vā*). An arrow smeared with it and covered with hemp and the bark of *trapusa,* is a (means of) setting fire. The destructive potentiality of these fire-causing means was immense and was called divine calamity (*daivapīdanam*). Indians had thus made considerable progress in developing fire powder and its use for the purpose of war. It is, however, notable that the *Arthaśāstra* has not mentioned any *nālikā* or gun-like contrivance to launch fire-causing devices. Animals, birds and arrows were used as carriers of fire.

Divine Element

An interesting aspect of the system of Indian weapons is that some sort of divinity was always attached to them. The *Rāmāyaṇa* says that weapons were devised by Jayā and Suprabhā, two daughters of Dakṣa Prajāpati.[114] Earlier, in a *Brāhmaṇa* text, the gods are credited with the creation of the arrow—Agni providing for arrow-head, Soma the socket, Viṣṇu the shaft, and Varuṇa the feathers.[115] Significantly, in the Vedas, Epics, and Purāṇas, every weapon is associated with one or the other god. *Cakra* (quoit) was the weapon of Viṣṇu, who was called Cakrapāṇī, *Śula* (trident) was the weapon of Śiva, who is also known as Śulapāṇī. Indra was called Vajrapāṇi after his weapon *vajra* (thunderbolt). *Paraśu* (axe) was the weapon of Paraśurāma. *Khaṅga* (sword) was born from the sacrificial altar of Brahmā, the creator. The supernatural weapons—*Brahmāstra,*

Agneyāstra, Nārāyaṇāstra, Pāśupatāstra, and *Vāyavyāstra* were associated with the gods Brahmā, Agni, Viṣṇu, Śiva, and Vāyu respectively. *Pāśa* was the weapon of Yama and Varuṇa. *Śakti* (spear) was wielded by the goddesses Durgā and Kārttikeya. In short, there was no weapon which was not related to one or the other god. This also explains the wide display of weapons in Indian temples.[116] Ancient Indians held their weapons in great esteem and worshipped them like gods.

The Epics and Puranas also mention many types of *divyāstra,* with magical powers. They could produce hallucinations, start a fire, bring rain, etc. It is difficult to give credence to such weapons in the absence of any plausible explanation of how they worked, though it is well-established that many highly advanced technologies of the ancient world have died out during the turbulent centuries.

Fortification and Siege Craft

For reasons of safety, early man lived in caves. Subsequently, he built houses which gave rise to villages and towns. In his search for security, he set about raising walls circling the villages and towns. It is said that ancient Egyptians raised these walls up to a height of 120 feet. The Great Wall of China (of the third century BC) was 1,400 miles long, 17 feet thick and 20 feet high.

Importance of Forts

The importance of forts for the security of the state had been a subject of debate among the military thinkers in early India. According to Pārāśara, any calamity that befell the fortified town was much more serious than that suffered by the territory lying outside the fort, because the treasury and army both were located inside the fort. Further, the people residing inside the fort were more faithful to the ruler.[117] Kauṭilya, however, considered a threat to the countryside as more serious, as the fort, treasury and the army depended on the people residing there.[118] The school of Piśuna, on the other hand, believed that a threat to the treasury was more serious than one to the fort, because the building, maintenance, and repair of the fort depended on the treasury. Kauṭilya, disagreed with Piśuna, stating that a threat to the fort was more serious, as in the absence of a fort the treasury would fall in the hands of the enemy.[119]

According to Manu, an archer protected by a fort could fight one hundred adversaries and one hundred archers could beat back ten thousand adversaries.[120] Śukra also follows the example of Manu in emphasizing the importance of a fort.[121] Kauṭilya considered the fort a vital limb of the state, as the ruler could stay safely inside it.[122] Kāmandaka considered a ruler without a fort as weak as a cloud before the wind.[123] *Yuktikalpataru* says that the power of a ruler is enshrined in his fort.[124] Manu believed that *Giridurga* was the best of all forts,[125] but Bhīṣma considered *Naradurga* the most secure.[126]

History

The history of fortification in India can be traced back to the Chalcolithic Age. At Kot Daji, near Mohenjodaro, a fortified town of prehistoric date, with a strongly walled citadel provided with rectangular towers of stone and mud brick has been discovered.[127] The remains of pre-Harappan Amri and Kulli culture from south Afghanistan also attest to the existence of forts.[128] The excavations at Harappa and Mohenjodaro have revealed the existence of lofty citadels.[129] The Harappan site of Kalibanga in Rajasthan, also reveals the existence of a citadel.[130] Perhaps the Ṛgvedic references to forts (*pura*), which the Âryans destroyed during their march through India belonged to the founders of Harappan civilization.[131]

After the Âryans settled in India, they too built forts, perhaps in imitation of the Dāsas and Daşyus, whom they had vanquished in war. These were probably mere places of refuge against attack, and comprised of ramparts of hardened earth with palisades and a ditch.[132]

Remains of a fort dated around the sixth century BC have been unearthed from Rajgriha. This town was well-protected by a cluster of hills. These natural defences were further strengthened by artificial fortifications. There were two lines of walls around the city, the length of the inner wall being four and a quarter miles. According to a report of the Archaeological Survey of India:

> The faces of the walls are built of massive undressed stones between 3 to 5 feet in length, carefully fitted and bounded together. . . . No mortar or cement is visible anywhere in the stone work. . . . From the fact that whenever the height of between 11 to 12 feet is reached, the walls are

invariably finished off with a course of stone work, and that there are no fallen blocks of stone lying near, we may assume that this was the original height of the massive masonry. Above this substructure, there was no doubt a superstructure composed either of small stone work or of bricks baked or unbaked, or possibly of wood and stone or brick combined.[133]

The bastions (towers) were attached to the outer side of the walls wherever special strength was required, and 16 such structures have been discovered. Further, the outer wall was provided with stairs or ramps, built in the thickness of the wall along its inner face, in order to give access to the top. The defences were further supplemented by watch-towers erected at important points on the hills. The thickness of the wall ranged between 14 to 17½ feet.[134] Specimens of contemporary fortification have also been discovered from Unchdih,[135] Bhita and Ahicchatra.[136]

Mauryan Period

Classical accounts also furnish information about the system of fortification in India in fourth century BC. Almost every capital city was located inside a fort. The fortification of the city of Massaga has been described by Arrian as follows:

> An army of 38,000 infantry defended the city which was strongly fortified both by nature and art. For on the east, an impetuous mountain-stream with steep banks on both sides barred approach to the city, while to the south and west nature, as if designed to form a rampart, had piled up gigantic rocks at the base of which lay sloughs and yawning chasms hollowed in the course of ages to vast depths, while a ditch of mighty labour drawn from their extremity continued the line of defence. The city was besides surrounded with a wall of 35 stadia in circumference, which had a basis of stonework supporting a super-structure of unburnt, sun-dried bricks. The brick work was bound into a solid fabric by means of stones so interposed that the more brittle material rested upon the harder, while moist clay had been used for mortar. Lest, however, the structure should all at once sink, strong beams had been laid upon these supporting wooden floors which covered the walls and afforded a passage along them.[137]

The Greeks have referred to many more hill-forts of India in their accounts.[138] The towns in the plains were provided protection by the defensive works. According to Arrian, Sāngala, the capital of the Cathaeans, was strongly fortified by brick walls.[139] About the capital of Malloi, he says that it was very well defended by walls, and that within these walls there was a citadel with gates, towers, and parapet.[140] But the most important fort referred to by the Greeks was that of Pāṭaliputra, the capital of Magadha, situated at the junction of the Sone and the Gaṅgā rivers. It was a long narrow parallelogram in shape, measuring about nine and one-fifth miles in length (eighty stadia) and one-and-a-half miles (fifteen stadia) in breadth. It was defended by a massive wooden palisade, pierced by sixty-four gates and crowned by five hundred and seventy towers. The palisade had loop-holes for the archers to shoot through, and outside there was a ditch, thirty cubits deep and four hundred cubits broad. The ditch was filled with the water of the Sone river.[141]

The *Arthaśāstra* on Forts

A detailed account of the forts in ancient India is found in the *Arthaśāstra*. It says that:

> . . . in all four quarters, on the frontiers of the country he (ruler) should cause a nature-made fortress, equipped for fight, to be made; a water fort (either) an island in the midst of water or high land shut in by water, or a mountain fort (either) consisting of rocks or a cave, (or) a desert fort (either) one without water and shrubs, or a salty region, or a jungle fort (either) a marshy track with water or a thicket of shrubs. Among them, the river fort and the mountain fort are places for the protection of the country, a desert fort and jungle fort are places for foresters or places of retreat in times of calamity.[142]

As for the defence of the capital city, located at the confluence of the rivers or on the banks of a lake, he says that three moats shall be dug around it, at a distance of one *daṇḍa* (6') from each other, fourteen, twelve and ten *daṇḍa*s broad, three quarters and a half of the breadth deep, with arrangements for filling and draining out of water, while being stacked with lotuses and crocodiles.

At a distance of four *daṇḍa*s from the moat (innermost), a rampart should be built from the earth dug out from the moats. The outer side of the rampart should be planted with thorny bushes and poisonous creepers. The top of the rampart should be covered with rounded stones with chariot tracks made of trunks of palm trees. A parapet, with a height between eighteen and thirty-six feet (12 and 24 *hastas*) and the breadth half its height, should be built on top of the rampart with stone or bricks. Along the rampart there should be turrets, and between every two turrets, a square tower. Between each tower and turret, a high wooden board with holes and covers should be erected, big enough for three archers (to defend the ramparts using the board as protection). In between these structures, there should be strong wooden planks projecting outwards (to make boarding difficult). A passage (for soldiers to go out on attack), an escape door, and an exit door should also be built in an unassailable part of the rampart.

Various defensive structures should be made outside the ramparts to obstruct the enemy advance. These included a covered road strewn with knee breakers, a mass of pikes, pits, concealed traps, barbed wires, serpent backs, palm leaves, etc. The gateway should have a main door and a side door, and defences against ramming by elephants. The bridges over the moat in front of the gate should be removable. The details furnished by the *Arthaśāstra* highlight the following features of the Indian system of fortification:

1. Ramparts made of stone, mud or timber;
2. Ditches (three in number) spiked and filled with mud, sand, or flowing water;
3. Ramparts planted with poisonous bushes and crowned with several ring walls of bricks;
4. Ring walls with roofed walks, wide enough to accommodate patrols in both directions and square towers;
5. Drawbridges spanning the ditches;
6. The invaders had to overcome numerous obstacles before approaching the rampart.

This goes to prove that,

> ... apart from their fundamental grasp of all the advantages to be drawn from naturally defensible sites, it is clear from Kauṭilya that the ancient soldiers were familiar with the two basic methods of augmenting them: walls covered by flanking fire from regularly spaced towers; defence in depth provided by concentric rings of walls and moats with advanced outworks controlling the approach.[143]

Forts in the Epic Literature

Forts are often referred to in the Epics. Ayodhyā was a well-fortified city provided with strong gates and massive walls and protected by various *yantra*s and *śataghnis.* A fathomless moat encircled the ramparts of the fort.[144] Laṅkā, the capital of Rāvaṇa, was also protected by a similar fort.[145] The *Mahābhārata,* elaborating on forts refers to six types namely, *dhanva-durga, mahī-durga, giri-durga, manusya-durga, abu-durga* and *vana-durga,*[146] The Ādi Parva described the town of Indraprastha as surrounded by a wide moat, lofty walls, and numerous gates, each furnished with a couple of doors. An abundant stock of weapons promised a stout defence; the battlements bristled with sharp hooks and *śataghnis,* and also machines (*yantras*) of war, and the walls were manned along their length.[147] In the Śānti Parva, the rulers are advised to protect the gate (*dvāra*) with heavy machines and *śataghnis*.[148]

The way a fort was to be readied for defence is best described in the Epic:

> On the fort, *Pragaṇḍis* and *Ākāshjanis* (defensive structures) should be constructed, while the moats should be filled up and provided with concealed spikes and crocodiles. There should be secret gates for egress from the town, to be used in case of emergency. At the fort gates, engines should be constructed and *śataghnis* placed upon them and kept in hand.[149]

It is notable that the Indians do not appear to have known any engine of destruction like catapults, previous to this date. The Greek accounts clearly mention that Alexander succeeded in storming and capturing Indian forts and cities mainly on account of his engines. The Indians could not understand such contrivances and were often overawed by them. It is, therefore, likely that these instruments were borrowed by Indians from the Greeks.[150]

The *Manusmṛti* gives a similar classification of *durga*s, excepting that it uses the terms *nṛ-durga* for *manuṣya-durga,* and *vārakṣya-durga* for *vanadurga.*[151] The types of forts mentioned by the *Manusmṛti* also find mention in *Auśānaṣa Dhanurveda, Yajñavalkya Smṛti, Bṛhaspati Smṛti,* and *Viṣṇu Smṛti.* Of all types of forts, Manu considered *giri-durga* as the best.[152]

Forts of Foreign Invaders

After the disintegration of the Mauryan empire, India suffered many invasions and consequently, many parts of the country were ruled by foreigners like the Greeks, Śakas, Pahlavas, and Kuṣāṇas. These invaders may have introduced their own system of fortification in India. The process may have started as early as the fourth century BC, when Alexander founded many towns in north-west India,[153] and may have continued during the rule of Bactrian Greeks.[154]

Sirkap (Taxilā), built during early second century BC, provides an illustration of Greek fortification in India.[155] Its earthen wall, has been assigned by historians to the Greeks, while the stone wall which was built later to the Śakas, who ousted them. The wall is nearly three and a half miles in length, fifteen to twenty-one feet in thickness, and twenty to thirty feet in height. The core of the entire wall was made of random rubble in mud, while the facing wall was built of coarse rubble. On the north side of the city, the wall was buttressed on the outside by a raised berm of about 25 feet in width, and a number of rectangular bastions built at irregular intervals along its face. The berm, which was made to protect the foundations of the wall from possible undermining, was composed of rubble and mud. The bastions were two or three storeys high, while being hollow, and loopholed in the upper portion for the use of the defenders. The fort was perhaps provided with four gates, though only the remains of the northern gate have been discovered. It was so designed as to give protection to the city from a direct attack, by screening the city streets. A description of the contemporary Greek settlement of Sākala is given in the *Milindapraśna*, a Buddhist work. It was surrounded by a ditch and a rampart. The gates and towers of the rampart were built to be very strong.[156]

The remains of Kuṣāṇa fortifications have been discovered at Sirsukh, again a Taxilā site. The walls were made of rough rubble and were overlaid with limestone masonry of heavy diaper type. The thickness of the walls was eighteen and a half feet. Its base was supported on the outer face with a heavy roll plinth which had been added after the wall itself was complete so as to strengthen the foundations and prevent undermining.[157] This unusual feature is not noticed at Sirkap or any other contemporary Indian site. Perhaps this method of strengthening fortification was borrowed from Central Asia, the homeland of the Kuṣāṇas. According to Marshall, the fortifications at Sirsukh were built by Wema Kadphises, who may have adopted the idea of rectangular planning from Central Asia.[158]

A comparison between the Sirkap fortification of the Greeks and Sirsukh fortification of the Kuṣāṇas reveals certain similarities. At both sites, the upper storeys were generally made hollow with walls that were loopholed and were invariably provided with beams or galleries for stationing armed guards on the upper floor. The upper floors had open terraces and battlements.[159]

But the differences between the two are more marked. The walls of Sirkap betray Greek and Śaka influence as they were built of coarse rubble masonry, whereas the walls of Sirsukh were made of heavy diaper masonry, characteristic of Parthian and early Kuṣāṇa period. Second, at Sirkap only the upper portions of the bastion were loopholed, whereas at Sirsukh both the lower and upper portions were loopholed. Third, the bastions at Sirkap were rectangular in plan, but those at Sirsukh were semi-circular.[160] Further, in the fortification of Sirsukh the place of a flat berm is taken by a heavy roll footing.[161]

The traces of Kuṣāṇa fortifications are also evident at Kauśāmbī, where the entire fortification measured about four miles. The height of the rampart ranged between 30 and 40 feet. The entire rampart was characterized by a series of salients or bastions, the space in between being filled with rammed mud. Gates were invariably provided between the centre of the two salients. Traces of a deep moat surrounding the entire rampart could also be seen. Besides, at a distance of nearly a mile from the ramparts, the existence of some mounds suggests that they formed the outermost line of the defence system at Kauśāmbī.[162] This twofold defence system, as met in Kauśāmbī, has not been found anywhere else in India, suggesting that it was a foreign, perhaps Kuṣāṇa, contribution. In Gandhāra art, city walls and gateways are widely represented.[163] These bear a close resemblance to the fortifications at Sirsukh and may be related to the Scytha Kuṣāṇas with greater certainty.

Forts at Sāñcī

The forts represented in Sāñcī art truly represent the conventional Indian style.[164] In the *Arthaśāstra,* three moats (*parikhā*), plinth (*vapara*), parapet (*prākāra*), tower (*aṭṭalaka*), gateways (*dvāra*), and gate houses (*pratoli*) are considered essential ingredients of a fort, and these are generally depicted in the Sāñcī reliefs. To begin with, at Sāñcī a single moat is represented perhaps due to lack of space, though in the *Arthaśāstra* and some Buddhist works, three moats are recommended. The Sāñcī reliefs represent all cities as protected by a wall. The ramparts were built either of large bricks or of dressed stones or mud. The boundary wall on the upper architrave, furnished with battlements, appears smooth, as if plastered. A small part of brick rampart finished with caping and provided with regular and internal turnings is seen on the right side of the city gate of Kuśinārā in the War of Relics scene. On the other side of the gate, there appears a brick boundary wall topped by a staircase-like formation.

The presence of fighters behind these parapets indicates that defensive positions were provided inside the wall. Battlemented brick boundary can be seen in many scenes. The battlements surrounding these defensive walls are octangular in some cases and conical in others. Ramparts without battlements were also constructed.

As prescribed in literature, high towers (*aṭṭālaka*) at regular intervals were added to the rampart wall on the inner side, so as to keep a watch on the enemy and if necessary, fight them from a secured place. Such defensive towers are represented in the lower architrave of the southern gateway at Sāñcī. In Sāñcī reliefs, gate houses (*pratoli*) are widely represented. Normally, a gate house comprised a closed room at the top, a pillared accommodation at the centre and two bastions projecting from the rampart wall on the ground. The bastions were made either of brick or mud but at Sāñcī, these appear to have been constructed with brick and then plastered. The bastions have a regular window opening in the upper part with or without a dripstone on each outer side. From these openings, the defender could watch the movements of the enemy outside and could also shoot arrows and hurl missiles at enemy troops.

The tradition of building forts continued during the Gupta period. *Durgapāla* or *Koṭapāla* was the officer responsible for the protection of the fort. In the *Raghuvaṁśa*, there are references to the fortification of the capital as also the border areas. Able rulers ensured the proper defence of their forts before moving out on a victory campaign.[165] The Chinese traveller Hiuen-tsang, who visited India in the seventh century AD, found villages and towns well-fortified. The ramparts were thick and built high, the material used in construction being brick or tile (*khapri*).[166] When the Arabs invaded Sindh in the seventh century, they also found Indian cities well-fortified.[167]

South Indian Forts

In south India too, forts were built mainly for the protection of cities and towns. Ancient Madurā was protected by a rampart, built of undressed stones. It had four entry gates. The rampart was encircled by a deep ditch and surrounded by dense forest of thorny trees. The roads leading to the entry gates were so broad that many elephants could walk abreast. On both sides of the entry gate above the walls, weapons and missiles were stored for use against the enemy.[168] Many such fortified cities existed in south India.[169]

On the battlements of the great forts of Madurā, Karūra and Kāñcī, many curious engines were mounted to shoot arrows or to fling stones on those that besieged them. There were machines like the fishing rod and angle to catch and drag up those that approached the wall and with iron-like fingers, to sieze and tear them to pieces. Provision of such furnaces was also made from which hot oil and molten metal might be poured on those that attempted to scale the wall; while iron spokes and spears existed to shove down any that might succeed in mounting the rampart.[170]

The above review of forts in ancient India indicates that the forts were generally built on the banks of rivers or on the hills. A ditch or a moat full of water surrounded the fort. Next to the moat, after some spacing, stood the ramparts. The space between the moat and the fort was covered with thorny and poisonous bushes, while a bridge connected the moat with the gates which provided entry to the fort. The parapets built over the ramparts provided protection to the defenders from the arrows shot by the enemy. In between the parapets were towers, occupied by the guards of the fort, while between the towers, *machans* were provided to facilitate the attack on the assaulting troops.

Types of Forts

The *Mahābhārata* refers to six types of forts—*dhanva, mahī, giri, manuṣya, abda,* and *vana.*[171] The *Rāmāyaṇa, Manusmṛti, Agni Purāṇa, Matsya Purāṇa,* etc., also refer to some of these fort types.[172] The *Arthaśāstra* refers to four types of forts, namely, the *parvata, odaka, dhānva,* and *vana.*[173] The *Śukranīti,* however, refers to eight fort types—*pārikha, pārigha, vana, dhanva, jala, giri, sainya,* and *sahāya.*[174] The literature on forts continued to be produced and the *Mānasollāsa* and the *Vāstuśāstras* furnish detailed information on fortification in medieval India. A brief description of principal fort types of ancient India is given below:

Giri-durga, also called *parvata-durga,* was surrounded by hills and was made in the shape of a cave.[175] The *Mahābhārata* says that this fort located at a height, was provided with an adequate supply of water and was considered impregnable.[176]

Jala or *Odaka-durga* was encircled by water. It was of two types—*antardvīpa* and *sthaladvīpa.*[177] The former was like an island encircled by water on all sides whereas the latter, though encircled by water, was built at a height. It could be negotiated only by means of boats.[178]

Dhānva-durga was surrounded by sand on all sides.[179] Its two sub-types included *Nirudaka* and the *iriṇa.* The former was located at the centre of a big waterless desert, whereas the latter was surrounded by land laid barren by saline water.

Vaṇa durga was surrounded by thorny bushes and dense forests.[180] The *Arthaśāstra* says that it was either surrounded by marshy land or by thorny bushes. In the first case it was called *Khañjana,* and in the latter case *stambagahana.*[181]

Security of the Fort

As a fort was the best insurance for the security of the state, all possible measures were taken to protect it from siege, assault, scaling, mining, sabotage, etc. The *Mahābhārata* mentions some of the measures required as follows:[182]

1. To keep the fort well-stocked with foodgrains and weapons and to prepare tunnels for secret movement to and from the fort.
2. To stop all entertainment-related activity inside the fort. This included a prohibition and bar on music and dance concerts as also the eviction of such performers from the fort.
3. To destroy the bridges and dry the wells on the approach road of the enemy.
4. To stop the movement of boats, lay thorns in the ditches, and to spread nails on the road, as far as possible.
5. To restrict movement in and out of the fort.

The *Arthaśāstra* also recommends some aggressive measures including the scorched earth policy, mining, destruction of supplies, and attack in the rear[183] for defeating the siege laid by an enemy. There were many types of fixed machines which were exclusively meant for the defence of the fort. Stone was always a handy weapon for defeating a siege. In the fourth century BC, an Indian ruler used stones to defeat the siege laid by Alexander.[184]

Siege Craft

There could be no final victory without reducing the fort of the adversary. The Vedic Âryans had developed this art some 2,500 years ago. They applied the method of siege (*upasad*) or assault through the breached walls (*Prabhid*) to capture a fort. The *purcariṣṇū*, a device figuring in the *Ṛgveda*[185] may have been some kind of a battering ram used for assaulting a fort. *Agni* is often described as a destroyer of forts. The *Taittiriya Samhitā* speaks of the three citadels of the Asuras which were cleft by a shaft, whose point was Agni.[186]

Subsequently, many methods were devised to reduce an enemy fort. One of the methods was to lay siege of the fort, disallowing any supplies or help to the fort, and thus forcing the fort to capitulate. This method of reducing the fort was called *aparodha.*[187] Kauṭilya described various means of reducing a fort by the term *durgalambhopāyah.*[188] In the absence of supplies, the besieged army was left with no option but to surrender. In the *Mahāummaga jātaha* there is a reference to the siege of Videha by king Brahmadatta and its ultimate surrender.[189]

In the *Mahābhārata*, many methods for the destruction of forts are mentioned.[190] Kauṭilya has mentioned five means of taking a fort: instigation to sedition (*upajāpa*); drawing out the enemy by means of stratagems (*yogavāmana*), employment of secret agents (*apasarpa*); laying a siege (*parayupāsana*); and storming (*avamarda*).[191]

But before going in for harder options like a siege or assault, the invader could use other options like psychological war to frighten those inside the fort and to encourage his own men. This could be done by subverting the enemy, officials and devastating his territory. The second option was to draw the enemy out of the protection of fort clandestinely and kill him. The third option was to infiltrate the fort with trusted men, who after gaining the confidence of the besieged, could by betrayal weaken the captive fort from inside. The means of laying siege and assaulting the fort were to be adopted as a last resort only. An assault on fort involved activities such as cleaning of the surroundings, breaching of the walls, and setting the fort on fire. Another method of destroying a fort was by mining. By making a passage under the fort, the ramparts and towers could be demolished.[192]

While making an assault, perhaps bamboo ladders and battering rams were used. But one of the well-known methods employed was the use of elephants. In the Epics, the elephant has been called the breaker of forts.[193] A *Jātaka* story refers to the destruction of a fort by an elephant.[194] The *Arthaśāstra* also refers to this method.[195]

A fort could also be destroyed by setting it on fire. The *Arthaśāstra* has described in detail the use of birds and animals for this purpose, but it also cautions about the risks involved in using the means of fire.[196] As a preventive measure against fire, the *Mahābhārata* recommends the plastering of thatched roofs.[197]

It seems that some special weapons were exclusively meant to break open the gates of the enemy forts. One such weapon called *paridha*, which had the capability to destroy the city gates, is mentioned in the *Rāmāyaṇa*. It was hard like *vajra* and had iron nails on all sides.[198] But details are not available regarding the design or performance of any of the missile-throwing engines used in a siege.

It appears that the fort did not form a part of the overall military strategy in ancient India. It merely served as a shelter in times of distress. Its potentiality was exploited neither for proper defence nor for offence. In the Indian scheme of fortification, there appears no provision for seeking a breakthrough or taking the enemy from behind while laying a siege. This was one of the greatest weakness of the military system in ancient India.

Education and Training

How to fight better has been an important human preoccupation through the ages. In the Vedic age, an organized system of military training had been developed. In this connection, the observations made by Das are significant:

> We shall not, therefore, be wrong in inferring that every village had some kind of organisation for training men in the use of arms, the art of riding, physical culture, skilful driving of chariots, and the rudimentary arts of warfare. Horse-racing and chariot-racing were indulged in probably not so much for amusement, as for the necessity of developing and promoting a skill in horse riding and chariot driving. We may surmise that *Grāmaṇi*, who was both the civil and military leader of the village took a lead in the matter and organised his village contingent, not only for the defence of the village, but also for taking an active part in any war that the king might wage against a powerful enemy.[199]

Dhanurveda

In the Epic age, the term *Dhanurveda* had came to denote the knowledge of warfare (*yuddha-vidyā*). The pre-eminence of the bow in the Indian battlefield perhaps led to the term being used for all types of military knowledge.

Dhanurveda thus meant the knowledge of all kinds of weapons and warfare, including the bow.[200] It included education and training in arts relating to war, such as ascending and descending from a vehicle, running, jumping, releasing the weapon, advancing, and retreating.[201] The manner of wielding a sword, shield and mace, as also the art of disciplining elephants was included within this.[202] In short, military education and training meant a learning of the *Dhanurveda.*[203]

In the study of *Dhanurveda,* concentration and practice were considered important and the learning process was treated like a penance. Proper training enabled the soldier to maintain his mental equilibrium at times of crisis.[204] The Epic says that a smaller army, if trained well, is preferable to a large but untrained army.[205] Before Kauṭilya, some military thinkers had believed that courageous elephants, though fewer in number, were better than many dull elephants. The *Arthaśāstra*, on the other hand, held that dull elephants in good number are more useful, because courage can be instilled by proper training, whereas the numbers cannot be increased by any means.[206] It also maintains that a well-trained Kṣatriya army is far more useful than a large but untrained Brahman, Vaiśya or Śūdra army.[207]

In the Kauṭilyan scheme of warfare, there was no place for an untrained soldier. The Commander-in-Chief conveyed his instructions regarding the formation of battle array by means of signals, transmitted through trumpets, standards, and flags when the army was in the camp, on the march, or on the battlefield.[208] This implies that the troops were educated and trained in all military moves and all kinds of signals.

Kāmandaka has emphasized the need for regular practice if soldiers are to achieve excellence in fighting from mounts, such as the horse, elephant, and chariot, and also in the skill of bowmanship.[209] Śukra expressed similar views.[210] The Sangam literature also refers to the importance of horsemanship and target practice by the soldiers.[211]

System of Training

Basic military training was imparted specially to the children of Kṣatriyas at their place of dwelling. The Kaurava princes Dhṛṭarāṣṭra, Pāṇḍu, and Vidura received their basic military training under the tutelage of Bhīṣma.[212] After learning the basics at their dwelling place, the princes and the Kṣatriyas boys sought admission in some *āśrama* run generally by a Brahman, who was highly proficient in *Dhanurveda*. Rāma and Lakṣmaṇa learnt *Dhanurveda* in the *āśrama* of Viśvāmitra.[213] Great warriors like Bhīṣma and Karṇa received their lessons in the *āśrama* of Paraśurāma. Ācāryas Śukra and Bṛhaspati, the two great military thinkers, must have run *āśrama*s for the benefit of the Asuras and Devas respectively. It is notable that wars fought between the Devas and the Asuras were monitored by their respective *gurus*.

In reputed *āśrama*s, seekers of knowledge in *Dhanurveda* came from far and wide. In the *āśrama* of Kṛpācārya many princes, besides the Pāṇḍavas and Kauravas, received instructions in the art of war.[214] This was also the case in the *āśrama* of Droṇa.[215] Occasionally, instructors were appointed to train the princes within the state capital, but the students had to lead a regimented life in an *āśrama* like atmosphere. After completion of the education, the offering of valuable presents (*guru-dakṣiṇa*) to the teacher was customary.[216]

Taxilā was a great centre of military education and training in ancient India. Many *āśramas* run by top military thinkers of the age were located in this city. It is believed that Kauṭilya and Chandragupta, had both received their education at Taxilā. In a particular *āśrama* there, as many as one hundred and three princes belonging to various kingdoms were under training.[217] Some institutions provided special training in bowmanship.[218] Jotipala, a Brahman, was sent to Taxilā by the ruler of Vārāṇasī at state expense to master the art of bowmanship. The teacher was so impressed by his excellence that he offered him his chair of Ācārya.[219]

The Mauryans organized their army as a regular force, and trained and equipped it at state expense. It appears that the *āśramas* ceased to serve as military training institutions at this time. The complete silence of the Greek historians, the *Arthaśāstra*, and *Nīti* works about *āśrama* education corroborates this speculation. The *Kādambarī*, a work of the seventh century AD, describes an institution where the princes and nobles of the state received training. It was a huge complex surrounded by high walls and provided with big and strong gates. The area was provided additional protection by constructing a moat all around it, and there was only one passage for entry. Within the boundary wall on one side a big stable was located, and on the other side a gymnasium. Teachers of all disciplines were appointed in the institution after a rigorous selection procedure.[220]

In ancient India, knowledge passed from master to disciple. Ācārya Bṛhaspati had mastered the *Agneyāstra* (weapon that caused fire) and from him this knowledge passed on to Bhāradvāja, Agniveśa, Droṇācārya, and Arjuna, respectively.[221] Before imparting the knowledge of weapons, the master examined the eligibility of the person seeking it.[222] During the training, tests were conducted to assess the capability of students.[223] At the end of the training, a great show was organized in which students displayed their skills in weaponry.[224]

Training

In the Vedic age, military education may have included training in weapons only. But by the fifth century BC, mock fights, roll call, parade, marching through the streets, and other such manoeuvres had come to form a part of military training, as is evident from the Buddhist Nikayas.[225] In the Epic age, military training came to include almost all aspects of warfare.[226] The *Mahābhaṣya* refers to some training centres which imparted instructions in military subjects.[227]

In the *Arthaśāstra*, the need for military training is repeatedly emphasized. Soldiers of all the four arms attended regular training sessions during the morning hours. *Patyādhyakṣa*, *Āśvādhyakṣa*, *Hastyādhyaksa*, and *Rathādhyakṣa* supervised these training sessions. The overall supervision of such training was done by the Commander-in-Chief, though the king also attended these sessions.[228] The training curriculum included the mounting of a chariot, elephant, and horse and practice in the use of weapons. Hunting, too, formed a part of military training.[229]

The system of military training as followed in ancient India, is best described in the *Śukranīti.* Close combat, wrestling, exercise and nourishing food were included in the programme.[230] The king, sitting on a raised platform, presided, while his aides kept a close watch on the practice and exercises. The training was performed in accordance with the signals passed on by the trumpet.[231] The king himself practised with various mounts and exchanged his knowledge of *vyūha*s with the army commander during the sessions.[232] He increased his stamina by practising the use of weapons with warriors and hunting tigers.[233] It is notable that the king spent two hours and fifteen minutes in military training and some forty-five minutes in practising with the soldiers everyday.[234] Hunting took forty-five minutes,[235] whereas horse-riding, chariot racing, etc., consumed another forty-five minutes.[236] Thus, military exercises alone took some five hours of the king's time everyday. The officers who organised military training were called *Śatānīkas* and *Anuśātikas*.[237] The *Nītiprakāśikā* also has much to say on the subject.[238]

Hunting

Hunting formed an integral part of military training. Kauṭilya advises that a king 'should go to a forest containing game, for practising on moving targets.'[239] He considered this practice as necessary also because:

> . . . in hunting, there is exercise, getting rid of phelgm, bile, fat, and (a tendency to) perspiration, practice in hitting the targets of moving and stationary bodies, knowledge of mind of animals in anger, fear and condition of ease, and (only) occasional marching.[240]

Forests were reserved for royal hunting.[241] Hunting was both an exercise and an entertainment for the rulers. They used to enter dense forests full of ferocious animals accompanied by their army.[242] Occasionally, they moved into the forest alone. King Daśaratha killed Sarvaṇa Kumār during one such hunt.[243] It may be recalled that hunting was a favourite sport with Indian rulers as early as the fourth century BC. The ruler of Saubhūti maintained a good number of hunting dogs who were amazingly courageous. He presented fifteen such dogs to Alexander.[244] The art of Bhārhut and Sāñcī also represent some hunting scenes.

The Gupta rulers were very fond of hunting. On his gold coins Samudragupta is shown as aiming his weapon at a lion. Chandragupta II, in one of his rare issues, is depicted as attacking a lion with a sword. The coins of Kumārgupta are replete with hunting scenes.[245] According to Rosenfield, hunting was an Iranian theme which the Gupta kings borrowed to depict on their coins.[246] This appears true because in ancient India hunting scenes are exclusive to Gupta coins.

That hunting was a popular sport for the rulers is also evident from the contemporary literature.[247] Prince Harṣavardhana, while accompanying his brother on an expedition, spent many days outside the camp hunting lions, tigers, etc.[248]

Training in Weapons

Training in the use of weapons was an important part of *Dhanurveda.* Among the large number of weapons invented by Indians, the bow, sword, mace, spear and shield were the most widely used. They had also evolved a system of training for each of these weapons.

The bow was the most popular weapon in ancient India. For learning its use there were four basic stages called the *atama, prati, ayam,* and *asa* respectively.[249] In *atama,* the trainee learnt the technique of holding the bow; in *prati* the method of fixing the arrow on the bow, in *ayam* to aim at the target; and in *asa* the method of releasing the arrow. After this basic education, the trainee learnt the skills and postures related to bowmanship (*kodaṇda cāturī*).[250] Hitting a target, while mounted on a chariot, elephant or horse, required special training and practice. Hunting was considered useful for mastering this art.

The sword was also an ancient weapon and Indians had evolved a procedure for training in swordmanship. In the Epics, eight techniques of wielding the sword have been mentioned: *bhrānta, āvidha, udbhrānta, āpluta, prasṛata, sṛata, sampāta,* and *samudīrṇ.*[251] In the *Agni Purāṇa,* thirty-two techniques are mentioned.[252] Soldiers also learnt the art of fighting with the sword while mounted on horseback.[253] Other weapons, such as the mace and the dagger, had their own techniques which the trainee had to learn.

Soldiers were also trained in the use of the shield, as survival depended on the way the shield was used by a warrior. In the *Mānasollāsa,* five techniques of holding a shield are *mentioned—kapolaka, śrivatsa, bhūmaṇdala, tikacakra* and *dalaga.*[254]

Training of Animals

Man has been using animals for the purpose of war from the earliest times. It is not surprising, therefore, that Indians had devised means of training elephants, horses, camels, etc., for use in war. There were institutions which specialized in the training of animals for war. Bhāradvajā's *āśrama* was one such institution.[255]

The elephant was domesticated in India about 2,500 years before the beginning of the Christian era. In the Epic war, elephants were used and an officer designated the *Arālika* was responsible for their training,[256] though occasionally the mahout could also do it.[257] In the sixth century BC, there were training centres which specialized in training elephants for war purposes.[258] A trained elephant remained firm in the battlefield whereas an untrained elephant sulked under pressure.[259]

In the *Arthaśāstra*, the training of elephants was known as *sannāha karma.*[260] An official called the *Anīkastha*[261] supervised this training, which was imparted with the help of fakes made of skins. Elephants were trained in seven kinds of activities such as the following: *upasthāna, samvartana, samyāna, vadhāvadha, hasti-yuddha, nāgarāyaṇa* and *samgrāmika.*[262] In *upasthāna,* the elephant was trained to raise or squeeze body organs and cross over such hurdles as standards, bamboo poles, etc. In *samvartana,* it learnt to lie down, sit on the earth, and jump over ditches. In *samyāna,* it was trained to move in a straight, bent, or zigzag manner. In *vadhāvadha,* it was taught to kill men or horses with the help of its trunk, body or teeth. In *hastiyuddha,* the animal was taught to fight with other elephants. In *nagārāyaṇa,* the elephant was taught how to break open the doors, walls and chains. In *samgrāmika,* the elephant was trained to fight. The *Śukraniti* also refers to the training of elephants.

The horse was introduced in the Indian battlefield by the Aryans, and this could not have been possible without proper training.[263] In the Epic age, the horse trainer was called the *Granthika* or *Aśvabandha.*[264] In the *Arthaśāstra,* there is a detailed description of horse training which is generally related to movements such as the *valgana, nicairagata, laṅghana, ghoraṇa,* and the *nirostra.*[265] These movements meant jumping at a gallop, rotating at a centre, leaping, moving at a trot, and responding to signals, respectively. Each of these five moves comprised many sub-moves in which the horse was trained.[266] The method of horse training in India has also been referred to in Greek accounts.[267] The *Agni Purāṇa* has devoted a full chapter to the training of horses.[268] In the *Śukranīti*[269] and the *Mānasollāsa*[270] the training of horses is described in greater detail.

Camels and asses were also used in war. The *Arthaśāstra* recommends that during a campaign in semi-arid zones, these animals could be pressed into service.[271] Further, when there was a shortage of horses, bullocks could also be yoked to chariots. The *Śukranīti* enumerates the methods by which these animals could be kept under control.[272] Dogs were also used in war. In the fifth century BC, an army unit despatched by a subject Indian ruler to the Iranian king was accompanied by dogs.[273] During the invasion of India, Alexander saw a large number of ferocious dogs with the king of Saubhūti in north-west India.[274] There is no doubt that all these dogs were specially trained.

NOTES

* Editor's Note: For the sake of simplicity, the references given in Sanskrit in the endnotes of the original version have been deleted.

1. G. C. Pande, *Dimensions of Ancient Indian Social History*, vol. 2, p. 98.
2. *Ṛgveda*, vol. 6.7.2–4; for details on Vedic weapons, see A. C. Das, *Ṛgvedic Culture*, pp. 331–7; S. D. Singh, *Ancient Indian Warfare*, pp. 86–95.
3. G. C. Pande, *Dimensions of Ancient Indian Social History*, vol. 2, p. 110.
4. *Atharvaveda*, 11.3.7; 5.28.1.
5. V. S. Agrawala, *India as known to Pāṇini*, p. 420.
6. *MB*, Karna, 4.90.
7. *Nītiprakāśikā*, 2.1–13; A similar classification is given in *Mānasollāsa* (2.6.683).
8. *Agni Purāṇa*, 249.2.
9. *Arthaśāstra*, 2.18.
10. Ibid.
11. P. C. Chakravarty, *War in Ancient India*, p. 151.
12. J. Marshall, *Mohenjo-daro and the Indus Civilization*, p. 499. It is believed that the bow and arrow came into vogue in the barbaric age, but after the spear. It was perhaps a chance discovery. The Polynesians and Austrasians had no knowledge of this weapon. This proves that man had advanced ahead of the early barbaric stage when he first used the bow.
13. Macdonall and Keith, *Vedic Index*, vol. 1, p. 388.
14. *Śukrañiti*, 4.3.73–4.
15. A. C. Das, *Ṛgvedic Culture*, p. 332.
16. *Ṛgveda*, 10.18.9.
17. *Arthaśāstra*, 2.18.8.
18. J. W. McCrindle, *Ancient India*, pp. 220–21; also *Invasion of India*, p. 210.
19. J. Marshall, *Guide to Sanchi*, pp. 4-5.
20. *Agni Purāṇa*, 245.7–13.
21. P. C. Chakravarty, *War in Ancient India*, p. 154.
22. *Dhanurveda*, 1771; *MB* also refers to it.
23. *Arthaśāstra*, 2.18.11.
24. E. W. Hopkins, *Social & Military Position of the Ruling Caste in Ancient India*, p. 224.

25. Ibid.
26. J. Marshall, *Taxilā*, p. 547.
27. C. R. Sharma, *Excavations at Kauśāmbī*, p. 46.
28. McCrindle, *Ancient India*, pp. 220–21.
29. *Vaśiśṭha Dhanurueda*, pp. 5–7.
30. Yajurveda, 29.42; also Rgveda, 5.57.2; 10.103.3; 6.74.5.
31. *ME*, Adi, 55.37, Uddyoga, 59.12; Śalya, 61.9.
32. E. W. Hopkins, E.W., *The Social and Military Position of the Ruling Caste in Ancient India*, p. 218.
33. *MB*, Adi, 124.24.27.
34. P. K. Gode, *Studies in Ancient Indian Cultural History*, vol. 2, p. 66.
35. R. C. Kak, *Ancient Monuments of Kashmir*, pls 23.3, 28.14, etc.
36. V. Smith, *Catalogue of the Coins in the Indian Museum*, Calcutta, p. 43, pl. 9.
37. A. S. Altekar, *The Coinage of the Gupta Empire*, pls. 8.1–5, 10.11–15, 15.14–15.
38. G. Yazdani, *Ajaṇṭā*, pt. 4., pls. 10–3.
39. P. C. Chakravarty, *War in Ancient India*, p. 42.
40. F. C. Maisey, *Sāñcī and its Remains*, pls. 6.2, 9.2, 20, 27; also S. Piggot, *Prehistoric India*, p. 268.
41. J. Marshall, *A Guide to Sāñcī*, p. 152, fn. 3.
42. P. K. Code, *Studies in Indian Cultural History*, vol. 2, p. 72.
43. *Vedic Index*, vol. 2, p. 380; S. D. Singh, *Ancient Indian Warfare*, p. 28, fn. 5.
44. McCrindle, *Ancient India*, pp. 89, 221.
45. E. W. Hopkins, *The Social and Military Position of the Ruling Caste in Ancient India*, p. 208.
46. P. C. Chakravarty, *The Art of War in Ancient India*, p. 38; J. Fergusson, however, doubts the very presence of bit in the art of *Sāñcī. Tree and Serpent Worship*, p. 134.
47. Y. S. Agrawala, *Harṣacarita Eka Sanshritika Adhyayana*, p. 21.
48. J. W. McCrindle, *Ancient India*, p. 221.
49. F. W. Hopkins, *The Social and Military Position of the Ruling Caste in Ancient India*, p. 209.
50. F. C. Maisey, *Sāñcī and its Remains*, pl. 6, fig. 2; also pls. 2, 9, 15, 20; also A. Cunningham, *The Stūpa of Bhārhut*, p. 42, pl. 32.
51. A. S. Altekar, *The Coinage of the Gupta Empire.*
52. J. Marshall, Mohenjo-*daro and the Indus Civilization*, vol. 1, pp. 35, 494–9.
53. *Vedic Index*, vol. 1, p. 47.
54. *MB*, Śānti, 160.2; 160.4.
55. J. W. McCrindle, *Ancient India*, p. 221.
56. A. Cunningham, *Bhārhut*, pl. 32.4.

57. *Arthaśāstra*, 2.18.12.
58. J. M. Rosenfield, J.M., *The Dynastic Art of the Kuṣāṇas*, pls. 2, 2A.
59. *Arthaśāstra*, 2.18.12.
60. E. W. Hopkins, *The Social and Military Position of the Ruling Caste in Ancient India*, p. 230.
61. A. Cunningham, *Bhārhut*, pl. 32.4.
62. J. M. Rosenfield, *The Dynastic Art of the Kuṣāṇs*, pl. 2.
63. T. Sulirnirski, *The Sarmatians*, p. 29.
64. J. M. Rosenfield, *The Dynastic Art of the Kuṣāṇs*, p. 179.
65. J. Allen, *Catalogue of the Coins of the Gupta Dynasties*, pl. 12.
66. *MB*, Sabhā, 47.24.
67. *Agni Purāṇa*, 245.21–24.
68. Ibid., 249.50.
69. J. Marshall, *Mohenjo-daro and the Indus Civilization*, vol. 1, pp. 35, 497–8.
70. *Vedic Index*, vol. 1, p. 118.
71. *MB*. Ādi, 26.44.
72. J. W. McCrinndle, *Ancient India*, p. 221.
73. *Arthaśāstra*, 2.18.7.
74. F. C. Maisey, *Sāñcī and Its Remains*, pls. 6.2, 20, 27, etc.
75. J. M. Rosenfield, *The Dynastic Art of the Kuṣāṇas*, pls. 40b, 49, 62.
76. J. Marshall, *Taxilā*, p. 546.
77. J. M. Rosenfield, *The Dynastic Art of Kushāns*, p. 55; also see, T. Sulimirski, *The Sarmatians*, p. 29.
78. N. K. Dhavalikar, *Ajaṇṭā*, pl. 38.
79. J. Marshall, M*ohenjo-daro and the Indus Civilization*, vol. 1, p. 35.
80. *Arthaśāstra*, 2.18.6.
81. J. W. McCrindle, *Invasion of India*, p. 312.
82. E. W. Hopkins, *The Social and Military Position of the Ruling Caste in Ancient India*, pp. 245–6.
83. *Arthaśāstra*, 2.18.5–6; For details, see R. P. Kangle, *The Kautilya Arthaśāstra*, vol. 2, p. 132.
84. *Arthaśāstra*, 2.18.6; for details, see, R. P. Kangle, *The Kauṭilya Arthaśāstra*, vol. 2, pp. 131–2.
85. *Ram*, Yuddha, 3.13.
86. *MB*, *Āraṇyaka*, 284.31.
87. P. V. Kane, *History of Dharmaṣāstra*, vol. 3, p. 214.
88. A. L. Basham, *The Wonder that was India*, p. 133.
89. *Agni Purāṇa*, 236.61.
90. J. W. McCrindle, *Ancient India*, p. 221.
91. *Arthaśāstra*, 2.18.17; for details, see R. P. Kangle, *The Kauṭilya Arthaśāstra*, vol. 2, p. 133.
92. F. C. Maisey, *Sāñcī and Its Remains*, pls. 20, 27, 35.

93. Codrington, *Indian Antiquary*, vol. 59, 1930, p. 170; also N. Griffith, *The Paintings in the Buddhist Cave Temples of Ajaṇṭā*, vol. 1, figs 33–40.
94. *Vedic Index*, vol. 1, p. 383; vol. 2, p. 271.
95. *Ṛgveda*, 6.75.
96. *Atharvaveda*, 11.10.22.
97. J. W. McCrindle, *Invasion of India*, p. 108.
98. Ibid., p. 204.
99. E. W. Hopkins, *The Social and Military Position of the Ruling Caste in Ancient India*, p. 248; Also *MB*, Śalya, 31.55, Ādi, 26.31; Droṇa, 102.54–5; Bhīṣma, 19.30.
100. Ibid., *Virāta*, 50.20; Śalya, 31.54.
101. *Ram*, Yuddha, 55.23–4.
102. *MB*, Droṇa, 140.28; Karṇa 16.21; and Bhīṣma, 43.4.
103. *MB*, Bhīṣma, 102.22; Āraṇyaka, 38.16; Droṇa, 40.16, etc.
104. *Arthaśāstra*, 2.18.16–17; also 2.23.17.
105. R. P. Kangle, *The Kauṭilya Arthaśāstra*, vol. II, p. 133.
106. *Arthaśāstra*, 2.18.16.
107. *Mānasollāsa*, 2.6.562.
108. H. Russel, Robinson, *Oriental Armour*, p. 89.
109. A. L. Foucher, *Art Greeco Boudhique Du Gandhara*, pls. 202, 204, 292.
110. A. L. Marshall, *Taxilā*, p. 208, also p. 549; also see A. L. Basham, *The Wonder that was India*, p. 133.
111. T. Sulimirski, *The Sarmatians*, pp. 31–2; also see A. L. Basham, *The Wonder that was India*, p. 133.
112. *MB*, Droṇa, 95.35–8.
113. *Arthaśāstra*, 13.4.2c.
114. *Ram*, Bāla 21.15.
115. V. R. R. Dikshitar, *War in Ancient India*, p. 94.
116. For details, see Gopinath Rao, *Hindu Iconography*, vols. 1, 2, 3, 4, pls.
117. *Arthaśāstra*, 8.1.24–7.
118. Ibid., 8.1.28–32.
119. Ibid., 8.1.33–40.
120. *Manusmṛti*, 7.74.
121. *Śukranīti*, 4.6.15–6.
122. *Arthaśāstra*, 6.1.1, 7.15.
123. *Kāmandakīya Nītisāra*, 4.56.
124. *Yuktikalpataru*, p. 17.
125. *Manusmṛti*, 7.71.
126. *MB*, Śānti, 56.35; also 69.62–63; 59.51; 308.153–5; 58.18.
127. M. Wheeler, *Early India and Pakistan*, p. 106.
128. S. Piggot, *Pre-historic India*, pp. 115–6.
129. J. Marshall, *Mohenjo-daro and the Indus Civilization*, p. 282.
130. *Indian Archaeology*, 1960–1, pp. 31–2.

131. *Ṛgveda*, 1.130.7, 2.19.6, 1.53.7, 1.33.12, 1.61.5; also 2.20.7–8,4.27.1, 4.30.20, 3.12.6.
132. *Vedic Index*, vol. 1, pp. 538–9.
133. ASI Report, 1905–6, pp. 88–9.
134. Ibid.
135. *Indian Archaeology*, 1959–60, p. 46.
136. M. Wheeler, *Early India and Pakistan*, pp. 131–2.
137. J. W. McCrindle, *Invasion of India*, pp. 194–5.
138. Ibid., pp. 69–71, etc.
139. Ibid., pp. 117–8.
140. Ibid., p. 142.
141. Ibid., *Ancient India*, p. 205.
142. *Arthaśāstra*, 2.3.1–2.
143. C. Tadgell, *History of Architecture in India*, p. 8.
144. *Ram*, *Bāla*, 5.10–13.
145. Ibid., Yuddha, 3.12–13.
146. *ME*, Śānti, 86.5.
147. *ME*, Ādi, 199.29.
148. *MB*, Śānti, 69.45.
149. *MB*, Śānti, 69.43; also see C. V. Vaidya, *Epic India*, vol. 1, p. 263.
150. C. V. Vaidya, Epic India, vol. 1, p. 201.
151. *Manusmṛti*, 7.70–71.
152. Ibid.
153. G. Woodcock, *Greeks in India*, pp. 110–11.
154. J. N. Banerjea, *Comprehensive History of India*, vol. II, p. 152.
155. J. Marshall, *Taxilā*, pp. 113–4.
156. *Milindapañho*, p. 2.
157. J. Marshall, *Taxilā*, p. 218.
158. Ibid.
159. Ibid.
160. Ibid.
161. Ibid., p. 47.
162. G. R. Sharma, *Memoirs ASI*, no. 74, pp. 1–3.
163. H. Ingholt, *The Gandhāra Art in Pakistan*, pls. 48, 91, 103, 151,152, 464; also W. A. Zwalf, *Catalogue of Gandhāra Sculpture in the British Museum*, vol. 2, pls. 55, 161, 163–4, 176, 205, 214, 218, 323–4.
164. A. L. Srivastava, *Life in Sāñcī Sculptures*, pp. 50–52.
165. *Raghuvaṁśa*, 4.26.
166. S. Beal, *Travels of Hiuen-tsang*, vol. 1, pp. 142, 203–4; also vol. II, pp. 28–9, 231, 247, 324–25.
167. Elliot and Dawson, *History of India*, vol. II, pp. 142, 203–4.
168. V. Kanakasabhai, *The Tamils Eighteen Hundred Years Ago*, p. 12; also pp. 15, 24, 86, 100.

169. Ibid.
170. J. F. Fleet, *Indian Antiqumy*, vol. 6, p. 130.
171. *MB*, Śānti, 87.5.
172. *Ram*, Yuddha, 3.20–22; *Manusmṛti*, 7.70, *Agni Purāṇa*, 222.4–5; Matsya Purāṇa, 217.6–7.
173. *Arthaśāstra*, 2.3.1.
174. *Śukranīti*, 4.6.8,12.
175. *Arthaśāstra*, 2.3.1; *Devi Purāṇa*, 72.
176. *MB*, Śānti, 83.40.
177. *Arthaśāstra*, 2.3.1.
178. *Śukranīti*, 4.6.5.
179. *Arthaśāstra*, 2.3.1; also *Devi Purāṇa*, 72.
180. *MB*, Śānti, 56.35.
181. *Arthaśāstra*, 2.3.5.
182. *MB*, Āraṇyaka, 16; *Devi Purāṇa*, 72.
183. *Arthaśāstra*, 12.5.
184. J. W. McCrindle, *Invasion of India*, p. 199.
185. *Vedic Index*, vol. II, p. 417.
186. S. D. Singh, *Ancient Indian Warfare*, p. 126.
187. *Śabdakalpadruma*; also *Harivamśa*, Viśṇu, 118.81–5.
188. *Arthaśāstra*, 13.1.
189. E. B. Cowell, *The Jatāka*, vol. II, p. 243; vol. VI, pp. 200–07.
190. *MB*, Āraṇyaka, p. 268.
191. *Arthaśāstra*, 13.1–4.
192. *Arthaśāstra*, 13.4.9.
193. *MB*, Sabha, 54.10.
194. E. B. Cowell, *The Jātaka*, vol. II, pp. 64–5.
195. *Arthaśāstra*, 13.4.9.
196. Ibid., 13.4.14–22.
197. *MB*, Santi, 69.45.
198. *Ram*, Āraṇyaka, 26.9–12.
199. A. C. Das, *Ṛgvedic Culture*, p. 330.
200. *MB*, Bhīṣma, 70.9, 78.34, 86.38, Śalya, 21.15, Droṇa, 117.36–9, 169.1.
201. *Agni Purāṇa*, 249.1–5.
202. *MB*, Ādi, 102.17.
203. *Ram*, Bāla, 18.37.
204. *Saṁhyutta Nikāya*, vol. I, pp. 123–4.
205. *MB*, Bhīṣma, 4.26; Śānti, 103.20–21.
206. *Arthaśāstra*, 7.12.8–12.
207. Ibid., 9.2.24.
208. Ibid., 2.33.11.
209. *Kāmandaka*, 15.50.
210. *Śukraniti*, 4.7.362–64, 532–73, 454–61.

211. N. Subrahmanian, *Sangam Polity*, pp. 143–44.
212. *MB*, Ādi, 102.17.
213. *Ram*, Bāla, 27.28, 29.
214. *MB*, Ādi, 120.21.
215. Ibid., 122.41, 47, 123.9.
216. As *gurudakṣīṇā*, Droṇacārya asked his disciples to arrest and bring king Drupada before him. *MB*, Ādi, 128; Ekalavya presented his right-hand thumb as *gurudakṣīṇa*, to Droṇacārya.
    Ibid., 123.33–7.
217. E. B. Cowell, *The Jātaka*, vol. 5, p. 66.
218. Ibid., vol. 5, p. 66; vol. 2, p. 60.
219. Ibid., vol. 5, pp. 66–9.
220. *Kādambarī*, p. 58.
221 *MB*, Ādi, 158.26–7.
222. *MB*, Ādi, 122–24.
223. Ibid., 123.45–73.
224. Ibid., 124–6, In *Sarabhanga Jātaka* (vol. 5, p. 67), a competition among bowmen is described. Four bowmen fighting jointly could not injure Jotipāla whereas he alone injured all of them. Pānini (4.2.57) has termed such competitions as *prahasan Krira*.
225. B. C. Law, *Indological Studies*, vol. 4, p. 350.
226. *MB*, Sabhā, 5.109–10,123.7; also *Ram*, Bāla, 18.27–8,22.15.
227. *Mahābhāṣya*, 4.2.60, 5.1.59.
228. *Arthaśāstra*, 2.30–33; also 1.5.12.
229. *Arthasastra*, 1.21.23.
230. *Śukranīti*, 4.7.32–3; also 36–7.
231. Ibid., 4.7.734–6.
232. Ibid., 1.663–4.
233. Ibid., 4.7.34–5.
234. Ibid., 1.566–7; One *muhurta* lasted for 45 minutes.
235. Ibid.
236. Ibid., 1.559.
237. Ibid., 2.281–88.
238. *Nitiprakāśikā*, 6.58.
239. *Arthaśāstra*, 1.21.23.
240. Ibid., 8.3.46; *Karmandakiya Nitisara*, 14.25.
241. *Arthaśāstra*, 2.23, *Kamandakiya Nitisara*, 14.7.36, 14.28–42.
242. *MB*, Ādi, 63; also Āraṇyaka, 229,1–11.
243. *Ram*, Ayodhyā, 63:14–23; 49.15–6.
244. J. W. McCrindle,. *Invasion of India*, pp. 189, 280–81.
245. In this context see A. S. Altekar, *The Coinage of the Gupta Empire*, pls.
246. J. M. Rosenfield, *Dynastic Art of the Kuṣhāṇas*, p. 182.
247. *Śākuntalam*, p. 2; *Raghuvaṁśa*, 9.48–80; *Harṣacrita*, p. 132: *Kādambarī*, p. 7.

248. *Harşacrita*, p. 132.
249. *Agni Purāṇa*, 249–50.
250. Ibid.
251. *MB*, *Bhīşma*, 50.44; also Droṇa, 13.51–2.
252. *Agni Purāṇa*, 252.1–4.
253. *MB*, Ādi, 63.16; Śalya, 56.16–19.
254. *Mānasollāsa*, 4.1.14–20.
255. *Ram*, Ayodhyā, 91.55–7.
256. *MB*, Virāta, 2.7.
257. Ibid., Karṇa, 27.9.
258. E. B. Cowell, *The Jātaka*, vol. 2, pp. 31–4.
259. Ibid., vol. 5, p. 162; also vol. 2, pp. 64, 155, 280.
260. *Arthaśāstra*, 7.12.8–12.
261. Ibid., 2.32.16.
262. Ibid., 2.32.4; also 2.31.4–6.
263. *Ṛgveda*, 4.27.1.
264. *MB*, Virāta, 3.2–3.
265. *Arthaśāstra*, 2.30.32.
266. Ibid., 2.30.33–41.
267. J. W. McCrindle, *Ancient India*, pp. 89–90.
268. *Agni Purāṇa*, 288.
269. *Śukranīti*, 2.260–63; 4.7.85–337.
270. *Mānasollāsa*, 4.4.43.
271. *Arthaśāstra*, 9.2.50.
272. *Śukranīti*, 4.7.339–48.
273. Rapson, J., *Cambridge History of India*, vol. I, p. 305.
274. J. W. McCrindle, *Invasion of India*, pp. 280–81.

SECTION II

The Demigods on Horses?
Warfare in Medieval India, 900 CE–1700 CE

CHAPTER 5

The Striking Power of the Army of the Sultanate

K. S. Lal

The establishment and continuance of Muslim rule in India was primarily due to its army. The extension of Muslim political power in India, was not possible without conquest, and so the Turkish Sultanate was, by its very nature, committed to maintaining a strong army. The army of Ghaznavids and Ghorids, the founders of Turkish rule in India was a very effective and striking force, as their victories in India show. The army of the Sultanate (1206–1526 CE) was patterned on this prototype; it was almost a continuation of this model. It possessed a strong punch; it owed its punch to its men and mounts, engines of war and strategy, and to its military organization.

Men

The army of the sultanate could be roughly classified into three categories—soldiers in the permanent employment of the ruler, special recruits enrolled on the eve of an expedition, and the volunteers or Ghazis 'for no pay but a share in the booty, for participating in what was called a Jihad'.[1]

Soldiers in permanent service, and the king's bodyguards called Jandars,[2] were largely drawn from his personal slaves. The slave troops, or the slave system in the limited sphere of the army, will, therefore, receive our first attention. Thereafter, we shall study about the special recruits and about the volunteers. The process of their selection and training made the army of the Sultanate develop a great striking power.

Right from the days of Mahmud of Ghazni the core of the regular army was the slave force (ghilmān, Thamālik).[3] These were obtained as presents and part of tribute from subordinate states or enslaved during campaigns. Captured or imported as youths, they were broken in at an early age, and their minds could be moulded and then bodies trained for warfare. The crucial development of the period of the thirteenth–fifteenth centuries was almost the 'Universal extension of the Mamluk military system. To sustain the new principalities, slaves, imported as youths from peripheral regions were trained at the court of their masters to be a fighting and administrative elite loyal to them alone and their comrades in arms.'[4] The value of the slave troops lay in their lack of roots and local connections and attachment to the ruler by a personal bond of fealty. Slaves were collected from all countries and nationalities. There were Turks, Persians, Buyids, Seliuqs, Oghuz (also called Iraqi Turkmen), Afghans, Khaljis, Hindu, etc., in the army of Mahmud. The success of the Ghaznavids and Ghorids in India was due, besides other reasons, to the staunchly loyal slave troops.[5] This tradition of obtaining slaves by all methods and from all regions was continued by the Delhi Sultans. In his campaign against Katehar, Balban massacred mercilessly, sparing boys only up to the age of eight or nine.[6] The age factor is significant. As these slave boys grew in age, they could hardly remember their parentage of nativity, and remained loyal only to the king. No wonder that in the days of Alauddin Khalji, while the price of a handsome young slave was twenty to thirty *tankahs* and that of slave-servant ten to fifteen *tankahs*, the price of a child slave boy (*ghulām bachchagān naukāri)* was seventy to eighty *tankahs*.[7] As these prices were fixed by the Sultan himself, the importance attached by this warlord to young slaves is self-evident. Alauddin Khalji possessed 50,000 slave boys,[8] who, as they grew up, would have made his strong army stronger. Muhammad Tughlaq too obtained slaves in campaigns. Firoz Tughlaq's acquisition of slaves was accomplished through various ways—capture in war, in lieu of revenue, and presents from nobles. He had instructed his amils and jagirdars to obtain slave boys in place of revenue and tribute.[9] Writing both as a theoretician as well as an experience commentator on the Sultanate's slave system, Ziyauddin Barani says this about the slave soldiers' loyalty, devotion to duty and courage: 'They strive with their hearts and souls for the success of every enterprise. They hurl themselves like balls into running waters and flaming fires. Then it becomes necessary for the whole army (in emulation) to take the same path as they have done. The value of slaves (as a shock battalion) is obvious.'[10] In short, the medieval Muslim slave system was a constant supplier of loyal troops to the army of the Sultanate.

Another source of strength of this army was the constant inflow of foreign soldiers from Muslim homelands beyond the Indus. These may be called for the sake of brevity by the genesis (generic-editor's intervention) terms Turks and Afghans. The Turks came as invaders and became rulers, army officers and army men. The warlike character of the Afghans attracted the notice of conquerors to India who freely enrolled them in their armies. Muhammad Ghori, in his last expedition, brought ten thousand Afghan horsemen with him.[11] Indian sultans continued the tradition. They had a preference for homeland troops, or any Muslim warriors from the trans-Indus region. In the time of IItutmish, Jalaluddin of Khawarism, fleeing before Chengiz Khan, brought contingents Afghan soldiers with him. In course of time, many of them took service under Iltutmish.[12] Balban employed three thousand Afghan horse and foot soldiers in his campaigns against the Mewatis,[13] appointed thousands of Afghan officers and men for garrisoning forts like Gopalgir, Kampil, Patiali, Bhojpur and Jalali.[14] In the royal processions, hundreds of Sistani, Ghori, Samarqandi and Arab soldiers with drawn swords used to march by Balban's side. This indicates the constant influx of foreign troops into India.The Afghans had got accustomed to the adventure of soldiering in India. They joined in large numbers the armies of Mongol invaders as well as of Amir Timur when the latter marched into India. Like the Afghans, the Mongol (ethnically a generic term, again) soldiers too were there in the army of the Sultanate in large numbers. Jalaluddin Khalji (1290–96) came to terms with a Mongol invading chief and many of the latter's followers joined service of the Sultan. Under Alauddin Khalji, they were called neo-Muslims. The Persian element in the rank of officers and men was also prominent. Abyssinian slave-soldiers and officers became prominent under Raziyah.[15] The immigration of foreign troops continued without a break in the time of the Tughlaqs, Saiyyads and Lodis. Under the Saiyyad and Lodi rulers, Afghans of all tribes and clans were invited into India with high promises, and they flocked into India like 'ants and locusts'. In short, constant induction of foreign soldiers from Muslim lands, contributed to the strength and superiority of the army of the Sultanate.

Indians, or Hindus, too were freely enrolled. Ziyauddin Barani was against the recruitment of non-Muslims in the army,[16] but the Indian element was prominent in the army of the Sultanate which, according to Al Umri, 'consisted of Turks, inhabitants of Khata, Persians, and Indians'.[17] Right from the days of Mahmud of Ghazni, Hindus used to join Muslim armies[18] and lend strength to them.[19]

Most of the Hindus in the army belonged into the infantry wing and were called Paiks. Some of these were poor persons and joined the army for the sake of securing employment. Others were slaves and war-captives. The Paiks cleared the jungles and prepared roads for the army on march. The captives were sometimes used as 'cannonfodder' in battle.[20] But others, especially professionals, joined the permanent cadre of infantry for combat purposes. Barbosa says this about them (early sixteenth century): 'They carry swords and daggers, bows, and arrows. They are right good archers and their bows are long like those of England. They are mostly Hindus.'[21] Many famous Paiks hailed from Bengal. Their most important weapon was the dhanuk or dhanush[22] (about the efficacy of which we shall discuss in the section on weapons). Alauddin Khalji, Mubarak Khalji, and Firoz Tughlak were saved by Paiks when attacked.[23]

Then there were mercenaries or volunteers enrolled on the eve of a campaign. 'The volunteer element in the army was known by the name of Ghazi. The Ghazis were not entitled to any salary, but relied mostly on 'rich pickings from the Indian campaigns'. The victories of the Ghaznavids had attracted these plundering adventurers to their standards. The Ghaznavid tradition of enrolling Ghazi mercenaries was continued by the Turkish sultans in India.[24] Writing early in the reign of Iltutmish, Fakhr-i-Mudabbir describes a military review and mentions a body of infantry 'who have voluntarily joined the forces'.[25] On his way to Lakhnauti, Balban enrolled about 2,00,000 horsemen and infantry. Raziyah, when she marched with her husband Altuniah to recapture the throne, is reported to have headed an army composed mainly of mercenaries from the Khokhar and Jat tribes of the Punjab.[26] Right up to the Tughlaq times and beyond, mercenaries (Muslim, says Afif for Firoz's times) joined the army for love of plunder and concomitant gains. These enthusiasts too added strength to the regular army.

Enrolment in the regular cadre depended on a number of considerations like personal prowess, skill in weapons and family background. The Sultans believed in the theory of 'martial class'. Fakhr-i-Mudabbir advises that those whose ancestors had not been soldiers should not be made officers, Sawars or Sarkhails.[27] Ziyauddin Barani also expresses similar views.[28] However, recruitment seems to have been based on merit, and troops were enrolled after a hard and gruelling test. Describing the scene of the review and fresh enrolment before the Governor of Multan, which was an important centre of recruitment throughout the Sultanate period, Ibn Battuta says: 'The Amir was sitting on a big dias. . . . Near him was the Qazi and Khatib. On his right and left were military chiefs; the armed warriers stood high behind his head. The troops passed before him in review. There were many bows. When anyone came desiring to enlist as an archer in the army, he was given one of these bows to pull. . . . And if he desired to be enlisted in the cavalry a drum was placed. He would drive his horse and strike it with his lance. A ring was also suspended against a small wall. The horseman would make his horse run until he came abreast of it. Should he succeed in lifting it up with his lance, he was considered an excellent horseman. If one desired to enlist as a mounted archer, a ball was placed on the ground. The candidate galloped on horseback and aimed the arrow at the ball. His salary was fixed proportionately to his success in striking the ball.'[29] The learned and experienced chronicler of the Sultanate period, Maulana Ziyauddin Barani, realised the importance of recruitment after a thorough test and says, 'the *ghazis* and *mujahids* (holy warriors) should be tested in the art of horsemanship, so that other people, who have nothing to do with the art of war and belong to groups of artisans and other professions, do not find a place among them. The enrolment of amateurs among veterans throws the work of the army into disorder. To secure the increase and stability of the army, the officers ought to be select and distinguished men, well-born, brave and virtuous.'[30] In brief, the recruitment of troops was based on merit which was determined after a severe test.[31]

Like the procedure of recruitment, the process of training too was hard. If the Samanid traditions had not been given up in India, the training of a slave-soldier as described in Nizam-ul-Mulk's *Siyasat Nama* should have turned him into a veteran warrior in the course of few years. In the first year after his purchase, the *ghulam* (slave) was trained as a foot-soldier, and was never permitted, under penalties, to mount a horse. In his second year, he was given a horse with a plain saddle. After another year's training he received an ornamental belt, and so on. By the seventh year only was he fully trained and fit to become a tent commander.[32] The training of a boy slave recruit in the Sultanate might have been more or less similar. Details about such training are not available in medieval Indian chronicles, but Barani does hint at it when he speaks about Balban's trained soldiers (*tarbiyat-yafta lashkar*).[33] For experienced soldiers, enrolled in the fashion described by Ibn Battuta, constant campaigns, tournaments, sports, shikar and regular reviews were enough to keep them fit and alert.[34]

The Mount

The Sultanate's army comprised both cavalry and infantry. It had an elephant corps. Camels and ponies and other animals were also used for commissariat service. But the most important wing of the army which gave it immense power of punch was the cavalry.

Cavalry comprises the man and his mount. We have discussed the prowess of men; we shall now turn to the study of the Turkish Sultanate's horses. In India, only in some places of eastern Punjab like the Shiwaliks, Samana, Sunnam, Tabarhind, Thanesar and the 'Country of the Khokhars', good quality horses were found in sufficient numbers.[35] But these horses were inferior to the horses of West-Asia breed, and importation of war-horses from abroad became an imperative necessity for the Sultans of Delhi. Good quality war horses were responsible in good measure for the victory of the Ghaznavids and Ghorids in northern India,[36] But after the initial establishment of Muslim power, the supply of war horses occasionally got disrupted. The Khokhar region was in an imperfect state of subjection. Roads were infested with recalcitrant elements and Mongol marauders, and Balban had to undertake stern measures to clear the roads for caravans[37] and to obtain horses. Medieval chroniclers speak of Yamini, Shami, Bahri and Qipchagi horses as being in use by soldiers in India, and there was large-scale importation of horses into India from Arabia, Persia, Afghanistan and even the steppe lands of southern Russia, known as Tatars. This trade yielded so much profit that in peace time it was not normally cut off even by the Chaghatai Khans of Transoxianā and their deputies.[38] Thus apart from regular traders, even Mongol raiders and tribal groups sometimes sold horses for the Delhi army. Ibn Battuta, after describing his journey through the Crimea and his arrival at Azof writes: 'The horse in this country are exceedingly numerous and their price is negligible. . . . These horses are exported to India (in droves) each one numbering six thousand more or less. . . . When they reach the land of Sind with their horses, they feed them with forage, because the vegetation of the land of Sind does not take the place of barley and the greater part of the horses die or are stolen. They are taxed on them seven silver dinars a horse and pay a further tax at Multan, the capital of the land of Sind. In spite of this, there remains a handsome profit for the traders in these horses. The good horses are worth 500 (silver) dinars or more.'[39]

Besides making direct purchases from abroad, the sultans of Delhi also replenished their *paigahs* with horses of foreign breed obtained from defeated Indian princes, particularly those with access to the sea, as they imported such horses in large numbers. The south and Gujarat provided war horses in particular, and the Deccan expeditions of Malik Kafur were most successful in this respect.[40]

According to Ziyauddin Barani, Alauddin Khalji is said to have had 70,000 horses in the *paigah*s (in Delhi).[41] The Arab geographer Ahmad Abbas Al Umari states that Sultan Muhammed Tughlaq distributed to his retinue 10,000 Arab horses and countless others. Even Firoz Tughlaq, who is said to have neglected the army, maintained extensive *paigah*s.[42] In the later fourteenth century the *paigah* had become so large that it was divided between five establishments. One of these was situated within the palace at the capital, and the other four were all at short distances from Delhi.[43]

Horses, however, were a 'perishable' commodity, and deaths and even epidemics among them were common.[44] Therefore, war horses of foreign breed were constantly imported in India to keep the *paigah*s well-stocked.

These horses and the predominant place of cavalry in the army of the Sultanate gave it an advantage over that of the Hindus. Balban believed that with six or seven thousand horses he could lay waste the territories of Hindu rulers who possessed a hundred thousand foot-soldiers.[45] Individual Hindu kings' cavalry could not be as large as that of the central Delhi Sultanate.[46] An idea of the cavalry of the Sultanate can be had from the fact that when Kaiqubad made preparations to march against his father he mustered 100,000 soldiers at Delhi.[47] Alauddin Khalji had under his command 475,000 horsemen,[48] and Muhammad Tughlaq's cavalry is said to have consisted of 900,000 soldiers.[49] Of course, the size of the army varied from time to time. The Saiyyads were weak and the Lodis not so strong. But even in the newly formed kingdoms of Gujarat, Malwa, Jaunpur, etc., Muslim cavalry generally had an edge over the armies of the neighbouring Rajas.

The Hindus also imported foreign-breed horses. Since the ancient times the balance of trade was in India's favour, and India obtained precious metals in large quantities. But Indian kings paid foreigners in gold for importing one commodity in particular—war horses. About Malabar, which was situated far away from northern India, but was connected with West Asia by sea, Marco Polo says that no horses were bred there and 'thus a great part of the wealth of the country is wasted on purchasing horses' brought by merchants of Kis, Hormuz and Aden. The Hindus did not know the art of cross breeding, and why should the Arabs have taught it to them? Indians did not even give these precious mounts a proper diet, so that every year large numbers used to die and new ones were imported.[50] Wassaf says that in this way 10,000 horses were exported annually to Ma'ar, Kambayat and other western Indian ports and 2,200,000 dinars (220 of red gold for each) were paid for them.[51] The Indian kings also paid for all the horses lost during the voyage.

This is the evidence with regard to western and southern India. About the north, whose rulers encountered the Muslim invaders, little is known. It may be presumed that they obtained war horses from the Shiwaliks and the country of the Khokhars. These regions were not entirely subdued by Muslim rulers and were mostly not converted to Islam. But their horses were inferior in quality and not plentiful in supply. Therefore, the cavalry wing of Rajputs was not as strong as that of the Muslims. This fact may be the cause and effect of a phenomenon observed in medieval Hindu forts. From the construction technique of these citadels it appears that their armies were not cavalry-oriented. It would even seem probable that the infantry was regarded more important while the cavalry was neglected. One thing is clear: horses could not be stationed in the forts constructed on hill tops and medieval Hindu forts were almost invariably built on the tops of hillocks. This is apparent on an examination of the forts of Devagiri, Asirgath, Champanir and Raisen, which I have personally visited and studied in some detail. The citadel of Devagiri is situated on an isolated cone-shaped hill 640 feet high from the round. The rock is steep, and a moat is cut into the solid rock 50 feet deep perpendicular. There can be no question that Devagiri, both in design and construction, was one of the strongest forts of early medieval India,[52] and yet there is no path by which horses could go up and be stationed in it. There is a subterranian passage, leading to the top of the hill and into the fort, but it has stairs for ascent, precluding the ascent of the horses. Asirgarh too is situated on a very high hill and, but for the graduated gradient roads built by Akbar and developed since then, stationing of horses inside the fortress should have been impossible. Raisen, even with its modern approach roads and beaten tracks, would not permit ascent of horses. Similar is the case with Champanir.

Indeed, it appears that in the early medieval period the main wing of the army of the Hindu rajas was only infantry. The elephants were used by the important persons for riding in the battlefield and these, together with horses, were probably kept at the base of the hillock on which the fort stood. This was strategically unwise as the invader captured the mounts at the time of investment of the citadel.[53] It has been mentioned above that Pratap Rudradeva of Warangal 'surrendered' to Malik Kafur 20,000 horses,[54] and 5,000 fine horses were taken in plunder from the stables of the Pandya ruler. And there is no reason to disbelieve Amir Khusrau, Barani and Ferishtah. Would it then follow that most of these mounts were kept in stables at the foot of the fort? And they were for ceremonial occasions and were not always used for war purposes.[55] This would then mean that Hindu rajas did not attach due importance to cavalry.

On the contrary the sultans of Delhi, from the very beginning of their rule, had fortresses on ground level, or almost on ground level or like Siri, Kilughari, Tughlaqabad, Kotla, Firoz Shah at Mandu and in Gujarat—not to speak of Mughal forts of Agra, Delhi, and Allahabad—for efficient deployment of the cavalry. When Muhammad Tughlaq developed Daulatabad (Devagiri), he built new fort walls and bastions starting at the ground level. It would be a bold statement to make, but the Hindu rulers of the medieval period gave importance mainly to infantry and the elephants, and cavalry wing was developed only in course of time.[56] On the other hand, the cavalry was the main branch and the best source of strength of the army of the Muslim invaders and their descendants, the Turkish Sultans of India. It was but natural that in the regions of Central and West Asia, where good quality horses were found, their accoutrement and equipment—stirrup, horseshoe and saddle—should have been invented and developed. In India, in the painting of Ajanta, all horsemen are without stirrups. While some eleventh century bronze stirrups used by the Ghaznavids are preserved in the museums of Kabul and Ghazni, P. K. Gode affirms that there is nothing to show that the Rajputs used them in pre-Muslim times.[57] The evidence regarding the shoeing of horses and the military advantage of this in Indian conditions of the time is not available. The horseshoe may have been in use in India, but it is not seen in paintings and sculptures fixed as it is at the bottom of the hoof. However, the use of saddles by the Hindus cannot be denied. But the use of metal stirrups by heavily caparisoned cavalry (wielding lances and bows and shooting long arrows from horseback) made the Ghaznavid and Ghorid horsemen formidable in the battlefield. This tradition was inherited by the horse soldiers of the Sultanate.[58]

As against the cavalry of the Sultans, the Indian rulers depended for military strength on elephants. But even in this sphere, the Sultans became predominant in a short time. For they obtained for their *pīlkhana* elephants from all possible sources, as plunder, as tribute from subordinate rulers, or provincial governors, by purchasing from outside Muslim ruled territories, or by trapping them directly from the forest regions. There is, and will always be, a controversy about the real efficacy of the elephant in medieval warfare. It is on record that on many occasions Rajput princes lost in war because, at a crucial moment, the elephant they were riding ran away from the field of battle wounded or enraged. Mongol raiders continually attacked Indians in spite of the Delhi Sultan's deploying elephants against them. Nothing would be achieved by Nasiruddin, Ibrahim Lodi, and Rana Sangha against Timur and Babur, although the former had huge war-elephants. During the post-Aurangzeb period, when the use of cannons and large guns had become common, neither the Mughals nor the Marathas could check the onrush of foreign invaders in spite of their elephant corps.[59]

But in the Sultanate period the elephant occupied an important place in warfare. Heavily armoured, it could be used as a living battering ram for pushing down the gates of a fortress. Many of the strongest fortresses in India had elephant spikes upon their doors to hinder such form of assault. The elephant could also serve as a pack animal carrying a very large load. Its gigantic size created a feeling of terror in the enemy ranks. War-elephants could kill and destroy systematically.[60]

Naturally, the Sultans of Delhi tried to acquire as many elephants as they could. Mahmud of Ghazni had taken hundreds of them from India. According to Minhaj Siraj he had 2,500 of them; a *pīlkhānā* of his in Ghazni could accommodate 1,000 elephants.[61] Balban thought about them with wistful emotion and considered one elephant equal to 500 war horses.[62] However, the elephant corps in the Sultanate until the time of Balban could not have been large, but he and succeeding monarchs were very keen to obtain elephants from wherever they could. In fact, when Balban established Bughra Khan in Bengal, he laid it down as a condition that war horses would not be sent to Bengal until Bughra Khan regularly sent elephants to Delhi.[63] Alauddin Khalji got the largest number of elephants from the south.[64] Most of the elephants came from the Bengal, but south India and Gujarat imported elephants also from Ceylon. Bengal was an area where war-elephants were trapped locally. Firoz Tughlaq obtained elephants from Bengal, and hunted and captured many in Orissa.[65] He acquired Ceylon elephants (from jazair islands) also, and compensated the (Gujarati) traders for the animals killed in transit.[66]

However, the strength of the elephant corps in the Delhi Sultanate even in its heyday does not seem to be great. Al Umri says that there were 3,000 elephants in the *pīlkhānā* of Muhammad bin Tughlaq, but according to Simon Digby, a 'maximum number from 750 to 1,000 war elephants in the possession of the Delhi Sultans in the period of their greatest power in the early fourteenth century appears not unlikely.'[67] In such a situation the claim of Barani that the Sultans of Delhi had the monopoly of the elephants[68] is not correct,[69] although the Sultanate possessed greater resources than individual Hindu kingdoms. These kingdoms had also to surrender elephants to the Sultanate on many occasions. Therefore, it would not be indiscreet to presume that the Delhi Sultans possessed a larger number of war-elephants than their own provincial governors or independent Rajput rulers. This provided the army of the Sultanate added strength. At the battle of Killi (1299), Alauddin put many elephants in the field, and the Mongols are said to have been defeated because of this.[70] Timur's army was scared to fight against the army of Nasiruddin Mahmud as the latter had huge war-elephants.[71]

Weapons

We may now turn to discuss the superiority (or otherwise) of the weapons of the army of the Sultanate. As has been pointed out earlier, its most important element was heavy cavalry. It was armed with the bow for engaging in combat at a distance and with one or more weapons for hand-to-hand fighting—the lance, the short spear, the mace, the lasso. The most commonly employed weapon of close combat was the sword. Fakhr-i-Mudabbir gives clear primacy to the bow, the most effective of the weapons of the horseman, and next he emphasizes the superiority of the sword. Of the regional varieties of the bow in use, Fakhr-i-Mudabbir first mentions the Chachi (named after Chach or Shash, modern Tashkend) and the Khwarazmi, in use among the people of Transoxiana. He then commends to archers the bows of Ghazna and Lahore and and of the two proximate geographical areas. He mentions next the mountain bow found in certain foothills (probably Salt Range and the foothills of the Punjab Himalaya). These mountain bows were made wholly of horn and they were true in their aim. The last variety of bow which is mentioned is the Indian bow *(kamān-i-hindavī)*. It is these with which the Rajput armies faced the Muslim invaders and with which the armies of the sultanate were mainly equipped. It was made from cane (*nay neza*-male bamboo?), and its bowstring was also made from the bark of cane. Its arrows did not travel very far, but from a shorter distance it inflicted a very bad wound. Most of such arrow heads were poisoned. The conclusion to be drawn from this information is that the bows generally in use in the late Ghaznavid and Ghorid army, in addition to being considered superior to those in use in Central Asia, had a longer range than the bows mainly used by the Rajput opponents in northern India, but were not a decisively superior weapon to these. However, three types of archer's thumb-rings are mentioned by Fakhr-i-Mudabbir, all with clearly Muslim names. It is, therefore, possible that the thumb-ring may not at this time have been in use among the Rajputs.

If Fakhr-i-Mudabbir's evidence regarding the bow is indecisive, he is quite clear the Indians had superior techniques of materials for the manufacture of the sword. He mentions many famous varieties of swords,[72] but among them all the Hindi sword is the best and most lustrous (*gawhardāratar*). His preference for Indian swords is not surprising. Many references show the esteem in which they were held throughout the medieval Islamic world. Their export to such distant areas as Umayyad Spain and Seljuq Anatolia is attested. Fakhr-i-Mudabbir mentions several varieties of Hindi sword. 'these blades are cherished by the Ranas, Thakurs and men of the tribes (*mardum-i-qabail)* and they are very sharp for wounding.' By this last piece of information, Fakhr-i-Mudabbir makes clear that the best of Indian swords were also in the hands of the Northern Indian Rajput opponents of the Muslim armies. He also declares that there is no better lance than the Indian. . .[73] His evidence appears decisive in concluding that the Muslim conquest and ascendancy was not based on a technological superiority in weapons of close combat.[74]

But as resources of the Ghaznavids and Ghorids were superior to those Hindu rulers of the Panjab,[75] Muslim Sultans in India had better resources than the Rajputs. They had in their possession Punjab and Sind and the fertile Ganga-Yamuna Doab from the very beginning. With their superior resources, the Turks had developed a magnificent strategy of war, which had come down as a legacy from Central Asia to Indian Sultans. Fakhr-i-Mudabbir points out that the Turko-Persian principles and methods of campaigns, encampments and strategy were superior to those of the Hindus.[76] His detailed study of fighting patrols, proper seasons and times of attack, tactics of ambuscade, selection of the battlefield, arrangements of rank and file, protection of standard bearers, distribution of loot in war, etc., gives the clue to the success of the Muslim army. It gained constantly in experience by coming into conflict (and contact) with the foreign Mongol invaders.[77] Its use of the engines of war[78] like arrada, gargach, minjniq, Maghrabi, haqqaha (rockets), etc., the mobility of its cavalry and the expertise of archers had made it very powerful.[79] Moreover, from the time of Iltutmish to that of Firoz Shah great developments had taken place both in the field of strategy, and manufacture of weapons and engines of war. Alauddin Khalji's deployment of engines of war helped in the conquest of major parts of the Indian subcontinent. The *Sirat-i-Firoz Shahi* mentions some very interesting 'equipments, outfits and instruments for waging war'. These were kept stored in the royal Karkhanas and included traps, nets, noose and snare. In the midst of a hotch-potch of assortment of items 'we find a brief reference to such instruments as . . . *Bandiqa* (Venetian cross-bow for throwing stone balls); Faraqha Falakhun (slings made of rope for throwing stones); *kaman guruha* (large mounted cross bow); Harf-i-kilk (arrow with inverted harp points): Julahiq (balls of stone thrown by ballistas); Zand-i-atash (incendiary fire-steel), etc.[80] In view of the fact that evidence regarding the use of similar engines and weapons by Rajputs is conspicuous by its absence, their use by the army of the Sultanate assigns to it a superior position.

Weapons, equipments, instruments, etc., for waging war are not mentioned only in the *Sirat-i-Firoz Shahi.* There are manuals in the Persian language written right from the tenth century onwards dealing elaborately with art of warfare. These would have provided guidance to the Indian Sultans on military matters. The *Qubūs Nama* for instance, written by Kaikaus in the year AH 475 (1082-83 CE) has three chapters on 'On Buying Horses; 'On giving Battle to the Enemy' and 'The Art of Controlling an Armed Force'. Similarly Nizam-ul-Mulk's *Siyasat Nama* written in AH 485 (1092-3 CE) contains two short chapters on 'Having Troops on various Races' and 'On preparing Arms and Equipment for war and Expeditions.'[81] These are not very detailed works. But *Abdul Harb wa shujaat* of Fakhr-i-Mudabbir, written in India around 1206 CE, is an excellent treatise on administration in general and on military matters in particular. It contains chapters like 'Counsel regarding war' (Chapter 7), 'Horses, their peculiar features and their good and bad points (Chapters 8, 9, 10)'. 'Use of weapons' (II), 'Recruitment of soldiers and review of the army' (12, 13). 'Fighting Patrols and night attack' (14, 15). All the chapters right up to 34 deal with the theory and practice of war.[82] *Adabul Harb* itself has been succeeded by a number of similar treaties like *Fatwa-i-Jahandari, Sirat-i-Firozshah-i* and *Tuzuk-i-Timuri* (translated as *Institutes of Timur* by Davy). In this regard the Yesa of Chingiz too would have given guidance to the Sultans in warfare. The Rajputs were lagging much behind the Turks in this sphere. They have hardly any works on military science with the result that one has to reconstruct the chief features of their art of war with the help of casual references, the actual or mythical wars contained in the contemporary Hindu literature or inscriptions or gleaned from the Muslim sources themselves. For the early medieval period mention of officers like *pilupati* (Elephant Commander), *ashvapati* (Cavalry commander), etc., is found in Dhanapal's *Tilakmanjari. The Lekhapaddhati* (a collection of model inscriptions) mentions forty weapons.[83] Some details of these weapons and other aspects of Hindu art of war are preserved in *Kanhadade prabandh* of Padmanabh[84] which was composed in V.S. 1512 (1455 CE). Other historical works (and not military manuals) are of dates even later than this. The availability of so many works on the art of war with the Turks and their lack with Rajputs helped to make the army of the Sultanate a strong military organization.

Organization

In addition to all the factors mentioned above, one very important fact which has ever to be borne in mind is that all medieval chroniclers and political thinkers give the army a very important place in Islamic polity. Ziyauddin Barani declares: 'Kingship is the army and the army kingship'[85] that is, the main strength and sustenance of the monarch is the army more than anything else. So also say all others. The utmost importance given to the army is best reflected in its efficient upkeep.

The Sultan was the supreme commander of the forces, *de jure* and *de facto*. He may not have been conversant with law, he may have known nothing about revenue matters, he may even have been illiterate, but he had to be a warrior and commander for sheer preservation of his throne. For administrative purposes, the army was placed under the charge of the Dewan-i-Arz or Minister of war. He was a very important minister, next only to Wazir and considered his post as 'the guardianship of the empire'.

Army officers were very highly paid. According to Shihabuddin Al Umri, a Khan received 200,000 *tankahs*, each being worth eight dirhams (silvers coin). 'This sum belongs to him personally, and he is not expected to disburse any part of it to the soldiers . . . .' The Maliks received 60 to 50 thousand and an Amir from 40 to 30 thousand *tankahs*.[86] There was no system of budgeting in those days but there is no doubt that major part of the state revenue was expended on the army. If the salary of a soldier was not less than what was paid in Alauddin's days, the annual salary of Muhammad Tuglaq's 900,000 troops alone would have come to more than 200 million *tankahs*. High salaries to officers and to good soldiers naturally increased the efficiency of the army.

Good salary was not all. Periodical reviews of the army, whether in headquarters or in camp, kept the soldiers on their toes and their mounts in good shape. After Alauddin Khalji had reorganized his army, 'soldiers from the cities of the empire were tested before the Diwan-i-Azr in archery. Those who were good shots and also possessed good arms were confirmed.'[87] The Diwan-i-Arz maintained a descriptive roll of every soldier whether in permanent employment or recruited temporarily,[88] and this was the only way of ascertaining his identity in days when there was no photography. Under the Khaljis the system of branding the horse and keeping a written portraiture of the soldier was strictly observed.[89] The system of *dagh wa chihra* (cauterization and descriptive roll) was discontinued by Firoz Tughlaq but it was revied by Sikandar Lodi and reintroduced by Sher Shah in all elaborateness. It ensured that at the time of review no soldier could send a substitute and no horse could be presented twice, or replaced by an inferior one after the review. However, as good quality horses were costly,[90] and all the soldiers could not always afford to keep high breed horses, many of them greased the palm of the clerks at the Diwn-i-Arz to get a fitness certificates. Many others, in spite of repeated reminders, just did not appear for review.[91] Bribery did often succeed,[92] if not under strong rulers. Barani emphasizes the importance of review and says: 'It is necessary after examination to prepare a record of the horses and arms of the men twice a year. The soldiers should be examined by persons concerning whom there can be no suspicion of misappropriation or falsehood, so that there may be no tumult at the time of postings or during battles. This review (arz) should be at such times and places that it can be finished at one stretch. The order of review should be for all.'[93] The review could be done easily and systematically, for the army was organized on the decimal system. A Sarkhail commanded ten troops, and the heirachy of officers rose by decimal progression to units commanded by Sarkhail Sipahsalar, Amir, Malik, to the supreme command of Khan.[94] The review was elaborate and inspection of soldiers minute. According to Amir Khusrau it took fourteen days for the muster roll and inspection of the army that went to Warangal in 1309.[95]

If the demands on the soldier for efficient turn-out were exacting and if the punishments for desertion and disobedience were severe,[96] he was also very well looked after by the regime. A soldier's salary was fixed according to his merit, efficiency and effectiveness,[97] leaving no ground for grouse. Alauddin Khalji, however, seems to have paid a fixed salary of about 20 *tankahs* a month (234 *tankahs* a year). Although there is no mention of a pay-scale or rate of increment, the price freeze in his reign was done primarily for the benefit of the armymen.[98] In any case, twenty *tankahs* a month was no small amount. Some slave troops were given (in addition to pay?) free ration and clothing.[99] Many others, captains and soldiers, were assigned land in lieu of pay.[100] The plea of political theorists and the practice of many rulers was to distribute conquered land among Musalmans.[101]

For a soldier an expedition was also an economic venture.[102] Salaries, rewards and emoluments of the army personnel were good.[103] Occasional loot made them still better.[104] During the march and in camp, every care was taken to make the soldier happy[105] when Ziyauddin Barani recommended that 'the Ariz (Muster Master) should be kinder to the soldiers than a mother and a father,'[106] he was only reiterating what was already in practice. Balban's Ariz treated the troops kindly and helped serving men with money.[107] If an officer needed a small loan, it was advanced to him; if his horse got disabled, it was replaced. The advice of Alauddin Khalji to Malik Kafur on the latter's expedition to Warangal delineates the consideration that was shown to the troops.[108] A number of grocers and merchants used to accompany the army on the march,[109] and friendly kingdoms through which it passed also established markets to cater for its needs.[110] But there were occasions when provisions hoped for through plunder could not be obtained, and in the absence of a regular commissariat service, the troops suffered badly.[111] Sometimes, many soldiers unable to bear hardship or disappointed with the quantum of loot, deserted the camp or rebelled.[112] But such occasions were made rare by fear of dire punishments, the uncertainty of reaching home safely,[113] and the deployment of troops in the battlefield.[114]

Army career held promise of unlimited rise. Avenues of getting promotion and prospects of receiving recognition were always open. Apart from foreign soldiers who rose to become kings and nobles, Indian Musalmans like Malik Kafur, Khusrau Khan and Khan-i-Jahan Maqbul reached close to the throne, and men like Mallu Khan, Sarang Khan, Muqarrab Khan, etc., petty soldiers at the start of career, rose to become great nobles and king-makers. Since the soldier was the strong prop of the regime, he was its favoured child.[115] In society he was feared and respected because he performed police duties also.

It is doubtful if he could take his family with him on a campaign.[116] Occasionally even nobles were discouraged from taking women with them.[117] However, army men were sometimes provided facilities for communicating with their families when out on a campaign.[118] If no mishap occurred, the soldier returned home often laden with spoils of war. But if he got disabled, he could only hope for care and protection from his relatives in the joint family system because there was no disability or old age pension. However, Balban discovered, the ineffectives managed to continue on the rolls of the army by bribes and other kinds of subterfuges. Moreover, since there was no retirement age, an army man continued to hold his post and pay for life. Firoz Tughlaq realizing the difficulties and helplessness of old age, made the profession of soldiers hereditary.[119] This was good only for the soldier and his family, not for the army.

The Muslim army looked impressive. There were contingents of Turks, Persians, Indians and others. The soldiers had excellent horses, magnificent armour, and a fine costume.[120] A soldier usually carried two swords,[121] besides he had bows and arrows, mace and battle axes. The Muslim soldier was an enthusiastic fighter. Psychologically, he was a soldier of Allah. The word Jihad had a magic appeal for him. His enthusiasm for war was whetted by the promises of rewards, prospects of plunder and religious slogans.[122] Consequently, he exhibited great zeal and practiced extreme ruthlessness and cruelty.[123] This cruelty gave the army of the Sultanate superiority over indigenous forces because it inspired terror wherever it went. The *Turushka* has become a bogey and everywhere inspired a paralysing fear.[124] As Ruban Levy points out, 'the Turks have always been amongst the most active of Muslim peoples, and if they are not greatly given to pious exercise, they are bigoted believers in this faith and excellent fighters in its cause.'[125] The Afghans were equally ferocious. These and other Central and West Asian soldiers of 'Allah, the Merciful, the compassionate', were neither merciful nor compassionate and created consternation whenever they launched an attack. Balban in the thirteenth century held the conviction that no king could succeed against the army of Delhi, be he a Hindu Raja or a Rana (*Midanam ki pesh lashkar-i-dihle hech badshahi dast astd natawaned kard fikef rayan wa rangan i hinduan*).[126] The same impression is conveyed by Vidyapati's description of a Muslim army in the fifteenth century. 'Sometimes they eat only raw flesh. Their eyes were red with the intoxication of wine. They could run twenty jojanas within the span of half of a day. They used to pass the day with the (bare) loaf under their arm. (The soldier) takes into custody all the woman of the enemy's city. . . . Wherever they happened to pass in that every place the ladies of the Raja's house began to be sold in the market. They used to set fire to villages. They turned out the women (from their homes) and killed the children. Loot was their (source of) income. Neither did they have pity for the weak nor did they fear the strong . . . . They had nothing to do with righteousnes'[127] It appears on seeing the Turks that they would swallow up the whole lot of Hindus.[128]

The graphic description shows how awe-inspiring the army of the Delhi Sultanate was. The narratives of Persian chroniclers of the massacres of the people after a battle, loot and plunder, and making of captives and converts support this description. The victories of Mahmud of Ghazni, Iltutmish, Alauddin Khalji and Muhammad bin Tughlaq against the Rajputs generally proved to be difficult and ephemeral.[129] But massacres and destruction, desecration and plunder, portrayed as 'achievements' of the Sultans[130] by the chroniclers give the impression of the armies' superiority. Even Timur's victory against Nasiruddin was not easily achieved, but beheading of thousands of captives, and massacres at Delhi, Meerut, and Hardwar give his expedition the appearance of an avalanche.[131]

However, cruelty and ruthlessness, by themselves, do not make a force superior. Therefore, to categorically declare it superior to the Rajput army (again a generic term for the army of the Hindu rulers in various parts of the country) may not be fair. Comparisons between the two would not be scientifically correct because while much is recorded by chroniclers about the Muslim army of the Sultanate, little is known in detail about that the Rajputs. If Mohammad Ghori won the second battle of Tarain, Prithiviraj defeated him in the first. The Turks captured many important cities in northern India in surprise raids, but local resistance continued and hundreds of Hindu inscriptions claim victories for their kings. Battles between Muslim invaders from Delhi on the one hand and Rajput defenders on the other were always very hotly contested. For the Muslim army the going was tough from the very beginning; otherwise Fakhr-i-Mudabbir would not have declared that 'peace is better than war',[132] and 'as far as possible war should be avoided because it is bitter fare.'[133] Such statements from one, who while describing five types of warfare, considers war with the kafirs as the most righteous,[134] are not without significance.

In fact, the army of the Sultanate suffered from a number of weaknesses. One was its heterogeneous character. Sometimes troops of the various racial groups could not pull together well or be equally loyal to regime.[135] Recruitment of the army of sultanate continued both from within India and Muslim lands abroad. There were many racial groups, and sometimes many conflicting interests.[136] Ethnic and racial tension and jealousies were rampant in the Sultanate's army. Slaves for instance, made good soldiers but 'they are of one group and one mind and there can be no permanent security against their revolt.'[137] The Afghans had been freely employed by Muhammad Ghori, Iltutmish, Balban, the Khaljis and other Tughlaqs. Under the Saiyyads and Lodis the whole complexion of the army was changed from 'Turk' to 'Afghan'. The Afghans were brave, sometimes even reckless. But they lacked discipline and were difficult to control. They had a traditional devotion to their own class leaders—and their clans were many. All this was not conducive to discipline in the army. Armymen could easily shift their loyalties, more so because there was no law of succession to the throne.

Another weakness was that soldiers were habituated to plundering even in peace times. In war, loot for the Musalmans was justified,[138] but when there was no war the soldiers were enjoined to behave with the civilians and not to loot or destroy their property.[139] In course of time and exceptions apart, such also seems to have become the norm of behaviour.[140] The massacre of the people of Delhi by Amir Timur was a direct consequence of his soldiers' misbehaviour with the market people.[141] The phenomenon repeated itself during Nadir Shah's invasion. As a result sometimes the rowdyism of the army men brought discredit to the regime. Again, keeping a very large army on a permanent basis had to be ruled out for reasons of finance, security and convenience, and a large portion of the army of the Sultanate remained temporary with loot as its only source of sustenance. Alauddin's keeping an army of about five hundred thousand made him resort to collecting fifty per cent of the produce as land revenue even when the imperial resources were large and gains of loot and tribute from his conquests were immense. Other rulers were not financially so sound. The army, besides, could not all be stationed at Delhi; it was distributed all over the Sultanate under provincial governors and garrison commanders.[142] And they could make use of it against the regime itself if they chose to revolt.

Thus the weaknesses in the army of the sultanate were many. But since it won most of the battles and occupied the whole of the northern India in the thirteenth century and penetrated into the South in the fourteenth, its superiority must be acknowledged. This superiority consisted first in the slave system. The slave system provided the Sultanate's army with loyal soldiers. The process of recruitment and training was elaborate and it turned out excellent human material for war. Evidence about any similar training amongst the Rajputs, if any so existed, has yet to be found out. Another reason for its having an edge over that of the local rulers was the constant and unbroken arrival of foreign troops like Turki and Afghans. The keenness of Delhi Sultans from Balban to Bahlol Lodi to recruit troops from Muslim homelands at once shows their superiority as fighters. The Rajputs could not replenish their manpower from a similar source. That is why if and when the contact of the Delhi Sultans with Muslim homeland was partially or wholly lost (as for example, because of the Mongol upheaval in Central Asia), the Rajput princes could contain Turkish expansion in India as the history of the Mamelūke Sultanate shows. The Ghazi element was peculiar to the Muslim army. While its cupidity resulted in too much cruelty in warfare, it added a very zealous element to the fighting forces. 'Islam' gave them a unity of thought, interest and action. Man to man the Rajput was not inferior to the Turk, but on the basis of the evidence available, the army men of the Sultanate, on the whole, had an upper hand over the indigenous warriors. A highly caprisoned cavalry was another strong point of the Sultanate's army; good quality horses in India were scarce and had to be imported both in the South and the North. This placed Indian rulers at a disadvantage. The Turkish army had many engines of war. An elaborate army administrative system, constant inspection and reviews of troops too increased the striking power of the army of the Sultanate.

NOTES

1. Habibullah, *The Foundation of Muslim Rule in India*, Allahabad, 1961, pp. 262, 265.
2. Minhaj Siraj, *Tabqat Nasiri*, tr. Major Raverty, Bib. Ind., Calcutta, 1864, 2 vols., London, 1881, vol. I, p. 180.
3. C. E. Bosworth, *The Ghaznavids*, Edinburgh, 1963, p. 98.
4. Ira Marvin Lapidus, *Muslim Cities in the Later Middle Ages*, Cambridge Massachusetts: Harvard University Press, 1967, pp. 6, 44.
5. K. S. Lal, 'The Ghaznavids in India', *Bengal Past and Present*, Sir Jadunath Sarkar Birth Century Number, July-December 1970, pp. 131–52.
6. Ziyauddin Barani, *Tarikh-i-Firoz Shahi*, Bib. Ind., Calcutta, 1862, pp. 58–9.
7. Barani, p. 314.
8. Shams Siraj Afif, *Tarikh-i-Firoz Shahi*, Bib. Ind., Calcutta, 1890, p. 272.
9. Afif, pp. 267–72.
10. *Fatawa-i-Jahandari*, vol. I, English, tr. by Mohammad Habib and Afsar Begum, Allahabad: Kitab Mahal, n.d., p. 25.
11. *Makhan-i-Afghan*, N. B. Roy's trs. entitled Niamatullah's *History of the Afghans*, Santiniketan, 1958, p. 11.
12. Sir Olaf Care, *The Pathans*, London: Macmillan & Co., 1958, p. 135.
13. *Tabqat-I-Nasiri*, p. 315.
14. Barani, pp. 57–8.
15. In later times, they were obtained mostly through the sea route. In the war between Humayun and Bahadur Shah of Gujarat (1533), the latter entered into a treaty with the Europeans (Portuguese) of Surat, and having, through their assistance, raised a force of 6,000 Abyssinians, returned to Ahmedabad. Jawhar, *Takirat-al-Waqlat*, tr. C. Stewart, Indian Reprint, 1972, p. 7.
16. *Fatawa-i-Jahandari*, pp. 25–6.
17. Shihabuddin Al Umri, *Masalik-ul-Absar*, E and D, vol. III, p. 576.
18. Utbi, *Kitab-i-Yamini*, tr. Reynolds, London, 1858, pp. 335–6. Ferishtah, op. cit., I, p. 18.
19. Bosworth, op.cit., p. 107. Also article on Ghazavids by Longworth Dames in the *Encyclopaedia of Islam.*
20. The infantrymen were so placed as to bear the first brunt of the enemy's attack. Consequently, the temptation to flee was great. But they could not leave their posts, for on the field of battle 'horses are on their right and left . . . and behind (them) the elephants so that not one of them can run away' (Alqalqashiadi, *Subh-al-Asha*, tr. Otto spies, Aligarh, n.d.) p. 76.
21. Barbosa, vol. I, p. 181. It may be noted that Prince Alauddin Khalji, when he marched against Devagiri, had with him about 2,000 *paiks*, (Barani, p. 222).

22. Barani, pp. 52, 593.
23. Barani, pp. 273, 376–7.
24. E. G. Minhaj, *Tabqat-i-Nasiri*, p. 317; Barani, *Tarikh*, p. 80; Afif, op. cit., p. 289.
25. Fakhr-i-Mudabbir, *Adab-ul-Harb wa shujaat*, Hindi trs. from photograph copy of the British Museum MS by S. A. A. Rizvi in *Adi Turk Kalin Bharat*, Aligarh, 1956, fol. 109b.
26. Habibullah, op. cit., p. 265.
27. Adab-ul-Harb, fol. 49a.
28. Barani, *Fatawa I Jahandari*, p. 2.
29. *The Rehla of Ibn Battuta*, English tr. with commentary by Mahdi Hussain, Baroda, 1953, p. 14.
30. *Fatawa-i-Jahandari*, p. 25.
31. Barani, p. 102.
32. Ruben Levy, *Social Structure of Islam*, Cambridge, 1962, p. 74.
33. Barani, pp. 51–2.
34. Minhaj, p. 225; al-Qalqashindi, p. 75; Shams Siraj Afif, *Tarikh-i-Firoz Shahi*, Calcutta, 1890, pp. 317, 322.
35. Barani, p. 53.
36. Lal, 'The Ghaznavids in India', op. cit., pp. 131–52, esp. p. 137.
37. Barani, op. cit., pp. 57–8.
38. Simon Digby, *War Horse and Elephant in the Delhi Sultanate*, Orient Monographs, Oxford, 1971, p. 34; Barani, pp. 461–2; Lal, *Twilight*, p. 131, p. 329.
39. Simon Digby, op. cit., pp. 35–6 quoting from Ibn Battuta, French edn II, pp. 371–4; and Gibb's tr. II, Cambridge, 1958–9, pp. 478–9.
40. Pratap Rudradeva of Warangal making peace with Malik Kafur in AH 709/AD 1310 is said to have surrendered 20,000 Kohi and Bahri horses. In praise of these, Amir Khusrau writes, in his poetic extravaganza *Khazain-ul-Futuh*, thus: 'The seaborne horse flies like the wind on the surface of water, without even its feet becoming wet. And when the mountain horse steps on a hill, the hill trembles like a Hindi sword, (Amir Khusrau, *Khazain ul Futuh*, ed. M. W. Mirza, Calcutta, 1953, p. 101. English tr. by M. Habib entitled *Campaigns of Alauddin Khilji* (Madras. 1931), p. 72.

    On Malik Kafur's final Deccan expedition, an unspecified number of horses was surrendered by the Hoysala ruler (K. F. P., p. 138). In the plunder of the stables of the Pandya ruler, 5,000 fine horses had been taken, of the Yamani, Shami and Bahri breeds (K. F. P., p. 163). Annual tributes of such imported horses were also imposed upon the Hindu rulers of the Deccan. In 1717, the Warangal king was required, by Mubarak Shah Khalji, to remit annually to Delhi 1,000 horses as well as 100 elephants. *Nuh sipihr*, ed. Wahid Mirza, (Calcutta: Oxford University Press: 1948), p. 128.

41. Barani, p. 262.
42. Afif, pp. 339–40.
43. Ibid., p. 318, p. 340.
44. Sharafuddin Yazdi, *Zafar Namah*, Bib. Ind., 2 vols, Calcutta, 1885; 1887; vol. II, pp. 59–70.
45. Barani, p. 52.
46. *Tabqat-i-Nasiri*, pp. 215–6, Afif, p. 119.
47. Amir Khusrau, *Qiran-us-Sadain*, Aligarh, 1918, pp. 35, 47.
48. Ferishtah, vol. I, p. 200.
49. Ahmad Abbas, *Masalik-ul-Absar*, E and D, vol. III, p. 576. Al-Qalqashindi, *Subh-ul-Asha*, tr. by Otto Spies, Aligarh, n.d., p. 66.
50. Henry Yule, *Ser Marco Polo*, 2 vols, London, 1903, vol. II, p. 340.
51. Abdulla Wassaf, *Tajziya-ul-Amsar wa Tajriyat-ul-Asar*, better known as *Tarikh-I-Wassaf*, *c.* 1327, Bombay, p. 302.
52. Sidney Toy, *The Strongholds of India*, London, 1957, p. 33.
53. Barani, p. 23; Ferishtah, p. 95.
54. Barani p. 330 has 7,000; also see note 42.
55. Wassaf writes that 'a large number of horses were imported every year into the Malabar country; but they were not given proper diet but were fed on 'dressed gram and milk'. Once in a while, they were taken out for ceremonial or festive parades and made to run fast. Improper diet, undue rest, and then sudden exertion killed many horses and fresh ones were imported year after year (Wassaf, op. cit., p. 302).
56. Recently, some equestrian statues have been discovered at Gool Village, 210 km north of Jammu. These are important as they depict the elaborate harness of the horses and robes and armour of the cavaliers. They clearly show that cavalry was in vogue in Kashmir Valley in medieval times. But we are not sure about the date of the statues. Vidya Ratan Khajuria, former Curator of the Dogra Art Galary of Jammu, places these in the pre-muslim period and says that they are not less than 700 years old. On the other hand K. N. Shastri, former Excavation Assistant of the Archaeological Survey of India, thinks that they belong to the period of Maharaja Gulabsingh (1792–1857). Gool is located at an altitude of 2,100 m in the mountain recesses, but is connected through a 50 km road with the Jammu Srinagar highway. The find is interesting, but there is nothing surprising about the use of horses for war purposes in Kashmir and north-west Punjab. Horses were always available in these regions. However, these statues do not prove that cavalry was an important wing of Rajput army throughout northern India in the Sultanate period. For details see *The Times of India*, 5 July 1977.
57. P. K. Gode, *Studies in Indian Cultural History*, Poona, 1960, vol. II, p. 76.
58. Alberuni makes a very interesting statement which gives a point of vantage to the cavalrymen from abroad. Writing about 'the strange

habits of the Hindus,' he says. 'They ride without a saddle, but if they put on a saddle, they mount the horse from its right side .... They fasten the Kuthara (i.e. the dagger) at the waist on the right side' (*Alberuni's India* by Edward C. Sachau, London: Routledge and Kegan Paul, 1910, 2 vols, vol. I, p. 181).

If the Hindus mounted the horse from the right side, they must have swung the left leg to do so. In that case, any weapon worn on the left side would have obstructed the process of mounting and naturally, as asserted by Alberuni, they wore the dagger or the sword on the right side. This could not have been drawn out of the scabbard with as much agility and ease with the right hand as any weapon worn on the left side. If true, this was definitely disadvantageous.

59. Nadir Shah is said to have remarked: 'What strange practice is this the rulers of Hind have adopted? In the day of the battle they ride on an elephant and make themselves into a target for every body?' (Rao Dalpat Singh, *Malahat-i-Maqol* cited by W. Irvine, *The Army of the Indian Moghuls*, London, 1903, p. 177. Irvine adds: 'long before the Moghul empire fell into decay, they (elephants) had become principally beasts of burden or means of display, and their role in the day of battle was comparatively insignificant,' (Ibid., p. 176).
60. Barbosa, *The Book of Duarte Barbosa*, 2 vols, London: Hakluyt Society, 1918–21, vol. I, p. 118.
61. *Tabqat-i-Nasiri*, p. 10; tr. 1, p. 83.
62. Barani, p. 53.
63. Ibid.
64. In 1308–9, 17 elephants were taken by Kafur in his sack of Devagiri (Barani, p. 326). Next year, he got 100 elephants from the Rai of Warangal (*Khazain-ul-Futuh*, p. 101). In the campaign in 1310–2, the total number captured was 512 to 612 (Barani, p. 333; *Khazain*, p. 161).
65. Afif, pp. 163. 167*ff.*
66. Ibid., p. 486.
67. Simon Digby, p. 59.
68. Barani, p. 594.
69. Sultan Muhamud Sharqi of Jaunpur marched against Delhi (1452), with a thousand elephants. (Ferishtah, vol. 1. p. 157; vol. II. p. 308; Lal, *Twilight*, p. 135).
70. Isami, *Futuh-us-Salatin*, p. 260.
71. Lal, *Twilight*, pp. 23–4.
72. *Adab-ul-Harb*, p. 69; also Rizvi, *Uttar Timur Kalin Bharat*, Aligarh, 1958, p. 177.
73. *Adab-ul-Harb*, p. 107a.
74. The above two paragraphs are based mainly on Mudabbir's *Adab-ul-Harb*, ably analysed by Simon Digby, pp. 15–20.
75. Lal, 'The Ghaznavids in India,' pp. 131–52.

76. *Adab-ul-Harb*, fol. 112a.
77. 'The Mongols understood the art of feigning retreat, of envelopment and of surprise, and, as battle after battle was fought against nations employing different methods of warfare, the sum of their experience had made them invisible (invincible; editor's intervention).' (P. M. Sykes, *A History of Persia*, 2 vols, London: Macmillan & Co., 1915, vol. II, p. 85.) The Sultan of Delhi had to deal with descendants of such warriors and gained new experience in warfare.
78. Ibid. has detailed notices on fols. 115–56.
79. Thomas, *Chronicles of the Pathan Kings of Delhi*, London: 1871, pp. 78–9.
80. S. M. Askari, 'A study of the rare Ms. Sirat-i-Firoz Shahi' *Journal of Indian History*, vols I and II, April 1974, Pt I, p. 127, p. 146, esp. p. 139.
81. M. S. Khan, 'The Life & Woks of Fakhr-i-Mudabbir', *Islamic Culture*, April 1977, pp. 138–40.
82. *Adab-ul-Harb*, fols. 66–190; Rizvi's tr. pp. 257–72.
83. *Lekhapaddhati*, Baroda, 1925, p. 97.
84. *Rajasthan Through the Ages*, vol. I, ed. Dasrath Sharma, Rajasthan State Archives, Bikaner, 1966, p. 710*ff.*
85. *Fatawa-i-Jahandari*, p. 22.
86. Massalik, E and D, vol. III, p. 577.
87. Barani, p. 319.
88. *Adab-ul-Harb*, fol. 107a, 110a. Masalik E and D, III, p. 576.
89. Barani, p. 145.
90. *Al-Qalqashindi*, p. 47.
91. Afif, pp. 299–301.
92. Afif, p. 57.
93. *Fatawa-i-Jahandari*, p. 25. Mohammed Habib appends a note saying': Our authorities often refer to soldiers coming for arz or review to Delhi. Standing on the Tughlaqabad fort one can see a space of several square miles enclosed by a crumbling wall. Very possibly this is the spot where the review was held. The review had to be finished at one stretch to prevent the arms, and possibly also the horse, of one trooper being presented again by another.
94. Barani, p. 145: Hajiuddabir, *Zafar-ul-Walih, An Arabic History of Gujarat*, ed. Denison, Ross, 3 vols., London, 1910–21, p. 782; *Khazain-ul-Futuh*, tr. Habib, p. 58.
95. *Khazain-ul-Futuh*, tr. Habib, p. 58.
96. Barani, p. 253; Afif, p. 173.
97. Ibn Battutah, (M.H.), p. 14.
98. Barani, pp. 303–4; also Lal, *History of Khaljis*, pp. 217–9.
99. Masalik, E and D, vol. II, p. 577; also al-Qalqashindi, p. 71.
100. Barani, p. 80; Afif, pp. 94–6.
101. *Adabul-Harb*, fol. 156a; Barani, p. 327.

102. Afif, p. 57.
103. Abas Sarwani in Roy's tr. of *Makhzan-i-Afghana,* pp. 67–9. Dorn, *Makhzun-i-Afghani,* London, 1829, p. 44.
104. Ferishtah, *Tarikh-i-Ferishtah,* Lucknow. Nawal Kishore Press, 1865, 2 vols; vol. I. p. 162. Yahiya Sarhindi, *Tarikh-i-Mubarak Shahi,* Bid. Ind., Calcutta, 1931, p. 188.
105. Afif, pp. 144, 201.
106. *Fatawa-i-Jahandari,* p. 24; also *History of the Khaljis,* pp. 237–8.
107. Barani, pp. 115–6, 328.
108. *Adabul Harb,* fol. 110a; Barani, p. 327.
    Fatawa-i-Jahandari, p. 24.
109. Afif, p. 290.
110. Barani, p. 328.
111. Afif, p. 88.
112. Barani, p. 253; Ibn Battuta (M.H.), p. 86; Afif, pp. 224–5; Sarhindi Yahiya, *Tarikh-i-Mubarak Shahi,* p. 76.
113. Afif, p. 201.
114. Al-Qalquashindi, p. 76.
115. Barani, *Tarikh,* p. 102; *Fatawa-i-Jahandari,* p. 21.
116. That is how Alauddin could punish at Delhi the women and children of the troops which had mutinied at Jalor on their way back from the Gujarat campaign (Barani, p. 253; also Afif. p. 173).
117. When he was planning action against Ainul Mulk Multani, Muhammad Tughlaq ordered that no women should remain with the nobles. As a result no women remained in the camp, not even with Sultan, I.B. [M.H.], p. 106. *Adab-ul-Harb,* fol. 47a, also advises against taking women on expeditions.
118. Firoz Tughlaq provided this facility, (Afif, p. 173).
119. Afif, pp. 302–3.
120. Masalik, E and D, vol. II, p. 576.
121. H. A. Gibb, *Ibn Battutah,* p. 216; Ibn Battutah (M.H.), p. 108.
122. Afif, p. 201.
123. Adab-ul-Harb, p. 115a, p. 158b. After the massacre in Bengal, even Sultan Firoz Tughlaq had begun to weep (Afif. p. 121). But such kind-hearted Sultans were few.
124. Habibullah, op. cit., pp. 72–3.
125. *Social Structure of Islam,* op. cit., p. 25.
126. Barani, p. 52.
127. Vidyapati, *Kirtilata,* Allahabad: Indian Press, 1923, pp. 70–72.
128. Vidyapati, op. cit., pp. 42–4. This impression was shared by many, including Padmanabh, as cited in *Rajasthan through the Ages,* p. 639.
129. Barani, p. 279; *Khazain,* tr. Habib, p. 48.
130. Ibid., p. 49; James Tod, *Annals and Antiquities of Rajasthan,* ed. W. Crooke, 3 vols, Oxford, 1920, vol. I, p. 311.

131. *Mulfuzat-i-Timati,* I and D. vol. III, p. 441.
132. Fakhr-i-Mudabbir, *Abadul Harb wa Shuiast,* fol. IIIa.
133. Ibid., fols. 66a–b.
134. Ibid., fols. 131a–132a.
135. Fakhr-i-Mudabbir, *Tarikh-i Fakhruddin Mubarak Shah,* ed. Denisen Ross, London, 1972, pp. 31–2.
136. Afif, p. 223. al-Qalqashindi, p. 66.
137. *Fatawa-i-Jahandari,* pp. 25–6.
138. Ibid. fol.a. 154b.
139. Ibid., fol. 117a.
140. Amir Khusrau, *Khazainul Futuh,* Habib, trs. pp. 58–9.
141. Sharafuddin Yazdi, *Zafar Nama,* Bib. Ind., Calcutta 1885–99, II, p. 186, *Zafarul Walih,* III, p. 907.
142. al-Qalqashindi, pp. 66–7. Also Ibn Battuta (M.H.) p. 26.

CHAPTER 6

A Phase in Mughal-Assam Relations: Rājā Rām Singh's Futile Expedition (1668–71)

J. N. Sarkar

The phenomenonal *blitzkrieg* of Mir Jumla, Aurangzeb's General and Governor of Bengal within the brief space of just a little more than a year, in Assam, which had so long defied all attempts at subjugation, proved to be a pyrrhic victory. The turn of the tide came within less than five years, as the Āhoms recovered Mughal Kāmrūp. In this article, new light has been thrown on Rām Singh's expedition as described in Sir Edward Gait's *History of Assam*, Acharya Jadunath Sarkar's *Aurangzib*, S. N. Bahattacharyya's *History of North-East Frontier Policy of the Mughals*, S. K. Bhuyan's *Lāchit Barphukan & His Times* and P. Gogoi's *The Tāi & the Tāi Kingdom.* It is based on a synthetic use of Persian chronicles, *farmāns*, Āhom and Assamese *Buranjis*, Rājasthāni records, accounts of foreign travellers, gazetteers, and maps.

Learning of the loss of Kāmrup on 13 Rajab 1077, 19 December 1667, Aurangzeb decided at once to retrieve imperial prestige and regain lost dominion to chastise 'the wicked tribe' of the Āhoms, who 'had a second time audaciously crossed their own frontier'. He commissioned Rām Singh of Amber, son of the distinguished General Mirza Rājā Jai Singh and a Commander of 4,000, to lead an invasion of Assam. The expeditionary force had as its basic force, i.e. the original imperial allotment, 4,000 troopers in his own pay, 1,500 *āhadis* (gentlemen-troopers), and 500 *barqandāzes* (imperial artillerymen). This nucleus was gradually augmented by 30,000 infantry (given by the Emperor), 21 Rajput chiefs (*Thākurs*), with their contingents, 18,000 cavalry, and 2,000 troopers of the Bengal command. A Koch Bihar levy with 15,000 archers and shieldsmen came as auxiliaries. On water he had only 40 ships. The Rājput General was accompanied, according to custom, by Rashid Khān, the late *faujdār* of Kāmrūp, conversant with the language and customs of the Āhoms. The Sikh Guru, Tegh Bahadur, accompanied the Rājā from Patna. At Dacca Shāista Khān, Mughal Viceroy in Bengal, received him cordially, gave him sound advice and offered him help. But the Viceroy was himself, if we believe the Assamese chronicles, in favour of an independent Assam and was not very optimistic about the success of the Rājā. The collection and transportation of the vast Mughal army took time. Hence, though Rām Singh was sent off by the Emperor on 27 December 1667, he advanced through Khuntaghat and reached Rańgāmāt, the frontier garrison town, only in February 1669.[1]

Rām Singh's advance naturally produced different reactions among the Mughals and the Assamese. Learning of it from Shāista Khān, the Viceroy of Bengal, the Emperor expressed satisfaction in a *farmān* dated 5 Shawwal 1079/26 February 1669 to his General at his progress according to schedule. He was directed to advance quickly towards the target, conquer *thānāh* Gauhāti and other *thānāhs* previously held by (Sayyid) Firoz Khan and (Sayyid) Sātār Khān, and then provide for their proper security. All this, the *farmān* went on, would rebound to his credit and prestige. On the other hand, the *Āhom Buranji* ascribed Rām Singh's advance to his unwillingness to stay in the territory 'devastated and plundered' by Mir Jumla and Rashid Khān.

Rām Singh perhaps thought that he would gain his end by pacific means. But his letters and messengers to Assam (*c.*March–April, 1669) failed, as will be explained later, on to make the Assamese leaders relent. So he decided to advance in 'Baisakh' (i.e. April–May 1669). Leaving a contingent of *mansabdārs* at his base at Rańgāmāti for safeguarding communication with Bengal, the Mughal General successfully advanced along the north Brahmaputra valley till he reached Suālkuchi (April 1669). Occupying the territories west of the Manās (Mānāhā River), he crossed it unopposed, captured two enemy posts at Chenga and Tapera, encamped at Baruāmukh, and occupied Hājo without a fight (and finally reached the Bar Nadi river). Rām Singh's initial successes, though not decisive, were surprisingly easy and he felt elated that his advance was comparable to the triumphal march of Mir Jumla up the river Brahmaputra.[2]

Assamese Defensive Strategy

Why was this so? To understand this, it is necessary to review the situation in Āhom camp. The deputation of Rām Singh marked a new phase in Āhom–Mughal relations. Unlike Assam's previous offensive war of recovery, the present was essentially a defensive war to retain possession of the recovered territory of Kāmrūp. The Āhom commanders posted in strongholds near Manās (Mānāhā) river attempted opposition in a few skirmishes but had to fall back. Assamese sources attribute this to havoc, caused by the Rājput General's 1,000 war-hounds. These snatched Assamese soldiers away under the screen of artillery smoke from the fighting ranks but could not be easily disposed of singly or in twos, as these did not come in packs. But the real reason lay in the unpreparedness of the Āhoms to resist the invader. Realizing the futility of the opposition at the frontier posts, their General, Lāchit Barpukhan, adopted the new strategy of: (i) evacuating them one by one, and leaving all territories west of Hājo to their fate; and (ii) concentrating on the defence of Gauhāti and the strategic centres around it, so as to lure the unwary Mughals to the well-guarded Gauhāti sector. This corresponds to what is known in modern warcraft as 'strategic retreat.' In pursuance of this policy, the Barphukan withdrew the Āhom forces from Agarāguri to Sarāighāṭ.[3]

The Assamese general displayed vigilance and circumspection in completing their preparations. The mature deliberations of the war council were committed to writing to form a staff manual.

(i) Lāchit Burphukan issued an order enforcing discipline. One must steadfastly hold to his charge and perform his assigned duties with the scheduled time on pain of death. His own maternal uncle was executed for negligence and delay in completing a rampart at Śrighāṭ on the north bank of the Brahmaputra (henceforth known as *Māmui katāgarh*) within a fixed date. Lāchit's outburst on this occasion has become classic: 'My uncle is not greater than my country.' The new sense of values, implied in his priority of public duty to private considerations, inspired the Āhoms. The spartan severity of action, claimed by the Barphukan, had to be sanctioned during the emergency by the king even though it violated a royal prerogative.[4]

(ii) Second, the fortifications of Gauhāti fort needed to be made impenetrable, with fresh ramparts on both banks of the Brahmaputra and with army dispositions on a new basis. In Assam, a unit of command was called a *pāli.* Each commander had a quota of troops with required number of weapons, ammunition, and provisions. On hill-tops, spurs, and ridges a soldier was posted at every 13½ feet and on the earthen ramparts in the plains after every 9 feet. Besides, each commander had under him a few commandos (*chorbācha*s, lit. choicest spies) to collect all information about the enemy, to ensure the safety of their detachment, and to perform acts of extraordinary courage and tact. The *pāli*s covered the entire line of fortifications on both banks of the river without any break or loophole. Now the *pāli*s were reorganized to deal with the invasion of Rām Singh. A soldier was to get the irreducible minimum in equipment—kit, uniform, and armoury. The length of each *pāli* and the number of bastions, and different types of guns to be mounted on each, were fixed. The relative distances of the hills and the ramparts were recorded after careful measurement. The materials needed to erect forts on sand were minutely prescribed. A commander was put in charge of a fixed portion of the fortified zone. The south bank was under the direct command of General Lāchit Barphukan with his camp at Andharubāli between Itākhuli (Sukreshwar Hill) and Kāmākhayā hill in modern Gauhāti. He had two *pāli* leaders under him on land and three naval commanders to guard the river on the south bank. The north bank was under Prime Minister Ātan Burhāgohāin with his headquarters at Lāthiā Parvat, 12 *pāli* leaders on land, and two naval commanders to guard the waters on the north bank. Further, there were a few more whose *pāli*s could not be ascertained.[5]

(iii) Sham Āhom negotiations: During 1669–70, sporadic fighting alternated with peace proposals. Though unnerved for a time by the overwhelming numbers of the Mughal army for the safety of the king, safety of the people, and safety of the posterity, Lāchit Barphukan planned to devise the best measures to counter the enemy. The Āhoms wanted time to complete their preparations—

construction of fortifications and raising the sand embankments of the Brahmaputra to prevent enemy landings from ships. The best way to gain it was through the old device of delaying tactics through opening sham peaceful negotiations. So when Rām Singh sent a letter through a messenger named Shaikh Lādi (Lodi?) for surrendering the conquered territories and for paying tribute in the past, the Barphukan adopted a shrewd diplomatic game that was a masterstroke of policy. Observing that whichever party gets victory will gain, he sent with the Mughal emissaries two or three messengers to the Mughal General, addressed as 'Bhai Rajah' (Brother King) to enquire why he was invading Assam and to emphasize pacific settlement of disputes, if any.

The straightforward Rajput Rājāh sent another mission of 14 members under Syed Firoz Khān to the Barphukan along with the Assam emissaries, demanding the restoration of the limits of territory up to Barnadi and the Asurār. Ali fixed in the treaty of 1639, i.e. Assam was to evacuate the territory west of this line. Further, the Āhoms were to release three Sayyids confined by them, Sālār Khan, Pahār (son of Firuz), and Hussain. If not, Rām Singh would advance from his base, the fort 'Phabung' (?). After a patient hearing, the Barphukan replied that he must necessarily abide by the order of his king.[6] This correspondence gave the Āhom general the much desired time for completing his army dispositions. He could now afford to send an 'evasive but determined' reply through Firuz Khān: 'Gauhāti and Kāmrūp do not belong to the Mughals. We took possession of the place by driving out the Koches, but lost them for some time through ill-luck.' He avowed that the Assamese were prepared to fight to the last as God had been 'pleased to give them back to us'. This bold and tactful yet dignified reply was a 'landmark' in Assamese diplomatic history.

The Āhoms Repulse Rām Singh's Attacks

Realizing the ineffectiveness of peace negotiations for the time being, Rām Singh advanced further east. The Persian chronicles are wholly silent on his inconsequential activities, while the sequence of events in the different *Buranjis* is divergent and hence confusing. Moreover, the Āhom–Mughal conflict was in the nature of tug-of-war, characterized by ups and downs, and alternate gains and losses of forts and their environs. The same places changed hands several times. Hence, it is extremely difficult to fix the exact sequence of events. A clearer account would perhaps be possible if we follow the course of activities on the two banks of the river Brahmaputra. Again, without entering into the intricate details of all the individual engagements and all names of commanders and captains on either side, which is neither possible here nor desirable for reasons of readability or brevity, we may refer only to some of the more important episodes only after a critical examination of the dates and details given in the *Buranji*s and Aurangzeb's *farmān*s to the general.

As Rām Singh 'prepared to enter our country', the *Āhom Buranji* comments, 'he divided the work between his men'. The Mughal army was arranged in four divisions for forcing the fortifications of Gauhāti at four places as follows: (a) the north bank under the General Rām Singh himself in front of the Āhom fortifications; (b) the south bank under 'Ali Akbar Khān'. Mir Sayyid Khān (Sayed Mirā of Buranji), Rājā Indrāmani (Indrāman?). Rājāh Jay Nārāyān, and Marul (?) Khān Sardār; (c) the Sindurighopā entrance to be guarded by Jahir (Zahir?) Beg, Kayam (Qeyām?) Khān, Ghanashyām Bakshi and three Baruāhs of Koch-Bihār—Kavisekhar (Kishore). Sarveshwar and Manmatha—with the shieldsmen and archers numbering 15,000; the Koch contingent was wiped out; (d) the waters to be guarded by naval commanders—Mansur Khān, Latif Khān, Rasip (? Sharif) Khan, Iswarpati, some *firangis* (Europeans), and one Kapidan Rājāh.

But the effect of the Barphukan's astute diplomacy was soon discernible on the subsequent course of events. Rām Singh's advance was perceptibly slowed down. In the *Uttarkol,* i.e. on the north bank of the Brahmaputra as he pressed forward from Jogiguphā to Hājo and thence nearer the Āhom fortifications to the sands of Koolihāṭi, and Sualkuchi, he had to face stiffening opposition. The sieges of Agiathuti, Rangmahal, Akur Āli and Sarāighāṭ (Śrighāṭ) were either prolonged or unsuccessful or indecisive. The General himself pressed the siege of Agaiāthuti (Chaitra 21, 1590 Śaka or about 3 April, 1669). The Rājput General's nephew (*bhatijā)* was killed in a skirmish. But the result was indecisive. Entrusting the siege of Agiāthuti to some of his lieutenants with adequate forces, the General advanced in triumph to Sarāi (Amingāon) or Śrīghāt fort of the Āhoms (where Rashid Khān had already been deputed) and entrenched at a distance of cannon shot from the Assamese fort. Setting up two forts, he besieged Śrīghāt. But the Mughal cause was weakened by the in-subordination of Rashid Khān, a *mansabdār* of 3,000, and, as he was expelled from the camp, for his suspected treasonable collusion with the enemy. Moreover the two Mughal forts were countered by two Āhom forts set up by Dihingiā Bargohāin. Finally the Mughals were completely encircled by the Āhoms according to the Barphukan's consultation with the *dāngariās.* Without being perturbed Rām Singh himself sought to advance Sarāi (i.e. Āmingāon) by digging underground passage but the Āhoms filled the surrounding moat with water. Then Rām Singh's cannonade from guns mounted on temporary platforms caused breaches in the walls but these were repaired immediately. The general, however, had to retreat on account of the counter-cannonade of the Āhoms.

The Mughal besiegers of Rangmahal, the frontier post (under Rām Singh himself), reeled before the vigorous charge of the entire defending garrison dashing out of the fort and had to retreat to Hājo. Rangmahal was reinforced at royal command. Similarly, the besiegers of the Āhom fort of Akur Ali were wholly surrounded and had to retreat to Pāndu. However, the Mughals attacked Hurāmati fort (then under Guimeliā Bargohāin).[7]

In *Dakhinkol,* i.e. on the south of the Brahmaputra, too, the Āhoms continued their aggressive activities. Two, Hāzarikās inflicted losses on the Mughals in manpower, guns, and shields (the Burhāgohāin re-occupied the fort called Ching (?) from the Mughals and constructed a fort at Lathia). A contingent deputed by Burhāgohāin, accompanied by the Barphukhan, plundered and occupied the Mughal fort Phrenbār. Rām Singh at first commissioned two Rājās, Indradaman and Jainārāyaṇ (grandson of rājāh Parikshit) along with Sayyid Mirā to seize the Āhom outposts, with the Mughal fleet (under Iśwarpati, the *firangis* or Europeans and one *amir*) standing by for succour. The two rājās occupied Luthuri (or Luthāri), built their own stockades at Phrenbār, and invested Pāndu. However, in their naval battles with the Āhoms, they lost two ships. This necessitated the advance of the Mughal general himself to the south. The Mughals could make a breach at Rāṅgaliburuz near it on the fifth day. But thanks to the prompt report of the ever-vigilant Rājā of Rāni and the state of preparedness of the defenders, the local commander, Luthuri Chetia Rājkhowā, had it repaired quickly so as to amaze the Mughals. Twenty-four Mughal cavaliers advanced from the forts Luthuri and Thangdin (?) to plunder the Āhoms and were opposed by an Āhom party that was joined by the Burhāgohāin. The Mughals then resorted to an artillery duel *(barahilair juddha)*. The *Āhom Buranji* describes it as a 'terrible battle'. It proved to be a veritable disaster for the Mughals, who had to retreat. A few fugitives had their fingers sliced off and they were sent to the Barphukan and then to the king, who rewarded the Rājā of Rāni (Bāiśakh, April–May).[8]

At this stage, the war changed its character from a pure military confrontation to an epistolary exchange, marked by an enjoyable repartee. The Rājput general never forsook his earlier recourse to negotiations. This, side by side with his inconclusive aggressive activities, he renewed demand for the evacuation of Gauhāti in the interests of cows and the Brāhmans of Assam through his envoy, Daivakinandan, dwelling on the valorous deeds of his predecessors and sending a bag of poppy seeds (*āphuguti ek topolā*), denoting the vast numbers of his army. His Āhom counterpart replied through his two envoys, Nim and Dikhumukhiā Rāmcaran, that the evacuation would depend only on a mutual agreement between the 'Swargadeo' and the Pādshāh, sent a stone slab (*patā*) and a tube of sands (*bālir chuṅgā*), implying that while the poppy seeds could be crushed on the slab into a watery paste, his men were not only as 'numerous' but 'as indissouluble as the sands'. 'This', ran the Barphukan's laconic message, 'is the characteristic of our soldiers' (*āmār sainyar eney lakshan*).[9]

Four months of the rainy season of 1669 and the accompanying floods brightened the prospects of the Āhoms and darkened those of the Mughals. In Jyaiṣṭha (May–June 1669), the Mughals under Rājā Sujān Singh and Rājā Rup Nārāyan were defeated at Kāljor hill by Miri Sandikoi Phukan in a nine day duel and had to retreat. After this abortive attempt, the Mughals set up a fort at Duimuni and tried to enter Gauhāti through Darrang under Bahlol Khān, Prān Nārāyan, Kaviśekhar Baruā, and Rājā Sujān Singh, while a contingent of 2,000 cavalary, 200 infantry, and 200 musketeers under Khataj Kan (Khwaja Tāj Khān?) and Rājā Sur Sing attacked Bānhbāri at the mouth of the Barnadi opposite Gauhāti. An attempt was made to mine the palace of Rājā of Darrang. But again, the Rājā of Rāni foiled them by giving timely warning of this move to the Barphukuan and by luring them into a narrow pass between two hills and then suddenly attacking them, thereby causing numerous casualties and heavy losses in provisions and other materials. The hill-men of Dimaruā also joined those of Rāni in resisting the Mughals, who had to retire to Dalibāri. Nor did the Mughal navy fare better than the land forces. The naval division of Mansur Khān was blocked at Pāniduār and after suffering severe casualties and losing two ships, retreated from there.

The rains had, in fact, compelled Rām Singh in Āṣādh (June–July) to withdraw from Agiāthuti with the main army to Hājo and bring down the fleet from the Hājo River to Suālkuchi on the right (north) bank of the Brahmaputra, 6 miles west of Pandu, so as to retain communications with it. In the north the Mughals retreated to Rangmahal from Harālu (?).[10]

Reports of repeated failures of Rām Singh reached the emperor through the account of the province of Bengal sent by (Wazir) Ja'far Khan. In a *farmān* dated 10 Rabi I 1079 (3 August 1669), the emperor appreciated the general's honest endeavours for the capture of Gauhāti fort with the army, artillery, and boats given to him by Shāista Khān. But he expressed his dissatisfaction at the general's slow progress on account of the heavy rains which had compelled the latter to halt at Agiāthuti, and at his failure to send a report to himself as ordered before, However, the emperor evidently realized (perhaps too late) that the expeditionary force was inadequate and made suitable arrangements to augment it in different ways. For the emperor urged on him to press on the final occupation of Gauhāti after the rains and supply of provisions with the reinforcements in men, animals, materials, cannons, ammunitions, and weapons of war which would soon be dispatched by Nawāb Shāistā Khān, from Dacca with Muzaffar Khān, the superintendent of the boats and Jalāluddin and the superintendent of the artillery. The general was further directed to firmly and confidently stay with the army at that suitable place near Gauhāti fort till the end of the rains and floods, and then press on its capture with 'full exertion and unbending endeavour'.[11]

The imperial *farmān* seemed to have spurred on the Mughal general to fresh action, even under the unfavourable circumstances. The siege operations thus continued under his officers with troops deployed suitably in villages.

Dissatisfied with the progress of the Āhoms, as reported by the Barphukan after a consultation with the *dāṅgariās*, the aggrieved Āhom king now urged his Prime Minister Ātan (Burhāgohāinpariā Phukan) and General Lāchit Barphukanpariā Phukan to launch an all-out attack on the Mughals on land and water. The Āhoms, under Sāiringiā Phukan, Dihingiā Phukan, and Guimeliā Bargohāin Phukan were ordered to construct a fort at Āgiāthuti ghat[12] near the Mughal fort (of Āgiathuti). It was placed under Ātan Burhā Gohāin. The Barphukan and the Kāliabariā Phukan set up a fort at Elāmung, north of Gauhāti. The Mughals attacked the Āhoms on land and water, but were themselves repulsed in a bloody engagement, on water by Ātan Burhāgohāin and Bhebā Phukan and on land by three Rājkhowās. Not only did the Mughals suffer numberous casualties but they also lost three stockades at Banpinkā,[13] west of Hājo.

Proceeding via Āltāmui to Agiathuti, the Bar Phukan directed a strong force to attack the Mughals on water and land. Asing or Ashinden Dihingiā Gohāin (grandson of Mājumelliā Gohāin), commanding the naval forces, halted at Sessa, while Lācham Abhoypuriā Rajkhowā (grandson of Bārgohāin), Nadarden, and Dihingiā Phukan and all Hāzarikās advanced on land. The Barphukan also advanced with a fleet. Then, a joint attack on land and water was organized against the Mughals by the (grandson of the) Dihingiā Phukan and Nadarden on land and by the Barphukan on water. A large number of Mughals were captured with their horses, and domestic animals, and articles and many were massacred at Āgaiāthuti.

The moral effect of this first Āhom victory was very great. However, the Āhoms were soon worsted when Rām Singh came in person, and Ashingden retreated. The Assamese land army, including Marān Hāzarikā, the grandons of the Bārgohāin, was massacred by the Mughals, and sailors jumping into water were killed by gunshots. They lost several war boats and four elephants. The Barphukan sought to save the situation with Nadarden but they were overpowered by a Mughal naval attack on the Sessa river. This compelled the Barphukan to escape to (?) Nāngken fort with the *Kāri*s (archers) and *Hājuā*s, leaving all ships behind. The king issued a stern reprimand to the Barphukan, with a threat of punishment if 'my army was killed without fighting' and if any one 'refrained willingly from fighting', for negligence in not making an enquiry about or recovering the ships and for abiding by 'my advice'. The Barphukan rightly pleaded his innocence, avowing that though he was 'ready to fight', there were 'none to proceed by water', that he had got a large number of captives and considerable spoils for delivery to the king. Judging from the Barphukan's ever loyal service, the king's assessment of his conduct must be deemed to be over hasty.[14]

Gohain phukan, the commander of Rangmahal fort on the north, at first suffered a reverse from the Mughal besiegers, advancing under cover of tall screen plates attached to the legs of horses and then coming out at the onset of a hand-to-hand fight. But the tables were soon turned when he adopted a new device in reforming the phalanxes which proved impenetrable—the ordinary soldiers with black uniforms remaining behind four outer rows of elephants with screened *howdah*s with spearmen, musketeers, and archers in each column. Hence the besiegers had to withdraw. The Āhoms also sought to recapture Luthāri, repulsed an attack on Akur fort, and recaptured Chenga and Phrenbār forts. In the series of naval fighting during August–September 1669, the Mughal war boats, carrying 16 cannon each, attacked the river stockades of the enemy. The Barphukan himself inflicted heavy casualties on the Mughals.[15]

As part of their defensive programme the Āhoms supplemented their open engagements with harassing gurerrilla tactics (*dagā yuddha*), specially in September 1669, which sorely tried the patience of the invaders. Swooping unawares on the latter from the secret hide-outs in jungles and on hill-tops or from their forts at midnight, the guerrillas would invest the Mughals, and if repulsed, hurriedly retreat. On the north bank, Premier Ātan Burhāgohāin organized from his base at Lāthiā fort a harassing campaign with his daring commandos or eavesdropping spies who sneaked into the Mughal camp at night after the commanders had drugged themselves to sleep by smoking *bhāng* and *dhaturā* through pipes of the *hookāh*s (hubble-bubble) and purloined treasures, money-bags and even the very silver *hookāh*s. Such activities resembled the 'hit and run' tactics of modern-day guerrillas. The Rājput general condemned such night activities as cowardly and dishonourable 'thieves' affairs', which lowered the dignity of warfare. But the Assamese justified these by saying that only lions fought (fight; editor's intervention) during night. In protest, Rām Singh withdrew from fighting during October 1669–March 1670. Rām Singh's moral protest had no material impact on the Āhom tactics. It merely delayed the issue. From the practical point of view his attitude was untenable.

However, guerrilla tactics and pilfering had their limitations. They could merely fatigue but never repulse and expel the opponent permanently. This could be done only in open encounters on land. But this was neither wise nor possible. The Assamese soldiers were mostly infantry men, dreading the fury of trained cavalry charges. Hence, the Assamese war council decided only in favour of naval fights to which the Mughals were to be lured. As the Āhom commanders hesitated to resort to a decisive showdown, the Barphukan's loyalty became suspect before the king.

After the rains, the Mughals resumed their activities but these proved to be futile. They lost a double engagement near Sindurighopā. They failed to blow up the enemy fort of Pāndu by mine on account of the alertness of its commander, who had the dismantled portion repaired quickly. The Assamese not only foiled a Mughal attempt to destroy Sārāighāṭ (Śrīghāṭ) fort but also demolished four Mughal wooden stockades, captured a half complete fort near Lāthiā, and seized munitions and a few prisoners. A Mughal contingent sailing up the Brahmaputra to attack Darrang was lured to a hill-pass by the Queen Mother of the Rājā at a secret hint from the Barphukan and cut down.[16]

Ālāboi

After the battle of Banpinkā, the exasperated Mughal generals again approached the Āhoms for a settlement. It was an unusual approach. To avoid further useless loss of human lives on both sides, the Rājput rājā invited the Āhom king to a duel, undertaking, in case of defeat, to withdraw from Assam with his entire army and boats. Presumably he was confident of his own gladiatorial capacity and hence of victory. In other words, he expected the Āhom king, if defeated, to restore the boundaries of 1639. Otherwise his own stern taskmaster would never have tolerated his unauthorized twist to the military campaign. The general's letter, sent through a mere emissary and not a formal envoy, evoked rightful scorn from the Barphukan who sent him back unaccompanied by any envoy, with the taunting reply that the Āhoms were 'ready to meet' the general in war and were 'not afraid of him'.

Thereupon, the general sent an envoy (*kataki*) named Jadu Indra with a letter to the Barphukan, demanding the release of several Mughal captives. The latter curtly returned the Mughal envoy and 'fettered' three captives, informing his king of all these events. The latter refused to accept the Mughal general's invitation for a duel on the grounds that it would be beneath his dignity, as Rām Singh 'is a mere servant and has no umbrella over his head'. Emboldened by recent victories, he was loath to delimitation. He sent four agents to direct all Phukans and Baruas to emerge from their forts and fight the Mughals.[17]

Now, the Mughal general again resorted to pacific negotiations. At first came his envoy (*kataki*), Phupaimung, and then a messenger brought his three letters, probably for the king, the Burhāgohāin, and the Barphukan. The last one seemed to be willing and sent a proposal to the king for orders, otherwise the Mughals could not have come up and encamped near the Assamese without any engagement. Perhaps getting apprehensive of the delay in getting a reply, the general again sent two envoys with presents.

Chakrāyudha left the matter to the discretion of his four high officers (*dāngariās*). The latter, in their turn, consulted the six Phukans. The unanimous secret decision of the Āhom war council was to avoid fighting on land and facing the sure rout of the Assamese infantry before the massive Mughal cavalry charge and to manoeuvre the Mughals to a naval encounter. Meanwhile, the king had received exaggerated reports about his general's dilatory methods and smelt something foul. Unmoved by the Premier's efforts to file away this suspicion, the impatient king even threatened to punish his General and Commanders in case of further delay in launching offensive operation.[18] It was most probably the most trying moment in the Barphukan's life. He could not but obey the king's order. Yet he knew that, just as 'It would be difficult to come out unscathed if one pokes into a nest of immature hornets', an attack on the Mughals concentrated at one place and staying with vigilance and circumspection (*Bengāl ekethāi hoi sābdhāne āche—kenchā rarlak jekāle gā sāribalok tān haba*) near Ālāboi hill, skirting a vast, open plain between two rivers, the Brahmaputa and the Sessa (near Dalibari) would be suicidal for the Assamese infantry that was always shy of the cavalry. His loyalty to the king overcame his duty towards his army. The order of the supreme head of the state superseded the judgement of the man on the spot.

The final upshot of this three-act open encounter could, therefore, be easily visualized. While Rām Singh's approach was essentially psychological, marked by pride, cavalry, and then revenge, the Assamese took recourse to diplomacy, deception, and misrepresentation, probably to overcome their basic weakness. The Rajput General insultingly challenged the Assamese to an open fight and sent a force of only 10,000 under Mīr Nawāb so as to get credit for a victory over a numerically superior Āhom host, reported by the Barphukan's messenger to be 20,000 strong. The Mughal van was, however, commanded by a woman warrior in male attire, named Madanāvatī, so that the defeated Mughal army would not be disgraced and the victorious Assamese would not be entitled to any honour. On the other hand, the Āhoms actually had sent 40,000 men, i.e. double the reported figure, adopted a century-old anti-Koch device of having a 'Brahman' vanguard (i.e. dressing their archers and musketeers as Brahmans) so that the Rājputs would desist from killing them.

In the first stage Madanāvati caused havoc by her elusive and invulnerable swiftness, dispersing the first four Āhom lines with heavy losses. The Barphukan tackled this by digging trenches where his fighters were concealed for attack. A Rājput diversion to cross the Brahmaputra was countered and Madanāvati was killed by a bullet on its bank. In the second stage, Mīr Nawāb's men were routed and he himself was captured and was kept under guard.

But the success of the Āhoms was short-lived. The nemesis came in the third stage. Before they could return to their forts with their captives and spoils, Rām Singh, enraged at the deception of the enemy, let loose upon them his veteran horsemen, equipped with machines (*yantras*) and long shields, which wrought a terrible carnage. Ten thousand Āhom stalwarts, each of whom was 'a pillar of strength' to the Barphukan, lay dead on the plain. Rām Singh exultingly commented: 'Look at the rashness of the Assamese, they venture to fight on the plains with Amber horseman' (20 Sravaṇ, Thursday, Śāka 1591, about 5 August 1669).

The Āhom general was deeply perturbed. He was, however, consoled by the Premier, and sought outwardly to minimize the loss before his counterpart as the loss of one detachment only, caused by 'an unauthorised diversion' of some border chieftains, with a sevenfold-strong army still in readiness. This serious loss of the Āhoms did not, however, mean a decisive gain for the Mughals, as it was 'a mere isolated triumph.'[19]

Reports of Rām Singh's successes, particularly at Ālāboi (August 1669), and of his efforts at encircling the suburbs of Gauhāti fort reached the emperor through Shāista Khān, Governor of Bengal. So the emperor was pleased, on the occasion of 'Id festivities in the thirteenth year of his accession to raise the General's *mansab* from 4000 to 5000', i.e. from *chahār hazāri* to *panj hazāri*, by a *farmān* dated 7 March 1670. It contained imperial directives to the latter for the future. If investment was possible, he was to advance further and conquer Gauhāti. If not, he was to devastate the land, plunder the inhabitants, and encamp on elevated places so as to avoid the sufferings of the previous year's rainy season and where supply of grain and provisions for the army would be easily available.[20]

Peace or War?

This resounding victory might have spurred the Mughal general on to further exploits over the weakened enemy. There were also the distant but ever-present imperial dinnings and threats to constantly goad him to action. But months of hostility had rolled on, yet not an inch of territory had been surrendered. The resolution to resist was ever-present among the Āhoms but it was sugar-coated with professions of unending friendship. The general was faced with a dilemma which he could not solve: to attack or retreat? Thinking that the Āhoms would now be weakened perceptibly and hence psychologically chastened by the Ālāboi disaster, the Rājput general felt encouraged to press his demands for delimitation. Without entering into a bewildering maze of details regarding exchanges of missions between the two sides, it will suffice to say that both were eager for peace. 'News for negotiations' over it was broadcast among the Āhoms. The Rājput general's definite proposal to his Āhom counterpart included the Assamese evacuation of Gauhāti and the status quo of 1639 in return for an indemnity of 3 lakh of rupees to cover the expenses on the fortifications, terms which the general considered to be overcomplimentary. After consulting the Premier, the Burhagohain, then at Lāthiā hill, the Barphukan expressed his inability, as a servant of the king, to commit himself without the latter's order, adding a sting that the Rājput Rājā's return without a decisive victory over the Āhoms would not rebound to his honour. However, the latter continued to press his demand for the evacuation of Gauhāti for the sake of mutual interest.[21]

Thus, Rām Singh's diplomatic missions in the time of Chakradwaj Singha ended in smoke. So Rām Singh next tried two other traditional methods of dealing with an enemy—dissension and corruption. The first took the form of epistolary diplomacy. By sending to one Āhom leader 'arrow messages' of allegations of a secret compact for easy passage of Gauhāti against another, aptly called *bheda-patra* in one *Buranji*, Rām Singh sought to influence the Phukans and Rājkhowās by freely distributing bribes—gifts, cash, and ornaments. But neither device bore any fruit. The cohesion of the leaders was too solid to be dissolved. Their patriotism was too genuine to be tainted. A gem-studded necklace (*bākharpatā kanthābharan*) was presented by Rām Singh through the Mādhavcharan *kataki* along with other presents to the Barphukan, but the latter did not wear the necklace. Even Rām Singh's envoy, Pandit Rāi, a diplomat of the first water, accompanying Mādhav, to repeat his old demand, failed to make the Āhom general budge an inch from his stand that any settlement, to be stable, must require the ratification of the sovereigns of the East and the West.[22]

It was during these critical days of peace negotiations that Chakradhwaj Singha died and was succeeded by his brother

Udāyaditya Singha (1670). Though lacking the inspiring, spirited zeal of his predecessor, the new ruler was quite able to conduct the civil and military affairs of the kingdom. Due to the long and continued hostilities, the Āhom kingdom was seething with discontent and the commanders believed that Rām Singh would not leave their country without achieving the task imposed on him by Aurangzeb. Hence, some Assamese commanders, including even the Barphukan, contemplated the acceptance of the status quo of 1639.[23]

When the Burhāgohāin and the Barphukan broached the matter of peace negotiations with the Mughals, the new king also expressed his willingness to settle the boundary question. In accordance with the consultation with the *dāngariās*, the Barphukan sent two envoys to the Mughals for the purpose.[24]

Rām Singh also now renewed his diplomatic efforts aimed at the recognition of his demand, regarding the frontiers of 1639. Negotiations made some progress. He wrote letter of friendship (only the year Śaka 1591, i.e. 1669–70 is given, but no date) through his three envoys—Mirā (i.e. Mir), Rāmhari Kārji, and Pandit Rāi—to the Barphukan referring to the relation between the latter's father and Allah Yār Khan and repeating his earlier demand of abandonment of Gauhāti in return for peace. The Barphukan was apparently agreeable, for he replied in an undated letter of the same year through his two envoys, Nim (Pāchipālai of BKK) and Rāmacharan, requesting the general, if willing to continue the tradition of friendship of 1639, to send these three envoys back. The two Assamese envoys were given a very warm reception and presented with sandal paste in a golden cup and betelnut in a silver tray. Rām Singh was at first willing to do so when the Assamese conveys conveyed this news to the Barphukan and the latter to the king; both of them arranged to receive the Mughal envoys with due éclat—silver and gold cups, trays and dishes, embroidered cloths and canopies.

Events appeared to be moving towards a favourable culmination. But the Mughal general, bewildered at first at the devious nature of Āhom diplomacy, came at last to entertain doubts about the bonafides of the Āhom commanders, who were apparently eager to bide their time. So the Mughal general changed his mind, complaining to the envoys that the Assamese were sending envoys again and again but no useful work was done (*bār bār ukil pathāon kām to eko hāsil nahoi*). He pressed for the evacuation of Gauhāti and the release of the son of Sayyid Firuz (Khān) and Sayyid Sātār (Khān), affirming under most solemn oaths that he had no other demands.[25] But though the Mughal general was evidently in extreme duress and in a highly tense mood, he sent this most important message to the Barphukan orally through Assam's envoys, Nim, and Rāmcharan. Neither any envoy nor any letter was sent from the Mughal general. It was a violation of diplomatic etiquette and hence a blunder on his part. The Āhom king commented that when Rām Singh had not sent an envoy, the Barphukan need not send one, and prohibited the dispatch of presents for receiving the Mughal envoy Pandit Rāi.

Expressing dissatisfaction at the Barphukan's acquiescence in the proposal and procedure of retreat from Gauhāti, the king left the matter to the decision of the *dāngariās.* All except the Burhāgohāin, the Assamese Prime Minister, concurred in the proposal. He was the lone but the most notable and effective dissenter. His cogent and eloquent arguments turned the scales. A voluntary surrender of Gauhāti would mean that the resistance offered and the sacrifices made by the Assamese so long would go in vain. It would render Assam's past efforts and expenses a meaningless drain of the country's manpower and resources. There was no guarantee, he pointed out, that the emperor would ratify his general's arrangements. Moreover, Rām Singh's terms and stipulations even though backed by oaths, if not ratified by Delhi or honoured and implemented by another nawāb, i.e. his successor in Assam as commander or governor, would be lacking in sanctity. It would be nothing more than 'a highway made of ashes'. Voluntarily vacating Gauhāti would inevitably lead to eventual withdrawal or expulsion of the Āhoms even from Garhgāon and hence to a logical thrust or retreat to Nāmrūp. Gauhāti, therefore, must never be abandoned even if the emperor made similar promises. Finally all, including the Barphukan, too, came to see reason. Agreeing with his Prime Minister, Udāyaditya asked his commanders to fight till victory. The Burhāgohāin, in his turn, continued to harass the Mughals by plundering their treasure and property by guerrilla methods.

Within a few months, by Vaiśākh (April–May 1670–71), a fort was constructed by Barpātra Dāngariā at Kurua (on the north bank) on royal order. When Rām Singh wanted the matter to be expedited, the Barphukan cleverly wriggled out of his previous willingness by pleading absence of royal order on fixation of the boundary from Kālikājān.[26]

Rām Singh's high hopes of a diplomatic or pacific settlement soon ended in smoke. The failure of the peace negotiations was due to a combination of several factors. To Rām Singh this was due to the evasive and delaying tactics of the Āhoms, concealing their real objective beneath sweet professions of a goodwill mission. What appeared to be inscrutable to the straightforward and credulous Rājput could have been divined long before at the very outset of the campaign by a shrewder general. Again, it must be admitted that he himself was guilty of unseemly conduct in exhibiting a bluntness that was certainly mistaken and cost him dear. He might have spoken the truth plainly to the last batch of Āhom envoys but he violated diplomatic courtesy in not returning an envoy. It is easy to accuse the Āhoms of prevarication. But what they did was for their *patriā*. They could not reasonably be expected to forego what they had won through blood and toil. In fact, the Assamese were not expected to voluntarily forego Gauhāti, the capital of Kāmrūp, enjoying natural and human fortifications as well as strategic centres around like Pāṇdu, Āgiāthuti, and Śrīghāṭ. Too late did Rām Singh realize this fundamental truth.

Another unfavourable factor for the Mughal general was the attitude of his own master. Report of his endless dallying with the Āhoms for a settlement and of Mughal losses on skirmishes must have reached Aurangzeb. He came to realize, from the letters of Shāistā Khān and Ja'far Khān Wazir (deceased), that the chances of the capture of Gauhāti fort were slowly receding and that dispatch of further reinforcements would be futile. So by *farmān* of 20 July 1670, the general was ordered to send Askar Khan and several other captains with their contingents back to the imperial court, but he himself was to stick to this post at Rangāmāti during the rainy season with a suitable army for safety, keeping watch over the borders and to act according to the prescriptions of Shāistā Khān after the rains.[27] Evidently, Aurangzeb had lost all trust in his general.

Meanwhile reinforcements in the shape of a few war vessels and three imperial officers ordered earlier came with the energetic cruising admiral, Munnawar Khān, zamindar of Bengal, to strengthen the Rājā's flagging resources. But Aurangzeb's caustic message, conveyed through the admiral, that Rām Singh was sent to fight and not to make friends with the Āhoms, cut him to the quick. Though disheartened (*biman*) by reports of Aurangzeb's veiled contrivance to kill his son (Krishna Singha), and letters of warning from his mother and wife not to disturb the country where religious music and recital of God's name (*nām saṃkīrtan*) were universal, where cows and Brahmans (*go-Brāhmaṇ*) were duly protected, and where Mir Jumla died soon after conquering it, the Kachchwahā Rājā, true to his salt, girded his loins, casting off his war weariness and futile pacific overtones. He moved along the north bank of the Brahmaputra to 'Kamden' (near Suālkuchi) and therefrom with ships with artillery and archers under *sardār*s to Śitāmari'. Detachments were also sent to Darrang and Dakhinkol.[28]

Sarāighāt

Learning of Rām Singh's latest bold, quick, and expansive offensive on both sides of the Brahmaputra, the Āhom king ordered his commanders to repair, garrison and strengthen all the fortifications on land and water at once. The Burhāgohāin (then at Kāthālbāri) was commanded to proceed from Sāmdharā to Sāraighāṭ (Śrīghāṭ) immediately with a strong force of 20,000. The Barphukan was ordered to come up. 'The Assamese hurried both from north and south.' On land, their attack was led by Lāsām Abhoipuriā Rajkhowa and Gohāin Rājhowās and other Rājkhowās, Phukans, and Hāzarikas. It was a 'terrible battle', as both Āhom *Buranji*s concur. This compelled Rām Singh to retreat towards the Juria hills (west of modern Gauhāti) for safeguarding his line of communications, leaving a few officers in the forward positions held. Giving the futile peace moves decent burial, Rām Singh now resolved to try the last alternative open for him to force a decisive encounter by a direct attack on Gauhāti. It was vulnerable only through one small break in the rāmparts at Āndhārubāli (Āndhari) sandbanks between Barphukan's base at Itākhuli (Sukreshwar hill) and the Āmarajuri ferry ghat at the foot of the Kāmākhyā hill. The Rājput general planned to enter Gauhāti through the breach with a body of men and horses, to be transported on boats across the Brahmaputra. But the breach was quickly repaired and the Mughal vessels had to retire to the north bank.[29]

No doubt the scene shifted from Gauhāti. But the situation was unfavourable to the Assamese. The soldiers were disheartened. Both their general Lāchit Barphukan, and Admiral were then seriously ill and so Narā Rājā (Hazārikā), son of Miri Sandikoi, was placed in chief command (as Neog). A double encounter ensued on land and water near Aswakrānta (opposite Gauhāti), where the Assamese pursuers had moored their ships. The Assamese, under Lāluk Bargohāin Phukan and Hazārikās, worsted the Mughals on land. But the Mughals *nawwāra*, advancing from Juriā to Aswakrānta, compelled the cannonading Āhom navy rushing from Āmrajuri under the Pāniphukan Alan Hazārikā and Ashingden, grandson of Dihingiā Bargohāin, to retreat to Barhilā, north of Śrīghāt. This is in turn disheartened the land army, which also retreated to avert encirclement. The situation was so critical that Barneog Hazārikā, the keeper of Pāndu, sought Lāchit's advice. The Barphukan sought to raise the dwindling morale of 'all land and naval forces' by proclaiming through his messengers, 'Tell my soldiers that I have bought a slice of land on the Chila by paying only four cowries; I am not leaving the place now, as my term of life is not yet over; and if I go at all, I will do so only after my people have gone.' He implied that he was determined to fight. Nara Hazārikā, advancing from Sindurighopā to Aswakrānta, appealed to the soldiers in the name of the king, saying: O ye my men, you may retreat only if you want to sprinkle poison on a platter of gold (*rājya, or sunia kanhita biha dhal note bhaq*). At this, the king reinforced him with 100 men. But such impassioned appeals proved unavailing. In the universal craze for flight, some boatmen sought to sail upstream with the loaded boats of the Burhāgohāin (then at Lāthiā or Lataria) and of the Barphukan from the scene of action, Latāsil. The spirited Barphukan, witnessing the battle from his sickbed, in the gatehouse (*bātg-har*) of his Itākhuli camp and collecting information of every moment (*tile tile vārtā loichhile*), sought to instill courage among his faltering men by shouting that he would prefer death at his station to desertion. Not a moment was to be lost in launching the attack. Yet the general had to wait for what seemed to be an eternity for the astrologer Achyutanand

Doli's verdict. His army was on the verge of extinction and with it the country's independence too would disappear. Suffering unbearable pain—physical—and mental and losing patience, he even threatened to kill himself. Then, with the auspicious moment pronounced, the sick general, helped by Nodai of Kharangi, boarded a boat with six other war vessels to launch a counter-attack with artillery by rallying the army and navy. The sight of their ailing general conducting operations notwithstanding high fever, instilled courage among the wavering Āhom fighters who now swelled his fleet from both banks. Reinforcements also came under the Sāringiā Phukan, the Neogkataki and many Hazārikās from Rangmahal. Now, the Assamese warships smashed into the thick of the Mughal fleet, then stationed on the waters at Āmrajuri, the northern bank of the river opposite Kāmākhyā hill.

It was keenly contested battle (*tayā-mayā-raṇ*). One fought for aggression and glory of victory. The other fought for life and *patria*, the independence of country. The issue was a foregone conclusion. The Mughals could not stand the well-planned and well-conducted Āhom attack. The right-angled triangle of the Brahmaputra (Itākhuli–Kāmākhyā–Aswakrānta region) became a complicated tangle of boats and men battling to save themselves from drowning. The Assamese spanned the Brahmaputra by 'bridge' of boats (*nāote bharhi di*) placed side by side. They also resorted to wily trick, combining a frontal charge with a surprise attack from behind, that proved decisive. The Barphukan pretended to attack the Mughal fleet from the front with some men on a few ships and lure it forward and then stabbed it from behind with the main army and fleet. Unaware of the danger lurking in his rear Mughal admiral, Sarif (Sharif) Khān, smoking his *hookā*, advanced forward, only to be killed by a gunshot from behind. The suddenness of the event threw the entire Mughal fleet out of gear and it retreated. The panic-stricken army could not be recalled to order. This marked the end of the battle (*Lākni Dāprāo*, 1592–3), Chaitra, middle of March 1671). For the Mughals, who suffered heavy casualties with three top-ranking *amirs*, 4,000 dead and wounded, it was not merely a defeat but a disaster.

In his hour of victory, Lāchit Barphukan behaved with a noble sense of idealism and dignified moderation. The Mughals were pursued three miles to Pāṇdu and then up to the Mānāha

(Manās) river, Assam's western frontier which was to be guarded, but strict orders were issued to the pursuers not to harass them by shooting guns or arrows. Refusing to tarnish the fair name of the king and ministers (*swargadeare pātrāmantriro jasasyā*) by spoliation of the fugitives who had fought for one year, he rejected the frontier guards' (*chakiāls*) suggestion to that effect. But he never gave way to complacency. For he also rejected the proposal of some Phukans and Rajkhowās to attack the retreating Mughals as unwise so as to avoid a second Ālāboi. Apprehending the retreat of the Mughals to be a mere ruse, to be followed by a second attack, the general ordered relays of messengers to be posted at short distances (*Khāpe khāpe manuha thabi*) to report to him quickly on the movements of the enemy while the Burhāgohāin and other commanders especially at Barepaita, Bhogpur and other places remained ready for action. Hence, the main Mughal force could retreat with difficulty and halted at Pachariā, south of Hājo. The Āhom (under Ghorā Kunwar of an outpost on the Chechanai river east of Hājo) secured another victory by a surprise attack on land and water on the retreating party of the Mughals, who were all killed. The Mughals in Darrang were also worsted.[30]

However, even at this stage, Rām Singh did not give up all hope and planned to encircle the Āhoms from the back by planning an attack on Desh Rāni in *Dakhinkol* under Rājāj Indradaman, Ismān (Usman?) Khan, Rājā Barnadiā, Jainarāyan and others. But thanks to the efficiency of the spies and the vigilance of the Rājā of Rāni, the plan was detected and scotched by the Barphukan, who sent a force under Marangikhowā Gohāin, Gajpuriā Rajkhowā (of Lānphima family), Lāsām (of Bargohāin family), Nadarden, and a few Hazārikās against the Mughals, though the latter were reinforced. The Gāros, under their Rāni, won over by the Assamese army with presents, and the hill-men retaliated on the Mughals for their acts of arson on their buildings. The latter, in turn, attacked Pāmali fort, then under Rangāi and two others, but had to retreat before an Āhom counter-attack. The Rājā of Rāni killed a few Mughal invaders at Kapili. A Mughal supporter, the son of Rāja Barnadia, was sent to Garhgāon. The remainder of the invaders escaped to the mouth of the river Haran (Hari) and sailed down the Kallang and the Brahmaputra to join the main army. Weakened by such repeated defeats and consequential losses and losing all hopes of recovering imperial grace by defeating the lord of Assam, Rām Singh bent his way back, 23 Chaitra, Śaka 1952, about 5 April 1671 from Kāmrūp to recross the Manās river and return to Rangāmāti. One is reminded of a similar retreat of his father, Mirza Rājā Jai Singh I, after his failure in Bijāpur in 1667.[31]

This brilliant victory of the Āhom at Sarāighāṭ, however, came to be clouded by a misfortune. Lāchit Barphukan, the hero of Sarāighāt, who had literally staked his life and honour, died at Kaliābar soon afterwards (April 1672), just as Nelson, too, died after his victory. But the assessment of S. K. Bhuyan that Sarāighāṭ was Assam's Trafalgar[32] is not wholly accurate, as Nelson died in action, while Lāchit died a year later.

Sarāighāṭ left an undying legacy of unflinching bravery and unalloyed patriotism of the Assamese. Lāchit became the symbol of Assamese nationalism, if we may use that term in that age. Sarāighāṭ, again, avenged Ālāboi. A small state like Assam had humbled the mighty Mughal empire in its palmy days. The battle of Sarāighāṭ holds a memorable place in Assamese history and legends. It was, again, a decisive battle in the history of Assam. The victory conferred some tangible gains to the defenders. Not only was the Mughal offensive hurled back for good, but the results of the sacrifices of the Assamese, past and present, were also preserved . . . the retention of Gauhāti and Kāmrūp. Darang and Beltalā were also lost to the Mughals. True, a stealthy effort was made 10 years later to penetrate into the same area through the back door, but the tide of self-confidence and territorial patriotism, engendered at Sarāighāṭ, was strong enough to sweep away everything that was anti-national. If Sarāighāṭ hurled the Mughal invaders in a defensive war, Itakhuli completed its work, 12 years later, in an *offensive war*.

Overjoyed at the news of the retreat of Rām Singh, forwarded by the Barphukan, Udāyaditya heaped presents on the Barphukan, and issued orders for the settlement of the conquered territory. Kāmrūp was annexed to Assam and its frontier outpost was pushed west to Hādirā opposite Goālpārā. Two tributary rājās were set up. Sūrya Nārāyāṇ, son of Mahendra and grandson of Bali Nārayāṇ in *Uttarkol*, i.e. in Darrang, and Gandharbha Nārayāṇ in *Dakhinkol*, (i.e. in Beltalā). For the defence of Upper Assam the king issued necessary orders to Burhāgohāin, all officers cooperating. To guard the way thereto, the Barphukan specially stationed the Bar Gohāin and the Bar Baruā. The Āhom commanding officers at Gauhāti and further down up to the Manās (Mānāhā) river had to remain alert to prevent any recurrence of a foreign invasion. They remained fully prepared for any eventuality. But nothing happened for some time.[33]

The gains to the Āhom from Sarāighāṭ meant losses to the Mughals—material and moral. But more damaging than the first was the second. It not only exposed the inner rot that had crept into the military machine, but also tarnished Mughal honour. Rām Singh's rout at Sarāighāṭ and retreat therefrom, duly reported by Hāji Mir Ghazar Beg, the Assam reporters, so angered the emperor that he at once demoted the Rājput general by 2,000 and ordered his recall. However, the crestfallen Rājput general waited at Rangāmāṭi till 1676 for a chance to invade Assam again. But in vain. The Mughals could not take advantage of the internal political chaos in Assam (1673–81), partly because of Aurangzeb's preoccupations in the north-west (*c.*1672–5) on account of the Afghan rising and in the Deccan on account of Shivāji's dazzling successes, and partly because of Aurangzeb's suspicious and ungenerous treatment towards Rām Singh and his family.[34] In February 1676, Rām Singh was recalled from Assam. He was directed to return after making over charge to the person recommended by *Umdat ul Mulk* (Shāista Khān) in the *thānāh* of Rangāmāṭi. Accordingly, he made over his charge to Abu Nisār Khān and had audience with emperor on 22 Rabi ul āwwal, 1087, Thursday, 25 June 1676.[35]

Reflections on Rām Singh's Failure

Once Aurangzeb accused Rām Singh for slackness in conducting the Assam campaign, because the latter was engaged in peace negotiations with Assam. 'I commissioned him to fight Assam, not to make friends with the people there.' The general stoutly pleaded his own defence, 'I have not refrained from fighting but it has proved useless. As there are no fields, fighting by spears, shields and guns is an impossible affair. The Assamese have erected an impenetrable wall of defence on both the banks. There is the possibility of naval fight only.'[36] Subsequently, on his return and in reply to the emperor's query, Rām Singh attributed his dismal failure after a few years strenuous efforts to three factors—the hills surrounding the country, the big fortifications of Assam, and the valour and skill of the redoubtable Assamese. Rām Singh did not allude here to the rivers and floods which impeded his advance, but emphasized that the hills dictated the strategy of Āhom fortifications and that the Assamese were not only courageous and formidable but highly skilled in the martial arts. Individually, each item represented a correct statement of fact.

Yet taken together, this does not appear to be a wholly correct explanation to a modern historian. A truer explanation would be found in the contrast between the conditions of Assam in 1661–63 and in 1669–71. In the time of Mir Jumla the first two factors were wholly present, but the third only in part. The courageous and skilled Assamese were there, of course, but they did not wilfully display their grit. The wells of Āhom doughtiness seemed to have suddenly dried up. Jaydhwaj's Assam was suffering from internal corrosion. So Mir Jumla had hardly to fight to recover Kāmrūp. His way was virtually greased, so to say, by discontent in the Āhom army. On the other hand, Chakradhwaj's Assam was renovated, revitalized, and made resolute to driving away the foreigners. A question arises in the mind of the reader—what would have happened if Mir Jumla had come in 1669?

It is, therefore, necessary to compare the two contending armies as regards the spirit animating them, their respective organizations and methods. The fundamental factor was that the contest was between two opposed principles or ideologies. While the Mughals came only for imperialistic expansion, the Assamese fought for life and liberty, the government carrying the people with them. It was a conflict between imperialism, championed by loyalist Rājput honour on the one hand, and the revived spirit of patriotism or, if we may call it, conscious nationalism, on the other. Surveying the vast assemblage of the Mughal hosts, Lāchit Barphukan could not restrain his tears and his monologue has become classic in Assamese *Buranji* literature: 'It is a tragedy that my *country* is facing this dire catastrophe, during my *Phukanship*. How will *my king* be saved?' How will *my people* be saved? And how will *my posterity* be saved? (Italics mine).[37] The general's spirit animated the entire army of Assam. Even Mir Jumla had some ambitions of his own to earn everlasting renown as a world conqueror. Rām Singh had, apart from loyalty, no idealism to inspire him, over and above promotion in service. This basic weakness in the Mughal position affected the final issue of the war, notwithstanding isolated triumphs of the Mughals.

This brings us to the question of leadership. Napoleon I used to say that in war it was not *men* that counted, but *the man.* The Āhoms were directed by a heroic and dedicated triumvirate—the King, the Prime Minister and the General. The autocratic Chakradhwaj Singh was always there to encourage and inspire his men. But the Mughal emperor was too far away from the theatre of action to influence the war except by orders, which took time to be implemented. Sometimes Chakradwaj's orders overruling his men on the spot did not produce happy results as at Ālāboi. But usually he had complete confidence in his ministers and relied on the sober statesmanship of Ātan Burhāgohāin, the Prime Minister, and the inspiring generalship of Lāchit Barphukan. Mughal gold could not seduce these constant hearts. The one occasion of the king's unfounded suspicion of his general's loyalty was quickly removed by the sagacious advice of the Premier. The Mughals had to admit the qualities of the Āhom leadership.

But Aurangzeb had no trust in the Rājput general of his choice. His deputation to the dreadful country of Assam was a measure of punishment for his suspected instrumentality in Shivāji's escape from Agra (and also of Tegh Bahādur). The epistolary warnings for the Rājā's widowed mother and wife, reminding him of the fate of Mir Jumla and the dark intentions of the emperor and the apprehension of misfortune evidently so dispirited him as to seek the advice of the Sikh Guru Teg Bahādur. The subsequent maltreatment of the emperor towards his son, Krishna Singh, disheartened him all the more. It must, however, be admitted that, though disaffected, Rām Singh was certainly never disloyal. He cannot be accused of being in any way lukewarm in his duty for this reason. True, he was valorous, able, and possessed some tact. He has been described in the *Maāsir-i-Alāmgiri* as one of the great and eminent nobles of the (Mughal) court.[38] But he lacked the ripe diplomatic acumen of his father and the grit, the dogged determination, and the enormous resources of the enterprising Mir Jumla. In the light of experience gained from the Mir's campaigns in the north-eastern frontier, it is doubtful if Aurangzeb's choice of Rām Singh was really sound. The history of the past invasions of Assam and the experience of the latest one of Mir Jumla were there before the emperor to acquaint him with the difficulties of an expeditionary force of Bengal going to attack Assam. The problems to be faced, the difficulties arising from the foul climate, heavy rainfall and floods, and geography—hills and rivers causing stupendous transport problems—were not unknown to the emperor.[39] The invaders had to sail upstream against strong currents, requiring the boats to be towed up. Their land forces had to cut their way through reeds, forests, and marshes. In either case, progress would be slow. Add to this the difficulties caused by the resistance of the invaded peoples, now conscious of their strength. All these difficulties, natural and human, required a superman to tide them over. Rām Singh lacked in leadership. Unlike Mir Jumla, he could not fathom the real motives of negotiations, namely, to gain time for the completion of fortifications. The Assamese *Buranji*s attribute boastful utterances to Rām Singh, proud of his descent from Māndhātā, Man Singh, and Mirza Rājā Jai Singh, and conscious of his own worth and greatness.[40] But unlike his reputed ancestors, and unlike Mir Jumla, Rām Singh was a mediocre general, who exhibited his helplessness before the Assamese ministers and admitted his utter incompetence in his actions and utterances. We are told in several *Buranji*s that Rām Singh was profoundly impressed with the statesmanship and generalship of the Āhom premier and the general, who admittedly used him as a 'toy', with the intricate and impenetrable fortifications of the Assamese at Gauhāti, which Rām Singh could not batter down. He often described these to possess 'the shape of *Yantras*' (machines), in which he could detect no flaw (*chhidra*). 'Forts have been constructed by the Āhoms', he told Rashid Khān, 'on tops of hills, and the outlying plains are also too narrow for the purpose of an open engagement. It is for this reason that the Assamese had proved invincible in their wars against foreigners. The fortifications are circular in shape, and to reach fort there are three passages. The enemy is beyond the reach of our heavy artillery; and there is no opportunity of fighting with arrows and guns. Their ministers, commanders and infantry are all to be admired for having constructed such an impregnable wall of defence.'[41] He was even reported to be overcredulous in believing that the Assamese had *rākṣasas* (demons) who fought only at night. All this could imply that Rām Singh came to develop an inferiority complex which was fanned by Assamese envoys (*kataki*s) and even by his own.[42] Admiring the valour and the skill of the redoubtable Assamese, Rām Singh exclaimed: 'Every Assamese soldier is expert in rowing boats, in shooting arrows, in digging trenches, and in wielding guns and cannon. I have not seen such specimens of versatility in any other part of India.'[43] Such an attitude implied loss of morale and destroyed all chance of success. The general, who at first proudly announced his reputed ancestry and the excellence of the Amber horsemen, had ultimately to own to self-humiliation at the end. 'One who comes to fight against Assam should be thrashed on the cheek by scavengers with their broomsticks.'[44]

So even without doubting the sincerity and loyalty of Rām Singh, the fact remains that he was not quite suitable as a general who could lead his men to victory in a country like Assam. The Mughal cause was rendered hopeless on account of the inadequacy of the expeditionary force, for which Aurangzeb was responsible. Initially this might have been small, but gradually it is swelled from various sources, as discussed before, that the Āhom general was unnerved when he first sighted the Mughal army. But the Assamese were 'a nation in arms', who could easily be mobilized at short notice. This enabled them to soon outnumber even the vast numbers of Rām Singh. The latter estimated the opposing army at about 1 lakh in December 1669. This might have been even more, for the Āhom general posted one armed soldier at a distance of 13½ feet on the hills and 9 feet on rāmparts on plains throughout the entire ring of fortifications on both sides of the Brahmaputra. On the other hand, reinforcements for Rām Singh were not only infrequent but very sluggish in coming up. Handicapped by comparative numerical deficiency and knowing that his losses would be seldom replenished, Rām Singh had necessarily to avoid resort to 'indiscriminate and unprofitable attacks'.

Again, to succeed in Assam, a land full of rivers, streams, and *nala*s, the invader must be supreme on water. Unlike Mir Jumla who had initially 323 warships, manned by Portuguese, English, and Dutch sailors, Rām Singh had at first only 40. He might have augmented his fleet by the capture of Assamese ships and control of two famous dockyards near Hājo (e.g. at Rāmdia and at Suālkuch). Once he sent a fleet of 500 boats with 'sixteen-mouthed' prows and carrying guns. Nevertheless, the Assamese now had mastery over the water down to Manās (Mānāhā) river. The strength of their fleet at Gauhāti is not definitely known. But it must have been adequate. Their navy was not only numerous but also powerful, owing to the vast forests, abundant number of dockyards (*nao-sāli*) and the boat building and boat plying activities organized by two guilds (*naosalla khel* and *naobaicha* khel). The Āhom mastery over the water was indisputable and the Mughal crash at Sarāighāṭ became inevitable because of this.

The inadequacy of the Mughal armed and naval forces was aggravated by Rām Singh's insufficient resources. While Mir Jumla had with him the entire resources of Bengal of which he was the Viceroy, Rām Singh had to depend on occasional reinforcements only ordered from Delhi or through Shaistā Khān, then Viceroy of Bengal, which cannot by any means be regarded as adequate.

The grim potentialities of this situation were rendered darker by insubordination and internal dissension. In accordance with the general custom of the Mughals to send two generals in a campaign, the emperor deputed Rashid Khān to accompany Rām Singh as his second-in-command, but in reality as a check on the latter. However, by his arrogance, love of power, insubordination, and disloyalty, Rashid Khān weakened the army instead of strengthening it. The ex-*faujdār* of the Mughal Kāmrūp, who had enjoyed independent command, lived in viceregal splendor, and been accustomed to be treated as 'all in all' by the Āhoms, could hardly brook a position subordinate to the Rājput general. Rashid Khān claimed equality of rank with the latter, e.g. in the number of times in beating the drums (*pancha shabda naubat*). The Khān blatantly refused to take orders from or cooperate with his chief. Enjoying a musical entertainment, he declined to attend an urgent military consultation after some reverse in the Agiāthuti-Sarāi sector (*c.*April 1669). More serious than refractoriness was his unreliability. He was found to be in secret correspondence, implying some collusion with the Āhoms, who were at least believed to have a friend in him. So at last Rām

Singh expelled him from the Mughal camp after having cut his tent-ropes.[45] The affair shows that, unlike Mir Jumla who had able and loyal lieutenants like Dilir Khan and Farhad Khān, Rām Singh had none.

Such a situation arising from indiscipline was unthinkable in the Āhom army, which fought as one man like a monolithic pillar. Rām Singh's encomium truly represented the situation in the Āhom army: 'One single individual leads all the forces' (*eke ādmiye sakālo send chalaite pare*).[46] The army dispositions were made on a regional basis for greater control but there was unified command. Discipline was rigorously enforced almost with spartan severity and none could go against the general. Any remission in performance of one one's duty was made a capital offence, which could be awarded by him without waiting for the king's sanction on account of the emergency. The decapitation of his own uncle, found negligent in constructing a fort, on the principle that 'my uncle is not greater than my country', bred a high sense of value in performing one's duty.

About the working of the Mughal espionage system in Assam, we hardly get anything from Persian sources. But some incidental details gleaned from Assamese sources would imply that it was poor and not very efficient in practice. Rām Singh, of course, tried to collect information about the Āhom army from his own envoys as well as theirs. In the battle of Sarāighāṭ, the negligence of Mughal espionage was displayed when Sharif Khan, enjoying his tobacco pipe on his ship with his back against the enemy, was shot dead near Āndhārubāli. The general system of security in the Mughal camp was so bad that the Assamese guerrilla could purloin bags of money, weapons, and even the silver hookahs which the nobles were smoking before sleep.

On the other hand, the Assamese espionage was efficient. Their spies followed Rām Singh's army right from Delhi. His departure from Dacca was also duly reported by spies to the Āhom general, Lāchit. The repeated visits of Assamese envoys to the Mughal camp during peace negotiations were utilized by them for the collection of vital military information which was passed to their superiors. Rashid Khān's friction with his general was reported by Nim to the Barphukan. Even travellers were used for this purpose. Thus

Hangal-bhanga Laskar, living in Rām Singh's camp, on his way to Gauhāti was made to disclose Rām Singh's demoralization to the Barphukan.[47]

The imperial offensive could not counter the defensive strategy of the Āhoms for a protracted warfare. The Mughals were strong on land on account of their cavalry and the Assamese on water with their navy. Hence, the struggle was really comparable to that between an elephant and tortoise (*gaja–kachchap*) or between a tiger and the crocodile. The Assamese displayed extraordinary foresight and conceived of every eventuality from before. So they were satisfied with not only gearing their war machine to immediate needs of defence by procuring soldiers, sailors, and materials like boats, arms, and provisions, but also in having surplus stores of these for prolonged resistance. Strong in naval power but shy of cavalry, equating one Mughal horseman with 10 *paik*s of their own, the Assamese found their salvation in avoiding open encounter with the Mughals. Hence, their strategy was to allow the invaders easy passage from the frontier and lure them to the environs of Gauhāti, which was made impenetrable with strong fortifications on both banks of the Brahmaputra. Here their superior navy would smash the Mughal army, depending on the fleet. Thus, unlike the days of Mir Jumla, the Assamese policy of strategic retreat was now based on a clear grasp of the realities of the situation. Their dilatoriness was measure not of weakness but of strength. It was the only way to perfect their own preparations and wear out the invaders. Their guerrilla tactics and night attacks were so harassing that Rām Singh condemned them as tricks of 'thieves'. The morale of the invaders was further destroyed by a clever use of propaganda. Thus, the failure of Rām Singh was a foregone conclusion.

* Editor's Note: Unlike in the original version, the endnotes in this reprint have been arranged chronologically.

Notes

1. Before the departure of 21 Rajab, 1077/27 December 1667, the emperor presented the rājā with a *khil'at*, a horse with gold trappings and a jewelled dagger with a pearl belt. A.N. 1068–9; M.A. 65; Tr. 43: AB 204 (warships) BKK, ii, pp. 38–9. The date of Rām Singh's arrival at Rāngāmāṭi is given 'in *Lākni Kāmut* month Dinshi'. This gives the year

1590–91 Saka. (AB p. 203). G. C. Barua is correct in equating the month with Falgun (February–March) but wrong in equating the year with 1670.

2. Reactions: Auragzeb's *farmān*, written by Jafar Khān Wāzir *San-i-julus* 12, Rajasthan Archives, Bikaner, New No. 110. AB 204 (devastated 'Shupha' territory). Advance: PAB, 140, 1977, pp. 108–9 (Chaitra, 1593 Saka, March–April 1672, evidently wrong); BKK, ii, p. 40. *Manasabdar*s at Rangāmāṭi: Nāsir Khān, Rājā Jai Singh, Rājā Śib Singh, Tāj Khān and others. AB 205 (Baisākh). *Baruāmukh*: evidently Barbarooāmukh will, in *mauza Rāmdiāh*, approximately 3 or 4 miles north-west of Hājo. Chengā, about 9 miles east of Barpetā. *Taperā*, evidently Tapabāri village in *mauza* Rāmdiāh, west of Hājo, (see *Lāchit* 54; Bhattacharya 369).
3. Rājput war hounds, MS. AB No. 12; *Lāchit*, 44–5; Aran, 68. Āhom 'strategic retreat' in BKK, ii, p. 39; AB 203. *Āhom* disposition: Learning of the arrival of the Mughals from the report of Bairagi Jayanti, the Āhom rājā deputed three Dangarias, Phukan, Rajkhowas and others to face the invader—Burhagohain at Sarāi, Har Gohāin at Pāṇdu, Bagchowāl Barpātra Gohāin at Kuruā, Kaliābariā Phukan at Asurār Ail (PAB, 1977, pp. 107–8).
4. Āhom strategy: (a) Lāchit's severity, Sarbeswar Barua, *Lāchit Barphukan in Jivanī-Saṅgraha*, I, p. 92; Kirtinath Bardoloi, Sandipika (extract from an old Buranji) 1933, p. 155, quoted in Bhuyan, *Ātan*, 67–68; *Lāchit*, 37; MS AB. No. 12; PAB 148; AB 205 (*mānuikatāgarh*).
5. Fortifications: U. C. Lekharu, List of military outposts and fortifications of Assam, compiled about 1681 (fragmentary); Āvāhan, ii, pp. 248–50, 441–50; postings in different parts of Gauhāti, SMAB, pp. 93–4; MS. AB. No. 5, p. 12; details of equipment of each soldier, AB 205f; Lila Gogoi, *Saraighater Yuddhar Kata*, pp. 2–3; Bhuyan, *Lāchit*, pp. 37–47, *Pāli*s, *Chor-bacha*s and commands on both banks; *Ātan*, pp. 64–5; Ramesh Ch. Barkakati, 'Sarāighāṭer Yuddher Yuja', *Assam Sahitya Sabha Patrika*, 1965, pp. 18–9; Benudhar Sharma, p. 37.
6. Exchange of missions: KB, pp. 92–3 gives the date Faigun Śaka 1590 (March–April 1669); SMAB (old), p. 113; new; AB. 204. The *Buranji*s do not agree on certain detals. While most of them refer to two Assamese *Katasi*s (Batārgayān Sundar [Sondar] and Komorukhowa) to Rām Singh, the AB refers to three but names only one—Hundrar, i.e. Sundar. Again, Rām Singh sent Firuz Khān and Pāchipālāi from Kuragusi (?) according to AB. But from Jogiguphā according to KB. Possibly Pāchipālāi was the third Assamese emissary. Lāchit Barphukan told his messengers, 'There are four ways of political conduct—conciliation (*śam*), gifts *(dan)*, division (*bheda*), and rupture (*daṇḍa*), and the sancity of the different books on the subject has always been maintained. He alone is considered to be a knowing man if he realizes the circumstances of

a particular situation. SMAB (old), pp. 113; LXX, (new), p. 94; XI, vii (detailed); PAB, 1977, p. 108.

Some *Buranjis* like KB and SMAB state that Rām Singh urged that in case of non-compliance with his demands, the Barphukan, the son of the Barbarua, should 'fight for an hour' with him, the grandson of Rājā Māndhātā (i.e. Mān Singh) and even offered to supply any deficiency in provisions. It is not clear how such a duel would fulfil the objective of Aurangzeb's expedition. The Barphukan is reported to have continued that instead of fighting for an hour, the Assamese were prepared to fight to the last as God had been 'pleased to give them back to us'. As for provisions, it was for the Mughals, weary after their long journey, to be short of these; the Assamese king had enough and to spare.

7. I have found it difficult to agree with the sequence given in Bhattacharyya and Bhuyan at places. Gait is very brief and so not very helpful. Activities, AB, 208; BKK, ii, pp. 39–41; MS, AB nos 5, 12; SMAB (old), pp. 113–5, *Lxxi–Lxxii* (new), pp. 94–5, xivii; PAB (old), pp. 139–40, 1977, pp. 108–9 (two hour duel, p. 110; *Durbin*, p. 37; *Lāchit*, pp. 51–2, 54; Atan, pp. 70–1; Bhattacharyya, pp. 370–2).

The overall command of the Mughal *nawwara* was entrusted to Dai Sālāmkha (?) and Shekh Buhuni, according to BKK, ii, pp. 39–41. But the AB enables us to correct the second name as Shaikh Muhudi.

Additional details of activities in north bank are available from AB, pp. 204–6 (a) Rangmahal fort under the Barphukan, Sāringiā Phukan, and Silani Deka, reinforced by the Burhāgohāin; (b) *Akur Ali* besieged by Jainārāyan and another (Badsā Musalman Rājā?), defended by Barphukan and Āhataguriā Rājkhowā; and (c) Mughal besiegers of Sarāighāṭ included Anat (Anant?) Singh, Kehit Singh, Rshid Khā Sawlung (Rashid Khā, Kamike Hurarām(?) Kumakr Harirām or Harerām), Hari Kaji (Kārji ?) and (Rājā) Indradaman. Defence party included Makā, Sadrāi, Kāsi Bukruphan, the son of Lakāitam, Khutāi, Lakat, and six Hazārikās. *Sindurighopā*, nearly 8 miles east of Hājo and 5 miles west of Gauhāti *Koolihāti* or *Koolhāti* approximately 3 miles south-east of Hājo. *Akur* is evidently Augardi in *mauza* Uttar Bar Khestri, west of Hājo (*Lāchit*, pp. 55–7; Āran, pp. 71–2; Bhattacharya, p. 370 (loss of 2 Mughal ships); Gait, p. 156.

8. Activities in Dakhinkol: AB, pp. 206–7 (names of Āhom captains). Assam contingent opposing Mughal cavaliers included Luthuri, Lādām, son of Khuntai, Mandām, Lāsām Chaodang Baruā (of *mungkangiā* Āhom clan), the Kongar Bars, Hu Garn of Lāhbakāi family, and Lātum Saika of Lukkhakhuan family. Ibid. Luthāri Chetiā Rājkhowā was assisted by Dolākāshariyā Baruā, Tekelā, Chowdāng, and Luthāri Rājkhowā. Luthāri, probably Lataria in *mauza* Choomoreeā, Kāmrūp district Phrenbār, probably Paerengā in *mauze* Nij Boko, south of Choomoreeā. See *Lāchit*, p. 45; Bhattacharya, pp. 369–70.

9. Devakinandan's mission, in SMAB, op. cit.; *Satsari*, pp. iii, 96–7. The greedy Rāmacharan who took a gift of two flying wooden birds from Rām Singh was punished, SMAB, op. cit.; PAB, op. cit. Lachit, pp. 47–50, p. 55; Atan, pp. 69–70; Bhattacharya, p. 368, Gait (2nd edn), p. 155; Lila Gogoi, *Sarāighāṭer, Yuddhar, Kathā*, p. 16.
10. BKK, ii, pp. 41–2; AMAB (old), p. 116; (new), pp. 96–7; PAB, pp. 142–3; 1977, p. 110; MS, AB, nos 5 and 14; Satsari, p. 98; Sadr Amin, p. 49; *Durbin*, pp. 44–5: MS, Chr, AB; Mughal withdrawals, p. 207; *Lāchit*, pp. 53–4; Ātan, pp. 71, 75; AB, p. 207 wrongly places Rangamahal in the south.
11. A *farmān* dated 10 Rabi ul awwal, 12 Julus (AH 1079), i.e. 3 August 1669. This date given in the Handbook of the Rajasthan State Archives, Bikaner, (new) No. 111 is confusing.
12. *Lāchit* slew his own maternal uncle for negligence in constructing the Āgiāthuti Gauhāti Rāmpart. It was then speeded up in record time for action, to the surprise of the Mughals.
13. AB, pp. 207–8; BKK, ii, p. 44. Banpika is probably Banpara in Barkshetri *mauza*, west of Hājo.
14. AB, pp. 209–11, gives names of Āhom contingents; Bhattacharya, p. 373. Bhuyan gives the entire credit to Dihingiā Phukan for the victory for the joint land and water attack near the Bessa river. But he has not given any authority. The BKK gives a different story, as given in the text.
    Elamung is perhaps to be identified with Langa villa in Barbangsar *mauza*, nearly 5 miles north of Gauhāti. *Banpinka* is perhaps Banpara in Barkshetri *mauzā*, west Hājo.
15. MS, AB, No. 12; BKK, ii, pp. 41, 44–5; AB, p. 205 (near Akur Ali); PAB, pp. 142–3; SMAB, p. 96, *Lāchit*, p. 55.
16. Guerrilla tactics, MS. AB. No. 12; *Lāchit*, pp. 56–8, pp. 62–3 (names of Ātan's commandos); Ātan, pp. 71–2; Storia, ii, p. 7 (*bhang* in powder) *Dhatura*, a stronger substitute for hemp *Lāchit*, p. 63; Ātan, p. 73.
    Autumn activities: PAB (old), pp. 142–3; 1977, iii; SMAB (new), p. 96; Bhattacharyya, pp. 372–3.
17. Duel, AB, pp. 208–9; BKK, ii, pp. 45–6; Gait, p. 156 (very brief); Rām Singh's letter, sent throough Hunbar (Sonbar) Nadial, runs thus: 'I wish that we both the kings, should fight with each other. . . in presence of our armies. I am the son of Jay Singh and a descendant of Māndhātā. I am Rājā Rām Singh. . . I have kept every thing ready for the context.'
18. Āhom reactions to Mughal proposals, details in AB, pp. 211–2; BKK, ii, pp. 48–9 (threat).
    Allegations against Barphukan, KB, p. 94 (*Durbachan*). Details in *Lāchit*, pp. 63–4, based on MS, AB, Nos 12 and 15. Bhuyan has collected (op. cit., pp. 58–62) instances of Rām Singh's over credulousness to propagandist stories of Āhom invincibility, sedulously circulated before him by different Āhom envoys of Rani (Rām ?) Kātāki, Kaliā Kataki,

Bhakatdāh Dhuli, and Churāmani *daibanga* (astrologer). These were checked by his own envoy Panditrāi's remarks. The sequence of Mughal peace mission and the names of the Mughal envoys and messengers and those of the return Āhom counter parts are differently given in different *Buranjis*. Even in the same *Buranji* this is not very clear. Their identification has become, therefore, difficult.

19. Battle of Alaboi, SMAB, p. 97 and introduction p.i. (similitude of hornet). MS, AB, Nos 5, 14, 15, 12; PAB, p. 149, KB, p. 94 (date), Rām Singhar Yuddhar Kathā (MS, p. 334, DHAS) in Gogoi, p. 468, SMJC, pp. 116–7. Curiously enough, neither the BKK nor the AB makes any reference to this battle by name. Mir Nawab was captured by Luthuri Rājkhow. The latter had misguided Dilir Khan in the storming of Simlāgarh and later was taken by Mir Jumla as a captive. It was at the intercession of Mir Nawab that he was released. But now he refused to help the Mir for fear of his own family (MS, AB, No. 12, MU, Tr. I, p. 500.

Ātan Burhāgohāin consoled the Barphukan by inspiring words. '. . . such a reverse should never shake your confidence in our ultimate victory. Eventualities of this character are normal in a protracted warfare. When you agitate the waters of a pond for catching large fishes the fish-catchers will be pricked by the thorny scales of the smaller fries. You should judge your success by the number of large catches' (*Lāchit*, pp. 63–70, Ātan, pp. 73–4 quoting MS, AB, Nos 5 and 15).

20. *Farmān* written by Ja'far Khan Wazir dated 24 Shawwal, 13 Julus (i.e. AH 1080), see Descr. *List of Farmans*, etc., p. 19. No. 112, Rajasthan State Archives. The *farmān* exhibits Auragzeb's spirit of vendetta against Assam. According to *Maasir-i-Alamgiri*, Text 97, Tr. 61, the order was passed 'on condition of servicing in Assam' on 13 February 1670. The difference in date appears striking. Probably it took some time to issue the *farmān*.

Bhattacharyya's surmise that Rām Singh advanced early in March 1670 seems to be wrong. It must have happened in April or May. Bhuyan's date, March 1669, for the rājā's promotion on occasion of the emperor's birthday (*Lāchit*, p. 51) is also wrong. Aurangzeb's 54th lunar birthday fell on 15 Zilq, AH 1080 or 27 March 1670 (MA), p. 98, Tr. 61.

21. For prolonged peace negotiations, the two Āhom *Buranji*s virtually agree, BKK, ii, pp. 49–51; AB, pp. 211–2. But their accounts differ in some respects with other Assam *Buranji*s, PAB, pp. 144–6, 1977, 111*f*; SMAB, pp. 97–100; KB, pp. 94–6, *Sātsari*, iii, pp. 95–6; *Lāchit*, pp. 70–2, Ātan, p. 745; Bhattacharyya, pp. 374–5. As previously, the sequence of missions and names of the envoys differ. The Mughal general sent two envoys—Panditrai and Kavisekhar (Paritrāi of Parkshitrāi and Hamikar or Samikar of BKK and AB)—to the Barphukan, requesting him to send a *bhālo mānuha* (good man), i.e. a duly accredited envoy. The latter sent a return mission under Dikhumukhiā Rāmcharan and Kaupatiā

Mādhavacharan (or Pāchipalāi of BKK and AB) and insisted that any proposal for peace must be preceded by the despatch of 'a responsible man with definite proposals' (AB, p. 212,) a good man of theirs as hostage to us' (BKK, ii, p. 50). The four envoys discussed the matter and agreed that both sides were anxious for peace. Agreeing with the Barphukan's view, Rām Singh deputed Ahianda Misir (?) (name only in BKK, and AB), along with the Āhom envoys to convey his proposals to the Barphukan. The latter sent his reply as a royal servant through Mādhavacharan, while the Panditrai conveyed the rājā's renewed demand.

22. Rām Singh's epistolary diplomacy and ruses, to create rift and diplomatic bribery, etc. SMAB, pp. 98–9, PAB, 1977, p. 112; *Sārsari*, iii, pp. 97–8 (*Bhedapatra*), *Lāchit*, pp. 63–5; *Ātan*, p. 73; Bhattacharya, p. 272.
23. Bhuyan says that 'the exact reason for this decision of the Assamese commanders is not known' (*Lāchit*, p. 76); perhaps the prevailing discontent in the country appeared to them to be a sufficiently strong reason.
24. Udāyaditya is reported in the two Āhom *Buranji*s to have significantly observed, 'My brother and I wished the Musalmans to send good katakis, to settle the boundary of our country but no action had proceeded' (AB, p. 213; BKK, ii, 51). It is true that there was a stalemate. But the previous role of the new king is not referred to in any source.

    The two Āhom envoys, Kaupatia Kazarika and Madhavacharan, sailed on 20 ships for talks. Ibid.
25. 'If I demand more than this,' swore Rām Singh, 'this sword in my hand which is like Parameswari or the Supreme Goodess will cause my annihilation; and this pearl-chain on my neck—a veritable Maha Lakshmi—will desert me for good, and my fourteen generations will go to hell. If my words are not believed let us proceed to the temple of Mādhab on the bank of the Lauhitya where I am prepared to solemnly affirm my oaths. If my brother the Barphukan agrees to this proposals he shall be given whatever he shall desire.' (Message sent through Nim and Rāmcharan without letter or envoy. MS, AB, Nos 5, 14 and 15 quoted in *Lāchit*, pp. 75–6; SMAB, p. 100; PAB, 1977, pp. 113–4. Both AB, p. 213 and BKK, ii, pp. 52–3 (another version of Rām Singh's talks) write only two Mughal envoys including Paritrai (Parikshit Rai) and another man, coming on 12 ships for parleys. KB, p. 4 refers to Mir and Rāmhari Kārji' SMAB (old), p. 119; (new), p. 100 to three, adding Panditrai. Details of letters dated Saka 1591 (1669–70) without dates between Mughal and Āhom generals; KB, pp. 94–6.
26. The Assamese *kataki*s who conveyed Barphukan's message were Rangāchila and Rāmcharan. BKK, ii, pp. 52–3; AB, pp. 213–4; KB, pp. 96–7; MS, AB, p. 14; *Lāchit*, pp. 76–7; Ātan, p. 76. It is very strange that Rām Singh expressed his desire 'to have some *dābtaroāls* (a kind of sword)' now to the *kataki*s. Lāchit Barphukan's reply to the Mughal

general and the Barhā Gohāin's arguments on the question of evacuation of Gauhāti clearly emphasize one point of contemporary diplomacy—that no agreement of a local general without prior consent or sanction of the government concerned would be effective. 'It is through the pleasure of the Swarga—Mahārājā of "Udayagiri", i.e. of the East and the Padishah of "Astagir", i.e. the West the Gauhāti can be given by me and Bengal by you. Their friendship will subsist as long as there remain the moon and the sun. Why should the masters respect the independent stipulations of their subordinate?' The Burā Gohāin asked pertinently: 'If we now abandon Gauhāti, why did we not do so before? And why did we fight at the cost of much war provisions? Rām Singh seeks the frontier by making solemen promises. Even if we honour these will Padishah do so? Where will we go if he does not ratify these? Where, again, will we stay if we abandon Gauhāti with its fortifications?' SMAB, (old) p. 120; lxxiv; (new) pp. 99–100; AB, p. 214.

27. *Farmān* written on 12 Rabi ul awwal, 13 Julus (i.e. AD 1080/20 July 1670. Desc. List Rajasthan Archives no. 113 is wrong in equating 13 Julus with 1081. It should AD 1080.
28. It was not Rashid Khān who brought Aurangzeb's caustic message of censure as stated by S. K. Bhuyan but Manoharkhā or Khān (respectively of BKK, ii, p. 54 and AB, p. 215); SMAB, (old), p. 121; (new), p. 100. Several *Buranjis* refer to Aurangzeb's asking Rām Singh's son to wrestle with two tigers within an enclosure and the latter's success in killing them; to the emperor's attempt to convert him and to the appeals of the rājā's mother and wife. KB, p. 94, names of five sardars (Mahābat Khān, Phārarāi Khān (?) Jainārāyaṇ, Prānnārāyaṇ and Chandranārāyaṇ) in AB, p. 215; SMAB (old), p. 121; (new), pp. 100–1; PAB, 147(1977), p. 114; MS, AB, No. 7 in *Lāchit*, pp. 77–8; Ātan, pp. 76–7.

    The entry of the Mughals into Darrange was regarded as a *casus belli* by the king (AB, p. 214; BKK, ii, p. 54).

    Kāmden is probably Kandalpala in Saru Bangar *mauzā*, south of Hājo. Sitamari (Sitāmani in BKK, ii, p. 54 and Bhattacharya) is Sheetomahru nearly 34 miles north-east of Gauhāti on the left bank of the Brahmputa, district Nowgong (Bhattacharya, p. 375; Gait, 157).
29. PAB, p. 148, 1977, p. 114 Āhom dispositions; KB, p. 93; AB, pp. 214–5, SMJC. 122. Aswakrāntā temple is located on a rock on the north bank of the Brahmaputra opposite of Gauhāti. Juria hills, probably the hills to the west of modern Gauhāti (Bhattacharyya, p. 375). Rām Singh had learnt of this venue for attacking Gauhāti from his envoy Panditrāi. The sandbank (Ānhārubāli) stretched north of the present strand road of Gauhāti running parallel to it. The rāmpart on the bank existed up to the eighteenth century, after which it was eroded (*Lāchit*, p. 73; Ātan, p. 75).
30. Battle of Sarāighāṭ (PAB, pp. 147–50; 1977, pp. 114–6; SMAB, pp. 101–

3; AB, pp. 215–7; BKK, ii, pp. 54–7; *Deodhāi*, AB, xix, p. 168. (Lāchit's inspiring exclamation and dependence on astrological forecasts, MS, Chr; SMJC, pp. 122–3; SKDAB, p. 31 (date different by two days); *Sarāighāter Yuddhar Kathā*, pp. 25–6, *Durbin*, pp. 47–51; *Lāchit*, pp. 73–4, pp. 78–87; *Ātan*, pp. 75–6, pp. 77–8; Bhattacharya, pp. 376–7, Gait.

31. For Aśwakrāntā, see M. Neog, *Pavitra Assam*, pp. 232–3. *Barhila* is probably Barhata in *mauzā* Patidarrang, north of Śrīghāṭ. *Pachariā* is located in *mauzā* Saru Bansar, south of Hājo. River Chechanai or the River Seinsa in district Nowgong. It is marked River Chencha in Robinson's map. River Kapili meets River Kalang near *thānāh* Jāgi, district Nowgong, nearly 18 miles due south of Sheotāmhree and 30 miles due east of Gauhāti. River Harān or Hari of River Nanal meets the Kalāng at Rahā, about 29 miles south-east of Sheelomaree and 16 miles north-east of Jāgi.
32. The *exact* date of the death of this patriot is not known. SMAB, p. 103; SKDAB, p. 32, dates it during the Dafla War. Comparison with Trafalgar (*Lāchit*, p. 87).
33. AB, pp. 217-8; BKK, ii, pp. 57–8. These *Buranjis* attribute the comparative lull to fear of the Mughals at Rām Singh's defeat. But the true reason was Aurangzeb's preoccupation in the north-west and the Deccan. Gait thinks that 'possibly' these wrongly refer to Chandra N. instead of Surya N. (1570).

    It is, however, difficult to agree with S. K. Chatterjee, *Place of Assam in History and Civilization of India*, pp. 46–7, that as a result of Sarāighāṭ, the Mughals gave up the idea of spreading (from Assam) to Burma, Tibet, and China. Mir Jumla had similar ambitions, no doubt, but it is not known whether Aurangzeb had too.
34. Sarkar, *Aurangzeb*, iii (Rām), (Afghan rising), iv (Shivaji); Ātan, p. 79; Bhattacharya, pp. 380–1 (treatment towards Rām Singh); *Lāchit*, pp. 118; *Annals* of *Delhi Badshahate*, p. 164 (for Ghazar Beg).
35. *Farmān*, 16 Zilhija, 1086, 21 February 1676, No. 115; *Memorandum*, Jaipur archives; *Lāchit*, App. II, MU, pp. 301–3; *Storia*, ii; JSAB, 1872, p. 154. Seven Assamese gentlemen, accompanied Rām Singh—(a) uncle of Gokul Chānd Barua of Kāmrūp; (b) Jayānanda Qānungo; (c) Kāmeshwār Choudhary of Baushi; (d) & (e) Kehirām Patowāry of Khetri and his brother; (f) Kandarpeswar Choudhary, and (g) Kailyān (? Kalyān).
36. To the imperial message: *'Taka moi Āsāmar juddhaloi patha lon, Āsām sahit prīti karibaloi pathowī nāi,'* Rām Singh replied, *'Juddha kari chālon, Juddhata nawāri; bandug, yāthi, barchhir, juddhao prayojan nai; moidan nahai uttare dakshine behugarh karile kintū pāniye eti juddha āehhe' SMAB*, para 237, tr. in *Lāchit*, pp. 157–8.

37. MS, AB, No. 12; *Lāchit*, p. 47.
38. MA, p. 65, tr. 43, *Storia*, ii, p. 153; *Padshah B*, paras, 116–20.
39. Aurangzeb is reported to have observed, while deputing Rām Singh '*Āsāmar yuddhalai gale kono nawab phiri nāhe. Kata bā banata mare, Kato āpuni mare, Si thair bis pāni, bis bātās boi. Sankat jāgā parbati garh*' (No nawab return from war in Assam. Many die in the forests, many die as matter of course. At the place the water is poisonous, air, too, is foul. The hill forts are full of peril). PAB, 1977, p. 107.
40. E. G. 'I, Rām Singh, grandson of Rājā Māndhātā, have taken the field in person.' Even I, Rām Singh, present on the spot, could not detect any flaw' (SMAB, pp. 94, 102, *Lāchit*, p. 48).
41. PAB, 1977, p. 116; SMAB, p. 100; *Lāchit*, p. 157.
42. A late *Buranji* of the eighteenth century puts the following eulogium of the Āhom generals in the month (probably mouth; editor's intervention) of the envoy of Rām Singh in reply to the latter's query. Panditrāi told the rājā, 'The Barpātra Gohāin, Burāohāin and the Barphukan have all impressed me as wonderfully capable commanders presenting a rare combination of beauty, accomplishment, valour and wisdom. As to the Burāohāin he is young in year, fair and handsome in features, sober and deep in intelligence, dextraous in all matters, and he rivals all others in the soundness of his counsel.' Rām Singh commented, 'It is really wonderful that a man can be so intelligent at this tender age.' The envoy remarked, 'The Burāohāin is also an arch diplomat.' Rām Singh asked in surprise, 'Who will be able to cope with such a minister when he comes to years? Pride should be the heritage of that land where such a counsellor has taken his birth' (MS, Assam *Buranji*, No. 15, from Suhungmung Dihingia Rājā to king Prāmatta Singh, 1497–1751, now in DHAS (see Bhuyan, *Lāchit*, p. 61). More passages of similar content may be found in other *Buranjis*.
43. H. C. Goswami, *Sarāighāṭer Yuddha Usha*, i, p. 239, quoted in *Lāchit*, p. 83.
44. MS, AB, No. 15 in ibid.
45. PAB, 1977, p. 110; SMAB, p. 96; MS, AB, No. 5 in *Ātan*, p. 70. Gait finds a fault with rājā for 'quarrelling' with Rashid Khān.
46. SMAB, p. 102.
47. PAB, 1977, p. 109; SMAB (old), pp. 112–4, MS, AB, No. 5; *Lāchit*, pp. 50–4.

CHAPTER 7

Guerrilla Warfare in Medieval India

Jagadish Narayan Sarkar

Guerrilla warfare differs from conventional or regular warfare in almost everything—conception, organization, armament, equipment, supply, strategy, tactics, leadership and command. The concept of modern communist revolutionary guerrilla warfare of the Chinese or Cuban stamp may be new. But orthodox guerrilla or irregular warfare is neither a communist invention nor a revolutionary movement nor yet a development of the present century. It has a long history. For centuries light, irregular troops, separate from but supporting the regular army in defence of the homeland, known as guerrilla fighters or partisans, have fought against and harassed invaders and oppressors in widely separate countries in Asia, Europe, America and Africa. It was used against the Romans in Britain; against Britain during the American Revolution (under Francis Marion); against France in Spain and Portugal during the Peninsular War; and in Russia during the Napoleonic War; by China against Britain in 1841–2 (Opium War) and 1850–64 (Taiping War); by the Boers in South Africa; by the Russians during 1918–20; by the Arabs against the Turks during World War I in the Middle East; by Abyssinia against Italy in 1935–6; by European countries occupied by the Germans; by Far Eastern countries occupied by the Japanese during World War II; by the Burmese; and in Vietnam, Algeria, Cyprus, Cuba, and East Pakistan (Bangladesh) in the present century. The term 'guerrilla war' means 'small war' and is derived from Spanish 'partides' or partisans. In international law, 'Guerrilla warfare consists in hostilities conducted in territory occupied by the enemy, by armed bodies of men who do not form part of an organized army. As they lack the force necessary to meet the enemy in open battle their operations are to a large extent clandestine and sporadic. They are usually composed of the remnants of the defeated army and of inhabitants who organise themselves for the purpose of harassing the enemy and destroying his communications' (Oppenheim). Partisan war is a weapon of a militarily weak nation against a powerful aggressor. Often branded as primitive, guerrilla war may, in fact, prove to be more sophisticated than orthodox war.[1] A distinction is sometimes drawn between guerrilla war and guerrilla type of warfare. Tribal war and steppe war belong to the second category. During tribal wars in early Islam the ordinary method of fighting was the raid—a sudden charge followed by prompt retreat and sudden return (*Karr u farr*, lit. return and fight).[2] Again, the mobile and frugal nomads of the Eurasian steppes, skilled in steppe warfare (*alat-i-jang-i-biyaban*) and mounted archery avoiding pitched battles and indulging in 'hit and run' tactics, always put the professional armies of civilized and settled powers like the Ghaznavids at a disadvantage, because the latter were unable to use their better tactical knowledge and fire power.[3]

The fundamental principle of guerrilla warfare is to preserve oneself and destroy the enemy. The basic maxims of guerrilla warfare were best formulated by Mao-tse Tung and these reveal the deep influence of Sun Tzu. These are six in number, namely:

1. using initiative, flexibility (by dispersal, concentration and shifting of position) and planning (in conducting offensives within defensive, battles of quick decision within protracted war, and exterior line operations within interior line operations);
2. coordination with regular warfare, in strategy, campaigns and battles;
3. establishment of base areas or strategic bases, in mountains, on plain and river–lake–estuary regions, though guerrilla warfare behind enemy lines is fought without a rear. Places occupied alternately by the enemy and the guerrillas are guerrilla zones which are transformed into base areas. This depends on certain conditions: (a) guerrilla leaders to build up an armed force in three stages—guerrilla units, guerrilla

formations and regulars; (b) the armed forces are to be used in coordination with the army; (c) the masses are to be aroused and armed; (d) the area must be extensive, mountainous areas being most suitable for base areas; and (e) money and grain are to be supplied to the guerrillas.

The base areas have not only to be extended to shake enemy morale by confining them to a few strongholds and cities and along the main lines of communication, they have also to be consolidated by organizing the people and training the units for protracted warfare. Expansion and consolidation should go together and be used alternately according to time and circumstances. The enemy and the guerrillas encircle one another respectively. The former encircles the latter in two ways: (a) by assuming strategic offensive operating on exterior lines while the guerrillas are on the defensive operating on interior lines; and (b) by surrounding each guerrilla base area in his rear. On the other hand, the guerrillas also encircle each advancing enemy column by taking the offensive in exterior line operations. All guerrilla base areas in the enemy's rear play very important strategic role in their efforts to 'dominate the spaces'.

4. strategic defensive and strategic offensive (i.e. counter-offensive) by the guerrillas within the nationwide war. The enemy attacks the guerrilla base areas and then seeks to consolidate the occupied areas and wipe out the guerrillas. The latter should smash the successive advancing enemy columns while the main force launches repeated surprise attacks, especially in ambushes and encircles the enemy occupied places. The enemy burns towns and villages as it retreats. But this deprives him of food and shelter in the next offensive. The guerrillas without relaxing, should destroy enemy communications and support the regulars, be vigilant and turn, if necessary, to strategic defensive (this happened in Bijapur and Assam);
5. development of guerrilla warfare into mobile warfare, in a protracted war. Guerrilla units should be gradually transformed into regular forces by increasing the numbers and improving the quality in organization, arms, techniques and tactics;

6. correct relationship of command. This means centralized strategic command (i.e. state planning and directions and coordination with regular war) and decentralized command in details, i.e. campaigns and battles. The higher levels must neither be negligent nor monopolise power; the lower levels must neither usurp authority nor lack initiative. Within unified strategy, guerrilla warfare is to be carried on independently in dispersed operations.[4]

In medieval India, some of the basic principles of irregular, partisan or guerrilla warfare were known, though in an inchoate form, and as resistance movement, not as revolutionary movement. The *Sukranitisara* lays down: 'One should subjugate the enemy through protracted processes by which provisions were cut short, food and fuel are diminished and the subjects are oppressed.'[5] The word *Qazaqi* (from *Qazaq*, a Cossack, a partisan, light-armed soldier, highway robber) means guerrilla warfare, free-booting or brigandage. It was used in the sense of a loose attack, followed by retreat,[6] The Rajputs, the Ahoms, the Marathas, the Sikhs and the Deccanis, who were comparatively weak and ill-equipped militarily, adopted this form of warfare against the Mughals. Their tactics and principles were similar in some ways to those of the modern guerrillas, though the latter are undoubtedly more ramified and developed than the former, and the ideological content of the latter was lacking in the former.

The medieval Indian guerrillas, like their modern counterparts, turned the conditions of terrain and climate and their own society against the enemy in order to obstruct him, but they themselves were not deterred by terrain or weather. Rugged or forest country was most favourable for security and surprise, notwithstanding some difficulties in getting supplies and reaching targets. The geographical and social features in Rajputana, Assam, Maharashtra, the Punjab, Ahmadnagar and Bijapur favoured this sort of warfare. The medieval Indian guerrillas used initiative and flexibility by dispersal, concentration and shifting of position.

After the battle of Haldighat, Pratap Singh, numerically inferior to the Mughals, resorted to guerrilla warfare which suited the country and the Bhils admirably. During their war in the time of Aurangzeb the Rajputs, unable to resist the Mughal artillery, manned by European gunners and 'hopelessly outclassed' on the plains, abandoned the low country and retired to the hills.[7] During the rainy season in Assam, comparable to the Russian winter, when 'streams took the ways of oceans and *nala*s looked like rivers', the Mughal horse, the terror of the Ahoms, was paralysed in the flooded or muddy ground. The Ahoms were then emboldened to indulge freely in their harassing tactics against Mir Jumla's army.'[8]

Geography, race and circumstances made the Marathas adept in enveloping and harassing tactics. Orme writes about them as follows: 'The strength of their armies consists in their numerous cavalry, which is more capable of resisting the fatigue than any in India: large bodies of them having been known to march fifty miles in a day. They avoid general engagements and seem to have no other ideas in making war, but that of doing as much mischief as possible to the enemy's country. . . . The rapidity of their motions leaves the prince, with whom they wage war, little chance of striking a decisive blow against them or even of attacking with effect any of their detachments. . . .' Powerless against walled and provisioned cities and artillery guarded camps, they used to cut off supplies but avoided a pitched battle (as was the Rajput practice). Their light cavalry 'more numerous than ants and locusts', acted as predatory horses (*ghanimi fauj*), like the light forayers of Scotland. Their efficiency depended on their mobility, speed, secrecy in movement and ability in quick dispersal and combination, avoiding pursuit (e.g. Shivaji's tactics at Dindori, 1670). Towards the end of the seventeenth century (*c.*1690) they encamped in obscure and inaccessible places during the rainy months. Their bands did not hold together throughout the year, but dispersed to their homes at the close of the campaigning season of six months (October to April). Fortifying out of the way places, they remained encamped in the shelter of woods and cut off Mughal detachments.'[9]

During the fourth Abdali invasion (1736) the Sikhs, unable to meet the invader openly, undertook mass flights to hills, jungles or deep ravines which were inaccessible to the invaders.[10]

Complex mechanical devices or logistics are not essential for the success of the guerrillas. The problem of logistics is directly solved by the capture of enemy weapons, equipment and ammunition. They establish certain base areas or strategic bases in mountains, on plains and river–lake–estuary regions. But they fight behind enemy lines without a rear. Behind the enemy lines, guerrilla warfare 'cripples the enemy, pins him down, disrupts his supply lines, and inspires the regular forces and the people throughout the country'. Strategically, 'it reverses the normal process of fighting by avoiding battle. Tactically, it evades an engagement which is likely to be lost. But it must ever be dynamic. It is never static. The tactics of the guerrillas are distraction, surprise and mobility. Sudden, sharp, vicious and short are their attacks. The enemy is harassed and confused. Adept in the arts of simulation and dissimulation, the guerrillas' target is the mind of the enemy and the will of its leader rather than the bodies of its soldiers.' Thus do they retain their initiative and seek to carry out the first law of guerrilla war—to preserve oneself and destroy the enemy. Its distinctive principle is 'hit and run' (or better 'tip and run')—to distract, disturb and demoralize the enemy. 'Running away', to lure and trap the enemy, may in effect be offensive.[11]

Some of these characteristics are traceable in the activities of the medieval Indian guerrillas. When Emperor Aurangzeb retired to Ajmer (March 1680) the Rajputs in Marwar 'made raids, cut off supply trains and stragglers and made the Mughal outposts extremely unsafe', and created 'a terror of their prowess'. The Rathor bands spread over the country, appearing unexpectedly in different quarters and scoring a success wherever a Mughal outpost was weakly held, closing the trade routes, and keeping the land in perpetual turmoil. No great pitched battle was fought, but the Mughal general was distracted by the ever present alarm and the necessity of reinforcing threatened points in time; his divisional commanders were worn out by their ceaseless marches and counter marches in the vain attempt to clear the country of the elusive Rajput bands and keep the roads open for traffic. All parts of Marwar, Jhalor and Siwana in the south, Godwar in the east, Nagor in the extreme north, and Didwana and Sambhar in the north-east, were invaded by Ajit's partisans in turn, always by surprise, and sometimes oftener than once.[12]

Mirza Rajah Jai Singh's dispatches during the Bijapur campaign (1665–6) show that the Deccanis evaded the charges of the Mughal heavy cavalry but harassed them by their 'Cossack' or guerrilla tactics, forming four divisions and fighting loosely. The Bijapuris made sudden and harassing raids on the imperial dominions and dislocated the latter, without coming face to face in a decisive engagement.

When charged by the Mughals, the Bijapuris used to abandon their camps, disperse to different directions and take to their heels. In accordance with 'the usual practice of the Deccanis', they divided and sent a group to the right as well as to the left and other groups spread themselves on different sides. Thus, by fighting behind the enemy lines and virtual encirclement, they galled the imperialists severely from the two wings and the rear (27 December 1665). The next day, the Bijapuris came in two groups, one being in front and another behind. Subsequently, they even pressed Jai Singh hard and made an attack on his person.[13]

The Ahoms were also superb in guerrilla warfare. They would sally out of their forts only during night and make surprise attacks on the enemy, besiege them, if possible, and would retreat if repulsed. Never daring to face the Mughals under Mir Jumla (*c.*1661–3) in an open engagement, they took recourse to guerrilla tactics, organizing surprise raids and night attacks, hindering enemy supplies and killing any stray person searching forage or firewood. The Āhoms, avoiding a pitched battle, concealed themselves here and there, and, mustering from different sides, made night attacks on every *thana* and intercepted the transport of provisions by water from Lakhau to Garhgaon. By using 'blood drinking' arrows the Ahoms made movements of the Mughals, even between Mathurapur and Garhgaon, impossible without the protection of a troop of archers. Subsequently, emboldened by the failure of Farhad Khan's mission, the audacious Ahoms now completely closed all the roads. None could come out of his *thana*; no help could be sent to it from outside. So Mir Jumla withdrew all the *thanas*. The Ahoms launched successive night assaults on the capital, Garhgaon.[14]

The Sikhs also adopted guerrilla tactics. Banda did not face the imperialists in an open battle. After his death, the Sikhs continued to create disturbances, plunder caravans, and withdrew to the hills and impenetrable forests. The armies of Nadir and Abdali, laden with spoils, were plundered in the rear by the light cavalry bands of the Sikhs.[15]

About 1690 the Marathas avoided pitched battles, except when they had to relieve a fort, nor did they stay long within easy reach of the Mughal armies. Palkhed was a classic example of what the predatory horse, when led by a genius, could achieve in the age before light artillery. During the Palkhed campaign (1727–8), Baji Rao, then the ablest exponent of the light foray tactics of the Marathas, plundered the Nizam's both flanks, disrupted the arrival of provisions and attacked the Deccani army when crossing a ravine or stream. But he fled when fighting began and engaged in 'Cossack-like' tactics.[16]

As in the modern times, so in medieval India also, the basic secret of the progress of guerrillas, nimble as mosquitos, was ubiquity plus intangibility. In order to confuse the enemy, they substituted for the principle of concentration that of 'dispersion' or 'fluidity of forces', operating in minute particles so as not to present a target, yet coagulating like 'globules of quicksilver' to overwhelm weakly guarded objectives.[17] Speaking of Jai Singh I's campaign in the Bhima–Maujira region (February–June 1666), the author of the *Alamgirnamah* describes the Bijapuri guerrillas in the same way as Liddell Hart does above. 'As the elusive enemy could not be caught in one body, nor crushed once for all, but they scattered like quicksilver, and the imperialist who were encumbered with a camp and heavy baggage could not pursue them for any long distance.' This is also corroborated by Jai Singh's despatches. Under the leadership of short-sighted lliyas, well-known as Sharza and Siddi Masaud, Azjz and Dalil and others, the enemies invaded the imperial dominions and raised tumult; many of them took shelter in the fort of Bijapur. They did not make themselves prominent in any place. These methods practically paralysed the vast Mughal army. The Mughals now retreated to expel the Bijapuri raiding parties. Iliyas and his archers left the imperial territories and re-entered their own devastated *taluqs*.[18]

Again, guerrilla operations in medieval India were necessarily as decentralized as in modern times. Waged by a few, guerrilla war rests on the support of the many. The people support, care for, hide the guerrillas and spy for them. They act as their storehouse, repair shop and as 'voluntary eyes and ears'. The people must be won over to aid the guerrillas by giving them intelligence and supplies and denying them to the enemy. So organization, instruction, agitation and propaganda are not less important than fighting. According to Mao-tse Tung, guerrillas are to the people what fish is to the water. Thus do the guerrillas buttress the 'menacing and majestic power' of a people's war.[19]

The part played by the people to help the guerrillas in medieval India may be judged from the following instances: in the rainy season in Assam, the Ahom guerrillas incited the villagers who had already submitted to the Mughals as at Dewalgaon. An Ahom host 10–12,000 strong retreated from Deopani after the fall of its leader. The ryots, who, professing obedience to the Mughals, were living in the environs of Garhgaon, Mathurapur and Abhoypur, began to desert their villages. During Aurangzeb's Rajput war, the entire country of Marwar was invaded by the partisans of Ajit Singh in turn, always by surprise and often more than once.[20] The Sikh leader Banda must have had considerable local support in the plains. About the activities of the Sikhs in 1714, Khafi Khan writes thus: 'The violence (of the Sikhs) passed all bounds. The injuries and indignities they inflicted on Musulmans, and the destruction of mosques and tombs, were looked upon by them as righteous meritorious acts. They had built a fort at Gurdaspur in the Punjab, ten or twelve days' journey from Delhi, and extended its limits so that fifty or sixty thousand horse and foot could find protection. They strengthened the towers and walls of the place, took possession of all the cultivated land around, and ravaged the country from Lahore to Sihrind, otherwise called Sirhind. . . . The infidels on several occasions showed the greatest boldness and daring, and made nocturnal attacks upon the imperial forces.' A modern writer thus describes their tactics: 'Abdali failed to put down the Sikhs because they refused to meet him on his terms. They were everywhere and yet elusive. . . . Fighting the Sikhs was like trying to catch the wind in a net.' The Sikhs were able to resort to these tactics because the people were behind them.[21]

One characteristic of modern guerrilla warfare, as laid down by Mao-tse Tung, is coordination with regular warfare, in strategy (e.g. harassing the enemy's rear and hindering transport), tactics and battles (getting information, acting as outposts and sentinels).[22] Let us see how far this was manifested during the medieval period. During the Mughal invsion of Bijapur in 1665–6 there was regular fighting besides guerrilla warfare. When charged by the Mughal captains, the Bijapuris dispersed and the Mughals began their return march to the camp.[23]

The Maratha captains individually carried on a guerrilla warfare, causing the greatest loss and disturbance to the imperial territories. The Mughals did not know what point to defend, nor where to find a vital enemy position for attack. Countless bands of mobile Marathas covered vast distances and attacked the most unexpected quarters. Universal unrest prevailed throughout the Deccan. Besides the (regular) divisions under the three generals numbering 60,000–70,000 thousand cavalry and the king's own contingent of 10,000 there were roving bands of 15 to 20 thousand. They fought their way to Maharashtra, levying *chauth* from the imperial provinces, driving out the Mughal outposts, and strengthening their own forts and strategic points (*nake jaga*).[24]

One important aspect of modern guerrilla warfare is the relationship between strategic defensive and strategic offensive. The enemy adopts converging attacks to wipe out the guerrillas. How far was this exemplified in medieval India, if at all? During Jai Singh's invasion of Bijapur, 1665–6, while the Bijapuris followed their Cossack tactics, the Mughals had to be always prepared for a dual task, making aggression on the Bijapuris and at the same time being on the alert to resist their sudden swoops. A single army found it extremely difficult, if not impossible, to keep its eyes now ahead and now behind. As Jai Singh wrote to Aurangzeb: 'To me it is crystal-clear that two armies are necessary for the purpose of protecting imperial territories. . . . When we advance for punishing the enemies of the empire and conquering territories of the hypocrites, another force should be left on this side (i.e. behind). The objective of both the armies is really for the purpose of the advance. Although it is probable that at the time when the imperial dominions are denuded of the victorious army, being engaged in devastating their territories, the accursed enemies might not turn their attention towards this side; yet if they do so, both the armies, those who are advancing and those with me, would fall upon them. In the event of the enemy's not turning to this side, both the armies would, in unison, punish them adequately. If they divide themselves and raise tumult on two sides, these two armies of ours would adopt remedial measures against them.' Jai Singh is formulating here what may be described as principles of anti-guerrilla war, aiming at severing the guerrillas from their base and opposing the guerrilla with their own tactics.[25]

The development of guerrilla warfare into mobile warfare, which has been stressed by Mao-tse Tung, cannot be perfectly illustrated during medieval India. But some approach towards it is traceable in the activities of Santaji Ghorpare (d. 1697). Towards the end of the seventeenth century, he supplied 'the classic example of the early Maratha type of warfare.' Combining Parthian tactics with guerrilla warfare, he was a perfect master in making night marches and surprises, and also in covering wide distances quickly. With an inborn genius for handling large bodies of men, he combined their movements over wide areas with an incredible accuracy and punctuality, paralleled only by Chengiz Khan and Timur. He could promptly change his own tactics in the light of every change in the enemy's plans and condition, and organize combined movements without the risk of failure.[26]

Another feature of modern guerrilla war is correct command. As guerrillas act independently, command cannot be too highly centralized. But their activities must be coordinated. Hence, command is to be centralized for strategic purposes and decentralized for tactical purposes. Leadership must be imaginative, intelligent, bold and at the same time, unified. Here also, only some resemblance can be traced in Maharashtra. After the execution of Shambhuji, Rajaram instructed the Maratha chieftains to ravage the country. The latter 'hovered round the imperial armies and were exceedingly daring.' Prominent among them were Santaji Ghorpare and Dhanaji Yadava, both experienced warriors commanding about 15–20,000 cavalry. Their leadership was accepted by other Maratha chieftains and the Mughals suffered great losses. Santaji's tactics succeeded partly because of his incredibly mobile troops and partly because his subordinates carried out his orders punctually to the minute. Demanding implicit obedience from his officers, he enforced the strictest discipline in his army on pain of severe punishment. Santa was thus able to crush Qasim Khan in November 1695, at Dodderi.

'Santa, more especially, distinguished himself in ravaging the cultivated districts and in attacking the royal leaders. Everyone who encountered him was either killed, wounded or made prisoner; or if any one did escape, it was with his mere life, with the loss of his army and baggage. Nothing could be done, for wherever the accursed dog went and threatened an attack, there was no imperial *amir* bold enough to resist him, and every loss he inflicted on their forces made the boldest warriors quake.' Accompanying the Maratha army for plunder, and recruited from various parts of India irrespective of race, religion or caste, the Pendharis resembled the Cossacks in their customs and movements.[27]

These details would show that the medieval Indian guerrillas were aware at least of some of the principles of modern guerrilla warfare, though the necessary conceptualization might have been lacking. They used initiative, flexibility and planning. They made flexible use of troops by dispersal, concentration and shifting of position. Some degree of coordination with regular war and guerrilla encirclement of the enemy were also then present.

NOTES

1. The term means 'small war' and is derived from Spanish (*partides* or partisans). *Ency. British*, 1968, X, pp. 100–4; *The Guerrilla—And How to Find Him*, Selections from Marine Corps Gazette, ed. Lt. Col. T. N. Greene, 1962; Abdul Haris Nasution, *Fundamentals of Guerrilla Warfare* 1965, pp. 11–6; Mao-tse Tung and Che Guevara, *Guerrilla Warfare*, pp. 68–2; Oppenheim, *International Law*; Mao-tse Tung: *On Revolution and War*, ed. M. Rejai, New York, 1969.
2. Ibn Khaldun, ed. Ouatremere, vol. II, p. 86; Levy, *Social Structure of Islam*, p. 428.
3. The civilized Chinese were at a disadvantage before the Tiu Kiu in the seventh century (AD 617). The Ghaznavid army, under professional Turkish soldiers, was worn down by the nomad Turkomans to whom the steppe was their 'father and mother' and who excelled the former as regards encampment, supply of drinking water, fodder for camels and lack of heavy equipage. Steppe warfare required lightness and mobility which the Turkoman riders, fighting as a self-sufficing unit, had. The Ghaznavids lacked mobility and depended on strong bases and towns for food, fodder and war materials. Without wasting time to reduce these, the ill-equipped nomad raiding parties devastated the agricultural areas of the countryside, starving the people and dislocated the caravan traffic to which Khorasan largely owed its commercial prosperity. Bosworth, *The Ghaznavids*, pp. 246–8.

4. Sun Tzu, Griffith, pp. 66–9, Introduction Section VI, pp. 45–56; Mao-tse Tung, *On War*, pp. 69–93.
5. *Sukranitisara*, tr. B. K. Sarkar, Ch. IV, Sec. VII, 11, pp. 572–3; *Kamandaka Niti*, XVI.
6. Irvine, *Army of the Indian Moghuls*, p. 240, German partisans were called *bandite*s or bandits. The Nizamshahis and Malik Ambar developed guerrilla fighting and predatory warfare (*bargigiri*); Radhesham, *History of the Kingdom of Ahmadnagar*, pp. 280, 376.
7. Sarkar, *Aurangzib*, p. iii.
8. J. N. Sarkar, *Mir Jumla*, p. 253.
9. For Marathas, Sen, *Military System of the Marathas*, Chapters 1, 4. 8; Sarkar, *Aurangzib*, p. v, 159; *Military History*, pp. 157–68; App. I; *Shivaji*, pp. 176–8; Chitnis II, p. 43.
10. For the Sikhs, Irvine, *Later Mughals*, vols 1 and 2.
11. Mao and Guevara, *Guerrilla Warfare*, Introduction, pp. 6–10; 21–2, 101; Liddell Hart's Introduction, p. xiii; Clausewitz, *On War*, vol I, Book VI, pp. 346–7 (Bases); Nasution, pp. 38-41 (enemy arsenals).
12. For Rajputs, Sarkar, *Aurangzib*, pp. iii, pp. 339–47.
13. *Haft Anjuman* (Benares Ms.) 85b, 86a, 86b, 87a, 88, 92a; J. N. Sarkar, *Military Despatches*, pp. 111–3, 115, 120–1, 143; *Auranzib*, p. iv.
14. Talish, *Fathiyya i ibriyya*, pp. 75–8, 86–91; Assam Buranji (Sukumar Mahanta), pp. 96–7; J. N. Sarkar, *Mir Jumla*, pp. 241, 252–7; Gait (new), p. 253.
15. Irvine, *Later Mughals*, vols 1 and 2, Khuswant Singh, Chapter 8.
16. Sarkar, *Aurangzib*, vol. V; *Military History*, p. 143.
17. Mao and Guevara, *Guerrilla Warfare*, p. xiv.
18. *Alamgirnamah*, 1018; Sarkar, *Aurangzib*, pp. iv, 142; *Haft Anjuman*, 85b, 86a.

    A people's war, like a kind of nebulous vapoury essence, should never condense into a solid body; otherwise the enemy crushes it. Clausewitz, *On War*, vol. I, Book VI, p. 346.
19. Liddell Hart, op. cit., p. xv. When backed by the sympathy of the masses, guerrilla warfare 'tends to be most effective if it blends an appeal to national resistance or desire for independence with an appeal to social and economic discontent, thus becoming revolutionary in a wider sense.' Ibid.; also p. 12; Nasution, pp. 33–8.
20. Talish, pp. 79–80; *Buranji from Khunlung and Khunlai*, pp. 702–3; J. N. Sarkar, *Mir Jumla*, p. 254; Sarkar, *Aurangzib*, pp. iii, 347.
21. Khafi Khan, E and D, p. vii; Khushwant Singh.
22. Mao-tse Tung, *Guerrilla Warfare*, tr. S. Griffith, pp. 69–77; Nasution, pp. 17–22.
23. *Haft Anjuman*, 86a–b.
24. Sarkar, *Aurangzib*, pp. v, 158–9, based on Chitnis, pp. ii, 43–5.

25. Mao-tse Tung, op. cit., *Haft Anjuman*, 91b–92a; J. N. Sarkar, *Military Despatches*, p. 121; Nasution, pp. 54–66.
26. Mao-tse Tung, op. cit.; Sarkar, *Aurangzib*, vol. V, p. 105.
27. Mao-tse Tung, pp. 27, 81; Nasution, pp. 51–4: Khafi Khan, pp. ii, 446; Sarkar, *Military History*, pp. 159–62. Dodderi is in Chittaldurg division of Mysore.

CHAPTER 8

Origin and Development of Gunpowder Technology in India: AD 1250–1500

Iqtidar Alam Khan

The introduction and early development of pyrotechny and firearms in India is a much debated subject regarding which divergent views have been expressed by modern historians. But, unfortunately, this discussion has generally remained at the level of chauvinistic speculations based on fanciful meanings attributed to the texts. After Elliot's well-known note 'On Early Use of Gunpowder in India', published more than a hundred years back,[1] the only other serious study on the subject is represented by P. K. Gode's papers which he wrote between 1939 and 1958.[2] While rejecting outrightly the ridiculous notions regarding existence of firearms in the 'age of *Mahābhārata*', Gode has shown, with the help of numerous early Sanskrit texts, that pyrotechny and firearms were already in use in the Deccan, Gujarat, and Vijayanagar empire from the middle of the fifteenth century. By comparing the formula of gunpowder given in the Chinese texts with the one recorded by Gajapati Prataparudradeva (AD 1479–1539), Gode has established that 'the formulas for the manufacture of fireworks were brought to India by China'.[3] These conclusions of Gode demolish Elliot's thesis in both of its important aspects, that some kind of combustible substance akin to gunpowder was known in ancient India but it fell into disuse before 'we reach authentic history', and that in the late fifteenth century the technology of gunpowder and firearms was imported into this country from the West. However, on the whole, Gode has confined his research to pinpointing the evidence suggesting the existence of firearms in India during the fifteenth century. He has not attempted a systematic analysis of the evidence collected by him so as to be able to find answers to some of the vital questions relating to the introduction and development of firearms in India.

One important question that has remained unanswered is whether any kind of firearms were developed in India indigenously, prior to the introduction of cannon and matchlocks from the West in the second half of the fifteenth century. It also needs to be explained as to what inhibited the use of gunpowder for military purpose in general and of firearms, especially cannon and matchlocks, in particular, on a large scale in northern India before 1526. Another vital aspect requiring further investigation is the impact of the introduction of firearms on the nature of the power structures that existed in India during the sixteenth century. Would it be correct to assume, as suggested by Barthold,[4] that the Mughal imperial expansion and high degree of centralization achieved under Akbar were, to a certain extent, related to Mughal superiority in firearms over other ruling groups and to a policy aimed at establishing the total monopoly of the central government over the manufacture and use of firearms?

In this article, while introducing some new evidence derived mainly from Persian chronicles that tends to push back the date of the introduction and use of gunpowder in India to the middle of the thirteenth century, an attempt is made to trace the development of this new technique in some of its aspects in India down to 1530. The discussion in this paper is mainly focused on the following three aspects of the subject: 1. the development of pyrotechny; 2. the use of gunpowder in siege operations; and 3. the development of *ban* (rocket). Here, these aspects are taken for brief comment in the same sequence as they are listed. This sequence corresponds with the chronological stages in the development of gunpowder technology in India.

Before commencing a proper discussion of the aspects listed above, it is necessary to take note of the difficulties involved in interpreting certain vital pieces of information contained in the *Tārīkh-i Firishta* (compiled in 1606–7) regarding the introduction and development of gunpowder technology in India. The *Tārīkh-i Firishta* contains definite statements suggesting the display of pyrotechny in the Delhi Sultanate in 1258 and possession of firearms by the Vijayanagar empire in 1365. On the authority of *Tuhfatu's Salāṭīn* by Mullah Daud Beduri, an early chronicle no longer extant, Firishta further informs us that it was around 1368 that the Bahmanis first acquired firearms which were manned by Europeans (*Firingīs*) and Ottoman Turks (*Rūmīs*).[5] There is, however, one obvious difficulty about this evidence. Firishta being an early seventeenth century chronicler and being well-known for his weakness to occasionally present information gleaned from earlier sources in a tendentious manner, cannot be fully relied upon. Briggs has, therefore, a strong case when he expresses doubt about validity of the above evidence.[6] But many of Firishta's other statements about the earlier history, which would have otherwise appeared equally far-fetched, are fully endorsed by contemporary sources. One such case is his reference to the mining of the forts of Bhatnair and Meerut by Timur in 1398, which is corroborated almost literally by Sharfuddin Ali Yazdi.[7] In view of this peculiar nature of Firishta's account, it would not be correct to reject outright all his statements suggesting familiarity with and actual use of pyrotechny and firearms in different parts of the Indian subcontinent at such an early date. To be on the safe side, even such of his statements as are not corroborated by any of the extant contemporary sources and sound on the surface improbable should not be ignored altogether. It may, therefore, be suggested that before Firishta's evidence regarding the display of pyrotechny at Delhi in 1258 and the use of firearms by the Vijayanagar empire and Bahmanis in 1365 and 1368 respectively is finally disposed of as unacceptable, it should be scrutinized carefully in the light of more reliable evidence relating to the spread of gunpowder technology in India as well as in the neighbouring regions. In the ensuing discussion, wherever it has become necessary to reject or accept any of Firishta's statements, we have adhered to this rule.

There exists definite evidence suggesting possession of some kind of gunpowder devices by the Mongols from the second quarter of the thirteenth century onwards. This, in turn, makes it plausible that the gunpowder technology in its early form came to north-western India as early as at the first half of the thirteenth century and that it was brought here by the Mongol invaders. But before one proceeds to study the dissemination of gunpowder technology in north-western India during the Sultanate period, it would be appropriate to discuss the evidence that we have regarding the use of gunpowder devices by the Mongols. This evidence is mainly derived from two contemporary Persian chronicles of the early history of the Mongol empire; *Tārīkh-i Jahān Gushā* by Alauddin 'Ata al-Juwaini (compiled in AH 658/AD 1260) and *Jami'al-Tawarikh* by Rashiduddin Fazlullah (compiled in AH 704/AD 1304–5).

A clear reference to a gunpowder device for breaching fortifications occurs in Rashiduddin Fazlullah's account of one of the Mongol invasions of China during Ogedei's reign (AD 1229–41). Describing the siege of a city in China, he states:

> They (the besiegers) deployed many *manjanīq*s (*mangonel*s) and *nardubān*s (stairs) against the rampart. The *naqqaban* (miners) fixed *changs/chunak*s in the foundation of the wall.[8]

From this description, it appears that *changs/chings/chunak*s were gunpowder charges meant to be exploded in the foundation of a rampart. In Persian, the expression used by Rashiduddin Fazlullah for this weapon in all its three variants (*changs/chings/chunak*s) would mean either a beak-shaped or claw-shaped containers carrying gunpowder charges and that it was possible to ignite the charges within these containers after having them fixed in the foundation of a wall. Apparently, the technique of exploding large mines containing several hundred *mans* of gunpowder had not yet come into vogue. This early technique may have been dictated by the non-availability of sufficiently large supplies of gunpowder.

There is yet another passage in *Jami 'al-Twārīkh* which testifies to the mining operations of the Mongol armies in the Sistan region during Mengue's reign (AD 1251–8). Referring to the suppression of Qaracha, a Turkish chief of Khurasan, Rashiduddin Fazlullah writes:

> Qaracha, fleeing from Kalbalad, sought shelter in the fort of Sistan. Tayir Bahadur proceeded to besiege him. For about two years he was digging trenches until it was reduced.[9]

In this passage, reference to mining operations that continued for more than two years before the fort of Sistan was reduced indicates the use of a technique involving comparatively smaller charges. It suggests the same kind of devices as the Mongols are reported to have employed in China. Thus one can assume that, as early as the middle of the thirteenth century, the Mongol armies operating on the north-western frontier of the Delhi Sultanate were using gunpowder.

It is difficult to guess the specific features of this device. There is a rather problematic passage in *Tārīkh-i Jahān Gushā* which may be interpreted as alluding to it. In this passage, Juwaini refers to the recruitment of experts (*ustādān*) from China for preparing war equipment at the time of Hulaku's setting out to invade Iraq and Syria. According to Juwaini, on this occasion the services of one thousand families of Chinese mangonel experts (*yak hazār khāna-i-khātāi manjanīqī*) were actually procured 'for processing the touch-holes in the hollow (pieces of) stone making them big enough for cable (of match?) to pass and for straightening the arrows of mangonel (*manjanīq*) by adding sinews and applying glue (to them) so that on rising from below these should not take a retrograde (course).'[10] The first statement in this passage seems to refer to some kind of gunpowder device consisting of a hollow piece of stone having an opening on one side. Apparently mouth-holes were drilled into it for passing cables of match. The Chinese experts recruited on this occasion were perhaps commissioned to widen the mouth-holes already drilled. But this interpretation of the text becomes possible only if the expression *ba zakhm-i-sang* (literally meaning 'blows of stone') in M. M. Qazwini's edition is read as *ba raḥm-i sang* (figuratively meaning 'into the womb of stone'). The meaning of the printed text becomes obscure because of the expression *ba zakhm-i-sang*. As John Andrew Boyle has followed Qazwini's version of the text, his translation tends to run into difficulties.[11] For example, in translating the expression *sūrākh-i sozan* as 'the eye of the needle', Boyle has ignored an additional meaning of the *sozan*, that is 'pricker of a gun', from which has been derived the term *sūrākh-i soz*, denoting 'mouth-hole of a fire-arm'. It may be argued that the expression *sūrākh-i sozan* is used in this passage in the same meaning as *sūrākh-i soz* and that the latter term is only a modified from the former.

It seems that the problematic nature of the text has goaded Boyle to take liberties with the construction of the two distinct statements occurring in this passage. The two statements are joined together with a simple *wa* (and). There is no word or twist of expression in the original text to justify Boyle's assumption that the second statement pertaining to the 'straightening of the arrows of the mangonels' qualifies the preceding one in which the expression *ba zakhm-i sang/ba raḥm-i sang* occurs. Apparently, he has been induced to render the second statement a qualifying sentence ('having fastened the poles of mangonels so firmly, etc.') as it tends to support his rather loose translation of the expression *ba zakhm-i sang* ('with a stone missile'). Similarly, Boyle's translation of the last line of this passage seems to be slightly off the mark. By implication he has made a distinction between 'the poles of mangonels' (*tīrhā-i manjanīq*) which were fastened 'so firmly' with sinews, etc., and the 'missiles', which were 'aimed from nadir to the zenith'. From this an impression is created that while 'the poles' fastened were a part of the launching pad, the missile itself was a piece of stone. On the other hand, from the text it is quite clear that arrows processed by the Chinese experts were the missiles and not the poles of the *manjanīq*.

It is on these grounds that one may suggest a reconsideration of Boyle's translation of this passage. However, the alternative interpretation suggested above also suffers from one noteworthy discrepancy. The use of the expression *ba raḥm-i sang* in the context in which it would be placed in the text appears outlandish. Though not entirely misplaced, this expression does sound a bit odd. A more appropriate expression in this context would naturally be *dar raḥm sang.*

In any case, the above evidence put together clearly points to the use of some kind of gunpowder devices by the Mongols as far back as the second quarter of the thirteenth century. They appear to have borrowed the skill to use gunpowder from the Chinese. On this basis, one may guess that the skill to manufacture and use gunpowder was first introduced in north-western India during the thirteenth century by the Mongol invaders.

It seems that the earliest form in which the use of gunpowder was introduced in India was pyrotechny. If Firishta's evidence for Nasiruddin Mahmud's reign is accepted, pyrotechny may be considered as already in vogue in the Delhi Sultanate towards the middle of the thirteenth century. According to Firishta, in 1258, during the reception extended to Hulaku's envoy, there were present three thousand carts, carrying pyrotechnical devices (*sih hazar 'arrādā-i ātishbāzī*). The Mongol armies operating on the north-western frontier of the Delhi Sultanate were already using, since the second quarter of the thirteenth century, some kind of gunpowder devices. It would thus appear plausible that Firishta's mention of *'arrādā-i ātishbāzī* in the passage referred to above is a genuine piece of evidence derived from one of the numerous extinct sources used by him for the history of the Delhi Sultanate and that the term *ātishbāzī* is used here in its real sense, that is, pyrotechny, and it is not Firishta's substitute for some kind of naphtha device. A large-scale display of *ātishbāzī* on this occasion might have been deliberately planned to impress the Mongols that the Indians had already achieved considerable skill in this new technique.

However, an unambiguous and contemporary mention of pyrotechny in the Delhi Sultanate dates from Firoz Tughlaq's reign (1351–88). Describing festivities on the occasion of *shab-bārāt* (*bāzīhā-i shab-bārāt*) at Delhi, Afif describes the 'bursting' of 'flower scattering rockers' (*hāwāihā-i gulrez 'anbarbez mī bakht*) which is not only a clear description of pyrotechny, but also indicates an advanced stage of skill.[12] We have yet another detailed and equally reliable description of pyrotechny in *Ma 'āsir-i Mahmūd Shāhī*, a chronicle of the Khaljī kingdom of Malwa compiled in AD 1467–8. A display of fireworks organized by Sultan Mahmud Khaljī I in AH 846/AD 1442–3 at Shadiabad (Mandu) is described in the following words:

> The fire-workers *(ātish bāzān)* (shot and) landed fire-arrows (*tīr-i ātishīn*) on the Sun. Contrived images of giraffe, elephant, tiger, camel and other objects were displayed inside the fire-spitting *charkhs* (wheels) and these were made to dance (as well).[13]

This description leaves little doubt that the display was of pyrotechny and not of naphtha. Without the use of gunpowder, the depicition in fireworks of moving image is not possible. Abdul Razzaq's description of fireworks in the Vijayanagar empire is incidentally of the same date as that of *Ma 'āsir-i Mahmūd Shāhī* for Malwa, that is AD 1443. In the light of the irrefutable testimony of the latter source indicating that at this time pyrotechny was known in Malwa, Gode's interpretation of Abdul Razzaq's evidence as a description of pyrotechny should prevail over Elliot's view that it was the work of naphtha throwers.[14]

There also exists evidence indicating that the use of gunpowder in its earliest form, namely pyrotechny, was known as far back as the first half of the fifteenth century in Kashmir and Bengal as well. Nizamuddin Ahmad (writing in AD 1594), followed by Firishta (writing in AD 1607), furnishes specific information relating to the existence of pyrotechny in Kashmir during Sultan Zainul Abidin's reign (AD 1422–72). According to Nizamuddin Ahmad, Habib, a distinguished expert of pyrotechny in Sultan Zainul Abidin's service, assisted the latter in compiling a treatise on pyrotechny. Firishta credits Habib with inventing a number of pyrotechnical displays. Both these authorities hold that *tufang* was introduced in Kashmir by Habib. In the light of contemporary evidence testifying to the use of gunpowder for display of fireworks in the Delhi Sultanate during Firuz Tughlaq's reign and in Malwa and the Vijayanagar empire during the first half of the fifteenth century, the above specific evidence furnished by Nizamuddin and Firishta about Kashmir may safely be accepted reliable.[15]

Apparently, the tradition of pyrotechny in Bengal also dates back roughly to the period when it came to the Delhi Sultanate. Writing in 1529, Babur records that the Bengalis had a reputation for *ātishbāzī*.[16] It suggests a long tradition of pyrotechny in Bengal before Babur. This impression is further strengthened by Gode's discovery that *Kautukacintāmaṇi* by Gajapati Prataparudradeva, the earliest known Sanskrit treatise containing formulae of fireworks, was compiled on Orissa.[17] Moreover, the Chinese traveller, Mahuan, writing in 1406, speaks of 'guns' as one of the items exported from Bengal.[18] The use of the terms 'guns' in the English version of Mahuan's travel is either a slip of translation or it has resulted from the Chinese traveller's inability to find a suitable term for describing *bān* which, apparently, was a weapon developed indigenously in India. I am thus inclined to believe that Mahuan, when he speaks of 'guns', is actually referring to *bān*s, which, it seems from Babur's description of the missiles fired by the Bengalis in the Battle of Ghaghara, were the only kind of firearms possessed by them on that occasion. In any case, Mahuan's incidental mention of some kind of firearms produced in Bengal goes to establish that the use of gunpowder was known in Bengal as early as 1406.

The available evidence, however, tends to suggest that one of the earliest forms of use of gunpowder in military operations, namely mining, did not become common in India till the second half of the sixteenth century. The earliest evidence about the use of mining technique in India relates to the sieges of Bhatnair and Meerut by Timur in AD 1398. Sharfuddin Ali Yazdi has given a detailed description of the laying of mines by Timur's forces and the panic and consternation of the members of the garrisons when they observed trenches being dug under the walls.[19] It indicates that already, by this time, people in northern India had become familiar with the devastating nature of this kind of operation. There is every reason to believe that the Mongol hordes who were invading north-western India frequently during the thirteenth and first half of the fourteenth centuries must have been using, from the middle of the thirteenth century, the mining technique for reducing forts. They are reported to have employed this technique in different parts of China and West Asia. There is no particular reason why they should have desisted from using it in India. Apparently, the familiarity of the people in north-western India with the devastating nature of mining operation indicated by Sharfuddin Ali Yazdi was the result of their experience of Mongol invasions that had continued unabated until half a century earlier. As far as this author could ascertain, the earliest reported case of the use of mines by an Indian power in reducing a fort relates to the siege of Belgaum in 1472 by the Bahmani forces commanded by Mahmud Gawan. This information comes from *Tārīkh-i Firishta*. The authenticity of this evidence is borne out by the specific nature of the details of this episode recorded by Firishta. His account shows that the chief of Belgaum was not familiar with the nature of mining operation. He did not realize the significance of trenches that were being dug by the Bahmanis for laying mines, till these were finally exploded.[20] This evidence further confirms the curious indifference of the Indian rulers towards the technique of mining. The use of this technique by the Bahmanis at Belgaum may be attributed to Mahmud Gawan's ingenuity and his Persian background. The persisting insufficiency of the Indians in the technique of mining is amply demonstrated by the crude manner in which it was put to use at Chittor in 1567. The operation cost more lives to the besiegers than to the besieged.[21] As late as the middle of the seventeenth century, according to Bernier, mining was 'imperfectly known among the Indians'.[22]

One of the earliest forms of the firearms known to Indians and perhaps the only one indigenously developed was *bān*, a rocket consisting of 'an iron tube of about one foot long and an inch in diameter, fixed to a bamboo rod of ten or twelve feet long. The tube being filled with combustible composition, is set fire to and being directed by the hand, flies like an arrow to the distance upwards of 1000 yards.'[23] When the British first encountered *bān*s during the Mysore and Maratha wars, they were greatly fascinated by this contraption. This kind of weapon was not known in Europe till Congreve introduced rockets made on the principle of *bān* into British service in 1806.[24]

In the list of various kinds of firearms developed in China, Tenny L. Davis and James R. Ware mention the 'flying fire spear (equipped with tubes)' used by Kin Tartars against the Mongols in 1232.[25] However, in the absence of detailed description of the weapon, it is difficult to guess whether it was a variant of the fire-arrow (*tīr-i ātish*) shot with giant cross-bows (*kamān-i ra'd*) or a firearm resembling *bān*. The view that Indians might have borrowed the idea of a rocket that could be used for military purposes from the Chinese is strengthened by Gode's discovery (already mentioned) that 'the formulas for manufacture of fireworks were brought to India from China'. In any, case this much seems certain that the *bān* was the earliest firearm adopted and developed by the Indians. Muhammad Baksh Ashob, a chronicler of the late eighteenth century, mentions that it was invented and first used in the *Dakhin*, which would perhaps denote the region originally covered by the Bahmani Empire.[26] There is no indication as to Ashob's source of information.

A rocket propelled by the use of gunpowder was originally conceived in India as a device of pyrotechny. This is indicated by the fact that in Gajapati Prataparudradeva's *Kautukacintāmaṇi*, the formulae for different kinds of *bān*s are given in the section devoted to entertainment. Again, a rocket with its Persian designation *hawāi* is mentioned in the description of fireworks displayed on the occasion of *shab-bārāt* during Firoz Tughlaq's reign.[27] The earliest mention of this device by its Persian designation *(hawāi)* as a weapon of war is to be found in *Ma 'āsir-i Mahmūd Shāhī* in the context of Sultan Mahmud Shah's military campaigns during AD 1435–67. This weapon is sometimes referred to by Shahab Hakim as *tīr-i hawāi*. In the account of a skirmish between the Rajputs and Sultan Mahmud Khaljī's forces near Mandalgarh (1443), Shahab Hakim states: 'Konbha used fire of naphtha (*ātish-i naft*) and *tīr-i hawāī*. A similar statement occurs in the description of yet another encounter between the two powers in AD 1456–7.[28] The construction of these statements suggests that *tīr-i hawāī* was not a device meant for throwing naphtha fire (*ātish-i naft*). It was also different from fire-arrow (*tīr-i atishīn*), which is listed as a distinct weapon. Afif's description of *hawāī* as a device that would emit sparks in a pattern looking like flowers lends further credence to the identification of *tīr-i-hawāī* with *bān* in its meaning of missile propelled by the detonation of gunpowder. This identification is further confirmed by Shahab Hakim's account of its use in 1460–1 to convey signals to the scattered columns of troops during the night. He states: 'During the night, (the king) ordered shooting of *tīrhā-i hawāī āstishbār* (fire-spitting *hawāi* arrows)'.[29] It is very significant that in this context the term *tīr-i ātishīn* (fire-arrow) is not used.

The *bān* is sometimes also termed in Persian chronicles of the sixteenth and seventeenth centuries as *ḥukka*. This is borne out by Abbas Khan Sarwani and Badauni's description of the accident at Kalinjar that caused Sher Shah's death in AD 1545.[30] Firishta also uses this term for the rockets which, according to him, were used in 1484–5, by the Gujarati forces at Champanir.[31]

From Babur's cryptic description of the missile-throwing devices used by the Bengalis in 1529, it can be inferred that these were some kind of contraptions of pyrotechny with which Babur was not fully acquainted. He describes the inaccuracy of the weapon without naming it.[32] On the other hand, his description of its impact—'they (Bengalis) fire not counting to hit a particular spot but fire at random'—is reminiscent of what Major Dirom has reported about *bāns* used by Tippu's forces:

They (*bāns*) make a great noise and exceedingly annoy the native cavalry in India who move in great bodies; but are easily avoided or seldom take effect against our troops, who are formed in lines of great extent and depth.[33]

Thus, it would be totally wrong to infer that the weapon described by Babur as being used by Bengalis in 1529 was a gun. This would, in turn suggest that when Babur generally refers to Bengalis having a reputation for *ātishbāzī*, he is actually having in mind their expertise in handling *bāns*.

In this context, Mahuan's testimony mentioning 'guns' as one of the items exported from Bengal as far back as AD 1406 needs to be explained.[34] If, in AD 1529, the Bengalis were having with them only *bāns* how is it possible that way back in AD 1406 they were producing 'guns' in large enough numbers to be able to export them? One possible answer to this question could be that the export item described by Mahuan as 'guns' was the same firearm to which a cryptic allusion was made by Babur and which, as we have argued, it is possible to identify as *bān.* For the use of the term 'guns' in the English translation of Mahuan's account, there can be two explanations. First, it could be a slip of translation. Second, it is possible that *bān*, being a weapon developed indigenously in India till the beginning of the fifteenth century, there did not exist a distinct Chinese word to describe it, which would naturally lead Mahuan to use an expression denoting the most common missile-throwing weapon known to him, that is, the Chinese equivalent of 'gun'. Similar confusion in the use of terms denoting guns and *bāns* seems to have existed in the sixteenth-century Sanskrit writings. A good example of such confusion in the use of the term *nālikā*, ordinarily denoting a gun, is used by Rudrakavi in one of his compositions of 1596. He depicts an iron ball (*āyasagolakaḥ*) containing sharp arrows and stones with which the weapon was charged *(nālikāvinihata).* Apparently, taking a wrong clue from the use of the term *nālikā* in the above piece, Gode has identified the weapon alluded to here as a cannon in which some kind of shells containing shrapnels were used.[35] But it is certainly known that cannonballs or shells that would explode on striking a target did not come into use even in Europe before the eighteenth century. Thus, the weapon described by Rudrakavi cannot be identified as a gun, though the term that he uses for it (*nālikā*) is the one that later came to be exclusively used for the same device. The greater likelihood seems to be that in the verse under discussion he is actually referring to that kind of *bān* which, according to Edward Moor's description, used 'to have a chamber' and would 'burst like a shell'.[36] From this discussion, on the one hand the plausibility of the inference that the firearms that were manufactured in Bengal around 1406, according to Mahuan, were actually *bān*s strengthened. On the other hand, it indicates that *bān*s containing chambers packed with sharpnels were already known in India before 1596.

NOTES

1. Elliot, *History of India as Told by its Own Historians*, Part VI, reprint, Allahabad, 1964, Appendix A.
2. P. K. Gode, *Studies in Indian Cultural History*, Part II, Poona, 1960. The following three articles are included: 'Use of Guns and Gunpowder in India from AD 1400 onwards' (first published in 1939); 'The Manufacture and Use of Firearms in India Between AD 1450 and 1850' (reprinted from *Bharatiya Vidya*, Part IX); 'The History of Fireworks in India Between AD 1400 and 1900' (first published in 1958).
   A short discussion on the use of firearms in India from 1526 onwards included in Jadunath Sarkar's *Military History of India* (Orient Longman, reprinted 1970, pp. 52–5) is also noteworthy. Sarkar makes a significant point in identifying Babur's firearms at Panipat as consisting solely of 'hand-guns and light pieces resting on forks'. But, on the whole, this note is too cursory and brief to deserve to be treated at par with the detailed studies of Elliot and Gode.
3. Gode, op. cit., p. 44.
4. *Iran*, ed. Minocher E. Dadrawala and tr. G. K. Nariman, Bomaby, pp. 48-9.
5. Cf. *Tārīkh-i Firishta*, ed. Nawal Kishore, AH 1321, Part I, vol. 73, pp. 290–1, 308. According to Firishta, Tuhfatu's *Salāṭīn* was compiled by Mullah Daud Beduri during the reign of Firuz Shah Bahmani (AD 1397–1422).
6. Briggs, *History of Rise of Mohammedan Power in India till AD 1612*, Part II, Calcutta, 1910, p. 434, cited by Elliot, op. cit., p. 466.
7. *Tārīkh-i Firishta*, Part I, p. 158; Maulavi Muhammad Ilahabad, ed., *Ẓafar Nāma* (compiled in AH 828/AD 1424–5), Part II, Calcutta, 1887, pp. 70–6, 130–1.
8. Rashiduddin Fazlullah, *Jami 'al-Tawārīkh*, ed. E. Blochet, Part II, London, 1911, p. 25.

9. Ibid., p. 38.
10. M. M. Qazwini, ed., *Tārīkh-i Jahān Gushā*, Part III, London, 1937, pp. 92–3.
11. '. . . and they brought from Khitai 1,000 household (*khana*) of Khitayan mangonelmen,who with a stone missile would convert the eye of a needle into a passage for a camel, having fastened the poles of the mangonels so firmly with sinews (*pai*) and glue that when they aimed from nadir to the zenith the missile did not return', *The History of World Conqueror*, Part ii Manchester, 1958, p. 608.
12. Afif, *Tārīkh-i Firūz Shāhī*, ed. Maulavi Vilayat Husain, Calcutta, 1890, pp. 365–7.
13. Shanab Hakim, *Ma 'āsir-i Mahmūd Shāhī*, ed. Nurul Hasan Ansari, Delhi, 1968, p. 51.
14. Cf. Gode, op. cit., p. 374; Elliot. op. cit., p. 466.
15. Nizamuddin Ahmad, *Ṭabaqāt-i Akbarī*, ed. B. De and Hidayat Hosain, Part III, Calcutta, 1935, p. 439; *Tārīkh-i Firishta*, Part II, p. 344.
16. *Babur Nama*, tr. A. S. Beveridge, London, 1969, p. 672.
17. Gode, op. cit., pp. 42–4.
18. Geo Philips, 'Mahuan's Account of the Kingdom of Bangala (Bengal)', *Journals of the Royal Asiatic Society*, July 1895, p. 532.
19. *Ẓafar Nāma*, Part II, pp. 70–6, 130–1.
20. *Tārīkh-i Firishta*, Part I, p. 252.
21. Cf. Abul Fazl, *Akbar Nāma*, ed. Agha Ahmad Ali, Part II, Asiatic Society of Bengal, p. 318.
22. Bernier, *Travels in the Mogul Empire*, tr. Archibald Constable, second edn revised by Vincent A. Smith, London, 1916, pp. 31–2.
23. Description given by Major Dorim cited in E. Moor's *Narrative of Capt. Little's Detachment*, 1794; cf. William Irvine, *The Army of the Indian Moghuls*, reprint, New Delhi, 1962, p. 149.
24. William Irvine, op. cit., pp. 148–9.
25. Tenny L. Davis and James R. Ware, 'Early Chines Military Pyrotechnics', *Journal of Chemical Education*, vol. XXIV, pp. 522–37, cited in Gode, op. cit., p. 39.
26. Muhammad Baksh Ashob, *Tārīkh-i Shahādat-i Farrukh Sīyar wa Julūs-i Muhammad Shah*, cited in *The Army of the Indian Moghuls*, p. 148.
27. Afif, op. cit., p. 365.
28. *Ma 'asir-i Māhmūd Shāhī*, pp. 57–86.
29. Ibid, p. 21.
30. Abbas Khan, *Tuḥfa-i Akbar Shāhī*, MS, India Office Ethe, p. 219*ff*, 101b–102a; Abdul Qadar Badauni, *Muntakhab-ut Tawārīkh*, ed. Ahmad 'Ali, Kabiruddin Ahmad and W. N. Lees, Part I, Bibliotheca India Series, pp. 371–2.
31. *Tārīkh-i Firishta*, Part II, p. 202.
32. *Babur Nama*, p. 672.

33. Cf. William Irvine, op. cit., p. 149.
34. *Journal of the Royal Asiatic Society*, July 1895, p. 532.
35. Gode, op. cit., p. 5.
36. Cf. William Irvine, op. cit., p. 149.

CHAPTER 9

Gunpowder and Empire: Indian Case

Iqtidar Alam Khan

The increasing use of firearms from the middle of the fifteenth century in different parts of world is often seen as a crucial factor in the rise of centralized monarchial states. In Europe, it was a manifestation of the overall weakening of the position of gentry, as against the king. This was a direct consequence of the increasing vulnerability of signioral castles to the field artillery maintained by the king and of the greater effectiveness of the musket-wielding infantrymen against mounted knights.[1] In the Islamic East, where the mounted archers were the mainstay of the imperial authority, this phenomenon appeared to have manifested itself in an altered form. The highly centralized empires of the sixteenth century like the Ottoman Empire, the Safavid Empire, the Uzebek Khanate, and the Mughal Empire in India are, for example, characterized by Marshall G. S. Hodgson as the 'gunpowder empires'. According to him, the changes promoted by the introduction of firearms in these states were not restricted to army organizations. The firearms also 'gave an increased advantage over local military garrisons, to a well-organized central power which could afford artillery'.[2] In this article,* such an impact is examined in the context of state formation in India, with a special focus on the Mughal Empire.

A primitive type of gunpowder artillery was already in vogue in different parts of India during the second half of the fifteenth century. Already by the middle of the century, there was known in North India a firearm with the designation *Kashakanjir* which threw balls 'by the extensive force of combustible substances (*darruha-i atishin*)'. It was in all probability a cannon. A weapon resembling the cannon is also reported in Kashmir. Srivara records that this weapon 'was called *tops*' in Muslim language while in the Kashmiri dialect 'it was called *kanda*'. He also alludes at its being made of an alloy.[3] This is also supported by allusions in two other contemporary texts, *Ma'asir-i Mahmud Shahi* by Shihab Hakim (1468) and *Riyazu'l insha* by Mahmud Gawan (1470) to the presence in Malwa and Deccan of *ra'd/kaman-i ra'd* (literally, lightening bow), which are identified by Firishta as proper cannons. According to one criptic description by Shahab Hakim, it was 'made from an alloy of copper'.[4]

The destructive capacity of gunpowder artillery of the fifteenth century, notwithstanding its primitive nature, was vastly greater than that of the mechanical devices of the earlier period. It is indicated by the contemporary descriptions of the sieges of Mandalgarh (1457) and Machal (1470),[5] as well that of Champanir (1485) recorded by Firishta (possibly copying, as was his wont, an earlier text).[6] This should explain why some of the forts known for their strength and solidity sometimes had to be redesigned in the fifteenth century. As was with the case with Vijaymandirgarh fort of Bayana, this redesigning was aimed at enlarging the enclosed space which could have been with the idea of making it difficult for a besieging force to aim its cannons at the built-up areas of the fort. Other similar examples from the Aravali tract is those of the forts of Mandalgarh and Champanir.[7]

The artillery pieces in India during the fifteenth century, being made uniformly of brass or bronze, were naturally very costly. These were generally beyond the means of most of the zamindars as well as the Rajput chieftains. The ruler of Mewar was perhaps one of the few exceptions among them.[8] These new weapons were processed in appreciable numbers only by the more prosperous regional kingdoms like those of Gujarat, Malwa, Bahmanis and Vijaynagara. Each of them is credited with overpowering the local chiefs of their regions by reducing their forts located in less accessible tracts. The reduction of these forts was apparently facilitated by the use of newly introduced gunpowder artillery which was as yet beyond the reach of most of the local chiefs.

It is, therefore, understandable that the appearance of gunpowder artillery synchronized with a distinct phase of internal consolidation leading to a limited territorial expansion in the case of more prosperous regional kingdoms of the fifteenth century. Internal consolidation, was always marked by the strengthening of the king's control over the nobles and, more importantly, by the suppression of local chiefs, some of whom hitherto enjoyed autonomous status on account of their large caste or tribal following and forts held by them in peripheral zones. This is evident from the history of Gujarat and the Bahmani Empire under Mahmud Begarha (1459–1511)[9] and Muhammad Shah (1463–82) respectively.[10] In the case of Vijayanagara Empire again the use of firearms is considered to be the most important factor behind its successes not only against the Bahmanis, but also 'against the enemies within', such as the powerful chiefs of the Tamil region.[11] These developments, in a way, tended to conform to Marshall G. S. Hodgson's view that the introduction of relatively expensive artillery would often lead to the growth of 'a well-organised central power'.

The impact of European gunnery introduced in India on a large scale in the beginning of the sixteenth century was, however, a much more complex process which I propose to examine here with reference to the rise and decline of the Mughal Empire.

During the sixteenth century, the heavy mortars produced in India registered a striking advance. This was a direct result of improved designs and casting methods learnt from the West through contact with the Portuguese as also through expertise brought in by Babur.[12] However, the problems like lack of mobility, proneness to accidents, slow rate of firing, and large consumption of gunpowder persisted causing a decline in their over all popularity. Already, by the middle of the sixteenth century, these had come to be treated as impressive exhibits probably meant to overawe the common people with the military prowess of the Empire, than for actual use in warfare.[13]

It is of interest to remember that in Babur's own descriptions of the battles of Panipat (1526) and Kanwah (1527), where he experimented with the deployment of firearms in the battlefield with some success, heavy mortars (*kazans*) are not mentioned. Though Humayun had deployed 21 mortars in the Battle of Kanauj (1540), these did not prove to be of much help.[14] Similarly in 1553, Islam Shah found it difficult to carry his mortars to Punjab for checking Humayun's anticipated advance thither.[15] In 1556, the entire park of Adil Shah Sur's slow moving mortars was captured by the Mughals before these could be deployed against them at Panipat.[16]

Under Akbar, heavy mortars did not figure prominently in the process of territorial expansion. Apart from the sieges of Chittor (1568) and Ranthambhor (1570), military operations leading to territorial acquitions in the early decades of Akbar's reign did not involve prolonged sieges requiring the use of mortars. The Mughal Empire's expansion during this phase was achieved primarily with the use of mounted archers supported marginally by light artillery and musketeers. In the second phase of territorial expansion under Akbar, during 1585–1601, again artillery was used sparsely, which was seemingly on account of the difficulty of transportation.[17] The eclipse in the popularity of mortars in the Mughal Empire temporarily ended during the decades when Aurangzeb was frequently faced with the task of attacking numerous hill forts in Deccan.[18] Acquisition of a large number of siege mortars in the Deccan towards the end of the seventeenth century, however, did not prove to be of much strategic advantage for the Mughals. They continued to be vulnerable to Maratha light cavalry resorting to hit and run tactics.

From the above, it is quite evident that the siege artillery of the Mughal Empire did not command 'the fateful significance politically' that is ascribed to the same category of firearms in a gunpowder empire of Hodgson's conception. Abu'l Fazl, no doubt, goes out of his way in characterizing artillery as an instrument of empire building[19] in words reminiscent of the theory of gunpowder empires but, the history of Akbar's military campaigns recorded by him does not bear out this characterization.

Two other firearms introduced from Europe in the sixteenth century were; (a) light cannons mounted on carriages; and (b) matchlock muskets. These, no doubt, were easily integrated in the prevalent form of warfare based on the use of mounted archery by adopting variable patterns of the battle plan of the Ghazis of Rum introduced in India by Babur (1526). In this battle plan, light artillery and musketry were protected by a barricade with gaps to facilitate the free movement of cavalry.[20] Both of these firearms appear to have contributed to the growth of the Mughal Empire as a centralized state. The matchlock musket particularly seems to have emerged as an instrument of centralization in so far as its use came to acquire special relevance to the centre's control of internal resources.[21] During the seventeenth century, on the other hand, dissemination of muskets among peasant communities also became a factor contributing to the militancy of disaffected rural population.[22] It would, perhaps, be useful to dilate separately on the status of each one of them in the Mughal system.

There was a distinct improvement in the basic design and general performance of the light artillery during the first half of the sixteenth century, which facilitated their deployment and effective use in the siege operations as well as open battles. The earliest specimens of these light cannons (*zarb-zan*) used by Babur (1526–30) were, in all probability, miniature replicas of his heavy mortars (*kazan*s). Subsequently, in the 1540s, the size of an average light cannon was reduced considerably. This was possibly aimed at improving the quality of casting within the constraints imposed by the use of manual bellows. It also economized on the quantity of the gunpowder consumed.[23]

The introduction, from Europe, of the art of making less costly wrought iron barrels naturally contributed to making light cannons much cheaper. Besides a considerable increase in the total number of light cannons possessed by the Mughals and their Afghan adversaries in North India, many of the local chiefs all over the country began to possess them in limited numbers. These light cannons, when combined with musketry, were generally perceived as effective in defending fortified positions. The enhanced military clout of the Rajput chieftains, controlling strongholds on the outer periphery of the Gangetic plain during the first half of the sixteenth century, may perhaps be linked to this development.[24] The exceptionally favourable terms offered by Akbar to the Rajput chieftains to induce them to join his service may be viewed from this perspective as well.

The Mughal response to the increased effectiveness of the light cannons was represented by their attempt from the very beginning, to enforce imperial monopoly on the production and use of every kind of firearms.[25] It also led to a drive on their part to increase manifold the number of light cannons in their arsenal. Under

Akbar, there was a concerted attempt to further improve and also to add to their variety. These improvements seems to have led to the division of light cannons cast in bronze/brass as well as those forged from wrought iron into two broad categories: *zamburak*s carried with king in the so-called 'artillery of stirrup' and still lighter pieces like *narnal*s and *gajnal*s distributed for deployment on the ramparts of the forts located in different provinces.[26]

Perhaps the most important innovation relating to military use of firearms in the Mughal Empire during the seventeenth century was the placing of light cannons on some kind of swivels mounted on camels.[27] It is likely that the notion of a light cannon fitted to a swivel on the back of a camel, the *shaturnal* (camel barrel), came to India from West Asia some time in the beginning of the seventeenth century. This cannon is described by Bernier as a 'small field piece'. Being better tuned to the requirements of battles fought with fast moving cavalry, *shaturnal*s often played a far more important role in action than the 'artillery of stirrup' represented by a comparatively small number of medium-size cannons mounted on horse-drawn carriages. The *shaturnal*s, were seemingly Indian and West Asian substitutes for the latest cast iron field guns of Europe with the significant difference that these, instead of rendering obsolete the dominant form of mounted combat, tended to give it added support. Despite the constraints imposed by the necessity of camels to kneel on the ground to open fire, the *shaturnal*s often proved to be more effective than the cannons carried on slow-moving carriages. The speed with which several hundred pieces of light cannon, capable of keeping up fairly rapid fire, could be moved from one point to another during the battle would, on many an occasion, be crucial to the outcome of a sharply contested action.[28] This is, for example, borne out by Mirza Nathan's account of the Battle of Daulabapur (1612)[29] and those of the battle of Samugar (1658) by Bernier and Manucci.[30]

The *shaturnal*s were of course not out of the reach for many of the rebellious Rajput chiefs and Marhatta *sardar*s defying the Mughals during the second half of the seventeenth century. But the rebels were certainly not in a position to deploy them in a matching strength. To this limited extent, it would appear, the increasing presence of the *shaturnals* in the field artillery, contributed to the Mughal Empire's holding on its own in the face of mounting rebellions down to the end of Aurangzeb's reign.

Matchlock muskets present in India from the early phase of the Mughal conquest (1526–56)[31] came to be regarded as effective weapons of general combat. As was the case at Panipat in 1526, these came to be used from behind barricades formed by bullock carts tied together in pairs for harassing the onrushing cavalry. The musketeers would sometime also provide cover during the battle to artillery carts on the move which appears to have been their role at Khanwah (1527).[32] This had a parallel in the muskets' singular contribution to the Ottoman victories over Shah Ismail at Chaldiran (1514) and over the Mamluks in 1517.[33] From the history of the Mughal Empire in India, many more instances can be cited to illustrate that sometimes a skilful use of muskets could prove to be of critical significance in deciding the outcome of a battle. This role of the musketeers would often tend to get enhanced in localized small-scale conflict.[34]

In this context, William Irvine's view that down to the middle of the eighteenth century, the bow and arrow was considered in India a much more effective instrument of combat than the musket,[35] needs to be viewed in its proper perspective. This view seems to be mainly based on a statement of Bernier, where he is comparing the 'astonishing quickness' with which the mounted archers discharged their arrows with the slowness of horsemen carrying muskets who obliged to dismount for firing a volley. There is no denying the fact that much more time would pass between each matchlock shot than between the shooting of successive arrows. But the simple point is that matchlock fire could hit much harder with a pellet and be effective up to a much longer distance; and thus frequency alone could not be the decisive factor. The musket fitted with matchlock when used from the ground in a skilful manner could prove to be a devastating instrument of war. Even a small number, of match lock men fighting from the ground, if deployed innovatively, could contribute to breaking up the onslaught of a much larger body of horsemen.[36]

The recognition of muskets as of an increasingly effective factor in warfare is reflected in the anxiety of the Mughal imperial authority to retain a large body of musketeers. The strength of the foot-musketeers in the service of the Mughal king rose from roughly 1,200 in 1526 to 35,000 around 1595.[37] Abu'l Fazl accordingly classifies musketeers (*banduqchis*) as part of the royal household (*manzil abadi*) and not as part of the army (*sipah abadi*).[38] It is understandable that along with artillery (involving heavy expenditure), comparatively affordable muskets should have been controlled exclusively by the Emperor. This would suggest that the muskets too were considered a major instrument of power. Leaving muskets entirely to the care of the nobles was evidently not considerable safe.

Under Akbar's *mansab* system, from the very beginning the officers were allowed to have in their contingents among *dakhili* foot-soldiers a party of foot-musketeers whose strength would be 12½ per cent of the total number of horsemen in the contingent. In other words, there would be present in each contingent one musketeer for eight horsemen. But on paper, these *dakhili* musketeers also were treated as personnel in the direct employ of the Emperor and were paid their stipends not by the officers concerned, but by the central treasury.[39] This system appears to have continued in the seventeenth century in a modified form. The term *dakhili* fell into disuse, but the officers often came to maintain a larger number of musketeers than prescribed under the rules framed during Akbar's reign. An inventory (*siyaha*) of the detachment commanded by Bahramand Khan in 1689 shows a ratio of one musketeer to five horsemen.[40] Sometimes, under Aurangzeb, select nobles were also allowed the rare privilege of recruiting foot-musketeers directly in their contingent; these would again be treated as being in the central government's service (*naukar-i-sarkar-i-wala*).[41]

There is some evidence indicating that from the latter part of Akbar's reign, the foot-musketeers came to partly replace ordinary cavalry as the instruments of the local control. The use of musketeers in village level operations could have been a much less costly affair than the cavalry troops of any variety as is suggested by the salaries of the two types of troopers. The difference between the salaries of centrally maintained *yakaspa sawars* and foot-musketeers (*sair piyada banduqchi*) ranged from 4½: 25 to. 6: 25.[42] Moreover, the total cost of equipping a cavalry trooper, even of the meanest order, the inclusive cost of a horse (with its apparel), weapons, and armour, would be quite considerable. This cost would be much higher than the cost of a musket and ammunition needed for equipping a musketeer.[43] Under Todar Mal's regulations of 27th R.Y./1582.3, the *jagirdar*s as well as the officials of the territory yielding revenues for imperial treasury (*khalisa*) could take the help of the imperial musketeers stationed in every locality under the command of an *amir-i-chakla* (commandant of *chakla*, a territorial unit within a province). For this assistance, they were made 'responsible for the collection of one *dam* per *bigha* of cultivated land for the maintenance (*nigahdasht)* of the musketeers. That this system was actually enforced in some of the provinces is borne out by the extant text of one of Akbar's orders appointing a *faujdar* in the province of Lahore.[44]

Many instances can be cited to illustrate the effective use of muskets by the Mughals against defiant rural populace as well as rebellious chiefs during the seventeenth century.[45] These go to clearly indicate that down to the end of Aurangzeb's reign, the matchlock musket played a conspicuously significant role as an instrument of local control.

Rapid dissemination of muskets in the countryside during the first half of the seventeenth century made the task of exercising local control and of ensuring the smooth flow of land revenue more onerous. Even a marginal improvement in the fighting efficiency of the disaffected peasants and *zamindar*s as a consequence of their access to muskets of even the most primitive type would become a matter of grave concern to the Mughal authorities. One response of the Mughal imperial system to this new situation was the creation under Jahangir (1605–27) of a corps of mounted musketeers called *barqandaz* among the centrally maintained *ahdi* horseman.[46] A few decades later, some of the senior nobles, for example, Mirza, Raja Jai Singh also came to enroll, possibly with the tacit approval of the imperial authority, in their contingents musket carrying horseman.[47] Down to 1658, one knows on Bernier's testimony, most of these *barqandaz* troops were *yak aspa* horsemen riding *yabu* or still more inferior mounts.[48]

This attempt at combining horsemanship with the use of muskets was obviously aimed at enhancing the striking power of the musketeers against the rural rebels, for whose suppression they are known to have been frequently employed in localized military operations since Akbar's time. The performance of mounted musketeers in a large-scale action like the Battle of Samugar (1658) would no doubt appear to be rather not very impressive as compared to that of mounted archers forming the bulk of opposing armies. This should not, however, blur one's view of the effective role that the *barqandaz* troopes often played in scattered operations. They came to be frequently used in the Deccan as well as in other regions against the dispersed resistance of the local authorities, particularly that of the Marhatta *sardars*. The effectiveness of mounted musketeers in dispersed fighting is borne out by a number of episodes recorded in *waqa-i sarkar Ajmer wa Ranthambhor* and *Mazhar-i Shahjahani*.[49]

Though the number of mounted musketeers in the contingents of select nobles (the Kachchwaha chief of Amber being one of them) may have increased appreciably during Aurangzeb's reign, but the muskets used by them as also by most of the *barqandaz ahdis* continued to be unwieldy matchlocks which could be fired only after dismounting. On the other hand, during the same period, some of the rural insurgents in north India, like the Jats of Mathura region, started using matchlocks[50] which were, in any case, more efficient than the crudely made arquebuses available to them till then. It could have been partly in response to this situation that there was created in the Mughal army a body of mounted musketeers possessing the skill of firing their muskets without dismounting. Islam Khan Rumi's *barqandaz* retainers were perhaps one such group. They are reported to have been the experts of the Ottoman style of fighting based on the use of muskets (*madar-i jung-iRumi bar banduq bud*).[51] It is likely that these new type of musketeer horsemen were armed with the Turkish version of European flintlocks. The specimen description of a flintlock reproduced by Anand Ram Kayath in *Siyaq-nama* (1696)[52] indicates that this musket was known in the Mughal military establishment during Aurangzeb's reign. But, as is evident from Bhimsen's description of Islam Khan Rumi's clumsy method of supplying gunpowder to his horsemen during a skirmish with the Marathas, the rigidity of the Mughal military organization based on a contract system did not suit this new form of warfare. Apparently, the new system required a more centralized organization of production, distribution and supply of firearms of different types which was practically ruled out in the *mansab* system of the Mughals.[53] It is, therefore, understandable that, despite there being strong reasons for shifting to the new form of musketeering, the flintlock musket and the skill of using it from horseback did not find wide acceptance in the Mughal Empire.

While concluding this discussion, one may reiterate that of all the different type of firearms introduced by Babur in India, the wide use of the matchlock musket, perhaps, had particular relevance to the centre's control of internal resources in the Mughal Empire. This is why muskets were considered 'honourable' not only when carried by the cavalry but also in the hands of ordinary musketeers firing from the ground.[54] The high status of the musket was reflected in Humayun's establishing in 1535 a rule that his leaving the *Diwan* would be announced by firing of a musket.[55] Significantly, Abu'l Fazl makes it a point to mention his hero Akbar's interest in this weapon and his being unsurpassed in making and handling it. In *A'in-i Akbari*, one of the three military skills prescribed for a commandant administering a province is that of shooting with the musket. It is put at par with horsemanship and archery.[56] It is, therefore, not surprising that the foot musketeers, though poorly paid as compared to the cavalry troopers, were allowed certain concessions like, for example, payment in advance of a part of the salaries which was not deducted during camapigns.[57] Their average stipends were always higher than those of the ordinary foot-soldiers of other categories.[58]

A similar situation obtained with regard to mounted musketeers. As early as 1636, *sih aspa* (three horse) and *chahar aspa* (four horse) *ahdi barqandaz* staioned in the Deccan were allowed to maintain one horse less than the number indicated by their ranks (*du aspa*). Till then, this privilege was not allowed to ordinary *ahdi* horsemen.[59] Again, additional payment to some of the horsemen in the contingent of the Kachchwaha chief of Amber during Aurangzeb's reign, on their equipping themselves with muskets (*azafa-ba-shart-i banduq*) also appears to point to the musket's special status as a weapon of war in the Mughal Empire.[60] Although, as Irfan Habib stresses, the main strength of the Mughals lay in their mounted archery,[61] the matchlock musket appears to have contributed from the very beginning significantly to the exercise of imperial control over disaffected localities or tracts.

Iqdar Alam Khan was formerly Professor of History at the Aligarh Muslim University, Aligarh.

*This article was presented as a paper at the Medieval History Section of the Indian History Congress Session, December 2004.

NOTES

1. Cf. Carlo M. Cipola, *Guns and Sails in the Early Phase of European Expansion,* 1400–1700, London, 1965, p. 28; Geoffrey Parker, *The Military Revolution: Military Innovation and Rise of the West,* 1500–1800, Cambridge, 1988, p. 8.
2. Marshall, G. S. Hodgson, *The Venture of Islam: The Gunpowder Empires and Modern Times,* vol. III, pp. 17–8, 26.
3. Ibrahim-i Qawam Faruqi, *Sharafnama-i Ahmad Munnairi* (1457–75), entitled *Farhang-i Ibrahimi,* AMU, Aligarh, Habib Ganj Collection 53/22, under *Kashakanjir.* See also Jonaraja, *Rajatarangini* (1459), tr. T. C. Dutt, *Kings of Kashmir,* Delhi 1968, pp. 105–6 and Srivara, *Jaina Rajatarangim* (1486), tr. Kashi Nath Dhar, New Delhi, 1996, p. 39.
4. Shihab Hakim, *Ma'asir-i Mahmud Shahi* 1467–8), ed. Nurul Hasan Ansari, Delhi, 1968, pp. 56, 87; and Mahmud Gawan, *Rayazu'l Insha* (1470), ed. M. Shafi, Lahore, 1941–9, p. 72. See also Iqtidar A. Khan, *Gunpowder and Firearms: Warfare in Medieval India,* New Delhi, 2004, p. 42.
5. *Ma'asir-i Mahmud Shahi,* pp. 85–9 and *Rayazu'l Insha,* pp. 72–4.
6. Muhammad Qasim Hindu Shah Firishta, *Tarikh-i Firishata,* (1607), vol. II, Kanpur, 1884, pp. 202, 251.
7. Cf. *Gunpowder and Firearms,* pp. 48–9.
8. *Ma'asir-i Mahmud Shahi,* p. 56. The chief of Mewar is reported to have supplied two *Kaman-i ra'ds* made of an alloy of copper (*half-josh*) to the ruler of Gagaraun in 1442–3.
9. See *Gunpowder and Firearms,* pp. 50–2.
10. Haroon Khan Sherwani, *The Bahmanis of Deccan,* Hyderabad, 1953, pp. 296, 323–4. The Bahmani Kingdom is described as attaining 'a height unequalled in the whole of its history' during the 'premiership' of Mahmud Gawan under Muhammad Shah Bahmani. Cf. *Rayazu'l Insha,* p. 72.
11. Burton Stein, in *The Cambridge Economic History of India,* eds., Tapan

Raychaudhuri and Irfan Habib, vol. I, *c.*1200–1750, Cambridge, 1982, p. 119.

12. See Iqtidar A. Khan in the *Journal of Royal Asiatic Society,* April 1999, pp. 27–32.
13. See *Gunpowder and Firearms,* pp. 94–5.
14. Mirza Haidar Doghlat, *Tarikh-i Rashidi,* MS, Aligarh University Collection, Aligarh Muslim University, no. 34, f. 351a.
15. 'Abdul Qadir Badauni, *Muntakhab-ut-tawarikh,* (1596), ed. Ahmad 'Ali and others, vol. I, Calcutta, 1869, p. 412.
16. Abu'l Fazl, *Akbar-nama,* ed. Agha Ahmad'Ali and 'Abd al-Rahim, vol. II, Calcutta, 1873–87, 36; Nizam al-Din Ahmad, *Tabaqat-I Akbari,* ed. B. De, vol. II, Calcutta, 1913, p. 131.
17. Cf. W. H. McNeill, *The Pursuit of Power, Technology, Armed Force and Society since* AD 1000, Chicago, 1982, pp. 95, 98. Attributes the 'precarious' nature of Mughal control in the Deccan to the difficulty of moving siege guns long distance overland.
18. *Gunpowder and Firearms,* p. 97.
19. *A'in-i Akbari,*(1598), vol. I, 1893, p. 82. See also *Journal of Royal Asiatic Society,* April 1999, p. 27.
20. Cf. A. S. Beveridge, *Babur-nama in English,* reprint, London, 1969, pp. 550, 568–9.
21. *Gunpowder and Firearms,* pp. 85, fn. 46, 150.
22. Op. cit., pp. 164–5.
23. Op. cit., pp. 74–9.
24. Op. cit., pp. 103, 120–1 f. ns. 43 and 44.
25. Op. cit., pp. 91–2. Compare *A'in-i Akbari,* vol. I, p. 82 and *Babur-nama* in English, p. 117.
26. *A'in-i Akbari,* vol. I, p. 82.
27. Francois Bernier, *Travels in the Mogul Empire,* 1656–8, tr. A. Constable, revised by V. A. Smith, London, 1916, p. 254.
28. Compare *Gunpowder and Firearms,* pp. 107–10.
29. J. N. Sarkar, *Military History of India,* reprint, Delhi, 1970, p. 89.
30. Bernier, p. 49; Nicolao Manucci, *Storia do Mogor,* 1656–1712, tr. William Irvine, vol. I, (London, 1907–8), reprint Calcutta, 1965, p. 254.
31. For an argument that muskets brought to India by Babur were matchlocks of Ottoman origin, see *Gunpowder and Firearms,* p. 143.
32. *Babur-nama in English,* pp. 468–9, 473–4, 557–8, 568–9.
33. David Ayalon, *Gunpowder and Firearms in the Mamluk Kingdom,* London, 1962, pp. 60, 88–9.
34. Yusuf Mirak, *Mazhar-i Shahjahani* (1634), ed. Pir Hasanuddin Rashidi, Part 2, Karachi, 1961, pp, 139–40. There is described a skirmish between a party of Mughal horsemen using muskets and a large band of Nahmardi tribesmen of *pargana* Schwan (Sind).

35. William Irvine, *The Army of the Indian Mughals,* reprint, New Delhi, 1962, p. 103.
36. Cf. Sidi Ali Reis, *Travels and Adventures of the Turkish Admiral Sidi Ali Reis,* tr. A. Vamberey, London, 1899, p. 37, A band of 30 foot-musketeers forced a large body of Rajput horsemen to retire.
37. *Gunpowder and Firearms,* p. 150.
38. *Ain-i Akbari,* vol. I, pp. 84–5.
39. Op. cit., vol. I, pp. 121, 134 Compare Shireen Moosvi, *The Economy of the Mughal Empire, c.1595: A Statistical Study,* Oxford Uuniversity Press, 1987, p. 223. She interpretes the text here differently.
40. *Selected Documents of Aurangzeb's Reign,* ed. Yusuf Husain Khan, Hyderabad, 1958, pp. 200–1.
41. For Maha Singh Bhadoria's request to be allowed such a privilege, see *Waqa 'i' Sarkar Ajmer wa Ranthambhor,* (1678–80), MS, Asafia Library, Hyderabad, *Fan-i Tarikh,* Aligarh transcript, pp. 417–8.
42. Irvine, *The Army of the Indian Mughals,* p. 173, Compare R. A. Alvi, *Studies in the History of Medieval Deccan,* Delhi, 1977, p. 30.
43. The lowest cost of the musket as given by Abu'l Fazl is half a rupee while the price of a horse is set at Rs. 2. Again, an ordinary handgun could be obtained for half the cost of an ordinary sword. Cf. *A'in-i Akbari,* vol. 1, p. 82.
44. Abu'l Fazl, *Akbar-nama,* vol. III, ed. Agha Ahmad 'Ali and 'Abed al-Rahim, Calcutta, 1887, p. 382. Cf. Abu'l Qasim Namakin, *Munshat-i Namakin,* MS, Aligarh Muslim University University Collection, 26, 675b.
45. Cf, *Gunpowder and Firearms,* pp. 153–4.
46. For a reference to *barqandaz sawar*s see *Tuzuk-i Jahangiri,* ed. Saiyid Ahamad, Ghazipur and Aligarh, 1863–4, p. 238.
47. For a reference to a *barqandaz sawar* serving in the contingent of a Rajput noble in *suba* Deccan in the year 1636, see *Select Documents of Shahjahan's Reign,* ed. Yusuf Husain Khan, Hyderabad, 1950, p. 25. Compare *Gunpowder and Firearms,* p. 152.
48. Bernier, p. 217. For musketeers participating in the Battle of Samugar (1658), he mentions three rates of payment: Rs. 20, Rs. 15 and Rs. 10 per month. These obviously are not the scales of foot-musketeers, who were never paid more than Rs. 6 per month. C. Shireen Moosvi, *The Economy of the Mughal Empire, c.*1595, p. 227. Yak *aspa ahdi*s were paid Rs. 20 per month.
49. This is borne out by a perusal of Jaipur Record no. 3833: '*uluja siphain,* in the Rajasthan State Achives, Bikaner.
50. Manucci, *Storia de Mogor,* 1656–1712, tr. W. Irvine, vol. II, London, 1907–8, reprint, Calcutta, 1965. p. 131.
51. Bhimsen, *Nuskha-i Dilkusha,* MS, Br. Library, Or. 23, f.66a.
52. Nand Ram Khayasth, *Siyaq-nama,* Lucknow, 1879, p. 154.

53. Athar Ali, *The Mughal Nobility under Aurangzeb*, revised edition, Delhi, 1997, p. xx was first to make this point.
54. For a contrary view see Stewart Gordon, 'The Limited Adoption of European Style Military Forces by the Eighteenth Century Rulers in India', *The Indian Economic and Social History Review*, vol. xxxv, no. 3; and Jos Gommans, *Mughal Warfare*, London, 2002, p. 161.
55. Khawar Shah bin Qibad al-Hussain (d.1565), *Tarikh-i Ilchi-i Nizam Shah*, MS, British Library, add. 23513, ff228b–229a.
56. *A'in-i Akbari*, vol. I. pp. 83, 196; see also 'Ali Ahmad Khan, *Mirat-i Ahmad*, ed. Nawab Ali, vol. I, Baroda, 1928, p. 167.
57. *Cf, Ruqq'a-i Hakim Abu'l Fath Gilani*, ed. Muhammad Bashir Husain, Lahore, 1968, p. 128.
58. *A'in-i Akbari*, vol. 1, pp. 82, 134; Shireen Moosvi, *The Economy of the Mughal Empire*, pp. 229–30. Cf. Irvine, *The Army of the Indian Moghals*, pp. 167, 173.
59. *Select Documents of Shah Jahan's Reign*, ed. Yusuf Husain Khan, pp. 24–5.
60. Several such orders are to be found in the bundle, *Siyaga ziayadtri wa kami daftar-i bakhshi, farsi*, 112911/11774, Sambat, in the Rajasthan State Archieves, Bikaner.
61. Irfan Habib, *The Agrarian System of Mughal Empire*, 1556–1707, second revised edition, New Delhi, 1999, p. 364.

CHAPTER 10

Gunpowder Artillery and Military Architecture in South India (15–18th Century)

Jean Deloche

The purpose of this article is to enquire whether the introduction of gunpowder artillery affected the military architecture of Indian forts. While in Europe walls and towers vulnerable to shot and mining were built at ground level, in India, on the contrary, tall and massive enclosures were being built until the end of the eighteenth century. The reason for this is probably that military engineers thought that the thickness of their masonry was sufficiently strong to resist siege engines, but this implies that the destructive capacity of guns was inadequate, a remark which raises the big issue of the nature of gunpowder artillery in the subcontinent.

In the Deccan, scattered on the ramparts of the forts, there are hundreds of guns which did not attract the attention of scholars but could be examined by specialists in metallurgical engineering. It is imperative that a physical examination of these weapons be carried out in order to find out what was exactly the existing state of metalworking and gunmaking during the medieval period and, thus, point out what was the effectiveness of Indian artillery.

Introduction

We know that the impact of gunpowder artillery on the architecture of the forts in Europe turned out to be of far-reaching significance. Profound changes in the art of static defence took place from the fifteenth century onwards. High walls and towers vulnerable to shot and mining were built at ground level, behind a deep ditch, in such a way that their masonry, invisible from outside, was well protected from shots by a glacis, in front of the counterscarp, sloping gently towards the open country.

In India, on the contrary, a striking feature of the fortifications is that tall and massive enclosures were being built until the end of the eighteenth century. With the progress of artillery, military engineers never considered lowering the curtain walls and the towers to reduce the surface exposed to missiles and to minimize their impact, as was done in the West, where the defence works consisted mainly of trenches and low extended parapets.

It is not easy to find an explanation for this choice. Engineers could choose between two solutions: they could either reduce or increase the command of the defensive works. In the first instance, the result would have been the reduction of the extent of view over the assailant, who could get closer to the fortification; in the second instance, the consequence would have been to increase the distance of visibility over the assailant and prevent him from making approaches, but this would have made the fortification vulnerable to artillery shots. Still they opted for the principle of the high command.

It is not because of tradition (high structures have always been symbols of strength and domination) that they adopted this defence system. If they continued building high curtain walls and towers, it is probably because they thought that the thickness of their masonry was sufficiently strong to resist siege engines. But the natural implication of this assumption would be that the destructive capacity of the guns used in the different kingdoms of India was inadequate, a remark which raises the big issue of the nature of gunpowder artillery in the subcontinent.[a]

This problem deserves a thorough analysis. We will here confine ourself to a few observations made during our fieldwork; while studying South Indian forts (it should be kept in mind that our survey was limited, as we could not cover them fully: the curtain wall round Bijapur is 10 km. in length!).

The High Command of the Fortified Positions in South India

As regards the south of the peninsula, particularly the Deccan plateau,[b] a careful examination of the fortified works[1] points out that during that period, towers tended to rise and to exceed the curtain walls in height; at certain places they have been elevated by several metres (at Solapur, Gulbarga); the most famous are at Bijapur, where the Firangi Burj, built in 1576, is 9 m. higher than the adjacent curtain walls, and at Golkonda, where the height of the lower portion of the Musā Burj (consisting of three storeys) is 18 m. from the bottom of the ditch.

It also shows that on most of the towers and at certain points above or behind the curtain walls, cavaliers (or platforms used as a support for the cannons), generally circular in shape, sometimes rectangular, square, or polygonal, were raised, providing the maximum of flanking fire. Among the various improvements carried out to strengthen the defence in this part of India, this is perhaps the most conspicuous innovation.

Cavaliers

The greatest cavaliers are found on the towers of the main enclosures (at Gulbarga, there is one that has a diameter of 14.80 m.); the smallest are on the towers of the low walls surrounding the rampart (about 5 m. in diameter); on the curtain walls, they have a diameter of 6–7 m.

At Bidar, behind the curtain walls, three independent massive towers were erected. One of them (Kālā Burj) is 10 m. high and 20 m. in diameter.

At several sites, high and solid isolated towers are found. They are rectangular or circular, accessible by staircases. At Naldurga, there is an enormous cylinder, erected in 1558, 27 m. high and 20 m. in diameter; at Bijapur, Haidar Burj, built in 1583, oval in shape, is 24 m. high; the most noteworthy is the Bālā Hisar at Gulbarga: it is a rectangular structure 54 m. long, 32 m. wide, and 19 m. high, and with two staircases.

As will be seen below, several of the guns found on these cavaliers are dated, most of them from the second half of the sixteenth century and the second half of the seventeenth century. As these towers existed before the installation of the cannons, it can be deduced that cavaliers were built from the middle of the sixteenth century to the eighteenth century, i.e. at a period when heavy artillery played a certain role in military operations in the Deccan.

Circular Gun Platforms

Upon these cavaliers there are large paved stone platforms, in the centre of which there are circular sockets to hold the pivot of the gun upon which the carriage revolved, and, at a distance from it, corresponding to the length of the gun, there is a channelled ring, cut into the pavement, in which the wheels of the carriage travelled; towards the back of the gun is a heavy segmental recoil wall, built back at a very short distance from the weapon, in order to counteract the recoil of the gun and prevent strain upon the pivot when firing. At some places there are several platforms of this type on the same tower, facing different directions: at Bijapur, on the Sherzā Burj, and at Gulbarga, on the top of Bālā Hisar, they are three in number.

Mode of Mounting Guns: The huge cannons weigh several tonnes, and are without trunions, so their barrels were possibly held to large balks of timer laid on the ground.

All the other guns are fitted with trunions resting on forks provided with a pivot, allowing the barrel to turn round (inside the socket mentioned above) on a horizontal and vertical plane.

Khan[2] mentions the extensive use, in north India, of light cannons resting on some kind of swivels fired from the back of camels, and, for the Deccan (ibid., pp. 109–10), following Cousens[3] refers only to light cannons (*jinjals*) working on swivels seen in the Firangi Burj at Bijapur, adding that 'these could be *relics* of Mughal times since the fort was taken over by the Mughals in 1686.'

This mounting of guns cannot be considered a vestige of north Indian influence, because it was widely distributed all over the Deccan much before the arrival of the Mughals: it is found in all the sites, whether the guns are large or small, long or short. At Naladurga, above the enormous stone cylinder built by Āli Ādil Shāh in 1558, on the two circular stone platforms, there are two cannons of this type.

Gunners firing light cannons from the ramparts were using them in a more simple manner. According to the French traveller de la Flotte, who was in south India in 1758–60, guns, when used in fortresses, 'are put on the very embrasure, or they are supported by two great movable timbers.'[4]

In Mughal miniatures drawn at Akbar's ateliers (1600), on the rampart of the north Indian strongholds, we see light guns put inside the crenels of the parapet or resting on two- or three-legged supports, as well as large cannons extending beyond the rampart through rectangular window-shaped loopholes, apparently without any stand.[5]

In these documents are also shown besiegers' guns mounted on two- or four-wheeled carriages having a platform with wooden planks on the sides and drawn by bullocks.[6]

In south India we have no evidence of this device, since no war scene is represented in Deccan paintings and no wooden structure of that period has been preserved. Wooden gun carriages upon which the barrel was permanently mounted were apparently not used in the Deccani forts for defence. As regards field artillery, we do not know how it was raised into position in siege operations against strongholds. Were the guns dragged unmounted along the ground towards the fort or mounted on wheeled carriages, as in Hindustan? It is probable that this last solution was adopted, at least during Aurangzeb's campaigns.

Guns Preserved in the Fortifications

Inside the forts of the Deccan, scattered on the ramparts or on these platforms, there are hundreds of guns that can be examined. In all the sites visited by us, except in Solapur, where the cannons rest on masonry supports in the garden of the fort, and in Naladurga, where some pieces are found at the entrance, guns are seen, lying in bushes or still in position on the platforms, some on their pivot.

The reason why they are still there is that they have not been removed after the Deccan forts were taken by the Mughals, because the fortified sites, having still a strategic value, were maintained by the new rulers and were provided with a garrison. On the contrary, in strongholds taken by the European armies during the Anglo-French conflict, indigenous cannons are usually not found, because they were taken away and dismantled. At Senji (Gingee), for example, in 1751, all the guns in the fort were pulled down from the hills by the French and convoyed to Pondicherry.[7]

Now these guns found in the old Deccan kingdoms did not attract the attention of scholars. It is indeed strange to note that there is no mention of them in all the learned articles written on warfare in medieval India. Obviously, except for the few pieces bearing inscriptions,[8–10, 11–15] experts on firearms are not aware of their existence. It is, therefore, urgent to consider them.

Design Features of the Guns

During our fieldwork we photographed and measured some of them, but not systematically. For the use of scholars, we have collected here whatever information has been published on the guns, particularly those bearing inscriptions, at Bidar, Bijapur, Golkonda, Parenda and Basava Kalyana, in the form of a table, mentioning the characteristics of the different weapons. Basically, two types of cannons are found in these forts (see Table 10.1):

1. the first type is the cast bronze cannon;
2. the second is the wrought iron cannon composed of iron bars yoked together by iron rings.

The most famous in the first category is the *Malik-i-Maidan* (Monarch of the field), at Bijapur, produced by a Turkish expert in the middle of the sixteenth century, made of an alloy of copper and tin, and weighing 55 tonnes.[16]

Among the notorious cannons of the second type, also at Bijapur, there are the *Lamcharri* ('Far-flier', 9.32 m. in length) and the *Landa Qassab* gun (weighing about 47 tonnes), both made 'of wrought iron bars of square section, laid horizontally about a core, and square section rings slipped on over these, one at a time, each being welded with the last while white hot'.[17]

As regards the guns of Bidar, Yazdani[18] while describing them in detail, does not mention the metal used for their fabrication; he just says that the 'large gun' in Mandu Gate has a highly polished surface and is built of bars of laminated metal, bound with hoops which have been 'welded together beautifully'.

The guns of Golkonda fort, described by Khwaja Muhammad[19] and G. Yazdani[20] were made, according to inscriptions, by the same man, Muhammad Ali Arab. The first author says that the *Qila Kusha* and Atish Bar guns are 'of bronze'; the second states that the Fath Raibār and *Azdāha Paikār* guns are 'made of laminated bars welded together and clasped with iron hoops'. R. Balasubrahmaniam tells

Table 10.1: Dimensions of a Few Cannons with Names, Date, Type and Places

Place	Name	Date	Type	Weight of the cannon (ton)	Length of cannon (m.)	Diameter of the muzzle (cm.)	Diameter of the bore (cm.)	Weight of the shot (kg.)	Powder
Bijapur	*Malik-Maidan* (Sherza Burj)	1549	Cast bronze	55	4.36	149	71.12	-	-
Bijapur	*Landa Qassab* (S. bastion)	1646	Wrough iron	47	6.57	13.4	49.53	-	-
Bijapur	*Lamcharri* (Hairder Burj)	1583	Id.	-	9.32	97.2	30.48	-	-
Bijapur	Other cannon (Haider Burj)	-	Id.	6.04	-	20.32	-	-	-
Bidar	*Ali Barid* (Mandu Gate)	1542	-	-	4.49	106	48.26	136	27.2
Bidar	*Fath Laskhar* (N.W. Cavalier)	1580	-	-	3.45	77.45	36.70	54.8	19.9
Bidar	*Top i-Haidari* (Lal Burj)	1596	-	-	3.65	83.2	36.80	-	-
Bidar	*Ali Barid* (Kala Burj)	1596	-	-	5.50	87.2	48.20	136	27.2
Bidar	Long Gun (W. plateau)	1569	-	-	8.83	53.3	15.20	-	-
Bidar	*Top-i- Mahmud Shahi* (Munda B.)	1591	-	-	-	-	-	-	-

Golkonda	*Azdaha Paikar* (Musa Burj)	1674	Wrought Iron and cast bronze	-	4.41	71	-	33.4	10.9
Golkonda	*Fath Raihbar*	1672	Cast bronze	-	4.94	66	-	33.4	11.2
Golkonda	*Dushman Kob* (Sampolia Burj)	1673	-	-	4.77	50.8	-	-	-
Golkonda	*Qila Kusha* (Baradari)	1666	Cast bronze	-	3.25	38	15	10.2	3.8
Golkonda	*Atish Bar* (Bala Hisar)	1679	Id.	-	5.18	48	18	12.5	4.1
Parenda	*Malik-i- Maidan* (N.E. bastion)	1663	-	-	-	-	-	33.4	11.1
Parenda	*Azdaha Paikar* (S.W bastion)	1660	-	-	5.20	-	-	16.7	5.6
Parenda	Gun (N.W. bastion)	-	-	-	5.00	75	30	-	-
Basava Kalyana	*Naugaj top*	-	-	-	-	4.70	60	23	-
Basava Kalyana	*Barid Shahi*	-	-	-	3.30	30	12	-	-

Sources: Bijapur: H. Cousens, *Bijapur*, pp. 29–33 and pls III et IV; Bidar: G. Yazdani, *Bidar*, pp. 35–6, 38–9, 42-3, 85 and pls XVII and XVIX; Golkonda: G. Yazdani, inscriptions in Golkonda Fort, in *Epigraphia Indica, Arabic and Persian Supplement*, 1913–4, pp. 55–6; Inscription on a gun at Golkonda, in *Epigraphia Indo-Moslemica*, 1935–6, p. 23; Ahmad Khwaja Muhammad, Some new inscriptions from the Golkonda Fort, in *Epigraphia Indo-Moslemica*, 1937–8, pp. 47–9; Parenda: G. Yazdani, Parenda; a historical fort, in *Annual Report of the Archaeological Department of His Exalted Highness the Nizam's Dominions*, 1921–4, pp. 19–20 & 24-5. Basava Kalyana: our own measurements. In the inscriptions, the weight unit is *jahangīrī* and *shāhājahānī*. They have been converted into kilograms and grams, following the equivalences given by I. Habib, *The Agrarian System of Mughal India*, Bombay, 1963, pp. 366–9.

me that he studied *Azdāha Paikār* in great detail and found that this is a bronze cannon, not an iron one, the inner bore being only lined with iron strips.

It is, therefore, imperative that specialists in metallurgical engineering look into the matter seriously. This is not the job of epigraphists and archaeologists (see also Table 1).

Cannon Balls

At all the sites, only spherical stone balls are found. At Parenda, in a store room they are nearly 300 in number. At Basava Kalyana, we measured one of them having a diameter of 45 cm. Nowhere are metallic balls met with. Perhaps, these projectiles were taken by the local inhabitants for their own use. Some specimens could be preserved in museums. Orderly investigations should be carried out in order to catalogue and analyse the finds.

Khan[21] specifies that the earliest reference to metallic cannon balls (cast brass shots weighing from 1.2 kg. to 12.6 kg.) in Mughal sources dates back to 1540, that the earliest allusion to the use of lead for making shots dates back to 1572; he adds that a large-scale switching from stone to metallic balls took place in the seventeenth century, but that finally the Mughals continued to use stone balls on a large scale in their cannons because it was much cheaper.

In the inscriptions carved on the guns, the weight of the shots as well as that of the powder is usually mentioned.

At Bidar, in the large guns, such as the two *Ali Barid* (dated 1569 and 1572), we find 136 kg. for the shot and 27.2 kg. for the powder, but we cannot say whether the projectile was a stone ball or a metallic object.

At Bijapur, the huge Malik-i-Maidan probably discharged shots of more than 200 kg. H. Cousens[22] writes that what was fired from this cannon was 'rather grape-shot or slugs, in the shape often of bags of dumpy copper coins, when nothing else was available'.

We may assume that the balls used in the lighter guns, manufactured during Aurangzeb's reign in Parenda and Golkonda, were metallic: the weight of their shots varies from 10.2–33.4 kg. and that of the powder used for discharging, from 3.8–11.2 kg.[c]

But it is probable that, until the end of the seventeenth century when military operations in the Deccan intensified under the reign of Aurangzeb, stone balls were mostly used. In a document dated to 1671, it is mentioned that 'military commanders in the field began to insist on only wrought-iron shots, which was bound to accelerate the process of gradual discarding of stone balls.'[23]

Effectiveness of Artillery

Whatever their shots, the damage caused by the large guns of the sixteenth century found at Bijapur and Bidar is difficult to assess. They must have impressed the troops more by the noise they were making than by the strength of their projectiles. Pietro Della Valle, the Italian traveller who was in south India in 1623, noticed that this type of cannon 'is useless for war and serves only for vain pomp.'[24] 'Moreover, we have to take into account a major problem: the lack of mobility of these pieces at the operational level. First, on the battlefield. How to position such heavy cannons (55 or 47 tonnes) so that, on firing, the discharged projectile will hit the target. Second, over long distances. Even dragged by a hundred pairs of oxen with several elephants to push behind, it must have taken months to convey such loads to their destination.

As regards field pieces of the seventeenth century, particularly those used during Aurangzeb's reign in his long campaign in the Deccan, they must have been effective on the battlefield, especially if metallic balls were used, but, in siege operations against forts, cannons were less successful in breaching stone curtain walls and towers, if, as noticed by de la Flotte[25], in the middle of the eighteenth century, the balls were of stone: these projectiles could only bounce off the walls without making any opening in the masonry.

Cannons have, in any case, never been the determining factor in the sieges laid by the Mughals in south India. As we know, the fate of most of the fortifications in the Deccan (and in India), was usually not decided by artillery, but by diplomacy or bribery.[26]

We are now in a position to answer the question asked in the Introduction. Actually, Indian military engineers opted for the principle of the high command, raised curtain walls, and towers, and did not bother to reduce the surface exposed to projectiles, because they knew that guns could not cause great damage to stone walls, i.e. that fortifications could withstand the siege technology of the day.[d] This does not mean that the impact of gunpowder artillery on military architecture was negligible. The examination of the fortified works points out that, with the development of firearms, various improvements were carried out on curtain walls, towers, parapets and gateways,[27] but this is a different aspect of our subject.

Conclusion

In conclusion, we would like to emphasize the need for a physical examination of firearms in India in order to find out what exactly was the existing state of metalworking and gunmaking during the medieval period. Almost all the books and articles written on artillery are based on literary sources, which are always difficult to interpret.

Systematic technical studies and chemical analyses on the weapons have to be carried out in different parts of India, so as to determine the nature of metal used in the fabrication of the guns (cast-bronze, wrought iron, etc.), the workmanship of their barrel (straight and smooth, of constant internal diameter), their capacity to withstand the explosion of the charge without cracking, the nature of the projectiles (stone, iron, cast iron balls), of the powder, and thus reveal the measure of the gunsmiths' skill.

Investigations should also be made on the ballistic characteristics of the cannons in order to give an estimate of their accuracy and range and, thus show (what is most important for historians) their destructive capacity.[e] Experts are exhorted to go and see the guns on site.

1. A careful examination of the cannons, still on their pivots, at Gulbarga and Basava Kalyana, is likely to throw light on the accuracy of aim of these weapons (at Gulbarga, to the north of the village, children come and play with a gun which they call *jhula tope*, because the pivot is so sensitive that they can have a swing). We would like to know whether the mounting of guns on fork and pivot was efficient, whether the angle of elevation could be easily adjusted, and finally, whether the wall, built a short distance behind the weapon, was able to counteract successfully the recoil of the gun and prevent strain upon the pivot when firing.
2. As regards the range of the guns, Khan,[28] depending on

Persian chronicles, asserts that the heavy mortars in the fifteenth century were very effective (which is doubtful), that a mortar made at Agra in 1527 had a range of 1,600 paces (1,219 m.), and another one, used in 1540, a range of a *farsak* (about 5.5 km.), a figure obviously exaggerated. Now, in the inscriptions found on the guns, the actual charge of the projectile is mentioned. Experts, by considering the length of the barrel, the diameter of the bore, the weight of the ball, and the quantity of powder used for projecting them, should be able to estimate the range and effectiveness of the cannons.

3. Lastly, we wonder whether the guns were normally aimed point-blank or a little above the horizontal. When it was necessary to use a high trajectory with an elevation of 45° or more in order to bombard hidden targets, did the engineers use mortars with a projectile containing a charge of powder exploded by a fuse? Literary sources keep us guessing; only experts, after examining the structures, will be able to tell us the real nature of the guns.

Notes

a. Before starting a careful examination of the weapons, we have to recollect what we know about gunpowder artillery in south India and keep in mind some points of reference. According to Iqtidar Alam Khan,[29] gunpowder appears to have come to India from China during the second half of the thirteenth century; a type of rocket was then adopted in Hindustan and the north of the Deccan during the second half of the fourteenth century; the use of gunpowder artillery increased from the middle of the fifteenth century and, after the arrival of the Portuguese in 1498 and Bābūr's invasion (1526), guns started playing a very significant role in military operations.

Regarding the Deccan kingdoms, it should be stated that, besides European or north Indian influence, the impact of West Asian gunnery, especially Ottoman technology, has been of far-reaching significance. The inscriptions of the last decade[30, 31] of the fifteenth century unequivocally point to the role played by Turkish engineers. The best example, as we know, is that of the famous Malik-i-Maidan, which was made by the son of a man called Hasan

Rumi.[32] Later, we find the names of Arab mechanics as gunmakers and among them the name of one Muhammad Hussain Arab, the maker of the Parenda guns[33] and Muhammad Ali Arab, the maker of some magnificent guns at Golkonda.[34, 35]

b. The best examples of this type of fortification are found on the Deccan plateau at Golkonda, Gulbarga, Naldurga, Parenda, Basava Kalyana and Daulatabad; the best documented are the strongholds of Bidar[36] and Bijapur.[37] Bidar fort was built in 1429, remodelled in 1461, and restored in 1565. In Bijapur, curtain walls around the city were completed in 1565.

c. Khan[38] suggests that the weight of a projectile, used at Herat in 1443, was 200 *man*, i.e. 1,200 kg. which appears implausible.

d. The Indian system was based on the accumulation and the great size of the obstacles opposed to assailants: mud ramparts in which shots buried and lodged themselves without doing any harm and hard stone revetments from which shots were deflected.

e. To evaluate gunpowder weaponry in India, European engineering should not be taken as the yardstick of Indian development. We cannot be satisfied with the opinion of European observers in the eighteenth century, who do not, as a rule, speak favourably of the Indian artillery, finding the guns 'cumbrous, ill-mounted and ill served'.[39]

Abbreviations

ARMAD: *Annual Report of the Mysore Archaeological Department*
ARADEHND: Annual Report of the Archaeological Department of His Exalted Highness, the Nizam's Dominions.
BEFEO: Bulletin de l'Ecole francaise d'Extrême-Orient
IAR: *Indian Archaeology, A Review*
MaSG: Maharashtra State Gazetteers
MySG: Mysore State Gazetteers

NOTES

*Editor's Note: For the sake of simplicity and brevity, the endnotes have been rearranged and the pictures accompanying the original article have been deleted in this reprint.

*Ecole Francaise d'Extreme-Orient, Centre de Pondichery, P.O. Box No. 151, 16 and 19 Dumas Street, Pondicherry 605001, India.

1. J. Deloche, 'Etudes sur les fortifications de l'lnde. IV. La fortification muisulmane dans Ie Dekkan méridional (XVe–XVIIIe siecle)', *BEFEO*, vol. 89, 2002, pp. 39–106.
2. I. A. Khan, *Gun Powder and Firearms, Warfare in Medieval India*, Delhi, 2004, pp. 107–8.
3. H. Cousens, *Bijapur and its Architectural Remains, with an Historical Outline of the Adil Shahi Dynasty*, Bombay, 1916.
4. W. Irvine, *The Army of the Indian Moghuls: its Organization and Administration*, reprint, New Delhi, 1962, p. 123.
5. I.A. Khan, *Gun Powder and Firearms*, pp. 102, 104–06.
6. Ibid., pp. 68, 111.
7. J. Deloche, *Senji (Gingi), ville fortifiée du pays tamoul*, Pondicherry, 2000, pp. 131–2, 225–9.
8. H. Cousens, *Bijapur and its Architectural Remains.*
9. H. Cousens, *List of Antiquarian Remains in His Exalted Highness the Nizam's Dominions*, 1900.
10. H. Cousens, *Notes on the Buildings and other Antiquarian Remains at Bijapur*; tr. of the inscriptions by E. Reatshek, Bombay, 1890.
11. G. Yazdani, *Bidar, its History and Monuments*, Oxford, 1947.
12. G. Yazdani, 'Inscriptions in the Fort at Qandhar', *Epigraphia Indo-Moslemica*, 1919–20, pp. 22–3.
13. G. Yazdani, 'Parenda: a historical Fort', in *ARADEHND*, 1921–4, pp. 17–26.
14. G. Yazdani, 'Note on the Survey of the Mudgal Fort', ibid., 1935–6, p. 227 and pl. IX–X.
15. G. Yazdani, 'Inscriptions in Golkonda Fort', *Epigraphica Indica*, Arabic and Persian Supplement, 1913–4, pp. 55–6.
16. H. Cousens, *Bijapur and its Architectural Remains*, pp. 29–30.
17. Ibid., pp. 31–3.
18. G. Yazdani, *Bidar and its History and Monuments*, p. 36.
19. Khwaja Muhammad Ahmad, 'Some New Inscriptions from the Golkonda Fort', in *Epigraphia Indo-Moslemica*, 1937–8, pp. 47–9.
20. G. Yazdani, 'Inscriptions in Golkonda Fort', in *Epigraphica Indica*, pp. 51–5.
21. I.A. Khan, *Gun Powder and Firearms*, pp. 88, 111, 113.
22. H. Cousens, *Bijapur and its Architectural Remains*, p. 29.
23. I.A. Khan, *Gun Powder and Firearms*, p. 113.
24. H. Cousens, *Bijapur and its Architectural Remains*, p. 30.
25. W. Irvine, *The Army of the Indian Moguls*, p. 123.
26. J. L. Jos Gommans & H. A. Kolff Dirk, *Warfare and Weaponry in South Asia*, 1000–1800, New Delhi: Oxford University Press, 2001, p. 36.
27. J. Deloche, 'Etudes sur les fortifications de l'Inde.IV. La fortification muisulmane dans le Dekkan méridional (XVe–XVIIIe siècle)', pp. 39–106.

28. I.A. Khan, *Gun Powder and Firearms*, pp. 48, 72.
29. Ibid., pp. 1–27.
30. G. Yazdani, 'Inscriptions in the Fort at Qandhar'.
31. G. Yazdani, 'Note on the Survey of the Mudgal Fort'.
32. H. Cousens, *Bijapur and its Architectural Remains*, p. 29.
33. G. Yazdani, 'Parenda: a historical Fort', pp. 24–5.
34. G. Yazdani, 'Inscriptions in Golkonda Fort', pp. 55–6.
35. Khwaja Muhammad Ahmad, 'Some New Inscriptions from the Golkonda Fort', pp. 47–9.
36. G. Yazdani, *Bidar and its History and Monuments*.
37. V. S. Sarma, *History and Antiquities of Raichur Fort*, Delhi, 1998.
38. I.A. Khan, *Gun Powder and Firearms*, p. 42.
39. W. Irvine, *The Army of the Indian Moguls*, pp. 116–8.

SECTION III

A Military Revolution in Early Modern India (1740–1849)?

CHAPTER 11

Military Structure of the Portuguese Navy in the Indian Ocean—The First Half of the 16th Century

Vitor Luis Gaspar Rodrigues[1]

Cabral's fleet has testified, in 1500, that the Indian Ocean was in fact a 'Moslem lake' where, according to Luis Filipe Thomaz, 'the second Islam, the peripheral, the Turkish and the Mongol Islam, coming from the steppe (. . .) had killed all Christianity in Asia which had, until then, played a relevant part in the trade dealings';[2] this had urged King Manuel and his counsellors to rethink about all the adopted strategy. In fact, the intended plan to conquer the near East and its following intervention in the spice trade through an alliance with the Christian kingdoms, which were presumably powerful, would crumble away. The king and his followers, aware of the true religion of the Indian subcontinent and conscious of their incapability to face, in terms of commerce, the Moslem forces in the Indian Ocean, and helped locally by several small kingdoms in the Malabar and the African East Coast eager to free themselves from their powerful neighbours, chose to confront their old enemy.

Once it was decided to blockade the Red Sea in order to strengthen the sea-route of the Cape, a Portuguese fleet was able to patrol, in 1502, the Indian Ocean and the Malabar Coast. Since then, the Portuguese policy would engage itself with the annihilation of the Red Sea trade and the maintenance of the gold trade in Soffala, reducing, consequently, Kilwa to a state of dependency, as well as imposing a trade treaty to Calicut.

The Portuguese naval force was thus established and became famous, through its surveillance at the Malabar seaports as well as the Babelmandeb Strait, for a number of military actions characterized by the capture of ships and cargo, which became a source of revenue to the king and his officers. During this first phase, which stretches out more or less until the beginning of Afonso de Albuquerque's government and is marked by the consignment of a number of strong fleets, the Portuguese, owing to a naval victory over the Mameluke fleet off Diu in 1509, were able to control the western Indian Ocean.

In less than ten years a new military power, mainly owing to the unquestionable superiority of its ships and the skill of its seamen, was thus able to become a great naval force in the Indian Ocean as well as in the Malacca seas when, in 1513, Fernão Perse de Andrade's fleet with only 17 ships managed to destroy the 90 ships' fleet of Pate Unuz, thus annihilating, for several years, the Jaus's naval forces in that area. Endowed with strong and seafaring warships (owing to the naval building techniques as well as the materials used) and having an artillery much stronger than the other military forces, Turks and Mamelukes included, the Portuguese began to take possession of the main trade routes, although they never succeeded in destroying the Red Sea route.[3] Moreover, according to Jose Alberto Barata, 'their ships were better equipped to face the weather conditions and dare to sail even during the winter season';[4] this fact was indeed very advantageous, mainly when they were forced to help any of their forts. Diu, for instance, was able to resist the Turkish and the Gujarati forces by virtue of the military help sent from Goa by D. Joao de Castro, in spite of the monsoon season.

Besides the superiority of the equipment found on the Portuguese vessels, a certified fact in high seas or trans-oceanic routes, a better bowline as well as a navigation by way of astronomic instruments could also be added which, according to Vitorino Magalhaes Godinho, would enable, them to absorb almost momentarily, the Indian Navy.[5] However, they were only able to retain all that knowledge through the high technology level the Portuguese navy had attained at its arrival at the Indian scene. On the other hand, the Portuguese had always known how to use the knowledge and the labour of the Asian populations to their own convenience; the decisive part taken by the 'gentile troops'[6] as well as by the 'casados' in the formation and the maintenance of the 'State of India' corroborates it[7]; G. V. Scammel, as well as other authors, aimed at underestimating the importance of the superiority of the Portuguese ships and artillery as a major factor for their establishment in Asia, in order to emphasize the role performed by the local forces acting under King Manuel's rule.[8]

Lastly, but not less important or even decisive, the Portuguese also presented a united front to a country politically as well as religiously divided. The fact that there was a viceroy or a governor of province endowed with exceptional powers and authority over all the Portuguese population in the Orient, as well as the foundation of a 'State of India', had also contributed to increase the military sovereignty of the Portuguese navy in the Indian Ocean. That same year, according to Castanheda, in order to achieve a better performance of the Portuguese vessels stationed in the Indian Ocean, two *Capitanlias-Mores* were thus created: the first one whose jurisdiction extended from Cape Guardafui to Cambay, and the second one from Cambay to Cape Comorin.[9]

With Afonso de Albuquerque, a new period begins, characterized by the development of the Portuguese expansion over the Persian Gulf and *Insulindia*, thus strengthening the power of the Portuguese navy. If the victory over Goa, Malacca and Ormuz as well as the surrender of the Zamorin of Calicut had turned the State of India into a 'network consistently established all through the Indian Ocean and politically structured',[10] it had also resulted in an increased military effort for the Portuguese crown, either in terms of men or ships.

Albuquerque's role in the renewal and improvement of his fleet was a very important one. He also ordered the building of a great number of vessels, better equipped to sail along the coast and more suitable to fight in rivers and estuaries in order to enable the Portuguese ships and caravels to manoeuvre in shallow and more tricky waters. [11]

Besides, while carrying out a policy of rationalization and efficiency of his settlement, he sent all the necessary military reinforcements and fleet to the fortresses. In 1511, when he set forth to conquer Malacca, he left in the western Indian Ocean 1,200 men and 18 ships distributed between Goa and Cochin, together with those consigned for the Red Sea blockade.[12] However, this could only be achieved because he was able to take possession of the ships from Diogo Mendes de Vasconcelos' fleet, who was sent from Portugal with the specific purpose to claim the great Malayan city.

After conquering the city, Albuquerque left there, under the command of Manuel da Lacerda, a fleet of ten ships of which some had already been built in India,[13] besides his garrison and crew, thus giving rise to the Southern Seas Armada, whose duty was to control its major trading routes. According to Gaspar Correia, the soldiers left there amounted to 500, men '300 in the fortress and 200 at sea with the exception of 120 who were taken by Antonio de Abreu to remain in Malacca when they returned'.[14] The outcome of this operation carried out by Albuquerque meant a remarkable increase in the number of Portuguese vessels sailing in the Indian Ocean between 1511 and 1515.

From the approximately 30 ships Albuquerque had in 1511, the entire Portuguese naval force in that region[15] grew to 45 in 1512, which gives us an estimate of the effort made to strengthen the fleets. On the other hand, we do not know this growth was due to an increase of seamen sent by the Portuguese crown. The details show that the number of ships pertaining to the *Carreira da India* remaining in the Orient decreased in the second decade of the sixteenth century.

This effort to endow the state of India with a navy suitably equipped to solve all problems which the enlargement of its area would pose would somehow be maintained by his successors, as the letter written on 30 October 1520 by Nuno de Castro would prove. He claimed to have a fleet of 79 ships and caravels, as well as 25 to 30 barges.[16]

This number would increase according to the interests of the Portuguese crown in the holdings scattered over the Indian Ocean as well as the Pacific coasts. In fact, the conquest of new areas on land led to the building of new ships, on the premises whenever possible, in order to support its garrisons and very often used as a means to serve the official as well as the private trading interests, in this case the interests of some unscrupulous captains. These small fleets, consigned to the defence as well as to the surveillance of the Indian Ocean's surrounding areas, co-existed with the fleets built in Cochin and Goa that sailed every year in order to patrol the Straits and the western Indian coasts.

According to *Relação dos navios que servem na India* prepared by the comptroller of the India's Treasury in 1522, the forts on the Malabar Coast as well as the neighbouring ones had only one *parau*; on the other hand, in Ormuz, Ceylon, and Malacca, small fleets consisting mainly of barges and *parau*s were dependent on the forts.[17] Two caravels and one brigantine were also stationed in Soffala and Moçambique in 1530; these were meant to patrol these waters subject to regulations.[18]

In addition, at the beginning of 1520, a captain and factor's position were also established on the Coromandel coast, which had at its service a small fleet to guard the coast from Paleate to S. Tomé of Mylapore as well as to grant free trading charters to the Asian navigation.[19]

Besides these regular fleets, which were somehow subjected to the seasonal rhythm of the monsoon, more or less detailed references to the organization of occasional fleets appointed to assist any part of the state or, when necessary, to take part in military expeditions, can be found in documents and chronicles. In such cases, the application for building civilian ships was very common; it was accomplished either through the distribution of incentives for the building and repair of ships suitable for rivers, or the assignment of captain to its owners. This fact confirms the double function of these ships, namely, economic and military by that time; these would remain as such through the forthcoming century.

With the increase of the Turkish threat in the Indian Ocean, mainly since the conquest of Bacora in 1546 and the expansion of the controlling region, Portuguese India became more and more dependent on the use of private ships as well as of vessels and men arriving from Portugal. According to Y. M. Godinho, this threat 'forced the sailing of important reinforcements in 1538: eleven great vessels sailed on the 8 April carrying 4,000 to 5,000 soldiers, some of whom were cavalrymen.'[20]

From Goa, which had become under Nuno da Cunha's government the political as well as the administrative centre of the

Portuguese empire, the leading fleets would sail away after having been chosen and the captains of the ships having been appointed. When the monsoon ended, the ships pertaining to the Northern Fleet sailed towards Cambay, Ormuz and the Strait but, according to Jose Alberto Barata, as the years went by, the number of vessels stationed at the entrance of Red Sea was diminishing. In fact, from 1540 onwards, the sea-route linking Cambay to the entrance of the Gulf was more guarded, a task the fleet stationed in Diu also performed as it fell to its surveillance of the Gulf of Cambay[21]

Among the fleets leaving Goa towards the south, the more important ones were: the Malabar Fleet assigned to control the commercial outflows of the pepper trade as well as the pirates; the Canara Fleet endeavouring to assure a normal amount of food supplies to Goa and to the northern fortresses; and the fleet guarding the coast from Cape of Comorin to Ceylon, thus protecting the ships carrying cinnamon as well as those arriving from the coast in the Bay of Bengal and the Southern Seas.

Besides these regular fleets, there were others whose sphere of action was more limited, also sailing away from Goa and returning once again during the summer. These fleets included, usually, lighter ships, sometimes rowboats and flatboats, appointed to inspect more efficiently the region nearer to the coast.

The increasing use of a Mediterranean type of ships on the main fleets of the Portuguese State of India was a growing phenomenon around the middle of this century. This order, which had occasioned vehement discussions between those backing the use of big ships and those defending use of rowboats,[22] had basically various concepts of naval war. On the one hand, it can be apprehended as the outcome of a better adjustment to the local problems; on the other hand, it seems to arise from the economic and political crisis that ravaged the Portuguese State of India as well as Portugal.[23]

Indeed, the cost and the time applied for the building of these ships together with a growing need to get more men might have induced the leaders of India's military policy to choose that solution. Perhaps the reason lies in the fact that towards the middle of the sixteenth century with the decline of the Turkish threat, a great naval power could not yet be found in the Indian Ocean that would cause the use of strong fleets.

Nevertheless, this bet involved a number of serious risks. On the one hand, because, as stated by D. Joao de Castro, it concerned slow ships while sailing in open seas and was not suited for great voyages and needed a big crew; on the other hand, this choice also meant the victory of the ancient techniques of naval war over the modern technical and tactical conceptions, which would soon be fatal for the Portuguese.

As they maintained the old tactic of attacking and boarding enemy ships using galleys and a few galleons (as the Turks had already done),[24] they became more and more dependant on the crew. Later, it would prove to be fatal when the Portuguese fleets confronted the ships pertaining to countries of northern Europe, specially the Dutch ones, as they used a tactic which aimed to affect the enemy with long range artillery. Never again would the ships be used as a means of transportation of men intended to attack the enemy through boarding, to become themselves the leaders of the combat with their cannons. The confrontation could not be more unequal.

NOTES

1. Researcher of the Centro de Estudos de Historia e Cartografia Antiga, Instituto de Investigacao Cientifica Tropical and follower of Fundação Oriente.
2. Luis Filipe F. R. Thomaz, *De Ceuta a Timor,* Lisboa, 1994, p. 174.
3. On this subject see also Charles Boxer, 'A note on Portuguese Reactions to the revival of the Red Sea spice trade and the rise of Atjeh, 1543–1600', *Journal of Southeast Asian History*, vol. X, Singapore, 1969, pp. 415–28.
4. José Alberto Leitão Barata, *Os Senbores da navegação Aspectos nauticos do dominio portugues no Oriente por meados do seculo XVI* (1543–70), Lisboa, tese de Mestrado em Historia Doscobrimentos e da Expansão Portuguesa apresnatada a Univasidade Nova de Lisboa, 1992, ed. policopiada.
5. Cf. V. M. Godinho, *Mito e Mercadoria, Utopia de Navegar, Seculos XIlI a, XVIII,* Lisboa, 1990. p. 319.
6. We use the word 'gentile' without any depreciative or ethnocentric sense. For Europeans, it means the mass of persons who do not believe one of the three religions of the Book: Christian, Jew or Islamic. In the Asiatic context, it is mainly appropriate to Hindus.
7. For a study about this subject see our work, 'Contributo das "tropas gentias" e dos "casados" para a afirmaçãio' e 'Mmanutenção do "Estado

da India" no seculo XVI', in *Actas da VII Reunião International de Historis da Nautica e da Hidrografia,* Viana do Castelo, 1994, no prelo.

8. Cf. G. V. Scammel, 'Indigenous assistance in the establishment of Portuguese power in Asia', in *Modern Asian Studies,* vol. 14, part I, Cambridge, February 1980, pp. 1–11.
9. Femão Lopes de Castanheda, *Historia do Descobrimento e Conquista da India pelos Portuguese,* II–I, Porto, 1979, p. 210.
10. Cf. Luis F. R. Thomaz, 'Estrutura politica e administrativa do Estado da India no seculo XVI', in *Actas do II Seminario d. Historia Indo-Portugesa,* Lisboa, I.I.C.T.-C.E.H.C.A., 1985, p. 519.
11. Castanheda, op. cit., III-LXXX, says that Albuquerque had built in 1512 30 *catures* to fight the Calicut army.
12. Letter from Albuquerque to Durate Galvãlo, dated end of 1511, in *Cartas de Afonso de Albuquerque seguidas de Documentos que as elucidam,* by R. A. de Bulhlão Patoe and H. L. de Mendonça, vol. I, Lisboa, Academia Real das Sciencias, 1884, pp. 396–7.
13. Cf. letter from Albuquerque to King Manuel, dated 20 August 1512, in op. cit., I, pp. 66–8.
14. Gaspar Correia, *Lendas da India,* vol. II, Porto, Lello e Irmao, 1975, p. 267.
15. Cf. letter from Albuquerque to Duarte Galvãlo (note 11), pp. 396–7.
16. A.N.T.T., C.C. , 1-9-126.
17. Cf. *Releção navios que servem na India,* dated 11 May 1522, in *Docummtos sobre os Portuguese em Moçambiqlle e na Africa Central (*1497–1588*)*, VI, Lisboa, C.E.H.U.–N.A.R.N., 1969, p. 92.
18. Cf. *Regimentot de Sofala,* dated 20 May 1530, in op. cit., pp. 362a, 366.
19. For a study about this subject, see Sanjay Subrahmanyam, 'O comercio e a bandeira: os Portuguese em Negapatão, 1530–1658', in *Comercio e conflito A presenca Portuguesa no Golfo de Bengala,* 1500-1700, Lisboa, ed. 70, 1994, pp. 87*ff.*
20. Arquivo de Simancas, *E* 371, de Luis Sarmiento, apud V. M. Godinho, op. cit., p. 366.
21. See Jose Alberto Barata, op. cit., pp. 74–7.
22. Ibid., pp. 321a–325.
23. About that economic and political crisis, see V. M. Godinho, 'Flutuações economicas e devir estrutural do sec. XV ao sec. XVII' in *Ensaio,* II, Lisboa, Sá da Costa, 1978, pp. 261a, 270; and S. Subrahmanyam, *The Portuguese Empire in Asia* 1500–1700, *A Political and Economic History,* London, 1993, pp. 80a–100.
24. About this subject, see Carlo M. Cipolla, *Canhõese Velas na primeira fase da Expansão Europeia,* 1400–1700, Lisboa, 1989, pp. 94a–97.

CHAPTER 12

Hyder Ali's Fleet

Surendranath Sen

One of the most formidable enemies the English had in India, was Hyder Ali, the able and energetic ruler of Mysore. He formed a steadfast alliance with the French against their common adversary. His son, Tipu, went farther and opened negotiations with many foreign potentates—Zeman Shah of Afghanistan, the Imam of Muscat and, last but not least, the Sultan of Turkey. His ambassadors received a warm welcome at Versailles and although these diplomatic efforts met with scant success, Tipu could very well claim to be the only Indian prince who took any interest in the world politics of his day. But an Indian ruler could not expect to form an effective alliance with Muscat or Constantinople unless he had a strong fleet at his command. Tipu, it is well-known, made an attempt to organize a good fighting fleet, but it will be a mistake to suggest that Hyder had failed to appreciate the value of a powerful navy. His English enemies were strong on the sea, his Portuguese neighbours still relied on their navy in their struggle with Indian states, even the Peshwa possessed a fleet of his own. When the conquest of the Malabar Coast put Hyder in possession of the famous ports of that region, he naturally aspired to extend his power over the sea, but our knowledge of his naval policy is extremely limited. We know that he had a fleet and we also know that his men-of-war were of no use to him in his war against the English. But when he actually undertook the organization of his navy and what agencies he employed for this purpose are not generally known. It is, however, not impossible to supplement our meagre knowledge on this subject with some scraps of information from unpublished Portuguese records.

Colonel Wilks mentions Hyder's fleet but once. In 1768, the Mysore admiral deserted his master's cause and joined the English.[1] Low gives the following account of this incident in his *History of the Indian Navy.*[2] 'Early in 1768, the Bombay Government fitted out an expedition, consisting of a squadron of their ships, with four hundred European troops and a large body of sepoys, to attack Hyder Ali's sea ports on the Malabar coast. The enterprise was completely successful. The expedition first made its appearance off Onore, or Honawar where Hyder Ali, the great ruler of Mysore, familiarly known at this time as Hyder Naick, had begun to prepare a fleet. He had, however alienated from his interest the captains of his ships by appointing as his admiral Ali Bey,[3] an officer of cavalry, who of course, was totally ignorant of nautical matters. The consequence was that, when the expedition appeared off Onore, Hyder's fleet, consisting of two ships, two grabs, and ten galivats, sailed and joined the English. Onore, and Fortified Island, at the mouth of the Onore river, were captured, and thence the expedition sailed for Mangalore.' Thus in 1768, his fleet proved worse than useless to Hyder. On land he could hold his own against his enemy, but on the sea he had the misfortune of witnessing his fleet going over to the other side. Hyder was not a person to be disappointed by a single disaster, however serious, and we shall see how he made a fresh attempt to recoup his loss and reorganize his navy.

If a contemporary Portuguese letter is to be believed, the numerical strength of Hyder's fleet was somewhat greater than that indicated by Wilks and Low. By 1763, Hyder had risen to sufficient eminence and a short biography of his was forwarded to Lisbon along with a letter, dated 26 January 1764. This brief but interesting sketch gives a fairly accurate account of Hyder's conquest of Kanara but does not say anything about his naval power.[4] In a letter, dated 23 September 1765, we come across the first notice about Hyder's growing power on the sea.[5] It runs as follows: 'The whole of this part of Asia [now] enjoys the benefit of a peace [which is] insecure, on account of the unbridled ambition of the potentates who rule this area: Our neighbours the Marathas and Haidar Aly concluded it during the last winter, and the freedom, in which the latter is, permits him to augment a fleet which has already begun to cause us some anxiety, and if at present we fear him as a pirate, we have reason to apprehend that time and luck may give him the power to ruin us. We know that his fleet now consists of thirty vessels of war and a large number of transport ships. It is commanded by an Englishman with some European officers.' In a letter, dated 12 December of the same year,[6] we again read of Hyder's increasing maritime power. It will not, therefore, be unreasonable to infer that Hyder first launched his fleet sometime between 1763 and 1765, and like many of his neighbours, employed European officers to command his navy. But it is a matter of surprise that his admiral should be an Englishman. Wilks and Low say nothing about the nationality of the admiral who joined the English so readily. Nor do we know whether the Englishman, mentioned in the letter quoted above, continued to hold his command till 1768. But apart from the discontent attributed to the appointment of a cavalry officer to the chief naval command, the ready rebellion and desertion of the fleet may very well be explained by the nationality of the admiral. It may be noted in this connection that not merely the English officers, but European commanders of other nationalities as well, deserted Daulat Rao Sindhia during the Second Maratha War. It is not unlikely that Hyder appointed Lutf Ali Beg to the head of his fleet because he could not implicitly trust the commanding admiral who happened to be an Englishman. But this is a mere conjecture.

We learn from a letter[7] addressed by Jose Pedro da Camara to Martinho de Mello e Castro on 28 December 1778 that Hyder was again building a large number of men-of-war and a Dutchman had been employed to strengthen the harbour of Bhatkal. The letter deserves quotation: 'I should particularly inform you that the Nabob Haidar Ali, aspiring to make himself as respectable on the sea as he is formidable on land, has ordered the construction of many sailing ships[8] in all the places of the south coast [which are] big enough for this great work. He has hitherto in the sea or in stocks eight three-masted ships which carry 28 to 40 pieces [of artillery] and a similar number of *Palas*, also in the sea or in docks, of lesser tonnage. For making a greater progress in the work and to provide necessary accommodation for building and preserving the most powerful fleet in Asia, he began this month to build a stockade above the water line in the gulf of Batical, which is situated near Onore on the firm land to the south, and is near the island of Angediva, with the intention of constructing a huge mole which will enclose a port, where, (at the full tide) it is said, a large fleet can anchor. The projected work also includes fortification for the defence of the port. It is being at present outlined according to its circuit inland; it will have an enclosure big enough for a large borough for the residence of numerous merchants of all nationalities who are expected to be attracted by the gift of convenient plots of the neighbouring lands and the loan of capital, which will ensure their establishment in that place where large warehouses for storing goods, articles and ammunition for a big marine, and factories for the work of a busy arsenal have been so well planned.' The letter proceeds to say that this great work was under the charge of a Dutchman named Joze Azelars, who was originally an ordinary shipwright in the service of the Dutch East India Company. He professed to be a skilled engineer when he entered the service of Hyder Ali, and undertook to finish the work in three years at an estimated cost of seventeen lakhs of pagodas. Jose Pedro da Camara, to whom we are indebted for this information, was of opinion that it would be impossible to complete the work in the stipulated period for lack of skilled workmen, and we do not know whether this grand scheme was ever realized.

We read in another letter (in the same bundle), dated 11 May 1779, that the work was not progressing satisfactorily. After giving a brief account of Hyder's annexation of the Krishna–Tungabhadra *doab*, the letter proceeds to say, 'the mole that the Nabob planned at Batecal, very near Angediva, is being built very slowly, because the Dutch director of the work encounters difficulties enough in the inlets of the bay and (experiences) greater opposition from the Brahmans who assist him as inspectors or overseers of that work. This is all that I can inform Your Excellency about the progress made by this terrible prince.'[9]

Hyder died in 1782, but before his death his fleet suffered another terrible disaster, as we learn from Captain Low. 'In the latter part of 1780, Sir Edward Hughes, while on the West Coast of India, dealt a fatal blow to the rising maritime power of Hyder Ally, against whom we were engaged in a life and death struggle. On the 8 of December, being with his squadron off Mangalore, the principal dockyard and naval arsenal of Hyder Ally, the Admiral saw two ships, a large grab, three ketches, and many small vessels, at anchor in the roads with the Nawab's flag flying on board them. He immediately stood in, and finding them to be vessel of force, and all armed, anchored as close to them as the depth of water would allow, and ordered the boats of the squadron to destroy them under cover of the fire of two ships of the Bombay Marine. This service was conducted with the usual spirit and activity of British seamen, and, in two hours, they took and burnt two ships, one of twenty-eight, and the other of twenty-six guns; one ketch of twelve guns was blown up by the enemy at the instant the boats were boarding her; another ketch of ten guns, which cut her cable, and endeavoured to put to sea, was taken, and the third, with the smaller vessels, were forced on shore, the grab only escaping into the harbour, after having thrown everything overboard to lighten her.'[10]

Thus ended the great projects of Hyder Ali, and the naval power of Mysore died in its infancy. Colonel Kirkpatrick was of opinion that Hyder had bestowed little or no attention on the organization of a fleet,[11] but the Portuguese letters, mentioned above, leave no doubt that Kirkpatrick's conclusion, based on negàtive evidence alone, can no longer be upheld. The earliest reference to Tipu's fleet was to be found, according to Kirkpatrick, in a letter[12] the Sultan addressed to Mir Ghulam Husain on 24 September 1786. The navy, says Colonel Wilks, 'was not finally organized on paper till 1796, and can scarely be deemed to have had a practical existence'.[13] The maritime hopes of Mysore perished with Hyder, and although Tipu established commercial relations with the Imām of Muscat, he did not succeed where his father had failed.[14]

NOTES

1. Colonel Wilks, *Historical Sketches of the South of India* (2nd edn), vol. 1, p. 331.
2. Low, *History of the Indian Navy*, vol. I, p. 153.
3. Lutf Ali Beg, according to Wilks.
4. Archivo Ultramarino, Officios dos Governadores, Maço 2, no. 12.
5. Officios dos Governadores, Maço 3, no. 44.
6. Officios Gos Governadores, Maço 3, no. 25.
7. Officios dos Governadores, Maço 5, no. 70.
8. Embarçacoens de gavia.

9. Archivo Ultramarino, Lisbon, Officios dos Governadores, Maço 5, no. 28.
10. Low, *History of the Indian Navy*, vol. I, p. 178.
11. *Select Letters of Tippoo, Sultan*, p. 415.
12. *Select Letters of Tippoo Sultan*, p. 414.
13. *Historical Sketches of the South of India* (2nd edn), vol. II, p. 267. It is, however, difficult to accept this statement of Colonel Wilks. In 1787, an alliance between the Portuguese and the Marathas was proposed against Tipu. Two articles of the draft treaty provided for Portuguese naval cooperation with the Marathas against Tipu's fleet. It is, therefore, clear that Tipu's fleet had a practical existence as early as 1787. Officios dos Governadores, Maço 20, no. 95. Biker, *Tratados da India*, vol. VIII, pp. 221–2.
14. Copies of four letters written at different times to one Raghuji Angria, who is described as Captain of Hyder Ali's fleet, are to be found in the Goa archives. These letters, however, furnish no information about the Mysore fleet except that a Hindu officer once occupied a high office in Hyder's navy.

CHAPTER 13

Limitations of Military Technology: Naval Warfare on the West Coast, 1650–1800

Anirudh Deshpande

The problematic of 'military revolution' opens the possibility of inquiring further into questions of historical needs of societies and the mentalities of the peoples involved in warfare. This essay examines the concept of 'military revolution' and tests its validity with respect to certain aspects of early modern Indian military history. It is argued here that the role of military technology in the military–naval history of the western coast of India, specifically in the eighteenth century, requires reappraisal. The author contends that the role of military technology in history can be fruitfully defined only in relation to interactive factors like geography and politics conditioning the environment of early modern warfare.

This foray is a preliminary examination of the concept of 'military revolution' propounded by Geoffrey Parker in relation to modern European, and conversely colonial, history. A study of the concept is followed by a test of its validity with respect to certain aspects of early modern Indian military history. Our conclusions of the matter lead to a reappraisal of the role of military technology in the military–naval history of the western coast of India, specifically in the eighteenth century. Our contention is that the role of military technology in history can only be fruitfully defined in relation to interactive factors like geography and politics conditioning the environment of early modern warfare. It is true that the problematic of 'military revolution' opens the possibility of researching further into questions of historical needs of societies and the mentalities of the peoples involved in warfare. At the same time, detailed military history and even salted narratives do enrich social history immensely.[1]

Let us first define the term 'military revolution'. The concept was named and examined first by Michael Roberts in 1955. In between 1560 and 1660 he singled out four changes in the European art of war as crucial. First, came a revolutionary change in tactics with emergence of massed archers and organized musketry. Second, the army size in most states grew markedly. Third, more complex and ambitious strategies were evolved to bring these armies into action. Finally, these factors in combination had an important impact on society. Soon after this, in 1956, Sir George Clark praised the concept in his Wiles Lectures at Belfast, helping it become a new orthodoxy in military history well up to the 1970s. Since then, however, historians have broadened the connotations of the concept by stressing the dialectic of the modern state and the evolution of military technology. In short, 'military revolution' now appears allied to certain significant developments in European history such as the formation of the modern nation-state, the industrial revolution and the age of expansion and reconnaissance.[2]

Interestingly enough, the thesis of 'military revolution' refers to the period before 1800 despite the several limitations experienced by warfare in it. Among several aspects of this concept in early modern Europe were the qualitative and quantitative improvements in artillery, consequent changes in the design of forts, the increasing dependence on firepower in actual battle and the rising importance of the infantry. At the same time, however, limitations, accepted by Parker, arose. Since artillery development was coterminous with improved fortification, siege and attrition evolved, making stalemate common: 'Most wars fought in Europe before the French Revolution were not brought to an end by a strategy of extermination, but through a strategy of attrition, via the patient accumulation of minor victories and the slow erosion of the enemy's economic base.'[3] In India too, decisive British engagements were fought against the Mysoreans, Marathas, and the Sikhs only in the late eighteenth and early nineteenth centuries. Similarly, on the Konkan coast before the late eighteenth century, attrition was more important than outright victory.

The 'military revolution' of the sixteenth and seventeenth centuries in Europe involving developments in military technology raised the costs of war tremendously, meaning that mercantilism and the growing nation-state had new challenges to answer. Most commanders preferred attrition to assault, for defensive technology aided by long range heavy cannon became a potent factor creating stasis in warfare. Contracting in recruitment and supply remained and matters of war were generally decentralized in nature. Similarly, standardization in uniforms and armament were desired but rarely achieved in practice. Europe still had to go a long way before attaining standing armies and an all-round proficiency in military affairs. Indeed, the early 'military revolution' made the state and economy preponderant in military history.[4]

During mercantile expansion, when land war usually produced stalemates, states often turned to naval power in search of decisions. Parker contends that failures on land deflected national strategy in Europe towards the sea. However, it can be added that as sea-borne trade grew after 1500, naval power became a prerequisite of successful maritime trade and brigandage. It can be argued with equal historiographical force that in a period marked by uncertain treaties, frequent piracy, and state-sponsored mercantilism, naval power emanated more from broader historical needs and the geographical placement of the Atlantic nation-states. In the sixteenth century, as Tudor shipbuilding attempts show, it had become clear that England or Holland could overcome the far-flung Spanish empire primarily through naval strength. In fact, the arena of forcing decisions had itself changed.

What possibly could sea power have meant in the age of the sail? In early modern Europe, no one equated sea power with an unhindered mastery over international waters. It is well-known that early trading companies were formed primarily to trade and not conquer. Their officials appreciated naval support without conceiving naval mastery over opponents. Most early modern European states were economically incapable of exercising an overwhelming naval supremacy on the high seas. Nonetheless, the era between the great discoveries of the 1490s and the 1840s when the Royal Navy was at its dominating best is often called the golden age of sea power.[5] The imperialistic eulogy of European and later British sea power, reflected most significantly in the works of Alfred Mahan, evolved in the late nineteenth century. Later, several authors revised the notion of sea power, pointing out the limitations inherent in Mahan's work which nonetheless displayed good strategic insight. Moving decisively away from 'salt water narrative' Graham, a noted scholar of sea power, asserts that in the 'eighteenth and nineteenth centuries sea power was probably most influential when it was least conspicuous. . . . Even in time of peace it functioned as a powerful instrument of diplomatic action and compulsion.'[6] Students of sea power now take a sober look at the immensely complex historical process which finally resulted in the naval domination of the East by the West. The navigational talent of medieval Asians have been recognized and appreciated. Historians for long have conceded that maritime trade in these regions much before the Europeans appeared was highly international.[7]

Between 1500 and 1800, the process of European naval warfare on open seas was marked by two important developments. First, a change in naval tactics became possible with the mounting of guns in the centre of ships. Second, with the help of naval superiority, European powers successfully dominated international waters. This was a 'great irony', for firearms were originally used at sea by the Chinese who stopped doing so from about 1550 onwards. In fact, as early as 1522, the Ming navy deploying artillery defeated a Portuguese flotilla off Tunmen delivering the captured Europeans to execution.[8] The Europeans took to sea-borne artillery from the fourteenth century onwards. The early advance of firearms on sea was slow and throughout the fifteenth century, ships intended to carry mostly anti-personnel pieces and light breech loaders. The galley permitted guns either in stern or stem but the change came with the Venetian galeass, a sail-cum-oar ship, 50 metres long by nine, carrying heavy guns at both ends and anti-personnel pieces along the sides. At Lepanto in 1571, this design was vindicated against the Turks.[9]

What really transformed naval warfare between 1450 and 1650 was the gradual evolution of the heavily armed sailing ship. During these years, experiments with sail plans and designs affording reductions in crew gathered momentum. First, as the galleys proved, experiments were made with light guns of about four pounder size. After 1500, heavy muzzle loading artillery pieces were mounted in the sides of the ships in specially designed gun ports and by 1588, England came to possess a navy with heavy guns. In Tudor shipbuilding drives, ships weighing easily over 500 hundred tons and carrying more than 50 guns were purpose built. These ships, made of several layers of reinforced planks, could withstand rough weather and heavy punishment and with refits, could last as long as 70 to 100 years. This capital gunship was slow and required large crew, but it brought into battle heavy artillery with devastating effect. Improvements in gun carriage designs, made to deal with recoil efficiently, aided this process and here the Atlantic powers proved resourceful. The 40 gun, 300 ton galleon frigate, an ace from the point of view of satisfying most of the needs of naval warfare, was perfected by the Dutch. For general purposes and especially commerce raiding, as the French were to prove later, the frigate was ideal. Combining speed, range, firepower and mobility, the frigates in the seventeenth century became the ships of the line and played a crucial role in the 'savage and prolonged naval rivalry' among the Atlantic states between 1588 and 1700.[10]

It is well-known that muskets and cannon played an impressive role in the Spanish conquest of America because the American Indians were virtually defenceless against such means of waging exterminatory wars. Europe could, however, gain an oceanic hegemony only after subduing the better armed Asian kingdoms in the nineteenth century. The territorial conquest of India was signally important for the final European supremacy in the East. Before the conquest of India in the nineteenth century, the 'military revolution' was tested to its full on sea as well as land. Since most of India was free of British control before 1800, the problems raised by the applicability of concepts like the 'military revolution' to Indian history appear rather complex. On sea too, matters were never as simple as they appeared in America, and Graham even contends that during the colonial domination of the eastern waters, the Royal Navy was never strong enough to ensure victory in any major battle without substantial support from outside.[11] Indeed, overenthusiasm for sea power has often led to a predating of British naval supremacy in Indian waters.

Specificity of Indian History

While important technological changes were sweeping over European maritime history, some easterners were not sitting idle. In the seventeenth century the Egyptians, in a bid for naval power under the Ottomans, tried in vain to resist the Europeans. In the latter half of that century, the Omanis rose to fame and in 1698 ousted the Portuguese from Mombasa. In India too, the Maratha navy was first formed and then expanded and on the Malabar coast the so-called Malabar pirates became active. The greatest challenge to rising European hegemony, according to Parker, who dismisses Indian naval resistance by mentioning the Malabar pirates, came from the Chinese captain Cheng Chengkung, better known as Coxinga, who, in the mid-seventeenth century, cut deep inroads into the Dutch monopoly from Fukien. By 1655 he had about 2,000 warships and 1,00,000 troops. Fortunately for the Europeans, he died aged 37 in 1662, leaving behind a son who continued resistance for another 20 years before finally being defeated by a Ching–Dutch alliance. This, according to Parker, established an equilibrium in Asian waters which lasted well into the nineteenth century.[12]

In India, following the Portuguese example, the English East India Company (hereafter Company) created a small navy to protect its trade. By 1615, this navy had become a permanent force of some 10 gurabs and galbats (local sail-cum-oar vessels convenient for coastal navigation) employing lascar crew and mounting some guns. It was in the latter half of the seventeenth century that the Company began to register a serious naval presence in the Arabian Sea. A variety of factors was responsible for this, including the acquisition of Bombay in 1665. The Company directors had been dwelling upon the strategic importance of Bombay from 1654 onwards although it is difficult to say why the Portuguese, with shipyards in Bassein, did not develop the superbly sheltered Bombay harbour into a maritime base. The Company lost no time in utilizing the services offered by Bombay and initially, technical expertise was imported from England. In 1669, for the purpose of conveying trade, work was begun on three small armed vessels at Bombay. The growing Maratha Navy and Shivaji's sack of Surat in 1664 also underpinned these early efforts. Soon, Warwick Pett of the celebrated Pett family of Deptford was appointed the Company's shipbuilder and orders were placed for necessary equipment in England. In 1670, orders were passed for the construction of two brigantines. At this stage, naval construction was aimed at building smaller and fast sailing vessels mounted with light guns to defend trade against local navies generally deficient in artillery.[13]

The measures taken during the late seventeenth century seemed to have enhanced English confidence on the western coast. By 1716 the Bombay Marine, as the Company navy was officially called, comprised a ship mounting 32 guns, four gurabs having 20 to 28 guns and 20 smaller gurabs and galbats carrying between five to 12 pieces each. This 'grab service', however, gave the Company enough courage to attack in vain some Angre strongholds in 1717. In 1722, to keep the pressure on an Anglo-Portuguese alliance, it also tried to besiege Alibagm an important Angre fort.[14] European naval presence on the western coast in this period was largely confined to the Company navies.

In the early eighteenth century the Company began to employ Parsi shipwrights regularly in Bombay, and soon realized that the forests near Bombay were rich in valuable timber and native artisans proficient in shipbuilding. The Bombay dockyard, thus established, functioned well into the second half of the nineteenth century. Dominated by the famous Wadia families it produced reputed ships, some of them being capital gunships for the Royal navy. The professional abilities of the Bombay dockyard were acknowledged by the chief engineer of the dockyard, Cursetjee, before the Parliamentary Select Committee in 1853.[15] But all this did not mean that the Marine had become a professional navy. Its officers were usually factory clerks performing military duty in search of prize, and crew composed of Europeans and lascars were generally drunk on the spirits sold to them at a profit by their officers. Drunkenness was so common and detrimental to the health of men and navy alike that in the 1730s express orders were passed, restraining the officers from selling liquor to the sailors. Similarly, to enhance efficiency, several incentives for the European sailors were announced, including pension for widows and compensation for disability.[16]

The Company was only one of the several powers trying to dominate the Arabian sea during the seventeenth and the eighteenth centuries. In this period, organized piracy was endemic in this region and exposed the limits of naval technology possessed by the Marine. The Malabar, Cambay and the Persian Gulf were natural bases of naval bands preying on unarmed and armed merchant men. In the middle of the seventeenth century, the elusive Sindanians were active on the relatively lesser known coast between Surat and the Persian Gulf. The Sidis of Janjira posed a constant threat near Bombay.[17] Spread out on the Konkan coast from the 1680s were the formidable Angre strongholds. Maritime brigandage was fuelled further by constant political rivalries which distracted indispensable naval strength. So when the tripartite rivalry between the Sidis, the Company and the Marathas escalated on the Konkan coast, freebooters became bold enough to attack large ships off the Malabar.[18] The stalemate in naval power was complemented by geography. On the western coast of India, the sailing season began after the monsoon but local navies with superior knowledge of local navigation could easily register some naval presence on the familiar coast even during the rains. The local practice of hauling up smaller ships on shore or moving them inland through estuaries and smaller rivers and then oiling them against the monsoon also helped conserve native naval strength. Limitations on improvised technology were also imposed by the shoal-ridden shallows of the littoral. Often, the Company's success was thwarted by shortsighted policies. Till the 1750s, for instance, lascars were discharged as soon as the monsoon began. It was later found that many of these men joined the enemies, bringing to them trained manpower and knowledge of English positions. The company shed its miserly attitude fairly late and began employing lascars permanently; this meant additional outlays on housing and maintenance in the lean season.[19]

Often, a combination of local powers made the Company's situation precarious. In 1689 the Sidi navy allied with a Mughal army blockaded Bombay, pushing the desperate English into piracy. Everyday piracy, in any case, was concealed in the euphemism 'to cruise'. Prize money and private trade were incentives enough for hungry seamen and greedy officers to indulge in piracy. The drawbacks of available naval technology were apparent in the struggle against the high sea pirates. Towards the end of the seventeenth century large, Arabic fleets employing pack tactics freely pillaged Diu and the Gujarat coast. Simultaneously, well-manned and heavily armed European 'rovers' appeared in the Indian Ocean. By 1698, these 'rovers' had become powerful enough to force various European companies to sink their differences temporarily. Heavy losses in Mughal shipping also prompted the

Mughal authorities to force the Europeans into accepting joint responsibility for curbing piracy. The Marine and the Royal Navy were not immune to the lure. Towards the end of the seventeenth century the crews of *Mocha* and *Josiah* murdered their officers and turned pirates, and Captain Kidd, commanding the *Adventurer* with 32 guns and 200 sailors, sent out from England to attack pirate strongholds in Madagascar, turned rover.[20]

The rise of high sea piracy hemmed in the Company's ships and the almost helpless Marine from one side. At the same time on the coast, the strength of the Maratha admiral Kanhoji Angre grew. Till the 1750s, the Company waged a fierce struggle against the Angres in which early modern military technology was stretched severely on the western coast of India. Around 1700, English naval weakness also stemmed from two factors. First, the Company was almost totally dependent on England for supplies of navigational equipment and guns. Second, the Royal Navy did not come to the Marine's aid soon enough, for only from the 1750s, as the Anglo-French rivalry intensified, did the East Indies Squadron become a permanent feature of the British presence in and around India.

Parker, after mentioning the growth of the Maratha navy in the 1650s, does not follow its history.[21] In 1690, Kanhoji Angre was appointed Deputy Commander of the Maratha navy which had 57 gurabs and 5,000 men at the time of Shivaji's coronation in 1674. The guns to this navy were supplied by the Portuguese and gunners were chiefly European deserters.[22] Between 1690 and 1700, when he became 'surkhail' of the Maratha navy, Angre began to trouble English shipping. His primary strength lay in his string of forts stretching south from Colaba to Suvarnadurg. He also enjoyed the political and military support of the mainland. In the first decade of the eighteenth century we find him in control of the Konkan, issuing *dastaks* on the lines of the *cartaz*.'[23]

The skirmishes between the Company and Angre dated from 1700 onwards, for the growth of Angre's power directly threatened the English, who were busy consolidating their hold over Bombay. Generally, Angre remained elusive. Since his navy comprising mainly gurabs lacking adequate firepower, could not face the Company's armed trading ships away from the coast, he usually avoided a direct line-to-line confrontation with the Company.

The Angre navy operated between the coast and the open seas and when attacked, resolutely slipped into shallower waters, often under the protection of guns mounted on coastal forts. Angre's forts mounted heavy cannon manned by international crew who were said to be regularly and well-paid.[24] Angre, however, went beyond the strategy of sea-borne guerrilla warfare. Like Tipu Sultan and later the Scindia in the nineteenth century, he tried his best to develop local military potential. Shipbuilding was encouraged in his domain and teak was sown in certain parts of the Western Ghats to overcome shortages of timber, but Portuguese help always remained uncertain. In the production of crucial artillery, the Angre strongholds seemed to have been deficient. This was nothing new, for during the eighteenth century, major formidable Indian powers like the Marathas and later the Mysoreans proved signally deficient in artillery.[25]

The Company launched its first serious expedition against Angre singling out Gheria, one of the strongest Angre forts, for attack in 1718. Almost complete intelligence about the place was conveyed to the English by a Portuguese defector but nonetheless the attempt failed. In November 1718, the Company invested Khanderi with forces appearing overwhelming for the time comprising 50 ships of all sizes, 2,000 sailors, hundreds of sepoys, and English soldiers. The small Khanderi garrison held out, beating back several inefficient English landings. The Company officers, apparently unaware of the lessons of the 'military revolution', turned out to be amateur commanders. The Company forces were incapable of effecting a successful siege either through the use of artillery or trained manpower. Finally, during both these encounters, the bulk of the Angre navy preferred not to give battle and steered clear into shallow waters and the thick fort walls proved impervious to English artillery. For defensive, essentially holding operations, such locally derived tactics were appropriate, but for the development of naval strength in the long term, despite the nationalistic projections of Malgaonkar, they held little promise.

The frustrating failures of 1718 pushed the Company into a desperate and premature offensive in 1720 against Gheria. The failure of artillery against the Angre forts prompted the Company to use the secret weapon called the 'phram' in 1720. Actually, the phram was a floating platform mounted with 48 pounders and the idea was to close in and shower devastation inside the fort from the sea without risking a costly landing. In the event, however, the phram sank and widespread drunkenness prevailed in the ranks due to the supply of free rum to boost morale. Next year another desperate attack, involving an Anglo-Portuguese alliance with the support of the Royal Navy for the first time, was launched against Colaba on sea as well as land. On land, at low tide, 6,000 infantrymen and 200 cavalry with 16 major artillery pieces were brought against Angre whereas from the sea, 300 big guns from 10 major ships incessantly shelled the fort. The alliance involved Europeans and African mercenaries, topasses, sepoys from Bombay, and even some Pathans. The coalition plan to storm the fort after heavy shelling from the sea failed because a column of Maratha cavalry under Pilaji Jadhav came to Angre's aid and put to flight the European land forces. Later Baji Rao, a friend of Angre, realizing the importance of Colaba, appeared on the scene, heading another strong Maratha contingent. Even the continuous cannonade from the sea in range as well as intended destruction was a total waste. Finally in December, the expedition was abandoned, and after considerable infighting had taken place between the English and the Portuguese, the European forces sailed for Bombay.

Between 1718 and 1721, three major expeditions at substantial costs to the Company's council at Bombay had been launched against Angre in vain. The intervention of the impressive artillery possessed by the Royal Navy in 1721 also failed to force the issue any further. Significantly enough, the unity of the Marathas also proved superior to the European coalition. It became clear that neither naval surprise nor superiority in artillery could result in a quick and decisive victory over Angre. Furthermore, Angre's personal leadership and better intelligence was an important factor the English had to contend with. The fact that the Portuguese were uncertain allies on both sides too did not make matters easy. In the stalemate thus ensured, Angre kept up a vigorous opposition till his death in 1729. It was not surprising that soon after that in 1730 the Company tried, without success, to enlist the support of the Bhonsales of Sawantwadi against the Angre strongholds.

During the 1730s, while steps were taken to make the Marine more effective and more ships were added to it, the Company began to take alliance diplomacy more seriously.[26] In the early

1730s, the Company first aligned with the Sidis against Manajee, one of the sons of Angre. Then, in 1738, it sent Captain Inchbird of the Marine to assist Manajee against his brother with money and stores. These diplomatic moves were accompanied by the usual cruising missions against the navy of the opposing Angre faction. However, the Marine commanders often lacked sufficient knowledge of local navigation and this allowed the smaller quarry to get away. Thus, on 22 December 1738, Commodore Bagwell failed to destroy a hostile Angre fleet which escaped into the Rajapur river near Colaba. They 'made off under his heavy broadsides, until he found himself with only four fathoms of water locked in by the rocks. Ignorant of the navigation he was compelled to give the signal for returning. . . .'[27]

Alliance diplomacy, more than the methods of the 'military revolution' against the Angres, finally began to pay. After Angre's death, his navy split between his sons Manajee and Tulajee. The latter refused to recognize the suzerainty of the Peshwa, who then allied with the English in 1755 to inflict the first serious defeat on the Angre strongholds. This time, artillery seems to have played some part in demoralizing the garrison in Suvarnadurg, but the decisive factor was the 10,000 strong Maratha storming force. The final defeat of Tulajee came in 1756, when a combined force of the Marine, the Marathas, and a well-equipped squadron of the Royal Navy under Admiral Watson first blockaded and then captured Gheria. This time, military intelligence was better and the Marathas proved to be indispensable allies. In February 1756, Gheria was taken after a five-day siege and the Angre fleet was burnt in the harbour. In fact, during the eighteen and nineteenth centuries, extensive boat burning was a feature of all successful anti-local or piratical expeditions launched by the British. After the elimination of the Angres as a formidable force till the end of the eighteenth century, local naval formations posed only a minor threat to growing British power in the region.[28] The process of attrition brought about by the peculiar balance of geography and political economy, and not primarily technology, which set in during the late seventeenth century on the western coast of India, finally resulted in an Anglo-Maratha victory over the Angres. In the ultimate analysis the Angre strongholds, deprived of political support from the mainland, were isolated and the local navy, bereft of bases, could not conserve itself. It is also important to note that in this period the Angres, Maratha protégés for long, failed to produce an ocean-going fleet capable of challenging the Europeans on the high seas. Similarly, the Marathas only half-heartedly looked at the sea for expansion.

It is true that in the eighteenth century the Europeans did acquire military superiority over the east specifically in terms of artillery, organized musketry, and the general deployment of firearms. But to overestimate this in comparison with economic and political factors would be to incline towards conceptual fragmentation and an undesirable disaggregation in analysis. After all, as the Mysoreans under Haider Ali and later Tipu Sultan with French help demonstrated, even Indian rulers could adopt modern methods of warfare. Later, victories over the Marathas at Assaye and Laswari were not easily won, proving that even the stubborn Marathas were learning. British superiority in revenues and the rise of the Sepoy Army were predicated upon Bengal. Similarly, an assessment of the economic role of Bombay in naval warfare must be made before the effects of the 'military revolution' on naval history in the Arabian Sea are talked about. Despite technical expertise of the British and several costly attempts, the coastal Arabs of the Persian Gulf could only be pacified in 1819–20.[29] From the seventeenth century onwards, the maritime Arabs made skilful use of topographical support, light, fast moving vessels like dhows, and pack tactics to keep British control at bay. No doubt, the British victory in 1820, made possible largely due to the men, money, and materials of the Bombay Presidency, was followed by extensive boat burning.

By 1800, the process of attrition was coming to an end with the resources of Bengal, Bombay and later the Punjab generally deciding the outcome of nineteenth century warfare in India. It is true that in the nineteenth century, with the development of steam, the railways and later the rapid firing guns, European nations acquired a long-term characteristic superiority over the East but even then, as the Afghan experience from 1839 to 1919 and the Mutiny of 1857 proved, superiority alone or even in combination with impressive economic resources was always qualified by imperatives of local histories. At least on the western coast of India in the seventeenth and much of the eighteenth centuries, factors like geography, politics, local tactics, and fort design as well as revenues seemed to have conditioned the experience of warfare more than the technologies associated with the 'military revolution'.

NOTES

Acknowledgements: This is a revised version of a paper presented at the National Institute of Sciences, Technology and Development Studies (NISTADS), New Delhi, on 25 April 1991. I thank Sabyasachi Bhatttacharya and Subrata Sengupta for commenting on its first draft. I shall forever be indebted to Anu for bearing with my idiosyncrasies while this paper was being rewritten in Cambridge during the winter of 1991–2.

1. A candid viewpoint on the subject is present in Geoffrey Parker, *The Military Revolution: Military Innovation and the Rise of the West,* 1500–1800. Cambridge, 1988. Interesting details are present in Paul Kennedy, *The Rise and Fall of the Great Powers: Economic Change and Military Conflict from* 1500 *to* 2000, New York, 1987, esp, pp. 16–139. Socio-anthropological implications of the rise of the West are very usefully portrayed from a near Marxist perspective in Eric Wolf, *Europe and the People Without History*, Berkeley, 1982. Anirudh Deshpande, 'Ideology and Culture'. *Mainstream,* July 4, 1987 is a sympathetic review of *Europe and the People Without History.* Hugh Trevor-Roper (ed), *The Age of Expansion*, London, 1968, exemplifies the Eurocentrim characteristic of most European writing on the subject. Roper's foreword tells us that, '. . . in the sixteenth century and the seventeenth centuries, world history was Eurocentric', and Europe was the 'dynamic element' and the 'motor of the process' of world history.
2. The Fontana 'War and Society' series is a shift in this direction. G. Best, *War and Society in Revolutionary Europe,* 1770–1870, Fontana, 1982, offers a comparative analysis of several states and cautions against overemphasizing technological factors. A critical survey of warfare during the colonial period is present in V. G. Kiernan, *European Empires from Conquest to Collapse, 1815–1960*, Fontana, 1982. The emergence of modern arms races, professional armed forces and the impact of total war on European society is analysed admirably by Brian Bond, *War and Society in Europe, 1870–1970*, Fontana, 1984.
3. Parker, op. cit., pp 24–43.
4. Best, *War and Society in Revolutionary Europe* and Bond, *War and Society in Europe* tell us that professional standing armies with academies and a trained officer corps were created in some European states not before the late eighteenth century.

5. See Parker, op. cit., pp. 82–114, for an assessment of European victory at sea. Statistically detailed information regarding naval developments in Europe is presented by Kennedy, op. cit., passim and pp. 100–39.
6. G. S. Graham, *The Politics of Naval Supremacy: Studies in British Maritime Ascendancy*, Cambridge, 1965, p. 1. The influence of Mahan, for example, can be seen in old style naval history such as G. Callender and F. H. Hinsley, *The Naval Side of British History 1485-1945*, London, 1952.
7. Graham, ibid, p. 33 points out that the Gujarati pilot of Vasco da Gama's ship Ahmad Ibn-Majid was responsible for some 35 treatises on navigation. The instruments Gama's ship did not surprise him either.
8. Parker, op. cit., p. 83.
9. For details see Trevor-Roper, op. cit., and Parker, op. cit, pp. 86–9.
10. Parker, ibid., p. 103.
11. Graham, op. cit., p. 27.
12. Parker, op. cit., p. 114.
13. Our account of the Company's early naval struggles is based on the following sources: *Materials towards a Statistical Account of the Town and Island of Bombay*, vol. 3, Administration, Bombay, 1894, pp. 203–56 comprising consultations of the Company directors and the Bombay Council from the 1680s to the 1780s. *Gazetteer of Bombay City and Island*, vol 2, Bombay, 1909. C. R. Low, *History of the Indian Navy*, vols 1 and 2, London, 1877, reprint, New Delhi, 1985. (This is an exceptionally detailed participant's memoir of the Company's Navy, including its history from the early 1600s to 1863.) James Douglas, *Bombay and Western India: A Series of Stray Papers*, vol. 1, 1893, reprint, New Delhi, 1985. Historically useful details of local sailing vessels are portrayed in the *Gazetteer of the Bombay Presidency*, vol. 2, Bombay, 1877. For further reference see the *Cambridge Economic History of India*, vol. 1, 1200–1700, Orient Longman, 1984, pp. 393–419. Company records of the time continuously referred to the Marathas and pirates active on the Konkan coast as Shivajees.
14. *History of the Indian Navy*, vol. 1, p. 90; *Gazetteer of Bombay City and Island*, pp. 275–6.
15. *Reports from Select Committees on the Affairs of the East India Company: First Report from the Select Committee on Indian Territories with Minutes of Evidence and Appendix*, 1852–3, Shanon, 1970, pp. 86–90.
16. *Materials Towards a Statistical Account of the Town and Island of Bombay*, consultations on marine matters. Despite all this, pay remained low and desertion was high. Attempts were often made to regain costly European drafts who were adept at handling artillery. Such measures often failed, for fugitives easily found employment at higher rates with native powers. Rough terrain, thick forests and the pursuer's ignorance

of local topography helped the deserters too. Marine surveying began only in the late eighteenth century and became intensified and 'scientific' only in the nineteenth.

17. D. R. Banaji, *Bombay and the Sidis*, Bombay, 1932, besides being an excellent monograph on the apparently enigmatic Sidis, is an example of superb Indian scholarship in late colonial India.
18. Low, op. cit., vol. 1, p. 71. In early 1683, a large ship. *The President* was attacked by Arabs manning two ships and four gurabs. The latter were destroyed by *The President*, which took the Muscat Arab prisoners who stated that they had been hired by Sambhajee to prey on the English. Sambhajee, however, denied any involvement in the affair.
19. Herbert Richmond, *The Navy in India*, London, 1931, p. 382. In fact, throughout the eighteenth century steps, were taken to counter desertion. According to the *Gazetteer of the Bombay Island*, p. 275, in 1724 an order was passed, holding the pay of all seamen two months in arrears. In 1754, the Mutiny Act was applied to the Marine, for, in 1748, a mutiny had occurred on *The Bombay* due to economic problems and the crew's homesickness. From the *Materials towards a Statistical Account*, pp. 203–52, we know that between the 1690s and 1780s, the authorities in Bombay were preoccupied with desertion. In fact, it was only in 1779–80 that the Board of Directors resolved to construct proper rooms for English sailors in Bombay.
20. For details of piracy see Low, op. cit., vol. 1, pp. 80–1; *Gazetteer of Bombay City and Island*, p. 274. There is nothing in A. C. Roy, *A History of Mughal Navy and Naval Warfares*, Calcutta, 1972 to suggest that Indian ships could stand up to the high sea pirates.
21. Parker, op. cit., p. 112.
22. Our account of Kanhoji Angre is also based on Manohar Malgonkar, *Kanhoji Angre, Maratha Admiral: An Account of his Life and His Battles with the English*, Bombay, 1959.
23. Soon the Company's Council in Bombay was deeply concerned about Angria the pirate. For details, see the following: *Materials Towards a Statistical Account*, p. 206, *Gazetteer of Bombay City and Island*, pp. 278–80. For a brief history of the Angre family, see *Maharashtra State Gazetteers, Kolaba District*, 1st edn, 1883, 2nd edn, 1964, pp. 57–129.
24. Malgonkar, op. cit., p. 100. According to his biographer, Angre had perfected the tactical manoeuvre of slipping away when faced with superior forces.
25. For a critical appraisal of Maratha military weakness and Tipu's artillery, see Satish Chandra, *The Eighteenth Century of India: Its Economy and the Role of the Marathas, Jats, Sikhs and Afghans*, Calcutta, 1986. Also see Parker, op. cit., Ch. 4.
26. *Materials towards a Statistical Account*, pp. 206–7.

27. Low, op. cit., vol. 1, p. 107.
28. *Materials towards a Statistical Account*, p. 221. Low, op., cit., vol. 1, pp. 133–4. *Gazetteer of the Bombay City and Island*, pp. 279–80. For details also see Douglas, *Bombay and Western India*, pp. 110–25. Douglas also wrote: 'Our readers would not thank us for a history of Kanhoji Angria's exploits. Each of the three great European nations in Indian waters had a shy at him and his family and each came of second best.'
29. Admiral Hughes, commander of the East Indies Squadron of the Royal Navy, thought Bombay to be indispensable to British success against the French; Admiral Hughes to the Governor and Select Committee of Bombay, 13 May 1784, India Office Records, Home-Misc, p. 174, cited in Appendix viii in Richmond, op. cit. For details also see Low, op. cit., vol. 1, Ch. 7. *Gazetteer of Bombay City and Island*, pp. 285–86. Graham, *Great Britain in the Indian Ocean: A Study of Maritime Enterprise 1810–1850*, Oxford, 1967, pp. 237–55.

CHAPTER 14

Military Synthesis in South Asia: Armies, Warfare, and Indian Society, *c.*1740–1849

*Kaushik Roy**

Following the rapid collapse of the Mughal Empire after 1707, the Mughal Successor States attempted to modernize their state apparatus and their armies. Both the Indian kingdoms and the British-led East India Company (hereafter EIC) attempted the construction of hybrid military organizations. How, then, can one explain the continuous military victories of the EIC? For opening up new dimensions on the military supremacy of the Europeans in Afro-Asia, the analytical tool of Military Synthesis might be more useful than the concept of Military Revolution or Military Evolution. This article focuses on the period from the 1740s to 1849.

> [M]any other states that have been disarmed have lost their liberties in less than forty years. No state, therefore, can support itself without an army.
>
> —Niccolo Machiavelli[1]

The rapid collapse of the Mughal Empire after 1707 did not result in a headlong decline of Indian society, polity, and economy. It is now an established view that the eighteenth century was not a 'Dark Age' in India. The political decline of the Mughal imperium resulted, rather, in an economic resurgence in certain parts of the subcontinent.[2] Recent research shows attempts by the Mughal Successor States to modernize their state apparatus and armies.[3] How, then, can one explain the continuous military victories of the East India Company (henceforth EIC)? This article attempts to answer this question. The article begins with the 1740s because that decade witnessed a series of decisive victories by the European powers against the Indian rulers; it ends in 1849, when the last indigenous military power was eliminated in Hindustan by the EIC. The focus is on war on land because India is a continental landmass: naval supremacy could not yield control over the subcontinent. Throughout history, only land powers like the Central Asian Turks were able to dominate India. Sea power enabled the British and French to protect their coastal enclaves against the Indian powers. But only when the EIC built up cavalry and infantry forces were the British able to conduct campaigns into the interior of the subcontinent.[4]

Military Techniques of Europe and Asia, 1740–90

Military Transformation in Europe

There is a consensus among West European and North American historians that as far as combat effectiveness is concerned, the eighteenth and nineteenth century European armies had a decisive edge vis-á-vis Asian armies. This was because of the culmination of certain trends that started emerging within the European armed forces in the preceding centuries. From the late sixteenth century onwards, north-west Europe experienced certain technological and organizational changes in the military sphere. These marked the genesis of postfeudal armies. Soldiers with uniforms, paid regularly in cash, and directed by a specially educated and technically skilled officer corps became common.[5] Late seventeenth-century western Europe witnessed the use of flintlock muskets and socket bayonets, which replaced pikes. The organization of the infantry into flexible tactical units like battalions, regiments, and brigades made continuous firing by the infantry, and manoeuvring in the field of fire, a possibility. The standard infantry tactic was a bayonet charge on the enemy after volley firing. Further, infantry got fire support from field artillery. The latter became effective due to standardization and increased mobility and accuracy. The invention of screws for elevating the guns gave them greater precision and raised their killing power. These innovations increased the firepower of the infantry–artillery combine, and gave it an edge in close quarter combat against cavalry.[6]

However, there is disagreement among scholars about the nature of these developments. One group of scholars whom I will call the Military Revolution School claims that north-west Europe witnessed radical and quick developments in the techniques of warfare, beginning in the early modern period. In 1955, Michael Roberts first coined the concept of 'Military Revolution' to accommodate what he perceived as marked innovations in the tactics, technology and training of West European armies. Roberts argued that, between 1560 and 1660, the Spanish *tercio* was replaced in prominence by a multiple number of small infantry units deployed in several lines. This allowed fuller exploitation of musket fire. In addition, infantry acquired mobile field artillery. All these required greater fire discipline and capacity to manoeuvre. This, in turn, gave rise to a professional commissioned and non-commissioned officer corps.[7]

Geoffrey Parker extended the time frame and scope of Roberts' Military Revolution. Parker asserts that the scale of warfare in West Europe rose considerably between 1500 and 1710. As the size of armies increased and weapons developed at a rapid pace, war became not only more lethal, but also more costly. This, in turn, gave birth to a complex credit network with long-term commercial and financial consequences. The net result was the genesis of capitalist centralizing states geared for maintaining and funding capital-intensive armies. Parker's greatest contribution is to link the Military Revolution that occurred in Western Europe with Western overseas expansion. While Geoffrey Parker writes that Europe experienced a single Military Revolution,[8] one of his followers, Clifford J. Rogers, has modified his thesis by claiming that that West Europe experienced a series of Military Revolutions from 1400 onwards. Rogers writes that in the fourteenth century an Infantry Revolution occurred, which resulted in the infantry becoming the decisive factor on the battlefield. The next century witnessed an Artillery Revolution which provided the disciplined and drilled foot-soldiers with fire support in the killing zone.[9]

The other group of scholars whom I categorize as the Military Evolution School, represented by Jeremy Black, asserts that Western Europe experienced a series of slow incremental developments in the art of warfare from the late Middle Ages onwards. Black attempts to point out that no radical change occurred between 1560 and 1660. He comments that the size of the armies and their firepower registered a linear growth in the seventeenth and the eighteenth centuries. Until 1799, centralized bureaucratic polities were absent in Europe, he avers. And marked technological developments in military hardware, he believes, occurred only in the nineteenth century.[10]

From the perspective of Indian history, it is noticeable that while the European powers were not successful in military encounters against the Indian powers in the seventeenth century, the military balance shifted drastically against the Indians in the mid-eighteenth century. For example, the Mughal cavalry defeated two British expeditions in Bengal in 1686 and in 1688; but from 1757 onwards, the British won a string of victories in Bengal and Bihar.[11] Again, in 1746, 450 French infantry armed with muskets and supported by two guns capable of firing 15 shots per minute defeated the *Nawab* of Carnatic's huge host, comprising cavalry armed with badly tempered swords and indisciplined infantry armed with matchlocks.[12] The supremacy of European military techniques seemed evident.

So, the Parker hypothesis (that Western armies armed with muskets and artillery, which were products of the Military Revolution, enabled the European powers to create empires in Afro-Asia)[13] seems to hold water. Following Parker's line, some historians dealing with South Asia have developed an interpretation which I will call the Limited Modernization School. The spokesmen for this approach assert that the Indian princely armies failed against the British-led EIC's Army because their modernization was limited.[14]

However, by analyzing the Indian military landscape more closely, we will see that the imported European way of warfare was inadequate to meet the varied demands of warfare and ecology in South Asia. Some European scholars accept the ineffectiveness of certain European military techniques in the extra-European world and highlight the role of indigenous assistance in the military penetration of the West in Afro-Asia.[15] The EIC emerged supreme because the British were able to strike a balance between the European elements of war and certain indigenous military techniques and utilize the natural, human, and animal resources of India in warfare. This I will call a Balanced Military Synthesis.

Due to gradual weakening of the Mughal central government, from the 1730s, the regional and local warlords started exacting duties from the European traders. The latter found this arbitrary and irritating. Hence, the European companies decided to acquire political power by subduing the local chiefs. Again, the regional warlords were engaged in fighting each other. Continuous civil wars forced the British and the French trading companies to enlist troops and fortify their settlements. Both the French and the EIC realized that if they were able to increase their hold over the regional chieftains, then not only would they be able to acquire more trading concessions but would also be able to push their European commercial opponents out of India. So, the French and the British offered their military expertise to the Indian rulers. In return for military aid, the Indian princes allowed these two European trading organizations to take over certain parts of their kingdoms. The British and the French found that revenue from these territories supplemented their profit from trade. The net result was to heighten their temptation to intervene more and more in the internecine struggles of the Indian rulers, which ultimately resulted in Anglo-French rivalry.[16]

Why did the British win against the French? The EIC, unlike the French, adapted its polity and military in accordance with the demands of South Asia's politics and ecology. Then, unlike the French *Compagnie des Indes,* the EIC was a profitable trading organization with a large cash flow and networks of credit. The French in India, under the Marquis de Dupleix, ran out of money and failed to pay their Indian soldiers.[17] After the elimination of the French threat, the EIC tried to annex more and more territories because trade was becoming unprofitable and the British were financing it by means of revenue collected from the land under Company control. This brought the EIC into conflict with the Indian powers.[18]

On the other hand, the Indian princes failed to integrate the imported Western art of war with the traditional Indian method of conducting warfare. The armies of the indigenous powers represented cases that I categorize as a Defective Military Synthesis. The Indian rulers' attempts to generate composite military machines collapsed due to failures at four levels—conceptual, institutional, economic, and political. The princes could not make up their minds whether to conduct the Western method of warfare (pitched battles) or traditional war (skirmishes, hit and run raids).

The Indian potentates also failed to construct the administrative fabric that was necessary to sustain their Westernized contingents. The Westernization programme also proved to be very costly for their exchequers. Finally, political challenges from within by the nobility forced the Indian rulers to go slow with their military reforms. To cap it all, India's traditional military culture also slowed down the process of Europeanization of the indigenous armies. Still, British victory was not a linear, inevitable process. There was no British *Blitzkrieg.* There were many ups and downs. The EIC's ponderous war machine took more than a hundred years to defeat the Indian rulers.

The Indian System of Warfare

Due to continuous development, the lethality of the European armies increased significantly in the early eighteenth century. Simultaneously, the combat effectiveness of the Indian armies underwent a drastic decline. In general, the Indian armies after the Mughal disintegration in the first decade of the eighteenth century experienced frequent treacheries. This was because, due to the disintegration of the imperial Mughal government, most of the troops were raised by the semi-autonomous chieftains on the basis of land grants (*jagir*s) made to them by the princes or the *Nawabs* (Mughal regional governors). The *jagirdar*s (holder of *jagir*s) were responsible for promoting and demoting the soldiers and feeding them from the revenue extracted from their *jagir*s. As a result, the soldiers were more loyal to the *jagirdar*s than to the princes.[19]

These private armies of the *jagirdar*s were incapable of tactical manoeuvre because they lacked regular subdivisions and a hierarchical command structure. Arms, accoutrements, and clothing were provided by the soldiers themselves, so there was no uniformity in their dress and equipment.[20] Since the cavalry lacked unit level training, combat often degenerated into individual displays of heroics.[21] Continuous drill and strict discipline were required for effective use of the matchlocks with which they were armed. Drilling the troops gave them confidence and a sense of unity, which in turn enabled them to coordinate their actions under enemy fire. For this, a permanent army was required. Since the Indian rulers maintained temporary forces which were raised with the aid of the *jagirdar*s during a crisis and then demobilized when the emergency was over, their infantry, though armed with matchlocks, was neither drilled nor disciplined. Hence, they proved to be more or less useless on the battlefield.[22]

The Central Asian horse archers (who were capable of waging high speed manoeuvre warfare) had vanished from the Indian order of battle because of the capture of the overland trade route to the horse markets of Central Asia by the Afghans after the collapse of Mughal authority in Kabul in the 1740s.[23] The Mughals depended on heavy cavalry, i.e. cuirassiers armed with long swords, for shock tactics. After the Mughal decline, even the cuirassiers made their exit from the Indian battle scene. Still, cavalry remained the most prestigious branch of service till the mid-eighteenth century.[24]

When the Mughal Empire disintegrated, two regional powers emerged from its ashes: the Marathas in Maharashtra and the Sikhs in Punjab. The Maratha peasants and landholders formerly had served in the armies of the Bijapur and Golkunda kingdoms. In the 1670s when the Mughals conquered these two states, the Maratha mercenaries under the leadership of Shivaji, a charismatic warlord, launched guerrilla attacks against the Mughals. Simultaneously, the Sikhs rebelled partly due to high Mughal taxation. The Sikhs were originally Jat peasants of Punjab who were converted to Sikhism by the 10 *Guru*s (spiritual leaders). The Sikhs were organized as a loose confederacy of *misaldar*s (chiefs). In the first decade of the nineteenth century, Ranjit Singh, the chief of the Sukherchakia *misl* (clan) united these *Misaldars*. He then established the *Khalsa* (Sikh) monarchy. In contrast, the Marathas, after the death of Shivaji, were organized under five chieftains who constituted the Maratha Confederacy. These five chiefs established hereditary families which ruled over five different regions. The Peshwa controlled Maharashtra and was nominal head of the Confederacy. Bhonsle was in charge of Orissa, Gaekwad controlled Gujarat, Holkar was in central India, and Sindia headed Rajasthan and north India.[25]

Both the Marathas and the Sikhs made extensive use of light cavalry in the early eighteenth century. Though their equipment and tactics differed, both the Maratha and Sikh cavalry followed an attrition strategy against their enemies. The Maratha light cavalry, armed with spears, conducted *ganimi kava* (predatory warfare).

Extreme mobility and the ability to make deep penetrations behind enemy lines characterized the Maratha cavalry. They could cover 50 miles in a day because the cavalrymen carried neither baggage nor provisions. The troopers and their ponies lived off the country.[26] Their operational aim was to avoid pitched battles with the enemy's army and instead to ravage the enemy's districts until the economy collapsed. In 1750, Bhaskar Rao, a general of Bhonsle, invaded Bengal with 20,000 cavalry. They carried out night raids, pillaging the Bengal *Nawab's* camp. They then destroyed the convoys which were bringing provisions to the *Nawab's* army. The Marathas followed a 'scorched earth policy', burning the neighbouring villages to prevent grain from reaching the enemy. The *Nawab's* soldiers were thus denied food, clothing, and conveyance.[27] However, the Maratha cavalry was ineffective against artillery and walled posts defended by trained musketeers of the European powers.[28]

As regards the equipment and tactics of the Sikh cavalry, George Forster, a civil servant of the EIC, wrote in 1783 that:

> A Sikh horseman is armed with a matchlock. . . . The predilection of the Sikhs for the matchlock musket, and the constant use they make of it, causes a difference in their manner of attack from that of any other Indian cavalry; a party from forty to fifty, advance in a quick pace to the distance of a carbine shot from the enemy, and then, that the fire may be given with the greater certainty, the horses are drawn up, and their pieces discharged; when speedily retiring about a hundred paces, they load and repeat the same mode of annoying the enemy.[29]

The tactics of the Sikh cavalry were similar to the Caracole tactics of the early modern German cavalry, in which successive ranks of horsemen trotted forward, discharged their pistols, wheeled back, and then retired.[30] But at the operational level, the Sikh cavalry conducted predatory campaigns like the Marathas. Colonel A. L. H. Polier had observed in the late eighteenth century that: 'they [Sikhs], particularly those on the borders, set off generally after the rains and make excursions in bodies of 10,000 horses or more on their neighbours. They plunder all they can lay their hands on, burn the towns and villages.'[31]

However, long-term sustained campaigning by the Indian armies was impossible because the Indian princes rarely paid their soldiers regularly. This, in turn, caused frequent mutinies. The net result was low military effectiveness. In 1789, the cavalry army of Mahadji Sindia, the Maratha chieftain, refused to fight any more because they had not been paid for three years.[32] Nevertheless, towards the end of the eighteenth century, due to the restructuring of the Indian militaries, their military effectiveness increased.

Defective Military Synthesis in the Indian Armies, 1770–1849

> At the moment war is declared there is so much to do that it is wise to begin preparation several years in advance. . . . I calculate on the basis of the worst possible case. . . . In war it is necessary to have sound and precise ideas. It is with safe and well conceived plans that we win wars. There is no man more pusillanimous than I when it comes to planning a campaign.
>
> —Napoleon Bonaparte[33]

The military confrontations with the European powers convinced the Indian princes that a radical transformation of their armies was necessary for survival. However, they were unwilling to completely imitate the European military system. They attempted to graft some components of the imported Western art of war on to the indigenous elements of warfare. The Indian rulers' objective was thorough Westernization of a significant portion of their militaries. This I will call Partial Europeanization/Westernization. The Westernized contingents were drilled and equipped on European patterns and administered by the emerging military bureaucracies. The Indian chiefs retained the traditional style infantry and cavalry, those in infantry and cavalry were equipped with indigenous weapons and neither disciplined in the Western style nor paid in cash. They were raised by the *jagirdar*s and can be categorized as irregulars. In addition to Partial Europeanization and retention of certain traditional elements of warfare, the Indian rulers also attempted innovation by introducing new elements of warfare, which were totally unrelated to the Western way of warfare. The net result was that the Indian rulers' attempt to mix the Indian and European elements of warfare did not gel into a coherent military system. At the tactical level, the Indian princes not only failed to assimilate certain crucial European techniques, but also retained certain indigenous components of war making that were either less effective than their Western counterparts or found no suitable application in the emerging new method of warfare. At the strategic level, the rulers dilly-dallied regarding the kind of war they would wage. Finally, at the grand strategic level, economic, administrative and cultural deficiencies further muddled their reforms.

Tradition and Transition in the Indigenous Militaries, 1773–1849

One characteristic feature of the post-Mughal armies of India was the induction of religious warriors. Their fanaticism enabled them to function as shock troops. In 1773, during the Battle of Barsana with the Mughal chieftain Najaf Quli, the Jats hired 5,000 Naga monks armed with muskets. Their leader was Balanand Gosain. In 1784, when Mahadji Sindia was campaigning in north India, his force included a contingent of Hindu religious warriors supplied by Himmat Bahadur.[34] Ranjit Singh, the ruler of Punjab from 1799 to 1839, recruited the *Akali*s (Sikh religious fanatics) as irregular cavalry.[35] However, being undisciplined, they were neither capable of manoeuvring collectively in the fire-swept battle zones nor able to discharge volley fire for the maximum effect. Hence, despite their raw courage, these religious warriors were no match for the Company's disciplined regulars.

The eighteenth century Indian rulers experimented by recruiting new ethnic elements. During the early medieval age, the Abyssinians had settled in Deccan.[36] Raghuji Bhonsle recruited them as irregular infantry.[37] During the Battle of Argaum on 29 November 1803, Bhonsle deployed 2,000 Arabs. Instead of using the irregular Arabs as skirmishers and sharpshooters, he made a tactical mistake in trying to use them as line infantry. The Arabs, though brave, were undisciplined. Hence, they could not withstand the volley firing and bayonet charge of the British infantry regiments.[38]

The Marathas retained the traditional Indian rockets known as the *bans* carried on the backs of camels. In 1779, during the First Maratha War, when the EIC's Army from Bombay tried to invade Maharashtra through the Western Ghats, the Marathas used *ban*s.[39] However, the rockets, still being at an experimental stage, were yet to become a decisive battlefield weapon. Instead of depending on the *bans*, the Marathas would have done better to rely wholesale on field artillery.

The *zamburaks* (light guns on camels), which were used by the Persians in the eighteenth century, were retained by the Sikh Army till its demise in 1849. The *zamburaks* were the Indian response to European horse artillery. However, the *zamburaks* were less mobile, and thus less manoeuvrable, than horse artillery. During the First and Second Sikh Wars (1845–6, 1849), the EIC's horse artillery came within 300 yards of the heavy artillery within the Sikh entrenched camps and, after destroying them, retired quickly. The rapidity of their movement prevented the *zamburaks* from catching up with them. In addition, the destructive power of *zamburaks* was inadequate, as they fired light shells.[40]

The irregular Sikh cavalry and infantry used the ancient Indian weapon known as *chakras* (war quoits). It was employed in close hand-to-hand combat. When thrown from a distance of 50 yards from the enemy, these weapons skimmed through the air and gave dangerous cuts. Enemy horses got confused by seeing such flying weapons.[41] Nonetheless *chakras*, the Indian near equivalent of European bayonets, were not as effective as the latter.

Partial Westernization and Military Effectiveness of the Indian Armies, 1780s–1849

The end of the second half of the eighteenth century witnessed Partial Westernization of the Indian military machines. This process occurred haltingly, in stages, but not merely because of cultural lag on part of the Indian rulers, as C. R. Boxer assumes. Boxer asserts that the Asian rulers had a strong cultural antipathy against using artillery effectively on the battlefield. Rather, they used artillery for increasing their status, by ceremonial firing during rituals like coronation ceremonies, etc. Randolf Cooper asserts that due to a unique military culture, the Indians considered warfare a sort of business enterprise. The Indians, according to him, lacked the will to fight to the death.[42] The Sikhs and the Marathas, however, were actually eager to absorb European components of the military system such as heavy cavalry, field artillery, and a professional officer corps. However, *realpolitik* hampered the Indian rulers' programme of Europeanization.

First, lack of an adequate number of European instructors was one of the principal reasons that prevented thorough Westernization of those contingents of the indigenous militaries set aside for Europeanization. Western military skill could be imparted to the Indian armies only through European military officers. The European officers gravitated towards the Indian kingdoms due to the prospect of high pay. But the British took all possible measures to thwart the inflow of European military specialists into the Indian kingdoms. After the EIC's victory at the Battle of Buxar in 1764, Clive and the *Nawabs* of Bengal and Awadh signed a treaty in 1765. The British inserted a clause that the *Nawabs* would never retain Sombre (a German mercenary officer whose real name was Walther Reinhardt) or any other European deserters. Moreover, the *Nawabs* were bound to deliver up to the British any Europeans who in future might desert from the EIC and enter their domains.[43] This reflects the EIC's fear of the combat effectiveness of the trained battalions of Sombre that had fought with the army of the Bengal *Nawab* Mir Qasim against the British at Buxar. By inserting the above clause, the EIC prevented Europeanization of the armies of Awadh and Bengal.

The Gurkha Kingdom of Nepal copied the infantry system of the EIC. The infantry were drilled and organized in battalions. Deserters from the EIC's Bengal Army taught the Gurkhas Western military discipline. In 1814, Nepal possessed 12,000 Westernized infantry. Against them, the EIC deployed 30,000 infantry and 60 guns. Due to their numerical and firepower superiority, the British won.[44] To stall further Westernization of the army in Nepal, the EIC forced a treaty upon the Raja of Nepal after the conclusion of the Nepal War in 1815. One of its principal clauses stated that the Raja of Nepal would never recruit or retain any European subject in his service.[45]

The secret of the professionalism of the Western officer corps lay in their education in military academies. Hence, the only way out for the Indian rulers was to set up institutions of modern secular learning and officer academies, where the Indian officers could acquire professional knowledge. But the Indian rulers, unlike the Russian Czarist and Ottoman regimes, failed to realize the role played by colleges in imparting professional knowledge to the officers.[46]

Again, those Asian rulers who attempted the assimilation of Western techniques of warfare met with serious obstruction from their nobility, who were the leaders of the traditional style military contingents. The nobility was jealous of the substantial perquisites and influence enjoyed by the foreign mercenary commanders at the courts of the Asian rulers. When Sultan Selim III tried to Westernize the Ottoman Army in response to the Russian military threat, he faced tough opposition from the Janissaries, the traditional Ottoman warriors.[47] Similarly, both Mahadji Sindia (head of the Sindia clan from 1769 to 1794) and his nephew cum successor Daulat Rao Sindia faced tough opposition from his *sirdar*s (Maratha *jagirdar*s) while implementing a programme of Europeanization. Due to their hostility, between 1788 and 1790, Mahadji failed to increase the number of infantry battalions from 2 to 10 as planned.[48] After being defeated in the Second Maratha War (1803–5) by the EIC, Daulat Rao tried to raise more Westernized infantry battalions. Many European officers engaged in lucrative private trade, which angered the nobility of the Indian rulers. In addition, the Indian soldiers of Sindia's Westernized infantry battalions hated the English and Portuguese officers placed over them due to their high pay and racial arrogance. In 1809, the Indian soldiers turned out the European officers from the battalions.[49]

In the 1830s, the Sikh *sirdar*s' (chieftains) hostility towards the European commanders in the Sikh Army increased. One way of showing hostility was to withhold the pay of the European commanders, especially during a period of resource crunch. Unlike the irregular Sikh cavalry, the Western trained soldiers were paid in cash on a monthly basis in imitation of the EIC. In 1834, many European commanders and their soldiers' pay remained in arrears for two months.[50] In the long run, this resulted in divided loyalties on the part of the latter. The irregular cavalrymen were mostly sons of the *sirdar*s and they opposed tooth and nail the introduction of Western style disciplined heavy cavalry.[51] This was also resisted by the *Akali*s who functioned as light cavalry of the Sikh Army during campaigns. They feared that Westernization of the Sikh cavalry would result in their discharge. The *Akali*s were respected by the common Sikhs because of their religious fanaticism and they were considered as spiritual leaders of the *Khalsa* (Sikh community). So even Ranjit Singh, the most powerful *Khalsa* monarch, failed to curb the *Akalis*. [52]

The traditional Indian military culture which existed for more than a millennium also hampered the indigenous rulers' attempt to raise Westernized infantry at five minutes before twelve. The culture of heavily armed, drilled, and disciplined infantry fighting shoulder to shoulder and geared for delivering a shock attack could be traced back to Classical Greece. Around 500 BCE, Greece came up with disciplined heavy infantry armed with long spears and known as hoplites. From the hoplites emerged the phalanx, under Philip of Macedon. The Romans modified the Greek infantry tradition by introducing the legion. After the medieval interregnum of the knights rampaging through west Europe on their horses, the Classical infantry tradition was revived during the Renaissance. Thus emerged the Spanish *tercios* and then Maurice of Nassau's battalions and regiments.[53] Thus, one could argue that the infantry component of Parker's Military Revolution (rise of drilled infantry armed with muskets) was as successful as it was in West Europe, because it could be grafted on to a preexisting infantry tradition. After volley firing, the infantry moving forward with their bayonets was a linear extension of the phalangists advancing in phalanx formation.

To the contrary, the gargantuan agrarian bureaucracies of Asia, such as China and India, lacked a military culture oriented towards disciplined heavy infantry. In ancient India, the shock arm was the chariotry. During the medieval era, elephants and mounted archers constituted the backbone of the armies. The social prestige associated with the cavalry prevented proper development of the infantry arm. The foot-soldiers remained local levies who were denied uniform dress, weapons, and regular pay.[54] One reason for the predominance of cavalry was the vast distances in Asia which could only be covered with fast moving light cavalry. However, in Western Europe, the theatre of war was more confined. Hence, foot-slogging infantry had a chance to intervene. Second, China, India, and Persia until the eighteenth century faced a threat from the nomadic horse archers of Central Asia. Till the sixteenth century, horse archery was more accurate and lethal than musketry.[55] Thus, disciplined infantry was an alien culture for the Asians and the 'cavalry mentality' of Asian warriors obstructed the genesis of infantry culture. As a result, during the eighteenth and nineteenth centuries, the Western trained infantry of the Indian rulers were not as good as the white infantry. Nor were white deserters available in India in large enough numbers to fill the ranks of the Indian rulers. Even the EIC's sepoys often broke in battle. A recent study shows that in most of the battles, the leading position was given to the British infantry regiments and the sepoy regiments formed the second line.[56] I am not hinting at white cultural exclusivity regarding disciplined infantry warfare. Given some centuries, the Indians might have absorbed the infantry culture properly. But this was not to be. The Indian rulers were bound to clash with the Europeans earlier. The Indian rulers' failure to generate high quality infantry should be seen in the wider context of the failure of the Chinese, Turks, and Persians to come up with effective Western-style infantry-oriented armies. So, how successful were the major Indian powers as regards Europeanization?

Mysore (1770s–99)

Mysore was a Hindu kingdom in south India which was ruled by the Wodeyar Maharajas. In the 1720s, Mysore's armed forces included matchlock-armed infantry recruited on a short-term basis. These were marginal peasants who joined the army to tide them over unfavourable harvests and when demobilized, returned to the land. The core of the army was light irregular cavalry and elephants.[57]

Mysore, under the stewardship of Haidar Ali and his son Tipu Sultan, clashed with the EIC over the issue of expansion in the Northern Circars and the Nizam's dominions. Haidar Ali was born in 1722. In 1749, he joined the Mysore Army. In 1761, he overthrew Chik Krishna Raja of the Wodeyar dynasty and became the ruler. Haidar Ali and his son Tipu Sultan Europeanized part of the Mysore force. Haidar Ali got the idea of Westernizing the force from his brother Mir Ismail, who was a general of the Mysore Army. In 1751, Mir Ismail purchased 2,000 muskets with bayonets and 6 cannons from the British Governor in Bombay. He enrolled 30 European sailors from the Malabar coast to train his gunners.

Mir Ismail thus created a corps of infantry armed with firelocks and bayonets and supported by field artillery. Haidar Ali imitated Mir Ismail's experiment on a larger scale.[58] In 1767, Haidar Ali's field army comprised 11,000 irregular cavalry and 12,000 infantry. About 8,000 of the infantry were armed with muskets and the remaining 4,000 with matchlocks. Their officers were mercenary Eurasians who had acquired military training under the French in Pondicherry. However, since the supply of such officers was erratic and inadequate, European prisoners of war were encouraged by Haidar and Tipu to train their regular infantry. Those who refused were tortured. Under Tipu, the proportion of infantry vis-á-vis cavalry increased in the Mysore Army. In the 1780s, there were 23,000 regular infantry and only 3,500 irregular cavalry. [59]

Maintaining the capital intensive Westernized military formations required a solvent economy. So, Tipu took certain steps to improve Mysore's economy. In 1788, he issued a circular claiming that agriculture was the backbone of the nation. To expand cultivation, Tipu offered *taqavi* (short-term loans) to the landless peasants. Again, when the farmers brought virgin land under cultivation, they were exempted from land tax for two years. In general, the moneylenders exploited the poor peasants. So Tipu opened certain banking houses which were controlled by a central bank at his capital, Seringapatam. The point to be noted is that the British introduced the banking system in India only in 1809. In 1795, the *mir asaf* (revenue commissioner) of Mysore ordered the *sadr*s (revenue officials) to prepare detailed lists containing information regarding the number of cultivators, condition of cultivation, etc. These lists were then passed to the Sultan's exchequer.[60] This was the beginning of a centralized fiscal system.

Besides a transition in the polity and the force structure, Tipu also initiated a doctrinal shift. While Haidar Ali ravaged British-occupied Karnataka by conducting manoeuvre warfare with the aid of his light cavalry during 1767 and 1768, Tipu reverted to positional warfare after his father's death in 1781. This was because the Mysore Army, under Tipu, became less mobile due to the dominance of the infantry–artillery system. With the help of French military engineers, Tipu constructed a fort at his capital at Seringapatam. The fort had a bastioned curtain wall and the river

Cauvery functioned as the wet ditch. He adorned this fort with 929 static guns and concentrated 22,000 of his 48,000 infantry within its walls. Seringapatam became the *schwerpunkt* of the British military operation in 1799.[61]

In response, the EIC's force became firepower heavy. The Company's Army deployed forty 18-pounders for breaching the walls of Seringapatam and seven 8 and 5.5 inch howitzers for plunging fire inside the fort's walls. In addition, there were fifty-seven 6-pounders for fire support for the besieging army against Tipu's infantry.[62] After Tipu's defeat, the Marathas challenged British power in Deccan.

Marathas (1790–1818)

> The chief strength of the Marathas is horse, the chief strength of Haidar infantry, cannon and small arms. From the one we have nothing to apprehend but ravages, plundering and loss of revenues for a while, from the other extirpation.
>
> —Lord Clive's letter dated 17 October 1766[63]

The deficit economy of Maharashtra forced the Marathas to launch plundering expeditions into Awadh, Mysore, and the Nizam's dominions. When these territories were brought under British control, war between the Marathas and the British became inevitable. The Marathas did not operate as a unit in the game of the subcontinent's power politics. The five hereditary chieftains (Peshwa, Sindia, Holkar, Gaekwad, and Bhonsle) frequently acted against each other. Shivaji, while fighting the European powers in Maharashtra and Gujarat during the second half of the seventeenth century, realized the value of infantry. So, he raised 12,000 infantry. However, they remained a sort of militia. They were husbandmen who were called to arms during campaigns. These footmen were not used in set-piece encounters but were used for garrisoning the forts.[64] The first Maratha chief to experiment with Westernized infantry was Peshwa Balaji Baji Rao. In 1760, the Peshwa enlisted Ibrahim Gardi, a Muslim mercenary soldier trained by the French, who raised 10,000 infantry organized in battalions[65]

The Peshwa faced opposition in purchasing cannon and munition from the Portuguese and the English officials in India.

So he established a cannonball factory at Ambegavan in 1765 and another factory at Poona for manufacturing cannon. However, these factories failed to produce state-of-the-art products. Worked by forced labour, they were neither economically productive nor technologically innovative.[66] A British officer, Major Dirom, wrote in 1793 about the low technological level of the Peshwa's army:

The gun-carriages, in which they trust to the solidity of the timber, and use but little iron in their construction, are clumsy beyond belief; particularly the wheels, which are low, and formed of large solid pieces of wood united. The guns are of all sorts and dimensions . . . although in every respect unfit for use. Were the guns even serviceable, the small supply of ammunition with which they are provided has always effectually prevented the Maratha artillery from being formidable to their enemies.'[67]

Mahadji and Daulat Rao Sindia were more successful than the Peshwa in producing artillery. One British officer who participated in the Second Maratha War expressed his anxiety about Sindia's force: 'It is in the Art of Artillery and Engineering alone that the Country Powers, have never yet been able to rival us, though of late years they have been making rapid strides towards it.[68]

Gradually, Daulat Rao's battalions reached technological parity with the Company's forces. Sindia's Western-style infantry battalions were equipped on the French pattern with 4-, 8-, and 12-pounder field guns.[69] Partial Europeanization among Sindia's troops was more effective than that of Tipu. After fighting the Battle of Assaye on 23 September 1803, the Duke of Wellington wrote to his brother Henry Wellesley about his opponents: 'Sindia's French [trained] infantry were far better than Tipu's, his artillery excellent, and his ordnance so good, and so well equipped, that it answers for our service. We never could use Tipu's. Our loss is great, but the action, I believe, was the most severe that ever was fought in this country.'[70]

Then what brought British victory over the Marathas? The Marathas not only failed to solve the doctrinal problem which they faced due to the Partial Westernization of their force structure, they also failed to create a Western-style officer corps. As a result, they had to pay heavily during their struggle with the British. At the beginning of the eighteenth century, when the Maratha Army was composed of light cavalry, they conducted long range mobile guerrilla raids. Though Sindia created regular infantry supported by field artillery, he also retained the traditional Maratha light cavalry. The infantry–field artillery combine could not conduct high speed guerrilla warfare. Hence, from 1790 onwards, there was a shift in the Maratha theory of warfare. With the Westernized infantry and field artillery, the Marathas decided to conduct pitched battles. But in such encounters, the Maratha cavalry had no role to play because they could not create a shock effect by charging simultaneously as could be done by the disciplined heavy British cavalry. The table on the following page shows that at Assaye, Sindia's infantry was only slightly more numerous than Wellington's soldiers. Sindia and Bhonsle's combined light cavalry totaled 35,000. But, they remained spectators in the ensuing battle.[71]

In addition, the officer corps of Sindia's infantry battalions disintegrated before the onset of the war with EIC in 1803. The British officers deserted just before the war, and the dismissal of the Eurasian officers on grounds of suspicion further exacerbated the situation. The Marathas lacked officers with requisite staff training to fill these vacant posts. Hence, unit level coordination was lost in the heat of the battle.[72] All these defects resulted in the Maratha defeat at Assaye.

On 23 September 1803, the Marathas had an appointment with history. As the EIC's force under Wellington advanced towards river Narmada, Raghuji Bhonsle joined Daulat Rao Sindia. From the very beginning, doctrinal differences paralyzed the Maratha war effort. Raghuji, with his 20,000 light cavalry and 500 camels equipped with *ban*s was for launching a guerrilla attack against Wellington's supply line which stretched back to Bombay and Hyderabad. But Daulat Rao with his trained infantry, wanted a set-piece battle. In the end, Daulat Rao's decision was implemented and in the ensuing battle, Raghuji's forces remained on the battlefield as interested spectators. The Maratha deployment was faulty. The Marathas fortified the village of Assaye and on its right flank, the infantry of Colonel Pohlman (a German mercenary in Sindia's service) was deployed. Assaye was surrounded by two small rivers, the Kaitna and the Juah. And due to the confined space, the Marathas could not bring into action their 35,000 irregular cavalry. Had there

Table 14.1: Decisive Battles Fought in the First Half of the Nineteenth Century

Name of Battle	Date	#Troops Deployed by Indian Power	#East India Company's Soldiers Engaged	Killed and wounded among Indian powers	Killed and wounded among EIC soldiers
Assaye	23 September 1803	10,000 infantry + 100 guns	8,900 infantry +1,600 cavalry	KIA= 428 WIA= 4,800	KIA=1,200 WIA=1,138 40% casualties among the British contingent of the EIC
Mudki	18 December 1845	2,000 infantry +22 guns	12,350 soldiers+ 41 guns	N/A	KIA=215 WIA=657 Total=872
Ferozeshah (This battle was the only one that lasted for two days.)	21-22 December, 1845	60,000 infantry +73 guns	35,000 soldiers	KIA=2,000 WIA=3,000	KIA=900 WIA=2,100
Sobraon	10 February 1846	30,000 infantry +70 guns	30,000soldiers +99 guns	KIA+WIA=10,000	KIA=320 WIA=2,063
Chillianwala	13 January 1849	20,000 infantry +60 guns	12,000 infantry + 3000 cavalry	N/A	Total Loss=89 officers +2357 men KIA=5% of the total force; WIA=12% of the total force

Notes: KIA=Killed in Action; WIA=Wounded in Action; N/A= Reliable figures unavailable. The Indian irregular cavalry did not take any part in these battles. Hence, their figures were omitted. The EIC's infantry denotes sepoys plus white soldiers.

Sources: Charles Gough and Arthur D. Innes, *The Sikh and the Sikh Wars: The Rise, Conquest and Annexation of the Punjab State* (1897; reprint, Delhi: Gian Publishing, 1986), pp. 77–8; Reginald Hodder, 'The Sikh and the Sikh Wars,' *Panjab Past and Present* 4 (1970), pp. 96–7, 100; Lieutenant-Colonel H. M. Sinclair, 'Second Sikh War: 1848–9,' *Journal of the United Service Institution of India* (henceforth *JUSII)*, vol. 28 (1899) pp. 233–5; Captain R. G. Burton, 'Battles of the Deccan,' *JUSII* 20 (1891) pp. 166–7; A. S. Bennell, 'The Anglo-Maratha War of 1803–5,' *Journal of the Society for Army Historical Research* (henceforth *JSAHR*), Autumn 1985, p. 154; Lieutenant Colonel W. D. Bird, 'The Assaye Campaign,' *JUSII*, vol. 41 (1912) p. 117; The Marquess of Anglesey, ed., *Sergeant Pearman's Memoirs* (London: Jonathan Cape, 1968) pp. 32, 51, 90–3; Colonel Lewis, 'Campaign on the Sutlej: 1845–6,' *Journal of the Corps of Royal Engineers*, vol. 49 (1849) pp. 156–8, 163–5; Ganda Singh, 'Colonel Mouton's Account of the First Sikh War: 1845–6,' *Panjab Past and Present*, vol. 15 (1981) p. 122.

been a wide ground, the cavalry could have harassed Wellington when he was crossing the Kaitna. Lack of space also prevented the Maratha cavalry from attacking Wellington when he was deploying his infantry and the rear of the EIC's army as it advanced towards Assaye. Divided command at the brigade level was another defect for the Marathas. Daulat Rao's Westernized infantry was under the command of Colonel Pohlman and Colonel Boliever. During the battle Boliever did not cooperate with Pohlman, whose seven battalions took the brunt of the attack, and Daulat Rao was not on the field to coordinate with the two brigade commanders. On the British side, meanwhile, Wellington led from the front and, in consequence, had two horses shot from under him.[73]

Still, the battle was no cakewalk for the British. Wellesley formed his infantry in two lines and the cavalry was kept in reserve behind them. The Maratha cannons immediately opened up. The leading regiment in the first line was His Majesty's 74th Regiment and it suffered heavily. The Maratha gunners were driven from their guns by bayonets. Then, the Maratha regular infantry started retreating. At that juncture, Wellesley threw in the 19th Dragoons, who cut them up.[74]

After the collapse of Daulat Rao Sindia's regular infantry–artillery combine at Assaye, Jaswant Rao Holkar reverted to the traditional *ganimi kava*. The British were overconfident that they would be able to checkmate the Maratha cavalry raids easily. Wellington, in a letter to Lieutenant-Colonel Thomas Munro dated 1 October 1803, wrote that the predatory war of the Maratha light cavalry could be checked by garrisoning the principal villages with matchlock-armed infantry.[75]

In response, Holkar's force structure underwent an innovation. Instead of depending totally on light Maratha cavalry, Holkar came up with an integrated force of light cavalry supported by about 200 light guns. This provided increased firepower for his cavalry force which raided British territories. Thus, Holkar was able to destroy Colonel Monson's battle group of 4,000 infantry.[76] Against Holkar's high speed cavalry warfare, the slow moving Company infantry and artillery had no answer. Holkar continued to carry fire and sword across west and north India till 1805.[77] He was also able to cut the supply lines of British General Gerald Lake's force which was shadowing him in north India. One British participant observed on 9 October 1804: 'Halt again! I fear grain is scarce and that this causes the delay—these infernal Marathas even cut off all communications.'[78] If Holkar had conducted this campaign when Sindia's Westernized infantry was in the field, the course of war might have been different. Thus, after the Second Maratha War, the Marathas were not extinguished. The Third Maratha War decided the issue in 1817–8.

As a reaction to the treachery of the European officers during 1803, the Marathas relied on an amalgam of *gamini kava* and positional warfare between 1817 and 1818. While the Maratha chiefs with their cavalry marched up and down, their bases remained hitherto inaccessible forts. For conducting predatory warfare, the Maratha chieftains hired the Pindari light cavalry. The Pindaris were soldiers demobilized from Awadh and Rohilkhand due to pressure exerted by the Company. The Pindaris, armed with 12-foot-long spears, ravaged and desolated central India.[79] The Marathas mobilized 78,000 cavalry and 27,000 light Pindari cavalry. [80]

In reaction, the Company mobilized a bigger army than was deployed during the Second Maratha War. Between 1803 and 1805, the British mobilized only 56,000 soldiers,[81] as against 110,400 soldiers in 1817–8. This time, the EIC deployed a large contingent of light cavalry for checking Maratha depredations and numerous heavy guns for taking the forts. Initially, Peshwa Baji Rao II decided to test his luck in a set-piece battle. As the EIC's 1,000 British and 2,000 sepoys marched towards the Peshwa's capital Poona, Baji Rao advanced towards them. In response, the EIC's force fortified the village of Kirkee. On 5 November 1817, the Peshwa sent 3,000 Arab infantry and 18,000 light cavalry under Bapu Gokla to capture the village. The thin red line formed a square. Due to an absence of artillery support, the undisciplined charge of the Arab infantry was easily beaten back by the 1st Bombay Fusiliers. A grape shot round killed Moro Dixit, the commander of the cavalry contingent. Due to the absence of a clear-cut chain of command, the leaderless Peshwa's cavalry retreated. In desperation, the Peshwa took refuge among the chain of forts along the hills in the Western Ghats.[82] While the EIC's troops were besieging the Peshwa's forts, Baji Rao

II's light cavalry was not able to achieve much. This was because the Maratha light cavalry received neither pay nor possessed any logistical back up. It was supposed to maintain itself by pillaging enemy territories. But in 1818, it was operating in its own homeland, worse, in the most infertile mountainous terrain of the Western Ghats. In addition, the light cavalry of the EIC made life impossible for them.[83]

How can one explain the lightning victories of the EIC against the Maratha forts between 1818 and 1819? The Marathas neglected to incorporate the latest European techniques regarding fortifications. The forts were defended by a round stone wall. Neither the *trace italienne* configuration nor Vauban's star-shaped fortifications for providing flanking fire were present. Worse, towards the end of the eighteenth century, the posts of the officials of the forts became hereditary. During their lifetimes, they absented themselves from their posts and appointed agents who carried on the duties of the offices. This not only reduced the Peshwa's authority over his subordinates, but the officials of the forts also became unprofessional. Again, most of the fortresses were garrisoned by matchlock men and *sowar*s who were not issued any uniform, equipment, etc. The fortresses mainly functioned as reserve depots for provisions and treasure. The big forts were administrative centres. Moreover, many Maratha forts were decorative rather than functional in the military sense. The architecture of the forts, through their gigantic size, represented the symbolic greatness of the chieftains' power. These forts were more or less adequate against the Indian culture of siegecraft. The Indian military officials captured forts by surrounding them and then bribing the officials to change sides. Another tactic was to starve the garrison. All these approaches were time consuming.[84]

But the British were able to capture the forts quickly due to the two scientific elements imported from West Europe: engineers and sappers plus heavy ordnance. The British took the fort of Hathras, thanks to a concentration of 44 mortars. In February 1818, a fort near Satara was captured with the aid of 5.2-inch howitzers. The Seogarh fort was located on such a hill that there was no road for dragging the heavy guns near the wall of the fort. The European engineers solved this problem by constructing a road under the covering fire provided by 8-inch mortars and then setting up several breaching batteries near the fort's wall. While these machines blasted the masonry, the garrison inside the forts, armed with matchlocks, had no chance to fight back.[85] This technique was used repeatedly to capture forts. When this process was completed in 1818, the Marathas passed into history.

Sikhs (1821–46)

After the collapse of the Marathas, the *Khalsa* Kingdom emerged as the chief competitor of the EIC. The Rubicon was crossed in December 1845 when the Sikhs crossed the Sutlej river and entered into British territory. The responsibility for war could be laid to both sides. After Ranjit Singh's death, continuous civil wars rendered the Sikh Kingdom weak. This in turn tempted the British Viceroy, Lord Hardinge, to extend the Company's frontier up to the Indus River by annexing the Sikh Kingdom. On the other hand, the *Khalsa* Army demanded higher pay and continuously harassed the Sikh chieftains and the members of the royal family. So, they decided to loose it on the British. Rani Jindan (Ranjit Singh's widow) and important officials like Lal Singh and Tej Singh encouraged the *Khalsa* Army to cross swords with the British.[86]

The Sikh force, before the advent of Ranjit Singh, was composed of cavalry under the command of various semi-autonomous chiefs.[87] Ranjit Singh was able to transform a part of the predatory levies of Sikh horsemen into an army composed of Western style infantry and artillery. The presence of European style infantry of the warlord George Thomas in Haryana and the failure of the Sikh cavalry against him convinced Ranjit Singh that Partial Westernization of the army was necessary.[88]

By 1838, Ranjit Singh's Europeanized contingent comprised 38,000 infantry and 4,000 gunners.[89] The qualitative improvement of the Europeanized contingent of the *Khalsa* Army was sufficient to cause consternation among EIC observers. In 1838, Ranjit held a review of his Westernized troops, ostensibly in honour of Governor-General Auckland's visit to Punjab, but really as an act of deterrence. On 6 December 1838, Auckland's sister Fanny Eden noted in her journal:

Ranjit had a review of his troops yesterday and all our people are in astonishment at his state of discipline, and the very superior way in which they performed their maneuvers . . . but I have a notion from what I can gather that our review was a remarkable poor piece of business, compared to theirs . . . I rode through a bit of their camp this morning and . . . I am rather afraid of them.[90]

Thanks to the strenuous attempts of Ranjit Singh, the Company's troops enjoyed no technological edge against the Europeanized contingent of the *Khalsa* Army just before the First Sikh War in 1845. Both the Sikhs and the Company's infantry used Brown Bess muskets, and the quality of Sikh artillery was equal to that of the Company's artillery.[91]

A modernized military system proved to be more costly. Consequently Ranjit Singh had to reorganize his fiscal administration in order to meet the rising military expenditure. Management of the revenue was put in charge of an Amritsar banker named Ramanand. He was also given the task of farming the salt mines. Bhowani Das, another official of the revenue department, established a pay office because the Westernized infantry had to be paid regularly in cash. The government derived its principal income from land. The state's share was 50 per cent of the gross product. Like the Mysore government, the *Khalsa* government also advanced *taqavi* to the poor peasants during famines. Around 1840, total land revenue collection came to about Rs. 17,500,000 per annum. Other government income came from excise duties, and town, transit, and custom taxes. The customs revenue came to about Rs. 2,400,000 annually. In order to increase the state's income further, Ranjit Singh encouraged the manufacture of silk in Multan.[92] Thus, by the 1840s, the state's income had increased substantially. In 1832, the total annual income of Ranjit Singh's Kingdom came to about Rs. 15,900,000 and in 1840, the total income of the state exceeded Rs. 20,000,000[93]

Nevertheless, some serious deficiencies plagued the Sikh Army, as several European military techniques were not properly integrated within the Sikh military format. The firing of the Sikh infantry was bad because the government allowed only a very small quantity of practice ammunition. Only 10 shots out of a 100 fell upon the target.[94] This proved to be a serious fault because the

EIC introduced target practice with ball ammunition at least twice a week.[95]

Ranjit Singh was able to Westernize part of his force with the aid of some European officers who filtered into India through Afghanistan. He had about 50 European officers on his payroll. The most famous among them were Claude Auguste Court, a French officer who trained his cavalry and artillery, and an Italian named Jean Baptiste Ventura, who trained the infantry.[96] Ranjit Singh was afraid that in case of war with the EIC, his European military advisers would desert him just as Daulat Rao's European officers had done. Thus, he attempted 'forced Punjabization' of his foreign officer corps. When appointed, the European officers were bound by oath to marry Indian woman and, if required, to fight against their own country. After Ranjit's death in 1839, most of the European officers were forced to leave the *Khalsa* army due to the hostility of the Sikh chiefs. For instance, Ventura was forcibly retired in 1843. The chiefs lacked staff training to fill the vacuum and there was intense rivalry among them. Hence, the European contingent within the *Khalsa* Army had neither trust from nor any respect for the Sikh chieftains. Just before the war with the EIC, the *Khalsa* Army was an organization without a head.[97]

The principal tactical deficiency of the *Khalsa* Army, like that of the Maratha Army, was the absence of an adequate number of Western style heavy cavalry which could be used effectively in conjunction with regular infantry during pitched battles. Ranjit Singh had hired Jean Francois Allard who, as a captain of cuirassiers, had fought with Napoleon at Waterloo. However, Ranjit Singh, due to the opposition of the *Akali*s and his nobility, never trained more than 2,000 dragoons and 1,000 lancers.[98] His successors continued to depend upon irregular cavalry. Henry Steinbach, a Prussian officer employed by the Sikhs, observed the following points about the Sikh irregular cavalry in 1846:

> The cavalry of the Sikh army is very inferior in every respect to the infantry. While the latter are carefully picked from large bodies of candidates for service, the former are composed of men of all sorts and sizes and ages, who get appointed solely through the interest of the different sirdars. They are mean-looking, ill dressed and as already stated, wretchedly mounted. Their horse trappings are of leather of the worst quality.[99]

Since the Sikh irregular troopers, like their Maratha counterparts armed at random with various types of weapons and lacking discipline, were unable to stand up in their stirrups to deliver a concentrated blow; they were no match in cavalry versus cavalry combat on the battlefield. As a result, the EIC's regular cavalry, assisted by the mobile firepower of the horse artillery and 6-pounder field guns firing grape shot (which were very effective between 400 and 1,000 yards), was always able to drive away Sikh cavalry and turn the flanks of Sikh infantry during the battles.[100]

The Changing Face of Warfare in Post-Mughal India

How did Partial Westernization among the indigenous powers change the architecture of military confrontations? The labour-intensive Indian militaries became capital intensive. The chief features of the battles fought were the absence of elephants as battering rams and of the horse archers who had dominated the Indian military scene from 1100 CE onwards.[101] The prominence of sabre-rattling and lance-wielding cavalry gave way to that of artillery and firepower-heavy infantry.

The battles that were fought during the first half of the eighteenth century were quite different from those of the first part of the nineteenth century. Not only did the size of the armies increase, but cavalry was replaced by firearms. On 9 April 1740, the Battle of Giria between the Governor of Bihar, Ali Vardi, and the *Nawab* of Bengal, Sarfaraz Khan, was mostly a cavalry encounter. Ali Vardi had 8,000 cavalry against the *Nawab*'s 4,000 cavalry. Ali Vardi used an elephant as a command vehicle. In March 1776, with 30,000 irregular cavalry, the Rohilla chief Zabita Khan attacked the Mughal chieftain Najaf Khan's irregular infantry. In this battle, Zabita Khan's cavalry functioned as the decisive arm which scattered Najaf Khan's infantry. Most of the wounds inflicted on the soldiers were due to arrows and sword cuts.[102]

But in the military encounters of the first half of the nineteenth century, most of the combatants who were killed and wounded were hit by artillery and small arms fire. This trend was consonant with eighteenth century European warfare.[103] The battles fought during the first half of the nineteenth century in India witnessed the impotence of the irregular cavalry against the infantry–artillery combination. In July 1801, at the Battle of Narmada, Jaswant Rao

Holkar deployed 10,000 light cavalry against Daulat Rao Sindia's four infantry battalions and 52 guns. Holkar's repeated cavalry charges failed to make any impact on Sindia's infantry–artillery system.[104] This was a case of an infantry–artillery centred Indian army beating another large cavalry oriented Indian force.

The increasing role of infantry and artillery in the battles fought between the Indian powers and the Company during the first half of the nineteenth century is evident from the earlier table. The duel between opposing regular infantry supported by field artillery constituted the chief feature of these battles.

Confusion and bloodletting were most evident during the storming of a fort. The final phase of the siege of Seringapatam was an example of Wagnerian drama. Tipu's defenders were firing and shouting *Alla Yar, Alla Yar.* After the EIC's breaching batteries did their job, the Company's soldiers crossed the ditch and the ramparts. A ball from an unknown British soldier pierced Tipu's skull. The wounded Mysore troops yelled for water. As the Company's soldiers entered the forts, terrified screams broke out from the *seraglio* (household). The women were first plundered and then raped.[105]

What about the soldiers' experience of battle? A British officer described the fiery charge of the Gurkhas during the Nepal War of 1814–5: 'a crowd of men rushing on in disorder like a pack of hounds in full cry, to the harsh sound of huge trumpets.'[106]

Battles were bloody and messy. On 18 December 1845, during the First Sikh War, about 10,000 Sikh infantry and irregular cavalry with 22 guns attacked 10,000 of the Company's infantry at Mudki. The Sikh cannonade was very effective. Trooper N. W. Bancroft of the Bengal Horse Artillery reminisced: 'round shot from the enemy's artillery began rolling and plunging among the horses' legs like so many cricket balls, but were not quite so harmless as they look, for they broke several of our horses' legs.'[107]

Sergeant Pearman of the EIC was also conscious of the dangerous Sikh artillery. About the Battle of Sobraon on 10 February 1846, Pearman wrote:

> They [Sikhs] soon returned the fire from the numerous batteries in their entrenchments. After a few shots to try the range, their practice became really admirable. . . . We must have been at the time from 1000 to 1200

yards from the enemy. . . . But a very short time had elapsed when their round shot shells and shrapnel came as fast as possible to our own batteries. . . . Such a cannonade and noise as was now taking place, no thunder was ever equal to.[108]

A Surgeon of the 29th Foot, named Ludovick Stewart, gives a chilling account from the sharp end of the encounter at Chillianwala:

I could not see ten yards for smoke. . . . The wounded were abandoned by the cowardly bearers. I drew my sword and tried . . . to stop the fugitives by entreaties, abuse, etc., but without success. I was knocked over, horse and all, by the crowd, and ridden over by a gun driver in a moment. I shall never forget it. . . . Others had ghastly sword cuts to be stitched up. Many a poor fellow had a leg or arm shot away and required amputation. The cries for water were incessant. . . . Lieutenant Metge, the smartest officer in the regiment, was brought in wounded by grape shot in the pit of stomach.[109]

Balanced Military Synthesis in the East India Company's Army, 1750–1849

Certain European military techniques like artillery (both heavy and field), disciplined firearms-equipped infantry, and heavy cavalry gave the Western powers an edge over their Afro-Asian opponents, but these were inadequate for gaining total military superiority in the extra-European world.[110] Absorption and accommodation of certain Indian military elements as part of the Western-oriented military machine and proper utilization of India's resources not only allowed the EIC to destroy Mysore, the Marathas and the Sikhs, but also enabled the Company to project military power outside South Asia.

Modern military forces require a modern state. Unlike the seventeenth century Russian kingdom, the Indian powers were not able to construct a modern bureaucratic state administered by a literate bureaucracy. The British imported elements of Western models of state structure. This enabled them to construct bureaucratic, revenue extracting government machinery, and thus, to maintain a big army permanently. On the other hand, the Maratha and Sikh *jagirdari* system of extracting land revenue, in which various chiefs fought among themselves over the surplus, created desolation, famine, and impoverishment within the Maratha and Sikh domains. As a result, even Mahadji Sindia had problems in paying his Westernized infantry regularly. Absence of a uniform taxation system and concentration of the manufacturing units in the hands of the big chieftains stifled the economic growth of the Sikh Kingdom. The resulting financial difficulties prevented these two Indian powers from providing an adequate amount of ammunition and artillery to their armies. By contrast, the Company state's political economy was able to generate substantial amounts of land revenue regularly, which in turn financed its military–industrial enclaves in South Asia.[111]

Western technology played a vital role in the conduct of warfare. Deployment of quantitatively and qualitatively superior field artillery was one of the principal reasons behind continuous British victories. In 1847, Major–General William Napier invaded Sindh. Two steamers conferred mobility upon Napier's invasion force by transporting them along the Indus River. Napier's force was composed of 1,350 infantry and 1,100 cavalry supported by four 9-pounders, two 6-pounders, two 24-pounders and two 12-pounder howitzers.[112] The Beluchi chiefs and their retainers, numbering 12,000 men armed with swords, shields, and matchlocks, took position at Miani. They also constructed a mud embankment. On 10 September 1847, Napier's 9-pounders opened up and blasted the Beluchi field fortifications. Under cover of artillery fire, His Majesty's 17th Regiment followed by the 1st Sepoy Regiment advanced towards the Beluchis. When the bewildered enemy started retreating, Napier unleashed the 9th Bengal Cavalry. The whole affair lasted for three and half hours and left about 800 Beluchis dead.[113] Once Sindh passed under British control, the next objective was Punjab.

In the battles against the Sikhs, whenever the EIC was unable to deploy superior field artillery, the goddess of victory threatened to leave them. On 21 December 1845, the Sikhs clashed with the EIC at Ferozeshah. The Sikhs had a larger number of heavy calibre guns, with which they surrounded their entrenchment. General Hugh Gough's frontal attack with infantry resulted in very heavy casualties. But, at the end of the day, the EIC's troops under Gough and Hardinge was able to occupy a part of the Sikh entrenchment.

However, Gough's troops were not only tired, but without any ammunition. Next morning, Tej Singh arrived from Ferozepore with fresh troops and 80,000 pounds of gunpowder. Hardinge was thinking of unconditional surrender. The fate of India was hanging in the balance. Thanks to Tej Singh's tortuous relations with the *Khalsa* Army's regimental commanders, the former departed after some minor skirmishes. The EIC's forces survived to fight another day.[114] The Second Sikh War (1848–9) involved several hard-fought battles. At the Battle of Ramnagar, Gough deployed 12,500 infantry and 3,500 cavalry against the force commanded by Sher Singh. Lacking sufficient field artillery, Gough failed to defeat the Sikh Army.[115] At the Battle of Gujerat on 21 February 1849, the tables were turned: Gough deployed 96 guns while Sher Singh lacked adequate field artillery. Gough's tactics were to fix the Sikh centre with his infantry and then to turn the enemy's flanks with heavy cavalry supported by artillery fire. Sher Singh's light cavalry armed with lances, was overwhelmed by firepower from the artillery.[116]

The Indian powers never managed to produce iron guns in adequate quantities. On the other hand, systematization of the production of artillery and munition and of its supply to the Company's forces was secured by establishing a chain of Western style arsenals.[117] These factories utilized raw materials from the subcontinent to produce military stores. To ensure a steady supply of raw materials to these arsenals, Clive imposed a Company monopoly on the trade in saltpetre (the essential ingredient of gunpowder) in 1758. The Company's traders were not to be taxed by the *Nawab's* officials, nor were any Indian traders allowed to buy saltpetre in Bengal, Bihar, and Orissa.[118]

Most of the EIC's British infantry and gunners were urban recruits, unlike the regular infantry of the indigenous powers. The latter recruited peasants without any technical skill. Hence, the Company's British regulars were more adaptive to technological changes than the peasant soldiers.[119] But white infantry were available only in small numbers. Further, they became easy victims of fever and cholera and India's hot and humid climate.[120]

The biggest British achievement was importing the European infantry system and then training the Indians as sepoys. Though the French started this practice, the British were more successful in extending the sepoy system. In June 1757, before the Battle of Plassey, Clive organized the sepoys into battalions with some European officers. He armed and dressed them in red jackets like those worn by the British troops. Every battalion had about 820 privates.[121] During 1759, each battalion was composed of 9 companies.[122] In 1764, 1,000 European soldiers supported by 6,000 sepoys defeated 40,000 soldiers of the *Nawab* of Awadh at Buxar.[123] By 1801, the EIC had recruited 120,000 sepoys. For a set-piece battle anywhere in India, the British could deploy 30,000 soldiers, of whom two-thirds were sepoys.[124]

Officers constitute the brain of an army. Unlike the Marathas and the Sikhs, the EIC was able to create a professional officer corps. In contrast to the indigenous rulers, it was able to transform a motley group of military adventurers into a self-conscious officer corps with its own corporate ethos.[125] Since there was a considerable cultural and linguistic gap between the white officers and the sepoys, the Company trained Indians as non-commissioned officers who functioned as a bridge between the white officers and the sepoys.[126]

Military imperatives made it necessary for the EIC to recruit irregular infantry, and in this regard it followed in the footsteps of the Indian rulers. The Company's infantry, operating in line formation and practicing volley firing, proved unsuitable in hilly terrain covered with forests. So during the Nepal War, it made use of 4,000 irregular Rohilla infantry. The recruitment of the Rohillas was a continuation of Maratha policy. The Maratha chieftain Jaswant Rao Holkar maintained 5,000 Rohilla irregular infantry in 1801. However, the EIC did not misuse the irregular infantry tactically as Bhonsle had. Instead of using them in pitched encounters, the British deployed irregular infantry as sharpshooters in skirmishing order before the regular infantry, arranged in linear formation. The irregulars were encouraged to use their initiative to take aimed shots at the enemy officers.[127] Ranjit Singh recruited Gurkhas because they made for excellent light infantry. They took advantage of the terrain to ambush the Company's infantry in rigid formation. Hence, after 1815, the EIC started recruiting Gurkhas as light infantry.[128]

Disciplined British heavy cavalry played a crucial role by repeatedly turning the flanks of the Indian armies in battle.

Nevertheless, due to the huge extent of the Indian theatre of operations, the military forces were stretched to the limit. This, in turn, required the maintenance of large numbers of light cavalry for reconnaissance, intelligence gathering and forage by every contending power. Inadequate numbers of light cavalry hampered both British military mobility in the subcontinent and Czarist military operations in Central Asia. The absence of such a cavalry force created difficulties for the Company's infantry–artillery-oriented military machine during the First Maratha War and in the campaigns against Haidar Ali.[129] Between 1781 and 1785, due to a lack of light cavalry and transport animals, the EIC's forces under General Eyre Coote were neither able to maintain themselves far away from the coast nor able to pursue the Mysore forces.[130] The Maratha and Mysore cavalry fought like the Crimean Tatars. In the seventeenth century, the Czarist army, like the EIC's force composed of infantry and artillery, had difficulty in coming to grips with the Tatars. Hence, Russia attempted a sort of Military Synthesis by employing the Kalmyk Mongol light cavalry to checkmate the Tatars.[131]

Similarly, the EIC, to check the depredations of Tipu's light cavalry, hired the Marathas, who provided 32,000 cavalry in 1792. By plundering Tipu's domain, they not only created logistical difficulties for the Mysore troops, but also diverted these supplies to the Company's Army.[132] In the long run, however, it was dangerous for the EIC to depend on the Marathas because of the probability of war with them. So, the EIC, like the Indian powers, started maintaining irregular cavalry for dispersed outpost duties. The big British horses were not suited for such duties and the British troopers found these duties very tiresome in India's hot climate. Moreover, the British found the Indian irregular cavalry much cheaper. The EIC recruited upper class Muslims from Awadh in this branch just as the Awadh *Nawabi* had done.[133]

The Skinner Irregular Regiment, commanded by the Eurasian Captain James Skinner, left Daulat Rao Sindia and joined the Company after 1803. Bishop Heber wrote in 1824:

> The commander of the party had a long spear with a small yellow pennon, the others had each a long matchlock-gun which they carried on the right

shoulder with the match ready lighted. . . . They are reckoned, by all the English in this part of the country, the most useful and trusty, as well as the boldest body of men in India, and during the wars both of Lord Lake and Lord Hastings their services and those of their chief were most distinguished.[134]

By accommodating India's animal and manpower resources, including the skills of the indigenous business community, the Company's commissariat system represented the most potent example of Military Synthesis. In 1791, due to a failure of supplies, Cornwallis had to retreat from Bangalore before Tipu's Army.[135] Both General Lake in north India and Wellington in the Deccan depended on the oxen taken from Mysore for carrying baggage, and on the *banjara*s (grain traders who supplied the armies in India from medieval times) for grain.[136] The *banjara*s mobilized 14,000 bullocks to provide provisions to Wellington's army as it advanced to meet the Marathas at Assaye.[137] On 1 April 1803, Arthur Wellesley (later Duke of Wellington) wrote to Lieutenant-General James Stuart: 'I have now in this camp 10,000 *Banjara* bullocks with full bags.'[138] For procuring and conveying supplies, the EIC also utilized Indian contractors and coolies. Parsi brokers of Bombay were tapped by the Company to build up stocks of grain and then coolies were hired to convey the grain to the various scattered detachments of Wellesley.[139] The EIC continued the Mughal tradition of using elephants for dragging heavy guns in roadless terrain. An amalgam of Indian manpower and animal resources with Western technology enabled the EIC to deploy surplus military power beyond the subcontinent. For operations in Punjab and further west, the commissariat maintained 20,000 camels for conveying the baggage of the army.[140] In 1824, during the First Burma War, steamboats transported Madras sepoys to Burma, but the Company used elephants for dragging 6-pounder guns through the jungles and hilly tracks of Arakan.[141]

Wellington was famous for crossing rivers and marching quickly in order to catch up with the Maratha cavalry. After the 1803 campaign, he commented to a fellow officer: 'I think we now begin to beat the Marathas in the celerity of our movements.'[142] One way he accomplished this was by crossing bridgeless rivers in Deccan. He employed basket boats which the Indians used for crossing streams; these were about 10 feet in diameter and 2 feet and 3 inches high.[143]

After the Sikh defeat at Ferozeshah in 1845, the Company's Army quickly crossed the Sutlej and moved into Punjab without giving any respite to the Sikhs to recuperate and reorganize any further defence. The British engineers forded the Sutlej quickly by employing indigenous techniques. The Sikhs crossed rivers in boats whose bottoms were made of thick cedar planks spiked together with siswoo wood. These boats, known as *chuppoo*s, were tied together to form a bridge. The British used them to ferry their infantry and artillery across the river,[144] and the Sikh Kingdom passed into history.

Military Synthesis was also evident in the sphere of military intelligence. Centralization of military and fiscal resources required prior collection of information about their distribution and the knowledge to determine their optimal use. With the collapse of the Mughal Empire, the Indian news writers turned to the British for patronage; and the EIC eagerly utilized them.[145] Further refinement of the intelligence set-up occurred when the British introduced the innovative institution of Resident. For diplomatic purposes, the EIC stationed one Resident in each *durbar* (court) of the Indian rulers. The Residents monitored the size and conditions of the princely armies, grievances of the nobility, etc.[146] Colonel John Collins, Resident at Daulat Rao's *durbar*, regularly passed on vital information regarding troop strengths and their deployments to Wellington.[147] This 'real time' intelligence enabled Wellington to move his troops accordingly before the decisive Battle of Assaye while the Marathas were groping in the dark regarding the advance of the EIC's troops.

Conclusion

The eighteenth and the first half of the nineteenth centuries constituted a crucial period in Indian history, coming as they did between the collapse of the Mughal imperium and the emergence of the British colonial system. This period witnessed both continuity and change. If we take a *longue durée* approach, then it is evident that the two elements which dominated the Indian military scene from the twelfth century onwards, i.e. war-elephants and horse archers, withered away. In their place came drilled and disciplined infantry equipped with firearms and field artillery. Forts of the Marathas became obsolete due to a rapid advance in siege artillery imported by the British. The *jagirdari* system was replaced by the battalion–regimental system administered by the quasi-centralized military bureaucracies.

The supremacy of Western warfare was not self-evident in India. The Indian rulers did not blindly imitate the Western military system but attempted, creatively, a selective assimilation of European elements of warfare. Their aim was to supplement traditional fighting elements with Partial Europeanization of the forces under their control. Both Indian kingdoms and the EIC attempted construction of hybrid military organizations. While the Indian rulers failed, the EIC succeeded. This happened because of several factors. The Westernization programme put a heavy strain on the economies of the Indian rulers. This was especially true for the Marathas. However, the principal problems were political and military. The Indian rulers were on the right track in maintaining irregular cavalry, which increased the operational reach of their armies, but failed to use it properly. They should have conducted both the Western and Indian methods of warfare simultaneously. When Sindia's Western modelled infantry met the Company's troops, Holkar, with his irregular cavalry, should have conducted an attritional guerrilla campaign against the Company's lines of communications which stretched back to Bengal and Madras. Pillage and plunder of the Company's territories would have reduced the colonial state's intake of land revenue, which in turn would have forced Viceroy Lord Moira to stop the war. But the rickety political system obstructed coalition warfare among the princes. Due to petty jealousies and internal hostilities, Sindia and Holkar could not coordinate their war effort for a joint attack on the EIC. Again, at Ferozeshah, the British emerged victorious from the jaws of certain defeat because civil–military tensions dogged the *Khalsa* Army.

While the Indian princes failed to realize the importance of Western-style cavalry and horse artillery for conducting pitched battles, the EIC understood this as well as the importance of light cavalry and irregular infantry for military operations in India. Besides the use of European elements of warfare like mortars, howitzers and horse artillery, the adoption of Indian light cavalry, manpower, and elephants as commissariat vehicles created a synergy which enabled the British to emerge as the chief power broker in South Asia.

Military Synthesis both in the case of the EIC and the Indian militaries was driven by an action–reaction dialectic. From the Indian case, one can also generalize that militaries get transformed only due to the pressure of external threats. To conclude, for opening up new dimensions on the military supremacy of the Europeans in Afro-Asia, rather than the concepts of Military Revolution or Military Evolution, it might be more useful to utilize the analytical tool of Military Synthesis.

Acknowledgements: I thank Prof. I. Kamtekar, Suhrita Saha, the *Journal's* three anonymous referees, and Dr Bruce Vandervort for their help in revising an earlier draft of this article. I was inspired by G. Parker's work on Military Revolution to write this article.

Notes

* Editor's Note: The map present in the original article is missing in this reprint version.

1. Machiavelli, *The Art of War*, translated by Ellis Farneworth, 1965; reprint, New York: Da Capo, 1990, p. 30.
2. Jadunath Sarkar, in *Fall of the Mughal Empire*, 1739–54, vol. 1 1932; reprint, New Delhi: Orient Longman, 1988, argues that the collapse of the Mughal Empire did result in a 'Dark Age' in India. While Sarkar represents the traditional view, modern research is represented by historians like Muzaffar Alam, who, in his *The Crisis of Empire in Mughal North India: Awadh and the Punjab, 1707–48*, Delhi: Oxford University Press, 1986, speaks of economic growth in north India during the first half of the eighteenth century.
3. Sanjay Subrahmanyam, 'Warfare and State Finance in Woodeyar Mysore, 1724–5: A Missionary Perspective', *Indian Economic and Social History Review* (henceforth *IESHR*), vol. 26, 1989, pp. 203–33; Jos J. L. Gommans, 'Indian Warfare and Afghan Innovation during the Eighteenth Century', *Studies in History*, vol. 11, 1995, pp. 261–80.
4. G. J. Bryant, 'The Military Imperative in Early British Expansion in India, 175–85', *Indo-British Review*, vol. 21, 1996, p. 20.
5. Martin Blumenson, 'The Development of the Modern Military', *Armed Forces and Society*, vol. 6, 1980, pp. 670–5.

6. James Michael Hill, 'The Distinctiveness of Gaelic Warfare, 1400–1750', *European History Quarterly*, vol. 22, 1992, p. 337; Bert S. Hall and Kelly De Vries, 'Essay Review—The "Military Revolution" Revisited', *Technology and Culture*, vol. 31, 1990, p. 502; Knud J. V. Jespersen, 'Social Change and Military Revolution in Early Modern Europe: Some Danish Evidence', *Historical Journal*, vol. 26, 1983, pp. 1–2; Michael Howard, *War in European History*, 1976, reprint, Oxford: Oxford University Press, 1977, pp. 61, 78; Hew Strachan, *European Armies and the Conduct of War*, 1983; reprint, London: Routledge, 1993, p. 33.
7. Michael Roberts, 'The Military Revolution, 1560–1660', in Clifford J. Rogers, ed., *The Military Revolution Debate: Readings on the Military Transformation of Early Modern Europe*, Boulder, Colorado: Westview, 1995, pp. 13–35. In medieval Europe, the infantry was deployed on the battlefield in a haphazard manner. But the Spanish Army organized their infantry in a deep square formation known as the *tercio*, which resembled the unwieldy Macedonian phalanx. Gustavus Adolphus increased the manoeuvrability of his infantry by deploying them in small units known as regiments, which were further subdivided into battalions. Gustavus was influenced by the Roman Army's legion, which was composed of several maniples. See Thomas Arnold, *The Renaissance at War*, London: Cassell, 2001, pp. 53–81.
8. Geoffrey Parker, 'The Military Revolution, 1560–1660-A Myth?', in Rogers, ed. *Military Revolution Debate*, pp. 37–54.
9. Clifford J. Rogers, 'The Military Revolutions of the Hundred Years' War', in Rogers, ed., *Military Revolution and Debate*, pp. 55–93.
10. Jeremy Black, *A Military Revolution? Military Change and European Society*, 1550–1800, Basingstoke, UK: Macmillan, 1991, pp. 93–5.
11. Lieutenant F. G. Cardew, *A Sketch of the Services of the Bengal Native Army to the Year* 1895, 1903; reprint, New Delhi: Today and Tomorrow's Publishers, 1971, pp. 2–32.
12. Michael Edwardes, *Clive: The Heaven Born General*, London: Hart-Davis, 1977, pp. 10–11.
13. Geoffrey Parker, *The Military Revolution: Military Innovation and the Rise of the West, 1500–1800*, Cambridge: Cambridge University Press, 1988, pp. 4–5, 115, 117, 125–36.
14. Pradeep Barua, 'Military Developments in India, 1750–1850', *Journal of Military History*, vol. 58, 1994, p. 616; Stewart Gordon, 'The Limited Adoption of European-Style Military Forces by Eighteenth Century Rulers in India', *IESHR*, vol. 35, 1998, pp. 229–45.
15. G. V. Scammell, 'Indigenous Assistance in the Establishment of Portuguese Power in Asia in the Sixteenth Century', in Douglas M. Peers, ed., *Warfare and Empires: Contact and Conflict between European and Non-Europecm Military and maritime Forces and Cultures*, Brookfield, Vt.: Ashgate Variorum, 1997, pp. 139–40; Jeremy Black, *War and the*

World: Military Power and the Fate of Continents, 1450–2000, 1998; reprint, New Haven, Conn.: Yale University Press, 2000.

16. Mark Bence-Jones, *Clive of India*, London: Constable, 1974, pp. 22–35; James P. Lawford, *Britain's Army in India: From its Origins to the Conquest of Bengal*, London: George Allen & Unwin, 1978, pp. 68–102; Indrani Roy, 'Some Aspects of the French Presence in Bengal, 1731–40', *Calcutta Historical Journal*, vol. 1, 1976, p. 91.
17. Bruce Lenman, *Britain's Colonial Wars*, 1688–1783, Harlow, UK: Pearson, 2001, pp. 99–100.
18. P. J. Marshall, 'British Expansion in India in the Eighteenth Century: A Historical Revision', *History*, vol. 60, 1975, pp. 40–1.
19. Jagadish Narayan Sarkar, *The Art of War in Medieval India*, New Delhi: Munshiram Manoharlal, 1984, vol. 62, pp. 81–82.
20. Shelford Bidwell, S*words for Hire: European Mercenaries in Eighteenth Century India*, London: John Murray, 1971, pp. 2, 4; Jadunath Sarkar, *Fall of the Mughal Empire: 1754–71*, vol. 2, 1934: reprint, New Delhi: Orient Longman, 1991, p. 174.
21. Fauja Singh Bajwa, *Military, System of the Sikhs during the Period 1799–1849*, Delhi: Motilal Banarasidas, 1964, p. 1.
22. Gommans, 'Indian Warfare', pp. 267–8; Steven T. Ross, *From Flintlock to Rifle: Infantry Tactics 1740–1866*, 1979; reprint, London: Frank Cass, 1996, p. 168.
23. Jos J. L. Gommans, *The Rise of the Indo-Afghan Empire, c.*1710–80, Leiden, Netherlands: E. J. Brill, 1995, pp. 4–5, 176–7.
24. Ghulam Muhammad, ed., *The History of Haidar Ali and Tipu Sultan: A Contemporary History*, by MMDLT, General of the Mughal Army, 1855; reprint, Delhi: Cosmo, 1976, p. 33; Ghulam Hussain Salim, *Riyazu-s-Salatin*, tr. Abdus Salim, 1903; reprint, Delhi: Iderah-I Adabiyat-i Delhi, 1975, p. 242.
25. R. C. Majumdar et al., *An Advanced History of India*, 1978; reprint. Madras: Macmillan, 1991, pp. 536–46; Khushwant Singh, *A History of the Sikhs*, 1469–1839, vol. 1, 1963; reprint, Delhi: Oxford University Press, 1977, pp. 63–184.
26. V. G. Dighe and S. N. Qanungo, 'Administrative and Military System of the Marathas', in R. C. Majumdar and Dighe, eds., *The Maratha Supremacy*, Mumbai: Bharatiya Vidya Bhavan, 1977, pp. 567–8.
27. Yusuf Ali Khan, *The Tarikh-I-Mahabatjangi*, tr. Abdus Subhan, Calcutta: Asiatic Society, 1982, pp. 27–36.
28. Jadunath Sarkar, *Fall of the Mughal Empire, 1789–1803*, vol. 4, 1950; reprint, New Delhi: Orient Longman, 1992, p. 85.
29. George Forster, *A Journey from Bengal to England through the Northern part of India, Kashmir, Afghanistan, and Persia and into Russia, by the Caspian Sea, 1782–84*, vol. 1, 1798; reprint, New Delhi: Munshiram Manoharlal, 1997, pp. 288–89.

30. Frank Tallett, *War and Society* in *Early Modern Europe, 1495–1715*, 1992; reprint, London: Routledge, 1997, p. 31.
31. Ganda Singh, 'Colonel Polier's Account of the Sikhs', *The Panjab Past and Present*, vol. 4, 1970, pp. 239, 243.
32. Jadunath Sarkar, *Mughal Empire*, vol. 4:1.
33. *Napoleon* on *the Art of War*, ed. and tr. Jay Luvaas, New York: Free Press, 1999, pp. 132–3.
34. Jadunath Sarkar, *Fall of the Mughal Empire, 1771–88*, vol. 3, 1938; reprint, New Delhi: Orient Longman, 1991, pp. 60, 180.
35. W. L. M'Gregor, *The History of the Sikhs*, 2 vols, 1846; reprint, Allahabad: R. S. Publishing House, 1979, vol. 1, pp. 236–7.
36. Muhammad, *Haidar Ali and Tipu Sultan*, pp. 21, 28.
37. Colonel G. B. Malleson, *The Decisive Battles of India, 1746–1849*, 1885; reprint, Jaipur: Aavishkar Publisher, 1986, p. 280.
38. Captain R. G. Burton, 'Argaum', *Journal of the United Service Institution of India* (hereafter *JUSII*), vol. 28, 1899, pp. 297–8.
39. J. G. Duff, *Histoy of the Marathas*, 3 vols. in one, 1863; reprint, Delhi: Low Price Publications, 1990, vol. 1, pp. 401, 2:261.
40. Colonel Lewis, 'Campaign on the Sutlej, 1845–46', *Journal of the Royal Engineers* (hereafter *JRE*) vol. 49, 1849, pp. 161, 164; Reginald Hodder, 'The Sikhs and the Sikh Wars', *Panjab Past and Present*, vol. 4, 1970, pp. 103–4; C. A. L. Graham, *The History of the Indian Mountain Artillery*, Aldershot, UK: Gale and Polden, 1957, p. 2.
41. Captain F. R. Lee, 'An Ancient Weapon of India', *JUSII*, vol. 41, 1912, pp. 189–92.
42. C. R. Boxer, 'Asian Potentates and European Artillery in the 16th–18th Centuries: A Footnote to Gibson-Hill', *Journal of the Malaysian Branch of the Royal Asiatic Society*, vol. 38, 1966, pp. 156–72; Randolf G. S. Cooper, *The Anglo-Maratha Campaigns and the Contest for India: The Struggle for Control of the South Asian Military Economy*, New Delhi: Foundation Books, 2005, p. 304.
43. D. C. Ganguly, ed., *Select Documents of the British Period of Indian* History, Calcutta: Trustees of Victoria Memorial, 1958, p. 75.
44. John Pemble, *The Invasion of Nepal: John Company at War*, Oxford: Clarendon Press, 1971, p. 26; 'The Gurkhas', notes by Lieutenant Colonel R. Sale Hill, with addenda by Charles Reid, in 'Ethnic Elements of the Indian Army, Records of Chief Commands, 1865–76, Notes and Minutes by Napier of Magdala', *MSS.EUR.F.*114, vol. 5, no. 4, Oriental and India Office Collection, British Library, London.
45. Ganguly, *Select Documents*, p. 228.
46. David B. Ralston, *Importing the European Army: The Introduction of the European Military Techniques and Institutions into the Extra-European World, 1600–1914*, Chicago: University of Chicago Press, 1990, pp. 175,

179; General Sir John Hackett, *The Profession of Arms*, 1983; reprint, London: Sidgwick and Jackson, 1984, pp. 56–64.

47. Stanford J. Shaw, 'The Origins of Ottoman Military Reform: The Nizam-I-Cedid Army of Sultan Selim III', *Journal of Modern History*, vol. 37, 1963, pp. 291–2.
48. Herbert Compton, *A Particular Account of the European Military Adventurers of Hindustan from 1784 to 1803*, 1892; reprint, Karachi: Oxford University Press, 1976, pp. 44–5.
49. T. D. Broughton, *Letters Written in a Maratha Camp During the Year 1809*, 1892; reprint, New Delhi: Asian Educational Services, 1995, p. 218; *A European Experience of the Mughal Orient*, tr. M. Alam and Seema Alavi, New Delhi: Oxford University Press, 2001, p. 5.
50. J. S. Grewal and Indu Banga, eds, *Civil and Military Affairs of Maharaja Ranjit Singh*, Amritsar: Guru Nanak Dev University, 1988, p. 123.
51. B. S. Nijjar, *Anglo-Sikh Wars, 1845–49*, New Delhi: K. B. Publications, 1976, p. 106.
52. H. M. L. Lawrence, *Adventures of an Officer in the Service of Ranjit Singh*, 1845; reprint, New Delhi: Rupa, 2002, p. 12.
53. Victor Davis Hanson, *Carnage and Culture: Landmark Battles in the Rise of Western Power*, New York: Doubleday, 2001.
54. Jeffrey Greenhut, 'Armies of India from the Aryans to the Marathas', *JUSII*, vol. 105, 1976, pp. 30–41; *The Seven Military Classics of Ancient China*, tr. Ralph D. Sawyer, Boulder, Colorado: Westview, 1993, pp. 2–16.
55. Dirk H. A. Kolff, *Naukar, Rajput, and Sepoy: The Ethnohistory of the Military Labour Market in Hindustan, 1450–1850*, Cambridge: Cambridge University Press, 1990. See especially Sun Tzu, *Art of War*, tr. Ralph D. Sawyer, Boulder, Colorado: Westview, 1994, pp. 33–126.
56. Channa Wickremesekera, *'Best Black Troops in the World': British Perceptions and the Making of the Sepoy, 1746–1805*, New Delhi: Manohar, 2002, pp. 130–86; Jos J. L. Gommans, *Mughal Warfare: Indian Frontiers and the High Roads to Empire, 1500–1700*, London: Routledge, 2002, p. 203.
57. Subrahmanyam, 'Warfare and State Finance', p. 215.
58. Muhammad, *Haidar Ali and Tipu Sultan*, p. 35.
59. N. K. Sinha, *Haidar Ali*, 1941; reprint, Calcutta: A. Mukherjee & Company, 1969, pp. 259, 262; Jadunath Sarkar, 'Haidar Ali's Invasion of the Eastern Carnatic, 1780', in Irfan Habib, ed., *Confronting Colonialism: Resistance and Modernization under Haidar Ali and Tipu Sultan*, New Delhi: Tulika, 1999, p. 23; A. W. Lawrence, ed., *Captives of Tipu: Survivors' Narratives*, London: Jonathan Cape, 1929, pp. 34, 50.
60. Muhammad Moienuddin, *Sunset at Seringapatam: After the death of Tipu Sultan*, New Delhi: Orient Longman, 2000, pp. 3–4; 'State Intervention in the Economy: Tipu's Orders to Revenue Collectors, 1792–

97, A Calendar', tr. by I.G. Khan, in I. Habib, ed., *State and Diplomacy under Tipu Sultan: Documents and Essays*, New Delhi: Tulika, 2001, p. 122.

61. Captain G. R. P. Wheatley, 'The Final Campaign against Tipu', *JUSII*, vol. 41, 1912, p. 254; B. P. Hughes, 'Siege Artillery in the Nineteenth Century', *Journal of the Society for Army Historical Research* (hereafter *JSAHR*), vol. 60, 1982, p. 45.
62. Wheatley, 'Campaign against Tipu', p. 255.
63. Quoted in A. C. Banerjee, *Peshwa Madav Rao I*, 1943; reprint, Calcutta: A. Mukherjee, 1968, pp. 86–7.
64. Jadunath Sarkar, *Shivaji*, 1919; reprint, Calcutta: M. C. Sarkar & Sons, 1961, pp. 359–60.
65. Lester Hutchinson, *European Freebooters in Moghul India*, Bombay: Asia Publishing, 1964, p. 12.
66. *History of the Regiment of Artillery: Indian Army*, Published by the Artillery Headquarters, Dehradun: Palit & Dutt, 1971, pp. 8–9; H. Fukuzawa, 'Non-Agricultural Production: Maharashtra and the Deccan', in Tapan Raychaudhuri and Irfan Habib, eds, *The Cambridge Economic History of India, c.1200–c. 1750*, vol. 1, 1982; reprint, New Delhi: 1991, p. 314.
67. Major Dirom, *A Narrative of the Campaign in India which Terminated the War with Tipu Sultan in 1792*, 1793; reprint, New Delhi: Asian Educational Services, 1997, pp. 10–11.
68. D. D. Khanna, ed., *The Second Maratha Campaign, 1804–05: Diary of James Young, Officer of Bengal Horse Artillery*, New Delhi: Allied, 1990, entry for 9 September 1804, pp. 7–8.
69. Jean Marie Lafont, 'Benoit De Boigne in Hindustan: His Impact on the Doab, 1784–95', in his *Indika: Essays* in *Indo-French Relations, 1630–1976*, New Delhi: Manohar, 2000, p. 179.
70. Antony Brett-James, ed., *Wellington at War, 1794–1815: A Selection of His Wartime Letters*, London: Macmillan, 1961, 3 October 1803, pp. 84–5.
71. Captain R. G. Burton, 'Battles of the Deccan', *JUSII*, vol. 20, 1891, pp. 166–7.
72. John Pemble, 'Resources and Techniques in the Second Maratha War', *Historical Journal*, vol. 19, 1976, p. 394; Randolf G. S. Cooper, 'Wellington and the Marathas', *International History Review*, vol. 11, 1989, p. 38.
73. K. G. Pitre, *Second Anglo-Maratha War, 1802–05*, Pune: Dastane Ramchandra and Co., 1990, pp. 61–78; H. C. Kar, *Military History of India*, Calcutta: Firma KLM, 1980, pp. 371–2.
74. Raghubir Sinh, ed., *Poona Residency Correspondence*, vol. 10, Mumbai: Gouranga Press, 1951, pp. 149–50.
75. Brett-James, *Wellington at War*, 1 October 1803, p. 83.
76. Khanna, *Diary of James Young*, p. 7.

77. A. S. Bennell, 'The Anglo-Maratha War of 1803–5', *JSAHR*, Autumn 1985, pp. 155–9.
78. Khanna, *Diary of James Young*, p. 35.
79. M. P. Roy, *Origin, Growth and Suppression of the Pindaris*, New Delhi: Sterling, 1973, pp. 23–6.
80. B. K. Sinha, *The Pindaris, 1798–1818*, Calcutta: Bookland, 1971, pp. 155–6.
81. Lieutenant-Colonel W. D. Bird, 'The Assaye Campaign', *JUSII*, vol. 41, 1912, p. 105.
82. George MacMunn, *Vignettes from Indian Wars*, 1901; reprint, Delhi: Low Price Publications, 1993, p. 70; idem, *The Armies of India*, 1911; reprint, New Delhi: Heritage Publishers, 1991, pp. 68–70.
83. Pratulchandra Gupta, ed., 'John Macleod's Private Journal during the Maratha War: 1817–8, *Bengal Past and Present*, nos. 192–93, 1982, p. 112.
84. Surendra Nath Sen, *The Military System of the Marathas*, 1928; reprint, Calcutta: K. P. Bagchi, 1979, pp. 79–95; J. Burton-Page, 'Study of Fortification in the Indian Subcontinent from the Thirteenth to the Eighteenth Century AD', *Bulletin of the School of Oriental and African Studies*, vol. 23, 1960, p. 514; Stewart Gordon, 'Forts and Social Control in the Maratha State', *Modern Asian Studies* (hereafter, *MAS*), vol. 13, 1979, pp. 1–17.
85. Dirk H. A. Kolff, 'End of an Ancient Regime: Colonial War in India, 1798–1818', in J. A. De Moor and H. L. Wesseling, eds., *Imperialism and War: Essays on Colonial Wars* in *Asia and Africa*, Leiden, Netherlands: E. J. Brill, 1989, p. 44; P. C. Gupta, 'John Macleod's Private Journal during the Maratha War, 1817–8', *Bengal Past and Present*, vol. 190, 1981, pp. 74–9.
86. W. W. Hunter, *The Marquess of Dalhousie and the Final Development of the Company's Rule*, Oxford: Clarendon Press, 1895, pp. 60–85.
87. Forster, *Journey*, vol. 1, pp. 285–6.
88. J. M. Lafont, 'Military Activities of French Officers of Maharaja Ranjit Singh', *Journal of Sikh Studies*, vol. 9, 1982, pp. 32–3.
89. N. K. Sinha, *Ranjit Singh*, 1933; reprint, Calcutta: Niva Mukherjee, 1975, p. 157.
90. Janet Dunbar, ed., *Tigers, Durbars, and Kings: Fanny Eden's Indian Journals, 1837–8*, London: John Murray, 1988, pp. 176–7.
91. Charles Gough and Arthur Innes, *The Sikhs and the Sikh Wars: The Rise, Conquest and Annexation of the Punjab State*, 1897; reprint, Delhi: Gian Publishing, 1986, p. 67.
92. Sinha, *Ranjit Singh*, pp. 139–46.
93. Charles Hugel, *Travels in Kashmir and the Punjab Containing a Particular Account of the Government and Character of the Sikhs*, tr. T. B. Jervis, 1845; reprint, Delhi: Low Price Publications, 2000, p. 403.

94. Henry Steinbach, *The Country of the Sikhs*, 1846; reprint, New Delhi: KLM Book House, 1978, p. 88.
95. Jac Weller, *Wellington in India*, London: Longman, 1972, p. 12.
96. Hugh Cook, *The Sikh Wars: The British Army in Punjab, 1845–49*, New Delhi: Thomson Press, 1975, p. 17; Khushwant Singh, *Ranjit Singh, Maharajah of Punjab, 1780–1839*, London: George, Allen & Unwin, 1962, p. 141.
97. H. L. Garrett and C. Grey, eds, *European Adventurers at Northern India, 1785–1849*, 1929; reprint, New Delhi: Asian Educational Services, 1993, p. 12; Ganda Singh, 'Colonel Mouton's Account of the First Sikh War: 1845–6', *Panjab Past and Present*, vol. 15, 1981, pp. 117–27; Sheo Narain, 'General Ventura', *Journal of Punjab Historical Society*, vol. 6, 1970, p. 70.
98. C. Grey, *European Adventurers*, pp. 80, 82.
99. Steinbach, *Country of the Sikhs*, p. 89.
100. Donald Featherstone, *At Them with the Bayonet: The First Sikh War*, London: Jarrolds, 1968, p. 3; N. K. Sinha, *Rise of the Sikh Power*, 1936; reprint, Calcutta: University of Calcutta, 1946, p. 151; Jac Weller, 'Wellington against Abrams: Where the Old Ways Better?', *Military Digest*, vol. 88, 1971, p. 53.
101. Jos J. L. Gommans and Dirk Kolff, eds, 'Introduction', in Gommans and Kolff, eds. *Warfare and Weaponry in South Asia, 1000–1800*, New Delhi: Oxford University Press, 2001, pp. 1–42.
102. Yusuf Ali Khan, *Tarikh*, pp. 13–6; Antoine Louis Henri Polier, *Shah Alam II and His Court*, ed. P. C. Gupta, Calcutta: S. C. Sarkar & Sons, 1947, p. 43.
103. Christopher Duffy, *The Military Experience in the Age of Reason*, London: RKP, 1987, p. 245.
104. Major Lewis Ferdinand Smith, *A Sketch of the Rise, Progress, and Termination of the Regular Corps of the Native Princes and Actions of the Late Maratha War*, Calcutta: J. Greenway, 1804, pp. 13–4.
105. Meadows Taylor, *Tipu Sultan: A Tale of the Mysore War*; reprint, New Delhi: Rupa, 2000, pp. 641–5; Kaushik Roy, *India's Historic Battles: From Alexander the Great to Kargil*, New Delhi: Permanent Black, 2004, pp. 117–8.
106. The quotation is from Colonel W. G. Hamilton, 'Ochterlony's Campaign in the Simla Hills–Some Further Notes on', *JUSII*, vol. 41, 1912, pp. 456.
107. George Bruce, *Six Battles for India: The Anglo-Sikh Wars, 1845–6, 1848–9*, Calcutta: Rupa, 1969, pp. 109–10.
108. The Marquess of Anglesey, ed., *Sergeant Pearman's Memoirs in India from 1845–53*, London, Jonathan Cape, 1968, pp. 52–3.
109. Mark Nicholls, 'A Surgeon in the Second Sikh War: Ludovick Stewart's Account of the Battle of Chillianwala', *JSAHR*, vol. 71, 1993, p. 220.

110. For the African case see John K. Thornton 'The Art of War in Angola, 1575–1680', *Comparative Studies in Society and History* (henceforth *CSSH*), vol. 30, 1988, p. 377.
111. *Sindia as Regent of Delhi, 1787 & 1789–91*, tr. Jadunath Sarkar, Mumbai: Director of Archives Government of Bombay, 1954, p. 1; Lieutenant-Colonel Valentine Blacker, *Memoir of the Operations of the British Army in India during the Maratha War 1817, 1818 and 1819*, London: Black, Kingsbury, Parbury, and Allen, 1821, pp. 28–9; Douglas M. Peers, *Between Mars and Mammon: Colonial Armies and the Garrison State in Early Nineteenth Century India*, London: I. B. Tauris, 1995; Sumit Guha, *The Agrarian Economy of Bombay Deccan*, Delhi: Oxford University Press, 1985, p. 168; J. M. Lafont, 'The Commerce of Punjab and Kashmir in 1832: C. M. Wade's Report to the East India Company', in Lafont, *Indika*, pp. 343–9; Marshall Poe, 'The Consequences of the Military Revolution in Muscovy: A Comparative Perspective', *CSSH*, vol. 38, 1996, pp. 614–5.
112. Charles Waddington, 'Account of the Battle of Miani', *JRE*, vol. 9, 1847, pp. 25, 28.
113. William Napier, 'Explanation of the Battle of Miani', *JRE*, vol. 49, 1849, pp. 65–70.
114. Khushwant Singh, *A History of the Sikhs*, vol. 2, *1839–1964*, 1966; reprint, Delhi: Oxford University Press, 1989, pp. 48–50.
115. Lieutenant-Colonel H. M. Sinclair, 'Second Sikh War, 1848–49', *JUSII*, vol. 28, 1899, pp. 229–31.
116. Ibid., and 'Discussion', *JUSII*, vol. 28, 1899, pp. 238–41.
117. Military Department, Proceedings of the Board of Ordnance, Letter from Captain Grant commanding at Buxar, to Ensign John Murray, Secretary to the Board of Ordnance, November 1775, p. 460, National Archives of India, New Delhi; Daniel George Robinson's letter to his sister, Ramgarh, 5 January 1847, in Alan J. Guy, R. N. W. Thomas and G. J. DeGroot, eds, *Military Miscellany I*, Stroud: Alan Sutton, 1997, p. 110.
118. James P. Lawford, *Clive, Proconsul of India: A Biography*, London: George Allen, 1976, p. 277; Ganguly, *Select Documents*, p. 62.
119. V. G. Kiernan, *European Empires from Conquest to Collapse, 1815–1960*, Bungay, Suffolk: Fontana, 1982, p. 15.
120. M'Gregor, *History of the Sikhs*, vol. 2, pp. 78–9.
121. Lieutenant-General S. L. Menezes, *Fidelity and Honour: The Indian Army from the Seventeenth to the Twenty-First Century*, New Delhi: Viking, 1993, p. 10.
122. Wolseley Haig, 'The Armies of East India Company', in H. H. Dodwell, ed., *The Cambridge History of India: The Indian Empire, 1858-1918*, vol. 6, Delhi: Sultan Chand in association with the Cambridge University Press, 1958, p. 155.

123. D. C. Verma, *Plassey to Buxar: A Military Study*, New Delhi: K. B. Publications, 1976, p. 92.
124. Stanislas Lefebvre, 'An Old French Memoir on India', *JUSII*, vol. 41, 1912, pp. 236–7, 240.
125. Raymond Callahan, *The East India Company and Army Reform, 1793–8*, Cambridge, Massachusetts: Harvard University Press, 1972, p. xi.
126. Lorenzo M. Crowell, 'Military Professionalism in a Colonial Context: The Madras Army, circa 1832', *MAS*, vol. 24, 1990, pp. 259–63.
127. Smith, *Maratha War*, p. 14; Colonel L. W. Shakespear, 'The War with Nepal: Operations in Sirmoor, 1814–5', *JUSII*, vol. 42, 1913, pp. 376–77.
128. Colonel W. G. Hamilton, 'Ochterlony's Campaign in the Simla Hills: 1814–15', *JUSII*, vol. 41, 1912, pp. 149–54.
129. G. J. Bryant, 'The Cavalry Problem in the Early British Indian Army, 1750–85', *War in History*, vol. 2, 1995, pp. 2–3.
130. Humphry Bullock, *History of the Army Service Corps, 1760–1857*, vol. 1, New Delhi: Sterling, 1976, p. 24.
131. L. J. D. Collins, 'The Military Organization and Tactics of the Crimean Tatars, 16th–17th Centuries', in V. J. Parry and M. E. Yapp, eds, *War, Technology, and Society in the Middle East*, London: Oxford University Press, 1975, p. 275.
132. Dirom, *A Narrative*, pp. 4, 9.
133. Seema Alavi, *The Sepoys and the Company: Tradition and Transition in Northern India, 1770–1830*, Delhi: Oxford University Press, 1995, p. 18.
134. M. A. Laird, ed., *Bishop Heber in Northern India: Selections from Heber's Journal*, Cambridge: Cambridge University Press, 1971, pp. 224.
135. E. W. Thompson, *The Last Siege of Seringapatam*, 1923; reprint, New Delhi: Asian Educational Service, 1990, p. 10.
136. Major H. Helsham Jones, 'The Campaigns of Lord Lake against the Marathas: 1804–6', *JRE*, vol. 8, 1882, pp. 69–70.
137. Burton Stein, *Thomas Munro: The Origins of the Colonial State and His Vision of Empire*, Delhi: Oxford University Press, 1989, p. 119.
138. Anthony S. Bennell, ed., *The Maratha War Papers of Arthur Wellesley: Jan.–Dec. 1803*, Stroud: Alan Sutton, 1998, p. 40.
139. Randolf G. S. Cooper, 'Beyond Beasts and Bullion: Economic Considerations in Bombay's Military Logistics, 1803', *MAS*, vol. 33, 1999, pp. 159–82.
140. H. M. Durand, 'Passage of the Indus by the Bengal Portion of the Army of Indus', *JRE*, vol. 4, 1840, p. 103.
141. George Bruce, *The Burma Wars, 1824–86*, London: Hart-Davis, 1973, p. 39; J. J, Snodgrass, *The Burmese War*, 1827; reprint, Delhi: Low Price Publications, 1993, pp. 1–60.
142. Brett-James, *Wellington at War*, p. 97.
143. Ibid., pp. 74–5.

144. Captain Yule, 'Some Account of the Passage of the Sutlej by the British Army in February 1846', *JRE*, vol. 49, 1849, pp. 177–82.
145. C. A. Bayly, 'Knowing the Country: Empire and Information in India', *MAS*, vol. 27, 1993, pp. 5, 25.
146. Michael H. Fisher, 'British Expansion in North India: The Role of the Resident in Awadh', *IESHR*, vol.18, 1981, pp. 72–3.
147. Anthony S. Bennell, *The Making of Arthur Wellesley*, Mumbai: Orient Longman, 1997, pp. 69–72.

SECTION IV

Military Confrontation and Collaboration in British India (1857–1947)

CHAPTER 15

The Recruitment of the Bengal Army: Beyond the Myth of the Zamindar's Son

James W. Hoover

During the last stage of the Revolt of 1857–9, a party of rebel sepoys retreating through the Terai forest sent an *arz* (petition) to Maharaja Jang Bahadur of Nepal. In the letter, the mutineers summarized their view of the army to which they had belonged, and their reasons for rising against their British officers:

> A century ago the British arrived in Hindoostan and gradually entertained troops in their service, and became masters of every state. Our forefathers have always served them and we also entered their service. . . . By the mercy of God and with our assistance the British conquered every place they liked, in which thousands of us Hindoostani men were sacrificed, but we never made any excuses or pretences nor revolted. . . . But in the year 1857 the British issued an order that new cartridges and muskets which had arrived from England were to be issued; in the former of which the fat of cows and pigs were mixed. . . . We and all our countrymen having united together, have fought here and there with the British for the preservation of our faith. . . . We have fought for two years in order that our faith and religion may not be polluted. If the religion of a Hindoo or Mussalman is lost, what remains in the world?[1]

The preservation of this document by the imperial government points to an interesting problem in the historiography of the Bengal army. The mutineers' *arz* presents a view of the political and social causes of the Revolt which the British themselves had come to hold. To the Victorian mind the story could be simply put: the sepoy Army, after decades of loyal service, became corrupted by religious 'feeling' and consequently a spontaneous revolt broke out, which later became a full-scale religious war. Significantly, the document also points out the fidelity of the sepoys prior to 1857, a claim widely accepted by historians despite much evidence to the contrary. In the decades preceding the Revolt, numerous British officers remarked that the normal state of the Army was one of 'discontent' or even 'mutiny'.[2]

Yet, as a soldier, the sepoy has won retrospective praises on all sides, and historians have maintained that the Mutiny was primarily either a religious war or an elite-led peasant revolt instigated by economic and political upheaval. All have approached the religious aspect of the struggle in abstract terms, employing only the ideology of orthodox Brahminical Hinduism to understand the spiritual concerns of those who took up arms against the Company Raj. Muslim participants have been treated as if all were Wahhabis dedicated to *jehad* against the *faringhi* Empire.[3] Almost nothing has been done to unravel the social history of the Bengal Army, particularly the connection between the sepoys in their cantonments and the villages from which they were recruited. A very stylized understanding of the social categories into which these soldiers fit has defined our understanding of the Army and its mighty challenge to British authority. That they were all the sons and heirs of Awadh landowners—all high-caste Brahmans and Rajputs—has been virtually accepted without question. Based upon this sweeping classification, reasons for insurgency have been set forth which would seem to be consistent with the discontent displayed by this class prior to the Revolt. This essay will examine some of the pieces of a very scattered puzzle which have come together to give us a more accurate sense of who the Company's sepoys were, both as soldiers and as peasants, and to what extent religion played a role in their decision to rebel in 1857.

Until recently, little serious analytical research was devoted the Company's armies, and most works on the subjects concerned themselves with the European officer corps, accepting traditional assumptions about the sepoys as valid. This oversight was consistent with trends in military history before the 1960s, when the interdisciplinary school of the 'new military history' emerged, with a greater emphasis on sociological issues rather than political or strictly military concerns. Amiya Barat's groundbreaking effort, appearing in 1962, has yet to be matched, and is most notable for bringing to light the problems within the service which the Army's unofficial propaganda had suppressed into the recesses of official archives. For instance, one does not find the sepoys languishing in squalid quarters in Philip Mason's *A Matter of Honour*, though Mason does take into account the factor of religion and its role in *esprit de corps*. In the latest major work related to the topic, Kolff casts strong doubts upon the traditional characterization of the Army as high caste, and clarifies for us the place of the sepoy in a long tradition of *Baksariya*, or a custom of military itinerancy among the surplus rural population of Awadh and Bihar. In this, he seems to expand upon the unsupported but insightful musings voiced by Eric Stokes in both his major works on peasant insurgency during the Revolt.[4] Yet Kolff falls short of providing a strong link between fact, idea, and conclusion, and one remains unenlightened about the nature of the bonds which connected the sepoy's varied world of village and cantonment, of caste and regiment, of religion and military duty.

Sadly, the pool of evidence is still relatively small, and as Rudrangshu Mukherjee observed in 1984, 'It is very difficult to find more specific quantitative statements [about recruitment] than "the Bengal sepoys were largely drawn from Oude", or that the sepoys . . . came "chiefly from Oude."'[5] Mukherjee's own search for a large body of pertinent data failed, and he was left to conclude that such evidence was not normally recorded, or, at best, kept 'in a haphazard manner' prior to the 1850s, which is startling when considered in the context of what was supposed to be, for the time and place, a modern, bureaucratic European style army.[6] Perhaps the largest single data set available concerning individual sepoys and their personal characteristics is a descriptive roll of deserters from the 22nd Native Infantry compiled at Berhampur in 1824.[7] This evidence has led Mukherjee to argue the importance of the 'area of taluqdar–peasant complementarity' which corresponds to Kolff's seat of *Baksariya* recruitment, the south-western districts of Awadh. 'Given the mass of statements about Awadh,' Mukherjee writes, and especially Bainswara, being the main recruiting area, there is no reason to surmise that the sample available from the 22nd N.I. is necessarily atypical.'[8]

I agree that the districts of south-western Awadh contributed more recruits to the Army than the other districts of that kingdom or of British India, as there are few direct references to sepoys who hailed from further north or east. However, if we accept such a constricted geographical area as the recruiting ground for an Army of at least one hundred and seventy thousand men, one must seriously question the ideal of the high caste. Company sepoys, for the upper echelons of the sacral hierarchy, could not have sustained a demographic burden of that magnitude over such an extended period of time.[9] At the very least, the term 'high caste', applied to sepoys, should be redefined with stronger reference to the socio-economic class of the recruits.

Demographics of Caste Recruitment

It is impossible at this point to entertain anything more certain than impressions about the demographics of the Bengal Army's recruiting ground. Before the annexation of Awadh, all statistics relating to the population of this region were broadly variable estimates at best, as represented by Montgomery Martin's gazetteer, *Eastern India*. In this work, co-efficients derived from small detailed samples were multiplied according to their proportion, then applied to similarly constructed estimates to produce a hypothetical aggregate. Martin attempted to portray the entire material culture of a district in quantitative terms based upon information drawn from just a few dozen families that was collected by Indian subaltern officials. The resulting figures, though not entirely misleading, owed much to the imagination of the statistician.[10] Thus, we cannot know how many high caste Rajputs and Brahmans inhabited the recruiting ground. We do know, however, which tribes predominated in this area, and it is not impossible to distill from these a select group of tribes which probably predominated in the Army as well.

The two most important Rajput tribes, in terms of sheer population as well as recruitment, were the Bains (or Bais) and the Chauhans, both thickly settled throughout the region.[11] In addition to these two great houses, the Army also relied heavily upon the Bhumihar Brahmans, whom Sherring estimated to be fifty to sixty thousand strong in Benares district alone, with thousands more in the adjacent rural districts.[12] Other significant communities, about whose contributions to the Army less can be said with certainty, were the Bachhgoti or Rajkumars of Jaunpur; the Bisen of Pratabgarh and Sultanpur—'fine specimen of the oriental yeoman...'; seventy thousand Raghbansis in Mirzapur and Azamgarh, 'ruined by the Permanent Settlement'; the Monas and Dirgbansis of Jaunpur, both enemies of the Raja of Benares; the Raikwars, re-establishing their power in the early nineteenth century after being crushed in the Rajput insurrection of 1751; and the Nanwag, Palwar, and Chaupat Khambh, together perhaps sixty thousand strong.[13] Forty-two additional tribes of lesser importance lived in the recruiting ground between 1800 and 1857, but many of these appear to have been those whom Kolff argues were crowded out of the *Baksariya* system when the military labour market of Hindustan became a buyer's rather than a seller's market, and opportunities were further reduced by Company's policy of systematic rural demilitarization.[15]

Given this sketchy information, it would be unreasonable to assume a population base for recruitment much greater than three or four hundred thousand, perhaps considerably less. What we can be sure of is the heavy impact which intensive recruiting had upon this demographic set. After the men of Bainswara and Salon flocked to the colours during the military augmentation of the late 1820s, the 'drain on the flower of the population (was) sensibly felt, there being in parts of Oudh, particularly between Sultanpur and the capital, not ten matchlocks where formerly three hundred could be mustered.'[16] Sleeman noted that 'from the estate of Rajah Hunmunt Singh in . . . Bunoda . . . there are one thousand sipahees in our service. From that of Benee Madho, in Byswara . . . there are still more.'[17] The former estate consisted of approximately 241 villages, the latter of 223, yielding a recruitment burden of four or more sepoys per village.[18] One must also bear in mind that large numbers of men from this same region were swelling the armies of Gwalior, Nagpur, Hyderabad, Alwar, and the Sikh Khalsa, not to mention the Awadh royal army and armies of other two presidencies.[19] Sleeman believed the population of these districts to have been literally decimated by recruiting.[20]

The High Caste Sepoy

Major-General Sir William H. Sleeman was one of the major

contributors to the image of a 'high caste' Bengal Army. He was fairly explicit about what he meant by the term, speaking of 'Rajput cultivators, who are among the bravest men in the world.'[21] He stated flatly, but without evidence, that 'three-fourths of . . . our Bengal native infantry are drawn from the Rajput peasantry of . . . Oudh . . . where their affections have been linked to the soil for a long series of generations.' He further believed this recruitment to be strictly voluntary, declaiming: 'Our Indian native army is perhaps the only entirely voluntary standing army that has been ever known . . . .'[22] His other contemporaries, however, were not so easily charmed by the willingness of these Awadhi peasants to fight under the Union Jack and perceived instead the causes and effects of an economic draft.

Frederick Shore, the 'rebel bureaucrat', noted that British officers did not have 'a correct knowledge of who (the sepoys) really were.'[23] The paucity of records which hampers research today seems to verify Shore's accusation. Yet one thing was certain—the British knew exactly who they wanted their sepoys to be. '. . . Only men of high caste and reasonably good social position—the younger sons of small landowners and large tenant farmers—could achieve the confidence and swagger that (British officers) wanted,' writes Mason, interpreting the prejudices which informed the romantic rhetoric of officers like Sleeman.[24] As the only Resident to the court of Awadh to tour the rural districts of the kingdom, Sleeman had first hand knowledge of the conditions prevailing in the recruiting ground, and he is frank enough about these in his travel narrative, although this must be recognized as a work of propaganda meant to influence government policy. But the same is true of other observers, such as Shore and Butter, whose conclusions about the motivations and social origins of recruits were decidedly different. While Sleeman mitigates the poverty of his Rajput cultivators, pretending that the sepoys considered themselves gentry fallen on hard times, yet still aristocrats, Shore speaks of

> a pretty general complaint that the men who have of late years enlisted are of an inferior stamp to those who formerly joined our army; nor is the complaint without foundation, although the men are of the same classes. But in common with the rest of their countrymen, they have sunk in the world in consequence of increased poverty, and have suffered the

depression of spirit and high feeling which is so universally occasioned by our system of government.[25]

During the Maratha Wars (1775–1819), zamindars sons had entered the British service, though the *Baksariya* system was never monopolized by the cavalier class, nor ever would be. After the defeat of the Pindaris, Army service offered few attractions to large-scale zamindars, most of whom left the service.[26] Such zamindars as one finds mentioned in sources, particularly by Sleeman, are scarcely more than independent cultivators, and a great many were probably sub-letting tenants.[27] Thus, it could scarcely be said that the Bengal Army was composed of zamindar's sons, or anything of the kind, except in the case of rare individuals.[28] Recruits were drawn from castes containing families who happened to be large-scale zamindars, but it was not true that tens of thousands of sepoys themselves were ever anything more than modest farmers at best.

For people of this class, enlistment in the Army was the only way to avoid a quick descent into poverty. Surgeon Butter, serving at Sitapur with the 63rd N.I. in the 1830s, found 'the acute and industrious Bainswaris' constrained to violate their own sense of dignity by taking up armed service. This was their only way of preventing the fragmentation of their estates due to over-population.[29] Sleeman considered the Army to be a social 'safety valve' for Awadh, channelling military manpower out of the hands of local warlords and into the service of the Company. Meanwhile the sepoys' pay, remitted home, augmented the local agrarian economy.[30] Nevertheless, Sleeman did not appreciate the problem of over-population and diminished resources with reference to recruiting.

Whether enlistment is to be understood as an opportunistic move on the part of the recruit, or as a desperate last resort, is debatable; more must be understood about the rural economy during this period. Even so, the adequacy of the sepoys' pay has been overestimated. Shore was not inclined to view recruitment as 'popular' for the same reasons that Sleeman thought it to be so; the former felt that many men who chose the Army would have rather remained nearer to home for less pay, were such opportunities available.[31] 'I wish to impress on my readers,' Shore concluded, 'that the sepoys are . . . [not] selected from any particular superior ranks of the people . . . but that they are from the lower classes . . . .'[32] Sleeman gives a romantic image of sepoy pensioners dwelling in 'honourable retirement . . . among their families and friends, where they form . . . fountains of good feeling towards the government . . . [32] Shore thought the sepoys served for unofficial privileges, mainly coercive powers, over other peasants. A tour of duty ruined the peasant in the sepoy: '(they) have learned nothing good from us, military discipline excepted, (and) their morality has been lowered by their acquiring no small portion of fraud and chicane.'[33] Shore's observation would seem to be borne out by examples drawn from Sleeman's own experiences with his retired paragons, who manipulated the British presence at Lucknow to seize rivals' estates. Indeed, the main reason for the sepoys' loss of their privilege of precedence in the civil courts was their frequent abuse of it.[34]

Kolff's thesis about the *Baksariya* system, the most important contribution to our understanding of the Army since Barat's work, supports Sleeman's view of the sepoy as opportunistic, but replaces the quaint and rather misappropriate title 'yeoman' with an indigenous term, *naukar,* someone who leaves home in search of service, ideally as a retainer.[35] Sleeman sees a kind of class category, while Kolff prefers an occupational one, military itinerant. In a sense, he combines the mutually antagonistic arguments of both Sleeman and Shore and unlike them, he does not really analyse the rural background of the Company sepoy. He does, however, understand the sepoy to be a peasant rather lower down the economic scale than the zamindar controlling several villages, or even only one.

The problem today remains the same problem which divided the Sleemans from the Shores: identifying who peasant recruits were in the above context. Kolff's work points the way by breaking through the rigid categories of anthropology which have defined our conception of the Awadh countryside for so many decades: village communities residing in virtual isolation and regulated almost entirely by caste structures. The 'village community' view was the paradigm upon which the British based their revenue settlements, but Kolff reminds us that the village was linked to a larger economy by *naukari* long before the British began transporting indigo, opium, and sugarcane to the world market. If we are to understand who the sepoys were, we must begin by obtaining as clear a picture of rural conditions as possible, taking into consideration as many social, economic, and political dimensions as the sources permit.

The Socio-Economic Background

At the centre of the recruiting ground in Bainswara, lay the estate of Daundia Khera, held in zamindari tenure by Rambakhsh Singh in the 1830s. It extended 'thirty miles ... east to west, and twenty miles ... north to south ....' The annual revenue was Rs. 300,000. Like other huge estates, this was parcelled out among numerous smaller zamindars whose farms were further sublet to tenant cultivators. 'One or two members' of these second class zamindar families lived on their farms, while 'the remainder [entered] the Company's other public services'. For this bottom strata of landlords, the 1830s were not prosperous times; Butter attests that their estates yielded perhaps Rs. 100, and 'afforded but a mere subsistence'. Ryots rented their tiny plots for from eight annas to two, three, or four rupees to the *bigha* (two-fifths of an acre). The overlord of Daundia Khera himself was an absentee, having his seat 'in a large country town on the Ganges' while eight or nine hundred 'followers' kept order on the estate and collected the rents.[36]

Few zamindar holdings in Awadh were as large as Daundia Khera, but the conditions prevailing there may be accepted as representative of the agrarian structure of the area. On the whole, Bainswara and Salon tended to be the most prosperous parts of the recruiting ground as well as the most densely settled and cultivated. It was in such districts, where land rights had suffered fragmentation, that the economic incentive to 'go on service' was likely to be strongest. Yet it was also in such populous areas that social structures, caste hierarchy in particular, were most important.[37] Over time, these districts had seen an inverse relationship arise between economic power and sacral standing as high caste landowning families crowded themselves off their own estates, yet retained or even improved their caste status. Over time, this status had become a saleable commodity in the local marriage market, as upstart low caste groups controlling wealth in the form of herds or craft monopolies sought alliances with higher caste communities.[38] In this way, the constituent elements of rural society negotiated military and economic alliances, most of which were aimed ultimately at control of the two most crucial resources of the area: land and labour.

Highly-organized fraternities *(bhaiachara)*, often forming co-parcenary communities, mostly Rajput and Bhumihar Brahman, thus formed the basic political unit. As Shore noted, relationships between these groups were defined more by marriage ties than by concerns about ritual pollution.[39] The village itself was not terribly important; there was no concept of a 'village republic'. In Awadh one village might be claimed by several *bhaiachara*, the subject of back country warfare and court intrigues for decades. It was also common for one village to contain numerous rival factions, ryots and artisans falling into ranks behind their patrons. Relationships with this class of non-landowning rural denizens were a form of mutual protection: Rajput and Brahman estate owners became a captive market for the monopolies of their clients, while the latter contributed their services to the maintenance of the estate. In a sense, their license to engage in their respective pursuits was guaranteed in return for services provided to the overlord classes.[40]

Tennant describes these relationships in considerable detail for one small estate north of Benares which actually belonged to a Bengal Army subedar. On the surface, the power of the subedar-landlord seems feudal, out of all proportion to what one might expect of an NCO. However, the extortionate revenue systems of both Awadh and British India, combined with the crushing usury of the *banias* and constant military reprisals against those slow to render their taxes, made the zamindar lifestyle a precarious one. Subedar Ram Jeet Singh's village grossed Rs. 1000, but netted him only 100; 'such are the profits of the farmer of five hundred acres to a man of rank who has under him several hundreds of ryots and tradesmen.'[41] The Subedar's decision to serve in the Army despite being a landlord becomes understandable when one considers the fate of such an estate after its division among heirs. Men like Ram Jeet Singh needed the additional income offered by the Army—but even more than that, government pensions and patronage—to secure the fortunes of their families for the next generation.

MILITARIZATION

In addition to the form of land tenure and the highly mobile but complex nature of caste, another key element of the sepoy's social background was the intense militarization of south-western Awadh. Even in a kingdom noted for its internal strife, this area was particularly infamous. 'The cannonading of forts and villages by the *chakledar*,' Butter wrote, 'is a sound very frequently heard, for days together . . . .'[42] It was noted that rural warfare had increased after 1814, but even before that date, Tennant wrote that 'rents are levied by an irregular banditti, under the denomination of an army, who drive away the whole of a village, burn the houses to the ground, and carry off the women and children.'[43] So uncontrolled was this fighting that rogue units of the Awadh army would attempt to ambush treasure caravans escorted by Company troops.

Such were the activities of the Awadh military, bolstering the attempts of the local *chakledar* (Nawabi procurator) to collect the revenue, much of which was destined for the coffers of the East India Company in the form of forced loans. South-west Awadh found itself in the eye of a storm of extortion, and the landlords and ryots learned and honed their martial skills defending their own villages and fields. But these skills were, as Kolff has shown, a commodity which could be exported.

After 1814, when leases were limited to one year, military reprisals and zamindar intransigence increased together; Butter's account of the region bristles with skirmishes between estate levies and *chakledar* troops. The great landlords carefully preserved tracts of jungle, particularly in river bottoms, as refuges from which a guerrilla war might be protracted until terms could be negotiated. In Bainswara, Kesri Singh maintained a private army of 1,000 matchlockmen, and twice defeated and killed the *chakledar*s sent against him; even in relatively quiet Salon, an inter-family feud put thousands of men into the field in 1832, and resulted in four hundred casualties.[44] Often fighting would cross the border into the Ceded Districts, and sometimes even involve Company troops. Bishop Heber, travelling to Lucknow during his tour of north India, was surprised when his personal attendants chose to arm themselves even though they were protected by a sepoy escort. One servant handed the Anglican cleric his pistols at night, commenting: 'In this country, one does not trust his own father.'[45] Weapons were produced locally—and cheaply in large quantities—as was gunpowder. The British had been careful to destroy such homespun armaments industries in their own districts, but the craft still flourished in rural Awadh.[46]

For the villagers, weapons were more than tools of self-defence in the deadly game of local politics. Parts of the area were still rather wild, offering opportunities for hunting and the odd encounter with a tiger. 'The villagers are good marksmen,' Butter noted with regard to their skill with firearms.[47] Seaton's regiment contained a man named Ramdeen whose passion for hunting was such that he dashed from the parade ground at once upon seeing his pet dog raise a hare from the nearby bush.[48]

Possession of weapons, particularly firearms, was what brought the *Baksariya* system to the fore among various early Mughal and Sultanate military systems. With their matchlocks, and later with British muskets, Awadhi sepoys brought the firepower revolution of eighteenth century Europe into Indian warfare. While they smashed the power of the Islamic states in South Asia and won an empire for the British, they also secured for themselves a monopoly over the military labour market of northern India that endured for three generations. Every army, even the Sikh Khalsa, was leavened with a contingent of Purbiya sepoys. In south-west Awadh boys grew up with weapons and war, and many who later wore the red coat may have already seen action in some local feud years before the British taught them how to march in close order and fire volleys.

Religion

Many have been content to believe that the sepoys were propelled into rebellion by a conservative and reactionary concern for their religious beliefs. In 1857, the rebels themselves declared several times that theirs was a religious war, a war brought on by messianic hopes of liberty and a widespread fear of apocalyptic defilement at the hands of the Christians. Society would be levelled in preparation for mass conversion by the spread of polluting substances such as the grease on the Enfield cartridges or bone dust in bazaar flour. Even before the Revolt, discontented sepoys of the 43rd N.I. at

Barrackpur reminded their British officers in a cryptic note that 'we will not give up our religion. We serve for honour and religion.'[49] Historians have always placed emphasis on these rather medieval complaints from the ranks, as if to distance the sepoys' fears from modern, Western reason and thus from reality. Concerns about issues of religious tolerance and stipulations of the soldiers' unofficial contract with the state are in thus manner transcribed as mere matters of belief, rather quaint at that, part of the lore of the inscrutable' Orient destined to be bludgeoned into the nineteenth century by modernity. There is little understanding that the sepoys' concern for their religion was a concern about a basic human right: tolerance of personal spirituality and freedom of worship and ritual practice. This much even a soldier was allowed. The same British officer who might hold strong opinions about the Oxford Movement or the rise of the Evangelicals at home were not always quick to extend the same indulgence to their Indian soldiers.

The British realized, of course, that the sepoys were concerned about their religious beliefs; numerous writers underscored the precarious position Christian Englishmen lived in, and how they ought to take care not to rouse the 'prejudices' of the population. Almost every mutiny which rocked the Madras and Bengal armies exhibited a prominent religious feature. However, the British did not see the sepoy's religion in its social context; individual soldier and civil servants were aware of the raw texture of folk religion in the districts, but the government's overarching policies and legal categories, including regulations, assumed that the *Laws of Manu* and the Koranic revelations were the unimpeachable social contracts of Hindustan. But what did the average sepoy actually hold sacred? How were the changes he saw before 1857 assimilated through the prism of his belief system?

Sita Ram, though his autobiography cannot be given the stamp of complete authenticity, may still have represented a large number of sepoys in both his religious training and experience, with the exception of his ability to read. Though educated by a family *pandit*, he nevertheless felt a need to perform rituals which disempowered his world and enabled him to make transitions from one state of being to another. We find his departure on *naukari* and his return from the wars always hinging on a ritual which either assures safety in the dangerous outside world or cleanses ritual impurities incurred during military service.[50] But his youthful interest in such things soon hardens into the realism of middle age; of his soldiering days, he writes: 'I have said the people of India worship power; they also love splendour, and display of wealth. Great impression is made upon the mass by this; much greater than the English seem to think.'[51] He pays the village Brahmans to restore his caste after each campaign with mounting cynicism, favouring the direct approach in his marital simplicity, scorning all tithing intermediaries, bureaucratic or spiritual.[52] His ideal is a king who is both father and God, and this, as Michael Fisher comments, was one of the religious ideals of the Awadh region.[53] With old age, Sita Ram returned to conservative orthodoxy, presenting his memoirs amid suitable invocations of various deities. But no doubt many soldiers found it necessary to orbit their religion at a distance while on service and leading the dangerous double life of soldier and peasant.

In nineteenth century Awadh, religion was an open-ended concept. The beliefs and practices of a given individual might include animism, a construction of ritual purity and pollution, notions of caste hierarchy, and relatively complex mysticism, simultaneously or by turns. This was true of Hindus and Muslims alike, and though the two groups tolerated each other, there was no syncretism. Muslims and Hindus might worship together at Sufi tombs and parade during Muharram, but their motivations differed.[54] Before the Revolt, far from describing the inhabitants of Awadh as fanatics, most remarked upon the virtual absence of any orthodox religious enthusiasm. Tennant wrote at the beginning of the century that '. . . the Brahminical rigour of discipline is somewhat abated [in Awadh] . . .', with a corresponding lack of respect for the ritual power of the Brahman priesthood.[55] The Wahhabis, having failed to interest the Lucknow elite in their zealous reformation, turned to the Muslim *ashrafs* of south-west Awadh only to be rebuffed by the zamindars of Salon, who expressed their intention to continue 'to follow the example of their fathers . . . in carrying tazias at Muharram, and in relieving and aiding the poor, the lame, and the blind . . .' Butter remarked that the 'religious excitability' of the Muslims of Awadh was less than that of any other Muslim community of north India.[56] Indeed, to the peasants, the religious were viewed with fear and disdain; wandering bands of Gossains, often armed and several thousand strong, were a periodic menace, and closer to home, the money-grubbing schemes of the village priest or shaman were a constant annoyance. Such scenes can scarcely be reconciled with the explosion of 'fanaticism' which the Victorians perceived in 1857.

For the Brahmans, religious devices were a means of achieving safety in a world filled with chaotic dangers. Rules and hierarchy organized and disempowered chaos, and cleansed the polluted world. The ideal was the peace of inaction. However, this theology, carried to its logical extreme, was untenable, and virtually the entire population compromised to varying degrees. Many chose to turn the Brahmanical system on its head, opting for a religion of empowerment by drawing upon the *shakti* forces of the goddess and less upon the inert legalism of the gods. The worship of most of the major tribes of the recruiting ground was essentially the worship of the goddess and the powers which She represented. The Smallpox Goddess, Debi, was particularly prominent, and her shrine near Unnao drew fifty thousand pilgrims during a nine day *mela* (fair) every March.[57] Animism and her shamanism was also involved in the daily religious experience while orthodox beliefs tended toward the mystical—Sufism or Bhakti—and not toward the South Indian Brahmanism as pictured by Dubois. And yet it was the rigorous south Indian model, with its sharply segregated categories, which informed the opinions of many British officers, and which continues to skew the ideas of some modern scholars with regard to the northern Brahmanism of the nineteenth century.

In south-west Awadh, religion was a vehicle of transcendence, enabling people to step in and out of their normal social roles, and to facilitate and regulate communication. Thus, religious practice tended to be either intensely personal or extremely public. In the latter case, particularly at the regional pilgrimage fairs (*tirthatan*), commerce was interwoven with devotion. Several hundred thousand people were likely to congregate for these *tirthatan,* and they became a means by which *banias* distributed local and imported products in an area where there were no large market towns or adequate lines of transport. Indeed, different pilgrimages tended to specialise in different commodities.[58] Wandering *faqirs* often doubled as traders, passing from one *mela* to the next. Charity was another major feature of the fairs—the recapitulation of traditional ties, with money and presents as the medium of the contract. At Ram Lila, Butter guessed that some fifty thousand gathered for a ten day festival 'during which charity [was] distributed by Brahmans and Chhatris to all comers.'[59] Even a Holi celebration by Company sepoys marching through Nagpur was incomplete without a ritual offering of 'a rupee or two on a clean napkin' to their British officers.[60]

A vicarious mixture of sacred and profane analysis at first glance: many have noted with cynicism the eagerness with which the mutineers used the greased cartridges against their British officers. Almost every writer has stressed the ritual dangers posed for Hindu and Muslim sepoys by the infamous Enfield cartridge and this is allowed to stand as an explanation for the subsequent actions of more than one hundred thousand men. Yet nothing is said about the readiness of Punjabi Sikhs and Muslims, who ought to have harboured the same reservations about the grease, to take up arms and fight for the Raj. How did the sepoy feel about the threat which the Enfield cartridge posed to his religion and caste?

The Enfield cartridge must be seen as one element among many in a long series of policies which threatened the sepoy's ritual status—and it should be noted that the sepoy was, by virtue of his occupation, suspect among his peers anyway. The Army had survived similar crises before—the introduction of leather cockades for the old turbans, the use of shakos instead of turbans, the transport of sepoys across the ocean, and the defiling campaigns in Afghanistan, Sind, and Burma. In almost every case, these orders were resisted, often with violence, occasionally by the mutiny of entire corps. Yet, the government was able to prevail over the troops. Nevertheless, British officers came to doubt the wisdom of trying to do with sepoys what they were accustomed to doing with European recruits—breaking traditional values and replacing them with new ones. It became a doctrine of the Bengal Army that the sepoy's religious opinions were so rigidly fixed that to tamper with them in any way would incite riot and rebellion.[61] Little attempt was made, however, to ascertain those opinions, and British officers were often shocked when their soldiers engaged in activities which were supposed to be defiling to Rajputs and Brahmans. It was often a surprise to learn that these high caste sepoys were not universally vegetarians, or that in daily practice, their veneration of the cow and horror of the pig displayed a considerably disparity between belief and conduct.[62] British officers did not understand that for the sepoy, religion had an economic component, and vice versa. Practical religion was concerned with one's place in the Cosmos, and one means of controlling the Cosmos was through the use of money, as in the case of buying high caste brides or low caste concubines. Serious discontent about religious issues in the Army was, as Mason points out, invariably accompanied by a crisis over pay or stoppages. It was not purely 'a matter of honour', though pride and prejudice had their place in these clashes. This had been the case with the most important mutinies in Bengal before 1857 that at Barrackpur in 1824, and those which occurred in Sind and the Punjab in the 1840s.[63]

When religious duty collided with military necessity, there was a common tendency to diffuse the situation by winking at traditional beliefs about pollution and justifying sin with an appeal to expedience or common charity. Mason draws our attention to the wounded Brahman who refuses James Skinner's offer of water, crying out: 'My caste! My caste!', and replying to the suggestion that 'no one would know that God sees me.'[64] No doubt, this incident or something like it did occur, but more common by far was the example given by Shore:

> During the attack [on] a fort on a hot day, two [British] officers had just procured a large earthen pot, full of water, out of which they had just drunk. At that moment, a sepoy came by, crying out for water: one of the officers offered him the pot; and on his demurring at first, observed, laughing, 'All's fair on service; you may get a bullet through your head next minute, and what will be your caste then? Quench your thirst, and make yourself comfortable while you can.' The man grinned, and took a hearty draught.[65]

This is what so many British officers meant by countering 'prejudice' with 'kindness'—creating a sense of gruff camaraderie, such as exists in every army, which allows the soldier, by invoking a sort of martial license, to overstep traditional moral codes.

> There is . . . a great deal of very convenient latitude on the subject of caste. If a man can persuade a considerable number to join him, he will do a great many things which he dared not have been guilty of alone. Strictly speaking the Hindu sepoys who have gone on foreign expeditions by sea have all lost caste; but who dare tell them so? They form too strong a party for any one to presume to hint at it, much less act upon the idea. On service they make no scruple of drinking from a (bhisti's) leathern water-bag, which they would never do on ordinary occasions.[66]

Such collective action in defence of 'honour' was an old theme in Rajput culture, predating British rule. The Rajputs of Awadh had used just such pressures to silence Brahmanical uneasiness about their practice of female infanticide.[67] Because of the temporal powers of the Rajput zamindars, and because Brahmanism was something of a trade in the spiritual as well, Brahmans could be manipulated easily enough by the more worldly sepoys. The men of a regiment stationed in Orissa in the 1830s smuggled one of their British officers, a man 'much beloved and respected', into the Juggernath temple, disguised as a sepoy. 'It was afterwards well-known; but as to the defilement of the temple, the Brahmins had sense enough to say nothing about it, as it might have diminished the presentation of offerings. . . .'[68] Attempts to subvert the loyalty of sepoys by appealing to their beliefs and superstitions fell on deaf ears during 'the years of victory' before the reverses in Afghanistan. No sense of loyalty whatsoever was felt toward the ruling family of Awadh prior to the annexation; there was no unrest in the Army as a result Colonel Low's palace coup of 1837, and it was a sepoy regiment which drove the Begum and her clients out of Lucknow.[69] That the situation could be so altered by 1857 indicates that some other great threat had combined with the ongoing religious difficulties to make the sepoy question his loyalty.

Land Reform

The nature of the threat to the sepoys' way of life was complex, but its essence lay in the economics of the agrarian structure. In 1857, opposition to the government's land tenure policy was expressed in religious and political terms. But these religious and political symbols—greased cartridges and dispossessed princes—around which action could rally, were given their dynamism by a direct connection with the peasant's means of subsistence. Between 'the years of victory' and the Revolt, Bentinck's reformist regime came to power, carried on by Dalhousie and Canning after a brief interval during the Afghan and Sikh wars. Key to the goals of this new style of Company rule was the massive revenue settlement of the North west Provinces, begun in 1802 by Henry Wellesley, but not pushed with vigour until Thomason's introduction of a new civil service ethos in the 1820s and 1830s. This much is well-known, but how did these reforms impinge upon the lives of the Bengal Army sepoys?

It has been argued by some that the sepoys revolted because they were of the same class which stood to lose at the hands of dreaded Regulation VII of 1822. In 1856, the Settlement was extended to Awadh with the Annexation. When first introduced, Regulation VII had proved too much for the existing bureaucratic infrastructure of British India—in the first nine years only 3,600 villages were settled in the Ceded Districts, and officials complained that at that rate they would require another forty to fifty years to fix the taxes of the North-West Provinces.[70]

Pressured by superiors for higher revenues to combat the Company's mounting debt (no small amount resulting from military expenses), settlement officers tended to 'screw the assessment up to the highest possible figure' and rely less upon any utilitarian system than upon what Metcalf has termed 'idiosyncratic estimates'.[71] Early revenue agents of the Company had favoured protecting zamindars—men such as Holt Mackenzie saw any policy of estate breaking merely 'frittering' immediate benefits among a swarm of 'needy' cultivators, who would all soon find themselves in thrall to *banias*.[72]

As it turned out, in the Upper Doab this was not generally what occurred; Rajputs lost their rights mostly to Brahmans, and only secondarily to *Banias*, while they themselves were driven into a 'sub-proprietary role'.[73] Metcalf has observed that in the districts north of the recruiting ground, transfers of land rights hurt zamindars and *pattidars* more often than they did *bhaiachara*, 'living for the most part off agricultural profits from their own home farm . . . .'[74] In Aligarh, rights changed hands not between castes, but within them; family feuds which in Awadh were settled with guns, were settled in British India with lawyers before the Sadr Diwani Adaulat.[75]

Regulation VII recognized two tiers of rights, or ownership—a top level of alienable taluqdari rights, and a lower level of inalienable rights belonging to the actual cultivators. The mass of sepoys and their families belonged to this latter tier, at least in the 1850s. But the intricacies of Regulation VII were not widely understood by peasants, and it should be remembered that sepoys liked to think of themselves as zamindars, albeit very small ones. They heard that zamindars were being dispossessed in the Upper Doab and west of the Ganges, and they assumed that they too would lose their land. Native officers stood to suffer most from any investigation of titles in Awadh: most sepoys who could properly be termed zamindars were of this rank and belonged to a group already displeased with service pay and conditions. The erosion of the native officers' status—the direct result of the increase in junior British officers—had coincided with repeated reductions of the native officers' pensions. At the same time, the pensions of common sepoys had increased. By the 1850s, the pension received by a native officer was in no way representative of his relatively high pay. Furthermore, as Sleeman had discovered, native officers had acquired lands through a variety of questionable means, and for them, their claims would be insupportable. Even where a landlord or *bhaiachara* defended justly held rights, the ordeal of the court battle could be financially devastating and extremely time-consuming.[76]

Fear of the land reform was not without foundation. It is not difficult to discern how even tenant cultivation were liable to be uprooted by the fall of their zamindar and patron, particularly in a society in which a large part of the economy consisted of ritual gifts exchanged between empowered and subordinate classes.[77] Few zamindars in south-west Awadh could keep out of debt, and the condition of the peasants was always precarious. Dalhousie, like many anthropologists today, believed that 'tenures in land . . . and the usages of the agricultural classes' were the same in Awadh as in the adjacent North-West Provinces, and he directed revenue officers investigating land tenures in April of 1856 to adopt the same measures for Awadh as were used in Allahabad and Aligarh. He added, ominously, that there was 'hardly any room for difference of opinion.'[78] The settlement of Awadh was to be completed by 10 May 1856, and the Treasurer, Martin Gubbins, was merciless toward the taluqdar class. Of 23,50 villages held by this group, Gubbins transferred 9,000 to various forms of ryotwari tenure, usually to co-parcenary communities.[79]

The new Governor-General, Canning, and the new Chief Commissioner, Henry Lawrence, both felt this summary judgement to be too severe. Lawrence thought Gubbins was 'destroying the aristocray' and that 'a dead level seem[ed] to be the ideal of many civil officers . . . .'[80] Those who stood to lose from the annexation had already decided to resist the British, and the Raja of Tulsipur in Gonda had two thousand men under arms already in April of 1856. He had not paid taxes to the King, and he would not pay the Company either.[81] Even taluqdars whose lands were held legitimately feared the demilitarization of their estates—a tremendous blow to their local prestige and power. Closer to the heart of the recruiting ground, the settlement fired old family feuds, the impoverished members of a clan siding with the revenue officers against their landholding relatives and rivals.[82]

Sleeman commented on the exceptional number of troops sent home on leave during the year of his rural tour. This was a cost-cutting measure by the Army, but whatever its fiscal effects, it also served to bring a third of the sepoys into close contact with their villages at a time when discontent was running high in the countryside as well as in the army occupying the newly-won Punjab. The effect of such a policy on the morale of the Army as a whole cannot have been benefical. Sepoys on furlough during the Annexation—and those who took part in the troop concentration during the transfer of power—no doubt brought word of rebellious activities in their homeland back to their cantonments. Of the regiments which mutinied at Delhi on 11 May 1857, one had been engaged only a few months previously in putting down refractory zamindars in the Terai.[83]

The Army had also absorbed several thousand soldiers from the Awadh forces into its regulars, as well as several Awadh local regiments in their entirety. These new troops whose bonds of loyalty to the Awadh elites were but freshly severed, and for whom the discipline of the British system must have been a rude shock, created an undercurrent of discontent wherever they were stationed. As long as Wajid Ali Shah was under house arrest near Calcutta, there were many who doubted the loyalty of the sepoy guards at Fort William.[84]

Conclusion

The purpose of this essay has been to begin the process of discovering who the sepoys were, of locating recruitment patterns and drawing conclusions about the connection between recruitment, social origin, religious orientation, and discontent with reference to the Revolt of 1857. It cannot, of course, explore even the religious element of pre-Mutiny Indian opinion regarding Company rule with any claim to do full justice to such a vast and varied topic. A complete account of the religious motivations of the sepoys would have to consider, apart from the sepoy's concerns as peasant, his relationship with the British officer corps as well. The collapse of personal relationships within regiments was perhaps even more catastrophic than the collapse of faith between the government and the people with the land settlement and other reforms, which seemed a repudiation of the social contract between *Sarkar* and ryot. Attention has been paid to sepoy–officer relationships by Mason in *A Matter of Honour*, but if one is to examine that issue in any depth, it is necessary first to understand the assumptions under which the sepoy operated, and how his village background constructed those assumptions. One must identify who the sepoys were as accurately as possible.

Religious issues, inextricably connected with land tenure issues, lie at the heart of any research into the social history of the Bengal Army. In Awadh, religious beliefs and practices deeply rooted in popular culture provided a theoretical framework and vocabulary in which complex economic and political concerns could be articulated, understood, and addressed. The men who joined the Company's service did not abandon the popular resistance tactics learned in their villages, continuing to use them to renegotiate their position within the Bengal Army.

Attempts to evaluate historical problems in isolation from one another, as if nineteenth century India had a modern, western bureaucracy with separation of religious creed and state constitution, serve no purpose, and are the invalidating core of most Marxist researches into the causes of the Revolt. More traditional interpretations suffer from the opposite extreme of embracing too closely untenable anthropological constructs of caste hierarchy, religious belief and practice, and economic relationships. One must consider a variety of local evidence in as much detail as possible, and upon this basis resculpt the flesh and bones of those who fought to raise up and then to tear down the East India Company.

NOTES

1. Rudrangshu Mukherjee, *Awadh in Revolt 1857–1858: A Study of Popular Resistance,* Delhi, 1984, pp. 150–1.
2. Amiya Barat, *The Bengal Native Infantry: Its Organisation and Discipline 1796–1852,* Calcutta, 1962, p. 185.
3. Fazl Lutfullah, an Indian civil servant of the post-Mutiny period, attempted to redress this problem early on, but for the British, Islamic 'fundamentalism' was a convenient scapegoat for the Revolt (see *Indian Antiquary*, vol. 10, March 1881, p. 69.)
4. Eric Stokes, *The Peasant and the Raj: Studies in Agrarian Society and Peasant Rebellion in Colonial India,* Cambridge, 1978, pp. 42–4. See also *The Peasant Armed: The Indian Revolt of 1857*, Oxford, 1986, p. 51.
5. Rudrangshu Mukherjee, p. 77.
6. Extensive recruitment records such as the Arz-o-Chehra are available for the Sikh Khalsa, for instance, but there seems to have been no central depository for such information in Bengal. The Sikh records provide detailed information for one-fifth of the entire Khalsa. See Fauja Singh Bajwa, *Military System of the Sikhs during the Period 1799-1849*, Delhi, 1964, pp. 134–5.
7. Rudrangshu Mukherjee, p. 78.
8. Ibid.
9. Strictly speaking, only regular infantry and cavalry were recruited from southwest Awadh. In the 1850s, the Bengal Army consisted of 74 regiments of regular infantry and 10 of regular cavalry, representing a recruitment burden of approximately 60,000 men. This means that the irregular and auxiliary units mustered about 110,000 troops, a figure which would have included the Punjab Frontier Force. The irregulars tended to find their manpower in the Upper Doab or the northern districts of Awadh, particularly among the Muslim mercenary bands settled there as colonists by previous dynasties.

10. For example see M. Martin, *The History, Antiquities, Topography, and Statistics of Eastern India*, vol. 2, London, 1838, Appendix, p. 12, where he attempts to estimate 'the extent to which the people of the northern part of the district of Gorukhpoor indulge in various intoxicating substances.'
11. M. A. Sherring, *Hindu Tribes and Castes as Represented in Benares*, vol. 1, Delhi, 1974 [reprint of 1872 edn], pp. 160–64. The Chauhans of the Upper Doab were considered superior, in sacral and political terms, to those of south-west Awadh. The Chauhans married their sons to the Bais, and daughters to the Ponwars. For the Bais see ibid., 192–8. There were three hundred and sixty sub-divisions of the Bais Rajputs.
12. Ibid., p. 44. The Maharaja of Benares was a Bhumihar Brahman. M. A. Sherring writes of this tribe: 'The Bhumihars are addicted to agriculture, a pursuit considered . . . beneath the dignity of pure, orthodox Brahmans. The word is partly derived from bhumi . . . land.' (p. 39). M. Martin adds: 'their manners are very similar to those of the Rajputs. They eat meat without its being offered in sacrifice; do not accept of charity (Dan), and are fond of a military life.' M. Martin, *The History, Antiquities, Topography, and Statistics of Eastern India*, London, 1838, vol. 3, p. 159.
13. Taken from M. A. Sherring.
14. Thomas Metcalf, *Land, Landlords, and British Raj: Northern India in the Nineteenth Century*, Berkeley, 1979, p. 51.
15. Donald Butter, *Topography and Statistics of the southern districts of Awadh*, Delhi, 1982; reprint of 1839, edn, p. 156.
16. William Sleeman, *A Journey Through the Kingdom of Oude, in 1849–50*, vol. 1, pp. 255–6.
17. For the size of these estates see Thomas Metcalt, pp. 178–9.
18. *Asiatic Journal and Monthly Register for British and Foreign India, China, and Australasia*, vol. 32, 1840, p. 115.
19. John Pemble, *The Raj, the Indian Mutiny, and the Kingdom of Oudh 1801–1859*. Hassocks, 1977, p. 41. 'One in ten of (Awadh's) Rajput and Brahmin population served as mercenaries all over the subcontinent.' This would be accurate if one assumes that all sepoys were drawn from landlord classes. But this was not the case. See William Sleeman, *Tour*, vol. 1, p. 288.
20. William Sleeman, *Rambles and Recollections of an Indian Official*, revised edn, Karachi, 1973, p. 366.
21. Ibid., pp. 624–5.
22. Frederick Shore, *Notes on Indian Affairs*, 2 vols, vol. 2, Londan, 1837, p. 438.
23. Philip Mason, *A Matter of Honour: An Account of the Indian Army its Officers and Men*, London, 1974, p. 125.
24. Frederick Shore, vol. 2, p. 23.

25. Barat, p. 150.
26. Sleeman, *Tour*, vol. 1, p. 21. Sepoy Miherban Sing of the 63rd N.I., for instance, was son of the Rathor zamindar Bhowani Singh of Golha. The village was attacked and seized by the bandit-zamindar Ghulam Hazrat, and the seizure recognized by the Lucknow court despite the sepoy's petition through the Resident. In another case (pp. 22–3), Sleeman met a Brahman whose grandfather had been killed at Bhurtpur in 1804; the sepoy's savings enabled the family to 'set up as agricultural capitalists in the village of Poorwa Pundit, on the estate of Kulunder Buksh. . . .' The zamindar plundered these sub-proprietors one night and made off with Rs. 2,755 in property, Rs. 277 in currency, and 107 gold *mohurs*—a considerable sum, possibly inflated to attract notice to the victim's petition. Sleeman lists several retired soldiers who had managed to collect a modest fortune of several hundred rupees, but none could claim control of more than one, or part of one, village.
27. Butter, *Topography and Statistics of the Southern of Awadh*, p. 156.
28. William Sleeman, *Sleeman in Oudh: An Abridgement of W. H. Sleeman's A Journey Through the Kingdom of Oude in 1849–50*, ed. P. D. Reeves, Cambridge, 1971, p. 94.
29. Frederick Shore, vol. 2, p. 415.
30. William Sleeman, *Rambles*, p. 369.
31. Frederick Shore, vol. 2, p. 440.
32. John Pemble, p. 41–3. About one hundred petitions were handled by the Assistant Resident at Lucknow every month.
33. Dirk Kolff, *Naukar, Rajput and Sepoy: The Ethnohistory of the Military Labour Market in Hindustan 1450–1850*, Cambridge, 1990, pp. 180–5. Kolff inflates the importance of the Bhojpuri dialect as an element of the *Baksariya* system of *naukari.* There is confusion in his argument about the geography of the recruiting ground, as he believes Shahabad to be the centre, but draws upon northern Bihar for much of his evidence. See ibid., pp. 191–2. The centre of the system was most likely Salon and Bainswara; all available evidence strongly supports this. The Awadhi dialect as spoken in Salon differed from that of Bainswara in that the former contained more Hindi words, whereas the vernacular of the latter resembled Lucknow Awadhi, with a profusion of Persian and Arabic loan words. (Butter, p. 167)
34. Butter, pp. 53–4.
35. Ibid., pp. 87, 156.
36. Shore, vol. 2, p. 484.
37. Ibid.
38. William Tennant, *Indian Recreations*, Edinburgh, 1803, vol. 2, pp. 200–1.
39. Ibid., pp. 183–4. The estate lay on the Dergauti River, thirty-six miles north of Benares, and the information was gathered by the zamindar

himself, at Tennant's request, during the summer of 1798. It forms one of the most detailed, and seemingly reliable accounts we have of a village economy in this region during that period. That this evidence has been overlooked is surprising.

40. Donald Butter, p. 102.
41. Seaton, p. 23.
42. Donald Butter, pp. 101–2.
43. William Tennant, *Indian Recreations,* Edinburgh, 1803, vol. 2, 245.
44. Butter, p. 79.
45. Reginald Heber, *Narrative of a Journey through the Upper Provinces of India,* 2 vols, vol. 1, London, 1828, p. 64.
46. Ibid., p. 4.
47. Donald Butter, p. 7.
48. Seaton, p. 38.
49. Mason, p. 273.
50. Sita Ram Pande, *Sepoy to Subedar,* Lahore, 1873, pp. 4–7.
51. Ibid., p. 68.
52. Ibid., p. 112.
53. Michael Fisher, *A Clash of Cultures: Awadh, the British and the Mughals,* Riverdale, 1987, p. 43.
54. Frederick Shore, vol. 2, p. 490.
55. William Tennant, pp. 260–61.
56. Donald Butter, pp. 164–5.
57. Ibid., p. 91.
58. Ibid., p. 89–91. Donald Butter estimated that as much as Rs. 100,000–150,000 worth of property might exchange hands at a pilgrimage fair. Cloth was sold at Dalamau in February and during the full moon of Kartik; at Surajpur near Daundia Khera, Gossains traded pearls and coral with Lucknow merchants; toys and sweetmeats were sold at Kolhaugar in Bainswara, and Lucknow-made trinkets at Debi's shrine near Unnao.
59. Ibid., p. 154.
60. William Barr, *March from Delhi to Peshawar, and from thence to Cabul,* Patiala, 1970 [reprint of 1884 edn], p. 81.
61. *Parliamentary Papers,* XIII (1831/32), 735–v. HC App. B. Colonel Pennington testified that 'treated kindly, (one might) rest assured of (the sepoy's) devoted attachment; but (one) must not interfere in their religion, nor in their prejudice regarding caste. Any wrong done to them on these points (could not) be atoned for by apologies or expressing regret.'
62. William Sleeman, *Tour,* vol. 2, pp. 301–2. See also Seaton, pp. 206–8.
63. Singh, pp. 157–8. Napier wrote to Wellington on 15 June 1850 that 'the Brahmins have been the leaders in every mutiny, in the last mutiny about pay, and which I may say, was general throughout the Bengal Army, though it appeared in six regiments only, all appeared to be governed by

Brahmins.' It is interesting to note the significance of Brahmans leading a mutiny 'about pay . . .'

64. Mason, p. 126.
65. Frederick Shore, vol. 2, p. 487.
66. Ibid., p. 486.
67. William Sleeman, *Tour*, vol. 1, pp. 311–25.
68. Frederick Shore, vol. 2, p. 487.
69. The 54th N.I.,—one of the regiments which mutined at Delhi in 1857.
70. William Metcalf, p. 59.
71. Ibid.
72. Ibid., p. 34.
73. Ibid.
74. Ibid., p. 136.
75. Ibid.
76. William Metcalf, p. 88.
77. William Tennant, pp. 183–200. Tennant describes these relationships in detail in terms of who in the village received various shares of the produce for different services.
78. William Metcalf, p. 59.
79. Ibid., pp. 169–170.
80. Ibid.
81. Ibid.
82. William Metcalf, pp. 176–7.
83. William Sleeman, *Tour*, vol. 1, p. 282. After the Sikh Wars, the government sent three hundred and fifty sepoys and native officers from every regiment on furlough; normally only twenty men per corps were permitted to be sent on leave at any one time. Apparently, many sepoys took this opportunity to press their often fraudulent claims at the Lucknow court.
84. Balcarres Ramsay, *Rough Recollections of Military Service and Society*, vol. 1, Edinburgh, 1882, pp. 245–6.

CHAPTER 16

Company Bahadur Against the Pandies: The Military Dimension of 1857 Mutiny Revisited

Kaushik Roy

Sunday, 10 May 1857 was the date. The day was quite hot. Towards the end of the afternoon, the Bengal Army's sepoys and sawars stationed at Meerut turned their muskets against their erstwhile white masters. It was the beginning of the general mutiny; the most dangerous of its kind, among the Bengal Army scattered from Punjab in the west up to Bihar in the east. The 1857 Uprising which resulted in blood, death and disaster for both the Indians and the British in the subcontinent had all the ingredients and grandeur of a Wagnerian drama. As the sun descended over the north Indian sky on that fateful Sunday only to rise next day, ironically it represented the temporary decline of the British power in South Asia. However, this temporary demise of British authority in north India lasted for more than a day, about a good part of the year.

The dominant historiography on 1857 tries to accommodate the event within an agrarian paradigm. The spokesmen of the agrarian paradigm could be divided into two schools. The school which gives agency to the British policy, I term them as the Imperialist School. One representative of this School, Eric Stokes, views 1857 as the consequence of agrarian policy of the Raj on north Indian rural society.[1] The second school, whose origin is more recent, somewhat forcibly emphasizes the popular character of the agrarian upsurge. Hence, the followers of this methodology could be categorized as belonging to the Subaltern School'.[2]

By contrast, the British writers of the colonial period gave special prominence to the military aspect of the 1857 Uprising.

Colonial British officers believed that the Rebels were defeated because of the moral superiority and cold steel of the European infantry. Field-Marshal Lord Roberts wrote in his memoirs '. . . the sepoys were no match for the British bayonets.'[3] He continues: '. . . that their strongest positions were inadequate against British pluck and determination.'[4] Lieutenant-General George MacMunn asserted, '. . . the rebels made determined attacks . . . at times to the very point of the defenders' bayonets, repelled again and again by the . . . 60th Rifles.'[5]

Modern historians have more or less chosen to ignore the military side of 1857. We have a chronological narrative of military operations from an amateur historian,[6] and only one book which tries to assess the structure of the Company's Army in Lucknow during 1857–58.[7] This article tries to fill the above mentioned historiographical gap by pointing out that the military nature of 1857 was vital but the colonial interpretation of the military aspect was inadequate. The aim of this article is to assess the military ineffectiveness of the Rebels by contrasting them with Company's troops.

Rebel Leadership versus Company's Military Leadership

Evolution of Rebel C3I

Sahib, ham log larai men bahut tez hain magar jang ka bandobast nahin jante.

—An old Indian officer to Roberts after the British victory at Delhi in 1857.[8]

Managerial limitations of the Rebels were exemplified in their C3I (Command, Control, Communications and Intelligence) arrangements. Leadership was concerned with inspiration and motivation. And for this reason, the rebel soldiers allowed Nana Sahib, the representative of the Maratha power at Kanpur and Bahadur Shah, symbol of the House of Timur at Delhi, to fill the positions of political leadership. However, command signified managerial functions like direction, coordination and effective battlefield use of the military assets. Besides commanding and controlling the military force, the commander was also responsible for assessment and dissemination of battlefield information. So, the Rebel troops rightly maintained a firm grasp over the C3I network.[9] One feature of the Rebel command structure which signified that artillery was held to be of supreme importance by the Rebels was the fact that Muhammad Bakht Khan, Subedar of the Artillery Regiment of Bareilly was appointed as the General commanding the Rebel Army at Delhi.[10] All these steps were in a positive direction.

However, there was gross tension within Rebel leadership, especially at Delhi. For the Rebels, this increased the 'friction of war', Bahadur Shah's favourite queen, Zinaat Mahal, was against the appointment of the princes to the command of the troop, since they were inexperienced in the art of war.[11] She was for the appointment of the former *thanadar*s and the *kotwal*s over the soldiers and to turn over the administration of Delhi to the *mufti*s and the *Sudder Amin*. The soldiers initially regarded Mirza Moghul, Bahadur Shah's son, as more dedicated to the Rebels' cause than the old emperor. Then, there was jealousy between Bakht Khan and Mirza Moghul. Further, the mutinous soldiery established a court (somewhat on the Revolutionary Soldiers' Committee of the Soviet style), where all policy matters were deliberated before being accepted.[12] Thus, a clear hierarchy of command structure for taking quick decisions on crucial issues was lacking at Delhi.

Beside the defective local command structure, at the grand strategic level, the Rebel leadership lacked pan-Indian unity. Worse, there was almost no coordination between the various regional commanders like the Begum of Awadh of the Lucknow theatre, with Tantia Tope in central India and Bakht Khan at the Delhi theatre. However, the Company possessed an ideal military command structure that was like a chain. At the top link of the chain was the Commander-in-Chief (Lord Clyde), who commanded all the forces spread over the subcontinent. He had below him a well-defined hierarchy of subordinates, one for each theatre.[13] For example, Havelock was at Kanpur, Neill at Benaras, John Lawrence at Punjab, *et al.*

Hence, as regards higher leadership, the prospect for the Rebels was indeed problematic. The situation was not much better at the regimental level. After rebellion, the sepoy regiments elected commanders from themselves. Quick promotions awarded to some of the rebel soldiers by their political superiors did not help matters. Nana Sahib promoted a *risaldar* named Jawala Prashad to Brigadier.[14] Since, they were non-commissioned officers and had no training in staff duties, they were not versed in operational matters and lacked experience to lead brigade sized formations (a brigade was composed of several regiments, and the ration strength of a regiment varying between 800–1,000 personnel). Most of the Indian officers had commanded companies (between 80 to 100 men) under the supervision of the British officers.[15] Further, most of the Indian officers were very old and thus physically and mentally inert. Due to the system of promotion in the Bengal Army on the basis of seniority, after about 20 years of service, some soldiers became non-commissioned officers. Some of the oldest serving sawars and the sepoys reached the starry ranks of Subedar-Major and Risaldar-Major at the age of 55 to 60.[16] For managing warfare (map reading, gun laying and staff duties), technical education was necessary. Most of them were illiterate while 60 per cent of the Company's white soldiers and the reinforcements that arrived from Britain were literate. Again, the reinforcements from Britain had 18 months' training behind them.[17] The Rebels had neither time nor institutions like the Military Academy of Addiscombe, etc., for training new officers in staff duties.

One could not expect any initiative from such persons who staffed the officer cadre of the Rebel Army. In addition, to remain in power, they had to follow populist policies. In other words, they lacked the coercive authority supported by the military code and the court martial apparatus for maintaining discipline among rank and file. Thus, gradually the rebel sepoys' corporate military identity evaporated and they were downgraded to a sort of militia. As their corporate coherence dissolved, their military effectiveness against the Company's regulars declined.[18] The resulting disintegration in the disciplinary apparatus raised the incidence of desertion. At Bareilly, after the uprising, almost, every day about 25 troops left for their home after plundering the rich men of the city .[19]

Technology and Command: Information Warfare in 1857

Thus it is said that one who knows the enemy and knows himself will not be endangered in a hundred engagements. One who does not know the enemy but knows himself will sometimes be victorious, sometimes meet with defeat. One who knows neither the enemy nor himself will invariably be defeated in every engagement.

—Sun Tzu[20]

By the word 'information' we denote all the knowledge which we have of the enemy and his country; therefore, in fact, the foundation of all our plans and actions.... This difficulty of seeing things correctly which is one of the greatest source of friction in war, makes things appears quite different from what was expected.

—Karl von Clausewitz[21]

Information is also military power. The importance of transmission of information from the commander to the battlefield units and vice versa so that the high command could respond rapidly to the changing dynamics of battle, i.e. Information Warfare, is not merely a hallmark of the Information Age of the late twentieth century, as some American theorists [22] seem to argue. Both the ancient Chinese warrior sage in 500 BCE and the hard-boiled Prussian philosopher of the nineteenth century writing about war realized it. Information Warfare, as we will see, played an important role in 1857 India and in this field also the managerial limitations of the Rebel leadership was further hampered by low technology inputs.

The Rebels brought out newspapers at Delhi for dissemination of information[23] as regards the current situation which, in turn, was necessary for keeping the morale intact. On 12 July 1857, in the *Delhi Urdu News,* Bakht Khan made the following declaration:

Let it be generally known to the persons living in the city and the country, such as chiefs of freeholds, pensioners, landholders of rent free estates, etc., that if, from anxiety for their incomes, they have hitherto continued on the side of the English, and have in anyway colluded with them by conveying intelligence or furnishing them with supplies, their having done so will not be considered inexcisable.[24]

The British maintained horse *dak* between Aligarh and Agra for rapid transmission of orders, and the *cassid*s (runners) supplemented this system. The Nawab of Fatehgarh responded by ordering his troopers to capture and execute the *cassid.* Since the Rebels enjoyed numerical superiority as regards cavalry, occasionally the imperial communications were cut. [25]

However, thanks to new technology, the British were saved. Command stands for effective communication within the various units of the armed forces. In case of mobile campaigns, when the forces were scattered over a wide area, command became extremely difficult. Innovative technological inputs like telegraph helped the Company to deploy a superior command structure that in turn functioned as a force multiplier.[26] The electrical telegraph comprised 4,000 miles of telegraphic wire and connected Calcutta with Peshawar, Agra with Bombay, and Bombay with Madras.[27] Quick information flow due to telegraph enabled the British to get inside the enemy's decision-making time cycle (also known as OODA loop) to generate new ventures at a faster tempo. The OODA loop meant—observe, orient, decide, and act.[28] The British military command was able to perform these four acts faster than the Rebel military leadership because the Company had telegraph at its disposal. Telegraph reduced the reaction time of the British military response. Robert Montgomery, the Commissioner of Lahore, knew about the Mutiny through telegraphy and immediately disarmed the 6,000 north Indian troops before the latter could learn about the Mutiny of their brothers and take steps.[29] The telegraph wire followed Lord Clyde's campaigns. Thus, he could contact the Governor-General at Calcutta, about 1,000 miles from his base of operations both during breakfast and dinner; Calcutta and Bombay about 1,409 miles distant, were within a few minutes' speaking distance by telegraph, and daily discussions for joint strategic planning were carried out. This, in turn, reduced the 'fog of war'. A mutineer pointing out to the telegraph wire before execution rightly declared: 'it is that accursed string that strangles us'.[30]

Feeding Mars

The Company's immediate task was to maintain its existing military bureaucracy and the next step was to expand it. The Rebels faced a much more daunting challenge. With an *ad hoc* rag tag leadership, the Rebels had to structure a military formation: a hard task in peacetime and almost impossible in times of chaos. The three ingredients of any military formation were: manpower to fill the ranks, money to feed and clothe the armed personnel, and finally, a transport net for deploying them to the theatres of war at the right moment.

Manpower

India had adequate manpower resources for filling the ranks of both the Company and the Rebel armies. The population of British India during 1857 was 380 milllon.[31] Just before the mutiny, the British Indian Army had 226,352 sepoys and sawars (including privates and Indian officers). Of them, there was about 9,532 Indian regular cavalry and 20,941 irregular cavalry. There were about 1,49,832 sepoys. In addition, the Company deployed about 6,170 European officers and 39,352 white troops. Of these, there were 20,884 infantry.[32] About 1,00,000 Indian troops supported the upsurge. Of them, 70,000 took direct part in the rebellion and the rest were fence sitters. The latter group was disarmed by the British and played no military role.[33]

Both the British and the Rebels recruited mostly from the countryside. The Rebels recruited their force mainly from Bihar and Uttar Pradesh, the two provinces under their control. The Company had the advantage of recruiting from a wider area like Punjab, west India and south India, since these regions were untouched by the Mutiny. Lord Dalhousie was suspcious of the *Purbiya*s (the Rajputs and Brahmins from Bihar and Awadh). They were called Pandies by the British due to the presence of large number of Pandey Brahmins who dominated the Bengal Army's infantry. So, Dalhousie tried to overcome this difficulty by enlisting a larger number of Gurkhas, Sikhs and Punjabi Muslims.[34] To reduce the dominance of the *Purbiya*s, the government, in 1856, ordered the Bengal Army to enlist between 100–200 Sikhs in each infantry regiment.[35] And these sorts of troops proved to be a salvation for the British during the stormy days of 1857. The British continued to procure the Gurkhas through the recruiting depot at Gorakhpur.[36] When the news of the Mutiny reached Punjab, it was John Nicholson who first mooted the idea of enlisting Pathans and Sikhs from Multan. John Lawrence and Herbert Edwardes procured Afridi tribesmen through their Khans and landowners.[37]

The heavy British horses were ill-suited for reconnaissance

and skirmishing. So the Company raised light cavalry from the Indians. The Indian cavalry proved excellent for outpost duties, escorting convoys, etc. Before 1857, the cavalry of the Bengal Army was recruited from the Pathans of Rohilkhand, Rajput Muslims of Haryana, and Jats of Hansi, Hissar, Bulandshahr, and Meerut. Mostly higher class Muslims like the *Shaikh*s, *Sayid*s, and descendants of the Mughals joined along with their retainers. Their hostility towards the British during 1857 could be termed, in Stokes' words, as the struggle of the decaying Muslim gentry of the western part of the north India against the Raj. Since they rebelled, the Company turned to the Punjabi Muslims.[38] Mounted police for internal security duties were raised from the Beluchis of Sind and Punjab[39]

In a way, the 1857 insurrection was also a caste war, a trial of strength between the British plus the low castes against the north Indian high castes. Contrary to the assertions of the Subaltern historiography as regards the role of the common people in the uprising, the low castes and the tribals sided with the British. Especially in Awadh, where according to both the Marxist[40] and Subaltern historiography[41] popular agitation was intense, the low castes remained loyal to the British. As the high caste levies in Awadh started deserting, the British recruited the low castes, and they remained loyal. Captain E. Hall raised the Awadh Levy and Lieutenant-Colonel H. Bruce filled the Awadh Police with the low castes. The Pasees (a low caste of Awadh) were enlisted in the Sapper Corps as their hereditary occupation was mining. The Rebels lacked sappers and the Pasees would have been of great help to them.[42] These marginal groups also played a very important role for the Company in serving as second line troops in the secondary theatres. The Gujarat Police Corps was recruited from the Bheels of Gujarat and the 1st Khandesh Bheel Corps enlisted its personnel from the Bheels of Khandesh. The former unit maintained order in Gujarat and the latter unit guarded the Company's lines of communications in central Indla.[43] The 44th Merwara Infantry Regiment, composed of the Mhair tribe of Rajasthan, remained loyal to the British despite provocation by the *Purbiya*s to rebel against the Raj. The 44th Regiment held the treasury and the arsenal at Ajmer against the rebellious 15th

Bengal Infantry Regiment during mid 1857, and thus prevented the spread of rebellion in Rajasthan. At that critical juncture there were no British troops in Rajasthan.[44] The Secretary of State for India himself acknowledged the vital role played by the marginal groups in the Company's war machine during 1857.[45]

By 1858 about 18 per cent of the British-Indian Army, i.e. about 17,309 personnel, were of low castes and tribes.[46] The low castes and the untouchables sided with the British probably because in the Hindu hierarchy they occupied a peripheral position and also because in the princely armies of pre-British India, they had no place. Again, military service with the British provided them economic security and a channel for upward mobility.

The Rebels made no significant attempt to enlist the low castes in north India, the region under their firm control, probably because the Indian officers of the Bengal Army's infantry regiments that had rebelled were mostly Brahmins and Rajputs.[47] Before 1857, when the Company tried to recruit some marginal groups, the *Purbiyas* who constituted more than 65 per cent of the Bengal Army, petitioned their British officers that due to their caste bias, they would not serve with the low castes.[48]

What was the social and regional composition of the 'loyal' British-Indian Army that the British raised to meet the Mutineers? The Madras Army deployed 2,600 cavalry. Most of the personnel were Muslims, recruited from Karnataka and Hyderabad. This army possessed about 43,000 infantry enlisted from the Muslims, Telingas, and Tamils from Karnataka, Mysore, and Tanjore respectively. About 11,000 infantry of the Bombay Army was recruited from the Marathas of the Konkan region. The Bengal Army's organization was in ribbons. Still, seven infantry regiments composed of about 7,900 men remained loyal to the British. Besides them, about 1,400 Sikhs and 1,200 Gurkhas of the Bengal Infantry also remained loyal to the British.[49] The Punjab Irregular Force, which bore the brunt of the struggle against the rebels, was composed of 14,692 Sikhs from central Punjab, 30,188 Punjabi Muslims from west Punjab, and 7,566 middle caste Hindus (Ahirs, Gujarsars, etc.) from eastern Punjab.[50]

Money and Provisions: The Sinews of Military Power

Both the Company and the Rebels tried to control the countryside for extracting food and revenue for maintaining the armed forces. The construction of redistributive machinery for supplying the soldiers with money and cash required the assistance of the *baniya*s and *mahajan*s. But, these two groups refused to cooperate with the Rebels as the Rebel regime was unstable and lacked credibility. Then, the Rebels were forced to loot and ransom the moneyed class. This could not ensure steady supply of stores and money, resulting in the dissolution of the rebel army.

When the troops mutinied at Bareilly, they elected Bakht Khan as their leader. His second, in-command was Muhammad Safi, the Risaldar-Major of the 8th Irregular Cavalry. By 31 May 1857, Bakht Khan was able to amass about Rs. 10,00,000. Bakht Khan's plan was to collect revenue from Moradabad, Shahjahanpur and Pilibhit, which would raise his fund to about Rs 30,00,000. Every day, 10,000 soldiers had to be fed. For this purpose, *ghee* (clarified butter), flour, and gram had to be bought. An account of the arms and ammunition ought to be kept. The troops in the Rebel camp were not expert at managing finance and in procuring supplies. So, whenever money was required to buy provisions or food had to be distributed, there was chaos. For keeping an account of the daily expenditure, Bakht Khan requested Durgadas Bandopadhyay, the Chief Clerk of the 8th Irregular Cavalry, to take up the job of treasurer. But, Bandopadhyay refused. Muhammad Safi tried to win him over by making high promises. Safi said that the Rebel government would give him a higher salary than what the sahibs provided him. A salary of Rs. 1,000 per month was fixed and Safi promised that after reaching Delhi, Bakht Khan would make him a minister with a salary of Rs. 2,000 per month. In addition, he would be given the honorary command of 100 cavalry. Still, Bandopadhyay resisted. This was because he had no faith in the unstable regime established by the Rebels and also due to his sense of honour. He could not bring himself to do *namakharami* (the concept of the loyalty to the salt giver was very strong among people of pre-industrial India) with the sahibs. Bakht Khan responded by keeping him under house arrest.[51]

In Bareilly, before 1857, Indian soldiers, British officers and the *baniyas* took loans from the banker Hiranand Seth. From his residence at Bhimani near Delhi, Hiranand Seth controlled his business ventures which sprawled over a large part of the subcontinent. At Bareilly only, the soldiers had taken a loan of Rs. 20,000 from Hiranand Seth. The Bareilly branch of his business was looked after by Hiranand's son, Jahurimal Seth. Immediately after the insurrection, about 25 sepoys, at Bakht Khan's order, raided Jahurimal's residence, put him under house arrest, and took away Rs. 40,000. Bakht Khan's order was that he could be released, provided he agreed to go to Delhi as a banker for the Rebels and advance a loan of Rs. 50,00,000 after reaching Bhimani. Jahurimal refused and, like Bandopadhyay, remained under arrest.[52]

Frequently, many rebel soldiers resorted to looting the houses of the *mahajans*. Though Muhammad Safi tried to curb this unauthorized looting by creating a mounted police force of about 100 sawars, things went out of control. The traders responded by closing their shops. The *baniyas* failed to buy provisions for the rebel troops from the bazaar. Due to heavy incidence of looting, the supply of *ghee* and flour from the countryside to the city also ceased. Hence, the Rebels suffered from logistical difficulties at Bareilly. When in the first week of June 1857, Bakht Khan ordered the *baniyas* to amass food that would supply the troops for at least 15 days, but they were able to provide stores for only seven days.[53]

All these commissariat difficulties delayed Bakht Khan's plan of marching to Delhi quickly and this ruined the Rebels' prospect of a quick victory over the emaciated Delhi Field Force. The Bareilly Brigade, composed of 2,300 combatants (much reduced by continuous desertions) and 1,000 carts containing baggage and plunder, was able to move into Delhi only on 1 July 1857. By this time, the Company's Field Force at the Delhi Ridge had also received 2,000 reinforcements from Punjab.[54]

Initially, at Delhi, the troops demanded daily allowance for food from the emperor. But when he replied that he had no funds, then Mehbub Ali Khan, an official of the emperor, was ordered to raise a loan from the merchants and bankers of Delhi for paying wages to the soldiers.[55] Mehbub Ali Khan agreed to pay 4 *annas* to a sepoy and Rs. 1 to a sawar per day. For each regiment, a writer was appointed for maintaining a nominal roll.[56] Later, Lala Mukand Lal was ordered to raise another loan from the merchants for paying the troops. To tide over the desperate financial situation, the Rebel government tried to fleece Lachmi Chund Seth by ordering his *gomustah* to accept the office of Treasurer. But he refused.[57] The resulting financial mismanagement and lack of discipline resulted in pillage and plunder by the troops. On 13 May 1857, the 38th, 54th and 74th infantry regiments plundered the shops of the cloth merchants at Chota Dureeba. The merchants responded by closing the bazaars, which further exacerbated the situation.[58] On 16 May 1857, the sepoys looted *Mahajan* Narain Das' house.[59]

The situation was no better in Nana Sahib's domain. Lala Shankar Das, a banker of Kanpur, was arrested by Nana's subordinate Nunee Nawab and released after paying the rebels Rs. 30. Then the Commissariat *Gomastah* of Kanpur, Lala Badri Nath, was arrested by Tikka Singh, Subedar of 2nd Light Cavalry, who demanded Rs. 3,000 from him. He was released only when a Khatri trader, a friend of Badri, paid the troopers Rs. 300 on 16 June 1857.[60]

This sad scenario should be contrasted with a case study of the superior British logistical venture. Unlike the Rebels, the British could fall back on the trained civilian bureaucrats, who were experts in bookkeeping and paperwork. One of the principal factors behind the successful British defence of the Lucknow Residency was the construction of a superior commissariat system, a feature which was absent in General Wheeler's entrenchment at Kanpur. From 24 October 1856 onwards, the Deputy Commissioner, with the aid of civilian officials, started buying up grain from the local sources. A far-sighted policy indeed. These grain traders cooperated with the British bureaucracy. The Chief Commissioner was assigned the task of preparing an inventory of all the supplies including rum, port and fodder for the baggage animals. Further, he was ordered to prepare an average of daily expenditure. Daily expenditure of grain was calculated to about 8,000 lb. The total strength of the garrison under siege was 3,420 soldiers. The scale of daily ration was fixed. Each British combatant received 1 lb. of meat and 1 lb. of flour with some salt. Along with the soldiers, many civilians were also cooped up within the Residency. There were about 700 European civilians (including women and children) and 600 Indian followers. A child over 12 years of age received 12 oz. of meat and those below that age received about 8 oz. of meat. Everyday a woman was served 6 oz. meat, 12 oz. *atta,* 1.5 oz rice, 1 lb grain and 5 oz. salt. Each Indian follower received 1 lb of *atta,* 2 oz. of grain and 25 oz. of salt. Initially, mutton and sheep were provided. But, when they were finished, the dead gun bullocks were used for meat. The siege lasted from 1 July 1857 till 17 November 1857. On 2 October 1857, the Residency had 2,80,000 lb. of grain. When the garrison marched out, it still had 1,60,000 lb of grain.[61]

When the Indian personnel manning the coercive apparatus of the state rebelled, the state structure collapsed. Then powerful landed magnates along with their followers engaged in plundering and robbing. What was the response of the Rebel government and the Company towards them? The Rebel officials demanded the *purwanah*s should be issued to all the rajas and the chiefs. This was because the rural landscape could be controlled only through such landed intermediaries. Not only would they supply Delhi with money and food but, in addition, they should raise new troops.[62] The Rebel government tried to enlist their support through a carrot-and-stick policy by appointing them in the new fledgling anti-British state bureaucracy and by a simultaneous show of force.

Moulvi Mohammed Ali, whom the Rebel government appointed as the police officer of Najafgarh, wrote to the emperor that the *Thankur*s, *Chowdhurie*s, *Patwari*s and the *Kanungo*s were made to explain the royal order that they should collect the revenue and after keeping their own prescribed share, would forward the surplus to the royal treasury. Nonetheless, Ali added, that these village officials would only pay if Mirza Moghul, with a regiment of infantry, demonstrated in their territories.[63] Shah Mul, a jat zamindar of Bijroal, plundered the *banjara*s and then burnt the *tehsil* of Burout. The Rebel government at Delhi appointed him the Subedar of Burout *parganah.* He was ordered to supply grain for the Rebel force at Delhi.[64] Then, the Rao of Dadree (a small town near Delhi) was ordered by the Rebel government at Delhi to plunder Meerut so that no supplies could reach the British.[65]

Similarly, the British also tried to retain control over the countryside for a steady supply of revenue and food grains. When the Mutiny broke out at Meerut, the government treasury had about Rs. 5,00,000. But, expenditure due to military supplies and payment resulted in a continuous drain. Due to breakdown of law and order, the Gujars attacked the rich Jat villages. And without military power projection, no revenue could be collected. Since the British field army was engaged against the Mutineers' regular force, the European gentlemen and Sikh stragglers from the Bengal infantry regiments were organized into the Meerut Volunteer Force for revenue collection. One trooper was a Civil and Session Judge of a district, another a retired Judge of Moradabad and another was a retired Deputy Commissioner of Punjab. The Meerut Volunteer Force was engaged in coercing the *lumburdar*s of each village of Meerut *parganah* to provide sheep and grain for the Company's force.[66]

The Rajas of Punjab provided vital service for the British in supplying food and garrisoning the rear areas for guarding, for which the hard-pressed Company could hardly provide troops. The Jhind Raja's troops garrisoned Rhai, an outpost in the rear area of the British Field Force at Delhi. This post functioned as a base depot where the troops could fall back for rest and recuperation.[67]

Transport

The Company had at its disposal a well-connected transport net which enabled the British high command to rush troops to threatened points swiftly. The Ganga and its tributaries were navigable and the British had access to steamboats. These boats came from Calcutta up to Kanpur. Moreover, Calcutta and Raniganj were linked with railways (a distance for about 120 miles).[68] The 84th Infantry Regiment moved up from Calcutta to Allahabad during late 1857 first by railways up to Raniganj and then by steamers.[69] Havelock at Kanpur received continuous reinforcements of manpower and food from Benaras through steamers.[70] This steady supply stream was one factor which prevented Nana Sahib's troops from overpowering the Company's contingent at Kanpur.

In 1857, there was a shortage of horses in Awadh. Even with money, one could not procure them.[71] Before the Mutiny, the government bought horses from north India (for equipping the regular Indian cavalry of the Bengal Army that ultimately rebelled) at Rs. 700 for each animal.[72] Mudud Ali, a soldier who was discharged from the Bengal Army before 1857 and later became a horse dealer, supplied some horses to Nana Sahib.[73] Nevertheless, thanks to British control over the high seas, the Company was able to import a large number of horses from Persia and the Cape.[74]

Military Hardware and the Conduct of Warfare

Once the armies were organized, they had to be given proper weapons. The Company enjoyed a technological edge against the Rebels both as regards small arms and artillery. The Rebels' cavalry had no carbines and most of the militia, which the rebels raised, were armed with matchlocks, which could not be fired during rainfall.[75] At times, the state of hardware of the militia was much worse. When in June 1857, Nawab Khan Bahadur Khan at Bareilly raised a levy, they were armed with swords and spears.[76] In Awadh, about 40,000 Muslims who belonged to the disbanded Nawabi Army joined the Rebels.[77] While the Rebels' regular infantry was armed with Brown Bess, the Company's European infantry was armed with Enfield rifles (a muzzle loader with a long three- grooved rifled barrel in order to impart spin in the .577-inch diameter bullet for greater accuracy) whose bullets had greater velocity, hence increased[78] penetrative power.

The cartridges were manufactured at the regimental magazines by the regimental khalasies.[79] The Military Department, under the Military Member of the Governor-General's Council, supervised the supporting services of the army. Under him came the Director General of Ordnance.[80] The imperialists were always nervous about associating the Indians in the artillery arm. The Court of Directors was against recruiting Indians in the artillery or their employment in the arsenals and the ordnance factories. Nevertheless, rapid expansion of the British-Indian Army in the first half of the nineteenth century forced the British government in India to recruit more and more Indians as gunners.[81] Still, the number of Indian gunners in the Sepoy Army was very low compared with the number of sepoys and sawars. Thus, the proportions of Europeans and Indians in the artillery branch was different as compared with the other two branches. In the artillery, the proportion of Europeans and Indians was 1.5:1. But in the cavalry and infantry, the proportion of Europeans and Indians was 1:8. Within the Bengal Artillery, there were 18 Indian Foot Companies and three Indian Horse Troops. Of these only six Foot Companies and one Horse Troops rebelled.[82] In total, from 4,300 Indian gunners, about 500 joined the Rebels, while the Company possessed about 7,700 British gunners.[83] The net result was that the Company possessed more gunners as compared to the Rebels. Since, the gunners required specialized training, the Rebels could not recruit them from the countryside.

Those Indian gunners who rebelled fired well[84] but lacked advanced ordnance pieces and adequate supply of munitions. The Rebels did not control any ordnance depot and maintained themselves with the stores acquired from the ordnance depots captured by them. They were able to capture the magazine at Kanpur. The guns and ammunition from this depot equipped Nana Sahib's force.[85] Nana made desperate efforts to cast guns. He floated a proposal that anybody who could cast a gun would be given a heavy reward. One craftsman who made a gun was given a lump sum of Rs. 100 by Nana.[86] Again, the Rebels of Lucknow were mostly armed with obsolete brass guns[87] (used mainly for ceremonial purpose) which belonged to the Nawab of Awadh.

When about 30,000 Rebels were cooped up inside fortress Delhi, how did 12,588 troops (Indians plus British) of the Company blast their way through?[88] This was possible because of the Company's superiority in siege artillery. The task of siege artillery was to breach the walls of the forts with the aid of round shots fired from heavy guns like the 18-and-24 pounders. Delhi was surrounded by a stone wall 16 feet high, 11 feet thick at the top and about 15 feet at the bottom. The wall had bastions which were provided with parapets about 12 feet thick and these were adorned with static guns fired by the Rebel gunners. Outside the wall was a ditch which was about 25 feet wide and 20 feet deep. To destroy this obstacle, the Delhi Field Force deployed five batteries. The Sami House Battery, with guns and howitzers, engaged the defenders of the Mori Bastion. The task of the Number 1 Siege Battery armed with five 18-pounder guns and one 8-inch howitzer was to blast the Mori Bastion. The Number 2 Breaching Battery with nine 24-pounder guns and two 18-pounder guns along with seven 8-inch howitzers destroyed the Kashmir Bastion and breached the wall near the Kashmir Gate. The Number 3 Breaching Battery, at a distance of only 200 yards from the wall and equipped with six 18-pounder guns and twelve 5.5, inch mortars, was designed to breach the wall near the Water Bastion. Finally, the Reserve Battery, with four 19-inch and six 8-inch mortars, fired plunging shots over the walls to harass the Rebels, thus obstructing their flow of reinforcements to those points of the wall that were breached.[89]

The Company's trump card was the availability of personnel trained in the scientific branches of warfare, i.e. the military engineers and the sappers. The British had about 110 engineers.[90] In front of Delhi, Lieutenant-Colonel Baird Smith was in charge of the engineers.[91] One engineer, Arthur Moffatt Lang, was in charge of the Punjabi sappers and pioneers. Their job was to construct and repair the parapets, revetments and embrasures of the batteries (gun emplacements). The embrasures were openings in epaulments (battery fortification) made of fascines (brushwood) and gabions (wicker baskets filled with earth).[92] The sappers, under the direction of the engineers, also trained the assault infantry on escalading (placing and climbing ladders over the walls during the attack).[93]

In the narrow streets of Delhi, the numerically superior rebel infantry used its muskets with deadly effect, taking advantage of the cover provided by the rubble and houses. The Company responded by evolving superior tactics made possible due to the availability of the sappers. The engineers blew up the walls of the houses and then the sappers advanced with sandbags with which a parapet was constructed. From behind the parapet, fire support was given to the engineers for blowing up the next house.[94]

In Lucknow, the Company's artillery superiority registered a quantum jump. In 1858, when Colin Campbell advanced towards Lucknow, his force deployed 54 field guns, 64 siege guns and of the latter, 6 were super heavy 68-pounders which were worked by the British sailors. To construct batteries for all these giants, the Company had 1,000 Indian sappers.[95] Since none on the Rebel side were well-versed in sapping techniques during the siege of the Lucknow Residency, the British proved far more superior in mining and counter-mining operations.[96]

In engagement after engagement, despite possessing numerical superiority, the Rebels were defeated due to inferior technology. On 22 December 1857, at Guilee near Alambagh at Lucknow, Brigadier Stisted, with 1,227 infantry, defeated a Rebel force composed of 2,000 infantry. This was possible because while the Rebels had four guns, Stisted was able to deploy six guns.[97]

On 11 January 1858, the Rebels attacked Jallalabad. Though the Rebels outnumbered Major-General James Outram's force by about 10 times, combined artillery and rifle fire from about 1,600 infantry posted inside the Alambagh and the Jallalabad pickets crushed the Rebel infantry assault. The horse artillery guns were smoothbore muzzle loading 6-pounder guns and were a source of mobile firepower in fluid battle situations. The four horse artillery guns opened up at a range of about 500 yards, and the 9-pounder field guns drawn by bullocks supplemented the horse artillery. During the next attack which was launched on 16 January, the Rebels tried a new infantry tactic. They send out skirmishers instead of coming in dense masses. They were allowed to come within 800 yards and then three field guns under Major Gordon discharged grapes. Shells from an 8-inch mortar supplemented the grapes. When the Rebels launched their cavalry to threaten the Jallalabad picket's rear, Major Olpherts' four horse battery guns turned them away.[98]

Again, the British evolved specialized artillery tactics during the relief of the Lucknow Residency because they possessed various types of guns and shells. While one battery of six 8-inch mortars under Captain Maude was engaged in counter-battery work, another battery composed of four 18-pounder field guns along with two 24-pounder howitzers used grape and shrapnel shells and they did heavy execution among the Rebel infantry. In contrast, the Rebels had no antipersonnel shells.[99]

Towards Counter-Factual Hisory

Was the defeat of the Rebels then inevitable? The answer is probably no. The Sepoy Rebellion began at the time, which for the British constituted the 'Worst Possible Scenario'. The mid-nineteenth century was a violent period in the Asian landmass. Along with the Mutineers in South Asia, 'Satan' was let loose in China in the form of Taiping warriors, who also represented themselves as holy soldiers with revolutionary ideology. In the end both in China and in India, the Taipings and the Rebels were defeated by European led Asian troops who enjoyed technological, tactical, and organizational superiority.[100] Still there were some opportunities for the Rebels to emerge victorious. The second Opium War had broken out in China in 1856. And this not only tied down a considerable number of white troops in China but also hampered the supply of reinforcements into the subcontinent.[101] The troopships took about four months to reach India from Britain.[102] The reinforcements from England reached India in substantial quantity only in November.[103] So, the Rebels had five precious months to destroy the British presence in India. What possible military alternatives existed in front of them?

In the arena of strategy and tactics, there was much space for the Rebels to experiment upon. As regards strategy, the Rebels ought to have followed what Liddell Hart terms as 'Indirect Strategy'. This involved both geographical and psychological indirectness to upset the opponent's balance. In other words, it meant attack where the enemy is not expecting and thus overturn his decision making structure. Even a small mass by such indirect attack could achieve surprise and raise the tempo of operations, making the enemy's all detailed planning irrelevant.[104] The Marathas under Shivaji and during the First Anglo-Maratha War were past master in this Indirect Strategy.[105]

The Rebels could have achieved decisive battlefield success by following this superior strategy. Simultaneous attacks at the enemy's weak points like the depots and hospitals, which the Rebels could have done easily given their superiority in cavalry, would have generated a synergy and this would have destabilized the British position. The Company would have been forced to dissipate its troops in manning its ever-lengthy lines of communications. And this could have weakened their main field army, thus setting the stage for the decisive phase. Such a stage might have been reached when due to continuous dissipation, the Company's field army would have been too weak to meet the Rebels' field army. However, the Rebels finally resorted to mobile guerrilla warfare in 1858, when the military balance had already swung against them.

Again, instead of following positional warfare, by flocking to Delhi and Lucknow, the Rebels should have resorted to manoeuver warfare by attacking Calcutta, the principal node of British power in the eastern rim of the British-Indian Empire. If the Rebels concentrated around Calcutta, then the Sikhs and the Pathans in British pay would have been unwilling to march in the uncongenial climate towards the swampy terrain of Bengal.[106] Moreover, longer distance would have further worsened the already acute logistical problems of the Movable Column from Punjab. Dust, distance and malnutrition could have taken a higher toll of especially the white soldiers. Further, sunstroke, agreed the contemporary British combatants, was a lethal enemy.[107] Like 'General Winter' in case of the Russians, 'General Summer' was the biggest friend of the Indians against any foreign invaders from time immemorial. The Rebellion broke out in summer, the worst possible campaigning season for the British. In 12 months, about 1,000 British soldiers in the force under the direct control of Colin Campbell at north India died from sunstroke.[108] If the Rebels conducted a mobile guerrilla strategy over a wider theatre of war, then the number of sunstroke cases for the British would have gone up drastically.

Another reason why the Mutineers should have attacked Calcutta and Bombay was that the British control over both the high seas and coastal waters enabled them to shuffle troops not only from the other presidencies to Calcutta, but also to receive vital reinforcements from Britain and her extra Indian territories through these two ports.[109] Water transport at that time was quicker than land transport. On 24 May 1857, the Madras Fusiliers arrived in Calcutta for their journey to north India. The 37th Company of the Royal Artillery came from Ceylon and the 37th Foot from Moulmein. The 64th and 78th infantry regiments came from Persia.[110] Then 5,000 troops destined for China landed at Calcutta and proceeded to north India.[111] The net result was due to continuous reinforcements, despite losses due to the rebellion, the strength of the white troops and engineers in mid-1858 came to about 63,000 men and 434 respectively.[112] Attacks on Calcutta and Bombay would have choked the British supply of vital reinforcements.

The Rebels in the western part of north India, instead of flocking to Delhi, should have attacked the weakly held British ordnance depot at Ferozepore and destroyed the heavy guns and the animal transport along with their carriages held there before the advent of the Movable Column from Punjab. This would have made the Punjab Movable Column firepower deficient and immobile, thus giving vital time to the Mutineers to consolidate their hold over the battlespace along the Ganga–Jamuna doab. The point to be noted is that in the end, the fort of Delhi fell to the Company's troops because the walls and bastions of Delhi were breached by the siege train which the British assembled along with elephants, camels and 700 carts at Ferozepore towards the end of July 1857. [113]

The Rebels of central India, especially Tantia Tope with the troops from Gwalior, instead of moving into the burning hell of Kanpur, should have moved towards the Bombay Presidency. Since the social and regional composition of most of the Bombay Army's infantry and cavalry was similar to the rebellious units of the Bengal Army, there was a high chance of the Bombay Army personnel sympathizing with their brethren in the Bengal Army. The Bombay Army was largely composed of Brahmins and Rajputs from north India (i.e. *Purbiya*s of the rebellious Bengal Army) and Marathas. The Bombay Army had 1,500 cavalry recruited from the north Indian Muslims, Rajputs and the Brahmins. About 11,000 infantry of the Bombay Army were *Purbiyas*.[114] Any advance of the Rebels towards them would have encouraged the north Indian soldiers to throw of the British yoke. The Maratha segment of the Bombay Army would probably have rebelled also if it had heard that Nana Sahib was trying to restore the Peshwaship. Unlike the Bengal Army, in the Bombay Army, young Indian soldiers were promoted on the basis of their military performance and not on the basis of seniority. [115] So, if the Bombay Army rebelled, then the Rebels would have acquired an excellent crop of young Indian officers full of determination and capable of seizing the initiative even under adverse conditions.

At the tactical level, instead of blundering into set-piece battles with the Companys firepower heavy regulars managed by staff officers, the Rebels should have followed mobile hit and run operations.[116] Instead of trying to eliminate the Company's force in encounter battles, an impossible task since the Rebel military leadership lacked staff college training, the Rebels should have focused on cutting the telegraph lines. And this tactic would have strategic effect by paralysing the Company's C3I network. At times, the Mutineers made sporadic effort in cutting the telegraph wires just as they did on the eve of the uprising at Meerut. And this positively aided the Rebels by preventing white reinforcements reaching Meerut, when the sepoys and sawars decided to throw off the foreign yoke. [117]

The Rebel superiority in light cavalry then could have been used with devastating effect for harassing British columns and their lines of communications. Rightly, Stokes asserts that the Rebels should have launched mobile guerrilla forces along the Grand Trunk Road, the principal artery for communications between Calcutta and the British military stations at north India. Such Rebel attacks would have been quite successful because the company's troops were transported in small penny packets by bullock carts and streamers.[118] The very existence of such a threat would have tied down so many troops of the Company along the Grand Trunk Road that the forces that could be deployed at the battlefields of north India would have to be drastically reduced. This would have resulted in an attritional campaign and the fate of the British in 1857 India might have turned out like the Americans in Vietnam of the 1970s.

Conclusion

However, contemplation can never bypass reality. Given the social composition of the rebellious Bengal regiments, the Rebels were in no position to enlist the support of the low castes. Nor could the Rebels do anything to thwart the British sea lines of Communications. So, the best chance of the Rebels was to conduct what the Prussian General Staff had termed as the 'Timetable War' before the enemy's superior resources turned the military balance against them.

On 31 May, a fleeting window of opportunity appeared before the Rebels. The fate of India was hanging in the balance. The situation was one of touch and go. The tactics of cutting telegraph wires and capturing the ordance depots guarded by weak garrisons would have paralysed the British lion. Instead of following the Fabian Strategy of avoiding the enemy's army and conducting a scorched earth policy, the Rebels went for the Clausewitzian strategy of annihilating the Company Army in a single decisive stroke. The gallant but under-armed rebel sepoys and sawars who were led by 'donkeys' tried to measure strength with the Company's field army equipped with state-of-the-art technology and managerial experts. After being defeated in battles, the Rebels shut themselves inside cities like Delhi and Lucknow, only waiting to be blasted into oblivion by British heavy ordance. By August 1857, for the British the worst crisis was over. The 'Goddess of Fortune' had left the Rebels and they had lost the one and only chance to alter the course of history. *Gotterdammerung*, for the Rebels, was beginning.

Acknowledgements: I am indebted to Suhrita Saha for her comments on an earlier draft of this essay.

NOTES

1. Eric Stokes, 'Rural Revolt in the Great Rebellion of 1857 in India: A Study of the Saharanpur and Muzaffarganar Districts', *The Historical Journal*, vol. 2, no. 4, 1969, pp. 606–27.
2. Rudrangshu Mukherhee, *Awadh in Revolt* 1857–1858, *A Study of Popular Resistance*, New Delhi: Oxford University Press, 1984; Tapti Roy, *The Politics of a Popular Uprising Bundelkhand in 1857*, New Delhi: Oxford University Press, 1994.
3. Field-Marshal Lord Roberts, *Forty One Years in India From Subaltern to Commander-in-Chief*, vol. 1, London: Richard Bentley and Sons, 1897, p. 156.
4. Ibid., p. 335.
5. Lieutenant-General George MacMunn, *The Indian Mutiny in Perspective*, reprint, Delhi: Sunita Publications, 1985, p. 156.
6. Christopher Hibbert, *The Great Mutiny India 1857*, 1978, reprint, Harmondsworth: Penguin, 1980.
7. Bruce Watson, *The Great Indian Mutiny: Colin Campbell and the Campaign in Lucknow*, New York: Praeger, 1991.
8. Roberts, *Forty One Years*, p. 329.
9. For a conceptual discussion of the C31 concept refer to G. D. Sheffield, 'Introduction: Command, Leadership and the Anglo-American Experience', in idem, ed., *Leadership and Command The Anglo-American Military Experience since 1861* London: Brasseys, 1997, p. 1.
10. Moti Ram, ed., *Two Historic Trials in Red Fort*, New Delhi: Roxy Printing Press, n.d., *Trial of Bahadur Shah*, p. 388.
11. S. Moinul Haq, ed., *Memoirs of Hakim Ashamullah Khan*, Karachi: Pakistan Histoical Society, 1958, pp. 390–1, 404.

12. Ram, *Historic Trials*, pp. 390–1, 404.
13. Sheffield, 'Command, Leadership', in idem, ed., *Leadership and Command*, p. 8.
14. G. W. Forrest, ed., *The Indian Mutiny 1857–58, Selections from the Letters, Despatches and other State Papers preserved in the Military Department of the Government of India*, vol. 3, 1902, reprint, Delhi: D. K. Publishers, 2000, Appendix, Deposition of Kanai Prashad, Mahajan of Kanpur, no. 16, p. cxxxv.
15. David Blomfield, ed., *Lucknow: The Indian Mutiny Journal of Arthur Moffatt Lang*, London: Leo Cooper, 1992, p. 67.
16. *Minutes of Evidence taken before the Commissioners appointed to inquire into the Organization of the Indian Army, Parliamentary Papers*, Cd 2515, 1859 (hereafter *Peel Committee*), pp. 15, 51.
17. Peter Stanley, *White Mutiny: British Military Culture in India, 1825–1875*, London: Hurst and Company, 1998, pp. 43, 111.
18. S. P. Mackenzie, *Revolutionary Armies in the Modern Era: A Revisionist Approach*, London: Routledge, 1997, pp. 113–4.
19. Durgadas Bandopadhyay, *Amar Jivanchant* in Bengali, 1925, reprint, Calcutta: Ananya Prakashan, n.d., p. 97.
20. Ralph D. Sawyer, *The Seven Military Classics of Ancient China*, Boulder: Westview, 1993, p. 162.
21. Karl von Clausewitz, *On War* in Caleb Carr, ed., *The Book of War*, New York: Modern Library, 1993, pp. 319–20.
22. Lieutenant-Colonel Douglas M. Macgregor, *Breaking the Phalanx: A New Design for Landpower in the 21st Century*, Westport: CT Praeger, 1997, p. 101.
23. Ram, *Historic Trials*, p. 397.
24. Ram *Historic Trials*, p. 405.
25. Field-Marshal Lord Roberts, *Letters Written during the Indian Mutiny*, reprint, New Delhi: Lal Publishers, 1979. Letters to mother, 27 October and 13 November 1857, pp. 85, 99.
26. For a glimpse of the concept of command see Martin Van Creveld, *Command in War*, Cambridge, Massachussets: Harvard University Press, 1985, pp.1–2, 4.
27. Arthur Mills, *India in 1858*, 1858, reprint, Delhi: Gian Publishing House, 1986, p. 171.
28. Sheffield, 'Command Leadership', in *idem*, ed., *Leadership and Command*, p. 3.
29. Charles Allen, *Sahib: The Men who made the North-West Frontier*, London, John Murry, 2000, p. 270.
30. William Wilson Hunter, *The Marquess of Dalhousie and the Final Development of the Company's Rule*, Oxford: Clarendon Press, MDCCCXCV, p. 199.
31. Ibid., p. 178.

32. *Peel Committee*, Appendix no. 17, Return showing the number of troops in the three presidencies immediately before the Mutiny.
33. Stephen P. Cohen, *The Indian Army: Its Contribution to the Development of a Nation*, 1971, reprint, Delhi: Oxford University Press, 1991, p. 35.
34. *Peel Committee*, p. 13; Hunter, *Dalhousie*, p. 214.
35. *Peel Committee*, Appendix no. 58, Lord Clyde's replies on the Organization of the Indian army, para 1.
36. *Papers Connected with the Reorganization of the Army in India: Supplementary to the Report of the Army Commission, Parliamentary Papers*, House of Commons, Session 2, 1859, Cd 254, (henceforth *Supplementary Report*). List of recruits levied at Gorakphur, p. 162.
37. Allen, *Soldier Sahibs*, pp. 226, 226-7.
38. Military Despatches from the Secretary of State, India Office, London, nos. 59, 77, 14 February and 24 February 1860, National Archives of India (henceforth NAI), New Delhi, *Supplementary Report*, pp. 274–5, 308; *Peel Committee*, Lietenant-General George Pollock examined, p. 5, Strokes, 'Rural Revolt', p. 47.
39. *Supplementary Report*, p. 47.
40. P. C. Joshi, '1857 in Our History', in *idem*, ed., *Rebellion 1857: A Symposium*, 1957, reprint, Calcutta, K. P. Bagchi, 1986, pp. 119–24.
41. Mukherjee, *Awadh in Revolt*, pp. 170-1.
42. Captain E. Hall, commanding Aligarh Levy, to Major, commanding at Saugor, Lieutenant-Colonel H. Bruce, Chief of Awadh Police to the Adjutant-General, Lucknow, Progs, nos 7 and 549, 9 January and February 1860, Military Department Proceedings, NAI.
43. *Supplementary Report*, p. 46.
44. Digest of Services of the 44th Merwara Infantry, 1818–1916, Origin of the Merwara Battalion, (NAI). This manuscript is without pagination and is organized under various headings.
45. Military Despatches from the Secretary of State, Charles Wood to the Governor-General, no. 73, 8 February 1861.
46. *Peel Committee*, Appendix no. 22, Return showing the Number, Caste and Country of the Indian Officers and Soldiers of each Regiment, Regular and Irregular of each Presidency, September 1858.
47. A. Bopegamage, 'Caste, Class and the Indian Military: A Study of the Social Origins of Indian Army Personnel', in Jacques Van Doorn, ed., *Military Profession and Military Regimes: Commitments and Conflicts*, The Hague/Paris: the Mouton, 1969, pp. 142–3.
48. *Report of Major General H. Hancock of the Bombay army* (hereafter *Hancock's Report*), Cd 2516, *Parliamentary Papers*, 1859, pp. 27–8.
49. *Peel Committee*, Appendix no. 22.
50. *Supplementary Report*, pp. 4, 14.
51. Bandopadhyay, *Jivanchant*, pp. 81–7, 108,
52. Ibid., pp. 87–9.

53. Ibid., pp. 97–8.
54. C. A. Bayly and Eric Stokes, eds, *The Peasant Armed: The Indian Revolt of 1857*, Oxford University Press, 1986, pp. 22–3.
55. Haq, *Ahsanullah Khan*, p. 5.
56. Ibid., p. 7.
57. Ibid., pp. 10, 12.
58. Haq, ed., Appendix, Copy of a Journal kept by Kedarnath, late Clerk in the Delhi Gazette Press, Delhi: 30 November 1857 and 13 May 1857, p. 37.
59. Haq, *Kedarnath's Journal*, 16 May 1857, p. 38.
60. Forrest, *Indian Mutiny*, Appendix, nos 18 and 21, Deposition of Lala Bhadri Nath, Commissarriat Gomastah at Kanpur and Lala Shankar Das, Banker at Kanpur, pp. cxxxiii, cxLvi.
61. Brigadier Humphrey Bullock, *History of the Army Service Corps: 1760–1857*, vol. I, New Delhi: Sterling Publishers, 1976, pp. 222, 225, 238–9, 243, 245–6, Appendix I, 249.
62. Haq, *Ahsanullah Khan*, p. 5.
63. Ram, *Historic Trials*, pp. 402–3.
64. Robert Henry Wallace Dunlop, *Service and Adventure with the Khakee Ressalah or Meerut Volunteer Horse during the Mutinies of 1857–58*, 1858, reprint, Allahabad: Legend Publications, 1974, pp. 45–6, 94.
65. Haq, *Ahsanullah Khan*, p. 9.
66. Dunlop, *Khakee Ressalah*, pp. 54–7, 64–5, 69, 96, 99.
67. Roberts, *Forty One Years*, p. 182.
68. MacMunn, *Indian Mutiny*, pp. 92, 100.
69. Ibid., pp. 104–5.
70. Ibid, pp. 110–1
71. Roberts, *Letters*, Letter to mother, 27 October 1857, p. 93.
72. *Supplementary Report*, p. 274.
73. Forest, *Indian Mutiny*, deposition of Kanal, Prashad, p. cxxiii.
74. MacMunn, *Indian Mutiny*, p. 198.
75. Dunlop, *Khakee Research*, p. 74–5.
76. Bandopadhyay, *Jivancharit*, p. 111.
77. Roberts, *Letters*, Letter to father, 1 November 1857, p. 95.
78. Lieutenant-Colonel Rufus Simon, *History of the Corps of Electrical and Mechanical Engineers*, vol. 1, New Delhi: Vikas, 1977, p. 31; Alexander Llewellyn, *The Siege of Delhi*, London: Macdonald and Jane's, 1977, p. 7.
79. Ram, *Historic Trials*, p. 394.
80. Simon, *Their Formative Years*, p. 13.
81. Ibid., p. 436.
82. Brigadier R. C. Butalia, *The Evolution of Artillery in India: From the Battle of Plassey to the Revolt of 1857*, New Delhi: Allied Publications, 1998, pp. 320–3.

83. *Peel Committee*, Appendix no. 17, *Hancock's* Report, p. 24.
84. *Peel Committee*, p. 17.
85. MacMunn, *Indian Mutiny*, pp. 97, 100.
86. Forrest, *Indian Mutiny*, Appendix no. 18, p. cxxxii.
87. Roberts, *Letters*, Letters to mother, 15 October and 13 November 1857, pp. 81, 98.
88. General Orders by the Commander-in-Chief, 23 November 1857, NAI.
89. Roberts, *Forty One Years*, p. 162; Major-General B.P. Hughes 'Siege Artillery in the Nineteenth Century', *Journal of the Society for Army Historical Research* (henceforth *JSAHR*), vol . LX, no. 243, 1982, pp. 129–30, 146–7.
90. *Peel Committee*, Appendix no. 17.
91. Blomfleld, *Lahore to Lucknow*, p. 55.
92. Ibid., 4 August 1857, 13 August 1857, pp. 59, 67, 68–9.
93. Ibid, *Lahore to Lucknow*, p. 78.
94. Llewellyn, *Siege*, p. 132.
95. Roberts, Letter to mother, 11 February 1858, pp. 132–3.
96. John Fraser, Captain Clifford Henry James' *JSAHR*, no. 243, autumn 1982, pp. 172–3.
97. Forrest, *Indian Militay*, Orders Issued by Major-General James Outram Alambagh, 23 December 1857, pp. 422–3.
98. Ferrest, *Indian Mutiny*, From Outram, Commanding in Awadh to General R. Mansfield, Chief of Staff of the Army, 12 January 1858. Outram to Mansfield, 17 January 1858, pp. 425–9; T.A. Heathcote, *The Indian Army: The Garnson of British Imperial India, 1822–1922*, Newton Abbot-David and Charles, 1974, p. 46.
99. Forrest, *Indian Mutiny*, Major V. Eyre, Commanding Artillery Brigade to Colonel R. Napier Alambagh, 8 January 1858, pp. 435, 439, 441.
100. Mackenzie, *Revolutionary Armies*, pp. 80–106.
101. Yu Sheng-Wu and Chang Chen-Khan, 'China and India in the Mid-19th Century', Joshi, ed., *Rebellion* 1857, pp. 338, 340–1.
102. *Hancock's Report*, p. 9.
103. Bayly and Stokes, *Peasant Armed*, p. 19.
104. J. J. A. Wallace, 'Manoeuvre Theory in Operations Other Than War, *Journal of Strategic Studies*, vol. 19, no. 4, 1996, pp. 207–23.
105. For an account of Maratha, '*ganimi kava*' (guerrilla warfare), refer to M. R. Kantak, *The First Anglo-Maratha War 1774-1783. A Military Study of Major Battles*, Bombay, Popular Prakashan, 1993, pp. 5–23.
106. V. G. Kiernan, *European Armies from Conquest to Collapse 1815–1960*, Suffolk, Fontana, 1982, pp. 47, 50.
107. Roberts, *Forty One Years*, p. 173.
108. MacMunn, *Indian Mutiny*, p. 217
109. Hunter, *Dalhousie*, p. 183.
110. MacMunn, *Indian Mutiny*, pp. 104–5.

111. Bayly and Stokes, eds, *'Peasant Armed*, p. 28.
112. Mills, *India in* 1858, p. 66.
113. Blomfield, *Lahore to Lucknow*, p. 56.
114. *Supplementary Report*, p. 45; *Peel Committee*, Appendix no. 22.
115. *Peel Committee*, p. 15.
116. Kieran, *European Armies*, pp. 48–9.
117. Bayly and Stokes, eds, *Peasant Armed*, p. 17.
118. Ibid., pp. 25, 27.

CHAPTER 17

Military Imperatives and Punjab's Agricultural Expansion

Rait K. Mazumder

Direct and indirect advantages accrued to Punjab because of its strategic importance as the frontier of British India and as the bulwark of its army.[1] The Russian threat could not be contained only by changing recruiting policy; an efficient logistical base to facilitate troop movement and provide the necessary ordnance was equally vital. This meant the creation of lines of supply and communication, the building of cantonments, and an administrative machinery which would enable swift and competent operations. This aspect of frontier defence resulted in a significant network of communications and markets for Punjab.

The colonization of canal colonies in the western districts of Punjab from the 1880s more directly benefited the recruited peasantry. The state gained from increased revenues, while the canal grantees, and Punjab agriculture in general, profited from significant increases in output. Punjab's agricultural boom was critically reliant on the development of this 'infrastructure' for strategic requirements.

Defence Strategy and Economic Infrastructure

The north-west frontier of the British empire was entirely along the ill-defined border of Punjab. The North West Frontier Province was created only in 1901, and consisted of the 'Pathan districts' on Punjab's frontier.[2] Therefore, all military requirements to protect the frontier had to be based either in the province or routed through it. Government orders from 1849 provided that the Board of Administration in Punjab was to maintain internal peace of the Province, and to guard the Western Frontier, from the northern borders of

Sindh to Attock, as also the whole Huzara territory'. Only Peshawar, on the entire frontier, was to be 'held by the regular army'.[3] The Punjab government controlled 500 miles of the border from Sindh to the Kohat pass; the 100 miles of the Yusufzai frontier; and the 200 miles from Torbeila on the Indus to the Jhelum at Kagan in Hazara. This was a total of 800 miles. The Indian army guarded just the Khyber.[4]

Military Works for the Frontier

The establishment of the Frontier Force was only one of the six provisions that Governor-General Dalhousie had deputed the Punjab administration to undertake in defence of the frontier. The others included the formation of posts 'along the entire frontier line', the 'construction or repair of Frontier forts', their armament and garrison, 'the construction of roads', and 'the establishment of cantonments for the troops'.[5] Table 17.1 shows the work undertaken by the department immediately after annexation.

In the early years of British rule, it was only to be expected that an unusual amount of activity would be centred around providing internal security and guarding the frontier. The government acknowledged that 'the great importance of Military work in these Territories will be perceived when it is remembered that some 55,000 Regular Troops are cantoned there, among which there are twelve European Regiments, with an aggregate strength of 12,000, and 3,400 European Artillery'.[6]

Table 17.1: Work Completed or in Progress by the Civil Engineer's Department, 1849–51

Type of buildings	Total	Cost (Rs)
Military buildings (incl. 6 forts, 29 fortified posts, 5 cantonments)	40	2,52,913
Civil buildings (incl. 13 court-houses, 11 treasuries, 27 jails)	51	7,25,313
Public buildings (incl. 3 dispensaries, 'various' conservancies, 1 salt mine)	4	85,504
Total expenditure		10,63,730

Source: PAR, 1849–51, p. 128. Conservancies included drainage in cities, filling marshes, bridging minor waterways, etc.

The expenditure on military works and roads by the Civil Engineer's Department amounted to 87 per cent of its cumulative expenditure between 1849 and 1856,[7] highlighting the military responsibilities of the Punjab government.

The major emphasis in securing the frontier was put on strengthening or building forts and fortifications along the long border. These activities were set in place as soon as the province was acquired. By 1853, defensive works were well in progress in Leria in Hazara, on the Kohat and Bahadur Khel forts in Kohat, on the Duleepgarh and Lakki forts in Bannu, on the Akalgarh fort, in the cantonments under construction in Dera Ismail Khan, and in Dera Ghazi Khan, and on the other forts on the Derajat frontier[8] covering the whole length from Hazara to Sind,

Of the main military stations in the province, Ambala, Ferozepur, and Jullundur in the eastern half of the province were in existence 'in a manner' before annexation.[9] The Lahore and Sialkot cantonments were built between 1849 and 1854, but after this 'important works' were carried on 'at Peshawur, Nowshera' Rawul Pindee, Mooltan, the Hill Stations of Kussowlie and Dugshaie, and the sanataria of Murree and Dhurmshala'. The arsenals at Ferozepur and Jhelum were built, the Kohat fort was almost completed during the same period, and new forts were planned at Multan and Attock. In addition, 'accessory works' were going on in the various cantonments.[10]

Road building, too, was a military activity at this time.[11] The construction of the 'military road' from Lahore to Peshawar 'first claim [ed] notice' of the Department though it built the Lahore–Multan and Lahore–Ferozepur 'military and commercial road[s]', constructed the entire Trans-Indus Derajat line connecting all the frontier posts on the Derajat, began the 'important military line' joining Attock to Kalabagh via Rawalpindi, and improved the difficult road through the Kohat pass into the Peshawar valley.[12]

Concerns over the frontier ensured that 'The Military Works of the province still form[ed] the most important class of those now being carried out by the officers of the Public Works Department' into the third decade of British rule,[13] and indeed into the twentieth century as well, even after the province was split. The activities of the Public Works Department demonstrated the significant interplay between the civil and military responsibilities of the Punjab government.

Roads

The Grand Trunk Road has been one of the most important public thoroughfares in Indian history. On annexation, 'The chief item on the programme which was soon drawn up [by the chief engineer] was the reconstruction of this ancient roadway right up to Peshawar to facilitate communication between the important military stations of Northern India.'[14] Other undertakings included 'Military Works' (the building of cantonments and forts), 'Public Works—for civil purposes' (roads and canals). Roads were classified as '1st—Military Roads', '2nd—Roads for external commerce', and '3rd—Roads for internal commerce', pointing to the Punjab government's priorities. The government further specified that, 'In this classification, the *primary* object is [to be] kept in view: lines designed directly for Military purposes may incidentally serve the ends of commerce; so, may commercial roads be occasionally be used for the transit of troops, stores and munitions.'[15] The object of the project is quoted at length to highlight the civil–military nature of the Grand Trunk Road in Punjab:

> From a political and military point of view its consequence can hardly be overrated as binding together all our important Northern Cantonments and maintaining communication with Peshawar, our greatest frontier station. In this respect it is of the greatest strategic importance to the Punjab and to India. But to the Punjab it confers another great benefit by forming a great highway, passing through the upper districts and the chief cities commanding the entrance to Hazara and giving access at several points to Kashmir. It thus constitutes a great artery from which numerous branches separate off in various directions. Lastly, it is the great outlet and channel for the import and export trade between India, Central Asia and the West.[16]

Arguably, the civil benefits were an afterthought, to justify the costs of meeting military needs. The total length of the Grand Trunk Road as initially proposed was 568 miles (between Delhi and Peshawar), and, as it was primarily for military purposes, it had to be an all seasons road.[17] The Lahore to Peshawar section was completed in 1853 with 103 'large' and 459 'minor' bridges, including 'floating bridges' of boats across the rivers Ravi, Chenab, Jhelum, and Indus. Another indicator of the military nature of the road was that it was built to provide the quickest possible access to Peshawar, the largest military base on the frontier.

Table: 17.2: Mileage of Metalled and Unmetalled Roads in Punjab, 1890–1912

	Metalled			Unmetalled		
Year	Punjab(E)	Punjab (W)	Total	Punjab(E)	Punjab(W)	Total
1890	1,986	632	2,618	17,862	6,388	24,250
1895	1,999	648	2,647	17,840	6,319	24,154
1900	1,932	668	2,600	17,663	6,386	24,049
1905	2,101	1,132	3,233	17,196	8,077	25,273
1910	2,599	1,240	3,839	17,724	7,812	25,536
1912	2,697	1,221	3,918	17,500	8,083	25,853

Source: Calculated from the *RERPI*, vol. 111, pp. 474–7.[18] E = East; W = West.

The next stage was from Lahore to the Sutlej river,[19] in the direction opposite to Peshawar. The Lahore to Beas stretch included a loop from Amritsar to the new cantonment town of Sialkot, joining the main Grand Trunk Road at Wazirabad. The Beas to Ludhiana section, constructed after 1857, passed through Phagwara and Jullundur—not the shortest way, but 'the best adapted both to the commercial and military needs of the Punjab.'

The final sector led from the Sutlej to Delhi via Ferozepore, Ludhiana and Karnal.[20] Karnal and Delhi were already connected, for the British had been entrenched in Delhi a few decades. The Lahore–Ferozepore section passed through Ferozepore cantonment, 'ignoring the city altogether.'

The Grand Trunk Road was the most ambitious road project in Punjab under British rule. It was not the only one. Increasing military activity on the frontier from the 1870s saw the mileage of roads nearly double from 1,036 miles in 1872–3 to 2,142 miles in 1892–3.[21] By 1912, Punjab had 3,918 miles of metalled and

25,853 miles of unmetalled roads (Table 17.2). The province had, moreover, 7.5 per cent of all metalled roads in British India, and almost a fifth of unmetalled roads by 1912,[22] the latter being a very high proportion in relation to Punjab's size and population. It was also officially recognized that there were 'very few' roads as compared to the total area of India, but that the frontier was 'better in this respect'.[23] In 1919, the Military Works Services maintained 2,090 miles of metalled and 1,049 miles of unmetalled roads in the province from imperial military funds.[24] Another indication that economic goals had not played the most crucial part in the development of this facility in Punjab was that in 'Punjab, West'—the half of the province closer to the frontier—the index number of metalled roads reached 190 by 1912, whereas it grew to 135 in 'Punjab, East' in the same period.[25]

In 1918 it was again reiterated that, 'On the Frontier where for military purposes roads are obviously vital to the defence of the Frontier, the roads have been improved by the Military Works officers who are hard at work improving them further.'[26] The connection with the army, begun in 1849, had only been strengthened over the next seven decades. The *Report on Roads* also noted that 'the railway facilities in India have lately proved totally inadequate for the country's needs and many towns on the North-West and Western Frontiers can with difficulty be supplied, there being no margin of carrying power left for emergencies or possible increase of traffic'. It recommended, 'both from a military and civil point of view', the improvement of the road system in British India.

Railways could be sabotaged and effective measures against local or trans-frontier emergencies could be seriously hampered. Therefore, 'To rely for transport in India, whether in peace or war, on railways alone, is a dangerous illusion.'[27] The railway provided much faster transport, yet the importance of the older mode of communication had not diminished.

Railways

Railroad construction in Punjab began in the 1860s and there was a dramatic rise in its expansion, some of which was directly related to increased military activities on the frontier. The government wanted to build the 'Great North Western Railroad' between

Calcutta and Peshawar with almost identical intentions as for the Grand Trunk Road.

> It is sufficient to say that the Punjab section will, in a Military and political point of view, be of more consequence than perhaps any other part of the Railway. Following generally the line of the present Grand Trunk Road, it will bind together the series of first-class Military stations held by the very flower of the Army, European and Native. It will connect the whole of these with the most salient point (Peshawar) of the most important of the several frontiers, by which the British Empire in the East is bounded. It will render the whole power of the Empire capable of being rapidly concentrated and brought to bear upon a sport of vital consequence to the politics of Central Asia and of the countries bordering Europe. Further, in a commercial point of view, the Punjab section will command a portion of the commerce between India and Central Asia.[28]

The railway in Punjab was so closely linked with military imperatives that the state eventually took over its operations.[29] The Punjab Northern (State) Railway was 'the first in India commenced under direct Government agency'.[30] In 1870, the Sind Railway, the Indus Steam Flotilla, the Punjab Railway, and the Delhi Railway were amalgamated into one company by an act of parliament, and the secretary of state for India considered putting this company directly under the Government of India rather than with any provincial government.[31] In 1886, all these lines were taken over by the government as the North Western Railway System.[32] Clive Dewey has shown that the first railways in the province connected the cantonments of Meerut (in the United Provinces) and Lahore through three others in Punjab—Ambala, Jullundur and Amritsar. The extension of this line to the frontier between 1878 and 1882 linked seven other cantonments.[33]

The logistical problems faced by Roberts during the Afghan campaign of 1878 spurred the extension of the Punjab Northern Railway's line across the Indus to Peshawar.[34] In 1880, Roberts recommended that the government 'bridge the Indus and complete railway [*sic*]' as one of the measures to contain Afghanistan.[35] It is no coincidence that all the 'frontier section (military)' lines of the North Western Railway date from this period. The first of these was ready in January 1880.[36]

Kitchener's tenure as commander-in-chief (1902–9) resulted in the 'Kitchener scheme' for the reorganization of the army. This included a proposal for the construction of three 'strategic railways': one along the Kabul river or across the Khyber, the Khurram Valley line, and the Bombay–Sindh railway to link India's largest port with its most sensitive frontier.[37] About the first two lines, officials acknowledged that 'we doubt whether it would have been proposed or sanctioned except for the purpose of facilitating a military advance to Kabul'. The Bombay–Sindh line was likely to be loss-making as well, and it was suggested that the secretary of state for India should therefore be given more details of its 'very great' military advantages, to induce him to sanction payment. Matters were delayed and it took the Third Afghan War in 1919 to provide the impetus to push the railway through the Khyber.'[38]

From just 410 miles in 1872, the railway network grew to 600 miles in 1882, nearly trebled to 1,725 miles in 1892, and increased by over 2,000 miles more by 1902 to stand at 3,086 miles.[39] Roberts, who had strongly advocated that communications were the most effective defensive measure, had (in 1893) 'the supreme satisfaction of knowing that I felt our North-West Frontier secure, so far as it was possible to make it so, hampered as we were by want of money. The necessary fortifications had been completed . . . and the roads and railways, in my estimation of such vast importance, had either been finished or were well advanced.'[40]

The capital expenditure on the 'frontier railways' from commencement of operations increased by over 700 per cent in 25 years. Table 17.3 details the expenditure. Significantly, all these railways were under the North Western Railway. Through the north-east frontier saw strategic road construction, Punjab alone benefited from such railways.[41] The military aspect of the railway in Punjab is also apparent in the accounts of the North Western Railway, where the capital account was divided into 'Military' and 'Commercial' sections.[42]

The following mileages were operated by the North Western Railway in 1910; Nowshera–Durgai—40.25; Kohat–Thal—61.75; Pishin Section—538.85; Sind–Sagar, etc.—616.19; Kalka–Simla—59.92; and the mainline—2416.64 miles.[43] Only the last two were not 'military' or 'strategic' or 'frontier' railways. In other words, of the total of 3,733.6 miles that the North Western Railway operated, more than a third was constructed to meet primarily military needs. Of the four non-commercial lines, three had negative 'net earnings',[44] that is, they cost more than they earned commercially. By 1947, abour 40 per cent of the North Western Railways' lines, nearly 1,500 miles, were 'military frontier railways'. They put the entire network in deficit.[45] These lines would not have been constructed if the normal commercial criteria of railway extension had been applied.

Table 17.3: Capital Expenditure Incurred on Military and Strategic Railways, 1884-1909

Section	Outlay to 1884–5	Outlayto 1909–10
North-Western Railway, Pishin Section	2,26,06,582	11,87,22,638
North-Western Railway, Sind–Sagar Line	3,92,863	5,77,13,714
North-Western Railway, Kohat–Thal Line	–	42,69,166
North-Western Railway, Nowshera–Durgai Line	–	25,94,931
North-Western Railway, Loi–Shilman Line	–	46,14,216
Total Outlay	2,29,99,455	18,79,14,655

By 1925, the North Western Railway alone consisted of 4,074.55 miles of 'open line', whereas the entire 'North Western Railway system' comprised 5,828.14 miles of open line.[46] The total open mileage of the 'commercial section' of the North Western Railway was 2,602.35 while the 'frontier section (military)' was made up of 1,472.20 open miles. Between 1910 and 1925, the proportion of military to commercial lines had increased further, the former now standing at 36.13 per cent of the total open mileage. Calvert summarized this: 'The great railway system of the Punjab has been moulded by two outstanding features: the great rivers, running south-west with their broad sandy beds and shifting currents, encouraged the builders to lay the lines roughly parallel to them towards Multan, so as to reduce the number of expensive bridges;

but military requirements required lines crossing these, running north-west to the frontier.' By the 1920s, Punjab had 660 railway stations and 'very few places' were more than 25 miles from a railway line.[47]

The significance of the North Western Railway System is better grasped in comparison with the other railway systems. In every year between 1880 and 1892, it had the highest open mileage of all the railway systems in British India.[48] In 1931, too, it was the largest, constituting nearly 23 per cent of the total open mileage in India, and operating a total of 7,092 miles. This was over 2,745 miles greater than the second largest, Eastern Indian Railways, which covered 4,347 miles.[49]

The expanding and vast rail network had repercussions upon the roads sector as well. 'It has usually been found in the Punjab that the construction of a new line leads to demands for road communication which have not been experienced before, and it is a remarkable fact that the districts which are the best served by Railways are identical with those which have shown the greatest activity in constructing metalled roads.'[50] Thus, even though constructed for strategic purposes, the rail network directly assisted the transport of non-military men and material and connected the agricultural regions with ports that brought general economic benefits to the province.

Post and Telegraph

Work on the telegraph network in Punjab began in the latter half of 1853 and by January 1855 Lahore had been connected to Peshawar, thus linking Calcutta with the north-west frontier, just as the road and rail systems had done. In 1855, the electric telegraph extended east to west along the Grand Trunk Road from Karnal to Peshawar, a distance of 520 miles. There were five telegraph offices—at Ambala, Jullundur, Rawalpindi, Lahore and Peshawar—which, according to the government, 'are indeed the five most important places in a Civil, Military, and Political point of view.'[51]

Another analogy between the telegraph and road network was the crucial importance of swift information transfer that the Government of Punjab realized during the disturbances of 1857.[52] This quickened the extension of telegraphy. By 1859 the connection to Multan was completed and the line extended from there to Karachi 'without a break'; a station had been opened in Amritsar; a branch line was constructed between Rawalpindi and Murree purely for military needs; Ambala was linked to Simla, where the Commander-in-Chief had his summer headquarters; and the electric cable over the Sutlej was completed.[53]

There were many expeditions against frontier tribes in the last decades of the nineteenth century. Each of them aided the extension of telegraphic connections along the border, linking the troops positioned there with the larger military stations spread over Punjab. The expedition against the Jowakis in 1877–8 led to the construction of 35 miles of 'flying lines' between Kohat and Peshawar;[54] the Second Afghan War led to the erection of 200 miles of wire for the Kohat Field Force, 140 miles for the Kandahar Field Force, and the line from Peshawar to Jamrud for the Khyber Field Force;[55] while 'Field Force Operations in Waziristan in connection with the delimitation of the frontier' in 1894–5 resulted in 70 miles of 'field wire' between Dera, Ismail Khan and Tank.[56]

The post and telegraph system grew alongside the railways and roads in Punjab,[57] following the Grand Trunk Road and, as Sarkar noted, 'providing instantaneous communication between all the large northern stations'.[58] The same was true for the postal service. Dak bungalows had been constructed by the East India Company at intervals on the Grand Trunk Road and were placed under the local executive engineer, while those near post offices came under the Post Master General.

The number of post offices in Punjab grew from 425 in 1870–1 to 4,257 in 1931, a 901 per cent increase, while the corresponding rate of growth for British India was 774 per cent.[59] In 1901, a post office served 93 square miles and 11,578 people in Punjab while the figures for British India were 115 square miles and 19,719 people, respectively.[60] By 1931, each Punjab post office served 52 square miles and 7,708 people while the respective averages for India were 74 square miles and 14,039 persons. Also, one letter box in Punjab covered 13 square miles and 1,917 persons, while the figures were 21 square miles and 3,902 people, respectively, for India.[61] As services improved, the differential remained.

Communications were also improved because of the canal colonies. By 1921, there were over 11 million acres of land irrigated by canals.[62] The Irrigation Department owned and worked a telegraphic system that connected every canal rest-house and every canal outpost at the headworks of a canal with the Canal Divisional Headquarters.[63] The canal colonies had their own telegraphic system, too. Punjab was covered under a vast network of communications that enabled the transfer of military and other information. Some of this information pertained to important agricultural matters relating to both the production and the marketing of Punjab's considerable agricultural produce.[64] The link between the army's requirements and its wider impact on the province's economy is apparent here as well.

Cantonments

A cantonment is, in its essence, an area of land reserved for military requirements. It is intended to contain accommodation for troops, residential houses for officers, store houses, and offices for the various military services, ranges and parade grounds. Further, as the necessaries of life must be provided with the minimum of difficulty and as on sanitary and disciplinary grounds it is essential that the troops should be denied unrestricted access to the towns and cities of the country, provision has in all cases been made for the establishment of bazaars within the limits of the cantonments. These bazaars have been administered under a special code of rules and have been kept under strict control.[65]

In theory, therefore, a cantonment was an enclave in a civil district, self-contained and in varying degrees self-supporting, the civil inhabitants being subject to taxation of a municipal character, the income of which was devoted to the maintenance of public services within the cantonment limits.[66] These army townships also aided in promoting commercial activity. They became markets that often blossomed into urban centres, particularly if the 'Bazaar has developed into a large town',[67] consuming much of the produce of the nearby countryside. Their existence was purely on account of military needs.

In 1919, it was decided that 'a permanent base should be established at Lahore, which is centrally situated for supplies for troops operating in the North West Frontier'. This base was to include a remount depot, a convalescent horse depot, a military grass farm, a stationery depot, a postal depot, a cattle purchase depot, a medical store depot, a Red Cross depot, a grain depot, an engineers' park, the Lahore Corps Lines (accommodation for troops), a supply depot, and a fuel yard 'with the necessary subsidiary services such as railway sidings, water supply, electric power, metalled roads, etc.[68] Some of these were purely military in character and would not have had much bearing for the wider economy of the district, but many would have resulted in direct dealings with the local economy (the military grass farm, the grain depot, and the cattle purchase depot, for example). A similar connection with surrounding areas would have been made in every cantonment.

By 1921 seven cities in Punjab were 'dominated by cantonments', where half or nearly half the population lived.[69] These included Rawalpindi,[70] Ambala, and Ferozepore. According to Dewey, Rawalpindi 'was so completely a creation of the Indian army that the role of military expenditure is beyond question: the defence budget dictated the pattern of its growth.' The army transformed the 'village of the rawals' into the third largest urban centre in Punjab, next only to Lahore and Amritsar. Ten other places were 'affected' by cantonments wherein a quarter of the people lived, or which had a minimum population of 5,000. Lahore, Jullundur, and Sialkot fell into this category. Then there were nine cantonments in the hills.[71] The above categories did not include places like Amritsar where cantonments were relatively small and had less influence.

Muree was a 'hill station' attached to Rawalpindi where British troops escaped the scorching Punjab summer.[72] The entire town grew because of the army; all roads leading to it were 'strategic.' The town itself consisted only of barracks or military buildings, its sanatorium was reserved for soldiers, and its only school was for the sons of British other ranks. The shopkeepers of Rawalpindi migrated to Murree in the summer with the soldiers. The army affected urbanization similarly in every cantonment.

The needs of Rawalpindi city and the cantonment were greater than could be provided within the district. Consequently, exports were 'small' and imports 'very large.' The market was large, but it catered to local needs and was not a centre of commerce. Therefore, 'Every kind of agricultural produce is in demand in Rawalpindi—

wood, fodder, milk, eggs, cattle, sheep and all the multifarious requirements of a large city and a great cantonment are brought in daily by zamindars and find a ready sale.'[73]

A cantonment was a permanent military camp that inevitably matured into a town. It influenced the surrounding areas. Its needs were those of a city, and it included markets where everyday goods and services could be traded. With the linking of cantonments by road and rail, a network of markets[74] emerged, enabling the Punjab farmer to sell some of his produce within the province. The presence of both a market and a transport system developed together because military stations had to be well-connected. While army needs dictated the expansion of these institutions,[75] they were not established to benefit the general populace of the province. The combination of a large market and a good system of transport and communications in a relatively prospering agricultural province could only have one outcome: Punjab's farmers did actually benefit hugely from the military importance of the province. As with the vast numbers recruited for the army from Punjab, this development of an infrastructure suggests the multiplier effects of military expenditure.

Strategic Considerations and Agricultural Growth

Military requirements were also connected with the expansion and commercialization of Punjab's agriculture. It is possible to suggest that the evolution of an agricultural boom in the province was promoted by the transport and communications network created by military needs.[76]

Expansion of Irrigation: Military Men and Canal Colonization

Perhaps the most significant input in agriculture during colonial rule was the massive extension of irrigation through the construction of the canal colonies. Even this activity had strong links with the army. From the mid-1880s, the province saw rapid economic growth and some major social engineering based on irrigation projects and the colonization of irrigated areas. Vast stretches of uncultivated land in the *doab*s of western and central Punjab were transformed into rich farming tracts. By 1936, the total area sown on only the permanently allotted land in the canal colonies had crossed 16 lakh acres—more than double the entire area irrigated by permanent canals in 1870.[77] The total area under crops in these colonies stood at nearly 32 million acres in 1922.[78] Table 17.4 shows the expansion of irrigation in the province over the decades.

Table 17.4: Acres Irrigated by Canals in Punjab, 1870–1940

Year	By Productive Works	By Unproductive Works	Total
1870	7,41,917	4,64,299	12,06,216
1880	6,98,631	8,67,246	15,65,877
1890	20,33,500	9,82,956	30,16,456
1900	46,42,852	13,57,699	60,00,551
1910	62,70,757	9,56,285	72,27,042
1920	95,05,633	7,68,057	1,02,73,690
1930	1,23,53,426	6,30,834	1,29,84,260
1940	1,27,37,000	8,51,000	1,35,88,000

Source: *Punjab Irrigation Report;*[79] M. M. Islam, *Irrigation, Agriculture and the Raj: Punjab,* 1887–1947, New Delhi: Manohar, 1997, Table C, p. 155 for 1940.

Notes: 1. 'Permanent' canals were called 'major' canals from 1887, and 'productive' from 1921 while 'inundation' canals changed to 'minor' and 'unproductive'.

2. Areas irrigated include both *kharif* and *rabi* harvests.

3. Figure for 'permanent' canals in 1930 included 7,25,668 acres in Bahawalpur state supplied by the Sutlej Valley Project, excluded in the following figure.

4. '1870' = 1870–71 and so on, in all the following tables.

The construction of canals opened up the tracts of the south-west, where inadequate rainfall and poor alternative irrigation had prevented noteworthy agricultural activity. Nearly six million acres of canal irrigated land here were converted into one of the most prosperous agricultural tracts of the subcontinent.[80] Between 1871–1936, the crop acreage in province had grown by 82 per cent,[81] whereas the per capita output of all crops in Punjab had increased by nearly 45 per cent between 1891 and 1921.[82] By the 1920s, in a 'normal' year the value of crops grown on irrigated land was between Rs. 40 crore and Rs. 50 crore, of which between Rs. 25 crore and Rs. 33 crore was 'entirely due to the canals'[83]

By 1931, Punjab had 99,29,217 acres irrigated by 'government' canals, the largest area in British India, representing 46 per cent of total irrigation by such canals. This was more than two and a half times greater than in Madras, the province second to Punjab in this category, but larger in total area. Punjab also had the highest irrigated area, constituting nearly half the total irrigated area of British India.[84] These figures are remarkably high because the province made up only 9.7 per cent of the total area of British India at this time.[85]

While there is no doubt about the importance of canal irrigation for the province the canals were also a means of strengthening access to resources for favoured classes, as the colonization pattern indicates. The canal colonies were ostensibly set up to ease demographic pressure in the central districts of Punjab by allowing agrarian groups there to move to the newly opened lands, and to set up ideal agricultural communities without tenants, if possible. It was hoped that this measure would aid agricultural improvements and increase productivity. The 'primary objective', however, was the expectation of financial returns from the investments. This was, in turn, based on the political economy of imperial relations between India and Britain, where the colony had to specialize in agricultural production to fuel industrial progress in the metropolis.[86] Imran Ali recommends that the real motivation for canal construction went further.[87] The state was trying to entrench itself in rural society, for land grants earned the loyalty of those so favoured even as it consolidated their status and authority. These people, in turn, were then expected to become vital props of the state. But military needs dictated the pattern of grants in later years, often at the expense of established government policy.

The largest category of grants was to 'peasant grantees', the others being 'yeoman' and 'capitalist' grants.[88] Peasant grantees could only belong to an 'agricultural caste'. Though there were some minor differences in the colonization patterns of the various colonies, the Chenab Colony is a good example of the settlement scheme. Colonized between 1892 and 1905, it was the largest project, in which more than two million acres were finally allotted. Of this, almost 36 per cent of the land went to the Jats alone. Arains received nearly 11 per cent and the Kambohs were granted 3 per cent of the land, while the Rajput share was 3.3 per cent. About 7 per cent of the land was distributed to 'elite castes' such as the Syeds, Qureshis, and Mughals among the Muslims, and the Brahmans among the Hindus. Moreover, all the colonists came from the central Punjab districts that the British associated with the best agriculturists of the province. In the earlier Sidhnai Colony, nearly three-fourths of the land had been allotted to the Jats, while in the Sohag Para Colony the Jat Sikhs alone received 38 per cent of the grants.[89] In no colony was the land designated for 'peasant grantees' allotted to non-landholding or menial castes.

Soldiers were given direct preference in allotments, in addition to a general partiality towards 'agricultural castes'.[90] In the colonies settled before the First World War, soldiers belonging only to these specified groups were granted land. They got about 1,60,000 acres of land in the Jhelum and Chenab colonies. In the Lower Bari Doab Canal, colonized between 1914 and 1924, an initial reservation of 1,03,000 acres had been made for military men. However, the compulsions of World War I led to a substantial increase in this figure for the province offered more land to the Government of India because of the large Punjabi contingent in the army. Finally, the amount allotted was 1,80,000 acres[91] and this went to war veterans instead of pensioners, as in the earlier colonies. Pensioners were not ignored; however, land was given to them from out of lands meant for civilian grantees! With newer colonies, the share of land allotted to military grantees increased. In the Nili Bar Colony, settled after 1926, this category alone received almost half as much land as that allotted to the entire civilian peasantry of Punjab.

The extension of the frontiers of agriculture led to an enormous increase in irrigation, in cultivated area, and in output. The direct benefits of these developments went to those who were privileged with land in the colonies. Production, productivity and profit were affected by the state's paternalistic policies, once again strengthening the hands of recruited peasants. In the words of one retired colonial officer:

> And (in Punjab) colonies were established, colonies in the Roman sense, whole districts or sub-divisions of small farmers, many of whom had served in the Indian army or whose fathers or brothers or sons had been

killed or wounded or had won distinctions. It was a policy that convinced soldiers that this was a good government to serve. It brought soldiers, and particularly Punjabis, together, emphasized their sense of difference from the rest of India, set them apart as friends and servants of the Raj.[92]

Crop Acreage

With canals, a tenfold increase in irrigation between 1870 and 1940 led to a corresponding increase in cultivation, as Table 17.5 shows. Particularly impressive is the third column, showing Punjab's percentage share in the total cropped area of British India. This share begins at expected 10 per cent level (which was the proportion of Punjab both in size and in population to British India). However, the very high investments in Punjab irrigation were not experienced in the same magnitude anywhere else in the subcontinent. Cultivation in the province grew at a faster rate than in the rest of colonial India. This is even more remarkable as Punjab was split up to form the North West Frontier Province in 1901. Thus, the slight fall in percentage share in 1911 was more than made up for in the following decades as canal irrigation spread throughout central and western Punjab.

Table 17.5: Total Acres Cropped and Total Revenue Demand in Punjab, 1871–1936

Year	Total Cultivation	% of British India	Revenue Demand (Rs)	% Increase
1871	1,79,28,140	NA	1,87,64,491	NA
1881	2,21,01,850	NA	1,91,91,755	2.28
1891	2,14,08,657	10.15	2,08,76,476	8.79
1901	2,43,55,227	10.71	2,62,52,892	25.75
1911	2,63,08,442	10.56	3,41,93,709	30.25
1921	3,18,33,537	12.41	4,90,58,563	43.47
1931	3,20,06,677	12.17	4,77,20,468	-2.73
1936	3,26,42,236	12.20	5,34,38,017	11.98

Source: *RAR: Agricultural Statistics of British India, RSCP,*[93] Revenue statistics from (L)rar.[94]

Notes: 1. Statistics for cultivated acreage were not available before 1870–1, whence it began to be included as Statement XXIX in the *RARs.* This was stopped by the 1890s, and the *RSCP* were published from 1901–2 onwards.

The data for the intervening period are from *ASBI.*
2. 'Total cultivation' = total of *kharif* and *rabi* cultivation together.
3. '% of British India' = the proportion of total cultivation in Punjab to a total cultivation in India[95]
4. The figures before 1906 are for 'harvested area', and for 'sown area' from that year on.[96]
5. In 1901, the North West Frontier Province was carved out of Punjab. The total Punjab acreage given for 1901 in *RSCP,* 1901–02 is the figure in Table 17.5; however, the sum total of the areas under various crops in Punjab in the same report adds up to 1,67,87,832 acres, or 7.38 per cent of British India. Therefore, the above figure probably includes undivided Punjab, though no mention is made of it in the said report. The total acreage from 1911 onwards was also equal to the sum of all crops cultivated, implying that these were correct and only included Punjab.
6. 'Revenue demand' was the government's calculation of the total that could be collected—the amount collected included assignments which meant that actual collections were slightly less than the demand.

It must be remembered that behind the development of canal irrigation and the extension of agriculture in Punjab lay one of the most critical colonial imperatives—revenue generation. This was the prime objective that spurred the huge government investment in irrigation.[97] As Table 17.5 shows, the revenue demand of the Government of Punjab increased with the extension of canal irrigation and agricultural expansion, slowly in the nineteenth century and then at a tremendous rate in the twentieth. Even though the hardships of the Depression years forced the state to reduce demand in 1931, Punjab agriculture was quick to bounce back and the government was again able to raise rates. Most of the increase was in the canal colonies, where new cultivation and more secure harvests enabled greater extraction of payment. Revenue collections in the canal-irrigated lands rose from less than 20 per cent of total government collection in 1913 to over 40 per cent in the 1920s. Revenue from the remaining lands stayed stagnant between 25 and 30 per cent in the period.[98]

While Punjab generally and some sections of Punjabis particularly profited, the state had not taken these initiatives for their sole benefit. The infrastructure of transport, communications and markets had grown out of military requirements, and the investment in irrigation was motivated by the state's need to extract more revenue. It was an invaluable coincidence, all the same, that the state's favoured sections, which included army personnel, also profited by these developments.

Acreage Under Cereals and Pulses

Cereals and pulses were together the most important crops in terms of the area cultivated as they made up nearly three-fourths of the total cultivated area in Punjab (cotton and sugarcane are dealt with later.) Table 17.6 shows the cultivation of cereals and pulses while Table 17.7 has Punjab's position in relation to British India.

Cereals and pulses show an increasing trend, particularly from 1901.[99] Punjab was never an important rice-growing region, for the climate and the diet of the locals did not support it. However, with the development of canal irrigation it was possible to cultivate it profitably,[100] and the acreage under it began to increase from 1911. Punjabis were wheat eaters and wheat was the most important crop. Wheat cultivation increased by 75 per cent between 1871 and 1936, underlining the crop's importance. It was 'the great colony crop', too, often making up over half the total cultivated area in the colonies and usually taking up more cultivated area than all the other *kharif* crops together.[101] The average yield of wheat increased by nearly 50 per cent in the irrigated tracts of Lahore and Delhi, as compared to unirrigated wheat.[102] By 1924, 49 per cent of all Punjab wheat acreage was irrigated.[103]

The scope for larger profitability, easier marketing,[104] and surer harvests led to the adoption of new varieties of wheat in the colonies after 1900, often replacing the traditional red-bearded Punjab variety to suit the demand in overseas markets.[105] The agricultural department made particularly vigorous experiments to develop better quality crops of wheat and cotton. By 1925, there were 11,50,050 acres of wheat under 'improved seeds'—8,89,920 acres were planted with Punjab-11 (introduced in 1913), 2,57,990 acres had 8-A (introduced in 1919), and 2,140 acres were under 'other' types. The director of agriculture calculated that the total *additional* income from the sale of these improved varieties over traditional types was nearly Rs. 84 lakh per annum.[106]

The increase in the acreage of wheat went together with the decrease in the cultivation of coarser grains like barley, jowar, and

Table 17.6: Total Area in Acres Under Cereals and Pulses in Punjab, 1871-1936

Year	Rice	Wheat	Barley	Jowar	Bajra	Maize	Gram	M&M	Total
1871	6,60,817	53,66,977	16,58,002	19,25,221	24,80,056	8,82,170	9,03,158	5,12,812	1,55,75,405
1881	8,68,821	65,96,505	16,16,790	23,38,889	28,95,012	13,36,511	16,18,435	4,07,279	1,91,71,678
1891	7,22,511	67,67,893	11,96,345	20,21,522	15,09,967	12,68,899	27,05,708	NA	1,83,04,229
1901	6,78,194	56,52,103	5,78,717	8,51,753	13,46,607	12,09,311	11,86,899	3,76,143	1,27,96,417
1911	5,13,731	97,25,494	13,39,097	5,54,234	11,55,046	9,55,348	40,99,894	2,19,963	1,93,78,585
1921	8,21,185	87,88,992	11,11,950	12,13,704	33,22,587	11,12,169	51,47,160	5,41,827	2,31,35,941
1931	7,99,028	90,79,613	6,29,480	10,13,634	32,32,886	10,04,431	55,46,685	5,37,784	2,28,16,099
1936	10,39,498	93,84,688	7,38,336	9,28,429	28,51,208	10,77.591	49,08,199	4,77,075	2,23,66,877

Source: *RAR, ASBI, PSCR*[107] 'M&M' = mung and mash; 'Total' = total for the cereals and pulses listed above and including 'other cereals' and 'other 'pulses', and is, therefore, not the total of the preceding columns.

Table 17.7: Punjab as Percentage of British India Crop Acreage, 1891-1936

Year	Rice	Wheat	Barley	Jowar	Bajra	Maize	Gram	Total
1891	1.14	33.53	34.43	10.04	14.57	40.19	33.53	NA
1901	0.97	30.38	9.31	3.90	10.20	19.51	12.13	7.23
1911	0.67	38.86	15.88	3.01	8.82	17.09	29.02	9.93
1921	1.03	39.23	15.11	5.01	20.90	17.56	34.19	11.30
1931	0.98	35.86	9.69	4.69	23.19	16.44	34.81	11.13
1936	1.27	37.18	11.30	3.87	24.90	18.10	31.07	10.96

Source: Calculated from figures for British India in ASBI, for the relevant years[108] and Table 17.9.

bajra, particularly after the development of canals.[109] The pattern for barley and jowar vindicates Banerjee's argument that the more profitable wheat and carton crops were substituted for these 'pre-canal staples'.[110] Maize, too, shows a similar trend though the difference in acreage is not as sharp, and there is an increase in acreage in the 1930s. By this time, Punjab was cultivating nearly a fifth of all maize in British India, while maintaining its position as one of the main producers of gram. Gram was popular in the canal colonies because its relatively low requirement of moisture and its regenerative effect on the soil were advantages in addition to its high price.[111]

Punjab was one of the major agricultural producers in British India and canal irrigation enabled it to strengthen this position. For a province that made up about 10 per cent of British India, Punjab cultivated around 11 per cent of total cereals and pulses in the country, having increased its share from 7.23 per cent in 1901. By 1936, Punjab's share of wheat, gram, bajra, and maize cultivation was a significant percentage of British India cultivation. The overall trend is summed up in the assessment for agriculture in Amritsar district:

> The net result [of canal extension] is a gain of over 12.000 acres in the average cropped area [per annum] combined with an improvement in the security and class of crops. Wheat, whether grown singly or mixed with gram, now covers 4,11,350 acres compared with 3,64,418 acres [in 1892]. Barley and pure gram are of much less importance than before, and the insecure pulses formerly grown over 40,000 acres now occupy little more

than 14,000 acres. Cane has fallen from 22,713 to 15,698 acres, but the cotton area has risen from 24,194 acres to 37,227 acres.[112]

Acreage Under Cotton and Sugarcane

Probably the most striking result of canal irrigation was the expansion of cotton cultivation, though sugarcane increased, too. Table 17.8 charts this remarkable growth.

Cotton cultivation epitomizes what the state had hoped for from the canal colonies. Not suited to most of Punjab because of its water requirements,[113] it was grown only in certain parts prior to the massive increase in canal irrigation. The productivity of cotton is said to have increased by 83 per cent in Lahore and by 100 per cent in Shahpur in irrigated tracts.[114] The total cultivated area under cotton rose by a huge 318 per cent between 1871 and 1936, though the major increase came from 1921, coinciding with the expansion of irrigation under permanent canals. Furthermore, Punjab's share of British India cotton cultivation reached nearly a fifth in 1936, starting out from a little over one-twentieth in 1891. What is even more significant is that by 1936 Punjab was producing nearly 35 per cent of the total cotton output of British India (see Tables 17.9 and 17.10), exhibiting the great production from the canal colonies.

Table 17.8: Total Area under Cotton and Sugarcane in Acres in Punjab, 1871-1936

Year	Cotton	% of BI	Sugarcane	% of BI
1871	6,95,108	NA	3.33,657	NA
1881	8,90,0,37	NA	3,77,320	NA
1891	5,00,299	5.65	3,63.976	11.74
1901	8.55.203	8.30	3,56,947	14.42
1911	14,62,500	10.04	2,98,296	12.38
1921	19,57,016	16.78	3,73,371	12.80
1931	21.59.722	14.91	4,74,655	16.52
1936	29,09,152	18.94	5,54,348	12.94

Source: *RAR*; *ASBI*; *PSCR*, Percentages calculated from British India figures in *ASBI*, for the relevant years. Details as in Tables 17.5 and 17.6. '% of BI' = cultivation in Punjab as a percentage of the total cultivated acreage in British India.

Wheat and cotton got the most particular attention from the Botanical Section of the Agricultural Department. The need to grow long-stapled American cotton had been frustrated by the local inability to adapt a strain that would grow in Punjab conditions until the second decade of the twentieth century.[115] However, in 1913, the Agricultural Department successfully introduced the 4-F variety at Lyallpur and 'by 1919 it was growing on half a million acres'. The market orientation of Punjab cultivators was evident as 'the Department could not supply the seeds fast enough to meet the demand, although *higher prices* than those of local seeds were charged'. By 1921, 285-F, 'another Lyallpur selection of American cotton'—hardier, more drought-resistant and higher yielding than 4-F—had been introduced. It was followed by 289-F, a 'still heavier cropper than either 4-F or 285-F'. Further improved varieties were being evolved, and the department had also introduced some 'greatly improved' *desi* (local) cottons. By 1924, over 10 lakh acres were under improved cottons.[116] The greatest impact was in the canal colonies, where acreage under American cotton grew from a few hundred acres in 1910 to 8,01,000 acres in 1930 and to 14,32,000 acres in 1940.[117]

Cotton had an additional effect on the local economy as ginning and pressing factories were established in the colonies. There were about 350 ginning factories by 1925. It was noted that there was no need for the government to encourage their establishment because the factories 'seem to spring up immediately, wherever they are wanted', attesting to the entrepreneurial spirit of the colonists.[118] American cottons could not be ginned by hand and this provided the stimulus in the growth of these factories. All of this ginned and baled cotton was exported to Bombay and Karachi; spinning was not possible in Punjab because of its dry climate.[119]

Canal irrigation, the development of improved varieties, the expanding facilities for marketing, wider networks of communications and transport, and the enterprising spirit of the canal grantees—all these led to a substantial growth of cotton cultivation and aided the development of some secondary sectors.

The Indian Sugar Committee of 1920 admitted that Punjab was outside the world's 'cane producing zone'. The cultivation fluctuated, as did the percentage share of Punjab, reaching a high of 16.52 per cent in 1931. Thereafter, the acreage cultivated rose in real terms, though it fell as a share of total sugarcane cultivation in British India in 1936. The figures for yield of sugarcane (Table 17.9), however, show that more was produced in each recorded year after 1911, perhaps indicating that profits from the crop were inducing more of it to be grown for sale than merely for utilization by the producer's family, and also that the yield per acre of the crop had increased.[120]

Sugarcane was not a profitable crop in some districts if the labour involved was paid at market rates. Under the prevailing conditions of the 1920s and 1930s it was 'unable to compete with such crops as cotton, wheat, *toria*, &c., grown in the canal colonies and in many other parts of the Province'.[121] Therefore, the fluctuations in cane cropping may be linked to the expectations of profit from cane (with labour rates worked into it).

Agricultural Production

The figures for the yield of crops exhibit the same trend as reflected in the data on cultivated acreage, as Tables 17.9 and 17.10 show Wheat, once again, establishes itself in premier position among the crops grown in Punjab. Though cultivated acres under wheat fluctuated as a share of British India output, the production of wheat increased by nearly 140 per cent between 1871 and 1936, which left the province with a share of 43 per cent of the total yield. This showed that the productivity of the crop was increasing and higher yield per acre was witnessed over the decade.[122] In terms of yield per acre in tons, Punjab began to perform better than British India from 1921, and by 1941 its yield per acre was 0.38 tons compared to 0.28 in India.[123]

Punjab's share of rice was so insignificant that production figures for the crop were not reported. The output of barley, jowar, and bajra and their shares of British India production echo the same trend as seen from the acres under cultivation for these crops, as do the statistics for maize and gram. The importance of cotton as a cash crop in Punjab and the growing significance of the province as a cotton producer are reflected in the production figures of the crop. The yield of cotton shows a tenfold increase in 45 years, and over a fivefold increase between 1921 and 1936.

Table 17.9: Yield of Selected Crops in Punjab, 1891–1936

Year	Wheat	Cotton	Sugarcane	Barley	Jowar	Bajra	Maize	Gram
1891	14,19,765	1,18,195	NA	NA	NA	NA	NA	NA
1901	20,05,611	2,20,255	2,39,105	NA	NA	NA	NA	NA
1911	38,09,000	2,41,000	1,61,200	3,82,000	68,000	97,000	3,66,000	11,26,000
1921	41,85,000	2,96,000	2,78,000	2,97,000	1,71,000	3,91,000	3,80,000	11,43,000
1931	27,60,000	5,38,000	3,68,000	1,61,000	96,000	4,60,000	3,80,000	10,80,000
1936	33,95,000	14,56,000	4,65,000	2,06,000	1,23,000	3,61,000	3,92,000	9,53,000

Source: *Area and Yield of Certain Principal Crops in India.*[124] All figures are in tons except cotton which is in 'bales of 400 Ibs.' North West Frontier Province excluded after 1906.

Table 17.10: Output of Selected Punjab Crops as Percentages of British India, 1891–1936

Year	Wheat	Cotton	Sugarcane	Barley	Jowar	Bajra	Maize	Gram
1891	23.30	6.96	NA	NA	NA	NA	NA	NA
1901	32.93	8.02	11.82	NA	NA	NA	NA	NA
1911	38.40	7.33	6.58	39.18	2.76	8.38	19.33	25.85
1921	42.57	6.60	10.63	9.49	2.64	14.81	15,46	26.23
1931	38.03	22.15	9.71	6.74	2.12	20.58	16.79	28.92
1936	43.20	34.78	7.60	8.91	2.67	18.89	21.35	24.97

Source: Calculated from *Area and Yield of Certain Principal Crops in India* (details as in Table 17.9).

The yield of sugarcane is also an increasing one—rising by nearly 95 per cent between 1901 and 1936—though the upward trend is particularly strong from 1921. Punjab was never one of the major sugar producing regions of India and the percentages of Punjab sugar yield prove just that. Yet, a look at the area under the crop (which fluctuated) and its output (rising continuously) shows that its productivity had risen in this period.

The Commercialization of Punjab Agriculture

The cropping pattern in Punjab changed over the last decades of the nineteenth century and the province began to grow crops based on their relative profitability in markets far and wide, rather than on the more immediate needs of personal consumption for subsistence. The process was most visible in the canal colonies, where the focus on cash crops led to a decline in per capita production of foodgrains in the province.[125] Table 17.11 shows the cropping pattern over the decades.

Wheat, cotton, and fodder[126] crops were particularly favoured, though sugarcane and tobacco too were produced for the prices they fetched. The most important factor in selecting the crop mix in the canal colonies was the price. As the *Settlement Report* of the Jhang and Gujera branches noted, 'the whole system of agriculture is essentially commercial, for the bulk of the produce being exportable everything depends on *Mandi* prices, and their fluctuations are watched with intense interest.'[127]

This is clearly reflected in the fall in the percentage of cultivated acres under cereals and pulses over the period covered, as cultivation of wheat and cotton increased. The share of total cultivation under all cereals and pulses fell from 86.88 per cent of total cultivation in the province in 1871 to 68.52 per cent by 1936. However, if we take wheat out of the equation (since it increasingly began to be grown for its commercial value from the mid-1880s), the percentage share of the remaining cereals and pulses of the total cultivation in Punjab fell from 55.82 per cent to 39.77 per cent over the same period. Rice cultivation began to show an increasing trend, even though it fluctuated. There was a sharp and continued increase after 1911 as cultivation rose by 5,25,767 acres between 1911 and 1936,[128] as a result of profitable cultivation through assured water supply

Table 17.11: Percentage Share of Selected Crops of Total Crop Acreage in Punjab, 1891–1936

	1891	1901	1911	1921	1931	1936
Rice	3.37	4.04	1.95	2.58	2.50	3.18
Wheat	31.61	33.66	36.97	27.61	28.40	28.75
Barley	5.58	3.45	5.09	3.49	1.97	2.26
Jowar	9.44	5.07	2.11	3.81	3.12	2.84
Bajra	7.05	8.02	4.39	10.43	10.10	8.73
Maize	5.93	7.20	3.63	0.35	3.12	3.30
Other cereals	9.86	1.00	0.04	0.68	0.56	0.47
Gram	12.64	7.07	15.58	16.17	17.33	15.04
Mung & mash	-	2.24	0.83	1.70	1.68	1.46
Other pulses	-	4.25	2.64	2.61	2.43	2.41
Total cereals and pulses	85.49	76.22	73.66	72.68	71.28	68.52
Oilseeds	4.12	3.69	6.08	5.23	4.20	3.49
Sugarcane	1.70	2.12	1.13	1.17	1.48	1.70
Cotton	2.34	5.09	5.56	6.15	6.75	8.91
Fodder	3.40	9.25	11.01	12.86	13.90	15.28

Source: As in Table 17.6. The above only includes crops which made up at least one per cent of total cultivation. 'Other cereals' in 1891 includes 'other foodgrains and pulses.'

in the canal colonies. Moreover, as seen before, both the acreage and share of total cultivation under the coarser cereals—barley, jowar, maize—declined over the period 1891-36. Gram fetched a high price and was a useful crop in the canal colonies as it helped the agricultural cycle, and its growing share of cultivation can be attributed to both these reasons. There was, however, a fall in the share of cultivation under mung and mash and other pulses.

The fall in share of foodgrains was mirrored in the increase under cotton, sugarcane and fodder crops. Cultivation under fodder crops rose hugely from 7,27,701 acres to 49,89,350 acres between 1891 and 1936,[129] and its share rose correspondingly quickly. Once again, increased and assured irrigation in the canal colonies had made it a suitable crop, and its high demand was also aided by the livestock requirements in the colonies, where individual grantees, military farms, horse runs and military dairies, and government cattle-breeding farms all had a growing need for fodder.[130]

The commercialization of agriculture, as indicated by production for the market, was noticed in other parts of India too, at different times.[131] The Punjab tiller was not forced to grow particular crops either by large landlords[132] or by creditors. [133] Most significantly, commercialization did not lead to 'de-peasantization' because colonists made a conscious choice, based on prices, to cultivate crops.[134] Furthermore, 'this province became one of the most market-oriented in the whole of Asia' because wheat, a food crop, was cultivated on profit based principles, too.[135] In short, commercialization improved the position of the zamindar cultivators of the province, with military groups witnessing a disproportionately greater gain in the canal colonies because of the preferential colonization policy.

Table 17.12: Profitability of Improved Cottons in Punjab, 1924

Type of Cotton	Out-turn mds/acre	Rate Rs./mds	Gross Income (Rs./acre)	Extra Income (Rs./ acre) Over Unselected Desi	Acreage	Total Profit (acres × extra income)
Unselected *desis*	6.0	15	90	-	-	-
Selected *desis*	7.0	16	112	22	67,400	14,82,800
4-F American	7.5	17	127	37	9,47,950	3,50,74,150
285-F and 289-F	7.5	18	135	45	16,370	7,36,650
Total gross profit						3,72,93,600

Source: Calculated from Milne's Evidence, p. 183.

Table 17.12 illustrates this in the case of improved cottons and reveals the profits made over unselected *desi* varieties (and not for all cotton produced) in the province in the year. Thus, the amount, nearly Rs. 3.75 crore, is the extra profit Punjab cultivators made by planting improved cottons. This is not the total profit made from the entire cotton cultivated. In the words of the director of agriculture: 'These American cottons have entirely altered the standard of quality of cotton produced by the Punjab, and have raised the price of land in the Province. They also put more money into the pockets of farmers in one year than has been spent on the Punjab Agricultural Department since it started.'

An idea of the amount of increase in agricultural earnings can be had from the following all-India figures. The price per tonne of wheat rose from Rs. 50 in 1875 to Rs. 76 in 1938 to Rs. 323 in 1946; that of cotton increased from Rs. 328 to Rs. 493 to Rs. 1,132, respectively; gram prices rose from Rs. 39 to Rs. 83 to Rs. 276, respectively; and sugarcane prices rose from Rs. 97 to Rs. 151 to Rs. 144, respectively. Consequently, the value per acre of wheat jumped from Rs. 15.95 in 1875 to Rs. 103.04 in 1946; that of cotton grew more marginally from Rs. 15.30 to Rs. 35.09; gram values increased from Rs. 9.32 to Rs. 65.96; and sugarcane rose from Rs. 125.60 to Rs. 575 per acre. [136]

The relative profitability of crops affected the respective shares of their cultivation. It was noticed that more cotton was grown in preference to wheat in the 'old established colonies'. It was forecast that 'there will probably be the same tendency in the new canals, but it all depends upon what the price of cotton is going to be and the price of wheat. The areas vary according to the price we find.'[137] Similarly, a fall in the price of cotton led to an 11 per cent increase in the cultivation of sugarcane in 1927 and 1928, and an increase of 11.5 per cent in 1932.[138]

The profit incentive worked even in selecting between types of cotton. The demand for improved *desi* varieties was lower in the canal colonies compared to 'the more profitable American cottons available', even though *desi* varieties were grown in the poorer canal lands where they were 'more profitable than Americans'.[139] Moreover, the grant of 7,500 acres of land in the Lower Bari Doab Canal to the British Cotton Growing Association was to facilitate the export of improved varieties to the Lancashire mills.[140] Hurdles to marketing the expanding output were removed when the Agricultural Department began auctioning produce from 1915, assuring a premium to cotton growers.[141]

Wheat cultivation and marketing, too, were determined by its prices. India was the fifth largest wheat producer in the world before World War I. According to a Punjab financial commissioner, the amount of Punjab wheat available in India depended on the prices in Liverpool; if local prices were high enough to offer profits superior to those obtained by shipping it to England, then larger quantities would be sold in Indian markets.[142] The government noticed that 'if stocks are low and prices in India sufficiently high, the wheat export may be checked, but if prices are sufficiently high in Europe to make the export of wheat profitable, it cannot be safely predicted that even low stocks would not be exported.'[143] The average value of exported wheat had increased from Rs. 168 lakh between 1886–95 to Rs. 880 lakh between 1912–4.[144]

The efforts of the Agricultural Department helped in the process of commercialization and in ensuring that the benefits were going to Punjab farmers. The introduction of 8-A wheat in 1919 'marked a very decided improvement in that cereal' and even millers in Britain wanted 'as much 8-A wheat as we could send.'[145] 4-F cotton seeds cost more than local cotton seeds but the great demand for the costlier variety 'was simply because farmers were getting larger profits by growing it than by growing their unselected *deshi* cottons.'[146]

The general trend was 'towards more intensive cultivation, and also a tendency to change over from subsistence to cash crops.' In Lahore, for example, between the settlement operations of 1912–6 and 1935–9, the total matured area under sugarcane grew from 0.7 per cent to 1.7 per cent, of cotton from 9.1 per cent to 13.3 per cent, of oilseeds from 4.7 per cent to 6.9 per cent; but wheat fell from 39.7 per cent to 28.7 per cent.[147]

Infrastructure and the Commercialization of Punjab Agriculture

Apart from the main business of supplying water and colonizing land on hitherto uncultivated tracts, the major benefit of canal colonies in aiding the commercialization of Punjab agriculture was providing a quick means of communication through telegraphy. The headworks of each canal had a telegraph system and this was used to disseminate information on prices. Bombay cotton prices were telegraphed to the main cotton markets in the canal colonies by the Agricultural Department from 1917, and the government bore all costs connected with this (about Rs. 20 per month per market).[148] The government was involved in non-colony areas too, and telegrams giving cotton prices in Bombay were posted in the 'more important cotton markets in the Punjab' three times a week from November to February.[149] Though cotton is the only instance of direct evidence of this nature, it is possible that it happened for wheat and other crops whose production and marketing were similarly dependent on prices external to Punjab.

With the emergence of the province as a major agricultural region of British India—and with the aim of maximizing production and marketing to optimize revenue collection—the government began to address these issues more directly. The extension of railway lines was seen to have the advantage of attracting all the marketable produce of the surrounding locality. The opening of the Lahore–Ajnala–Gurdaspur railway extension was lauded as it would redress the marketing of the produce of this fertile area, which had so far suffered because of 'the difficulty of putting it on the [railway]'. Similarly, with the possibility of canal construction in Shahpur and Gujarat districts, the railways were urged to ensure that lack of rail lines did not prevent marketing of surplus.[150] The new railway projects attempted to have the cultivators, at least in the plains, within 12 miles of their market town. 'Within this radius he should, with reasonably good roads, be able to market direct.' Moreover, road building was to be in conjunction with railway expansion to enable easier access to the railways.[151]

The Grand Trunk Road had aided commercial ventures from its earliest days.[152] The government bullock train went all the way to Lahore, carting 'a large amount of private goods and a considerable number of passengers' as well as its usual transport of government stores. 'Private companies' that, till 1856, had not taken their carriages beyond Karnal, now conducted business inside Punjab. As Sarkar noted, 'Incidentally a boon to commerce, this grand road-way had been constructed chiefly with the Military objective of linking together all the important military stations of the Punjab.'

The implication is that road and rail development stimulated economic activity. Dewey states that 'strategic railways' for military needs had a greater presence in Punjab than in any other part of colonial India, and that the economic effects of this promoted trade in these areas.[153]The records allow some measure of this. The section on the 'coaching traffic' of the North-Western Railway's balance sheet for 1910 had separate entries for 'ordinary passengers'

(Rs. 1,28,88,705), and 'military passengers' (Rs. 3,09,286), 'passengers luggage' (Rs. 2,54,085) and 'military baggage' (Rs. 30,204), and 'ordinary carriages, horses and dogs' (Rs. 1,38,579) and 'military carriages, horses and dogs' (Rs. 30,890). Similarly, the accounts for 'goods traffic' carried 'merchandise, general' (Rs. 2,33,00,859), 'military stores' (Rs. 1,34,458), 'revenue stores' (Rs. 5,50,262), 'coal for the public' (Rs. 4,01,480), 'coal for the railway' (Rs. 12,36,096), 'livestock, public' (Rs. 1,44,710) and 'military livestock' (Rs. 4,980).[154] This is not a complete list of the accounts, but a pointer to the relatively high amount of the civilian activity of the railways.

The railways enabled all the major agricultural tracts of the province to become easily accessible to Karachi (in Sindh and the nearest port to Punjab).[155] Similarly, the line from Rewari to Ferozepore directly connected Punjab to Bombay.[156] The opening up of the railway link to Karachi removed one of the main hurdles to export of Punjab crops outside India as it was the port closest to the landlocked province. However, the volume of traffic from Punjab in the 'record export year' of 1917 brought out the 'extreme difficulty' of handling such heavy export traffic with the existing capacity on the railways. It was, therefore, recommended that future reconstruction 'must take into consideration not only the volume of traffic already reached, but the further increase of traffic due to extension of irrigation in the Punjab and Sind. . .'.[157] Railway and canal extension would become complementary.[158] Railways and roads, in particular, had an important part in Punjab's external agricultural trade. 'Every mile of railway and road newly opened brings some fresh village within a comparatively easy access to these [overseas] markets and enables it to enjoy to the full the effect of a short harvest in the Argentine or Canada.'[159]

Another advantage that the vast transport network, particularly the railways, provided was the equalization of prices across the province. As early as 1892, it was noted that the difference between harvest prices obtained by zamindars in the villages of Amritsar district and the market prices in the city was 'steadily decreasing.'[160] In fact, 'Those [villages] lying near the railway can almost always, if they choose, command a price for their wheat which is only 5 per cent, lower than that ruling in the city.'[161] The price of wheat in the three important markets of Delhi, Multan, and Peshawar in 1861was Rs. 8, 16.50 and Rs. 29.25 per *seer*, respectively, but by 1901 the difference was negligible in comparison at Rs. 13.31, 14.35 and Rs. 15.12 per *seer*, respectively.[162]

The extension of the railway system spurred the growth of some agro-industries too. The opening of the Delhi–Ambala–Kalka railway in 1892 and the extension of the Southern Punjab Railway to Kaithal in 1899 provided a considerable stimulus to trade which enabled cotton ginning factories to come up at Samlkha, Panipat, Karnal, and at Kaithal near the railway stations. This was only to increase with the extension of the railways to Jind which 'opened up' a new part of Karnal district.[163] The railways gained too. It was thought that 'there is not a single one of the feeder line projects which have been carried out in recent years in the Canal Colonies and the Central Punjab, which is not working at a considerable profit.'[164] Between 1908 and 1924, the export of wheat alone by rail had increased by 213 per cent, from 6 lakh tones to 16.8 lakh tonnes.[165]

Cantonments have not been considered as yet. These became permanent markets in which a large number of troops and military animals were garrisoned.[166] Their requirements of food, fodder, and provisions would also have helped in absorbing Punjab's agricultural produce. It is not possible to give figures of demand and consumption in cantonments, but the fact that Punjab had the largest concentration of cantonments in British India suggests that the very presence of these military camps would only have aided the overall trends in provincial agriculture. Calvert sums it up succinctly: 'The expansion of agriculture, the construction of great works of irrigation, the introduction of railways and of metalled roads were all interdependent; railways and canals were built by government with the aid of borrowed capital, and the roads from the increasing revenue which the resultant expansion of cultivation brought in.'[167] In addition, there was the incalculable benefit of the goodwill of a prospering, recruited peasantry.

In brief, military expenditure on frontier defence resulted in the development of an infrastructure that sustained the huge expansion of agricultural production in Punjab. The province had come a long way from the early years of British rule, when surplus produce was wasted because of a lack of adequate marketing facilities.[168]

The extension of irrigation and the development of marketing and communication facilities remedied these defects and the change was seen to be dramatic:

> People nowadays find it difficult to understand the state of Punjab before the present great system of communications was created. There was little trade between village and town, little enough between neighbouring villages, and none of great value between places far apart. Each place consumed what it produced and could find no use for any surplus; a cultivator one year had little to sell and the next could not get a purchaser for his bumper crops. There was no outlet for any quantity above what the immediate locality wanted and so there was nothing to gain from producing it; in short, the cultivation of wheat was restricted by the lack of an export market, and it will be restricted again if the export market is put beyond the reach of the producer.[169]

From the last decades of the nineteenth century, production was not merely for local and personal consumption but was sent wherever the best prices were available, in India or overseas. This profit motive also altered the cropping pattern as traditional cereals were substituted by wheat and other cash crops. Prices and relative profitability played a crucial role in the selection of crops, and to this extent the commercialization of Punjab agriculture was neither 'forced' nor 'artificial'.[170] The agriculturists from central Punjab established on the colonies responded quickly to the market and gained most out of it, both in their home districts and as canal grantees. A disproportionate benefit of agricultural growth was going to particular sections of Punjabis—the recruited 'agricultural tribes'. Some of this they achieved by their own skill and initiative, but important privileges were provided by the state. Moreover, the province became extremely important for revenue collection, and profitability for both the Punjab zamindar and for the Punjab government was ensured. State, economy, and certain sections of Punjab society were closely linked to the great agricultural boom. The seeds were sown, literally and metaphorically, for an interaction of mutual benefit between state and society. Rural Punjab responded to the state's measures via its loyalism.

NOTES

1. An extended version of some sections of this chapter was earlier published as 'Military Imperatives and the Expansion of Agriculture in Colonial Punjab,' *International Journal of Punjab Studies*, vol. 8, no. 2 (2001), pp. 157–86. I am grateful to the editors for allowing its abridged reproduction here.
2. The province was created to bring 'the management of political relations with the trans-frontier tribes' under the 'direct control' of the Government of India. *PAR, 1911–2*, p. 26.
3. *PAR, 1849–51*, p. 35.
4. *PAR, 1851–3*, p. 29.
5. *PAR, 1849–51*, p. 48.
6. *PAR, 1854–6*, p. 62.
7. Ibid., p. 65.
8. *PAR, 1851-53*, pp. 148–9.
9. *PAR, 1854–56*, p. 81.
10. Ibid., pp. 62–3.
11. Details are given in the following section. It is mentioned here to show that military roads, too, were made by the civil government and should be included in the military expenditure of the Public Works Department, highlighting the full significance of this department's military activity.
12. *PAR, 1849–51*, pp. 128–30.
13. *PAR, 1867–68*, p. 54.
14. K.M. Sarkar, *The Grand Trunk Road in the Punjab, 1849–86*, New Delhi: Nirmal Publishers, reprint 1986, p. x; *PAR*, 1849–51, p. 128.
15. *PAR, 1849–51*, p. 128. Emphasis in original.
16. 'Administration Report, 1852–53 [*sic*], quoted in Sarkar, *Grand Trunk Road*, pp.11–12. Most likely, *PAR, 1851–3*.
17. Paragraph based on Sarkar, *Grand Trunk Road*, pp. 15–22.
18. There appear to be some discrepancies in the mileage, as later years sometimes show a lower figure. One of the explanations for this in *RERPI*, vol. III was, 'The records previous to 1901 were destroyed, hence the discrepancy in mileage cannot be explained' (Note (c) on p. 474). At other times, incorrect classification, usually of unmetalled as metalled, led to correction once the error was noticed, and it was appropriately updated in the next year. However, the broad trend of the figures and the argument based on them are not affected.
19. Sarkar, *Grand Trunk Road*, pp. 25–6.
20. Lahore to Ludhiana was connected by a 'double line': one via Ferozepore (military needs dominated) and the other through Amritsar and Jullundur (for commercial reasons). Sarkar, *Grand Trunk Road*, p. 25.
21. Himadari Banerjee, *Agrarian Society of the Punjab, 1849–1900*, New Delhi: Manohar, 1982, p. 70.

22. Calculated from *RERPI*, pp. 475, 477.
23. *Notes on Mechanical Transport*, 1917, p. 2.
24. *Administration Report of Military Works Services for the Year of 1919–20*, Appendix III, hereafter, *ARMWS*.
25. *RERPI*, vol. III, pp. 475–6. Most of the canal colonies were also built in the western half of the province.
26. Paragraph based on Montagu (Advisor on Mechanical Transport Services in India) to Quarter Master General in India, 10 April 1918. *Report on Roads*, p. 1.
27. Ibid., pp. 7–8.
28. *PAR*, 1854–6, pp. 51–2.
29. From 1900, the opening or extension of any railway line in Punjab had to be directly brought to the notice of the General Officer Commanding the district in which the work was being undertaken by the staff officer on the spot; the latter was not to wait for information by railway authorities. *Punjab Command Orders, 1990*, Command Order 187, p. 67.
30. *PAR, 1868–9*, p. 93.
31. *PAR, 1870–71*, p. 80.
32. H. Calvert, *The Wealth and Welfare of the Punjab*, Lahore: The Civil and Military Gazette Ltd., 2nd edn, 1936, p. 108.
33. Dewey, 'Military Expenditure', p. 139.
34. Roberts offered a contrary strategy to a 1885 Defence Committee on frontier matters: 'the majority of the members laid greater stress on the necessity for constructing numerous fortifications, than upon lines of communication, which I conceived to be of infinitely greater importance, as bringing all the strategical points on the frontier into direct communication with the railway system of India.' Roberts, *Forty-one Years*, vol. II, pp. 407–8.
35. Roberts to Foreign Secretary, India, 4 April 1880, *MP*, p. 183.
36. *History of Indian Railways—Constructed and in Progress Corrected up to 31st March, 1925*, pp. 146–7. Hereafter, *History of Indian Railways, 1925*.
37. Paragraph based on *Report of a Committee on Special Military Expenditure*, pp. xxix–xxxiii.
38. *MP*, p. xviii.
39. Banerjee, *Agrarian Society*, p. 70.
40. Roberts, *Forty-one Years*, vol. II p. 408.
41. *RERPI*, III, pp. 474–7.
42. GoI, Railway, Statistics, B, August 1911, no. 81/1, p. 1.
43. Ibid., pp. 1, 4.
44. Only the Nowshera–Durgai Line made a profit (of Rs. 17,46) in the second half of 1910. The Kohat–Thal Line had 'negative net earnings' of Rs. 69,160; the Pishin Section ran at a loss of Rs. 55.609; and the Sind

Sagar and constituent sections lost Rs. 18,255. These figures are only for the second half of the financial year 1910.

45. Dewey, 'Military Expenditure', p. 138.
46. Paragraph based on *History of Indian Railways,* 1925, pp. 145–7.
47. Calvert, *Wealth and Welfare,* p. 109.
48. *RERPI,* III, pp. 464–5.
49. The following is the mileage of the other railway system, which had more than 3.000 'open' miles: Bombay, Baroda and Central India—3,944; Great Indian Peninsula—3,725; Bengal-Nagpur—3.417; Madras and Southern Maharatta—3,229. *SABI, 1931–2,* Table No. 196, pp. 548–53. Some of these systems operated across larger geographical areas than the North Western Railway.
50. Secretary, PWD (B&R), GoP to Secretary, Railway Board, 14 February 1916. GoI, Railway, Statistics, B, April 1919, no. 187, p. 16/1–2.
51. Paragraph based on *PAR, 1854–6.* pp. 69–70.
52. '. . . it is indeed hard to describe *how useful* the Telegraph has proved to the Punjab Administration during the crisis of 1857. It may be truly said that, for months, the Military and Political correspondence of the Punjab Government was carried on by Telegraphs'. *PAR, 1856–8,* p. 28. Emphasis in original. Also, S. S. Thorburn, *The Punjab in Peace and War,* London and Edinburgh: William Blackwood & Son, 1904, pp. 186–7. Hereafter, *PPW.*
53. *PAR,* 1858–9, p. 390.
54. *Administration & Report of the Indian Telegraph Department for 1877–78,* para 60, Hereafter *ARITD.*
55. *ARITD, 1878–9,* pp. 11–4.
56. *ARITD, 1894–5,* p. 28.
57. In 1880–1, there were 808.87 miles of telegraph along roads and 238.2 miles along ralways in Punjab. Calculated from *ARITD, 1880-81,* Appendix I.
58. Paragraph based on Sarkar, *Grand Trunk Road,* pp. 48–9.
59. From *Annual Report on the Operations of the Post Office in India, for the year 1870–1,* Appendix I. Hereafter *JPOR* and *Indian Posts and Telegraph Department, Annual Report for the year 1931–2,* Appendix III(a), part I. Hereafter *IP&TDR.*
60. *IPOR, 1901–2.* Appendix I. A Punjab letter box served 39 square miles and 4,935, people whereas the Indian figures were 37 square miles and 6,386 persons.
61. *IP&TDR,* 1931-2, Appendix III(a), part II.
62. Calvert, *Wealth and Welfare,* p. 121.
63. Commissioner, Multan Division to Additional Secretary, Punjab, 27 June 1916, GoP, Commerce and Industry, A, August 1916. nos 34–5.
64. See the last section of this chapter.

65. *CRCR*, Appendix I, Annexure II, para 1.
66. *CRCR*, para 2.
67. *CRCR*, Appendix I. Annexure II, para 3.
68. *ARMS, 1919–20*, p. 9.
69. Paragraph based on Dewey, *Military Expenditure*, pp. 123–5.
70. 'The cantonment is the largest and most important in the Punjab, and perhaps in India' (*Rawalpindi DG, 1907*, p. 228).
71. Places 'dominated by cantonments' were Rawalpindi, Ambala, Ferozepore, Nowshera (Peshawar), Abbottabad (Hazara), Risalpur (Peshawar), Bannu, and Campbellpur (Attock). Districts in the NWFP are in brackets. Those 'affected by cantonments' were Lahore, Jullundur, Peshawar, Delhi, Sialkot, Kohat, Multan, Jhelum, Mardan, and Dera Ismail Khan. Cantonments in the hills were Dagshai, Kasaui, Jurogh, and Subathu in the Simla Hills; Bakloh and Balun (Gurdaspur); Dharamshala (Kangra); Cherat (Peshawar); and Murree (Rawalpindi). Districts in brackets.
72. Paragraph based on Dewey, *Military Expenditure*, pp. 130–1.
73. Paragraph based on *Rawalpindi DG, 1907*, p. 173.
74. The population of a selection of the cantonments (and not the cities) in 1921 was as follows: Rawalpindi—46,000; Ambala—48,000; Ferozepore—25,000; Nowshera—17,000; Lahore—25,000; Peshawar—25,000; Jullundur—12,000; Sialkot—15,000; Multan—12,000. From Dewey, *Military Expenditure*, p. 124.
75. 'It may be truly affirmed that, at the rainy season of that year [1857], if there had not been this good [Grand Trunk] road, if the line had been in the same condition as it was five years ago, the vast amounts of material and munitions of war could not have reached the scenes of action; and that, without this road, it might hardly have been possible to take Delhi, at least till the autumn of 1857. From this case we learn the paramount necessity of improving our means of military communications' *PAR, 1856–8*, p. 7.
76. Imran Ali, in specific reference to the canal colonies, questions how the Punjab economy could have 'experienced significant growth and yet have remained backward, or even have acquired through the very process of growth further structural resistances to change'. According to him, the political, military and revenue compulsions of the colonial state, and the uses that colony land were put to, lay behind this contradiction. See Imran Ali, *The Punjab Under Imperialism, 1885–1947*, Princeton: Princeton University Press, 1988, pp. vii, 237–44. The present book is not concerned with the long-term impact of colonial rule on Punjab's economy, but rather on the more immediate effects of it on recruited groups and the consequent perception among them that the state was beneficent, and with how military considerations affected Punjab. The

recruited peasantry benefited from the agricultural expansion, were particularly favoured in canal colonization, and this was another tangible reason for their support of the government.

77. 16,19,589 acres were sown on permanently allotted land in the canal colonies in 1936–7 while the total irrigation from all permanent canals in 1870 was 7,41,917 acres. *Annual Report on the Punjab Colonies, for the year ending 30th September 1937*, p. 30, hereafter *ARPC, 1937; Revenue Report of the Irrigation Department, Punjab, for the year 1877–78*, p. 2; hereafter *PIR, 1877-78* (Punjab Irrigation Report).
78. H. K. Trevaskis, *The Punjab of To-day*, Lahore: Civil and Military Gazette Press, 1931, p. 433.
79. *PIR, 1877–78*; *PIR*, 1881–82.
80. *Talbor, Punjab*, p. 39.
81. The total crop acreage in 1871 was 1,79,28,140 and had shot up to 3,26.43,277 in 1936 (*Report on the Revenue Administration of the Punjab and its Dependencies for 1871–72*) Statement no. xxix; hereafter *RAR; Report on the Seasons and Crops of the Punjab for the Agricultural year ending* 30th *June 1937*, Statement III; hereafter *RSCP*).
82. Talbot, *Punjab*, p. 39.
83. Calvert, *Wealth and Welfare*, p. 126.
84. The total irrigated acreage was 1.42.67,056 in Punjab and 2.87,28,580 in British India, *SABI, 1931–32*, Table No. 164, p. 467.
85. Calculated from ibid., Table 17.1, pp. 2–3.
86. See Islam, *Irrigation*, pp. 18-9.
87. Paragraph based on Ali, *Punjab*, pp. 13–4.
88. Paragraph based on ibid., pp. 45–7, 49–51.
89. These 'agricultural castes' were synonymous with the 'martial' races' that the army recruited from.
90. Paragraph based on ibid., pp. 32–3, 55, 114.
91. The eventual allocation to veterans in all the colonies, including the above figure, was over 4.2 lakh acres, granted to 6,000 commissioned and non-commissioned officers. Islam, *Irrigation*, p. 143. The accepted standard of allotment was 50 acres for commissioned officers, 25 acres for non-commissioned officers and men (Leigh, *Punjab*, p. 283).
92. Mason, *Matter of Honour*, p. 388.
93 Statement XXIX in *RAR, 1871–72, 1881–82*; *Agricultural Statistics of British India for the years 1891-92 to 1895–96*, Table A-3, 1901, vol. I, Table 3; 1911. vol. 1, Table 3; 1921, Summary Table No. A, and Table IV in 1931, 1936; hereafter, *ASBI*; *RSCP, 1901–2*, Statement II, thereafter Statement III in *RSCP, 1911–12, 1921–22, 1931–32, 1936–37*.
94. Statement I from *RAR*, 1871–72, 1881–82; Statement VIII-A from *LRAR*, 1891–92, Statement I from *LRAR*, 1901–92, and Statement IV from, *LRAR*, 1911–12,1921–22,1931–32, 1936–37.

95. Percentages calculated from figures for British India in *ASBI*, 1891–92 to 1895–96, Table A-3, 1898–99 to 1902-3; vol. I, Table No. 3, 1907–8 to 1911–12; vol. I, Table 3, 1921-22, vol. I, Table A, 1931–32, vol. I, Table IV, 1936–37; vol. I, Table IV, No. 5.
96. The figures are, therefore, not strictly comparable. However, their use in this analysis is very broad as the aim is merely to show the vast expansion of irrigation and cultivation over the decades. Also, the trends described are fully vindicated in Islam's *Irrigation*, where adequate measures have been taken to eradicate this problem for the more complex arguments attempted therein.
97. By 1945, the government had made a net profit of Rs. 128 million over its investments in Punjab irrigation projects. Islam, *Irrigation*, p. 136.
98. Richard C. Fox, *Lions of the Punjab: Culture in the Making*, Berkeley: University of California Press, 1985, p. 56.
99. The fall in 1901 was because of the separation of the North-West Frontier Province from Punjab.
100. Although wheat covered the largest area in the Nahri (canal irrigated) circle of Amritsar *tahsil*, 'rice [was] perhaps as important and as much valued' (*Amritsar AR*, 1892, p. 28). Rice continued to be grown on the same area in 1912, too, but the output had decreased over the previous seven to eight years because of reduction in supply of canal water. (*Amritsar AR*, 1912, p. 19).
101. Ali, *Punjab*, p. 224. Quotation from the *Upper Jhang Branch AR*, 1909 cited in ibid.
102. *RSCP*, 1906–7, Statement V.
103. Evidence of D. Milne, Director of Agriculture, Punjab in *Royal Commission of Agriculture in India*, vol. VIII, *Evidence Taken in the Punjab*, p. 184. Hereafter, Milne's Evidence and *RCAI*, vol. VIII, respectively.
104. Punjab wheat was in demand in Britain too, for it was ideal for baking and arrived on the market when wheat from other countries was usually unavailable, (Banerjee, *Agrarian Society*, p. 51).
105. Ali, *Punjab*, p. 224.
106. Milne's Evidence, p. 184.
107. Statement XXIX from *RAR, 1871–72, 1881–82*; *ASBI, 1891–92* to *1895–96*, Table A-3; *RSCP, 1901–2*, Statement II, thereafter Statement III from *PACR, 1911–12, 1921–22, 1931–32, 1936–37*.
108 *ASBI, 1891–92* to *1895–96*, Table A-3, *1907–8* to *1911–12* Table No. 3, 1921–22, vol. I, Summary Table No. A, *1931–12*, vol. I, Summary Table No. 4, *1936–37*, vol. I, Table IV, No. 5.
109. See Table 17.11.
110. Banerjee, *Agrarian Society*, p. 26.
111. Ali, *Punjab*, p. 229. For example, after 1920, it took up at least 7 per cent of cultivation in the Chenab Colony.

112. Junior Secretary to FCs, Punjab to Revenue Secretary, Punjab, 13 January 1915, p. 1 in *Amritsar SR, 1914*. For a similar trend in the 1930s, see *Lahore SR, 1939*, p. 3. Also see Table 17.11.
113. 'Cotton is produced, but the uncertainty of seasons which prevails in the Punjab will probably prevent its becoming a cotton growing country', *PAR*, 1849–51. p. 7.
114. *RSCP, 1906–7*, statement v.
115. 'In 1907, no official or trader believed that it was possible to grow long staple cottons successfully in the Punjab' as it had been tried 'many times in the past 100 years' but had 'consistently resulted in failures'. Milne's Evidence, p. 180.
116. Paragraph based on Milne's Evidence, pp. 180–2. Emphasis added. Milne further wrote that, 'That rate of spread of a single type (4-F) has no parallel, not even in America—as far as has been discovered.'
117. Ali, *Punjab*, p. 226.
118. Milne's Evidence, p. 213.
119. Paragraph based on Calvert, *Wealth and Welfare*, pp. 138–9.
120. Also see Islam, *Irrigation*, pp. 72–6.
121. Milne's Evidence, p. 185.
122. Punjab's share of wheat cultivation actually fell from 39.23 per cent of British Indian 1921 to 37.18 per cent in 1936. However, the share in output was 42.57 per cent and 43.20 per cent of British India, respectively, showing a higher yield in 1936 than in 1921, even though the share of cultivation had fallen. See Tables 17.6 and 17.10.
123. Karunamoy Mukerji, 'Land Prices in Punjab', in M. K. Chaudhuri (ed.), *Trends of Socio-Economic Change in India, 1871–1961*, Shimla: Indian Institute of Advanced Study, 1969, p. 543.
124. *Area and Yield of Certain Principal Crops in India, for various periods from 1891–92 to 1905–6*, pp. 39–42, *1898–99 to 1911–12*, pp. 10–3, 16–9, *Estimates of Area and Yield of Certain Principal Crops in India, 1925–26*, pp. 14–6, 23–7, *1935–36*, pp. 14–7, 26–30, *1938–39*, pp. 14–7, 26–30.
125. Islam, *Irrigation*, pp. 63–4; Ali, *Punjab*, p. 227.
126. Details follow.
127. *Jhang and Gujera Branches SR, 1925* quoted in Ali, *Punjab*, p. 227.
128. All references to actual acreage in this paragraph are based on Table 17.6.
129. Acreage of fodder crops from *ASBI, 1891–92*, Table A-3 and *RSCP, 1936–37*, Statement III.
130. Islam, *Irrigation*, pp. 70–1.
131. Indigo plantations in the eastern United Provinces and Bihar from the middle of the nineteenth century and cotton in the Deccan from the 1860s are just two instances.
132. Islam, *Irrigation*, pp. 71–2.

133. Mridula Mukherjee, 'Commercialization and Agrarian Change in Pre-Independence Punjab' in K. N. Raj (ed.), *Essays on the Commercialization of Indian Agriculture*, Delhi: Oxford University Press, 1985, p. 61.
134. Also see Banerjee, *Agrarian Society*, pp. 204–5; and Islam, *Irrigation*, p. 141.
135. Islam, *Irrigation*, p. 66. Wheat acreage increased with increase in price over the last decades of the nineteenth century while the Chenab and Sidhnai Canal colonies saw greater market orientation than the rest of Punjab. Himadri Banerjee, 'Growth of Commercial Agriculture in the Punjab During the Second Half of the 19th Cenrury', *PPP*, April 1978, p. 227. For details of the commercialization of wheat, cotton, and sugarcane, see ibid., pp. 228–53.
136. From A. Heston, 'National Income', *CEHI*, p. 427, Table 4A.2. The value per acre of the crops in 1875 and 1946 are at the prices in the respective years. Cotton values seem too low, but there is no explanation for it.
137. Evidence of W. P. Sangster, Chief Engineer, Irrigation Works, Punjab, *RCAI*, vol. VIII, p. 17.
138. Ali, *Punjab*, p. 227.
139. Milne's Evidence, p. 181.
140. Ali, *Punjab*, p. 226.
141. Islam, *Irrigation*, p. 69.
142. Calvert, *Wealth and Welfare*, p. 278.
143. GoP, R&A(A), December 1895, nos 7–9A, cited in Banerjee, *Agrarian Society*, p. 56.
144. Calvert, *Wealth and Welfare*, p. 281.
145. Evidence of T. A. Miller Brownlie, Principal, Agricultural College, Lyallpur, in *RCAI*, vol. VIII, p. 714.
146. Milne's Evidence, p. 180.
147. Paragraph based on *Lahore SR, 1939*, p. 3.
148. Milne's Evidence, p. 216.
149. Ibid., p. 221.
150. Senior Secretary to the FCs, Punjab, to PWD(B&R) Secretary, Punjab, 16 August 1915, paragraphs 5 and 6 in GoI. Railway, Project, B, April 1919, nos 187, p. 16/1–2.
151. Quotations from the evidence of K. G. Mitchell, Secretary, Communications Board, Punjab, in *RCAI*, vol. VIII, p. 505.
152. Paragraph based on Sarkar, *Grand Trunk Road*, pp. 47, 51.
153. Dewey, 'Military Expenditure', p. 139.
154. GoI, Railway, Railway Statistics, B, August 1911, No.74/1, pp. 18–9. Figures in brackets are value of goods carried in each category. The accounts are 'for the half year', suggesting the total for the year would be greater.
155. Banerjee, *Agrarian Society*, pp. 50–1.

156. *Report on the Material Progress of the Punjab for the Decade 1881–1891*, p. 21.
157. GoI, Railway, Way and Works, A, May 1920, nos 1–6, p. 2.
158. 'Railways were as essential to the big canals as canals have been to some of the railways.' (Calvert, *Wealth and Welfare*, p. 15).
159. *Lahore DG, 1916*, p. 147.
160. Amritsar was 'the most important market for wheat in the province' *Amritsar SR, 1940*, p. 3.
161. *Amritsar AR, 1892*, p. 18.
162. Banerjee, 'Commercial Agriculture', p. 277.
163. *Karnal DG, 1918*, p. 140.
164. GoI, Railway, Project, B, April 1919, nos 187P.16/1–2, para 5.
165. Calvert, *Wealth and Welfare*, p. 135.
166. The earlier section on cantonments gave the size of the human population in some of them, pointing to the size of the market these military stations had become.
167. Calvert, *Wealth and Welfare*, p. 107.
168. The very good harvests in the first three years of annexation, where production far exceeded consumption, could not be optimally utilized as 'there [was] not a sufficient market to secure its sale at remunerative prices.' Further, a lack of transportation and neighbouring markets meant that there was no place 'to which any great quantity of grain could be exported' *PAR, 1849–51*, p. 95.
169. Calvert, *Wealth and Welfare*, p. 280.
170. Banerjee, *Agrarian Society*, p. 204.

CHAPTER 18

Sailors and the Crowd: Popular Protest in Karachi, 1946

Anirudh Deshpande

The naval uprising of February 1946 was an event which galvanized various classes of Indian society against British imperialism. Unfortunately, unlike the Indian National Army (INA), it does not command adequate status in Indian historiography.* In this article, we study a storm centre of that significant event. The first section surveys the ratings' revolt, while the second analyses crowd action and tries to locate the crowd in its specific historical context. Finally, rumour in relation to protest and context is scrutinized.

I

> Everything has been overshadowed by the RIN Mutiny and its results.[1]

In Karachi, months before the uprising occurred, ratings, mostly from Bengal and Travancore-Cochin, had a Sailors' Association. A number of youths, affiliated to the All India Students Federation during their student days, took the lead in forming this organization, the main tasks of which included raising money for the INA relief funds[2] and conducting variety programmes for Durga Puja. Anil Roy, a leading member of these ventures and later the mutiny, explicitly mentions that the Sailors' Association 'never tried for [a] mutiny in Karachi though its aim was naturally . . . only to spread anti-British feeling among the ratings'.[3]

The news of the strike on His Majesty's India Ship (HMIS) *Talwar* in Bombay reached the ratings in the shore establishments of Karachi through newspapers on 19 February and was received with 'tremendous excitement' and 'suppressed jubilation'. However, the geographical location of Manora where these establishments were situated induced in the authorities some confidence for they 'did not show any sign of nervousness'.[4] According to another version the commanding officer (CO) of HMIS *Chamak*, Lieutenant Commander Chatterjee, upon hearing the news from Bombay, called a meeting of all the ratings and told them that they had nothing to do with the *Talwar* strike.[5] Nevertheless, the restive ratings of the Sailors' Association called a meeting of ratings from *Himalaya*, *Bahadur* and *Monze* (the shore establishments of Karachi) on the beach at Manora in the afternoon. This general body then decided unanimously to launch a mutiny and concluded that action against the British would commence on the 21 February. The programme of protest they chalked out was as follows: gathering at Keamari jetty, procession and demonstration through Karachi, invitation to the dock workers of Keamari to join the protest, shouting of slogans denouncing the British imperialists and urging the Congress and the Muslim League to unite, complete abstention from work, and finally, the attainment of Karachi-wide unity of ratings.[6]

But HMIS *Chamak* was not destined to lead the uprising for on Wednesday, 20 February, Indian sailors on board HMIS *Hindustan*, an old sloop anchored off Keamari jetty, rose in revolt.[7] Protesting against the insulting behaviour of the Captain and the executive officers, a dozen rebels disembarked, entered the city, and refused to return till the indicated officers were transferred.[8] During the day, ratings from HMIS *Himalaya*[9] joined these men and together they visited hotels in Keamari asking the owners to pull down shutters, and raised the slogans *Jai Hind* and *Inquilab Zindabad*. Later they traversed Jackson Bazaar in Keamari shouting similar slogans. Then, with cries of *Hindustan Azad* and *Jai Hind*, around 150 mutineers marched towards the railway station, proclaiming on the way that they were marching upon Delhi. [10] Thus they publicized their inspiration and intention. In the dense bazaar and harbour areas, they infused excitement among crowds which already possessed perceptions of the INA and 'Delhi Chalo'.[11] News of these incidents spread rapidly in such circumstances.

The news from the *Hindustan* led to another meeting of the Sailors' Association which decided to forge a Karachi-wide unity of ratings and to write slogans on the walls and posters. 'Hindustan Zindabad', 'Down with British Imperialism', 'Shed blood to get freedom', 'We shall live as a free nation', and 'Tyrants your days are over' were decided by the meeting as slogans needed for the hour.[12]

Next morning, the usually placid atmosphere of Manora was rent with slogans shouted by hundreds of young sailors:

> Although [*sic*] the streets the shouting of slogans continued. The small inhabitants of Manora never saw a scene like that before. They cheered us by clapping. Some even joined us . . . We were now at the Manora jetty. The most heartening job was done by the local boatmen who not only made a number of trips to ferry the ratings but refused to take any money from us. Their only request was 'Zalimo ko mar dalo'—kill the tyrants.[13]

When the ratings landed at Keamari, they were faced with the option of breaking through a well-armed cordon of British troops. In the meantime, incidents swiftly occurred on sea. A batch of ratings crossing to Keamari from the *Himalaya* jetty on Manora in local and motor launches ran into a British patrol boat. The latter ordered the ratings to go back and when the order was not heeded, opened fire, killing two ratings instantaneously and wounding some. Luckily for the *Himalaya* ratings, HMIS *Hindustan* from nearby opened up with its 12 pounders, driving away the patrol boat. After the patrol fled, about three to four hundred ratings with their dead and wounded boarded the *Hindustan.*[14]

The state, however, was well-prepared for an emergency. A strong military and police cordon was placed across the bridge connecting Keamari with Karachi and all boats were brought across to the Karachi side of the harbour. This was successful in preventing the 'mutineers from entering the city'.[15] The government moved according to warnings received from Bombay, where a close contact of the ratings with civilians had brought about an undesirable state of affairs for them. According to Governor Francis Mudie:

> If Bombay had not blown up a day or two earlier we would have been taken completely by surprise and I have no doubt that the ratings would have marched through Karachi and that, due allowance being made for the difference in size and turbulence of the two cities, the events in Bombay might have been reflected here.[16]

Anyway, since it was impossible to break through the army cordon, hundreds of ratings armed with hockey sticks demonstrated by shouting 'revolutionary slogans' throughout the afternoon. They were joined by the dock workers (imbued with and) displaying similar enthusiasm. On the other side of the cordon, an assembly of civilians watched the proceedings keenly. Towards evening, the rebels decided to return to their establishments to decide fresh programmes. Finally, they fixed a rendezvous with the enthusiastic dock workers, exchanged *lal salam* with them, and returned to Manora.[17] That night at Manora meetings were held, speeches made, and Urdu couplets were recited. The ratings kept chanting slogans late into the night. Around 11 at night on 21 February, ratings from the *Himalaya* brought disturbing news to the *Chamak*: the authorities had issued an ultimatum to *Hindustan*, which stood sovereign off the coast of Karachi, to surrender by 10 the next morning.[18]

The military high command had calculated well. They knew that during the ebb tide before noon, the *Hindustan* would sink to a lower and strategically disadvantageous position. In answer, the ratings manned the ship's guns. But they were no match for the well-placed enemy who concentrated heavy fire upon a single helpless target. Thus, after a brief spell of heavy, largely one-sided firing, the Indians surrendered. During this small battle, the rebels, for fear of hitting civilians, could not make full use of the fire power at their disposal.

In the meantime, ratings from Manora were trying to cross over to Keamari. Very few of them managed because the British army, 'had scared away all the boatmen (by) threatening to kill anybody who would come within a mile of *Hindustan*.' Some boatmen did ferry a number of ratings to Keamari, but at that moment everyone heard the firing between the *Hindustan* and the British troops: 'Three or four shells were fired in quick, succession. We knew these were from Hindustan. We shouted "death to the tyrants". The boatmen joined us. There was no trace of fear on their faces.' When these ratings reached Keamari, they were amazed to learn that everything was over:

The British troops were standing like a wall with fixed bayonets pointing at us. In choked voices we started shouting slogans. Some screamed in utter despair, while others went on striking their chests with both of [*sic*] their palms. [19]

When the ratings returned to Manora, they found it occupied by the Black Watch Regiment. By then, the revolt was over. The next day, on 23 February 1946, Roy, Kurian, Musa, and Harjinder, in faraway cremation and burial grounds, performed the last rites of their comrades killed in action. Roy calculated the number of dead as 14 and admitted that he did not know how many of the wounded died later.[20] Official reports gave varying figures of the dead and wounded. IB1 claimed eight killed and 37 wounded. IB2 claimed 12 killed and 30 injured. The Governor himself claimed that five ratings were killed and 36 wounded.[21]

At Manora, on 23 February, the ratings observed a complete hunger strike, protesting against the presence of British troops. Soon thereafter, many ratings, including the leaders, were arrested and transported to the Malir Camp outside Karachi. The Bombay rebels also surrendered on the same day. Thus, a memorable event of the Indian struggle against imperialism passed into history .

II

The context of the Karachi riot was predicated upon the nature of the city itself. Karachi, conquered by the British in 1843, till fairly recently, had a great economic, strategic, and administrative importance.[22] As a natural harbor, it was indispensable to the British. Moreover, Sindh and turbulent Baluchistan were monitored from Karachi. It was also a nodal point in the trade, involving up-country produce, especially wheat from Punjab.[23]

The original inhabitants of Karachi city were the Kulachees.[24] These Muslim fishermen had settled for long in Keamari. Later, from the nineteenth century onwards, Hindus, mostly Sindhis, moved in as traders. In 1947, Karachi was a small city developed around a natural harbor, with its business activity pivoted on shipping.[25] Consequently, the majority of its workforce, concentrated around the harbour, was engaged in loading and unloading ships, etc. Keamari was thus the stronghold of the Karachi working classes, for in it resided a differentiated group of dock workers, fishermen, porters, and ordinary daily labourers.[26]

In 1941, Karachi city contained 3,59,492 inhabitants,[27] of whom the majority were Sindhis, Punjabis, and Baluchis. The Baluchis and Makranis, a large tribal group in Karachi, spoke Baluchi in addition to other languages. The Makranis, a tribal group with negrito characteristics speaking Baluchi, were proud of their heritage and presumably had close kinship ties in Karachi and especially in and around Keamari. The Baluchis and Makranis, along with the Darzadas and Nakibs, were traditional emigrants to Karachi from the western wastelands of Makran and Baluchistan. The majority of them worked in Karachi as day labourers and lived in and around the harbour area.[28]

Karachi, unlike Bombay or Calcutta, was not a burgeoning industrial metropolis. Among its extremely limited industries, the most important in 1946 was cotton spinning. However, the limited number of cotton mills before 1947 were located in Landhi, some 16 miles away from the city proper.[29] Due to the 'small-scale' nature of Karachi before 1947,[30] no concentration of a large industrial working class took place in that city. As a consequence, the working classes in Karachi comprised fishermen,[31] who lived in their traditional village complex in Keamari, day labourers, porters, and the like who lived in or around the dock area. Though a Parel or a Girgaon was absent in Karachi, nevertheless its working classes were compressed into Keamari and the adjoining areas which saw most of the action on 20, 21, and 22 February and from where most of the rumours rose.

Karachi in the National Movement, 1942–6

In Sindh, the Muslims constituted an overwhelming majority. During the 1942 upsurge, it followed the pattern of Punjab and the North West Frontier Provinces (NWFP) rather than that of Maharashtra, Uttar Pradesh, and Bihar.[32] The Sindhi Muslim response to the Quit India Movement was similar to that of Muslims elsewhere in India:

> The remarkable thing about Hindu–Muslim relations during the Quit India movement is that nothing remarkable happened, the predictions of Congressmen, Muslim Leaguers, and British officials were all belied. Hindus did not terrorize Muslims; but neither did the Muslims join in the struggle. Most Muslims kept aloof, offering support neither to the nationalist uprising nor to their supposed British benefactors.[33]

Furthermore, Karachi was dominated by the Sindhi community which had historically developed a syncretic culture.[34] But after the war, when Pakistan loomed nearby and elections were round the corner, communal passions became active in Sindh. The Muslim League Ministry of Sindh was deeply resented by the Congress and the Hindu Mahasabha[35] and already in October 1945, communal bitterness was rising in Sindh: 'There are signs that the approach of the elections is being accompanied by increased bitterness in communal feeling. Inflammatory communal literature is coming to notice in Karachi, Hyderabad and Sukkur.'[36]

Although Karachi was also swept by the INA wave which was being directed by the Congress,[37] the League lent its own interpretation to the INA trials. Jinnah, in *Dawn*, launched a crusade against the victimization of Abdul Rashid and constantly referred to the Muslims as a community endangered on the one hand by the Raj and on the other by the Hindu Raj. Thus, even this pinnacle of anti-imperialism in the last of the climactic years of the Raj was not free of the contradictions characterizing the Indian National Movement. Karachi was no exception in this process; albeit the event under study contained a popular exposition of remarkable Hindu–Muslim unity reminiscent of earlier united anti-imperialist struggles.

The Crowd

The population of Karachi, concentrated around the harbour, became involved in the incidents happening on the RIN front on the day the revolt broke out at Manora. This passive but keen involvement was activated on Friday, 22 February, when firing between British troops and the *Hindustan* occurred. On the same day, the harbour areas teemed with military vehicles, ambulances, and lorries. Rumours appeared and spread quickly; 'crowds collected along the route taken by service vehicles and stoned military trucks, despatch riders, and troops. Indian military police were hooted and jeered at and a number of British troops were hit by stones. . .'[38] The army sealed the harbour and the dock, allowing nobody to proceed beyond the port trust buildings which were four miles away from Keamari.[39] Furthermore, from Thursday onwards the army, afraid of the ratings infiltrating into Karachi, began checking every vehicle which returned from Keamari.[40] Apprehension in the city began to rise and on Thursday itself, 'exaggerated accounts of these happenings quickly reached the town and the people became very excited. Crowds gathered at various points and stones were thrown at military vehicles.'[41] Spontaneous protest began on Thursday as the army sealed off the Keamari overbridge[42] from the harbour areas and prevented slogan shouting ratings from entering the town. The same day, the authorities confiscated all local dhows (boats) and brought them to the Karachi side of the harbour.[43] On Thursday evening and on Friday, the excitement in the city was in large measure derived from the interpretations of events given out to the general populace by the expropriated boatmen and fishermen. An Associated Press of India (API) correspondent, touring the area within three hours of the action, found Keamari village deserted with only frequent patrolling of British troops in jeeps and the nearby area strewn with stray bullets.[44] Had the army forcibly driven away the villagers or did they take to their heels at the sight of the former or the sound of action? British troops, with force and alarm moved, into Keamari on Thursday and stayed on till Sunday. This dislocated life and fishing, ferrying, loading, and unloading was suspended for at least three days.[45] This leaves no doubt as to why Karachi was most turbulent on Friday and Saturday.

Initially, the popular protest was spontaneous but on Friday, as students and leaders stepped in, it gained a wider legitimacy and a semblance of organization. On Friday, as flashes of firing were seen[46] and sounds of heavy gunfire heard,[47] 'in great excitement . . . most colleges shut at once, and processions of students were taken out in the town.'[48] Crowds attacked military vehicles in the port areas and along the routes taken by army lorries, ambulances, and jeeps carrying British paratroopers even before the students reacted. Almost simultaneously the Sindh Students' Congress, assisted by prominent local Congress leaders, took out a well-attended procession which was followed by a meeting in which INA and abusive anti-British slogans were raised.[49] The speakers who addressed the mass meeting were Swami Krishnanda, Kishan Lulla, Sital Devanathan, Ali Mohammed Makrani, and R. K. Sindhwa. Resolutions sympathetic to the RIN, critical of army action and demanding an impartial enquiry into the whole affair, were passed and anti-British speeches marked with an 'anti-racist strain' were made. Another well-attended students meeting was held outside the Law College and addressed by local leaders like Kirat Babani, Kishan Lulla, Ali Mohammed Makrani, and Mohd Hafiz Qureshi. [50]

In the evening, CPI held a meeting at the Id Gah which was attended by about a thousand people. Sobho T. Gianchandani presided and local CPl notables Asafjab Karwani, Kazi Mohd. Mujtaba, Avtar Kishan Angle, S. K. Dharmani, Govind Mali and P. H. Ghawali were present. In this assembly, 'provocative and dangerous anti-British' speeches were made. For instance, Mujtaba 'sarcastically' said that the British who could not face Germans could only shoot down Indians and Karwani, in a 'most objectionable' way, asserted that for a single rating's life, Indians would take 1,000 British ones. According to Gianchandani, Indians were proud of the ratings who were facing bullets to uphold national pride. It was maintained that the ratings had shown how the arms given to them could be really utilized, whereas the civilians were helpless, by and large, because they were unarmed and because of their inability to contact the ratings.[51]

This rhetoric 'had a visible effect on the audience',[52] the nature of which became obvious in the actions which followed. The meeting called on all communities to organize a complete *hartal* and for the labourers to go on strike the next day.[53] The leaders decided to take out a procession next morning to tour the factory areas and persuade the workers to strike.[54] Finally, the gathering dissolved with a resolution calling a mass meeting at noon next day at the Id Gah *maidan* (ground). At this stage, the local CPI leadership was taking a radical step as compared to the Congress, and their speeches were violent, compared to the milder tones set by the Congress.[55] The CPI leaders also calculated pragmatically and shrewdly and

> . . . appealed to all sections of the community, and the mass procession and meeting to have been held on the Id Gah maidan was scarcely likely to have passed off without any incident. *By deciding to hold their meeting at this place, they were obviously attempting to enlist Muslim sympathy.*[56] (emphasis added)

These developments, together with the news from Bombay, alarmed the government and generated a resolute official will to prevent disturbances.[57] In those tense moments, after having 'horrified' 'ordinary Indian opinion'[58] by its use of force against the *Hindustan*, the government retaliated swiftly. The District Magistrate issued an order under Section 144, prohibiting meetings and processions on Saturday, and had three prominent communist leaders arrested.[59] But these measures were unsuccessful in stemming the popular tide.

Rioting began on Saturday morning (when the RIN rebels in Bombay had already surrendered). Workers from workshops, presumably mechanics, artificers, fitters, and printers, observed a complete *hartal*, and students from schools and colleges collected in small processions and groups. Then these groups moved around the town obstructing traffic and persuading, peacefully or otherwise, shopkeepers to close their shops.[60] The CPI took out a procession of around 30,000 people[61] and the whole city was brought to a pitch of great excitement. These activities continued while Section 144 (according to which more than four persons could not assemble anywhere in the city) was in force, which suggests police abstention or collusion. This was highly probable because during the war, the police had to contend with rising crime and rebellion almost all over India despite being undermanned and at a considerable cost to morale. Police inertia in the initially crucial hours of Saturday can also be explained by a marginal note in a partisan source suggesting that 'police behaviour during the disturbances was excellent, even though there had just previously been some discontent among them about scales of pay'.[62] It seems that the police was not above post-war social discontent.[63] We will come back to the police later, but here it suffices to state that police indifference at the outset of the riot helped it gain momentum. Consequently, British troops were deployed to save the day for the government.

By noon, a crowd of thousands gathered at the Id Gah *maidan*.[64] Congress, League, and Communist flags were prominent and soon the crowd was swelled by the entry of a fresh communist procession. When the police (and now it acted!) tried dispersing the crowd, it retaliated by pelting the police.[65] At this stage, sensing the prevalent popular temperament, the party leaders began to waver. Even earlier, many communist leaders, heeding the alarm raised by the authorities, had backed out of the situation. On Saturday, many communist leaders decided against holding the meeting at Id Gah, but the crowd refused dispersal and instead attacked the police.[66]

The crowd, fuelled by the speeches of Friday, was willing to burst through what had become the fetters of organization, for 'all efforts to disperse them peacefully failed. . . and the crowd increased and resorted to violent stoning at every opportunity and without provocation . . . leaders had no control over the mob, and ultimately the police were forced to open fire.'[67]

The crowd, comprising students and various sections of the working class, certainly demonstrated determination and unity in action and audacity in behaviour:

> Hooliganism by *students and loafers* increased hourly, traffic was obstructed, *Europeans, Anglo Indians, and government buildings* stoned and people attacked and *forcibly deprived of their hats and ties*, which were burnt on the spot. A Police Officer was attacked by the crowd. . . .[68] (emphasis added)

The crowd, symbolically destroying British power and asserting its own identity, was in no mood to attend to the passivity now being preached by its erstwhile teachers.[69] The leaders, lacking any programme of struggle beyond rhetoric and confronted with a phenomenon they helped create but could not control, performed a volte-face on Saturday:

> During the disturbances, repeated attempts were made by party leaders, collectively and individually, to pacify and disperse the mob. They met, however, with no success whatsoever. A number of them, including Sir Ghulam Hussain Hidayatullah, were stoned by the crowd. These party leaders included some of the more peacefully inclined communists. A joint meeting was held of Communist, Congress and Muslim League leaders at the Swaraj Bhawan on Saturday afternoon to decide on measures to restore peace in the city. It is reported that they were unable to decide on methods to be used and no joint action was taken.[70]

In the afternoon British troops occupied the Id Gah, which had been transformed by the crowd into a centre of resistance.[71] 'The riotous crowds. . . composed mostly of youths, both Hindu and

Musalman, and hooligans',[72] now facing an enemy more formidable than the police, broke up into several groups, left the locality, and directed its attentions elsewhere. These smaller crowds attacked isolated police *chowkis*, post offices, other governmental buildings, and a European bank. Stray government servants were beaten up and letter boxes, and in one case a sub-post office, were set on fire. The armed forces opened fire on several occasions, killing four and injuring more than 22, and in crowd attacks on the police 53 policemen were injured, a few of them seriously.[73] According to Mudie, eight persons were killed and 18 injured when the police fired in self-defence and 'in defence of the police outposts, post offices, one revenue department building and the Grindlay's Bank . . . '.[74] Communist leader S. K. Dharmani and 10 Hindu youths were arrested under the Police Act for hooliganism.[75] The latter were arrested while they were trying to occupy the municipal department building.[76]

Communications in the city were paralysed for the day and the tramway workers observed a complete strike, much to the relief of the authorities.[77] By nightfall, the crowd disintegrated and vanished as students returned home and the workers too retired to their quarters. State control became absolute as the British army clamped down a successful curfew.[78]

A perusal of the rapidly occurring events of Friday and Saturday reveals that popular protest began spontaneously with the stoning of troops near the harbour on Friday. Then, students and party leaders intruded and political rhetoric became successful exhortation. Saturday was carried by the crowd, with the political leaders backing out. By Sunday, after two turbulent days, quiet began to prevail and finally by Monday, the troops were withdrawn and Karachi became normal.

Our survey clarifies that the crowd comprised school and college students, disaffected boatmen and fishermen (who by attire were singled out in reports as hooligans), workers from striking workshops, and most probably the day labourers from the harbour areas. In 1961, the total number of college students in Karachi was 1,747, of whom hundreds became students due to expanded opportunities after 1947.[79] This would mean that in 1946 at least hundreds of students, if not thousands, protested, and of these, presumably the older ones stayed on longer. Most probably, a few hundred college students played the most active leading part and the thousands mentioned in the reports belonged to the lower orders of Karachi.[80] Trade unions, with the probable exception of the tramway union, played no role in the upsurge. No report mentions them and even *People's Age* of the period is silent on them.

The newspapers, generally sympathetic to the RIN rebels, spoke hesitantly of the Karachi proletarians who so heroically rose to the occasion. The press, with few exceptions,[81] echoed the perspective of the national leaders. It condemned such disorderly conduct in police terminology and called it the product of a conspiracy by anti-social elements to establish *goonda raj* in contradistinction to the desired swaraj.[82]

In passing, we noticed police *chowki*s, a foreign (Grindlay's) bank, a revenue department building, and persons in western attire as the targets of popular fury. Against the historical background of nationalist struggle in India, the Karachi crowd, by attacking these symbols of alien rule was, in effect, destroying the Raj of its own perceptions. Far from being meaningless, false, or incorrect, this act was the outcome of mental aggregates formed in the life, and consciousness (thereby implied) of the participants. Popular violence was selective, not arbitrary, and though unplanned, signified the evolution of consciousness. And this is why a foreign bank, not others, was chosen for attack. Behind this may have laid the common nationalist discourse saying that the country was plundered by the British and the loot lay in their coffers.

The attacks on policemen, who embodied state power, and the snatching and burning of hats and ties, took place in a continuum within which the formation of a 'collective frame of mind had already taken place'.[83] The post-war upsurges remind us of the Quit India movement in their sharp demonstration of popular bitterness against the police. Such attacks can convey more meaning if the history of the urban/rural poor–police interaction is unearthed. Similarly, the scenario of wartime and post-war black markets brought about by soaring inflation and famine-like conditions awaits unfolding.[84]

Arson, including the snatching and burning of hats and ties, was common to Karachi and Bombay. But does this indicate something more than a cultural symbolic cremation of the Raj? Arson appears in riotous situations everywhere but its role (and analysis) varies with context. In our case, the crowds of the post-war upsurge were not guided by criminal instincts. Nor did they conform to the communal type which took over completely from August 1946. In Karachi those arrested for rioting were students, and reports nowhere attest the participation of identifiable criminals. In the reports a general cover term 'hooligan' sufficed when, in fact, no hooligans, i.e. those known to the police as bad characters, were either identified or arrested. Thus, official and much of non-official characterization of the crowd was prejudiced. So if mischief or 'malicious' intention was really absent, why did the rioters resort to arson? Burning was not criminal madness. It was the manifestation of the popular desire to punish the enemy by destroying those goods which were dear to him and which formed the 'symbol and basis of his power'.[85]

Arson, in this case, was both an act of cultural incantation and liberation. In unsettled times when opportunity arose, crowds, composed generally of the losers, gathered to settle scores with those perceived as their tormentors. In the hour of expected apocalypse, they, if only ephemerally turned the world upside down. As the crowds stripped and burnt ties and hats in small bonfires, it was as if they were celebrating. They created a moment such as would be talked about for long at tea shop gatherings, a moment when out of their usual dark backstage, they appeared under the glare and a moment immortalized in the tale each participant would carry of the event. And the event itself would signify historical victory, if only fleetingly.[86]

Our evidence does not substantiate the views aired by most, including Gandhi and Nehru, that during the days under study, anti-social elements were conspiring to subvert the normal course of attaining freedom. Without discounting the participation of criminals in these upsurges, it seems clear that these 'anti-socials' were subsumed under the prevalent collective mentality of the riotous heterogeneous crowds.[87] This collective mentality was not that of a usual group, but of an unusual social aggregate formed under specific circumstances.

The state and propertied classes have their own definition of crime, but crime characteristic of communal carnages or riots perpetrated in the name of religion and often with the involvement of well-known leaders was absent from Karachi and Bombay during these days. In fact, these crowds did not conform to the image of crowds carried in those days by the press, state, and leaders.[88] Not a single report from Karachi or Bombay mentions participation in abominable acts usually classified as heinous crime.[89] Indian factories and homes were not broken into, middle-class security was not threatened. The protest was political and anti-imperialist as far as the identification of enemies was concerned.[90]

Earlier, we noticed the moment in which the crowds were transformed into a 'state of crowd'.[91] That moment was the product of a specific historical conjuncture and one of the motives underlying its creation was rumour.

III

> Rumour is the process by which a collective historical consciousness is built. The collective interpretations resulting from massive rumours lead to commonly accepted interpretations of events, non-events, or acts of events. Hence . . . rumour tells us more about the mentality of the time of the happening than about the events themselves.
>
> —Jan Vansina[92]

Rumour has played a significant role at various times in Indian history.[93] The context of rumours in the case of the Karachi riots comprised:

1. The connection rumour had with the state;
2. The generation of collective consciousness in the short term; and
3. The relation rumour had with the specific topography of Karachi.

Reports mention numerous rumours and for this we must be thankful to the alarm raised by the popular upheaval which rocked the Indian subcontinent during 1945–6. In crisis and especially during popular disturbances, the Raj functionaries became acutely sensitive to bazaar gossip and premonition of impending turbulence led the more careful of them to record rumour. For our purpose, superintendent K. R. Eates certainly took his job as a sentinel of the Raj seriously, but Eates only stated the problem for us. He unknowingly transmitted the messages to us and it is up to us to decode them. Just as on the basis of disparate information we pieced a story together in the foregoing sections, so in this part, on the basis of rumour, we have tried to reconstruct the mentality of the Karachi rioters of February 1946.[94]

List of rumours circulating in Karachi on Friday, 22 February and Saturday, 23 February 1946:[95]

1. Indian troops in the embarkation buildings had refused food and were in sympathy with the RIN ratings.
2. The *Hindustan* had been sunk with 300 ratings on board.
3. The *Hindustan*'s captain was an Irishman in sympathy with the strikers.
4. The military had fired on the ratings first.
5. In Keamari Baluch, troops had refused to fire on the ratings and as a result had been disarmed and shelled in their lines by the British.
6. The police had fired on peaceful crowds.
7. Police firing had been indiscriminate and had been bought over by increased rates of pay.
8. British soldiers had treacherously fired at the naval ratings under cover of a white flag (newspaper news).
9. Indian soldiers had refused to fire on the ratings (newspaper news).
10. The *Hindustan* had been set on fire by incendiary bombs (special bulletin issued by the *Hindu*).[96]

Before analysing these rumours, a glance at the topography of Karachi will be in place. This will enable us to pinpoint the areas of conflict, the source of popular assemblies, and the attendant rumours. In Karachi, the zone of conflict under study lay in the littoral area of the town. Keamari contained a fishing village, a jetty, and a harbour and was linked to the city proper by a narrow overbridge. Adjoining the harbour were densely populated and market regions such as the Queen's and Empress market areas. 'The surroundings of the wharf and Keamari were the houses of the day labourers and porters of whom the bulk may have been, in 1946, composed of Baluch and Makran migrants.'[97] As Karachi grew during 1939–45, due to the development of maritime trade, the harbour areas were the ones most affected.[98] New Karachi was developed systematically only after 1947 and before it, as working class colonies did not exist, the workers crowded in close proximity to the harbour. Furthermore, fishing, ferrying and dock activity were the most important economic activities on the Karachi city and district coast. [99]

To sustain day-long activity, which mushroomed during the inter-war and war years, a host of allied economic activities seem to have developed in the harbour areas. Restaurants, hotels, tea shops, general shops catering to porters, fishermen, and traders and other visitors developed and came to stay. Similarly, wholesale fish merchants flocked to Keamari for we are told that the Karachi fishing grounds yielded rich hauls which were demanded in Karachi and its hinterland. [100] In other words, Karachi, harbour, given all its economic linkages, was a dense area humming with activity during daytime.

Karachi was a small town compared with Bombay and Calcutta, and as our sketch shows it was prone to a daily, if not permanent, demographic hypostasis occurring in the southern part of the town. The nerve centre of the city lay in the port area, and what better surroundings could be found for the creation of daily assemblies, which could, when the moment came, be transformed into sensitive volatile crowds. But the existence of a revolutionary crowd is underlined by an appropriate collective mentality which has been previously formed in a human aggregate. This means some dues must be found to determine the creation of an elementary preparedness before an external stimulus transforms the always available human aggregate into a turbulent mass.

The examination of the genesis and growth of popular mentality in Karachi in the long term is beyond the scope of this article, but in brief, we can explore two possibilities in this direction: one economic and the other political.

One of the main factors underlining Karachi's expansion during the war years was the increase of wheat exports from upcountry Sindh and Punjab.[101] Population statistics for Karachi district record a rise from 1901 to 1961, and a particularly sharp rise from 1939 to 1941 of 44.9 per cent. In 1941, Karachi city had a population of 3,59,492, leaving only 76,395 persons outside it in the district. This high level of urban concentration continued after 1947, for in 1961, 93.6 per cent of Karachiites were urban dwellers. The point is to stress that considering the high urbanizing tendency, it seems more than likely that during the war, 1939–45, the city experienced a heavy influx of people from the west and also perhaps from the north. Immigration from the east, before 1946, was constrained due to various factors, geographical location being one of them. It seems Karachi, like Bombay and Calcutta, acted as the local magnet during the war and the endemic grain shortage created during the years 1942–6.

This inflow of people swelled the Karachi labour ranks. As the war effort was stepped up after 1940 due to the German move eastwards, almost all the ports on the coast from Cambay to Suez experienced an upswing in economic activity. The importance of Karachi with the rest of India increased when in and after 1942 Britain was left with India as her major supply depot. Thus, the formation of the post-war Karachi crowds came to be predicated upon the logistics of war.

In 1945, the process of expansion was brought to a halt. Activity and opportunities dwindled and India was hit by famine-like conditions in 1945–6. Inflation spiralled and food shortage raised tempers universally. In Karachi, as the troops left, a variety of services became superfluous. Rapidly declining army procurements must have slashed demand for fish and other goods. In short, for millions of people all over India, but especially in ports, the end of a long and trying war brought no prospect of a secure future. The end belied millions of expectations and post-war retrenchment only added to this feeling of insecurity which mounted with the rapidity with which long lines were formed outside grain shops. Only tiny sparks were needed to fire this powder, and sparks which flew from political friction far above these lines more than often fell on this accumulated tinder. In this vortex Karachi too was swept away, and the INA trials were a part of this wave.

The INA issue had a tremendous psychological impact upon Indian minds in the year 1945–6. In this politically significant year, in many flashes, at popular levels, we find the spirit of the Non-Cooperation-Khilafat mass movements revived. The Calcutta upsurges of November 1945 and February 1946[102] and the Bombay uprising of February 1946 are in a sense significant events in Indian history. But even this peak of popular struggle failed to transcend the socio-religious boundaries which were cardinal to the Indian anti-imperialist struggle. In this sense, the question of a possible alternative from 'below' to the truncated settlement from 'above' in 1946–7 seems to be closed. The Indian national movement had developed in an ideological context in which operative categories like nationalist and communal were not mutually exclusive.[103] Only a class-based secular identity could have overcome this inherent antinomy in Indian nationalism. Movements seeking alternatives in terms of thought and being were in the making in Telengana and Bengal at that time. But the urban protests of the period were unable to break decisively the parameters of identification long established by Indian nationalism.

In 1945 almost all Indian political parties, to be in tune with the rising popular wave, came out in defence of the INA prisoners who became national heroes. The INA became a symbol of national unity against the British and in that atmosphere, popular action in response to stimulus from external groups, like students, quickly manifested itself in upsurge. Hence Mudie was partially right in observing that the Karachi episode occurred due to the rhetoric of Nehru and Aruna Asaf Ali, and 'all those who have preached violence and glorified the INA . . .'. But he exaggerated in maintaining that these members of the middle-class leadership created 'an atmosphere about that any attack on government is a patriotic duty *even though the* object of that attack is merely to destroy'.[104] (emphasis added) The 'atmosphere', however, was not primarily created by the leaders but by the effects of war and the attitude adopted by the government towards the INA men. In this case, we have also observed how this popular mentality behind the urge to 'destroy' was already made even before the leaders made their speeches.

Our observation indicates the ambiguous relation the masses

shared with the leaders. Hence Mudie, in his search for the culprit, was wrong when he said that personally he had little doubt that the communists were at the bottom of the trouble because, 'the 4-inch guns of the *Hindustan* probably convinced the leaders of the other parties that things were a bit tough for them.'[105] This was right as far as the officially perceived difference between the CPI and the Congress was concerned, and it seems the communists were more violent, in speech, than others but they nevertheless proceeded to the Swaraj Bhawan once the crowd got 'out of control'. Thus, the generality and spontaneity of popular action based upon a pre-formed collective mentality of upsurge eluded the administrator's eye.

In brief, the INA trial and the post-war economic conditions coupled with political rhetoric and the strikes in the Allied and Royal Indian Air Force (RIAF)[106] lent the emergent milieu in 1946 an aura of general collapse. The RIN uprising, with the postures adopted towards it by the British, made a decisive confrontation seem imminent and this raised hopes for change in the minds of millions. The economic and political situations, obtained after the war, thus met in a powerful conjuncture which instantaneously attracted the growing militancy of the ordinary people. In the lives of millions of working people, such were the moments when a choice between subjection and rebellion was made for: 'Even those who accept exploitation, oppression and subjection as the norm of human life dream of a world without them: a world of equality, brotherhood and freedom, a totally *new* world without evil.'[107]

Due to the post-war posture of the Congress and later of the other parties, regarding the INA trials, it may well have appeared to the masses that another mass nationalist upsurge was about to take place.[108] Here, especially in the younger elements of the crowds, the memory of 1942 must have played its role.

Such were the constituents of the context within which the Karachi riot and the rumours informing it made an appearance. Let us now try to grasp the consciousness these rumours reflected.

It was widely believed in Karachi that troops in the embarkation building had refused food and were in sympathy with the rebellious ratings. Although official sources claim that during the RIN revolt the Indian Army remained loyal, sources sympathetic to the rebels assert otherwise. According to Banerjee, the embarkation unit, a heterogeneous body, was the first to be affected by the uprising. On 21 February, none of these men reported for duty. Later they were arrested, put under guard and this information was relayed to the newspaper offices by a brave Pathan private.[109] But these men were not on a hunger strike. They struck work in the morning and were removed to a camp in the afternoon. In fact, at Drigh Road, the RIAF men went on a hunger strike in favour of the RIN and at Mauripur too, 450 RIAF men did the same on 22 February.[110] In popular perception, all these actions became merged and the attribute of one element was taken over by another. Thus, rumour distorted information to make it conform to collective mentality. Further, partially substantiated newspaper reports helped this process by lending social authority to popular belief.[111] Hence, news and rumour became inextricably intertwined.

Another accepted belief maintained that Indian soldiers had refused to fire on the ratings and that Baluch soldiers had been punished for disobedience. It is difficult to say what *actually* happened during those days. But from our point of view, the validity of the moment for popular mentality is important. It is immaterial whether Indian troops refused to fire or not, for the significant factor in our analysis is the fact that collective mentality believed it to have been so. The overwhelming presence of British troops in the harbour area and the blockade erected by them seems to have given rise to mass speculation that so many white soldiers were being used *because* Indian troops had become unreliable. Soon, this speculation became news because of the readiness to interpret generated by collective mentality already prepared by other incidents. The army, by sealing of the ratings from the general civilian assembly, created fertile grounds for common apprehension. Thus, heavy troop deployment involving large contingents of British troops along with heavy and medium artillery generated panic around the dock. Similarly, the confiscation of boats by the authorities and the desertion of Keamari village added, in a large measure, to the general state of panic created by the situation and as a consequence, popular imagination was fired into believing numerous instant stories. [112]

The Baluch troops case can be interpreted in two ways. The

Baluch, a recognized 'martial race', were well-known in Karachi for a variety of reasons'[113] and it is likely that the rumour mentioning the disarming and shelling of Baluch troops emanated from the large Baluchi component of the crowds. Crowd studies indicate that often crowds in action invent allies when actually none exist. Thus hope of victory is generated from the feeling dominating the moment. In Karachi, too, the pre-formed mentality of the rioters produced enough scope for wishful thinking.

Why Baluch and not the Gurkhas or others?[114] Precisely because the Baluch troops were locally known and perhaps some even had their kin in the crowd. They were familiar and since they were ethnically Baluch, it was generally believed that they would throw in their lot with the crowd. Hence ethnic loyalties guiding popular perceptions and actions during crowd mobilization and action cannot be ruled out in our analysis. However, in identifying the Baluch troops with the crowd, the rumour was explicit in formulation. It maintained that the Baluch troops were disarmed, taken to their lines, and shelled by the British. If analysed symbolically, this rumour unfolds an interesting process. First, the troops disobeyed orders, thus becoming identified with the crowd. They were than disarmed, i.e. alienated from their means of defence, and finally were slaughtered like goats. This theme of rebellion–expropriation–punishment was generated rapidly to suit the moment and the mood. In a flash, the crowd identified the Baluch with the RIN who too were being similarly punished. Thus, the imperative to defend their countrymen, being killed by the British, underpinned the creation of group solidarity in the crowd—what was happening to the RIN was also happening to the Baluchis and would happen to anyone opposing the British. In certain instances, this idea could discourage rebellion and yet in others it could, and did, lead to riot. The latter was decided by the development of collective sensibilities upto the point when such moments came. This explains why Karachi, sedate in 1942, exploded in 1946.

But were the Baluchis actually shelled? From where did the rumour derive legitimacy? During the hostilities between the *Hindustan* and the military, some 4-inch shells fired from the ship fell in the Baluch lines but did practically no damage.[115] The crowd surmised that shells had fallen into the Baluch lines and since in its view the RIN could never have shelled their brethren, it must have been the British who did it. And so, in a tense moment when accidentally some stray shells fell in the Baluch lines, they, like the pieces of a puzzle falling into place, acquired a meaning and instantly a story was born and believed. It was believed because the crowd, guided by pre-formed collective perceptions—in which the INA, RIAF, and RIN issues played important roles—expected the troops to support the RIN uprising and these rumours were simultaneously the products as well as the propellers of this mentality.

Somewhat similar in content was the rumour regarding the police. The crowd said the police had been bought over by increased rates of pay. The fact that it believed the police could be 'bought' emerged from its general characterization of the police force as an easily corruptible body. This conception emanated from everyday popular experience. The police undoubtedly must have treated Karachi as a lucrative proposition! But the rumour had a notion of betrayal attached to it. The previous section observed that the Karachi police, prior to this riot, had been restive regarding pay. It is likely that by way of casual conversation or press reports this unrest was made known to the commoners of Karachi. Such casual information went into the pool of popular memory. Further, we noticed that during the initial part of the upsurge, despite Section 144 being in force, the police did not act against the rioters. This probably generated an impression in the crowd that the police was sympathetic. Ultimately when the police, under pressure, did act albeit ineffectively, its 'true nature' was exposed to the crowd. This ambiguity in police behaviour was thus construed as a betrayal by the crowd. Believing this, the crowd proceeded to attack police stations and *chowki*s.

Among rumours current, three were about the *Hindustan.* One mentioned that the ship had been sunk with 300 ratings on board. Another claimed that its captain, an Irishman, was in sympathy with the rebels. The third stated that the ship had been set aflame by incendiary bombs. Let us recapitulate the incidents of Friday, 22 February, to analyse these rumours. In the first place, the harbour area was occupied by British troops who disallowed anyone within 4 miles of the dock. Second, from about 10 a.m., in citizens heard and saw heavy firing in the harbour. Third, after the firing, ambulances and lorries carrying the wounded and other ratings left the area. The battle became a military secret and to date we do not have single non-official eye witness account from the *Hindustan.* Nobody, in fact, knew what happened to the *Hindustan* during the exchange of fire.

This situation, facilitated by the topography of the area, created apprehension in the crowd assembled faraway from the actual battlefield. Further, as British troops kept vigil, till Sunday nobody was allowed near the quayside. This enhanced popular suspicion regarding the situation. Thus the state itself was instrumental in the emergence of rumours. Deployment of artillery, including a field gun, mortars and heavy machine guns had a tremendous visual impact upon the crowds.[116]

Panic was enhanced by the entry, into the crowd, of boatmen and fishermen from Keamari. Their boats too had been seized and hence, in their view, the only possible means of escape, for the ratings had vanished. And when in these circumstances heavy firing began, everyone was convinced that the *Hindustan* was being sunk.

The second rumour reflected a knowledge of the historical Irish–British rivalry. It most probably came from students aware of British history or from general perceptions of the Irish struggle handed down to popular levels by the nationalist ideology. In either case, the appearance of this exceptional rumour displays the mechanism of fabricating allies at work during crowd upsurges.

The third rumour also appeared in a special bulletin issued by the *Hindu* on 22 February.[117] Studies in crowd behaviour suggest that often the belief of the crowd in itself becomes rejuvenated by a feedback, into its information pool of knowledge, commanding social sanction and authority. In most literate societies, the newspaper, before the advent of the audio visual media, is generally considered an authentic source of news. Furthermore, the role of the Indian press during the anti-imperialist struggle lends basis to this idea. Hence the news from the *Hindu,* which most probably arose from popular perception of matters and then went back to the crowd, greatly strengthened the collective resolve of the crowd.

In this respect certainly, more important was the AIR broadcast made by the Flag Officer Commanding RIN *Godfrey* on the afternoon of 21 February, in which he categorically stated that the RIN would be destroyed if the mutiny continued. The whole country heard this 'submit or perish' speech.[118] These words immediately preceding the battle in Karachi deepened the sense of gloom prevalent and heightened popular fears regarding British intentions in dealing with the RIN. Thus, rumours mentioning the sinking and damaging of the *Hindustan* were not without substance, as shown in the public actions of the state during those dramatic incidents of February 1946.

The consciousness generated in the Karachi crowd and brought to the fore due to its interaction with an external stimulus led to an unorganized momentary upsurge. The spontaneous outburst converted the street into a temporary battlefield, but for various reasons could not be channelled into a wider movement. Another crowd which began to collect on Sunday 24 February was homogeneous and hence motivated by different group solidarity.

On Sunday afternoon, some 'Hindus' (?) attacked Sayed Haroon, the brother of Yusuf Haroon, a member of the Central Legislative Assembly, and tried to snatch away his tie and hat.[119] That evening, 'a crowd of Makranis were collecting to take revenge on Hindus, but they were persuaded to disperse'.[120] According to Mudie, after the assault on Haroon, the 'Muslims who had gathered to avenge Haroon' were, however, persuaded to disperse 'with the assistance of Sir Ghulam Hussain'.[121] This was the same leader who was stoned by the crowds only a day before!

The Sunday crowds, under control of their leader, was different from that of the Saturday crowd and similar actions on Sunday provoked the crystallizing of a distinctly different collective mentality from that of a day before. Even if we do not believe that the crowd on Sunday gathered to avenge their leader, nonetheless it displayed confidence in a leader. This separated its mentality from that of the insurgent crowd on Saturday. Thus, the formation and reformation of crowds in Karachi was a microcosm of a larger process which played on and generated a contradictory consciousness. The question here is not one of the fickle-mindedness of a sub-proletariat.[122] It is, rather, one that probes the problematic of the complexity of human consciousness which evolved through numerous social intricacies in a multidimensional national movement. However, the tackling of that question, which is open, calls for much wider generalizations lying beyond the purview of this particular study.

Acknowledgements: I must thank Sabyasachi Bhattacharya and Majid Hayat Siddiqui, for encouraging me and criticizing this paper at various stages.

NOTES

* For a history of the INA see the following: High Toye, *The Springing Tiger*, Bombay, 1962; K. K. Ghosh, *The Indian National Army*, Meerut, 1969 is by far the most comprehensive work on the subject. Articles by Sehgal, Dhillon, and Bose in Part V of N. R. Ray et al., eds., *Challenge: A Saga of India's Struggle for Freedom*, New Delhi, 1984. The statements of the INA officers on trial were published by the All India INA Enquiry and Relief Committee as *The I.N.A. Speaks*, Delhi, 1946. Netaji was looking and planning for a proper psychological movement for a revolution. For his ideas and moves in 1940–3 see Subhas Chandra Bose, *The Indian Struggle*, Bombay, 1967, especially pp. 357–463. On the Royal Indian Navy (henceforth RIN) see Banerjee, *The R.I.N. Strike*, Delhi, 1954; B. C. Dutt, *Mutiny of the Innocents*, Bombay, 1971; Anil Roy, 'Karachi Chapter' in N. R. Ray et al., eds, op. cit., and Anirudh Deshpande, 'The Royal Indian Navy Uprising and Popular Protest', 1946, unpublished M.Phil dissertation submitted to the Centre for Historical Studies, JNU, 1987.

1. Fortnightly Report (henceforth FR), second half of February 1946, Sindh, Home Department—Political, 18/2/1946, National Archives of India (henceforth NAI).
2. That the INA influenced the evolution of nationalist consciousness in various sections of the Indian armed forces after the war is evinced by the FR for Sindh between August 1945 and February 1946 as well as the *Transfer of Power*, vol. VI edited by Mansergh and Moon.
3. Roy, 'Karachi Chapter', (hereafter KC) op. cit., p. 606.
4. Ibid.
5. Subrata Banerjee, op. cit., p. 83; and the evidence of Chatterjee in Karachi Statements, a file containing petitions to the RIN Mutiny Commission of Enquiry, serial number 14, RIN Mutiny Papers, NAI.
6. KC, p. 607.
7. Ibid, p. 608; and Intelligence Bureau (IB) Home Department report titled 'Mutiny in the RIN and concerned disturbances', February 1946, Sindh (hereafter IB1), Home—Political 5/14/46, NAI, compiled by K. R. Eates, DSP, Sindh CID.
8. IB1.

9. There were five shore establishments in Karachi situated in Manora: HMIS *Monze* Local Naval Defence Base, HMIS *Himalaya* Gunnery School, HMIS *Bahadur* and *Dilwar* Boy's Training Schools, and HMIS *Chamak* Radar Training School.
10. IB1.
11. The impact of the INA on post-war polities has been noted well by Ghosh, *The Indian National Army*, pp. 198–251.
12. KC, p. 609.
13. Ibid., pp. 609–10.
14. KC, p. 610, and I.B. Central Intelligence Officer's report on 'The recent disturbances in Karachi for Home Department's information' (hereafter IB2), Home—Political, 5/14/46, NAI.
15. FR (Sindh), second half of February 1946.
16. Sir Francis Mudie (Governor of Sindh) to Wavell, 27.2.46, in N. Mansergh, ed., *The Transfer of Power*, 1942–7, vol. VI, London, 1976, pp. 1071–4 (hereafter *TOP*).
17. KC, p. 610; *lal salam* means red salute, a communist greeting.
18. KC, p. 612; and IB1.
19. This paragraph is based on KC, pp. 613–4.
20. KC, p. 615.
21. *TOP*, pp. 1071–2.
22. *Population Census of Pakistan*, 1961, *District Census report Karachi*, 1961, (hereafter *PCP*) Social Science Library, JNU, New Delhi, pp. 1–5.
23. The *Gazeteer of the Province of Sind B, Volume I Karachi District*, compiled by J. W. Smyth, L.C.S., Bombay, 1919 (hereafter *GKD*) supports the general information contained in *PCP.* Karachi was the civil, military, and economic centre of Sindh and the third port of India after Calcutta and Bombay. It was the maritime terminus of the whole system of railways that served Sindh. British Baluchistan, Punjab, and the Northwest Frontier of India. Between 1850 and 1917, Karachi developed as 'the key of Sind and of the Indus' due to consistent administrative effort (also see Appendix).
24. PCP, pp.1–29.
25. For an account of the administrative and engineering effort underlying the development of Karachi harbour see *GKD*, pp. 84–90, According to the *Gazeteer of the Province of Sind*, compiled by E. H. Aitken, Karachi, 1907 (hereafter *GPS*), pp. 85–153, Sir Charles Napier annexed Karachi and made it the headquarters of Sindh in 1843, Later, Sir Bartle Frere, as commissioner of Sindh from 1851 to 1859, settled the revenues in 1855 and initiated concrete steps to make 'Karachi and not Calcutta' the port of Punjab.
26. Information supplied by Mr D. S. Arora who lived in Karachi from 1934 to 1942 and now resides at Kashmere Gate, Delhi.

27. *Census of India*, 1941, *Simla*, 1943, p. 77.
28. *PCP*, section on history; *Baluchistan District Gazeteer series*, vols VII and VII-A on Makran and Kharan, Bombay, 1907, p. 69.
29. *PCP*, section on industry.
30. Ibid., also see *GPS*, pp. 388–400.
31. '*GPS*, p. 61: 'the fisher's craft has been carried on at and about Karachi from time immemorial on a scale so much in excess of local requirements that the salting of fish for export has also become a great trade'. Karachi fishermen were generally indebted to the Khoja and *bania* merchants who advanced credit mainly for boats and nets. Contractors owned godowns where salted fish and prawn was kept for export to east Africa, Burma, Colombo, China, and the UK.
32. During the Quit India movement Sindh, Punjab, the North West Frontier Province and many areas of south India were quiet as compared to western Maharashtra, the eastern United Provinces, and Bihar.
33. Francis G. Hutchins, *India's Revolution*, Massachusetts, 1973, p. 237.
34. The *GKD*, p. 101, describes Pir Mangho, popularly called Mugger Pir, a religious shrine, 10 miles north of Karachi in the following words: 'When the Pir died and was buried, his grave became a place of pilgrimage for pious Muslims from all parts of the country. But it is also a resort of Hindu devotees, who call it Lala Jasraj. This double character is common among the shrines of Sind: The Mussalman Lal Shahbaz is the Hindu Raja Bhartari and the Mussalman Kwaja Khizr is the Hindu Jinda Pir.'
35. FR (Sindh), first half of February 1946, Home—Political, 18/2/46, NAI.
36. FR (Sindh), second half of October 1945, Home-Political, 18/10145, NAI.
37. H. Dow (Governor of Sindh) to Wavell, 3.11.45, in *TOP*, p. 438. After October 1945 the Congress consistently supported the INA men, and Congress attempts to defend them were widely propagated.
38. IB1.
39. IB2 and *Dawn*, 23 February 1946.
40. *The Tribune*, 22 February 1946.
41. IB2.
42. This 1,200 feet long screw-pile bridge was built in 1865.
41. FR (Sindh), second half of February 1946.
42. *The Tribune*, 23 February 1946.
43. Firing occurred on Friday. This may have influenced the sensibilities aroused in devout Muslims in the town. According to *GKD*, p. 60, at Manora there was (and probably is) a tomb of a 'wonder-working Pir' which attracted crowds to an annual fair.
46. *Dawn*, 23 February 1946.
47. *The Tribune*, 23 February 1946.
48. IB2.
49. IB1.

50. IB1.
51. IB1.
52. Ibid.
53. IB2.
54. Ibid.
55. FR (Sindh), second half of February, op. cit.
56. IB2.
57. Forewarning from Bombay was thankfully acknowledged by Mudie. See *TOP*, p. 1072.
58. FR (Sindh), second half of February.
59. IB1.
60. IB1.
61. *Inspiring Story of the Historic RIN Uprising* by a victimized RIN striker, duplicate of a PPH pamphlet in the Archives for the documents of contemporary history, JNU, New Delhi, p. 10.
62. IB2.
63. Sumit Sarkar, 'Popular Movements and National Leadership, 1945–7', *EPW* annual number April 1982, mentions the police strikes of 1946. Wider generalizations regarding police behaviour during 1939–46 can, however, be made only after considerable research in this field is undertaken.
64. IB1.
65. IB1.
66. FR (Sindh), second half of February 1946.
67. IB1.
68. IB1.
69. Violence in Karachi was not as extreme as in Bomhay during the RIN uprising where a virtual upheaval of the 'have nots' occurred. In Karachi, mass participation was in the nature of an extended riot.
70. IB2.
71. The occupation of the Id Gah by foreign troops probably inflamed passions further.
72. IB2.
73. IB1.
74. *TOP*, p. 1072.
75. IB1.
76. *Dawn*, 24 February 1946.
77. Ibid.
78. *Dawn and The Tribune*, 25 February 1946.
79. *PCP*, pp. 1–41.
80. This fits in well with the general student-worker militancy of that period in Indian history.
81. Even the *People's Age*, which was by and large sympathetic to the Bombay working class, mentioned that during 'Bombay's three days of

Heroic battle', 'anti-socials' in some localities took 'advantage of (the) situation by organizing orgies of loot. . . . and senseless burning', *People's Age*, 3 March 1946. An attempt was thus made to dissociate a disciplined working class from some anti-social elements. In any case, the question who was 'organizing' loot and what was being looted and why was left unanswered by this organ of the CPI.

82. For example, to describe the crowd, the *Bombay Chronicle*, 24 February 1946 used terms such as 'frenzied crowds' and 'hooligans'. The crowd action was called a 'thoughtless orgy' of violence. Similar vocabulary characterized the *Times of India* reports.
83. Georges Lefebvre, 'Revolutionary Crowds' in Jeffry Kaplow, ed., *New Perspectives on the French Revolution: Readings in Historical Sociology*, London, 1965, p. 175.
84. Sumit Sarkar in 'Popular Movements and National Leadership, 1945–7, describes the post-war conditions and tensions. Lefebvre in 'Revolutionary Crowds' writes that 'no gathering' apart from lines formed outside bakery doors in large cities is more apt to be suddenly transformed into 'an assembly of rioters'.
85. Lefebvre, op. cit., p. 185.
86. In times of social crisis feeling of imminent change often becomes generalized and the so-called 'lower orders' too partake of this. Conditions in India from 1942 to 1947 were also critical and uncertain in many ways and the Indian crowd too participated in history within this context.
87. Lefebvre, op. cit., p.179, writes: Every human aggregate forms within society. It is true that, to become a part of it, the individual must provisionally break away from the social group to which he normally belongs; but he cannot for all that completely throw off the collective mentality of the group. The ideas and feelings which it involves are only pushed into the back of his consciousness. The degree to which this repression occurs depends upon the degree of heterogeneity in the aggregate.
88. See the brilliant discussion on the images, prejudices, ideas, and reality relating to crowds in George Rude, *Crowds in History*, New York, 1964. Also see E. J. Hobsbawm, *Bandits*, Harmondsworth, 1985 for a general formulation of popular notion of crime. While disagreeing with some of the author's presumptions, we nevertheless believe that amongst popular groups (both urban and rural), conceptions of 'straight' and 'bent' exist.
89. This usually refers to massacre, mutilation, rape, etc.
90. In contrast, a few months later, the complexion of the crowd activity was completely transformed. This shows that crowds, like other, and purportedly more conscious social aggregates, are prone to a change in mentality. Instincts of varying types can be aroused by different

moments, the creation of which depends upon factors often beyond the control of crowds.

91. Lefebvre, op. cit., p. 180 writes that the 'sudden awakening of the group consciousness, provoked by a violent emotion, gives the aggregate a new character which could be called the "state of crowd".'
92. Jan Vansina, *Oral Tradition as History*, London, 1985, p. 6.
93. Ranajit Guha has analysed the role of rumour in peasant insurgency in colonial India on the basis of pioneering works by Allport and Postman, Lefebvre, Hobsbawm, Rude, and Prasad in his *Elementary Aspects of Peasant Insurgency in Colonial India*, Delhi, 1983. pp. 251–77, Valuable analyses of rumours are to be found also in Shahid Amin, 'Gandhi as Mahatma: Gorakhpur District, Eastern UP, 1921–8,' in Ranajit Guha, ed., *Subaltern Studies III*, Delhi, 1984; and Anand A. Yang, 'A Conversion of Rumours: The Language of Popular Mentalities in Late Nineteenth Century Colonial India,' *Journal of Social History*, vol. 20, No. 3, 1987.
94. According to Lefebvre, op. cit., p. 184, the analysis of crowds also contains in large proportions, 'a study of the collective mentality.' Guha, *Elementary Aspects*, p. 252 cites Allport and Postman on the subject of riots: 'No riot ever occurs without rumours to incite, accompany and intensify violence.'
95. IB1.
96. Here, news is listed with rumour because most probably the newspaper accounts, due to official restrictions, were based on rumour. In that case, rumour by becoming news rejuvenated itself.
97. *Baluchistan District Gazeteer*, op. cit., p. 69 and pp. 53–136, for general ethnographical information. *GKD*, p. 9, mentions that the majority of migrants were labourers. See the *PCP*. section on history.
98. See Appendix and Raffat Khan Haward, 'An Urban Minority: The Goan Christian Community in Karachi,' in Ballhatchet and Harrison, eds, *The City in South Asia*, London, 1980, pp. 304–6.
99. *GKD*, p. 84; *GPS*, pp. 61–76; *PCP*, section on history.
100. *GPS*, pp. 61–76; *PCP*, section on economic activity.
101. *PCP*, chapter on Karachi city.
102. See Ghosh, *The Indian National Army*, pp. 198–251.
103. Harbans Mukhia, 'The Connotations of Indian Secularism,' 'Express Magazine,' *Indian Express*, 4 January 1987. For a brief review of Indian nationalism see Gyanendra Pandey' 'Questions of Nationalism and Communalism,' *Economic and Political Weekly*, 20 June 1987. In Karachi, the INA trials issue and League mobilization on it ran on communal lines and the Muslims of the Indian army were found attending Muslim League meetings. The stand taken by Jinnah on the demand for the release of Abdul Rashid in his newspaper *Dawn* tilted clearly towards an open communal position. The FR (Sindh) from October 1945 to February 1946 reported extensively on these matters.

104. *TOP*, p. 1073.
105. Ibid.
106. These preceded the RIN uprising.
107. E. J. Hobsbawm, *Bandits*, pp. 27–8.
108. For a sharp insight into the Congress image during the post-1945 period see D. D. Kosambi, *Exasperating Essays*, Pune, 1986, especially pp. 16–7.
109. *The R.I.N. Strike*, pp. 120–1.
110. IB1.
111. The IB1 reports that newspapers were spreading 'alarmist' news.
112. Lefebvre, 'Revolutionary Crowds', mentions suspicion, fear, panic, and hope as essential attributes of situations involving crowds in action. George Rude, *The Crowd in the French Revolution*, Oxford, 1959, pp. 221–5 writes that 'one of the most constant elements contributing to certain states of collective mentality, at all times and all places. . . is the element of panic-fear propagated by rumour', and that this panic arises from a 'threat, real or imaginary, to three matters of vital moment—to property, life, and the means of subsistence'. In Karachi, especially around the harbour, on 22 and 23 February 1946, these elements were more than present.
113. For instance, the Baluch Regimental Centre was situated in Karachi.
114. Banerjee, *The R.I.N. Strike*, p. 87 tells us that British troops were used after the Baluch and Gurkha troops disobeyed orders. However, his claim that the entire Indian army in Karachi during those days was on the brink of an armed rebellion can only be settled after more rigorous research. *The Inspiring Story of the Historic RIN Uprising*, p. 9 says that two platoons of the Baluch Regiment refused to board the *Hindustan* on 21 February.
115. *TOP*, p. 1072.
116. Visual impacts often produce images of the adversary. If an enemy appears very strong, given varying conditions, the psychological implications of the appearance may vary. In Bombay and Karachi during the RIN uprising, the appearance of state power, though menacing, seems to have spurred the collective resolve and solidarity of the working class.
117. IB1.
118. This relay was printed by all newspapers and in books and articles on the RIN revolt.
119. IB2 and *TOP*, p. 1072.
120. IB2.
121. *TOP*, p.1072.
122. E. J. Hobsbawm (*Primitive Rebels*, New York, 1965, pp. 108–25) has written instructively on the 'city mob' as a sub-political, sub-proletarian, and 'fickle'-minded group. The Indian proletariat has not freed itself from this 'fickle'-mindedness which Hobsbawm associates with a largely

pre-industrial sub-proletariat. The Indian case, by no means exceptional, raises the problem of defining proletarian class consciousness in the Indian as well as the general context.

SECTION V

Colonial Continuity and Post-Colonial Innovations: 1947–2005

CHAPTER 19

Indian Defence Expenditure: 1872–1967*

K. N. Reddy

The purpose of this article is to study the behaviour of defence expenditure in India over 1872–1967 on the basis of historical and empirical facts. In Section I, we explain the method and procedure followed in our study. In Section II, we trace the growth of defence expenditure in money terms and real terms and examine its growth in relation to total government expenditure and national income. In Section III, we analyse the reasons for variations in defence expenditure before and after the independence. In Section IV, we pursue a brief analysis of capital expenditure, and in Section V we note some of the observations.

I

Method and Procedure

The period under our study is from 1872 to that of 1967. All the estimates refer to the financial year ending 31 March. The expenditure series—defence expenditure and total government expenditure—vis-á-vis national income figures pertain to British India up to 1946-7 and the Indian union thereafter. As the area under British India had undergone changes, first when Burma separated in 1937, and second when Pakistan separated in 1947, the aggregate expenditure figures and national income figures are not strictly comparable. To provide comparability we assume that the per capita expenditure of government and per capita national income were the same throughout India, both in British India and the princely states.[1] The definition of government expenditure adopted in this study is based on the various earlier studies made for the United Kingdom,[2] Germany,[3] and Japan.[4] Government expenditure includes not only the purchase of goods and services but also transfers and subsidies. It excludes all expenditures financed out of proceeds to other sectors. Further, any expenditure is included only once, even though in the course of transfers from the centre to the states and the states to the centre an item might appear in the accounts of both. This is meant to avoid double counting. Although in the true sense of the term public expenditure includes the expenditure of central, state, and local authorities, we have excluded the expenditures of local authorities owing to paucity of data.

The defence expenditures series include the expenditures on revenue account and capital account. It must be remembered that until 1943 the capital budget for defence was not separated; all expenditure was shown in the revenue account only. Hence, capital outlay on defence appears separately from 1943 in the budgets of the Government of India.

The main sources for the construction of the expenditure series were 1. Reserve Bank of India, *Banking and Monetary Statistics of India* (1954), and its supplement (1964); 2. Reserve Bank, *Reports on Currency and Finance*; 3. *Combined Finance and Revenue Accounts*; and 4. the budgets of the central government.

Although in almost all the studies of public expenditure, defence expenditure has been related to gross national product (GNP), we have chosen net national product (NNP) at factor cost as our concept, not because of its greater relevance over GNP, but because of the non-availability of the latter in continuous series. In presenting the national income estimates considerable difficulty has been faced, for the historical statistics of national income over the entire period under study are not available officially. Official estimates of national income are available in continuity only since 1949 at current and constant prices in the *Estimates of National Income* issued by the Central Statistical Organization, Cabinet Secretariat, New Delhi, Government of India. Prior to 1949, estimates are available only for specific years—barring a couple of recent long-term estimates—and the methods adopted in estimating them differ widely from one estimate to another. Therefore, the problem has been to present a series of national income estimates for the period 1872–1948 with reasonable consistency. After careful assessment, although we had constructed our own series of national income,[5] we have depended ultimately on M. Mukherjee's[6] estimates for 1872–1900, K. Mukerjee's[7] estimates for 1901–48 and official estimates for 1949–67.

In view of the fact that the growth of government expenditure and national income in money terms gives an imperfect picture, we had to choose suitable price indexes to eliminate the influence of price changes. But the elimination of price changes confronted us with conceptual and statistical problems. Conceptual problems arose because there was no perfect method of choosing a deflator. Statistical problems arose because the data available for constructing the series were scanty. However, we have adopted the wholesale price index for the years 1872–1948, and the index implicit in the official estimates of national income in current and constant prices[8] for the years 1949-67.

II

Growth of Defence Expenditure alongside Government Expenditure and National Income

Defence Expenditure in Money Terms

During the period 1872–1967, defence expenditure per head of population increased from Rs. 0.82 in 1872–80 to Rs. 13.57 in 1961–7 (an increase of 1555 per cent). It can be seen from Table 19.1 that per capita expenditure on defence was roughly constant up to 1900 and increased largely in the decades of 1911–20, 1941–50, and 1961–7. The large increase during these periods was due to the involvement of India in major wars—World War I, World War II before the independence, and near wars with China and Pakistan in 1962 and 1965, respectively, after the independence.

While it is true that the rise in defence expenditure was associated with wars, it cannot be overlooked that the periods of war were also the periods of inflation. During the decades of 1911–20, 1941–50, and 1961–67, the price index with base 1948–9 moved from 22.3 to 52.5 (a rise of 135 per cent), from 32.2 per cent to 102.2 (a rise of 214 per cent), and from 111.1 to 154.6 (a rise of 39 per cent), respectively.[9]

Defence Expenditure in Real Terms

It can be seen from Table 19.1 that the expenditure per head of population had grown at a slower pace in real than in money terms over the period under study. Between 1872–80 and 1961–7, the per capita defence expenditure in real terms increased by only 104 per cent whereas it increased by 1555 per cent in money terms. But such comparison over a long period does not give a complete picture. Let us analyse the growth of defence expenditure in real terms from decade to decade.

Table 19.1: Growth of Defence Expenditure at Current and 1948–9 Prices: 1872–80 to 1961–7

Period	At Current Prices		At 1948–9 Prices			
	Total in crores Rs.	Per capita Rs. P.	Total in crores of Rs.	Per capita Rs. P.	As % of total Expenditure	As % of NI
1872 –80	16	0.82	96	5 .12	29.22	2.87
1881–90	19	0.90	119	5.77	27.03	2.69
1891–1900	23	1.02	123	5.43	30.09	2.71
1901–10	27	1.12	126	5.34	26.56	2.39
1911–20	57	2.31	168	6.71	36.63	2.87
1921–30	61	2.37	137	5.35	28.61	1.96
1931–37	47	1.68	187	6.68	26.44	2.48
1931–40	48	1.67	184	6.47	26.31	2.41
1938–47	205	6.76	390	12.96	40.54	4.68
1941–50	257	8.27	420	13.70	41.27	4.97
1949-50	209	6.17	202	6.12	22.56	2.45
1951–60	215	5.50	207	5.29	16.30	1.99
1961–67	640	13.57	489	10.43	15.74	3.38

The per capita defence expenditure in real terms increased from Rs. 5.12 in 1872–80 to Rs. 5.77 in 1881–90, and remained more or less steady for the following two decades. In the decade 1911–20, it increased to Rs. 6.71 and in the two following decades it declined to Rs. 5.35 in 1921–30, and then increased to Rs. 6.47 in 1931–40. The per capita defence expenditure rose to Rs. 13.70 in 1941–50. After independence, the per capita defence expenditure decreased in the decades immediately following, 1951–60 from the level of Rs. 13.77 reached in 1941–50 to Rs. 5.29, but it increased to Rs. 10.43 in 1961–7.

At this stage, it will be appropriate to ask if measuring the growth of defence expenditure in per capita terms does not understate the real increase in the country's expenditure on defence. It might be objected, with some justification, that the relationship between the defence commitment of a country and the rise of its population is, if anything, extremely remote. It might be more appropriate to observe the growth in defence expenditure after adjustment only for the price changes over the period under review. But the study of the growth of defence expenditure poses the problem of comparability of figures as the geographical area of India did not remain the same throughout this period.

However, we have attempted to overcome this difficulty by dividing the whole period into three sub-periods keeping in mind these changes: 1. 1872–1937; 2. 1938–47 and 3. 1949–67.[10]

During the period 1872–1937, defence expenditure in real terms increased from Rs. 108 crore in 1872 to Rs. 186 crore—an increase of 72 per cent. But during this period, there were years where the increase in defence expenditure was quite significant. The increase in total defence expenditure in real terms was gradual all through but in the decade of 1911–20, in which occurred World War I, from Rs. 96 crore in 1872–80, annual expenditure increased to Rs. 126 crore in 1901–10. It went up to Rs. 168 crore in 1911–20, but declined to Rs. 137 crore in 1921–1930, and again increased to Rs. 187 crore in 1931–7.

In the next period, 1938–47, which was also the decade of World War II, expenditure was Rs. 173 crore in 1938 and Rs. 285 crore in 1947. But in between there were years which witnessed the highest levels so far. Defence expenditure which was Rs. 228 crore in 1941 reached Rs. 616 crore in 1943, Rs. 665 crore in 1944 and Rs. 697 crore in 1945. This phenomenal increase, it must be understood, was due to the impact of World War II.

Next is the period 1949–67. During this period, defence expenditure in real terms increased from Rs. 257 crore in 1949 to Rs. 588 crore in 1967. During this period also, there have been years with peaks and troughs. The defence expenditure had already started declining in the preceding period and it touched the level of Rs. 148 crore in real terms in 1950. Thereafter, the curve of defence expenditure in real terms has been ascending from year to year, starting from Rs. 156 crore in 1951 to Rs. 276 crore in 1962. Then it spurted to Rs. 410 in 1963 and Rs. 662 crore in 1964. In the last year of our period, i.e. 1967, defence expenditure in 1948–9 prices stood at Rs. 588 crore. Interestingly enough, 1965–6, the year during which India was involved in war with Pakistan, was not the year of maximum defence expenditure in real terms.

As a percentage of total government expenditure,[11] defence expenditure moved rather differently. Throughout the British period, 1872–1947, it accounted for roughly 30 per cent of total government expenditure, with the exception of the periods 1911–20 (World War I) and 1938–47 (World War II) during which periods the percentages were 37 per cent and 43 per cent, respectively. In the period after independence, the proportion of defence expenditure to total expenditure decreased to 16 per cent in 1951–60 and 15.74 per cent in 1961–7. It is interesting to note that at a time when near-wars, threatening the sovereignty of the country, occurred during 1961–7, the relative proportion of defence expenditure to total expenditure declined, contrary to normal expectations. This has happened even though the outlay on defence in real terms increased during the period 1951–67 by almost four times. Clearly, the expenditure on categories other than defence has been rising at a pace faster than that of defence expenditure.[12]

Defence expenditure, as a percentage of national income, amounted to roughly 2.5 per cent during the whole pre-independence period, with the exception of the decades 1921–30, and 1941–50. It was the lowest in the decade 1921–30, and the highest in the decade, 1941–50. It was low in the former decade not due to any decrease in defence expenditure, but due to a rapid increase in the national income; it was high in the decade 1941–50 due to the occurrence of World War II. In the period after independence, the percentage of defence expenditure to national income has remained around 2 per cent except during the years after 1962. The percentage in 1967 was 4.35.

Thus, there has been a clear-cut demarcation in the pattern of growth of defence expenditure before and after independence. Before independence, while total defence expenditure in real terms was steadily growing decade after decade, every war—minor or major—pushed the expenditure to a higher level; per capita defence expenditure, percentage of defence expenditure to total expenditure, the percentage of defence expenditure to national income, all the three measures remained roughly constant with the exception of the decades in which the World Wars occurred. After independence (1950–67), while total defence expenditure in real terms increased fourfold in a matter of less than 20 years, per capita expenditure on defence rose almost threefold, and the proportion of national income spent on defence almost doubled, but the proportion of government expenditure incurred on defence remained almost constant. At the same time, it is interesting to note that the highest proportion of national income spent on defence in the period after independence, i.e. 4.74 per cent in 1964, was far below the highest level reached before the independence, i.e. 7.77 per cent in 1944, the penultimate year of World War II. If we were to consider the decennial averages, the proportion of defence expenditure to national income was the highest (i.e. 5 per cent) during the decade, 1941–50. What is not less interesting is that while in the decade immediately following, 1951–60, the proportion was 1.99 per cent, the corresponding proportion for the two decades ending with 1920 was between 2.39 and 2.81 per cent. During the decade 1921–30, the proportion was lower, i.e. 1.96 per cent. Clearly, the proportion before the independence spent on defence was rather high almost throughout the period of our enquiry.

III

Variations in Defence Expenditure—Before and After Independence

Up to the end of the nineteenth century, India was engaged in one war or the other to consolidate and extend the frontiers. Between 1872 and 1947, quite a significant number of wars were waged at the expense of India. Chronologically, the wars fought by the Britishers were:[13]

1. Perak (1875)
2. Afghan War II (1878–81)
3. Egypt (1882)
4. Sudan (1885–96)
5. Burma (1885–91)
6. Suakin (1896)
7. World War I (1914–9)
8. World War II (1939–46)

Defence expenditure was to be kept high not only during the actual years in which wars had taken place, but also in the years immediately following the wars. This was particularly so up to the first quarter of the twentieth century. Moreover, it was the policy of government that the 'Army should be kept in a continual state of preparedness for instant operations in the event of war or unrest.[14]

After the World War I, some attempt was made towards the reduction of defence expenditure. The Inchcape Committee, 1921 had recommended that defence expenditure had to be brought down considerably. In fact, it was brought down (in current prices) and at one stage (1934–8), when it was reduced to the level desired by the Inchcape Committee, both Sir George Schuster and Sir James Grigg, India's Finance Members, warned the Legislature that 'This figure could not be regarded as a new permanent level of defence expenditure.' It must be remembered that even this reduction in defence expenditure was brought about in a period when incomes and prices were depressed, and therefore the drop in real terms in defence expenditure was very little. In any case this drop was short-lived because with the outbreak of World War II the burden placed on India's shoulders was raised several-fold, particularly if one included the expenditure on behalf of and therefore recoverable from Britain.

The total defence expenditure (defence expenditure incurred on on her own account + defence expenditure incurred on behalf of Britain) which was Rs. 46 crore in money terms at the commencement of World War II (1939) increased to Rs. 298 crore in 1942; Rs. 593 crore in 1943; Rs. 774 crore in 1944; Rs. 689 crore in 1945; and Rs. 770 crore in 1946. From the commencement of the

World War II to the penultimate year of the War, it increased by 19 times (in money terms). During the same years, the proportion of national income spent on total defence increased by seven times. It increased from 2.4 per cent in 1939 to 14.3 per cent in 1946 (see Table 19.2). The largest proportion (16.4 per cent) of national income spent on defence was during 1943.

Table 19.2: Growth of Total Defence Expenditure (Defence Expenditure Incurred on Her Own Account + Defence Expenditure Incurred on Behalf of Britain) during World War II, and its Percentage to National Income at Current Prices: 1939–46

Year	Expenditure incurred on India's account (in crores of Rs.)	Expenditure incurred by India on behalf of Britain (in crores of Rs.)	Total (2+3)	Total defence expenditure as % of national income
1	2	3	4	5
1939	46.18	Nil	46.18	2.4
1940	49.54	4.00	53.54	2.2
1941	73.61	53.00	126.61	4.8
1942	109.93	194.00	297.93	10.1
1943	267.13	325.48	592.61	16.4
1944	395.86	377.87	773.73	15.2
1945	458.32	410.84	869.16	14.5
1946	395.32	374.54	769.86	14.3

It is interesting to note that the expenditure incurred by India on behalf of Britain far exceeded the total amount of defence expenditure incurred on her own account, assuming, of course, that the latter expenditure could be said to have been incurred on the genuine defence needs of India itself arising out of World War II, an assumption which would be strongly contested, in India. The percentage of recoverable war expenditure to defence expenditure on India's account was 8 per cent in 1940; 72 per cent in 1941; 186.7 per cent in 1942; and 121.8 per cent in 1943. During the other years also, it formed a substantial part in total defence expenditure.

No less interesting is the fact that the total defence expenditure exceeded the rest of the total government expenditure. It can be seen from Table 19.3 that the total defence expenditure was more than twice of the rest of total government expenditure after 1942.

Table 19.3: Total Government Expenditure Excluding Defence and Total Defence Expenditure in Current Prices—1940–46

(*Rs. in Crores*)

Year	Total Government Expenditure Excluding Defence	Total Defence Expenditure
1940	138.55	53.54
1941	141.32	126.61
1942	146.10	297.63
1943	217.09	592.61
1944	312.16	773.73
1945	313.73	869.16
1946	338.25	769.86

*Defence expenditure on India's account + defence expenditure on behalf of Britian.

The reason why one should take note of defence expenditure incurred on behalf of Britain is that then alone does one get the true measure of the extent of the burden borne by India during the War. The goods and services covered by the expenditure incurred on behalf of Britain constituted draft on resources available for current consumption in precisely the same manner as did the goods and services forgone for expenditure said to have been incurred for India's own defence. The mere fact that with respect to the expenditure incurred on defence on behalf of Britain, India accumulated corresponding credit balances with Britain does not mean that India incurred any less sacrifice in parting with the real resources it actually had to part with. Such an argument is as invalid as the one which might try to prove that the real cost of war can be shifted to the next generation through the mechanism of debt financing.

As for the growth of defence expenditure after independence, a case for increase in defence expenditure rather than decrease could be made in terms of the defence burden imposed on the country not by the mere fact of its becoming independent but by subsequent developments, i.e. the dispute with Pakistan over Kashmir and with China over Aksaichin.

Soon after the independence quite a significant number of events—communal disturbances, police action in Hyderabad and Kashmir, the integration of Part B States with the Indian Union in April 1950, the liberation of Goa, and continuous border disputes with Pakistan and China, particularly after 1960–took place and compelled the government to increase defence expenditure. It is worth while to note that the partition of the country on 15 August 1947 contributed to an increase in expenditure in the sense that it deprived India of the great advantage in defence strategy of an impregnable land frontier. A long land frontier has to be safeguarded.

IV

Analysis of Capital Expenditure

In this context, it is worthwhile to study the growth of capital expenditure on defence and its proportion to total defence expenditure, so that we could know the permanent assets created by the growth of defence expenditure. The capital outlay in real terms which was only Rs. 1.91 crore in 1950 increased to Rs. 18.48 crore in 1956; Rs. 42.01 crore in 1963, Rs. 90.88 crore in 1964, and Rs. 68.71 crore in 1967 an increase of 36 times over the period 17 years. As a proportion of total defence expenditure, the capital outlay increased from 1.21 per cent in 1950 to 11.69 per cent in 1967.[15] In other words, capital outlay has contributed to the growth of defence expenditure significantly.

The total capital expenditure spent on defence between 31 March 1948 to 31 March 1964 was Rs. 493.62 crore.[16] Out of Rs. 493.62 crore, Rs. 199.29 was spent on the army, including factories and farms; Rs. 107.68 crore was spent on the Navy; Rs. 93.85 crore was spent on the air force; Rs. 63.98 crore on stores and fixed installations taken over from the government of the United Kingdom on April 1947; and Rs. 28.83 crore on industrial development. In percentages, the army, navy; air force's stores and fixed installations and industrial development amounted to 40 per cent, 22 per cent, 19 per cent, 14 per cent and 6 per cent, respectively. These proportions were entirely different up to 1958; stores and fixed installations claimed the major proportion of capital outlay. Strictly speaking, 'stores and fixed installations' should be kept out of the picture in our analysis as its basis for inclusion in capital outlay stands entirely on different ground.

V

Conclusions

During the period under our review, the per capita defence expenditure in real terms increased from Rs. 5.12 in 1872–80 to Rs. 10.43 in 1961–7 (an increase of 104 per cent) whereas it increased in money terms from 82 paise in 1872–80 to Rs. 13.57 in 1961–7 (an increase of 1555 per cent).

As a proportion of national income spent, defence expenditure amounted to roughly 2.5 per cent during the whole pre-independence period with the exception of the periods 1915–20 and 1939–47. In the period after 1950, the proportion of defence expenditure in national income remained around 2 per cent, except during the years after 1962.

Before independence, all the three measures of defence expenditure—per capita in real terms, percentage of total expenditure and percentage of national income—remained constant except during the decades in which the World Wars occurred. After independence, while total defence expenditure in real terms increased fourfold (1950–67) in a matter of less than 20 years, per capita expenditure on defence rose almost threefold and the proportion of national income spent on defence almost doubled, but the proportion of total government expenditure incurred on defence remained almost constant. At the same time, it is interesting to note that the highest proportion of national income spent on defence in the period after independence, i.e. 4.74 per cent in 1964 was far below the highest level reached before independence, i.e. 7.7 per cent in 1944, the penultimate year of World War II.

NOTES

*Editor's Note: Two charts which are present in the original version of this essay have been deleted in this reprint version.

*The author is highly indebted to Professor I. S. Gulati for his help and guidance. The article is partly based on the author's PhD thesis, *The Growth of Public Expenditure in India*: 1872–1966.

1. Such an assumption is not without precedent. See Suphan Andic and Jendrich Veverka, 'The Growth of Government Expenditure in Germany since Unification', *Finanzarchiv*, January 1964, p. 175.
2. Alan T. Peacock and Jack Wiseman, *The Growth of Public Expenditure in the United Kingdom*, Princeton, 1961.
3. Andic and Veverka: 'The Growth of Government Expenditure in Germany since Unification', *Finanzarchiv*, January 1964.
4. Koichi Emi, *Government Fiscal Activity and Economic Growth in Japan: 1868–1960*, Economic Research Series 6, The Institute of Economic Research, Hitotsubashi University, Tokyo, 1963.
5. See K. N. Reddy, *The Growth of Public Expenditure in India: 1872–1966* (PhD Thesis), M. S. University of Baroda, August 1968, Chapter II.
6. M. Mukherjee, 'Growth of National Income in India', *Asian Studies in Income and Wealth*, eds., V. K. R. V. Rao and K. Ohkawa, Bombay: Asia Publishing House, 1965, pp. 71–103.
7. K. Mukherjee, *Levels of Economic Activity and Public Expenditure*, Bombay: Gokhale Institute of Politics and Economics, Asia Publishing House, 1965, p. 58. Table F.
8. Conventional series with 1948–9, p. 100.
9. Price index specially constructed for the purpose. It is the wholesale price index up to 1948, and the implicit indicator in the current and constant national income figures thereafter.
10. Actually the year 1948 should be included instead of 1949, but as the figures for 1948 pertain to only 7.5 months, we have taken 1949 into account.
11. It may be noted that the total government expenditure includes the expenditure of the central as well as state governments, as defined in the first section.
12. See K. N. Reddy, op. cit., Chapters VII, VIII, and IX.
13. See C. N. Vakil, *Financial Developments in India, 1860–1924*, Bombay, D. B. Taraporewala Sons & Co., p. 190, London, P. S. King and Sons Ltd., 1924, p. 126.
14. Inchcape Committee Report, p. 13, quoted by C. N. Vakil in his *Financial Developments in Modern India*, p. 112.
15. See Appendix, Table 2.
16. See Appendix, Table 3.

APPENDIX

Table 1: Defence Expenditure at Current and 1948–9 Price during 1872–1967

Year	At Current Prices			At 1948–9 Prices			
	Total in Lakhs of Rs.	Per Capita Rs. P	Index 1900–100	Total in Lakhs of Rs.	Per Capita Rs. P	Index 1900-100	Difference Expn. as % of Nl
1	2	3	4	5	6	7	8
1872	1,473	0.80	87	10,752	5.84	114	3.03
1873	1,459	0.79	86	10,062	5.45	107	2.82
1874	1,422	0.76	83	9,673	5.17	101	2.96
1875	1,439	0.77	84	8,938	4.78	94	2.36
1876	1,426	0.76	83	10,042	5.35	105	2.54
1877	1,487	0.78	85	10,115	5.31	104	3.36
1878	1,577	0.83	90	8,300	4.37	86	3.01
1879	1,612	0.84	91	7,902	4.12	81	2.42
1880	2,063	1.07	116	10,973	5.69	111	2.79
1872–80	1,551	0.82		9,640	5.12		2.81
1881	2,386	1.23	134	14,820	7.64	150	3.42
1882	1,504	0.76	83	10,231	5.17	101	2.29
1883	1,677	0.84	91	11,566	5.79	113	2.59
1884	1,602	0.79	86	10,898	5.38	105	2.58
1885	1,615	0.79	86	10,221	5.00	98	2.333
1886	1,913	0.92	100	12,108	5.82	114	2.67
1887	1,887	0.89	97	12,333	5.82	114	2.69
1888	1,981	0.93	101	12,948	6.08	119	2.97
1889	2,002	0.93	101	12,207	5.67	111	2.78
1890	2,042	0.93	101	11,736	5.34	105	2.58
1881–90	1,861	0.90		11,907	5.77		2.59
1891	2,040	0.92	100	11,724	5.29	103	2.64
1892	2,211	1.00	109	12,492	5.65	111	2.99
1893	2,301	1.03	1112	11,800	5.28	103	2.78
1894	2,273	1.08	110	11,963	5.32	104	9.61
1895	2,330	1.03	112	12,944	5.72	112	2.73
1896	2,452	1.08	117	13,853	6.10	119	2.87
1897	2,340	1.03	112	12,124	5.34	104	3.05
1898	2,614	1.14	124	11,465	5.00	98	2.22
1899	2,309	1.01	110	12,481	5.46	107	2.53

1900	2,125	0.92	100	11,806	5.11	100	2.69
1891-1900	2,300	1.02		12,265	5.43		2.71
1901	2,141	0.93	101	10,097	4.39	86	1.99
1902	2,218	0.95	103	11,035	4.73	93	2.27
1903	2,433	1.04	113	12,606	5.39	105	2.28
1904	2,520	1.07	116	14,000	5.94	116	2.59
1905	2,901	1.23	134	15,681	6.65	130	2.91
1906	2,734	1.15	125	13,602	5.72	112	2.60
1907	3,021	1.127	138	12,801	5.38	105	2.23
1908	2,887	1.20	130	12,233	5.08	99	2.60
1909	2,940	1.22	133	11,667	4.84	95	2.17
1910	2,867	1.18	128	12,742	5.24	103	2.22
1901-10	2,666	1.12		12,647	5.34		2.39
1911	2,890	1.19	129	12,960	5.34	105	2.13
1912	2,934	1.20	130	12,432	5.08	99	2.06
1913	2,935	1.20	130	11,787	4.82	94	1.89
1914	2,984	1.22	133	11,477	4.69	92	1.99
1915	3,065	1.25	136	11,437	4.67	91	1.92
1916	3,339 (5,589)	1.36 (2.28)	248	11,130 (18,630)	4.53 (7.60)	149	2.06 (3.40)
1917	3,769 (8,269)	1.54 (3.37)	366	10,988 (24,079)	4.49 (9.82)	192	1.59 (3.40)
1918	4,356 (9,606)	1.78 (3.92)	426	11,198 (24,694)	4.58 (10.08)	197	1.65 (3.50)
1919	6,672 (9,692)	2.72 (3.93)	427	14,136 (20,491)	5.76 (8.32)	163	2.42 (3.10)
1920	8,698	3.54	385	16,568	6.74	132	2.38
1911-20	4,164 (5,664)	1.70 (2.31)		12,411 (16,755)	5.07 (6.71)		2.01 (2.57)
1921	8,175	3.31	360	15,083	6.11	120	2.38
1922	6,981	2.80	304	14,544	58.83	114	2.12
1923	6,527	2.60	283	13,828	5.51	108	1.89
1924	5,623	2.22	241	12,197	4.82	94	1.70
1925	5,563	2.18	237	11,989	4.70	92	1.72
1926	5,600	2.17	236	13,146	5.09	100	1.91
1927	5,597	2.15	234	14,098	5.42	106	1.99
1928	5,479	2.09	227	13,801	5.26	103	1.95
1929	5,510	2.08	226	14,165	5.35	105	1.94
1930	5,510	2.06	224	14,577	5.45	107	1.95
1921-30	6,057	2.37	217	13,743	5.35		1.96
1931	5,430	2.00		17,460	6.43	126	2.34
1932	5,176	1.88	204	20,140	7.32	143	2.80
1933	4,674	1.68	183	19,156	6.89	135	2.68

1934	4,442	1.58	172	19,064	6.78	133	2.48
1935	4,434	1.56	170	18,552	6.53	128	2.45
1936	4,498	1.56	170	18,434	6.39	125	2.41
1937	4,545	1.56	170	18,627	6.39	125	2.23
1931-7	4,743	1.69		18,776	6.68		2.48
1938	4,735	1.60	174	17,344	5.86	115	2.16
1939	4,618	1.60	174	18,110	6.27	123	2.40
1940	4,954	1.69	184	17,083	5.83	114	2.10
1931-40	4,751	1.67		18,397	6.47		2.41
1941	7,361	2.48	270	22,860	7.70	151	2.78
1942	10,393	3.48	378	29,112	9.75	191	3.52
1943	26,713	8.88	965	61,551	20.46	400	7.41
1944	39,586	13.13	1427	66,531	22.07	432	7.77
1945	45,832	15.13	1645	69,758	23.03	451	7.62
1946	39,532	12.93	1405	59,447	19.44	380	7.33
1947	20,737	6.70	728	28,524	9.21	180	3.68
1941-7	20,446	6.70		39,032	12.96		4.68
1949	25,660	7.42	807	25,660	7.42	145	2.97
1950	16,081	4.28	465	14,756	4.19	82	1.68
1941-50	25,766	8.27		42,022	13.70		4.97
1949-50	20,870	5.85		20,208	5.81		2.33
1951	16,132	4.70	511	15,629	4.36	85	1.76
1952	18,113	4.98	541	16,526	4.54	89	1.82
1953	18,548	5.00	543	17,869	4.82	94	1.88
1954	19,646	5.21	566	18,800	4.99	98	1.87
1955	19,513	5.07	551	20,870	5.42	106	2.03
1956	18,982	4.85	527	19,939	5.09	100	1.90
1957	21,185	5.30	576	20,608	5.16	101	1.87
1958	27,965	6.87	747	26,735	6.57	128	2.46
1959	27,881	6.71	729	25,768	6.20	121	2.21
1960	26,697	6.29		24,478	5.76	113	2.06
1951-60	21,536	5.50	684	20,722	5.29		1.99
1961	28,094	6.48	704	25,287	5.83	114	2.11
1962	31,249	7.05	766	27,581	6.22	122	2.58
1963	47,391	10.43	1134	40,960	9.01	176	4.74
1964	81,611	17.60	1913	66,243	14.28	279	3.94
1965	80,580	16.96	1843	64,586	12.74	250	4.35
1966	88,476	18.23	1982	63,515	13.09	256	3.94
1967	90,859	18.27	1986	58,770	11.82	231	3.38
1961-7	64,037	13.57		41,992	10.43		

Note: During the years of World War I, the figures in brackets indicate adjusted figures, while the figures in direct line indicate official figures: the index numbers are for the adjusted figures.

The contribution made by Government of India (Rs. 150 crore) in 1918 towards the war cost of the United Kingdom is taken into account as defence expenditure, and is distributed over the war years in the ratio 15:30:35:20. Therefore, the figures in brackets show regular defence expenditure plus the contribution towards the war cost of the United Kingdom.

Table 2: Capital Outlay on Defence at Current and 1948–9 Prices: 1943–67

(*Rupees in Crores*)

Year	At current price	At constant (1948-49) prices	As percentage of total defence expenditure
1943	52.51	120.99	19.65
1944	37.46	62.96	9.46
1945	62.83	94.48	13.70
1946	35.09	52.77	8.87
1947	2.23	3.07	1.06
1948	—	—	—
—	—	—	—
—	—	—	—
1949	110.55	110.55	42.95
1950	1.95	1.91	1.21
1951	4.19	3.39	2.48
1952	10.17	9.28	5.61
1953	5.96	5.74	3.21
1954	10.16	9.72	5.17
1955	8.47	9.06	4.34
1956	17.59	18.48	9.26
1957	19.70	19.16	9.29
1958	22.93	21.92	8.19
1959	27.88	25.77	9.99
1960	36.11	33.07	13.52
1961	33.39	30.05	11.88
1962	22.95	20.26	7.34
1963	48.61	42.01	10.25
1964	111.97	90.88	13.71
1965	112.95	82.93	14.02
1966	122.58	88.34	13.85
1967	106.22	68.71	11.69

Source: Reports on Currency and Finance, Reserve Bank of India, Bombay.
Note: The Capital outlay for the year 1949 was abnormally high for the reason

that Rs.. 103.81 crore was spent on stores and fixed installations taken over from the United Kingdom on 1 April 1947.
Figures above the line are not comparable as they represent undivided India.

Table 3: Distribution of Capital Outlay on Defence to the End of Each Year since 1948–9 to 1963–4 in Current Prices

(Rupees in Crores)

Year	Estimated Balance Brought Forward on the 15 August 1947	Army Including Factories and Farms	Navy	Air Force	Stores and Fixed Installations taken over from the UK Govt on 1 April 1947	Industrial Development	Total
1948	–	–	–	–	–	–	144.16
1949	*144.16	2.19	2.69	1.87	103.81	NA	254.16
1950	*144.16	8.74	3.19	4.68	95.87	NA	256.66
1951	*144.16	14.68	3.93	9.44	88.71	NA	260.93
1952	*144.16	24.89	5.20	10.94	85.16	2.20	272.35
1953	*144.16	31.39	6.98	12.53	80.12	3.22	278.39
1954	*144.16	38.00	9.14	14.17	79.59	3.34	288.40
1955	*144.16	43.24	13.09	16.19	76.34	3.83	296.84
1956	*144.16	52.03	20.42	18.90	73.64	5.29	314.44
1957	*144.16	58.12	28.53	22.58	71.07	7.68	334.14
1958	*144.16	64.35	41.85	26.92	68.05	11.75	375.07
1959	*144.16	72.25	57.35	30.28	66.26	14.64	384.95
1960	*144.16	81.25	76.60	33.62	66.17	19.14	420.96
1961	*144.16	91.44	91.85	37.50	65.07	24.32	454.34
1962	*144.16	104.22	96.26	42.06	64.24	26.35	477.29
1963	*144.16	130.79	101.71	58.82	63.98	26.37	525.82
1964	*144.16	199.29	107.68	93.85	63.98	28.33	637.78

*Provisional

Source: Combined Finance and Revenue Accounts of the Central and State Government in India.

CHAPTER 20

Decentralization and Diffusion of Power in the Army Structures of India and Pakistan

Daljit Singh and Katherine Singh

> It was also interesting and pleasing to find that order of parade was actually the same as at Sandhurst, even to the adjutant riding his horse through the main entrance of the building at the end of the parade to the strains of 'Auld Lang Syne.'[1]

These are the words of Sir John Harding, a former General in the British-Indian Army. Spoken in 1955, they illustrate the continuity, at least in externals, of English traditions in the armies of independent India and Pakistan. One should not be deceived by outward appearances, however, for despite the somewhat 'romantic attachment' with the British past, the armies of India and Pakistan have undergone significant changes since 1947. It is the purpose of this article to analyse these transformations in organizational structure, recruitment patterns, and in civil–military relations. In doing so, we will discover how the military was utilized by the two nations to meet the demands of their respective internal and external policies.

Structure and Civil Military Relations Before 1947

The development of the present Indian army structure began in 1857 when the Governor-General-in-Council became the controller of all military affairs. The Commander-in-Chief of the army was the executor of military policy. Until 1905, the civil–military relationship was largely a cooperative one.[2] However, there was one prominent dispute which came to be known as the Curzon–Kitchener Controversy. During this constitutional crisis, Lord

Kitchener, the Commander-in-Chief of the armed forces in India, argued that the office of the Military Member on the Governor-General's Council was 'detrimental to military efficiency.'[3] The Military Member was equal in rank and status to the Commander-in-Chief and was 'responsible for the administrative work of the army, representing and issuing the order of the Government of India.'[4] The execution of any military policy required the concurrent approval of the Military Member. This Lord Kitchener resented. He proposed the unification of the offices of the Military Member and the Commander-in-Chief into one position—Commander-in-Chief in India and War Member in Council.[5] These suggestions were not favoured by Viceroy Curzon. He felt that such a move would be 'tantamount to the establishment of a military autocracy in the country.'[6] He believed that:

> The Government of India being invested by law with the supreme control of military affairs, it was imperative that it must possess an office of a ministerial establishment and an officer of high rank at the head of such a department, for the purpose of communication with the Secreatry of State, for the issue of orders, for the maintenance of continuity of administration, for the necessary adjustment of military requirements with other branches, and more especially with the Financial Branch of the government.[7]

The result of this dispute was that the Secretary of State for India appointed a committee to study military organization. As a result of the committee's report, Kitchener won a temporary victory. The position of the Military Member was abolished and replaced by a new Council Member in Charge of Military Supplies. All other matters concerning organization and military policy were brought under Commander-in-Chief Kitchener. However, in 1906, a new Department of Military Finance was created which was headed by a civilian from the Finance Ministry. This organizational format, which further strengthened civilian control, continues in India to this day.[8]

Further changes in defence organization took place in 1911 when the Department of the Commander-in-Chief and the Department of Military Supplies were merged into a single Army Department. This organization was retained until 1935. After that there were several name changes, but the structures remained much the same.

During World War II, the military arm of government was known as the War Department. It wielded extensive powers. With the end of the War, the name became the Defence Department, for the new members of the Viceroy's Executive Council were predominately Congressmen, and the Indian leadership disliked the old title 'War Department' and its connotations.[9]

The Indianization Process and Recruitment Procedure

Under pressure from the Congress Party, the Indianization of the army started in 1919. Before this time, the army was controlled exclusively by the British and no Indian was granted a King's Commission. There was an inferior class of commissions, the Viceroy's Commissions, which were given to native soldiers. Even so, an Indian officer could command no more than a platoon of Indian soldiers or Nepali Gorkhas.[10] Of course, Indian were never permitted to command British nationals. The Viceroy's Commission ranks were those of Risaldar, Subedar, and Jemadar. These Indian officers came up through the ranks and were equivalent to the junior and senior non-commissioned officers in the American and British forces.[11]

Following the announcement of the Montagu-Chelmsford Reforms in 1917. Indian participation in the government increased, and in addition, 10 King's Commissions or 10 seats at the Royal Military College at Sandhurst were reserved for Indians.[12] Although this quota was far too small to satisfy the demands of the nationalists, the Monetford Reforms did provide a major breakthrough for further Indianization of the army. By September 1945, the Government of India declared that 'in the future only Indians would be eligible for regular commissions in the Indian armed forces'.[13]

In addition to his dispute with Viceroy Curzon, Lord Kitchener is remembered as the chief architect of a policy of army recruitment based on the concept of the 'martial races'. Under this policy, preference was given to persons coming from specific geographic areas and religious communities. Among those who were to have a disproportionate share of army positions were the Punjabi Muslims, Rajputs, Jats, Sikhs, Gorkhas, and Pathans.[14]

Table 20.1

	Provincial Percentage		
Punjab	50	UP	15
NWFP	5	Madras	10
Nepal	8	Bombay	10
Bengal	2	Ajmer and Merwara	3
		CP Burma, Assam, Bihar and Orissa	5
	Communal Percentage		
Muslims	34	Sikhs	10
Hindus and Gurkhas	50	Christians and Others	6

Source: Aslam Siddiqi, *A Path for Pakistan*, Karachi: Pakistan Publishing House, 1964, p. 47.
*CP: Central Province

There was never a lack of army volunteers from the 'martial' communities, and most regiments had long waiting lists.[15] In so far as officers were concerned, most of the recruitment was from the upper and middle classes of the Punjab and Northwest frontier. Before 1925, officer corps was drawn almost exclusively from the wealthy, landed aristocratic families.[16] Furthermore, the British gave preference to candidates whose relatives had served in the army, thus perpetuating the 'martial races' policy.

Structural and Recruitment Changes After 1947

The Partition ended the long and common history of the Indian and Pakistan armies. The military forces were divided between the two nations on a three-to-one ratio. India received 16 cavalry regiments, 18 artillery regiments, and 82 infantry battalions. Pakistan's share was six, nine, and 45, respectively. Hardware, ordinance factories, and barracks were also allotted on a three-to-one basis.[17]

Independence brought obvious problems of military reorganization for both nations, but Pakistan's position was perhaps more difficult. All of Pakistan's army came from the Punjab and Northwest frontier. There were 1,50,000 men in the army divided into approximately 500 units.[18] The bulk of the armed forces was located in West Pakistan. As Ayub Khan noted in his autobiography:

> All we had in East Pakistan at the time of Independence were two infantry battalions: one of these had three Muslim companies, the fourth, a Hindu company, having been transferred to India. The other battalion had one Sikh company and one Dogra company, leaving us with only two more Muslim companies.[19]

It was under Ayub's leadership as the commanding General Officer that the first two East Pakistan battalions were formed in 1948 and 1949. Most of the personnel were gathered from fragments of former British companies.[20] Efforts to recruit Bengalis into the Pakistan army were little more than token gestures, however. Recruitment patterns were not changed substantially, and Bengalis continued to comprise a very small percentage of the army.

In July 1956, a quota of 2 per cent was fixed for East Pakistanis. Two reasons were given for this policy. First, Bengalis were considered unsuitable for army life, and second, East Pakistan was not considered to have had a martial tradition.[21] Obviously, these were the same arguments used by the British to justify the composition of the colonial army. An important, unstated argument for limiting the number of Bengalis was no doubt the fear that a strong contingent of East Pakistanis might, some day aid in a secessionist movement. According to Rounaq Jahan, some attempts were made to increase the Bengali representation in the navy and air force, and civil service, but in the army, 'East Pakistan's representation remained nearly as marginal as before.[22]

Since recruitment procedures and policies have a vital impact on efforts for national integration and nation building, the failure of the central government in Pakistan to make the army a national force was to have serious consequences. For years, the army representation issue provided fuel for the fire of East Bengal separatists. As early as 1948, some East Pakistanis were considering the West Pakistan army stationed in their wing to be an occupying force.[23]

The Modernization and Politicization of the Pakistani Military

At the time of independence, there was a great dearth of officers to meet the immediate needs of the new army. The requirement was for 4,000 officers, but only 2,500 were available. Of these, 500

Table: 20.2: East Pakistani Representation in Different Branches of the Armed Forces in 1963 (in percentage)

ARMY

Ranks	Authorized Representation	Actual Representation
Commissioned Officers	(No fixed percentage)	5.0 (a)
Junior Commissioned Officers	7.8	7.4
Other Ranks	7.8	7.4

AIR FORCE

	General Pilots	Duty Navigators	Technical	Adminis-trative	Educational	Overall
Commissioned Officers	11.0	27.0	17.0	31.0	13.0	17.0
Warrant Officers	–	–	13.2	45.0	11.37	13.2
Other Ranks	–	–	28.0	36.0	37.8	28.0

NAVY

Ranks	Technical	Non-Technical	Overall
Officers	19.0	9.0	10.0
Branch Officers	4.0	6.0	5.0
Chief Petty Officers	8.4	13.4	10.4
Petty Officers	21.3	14.7	17.3
Leading Seamen and Below	28.4	28.5	28.8

Source: Pakistan, National Assembly, *Debates*, vol. I, 8 March 1963, pp. 30-1.
(a) This does not include the Medical Corps in which East Pakistan representation is 23 per cent.

Our source is: Rounaq Jahan, 'Ten Years of Ayub Khan and the Problem of National Integration', unpublished paper delivered at the 66th Annual Meeting of the American Political Science Association, Los Angeles, California, 8–12 September 1970.

Table 20.3: Military Elite in Pakistan—July 1955

Officer Rank	East Pakistan	West Pakistan	Per cent of East Pakistan
Army	14	894	1.6
Navy	7	593	1.1
Air Forces	60	640	9.3

Source: *Dawn*, Karachi, 1 January 1955.

Our source is: Rounaq Jahan, 'Ten Years of Ayub Khan and the Problem of National Integration,' unpublished paper delivered at the 66th Annual Meeting of the American Political Science Association, Los Angeles, California, 8–12 September 1970.

officers were of good quality with adequate training and experience in World War II. The remainder was short service and emergency commissioned officers recruited for the war time army. Because of the actual officer shortage, the Government of Pakistan requested that British officers of the pre-independence army continue to serve in the Pakistani forces. Approximately 500 Britishers offered their services.[24] For the first three years, the Pakistan army was headed by an Englishman, General Gracey. On 17 January 1951, Ayub Khan became the first Pakistan Commander-in-Chief. General Ayub described this occasion:

> After nearly two hundred years a Muslim army in the subcontinent would have a Muslim Commander-in-Chief. I knew whatever traditions and standards were established would continue to guide the army for a long time. I was determined that I should establish the highest standards of professional work and in all my dealings with people. I was going to be entrusted with the job of organising a young army.[25]

As Commander-in-Chief, Ayub Khan accelerated the recruitment process, but soldiers continued to be drawn from West Pakistan, particularly from those Punjab villages which had traditionally provided manpower for the army.

The costs of building and modernizing the Pakistan army were high. The war with India in 1948 over Kashmir further handicapped efforts to improve the military. Over 80 per cent of the nation's total revenue was used to maintain the military apraratus.[26]

During the early Cold War Years, when the United States was looking for allies to help contain Russia and China, Pakistan was found to be willing to join in military pacts. By virtue of being a member of the Southeast Asia Treaty Organization and the Baghdad Pact, Pakistan acquired modern military hardware and advanced training for its military officers.

In examining the politicization of the Pakistan army, it seems that a significant factor was the tendency of the government to rely upon the military to establish order. This pattern became evident very early.

In 1953, Governor-General Ghulam Mohammad dismissed Prime Minister Khwaja Nazimuddin and did so with army backing.[27] In the same year, the army restored order to Lahore following the anti-*Ahmadiya* riots.

The following year, Ghulam Mohammad, again with military support, dismissed the first Constituent Assembly.[28] The Governor-General then named Ayub Khan to the Cabinet as Defence Minister. In 1954, General Ayub wrote a 'Short Appreciation of Present and Future Problems in Pakistan', in which he outlined fully his ideas about the constitutional form that Pakistan's government should take.[29] Finally, Ayub claimed that Governor-General Mohammad was prepared to hand over the government to the military and had placed the documents for the proposed changeover in General Ayub's hands. Ayub refused the offer.,[30] In May 1954, additional army troops were sent to Bengal when President's Rule was declared in the province.[31]

In 1956, General Ayub was once more requested to take control of the government. This time, the offer was tendered by Prime Minister Chaudhri Mohammad Ali.[32]

In 1957, the army undertook 'Operation Closed Door', a massive effort to curb smuggling in East Bengal. One effect of this campaign was to exacerbate the already unstable political situation in East Wing. Hindu members of the provincial assembly threatened to withdraw their support from the Awami League government if the army's programme was not curtailed.[33]

These incidents of army intrusion into civilian realms of concern, ranging from the restoration of order in Lahore to General Ayub's formulation of a constitutional plan, serve to illustrate how from

1953–8 the political atmosphere became more conducive to military control.[34]

Diffusion and Decentralization in the Indian Army Structure

Professors Susanne and Lloyd Rudolph have put a question to their readers in their excellent study of the Indian army: 'How is it that the Indian Military Services have played a limited professional role when in neighbouring Pakistan, also part of the old British Raj, the present regime is headed by a military man?'[35]

To understand why the army came to occupy the premier position in Pakistan and a secondary position in India, one must consider several factors. First, from the beginning there has been a divergence in Indian and Pakistan political experiences, with the Indians tending to adopt the parliamentary system and Pakistan favouring the Viceregal system. According to the Rudolphs:

> The Viceroy and Parliament, one autocratic, the other democratic, represent the two great traditions of modern politics which the subcontinent experienced under British rule. The difference between the role of the military in India and Pakistan are related to the fact that after independence Pakistan under Jinnah identified with the Viceregal tradition while India under Nehru embraced Parliamentarism. The English Viceroy and Governor-General headed an administrative state which, at its best approximated the ideal of Platonic guardians, paternal benign, and efficient. The Commander-in-chief stood second to the Viceroy under the British Raj powerful yet subordinate to the Crown's civilian representative in India. Representative democracy developed side by side with the Viceregal tradition. In Pakistan a kind of Viceregal government was toppled by a general who has tried to rid the state of parties, politics and politicians.[36]

Before independence, the British-Indian Army was constantly criticized by the leaders of the freedom movement. They insisted that the military was 'hopelessly feudal, inequalitarian, and caste bound.'[37] However, after 1947, the Government of India was not able to carry out its promises to eradicate the old military organization. In fact, the same recruitment procedures of the British Raj were maintained. This was due to India's involvement in the disputes in Hyderabad and Kashmir. These early conflicts forced the government to send the army into immediate action, and there was little time or energy for large-scale changes.

Those changes which did take place were to have an important impact upon civil–military relations. First, the office of the Commander-in-Chief of the army was abolished and replaced by the position of Chief-of-Staff of the army. The effect of this move was to place the top army officer on par with his counterparts in the air force and navy. Prior to independence, the Commander of the army had always been considered 'first among equals' vis-á-vis the other service officers. Second, the Minister of Defence became the head of the defence establishment with cabinet rank. Under the Viceregal system, the army Commander had held a set on the Governor-General's Council.[38]

To further de-emphasize the importance of the army, civilian secretaries in the Government of India, who had previously ranked lower than lieutenant generals, became the equivalent in status to full generals. In addition, generals were now required to approach the Defence Minister through the Defence Secretary. During British times, ranking army officers had direct access to the executive.[39]

Indian High Command

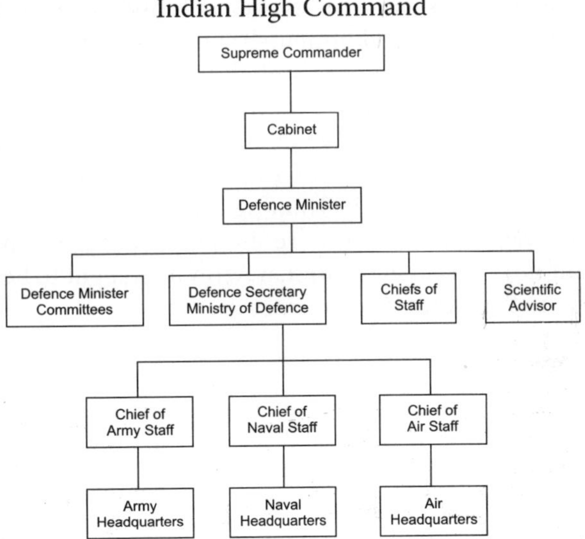

Source: M. K. Chopra, 'Democracy and Defense in India', *Military Review*, vol. 47, August 1967, p. 14.

Finally, several control committees, composed primarily of non-military officials, were set up. The most important of these was the Defence Committee of the Cabinet. The highest policy-making body for military matters, it was composed of the Prime Minister, the Minister of External Affairs, the Defence Minister, other ranking cabinet officials, and the three Chiefs-of-Staff. A second Defence Minister's Committee was chaired by Minister of Defence and also included the Minister of Defence Production, the Defence Secretary, the Scientific Advisor, the Financial Advisor on Defence, and the Chiefs-of-Staff.[40]

Following the Indo-Chinese War, public pressure prompted the establishment of the National Defence Council. Headed by the Prime Minister, the Council included prominent public figures, scientists, economists, and retired generals. The function of the Council was to advice the government on problems of national defence.[41]

In recent years, even more far-sweeping changes have come about. Selection procedures for military officers have been altered. In order to have a truly national army, the Government no longer adheres to the policy of giving preference to certain communities. For example, Sikhs are no longer allotted 'disproportionate numbers of officers' appointments'.[42] The training of officers has changed drastically. Now cadets of all three services receive joint instruction for at least two years at the National Defence Academy. The result is not only a basic general education for all new officers but a heightened awareness of the importance of inter-service cooperation.[43] During their training, the principles of civilian control of the administration are emphasized. Cohen maintains that: '. . . Junior officers in the Indian Army are taught to be political illiterates, and are content to remain so.'[44]

Conclusion

Although India and Pakistan inherited a common political and martial history, there was a great divergence in the civilian–military relationship after independence. The following factors predisposed the fusion of military and political power in Pakistan, on the one hand, and conditioned civilian control in India, on the other.

First, Pakistani politicians increasingly depended upon the army to establish order during riots and civil disorder. This helped to make the army the only institution which could provide stability for the nation.

Second, since Pakistan continued the old British system of making the Commander-in-Chief of the army the Defence Minister and a member of the cabinet, the army was given a direct entry into the political system. Generals like Ayub Khan were always in a position to view at close range the individual weaknesses and ineptness of politicians. They concluded that they could do a better job.

Third, the Pakistani fear of imminent war with India helped to boost its military expenditure and power. Before 1962, at least, India felt secure that it could defend itself against Pakistan without bolstering the role of the military.

Fourth, India was fortunate in successfully legitimizing parliamentary institutions and in having popular leadership. This created an atmosphere conducive to civilian control.

Finally, recruitment policy in Pakistan continues to encourage the dominance of one community and one section of the country. Therefore, whenever efforts were made to make the military more responsible to the majority, the reaction of the army was to further centralize and enhance its power.

NOTES

1. Field-Marshal Sir John Harding, 'The Indian and Pakistan Armies of Today', *Asian Review*, LI, July 1955, pp. 175–87.
2. Nagendra Singh, *The Theory of Force and Organization of Defence in Indian Constitutional History: From Earliest Times to* 1947, New York: Asia Publishing House, 1969, p. 235.
3. Ibid.
4. Ibid., p. 238.
5. Ibid., p. 240.
6. Ibid., p. 243.
7. Ibid., p. 245.
8. Stephen P. Cohen, *The Indian Army: Its Contribution to the Development of a Nation*, Berkeley: The University of California Press, 1971, p. 27.
9. Singh, op. cit., p. 253.
10. William Gutteridge, 'The Indianization of the Indian Army 1918–45: A Case Study', *Race*, vol. IV, May 1963, pp. 39–40.
11. Brigadier Cyril N. Barclay, 'The Indian Army', *Army*, vol. IV, 7 July 1967, p. 55.
12. Gutteridge, loc. cit.
13. Ibid., p. 46.

14. Aslam Siddiqi, *A Path for Pakistan*, Karachi: Pakistan Publishing House, 1964, p. 47. Cohen gives credit to Lord Roberts of Kandahar, the Commander-in-Chief of the Indian Army from 1885 to 1893, for introducing the recruitment policy of 'martial races' (Cohen, op. cit., p. 45).
15. Barclay, loc, cit.
16. Rounaq Jahan, 'Ten Years of Ayub Khan and the Problem of National Integration', unpublished paper delivered at the American Political Science Association Meeting, Los Angeles, September 1970, p. 5.
17. Singh, op. cit., p. 25. The Pakistan version is somewhat different. Siddiqi claims that Pakistan 'received eight Infantry Regiments, six Armoured Corps Units, eight and a half Artillery Regiments and 34 Engineering Units . . . . Pakistan's share of military stores worked to 163,000 tonnes. But actually it received only 30,000 tonnes', (Siddiqi, op. cit., p. 74).
18. Ibid., p. 77.
19. Mohammad Ayub Khan, *Friends Not Masters: A Political Autobiography*, New York: Oxford University Press, p. 22. There was only one member of the Indian Civil Service from East Bengal at the time of independence.
20. Siddiqi, op. cit., p. 78. Today, the East Bengal Regiment has only 2,000 soldiers divided into four or five battalions, whereas the West Pakistani Regiments have 15–20 battalions each. East Pakistan also has a paramilitary force called the East Pakistan Rifles, with 13,000 members (*The New York Times*, 27 March 1971).
21. Cohen, op. cit., p. 193. A West Pakistani student of mine agreed that there is no discrimination against Bengali entrance into the army, but that the Bengali physical stature is too small to qualify them in the examination into the officer corps.
22. Rounaq Jahan, op. cit., p. 8.
23. Ayub Khan, op. cit., p. 27. The brutal force which was used by the West Pakistani troops to crush the demand for Bangla Desh has further strengthened the Bengali belief that these forces were truly an occupying army and East Bengal was in fact a colony of West Pakistan. It will be a long time before East Bengalis will regard General Tikka Khan, Martial Law Administrator of East Pakistan, as their Muslim brother.
24. Fazal Mugeemi Khan, *The Story of the Pakistan Army*, Karachi: Oxford University Press, n.d., p. 22.
25. Ayub Khan, op. cit., p. 35.
26. Siddiqi, op. cit., p. 74.
27. See, for example, Ayub's advice to Prime Minister Liaquat Ali Khan in 1951 (Mohammad Ayub Khan, op. cit., p. 40). It should be noted, however, that in 1951 there was an attempt by army officers to seize control of the army and the government. Not much is known about this 'Rawalpindi Conspiracy', since the officers were arrested and tried in

secret (see Henry Frank Goodnow, *The Civil Service in Pakistan*, New Haven: Yale University Press, 1964, p. 106, *fn* 6).

28. Sayeed, *The Middle East Journal*, Autumn, 1959, p. 390.
29. Ibid.
30. Ayub Khan, op. cit., p. 52.
31. Goodnow, op. cit., p. 62.
32. Ayub Khan, op. cit., p. 54.
33. Sayeed, *The Middle East Journal*, Autumn, 1959, p. 396.
34. Also, one must take into account that Ayub's appointment as the Commander-in-Chief was about to expire on 16 January 1969 '. . . no doubt contributed to his removal of Mirza on 27 October 1958' J. C. Hurewitz, *Middle East Politics: The Military Dimension* (New York: Frederick A. Praeger, 1969), p. 186.
35. Susanne Hoeber and Lloyd L. Rudolph, 'Generals and Politicians in India', *Pacific Affairs*, vol. XXXVII, Spring 1964, p. 5.
36. Ibid., p. 7.
37. Cohen, op. cit., p. 170. Caste was an established part of the army organization under the British and it remained the same in independent India. M. S. A. Rao, 'Caste and the Indian Army', *Economic Weekly*, XVI, 29 August 1964, p. 1443.
38. Cohen, op. cit., p. 171.
39. M. K. Chopra, 'Democracy and Defense in India', *Military Review*, vol. 47, August 1967, pp. 9–15.
40. Dharm Pal, *The Indian Army*, India: Ministry of Information and Broadcasting, 1967, pp. 9–15.
41. Ibid., p. 94.
42. William Gutteridge, *Armed Forces in New States*, London: Oxford University Press, 1962, p. 13.
43. E. Halladay, 'The Indian Army Since 1947', *Army Quarterly*, vol. XXCVII, January 1964, p. 247.
44. Cohen, op. cit., p. 176.

CHAPTER 21

Negotiating Insurgencies: The Naga Imbroglio

Kanchan L.

End Game in Nagaland?

Is one witnessing the 'endgame' in Nagaland, the 'withering away' of a 50-year-old insurgency? A time frame of two years to resolve the Naga imbroglio was reported to have been arrived at during the latest round of negotiations at the highest level between Prime Minister Atal Behari Vajpayee and the National Socialist Council of Nagaland—Isak-Muivah (NSCN-IM) leaders Thuingaleng Muivah and Isak Chisi Swu in Osaka, Japan, on 8 December 2001.[1] The longevity of this insurgency and, more significantly, the phenomenon of persistent and high acceptable levels of violence, have made the Naga case unique among the various theatres of conflict in India. Even a cursory analysis of the Naga insurgency would indicate that certain specificities have led to consistent stalemates and consequently, to the intractability of the conflict.

Bernard Crick, analysing the 'high price of peace', explored the personality of a non-zero sum game in which all parties might gain, rather than one party's gain automatically entailing the other's loss.[2] This does not appear to be the trajectory of the ceasefire in Nagaland thus far. Each phase of negotiations has, in fact, led to the commencement of a complex confluence of factors and more critically, every abortive attempt at negotiating a durable solution to the Naga problem has tended to prejudice further negotiations, constructing greater resentment between the negotiating parties, as also a polarization vis-á-vis the negotiating structure.

Both the Union government and the NSCN-IM have accused each other of being disinclined towards a durable solution, and have thus contributed to a negotiating framework incompatible to an early and final agreement. Effective political processes require that parties make concessions in order to hold or gain power. Yet it appeared as though both the parties were adopting maximalist postures, projecting any kind of bargaining or concession as a 'failure' or 'defeat' among their respective constituencies. The NSCN-IM primarily perceived the ceasefire and negotiations as a new battleground—a different arena of political pressure. But, for an endgame to transcend the realm of a propaganda exercise, the NSCN-IM would have to significantly revise the concept of *Nagalim* ('Greater Nagaland').[3] As Bowyer Bell, reflecting on the 'concession framework', expresses it, 'everywhere the dream, however, must be adjusted, perceived differently if there is to be any negotiation. The zero-sum game must be replaced with an endgame'.[4] The critical point is that both the parties would have to explore new and more efficacious responses and engineer a move forward that escapes the traps of what has become the established orthodoxy.

The end game of a long drawn out insurgency is perhaps the most complex phase of transformation in an evidently complex process. In such a phase, conflicting parties need to avail themselves of the most appropriate process of dialogue to facilitate negotiations and also successfully negotiate a sustainable solution by constructing effective reward structures and political frameworks. The projected outcome must be one that would assuage both the parties: a potential win–win solution. In Nagaland, however, the stated positions of the two parties, have necessarily reinforced the intractability of the conflict and deepened the imbroglio.

However, while neither party was in the proximity of a possible consensus, they still deemed it fit to 'work together' and this was certainly one positive element in the negotiations. Nevertheless, there were grave deficiencies in the present process, with both parties moving in a sphere that manifestly lacked negotiating space. Indeed, they appeared discernibly to be negotiating *at* each other rather than *with* each other. The current dynamics proceeded within the parameters of what can at best be described as low-escalation negotiations, with an ever-present threat of renewed large-scale violence. There was no emerging convergence or confluence of positions and, consequently, the process lingered on without any substantial and visible end product.

The negotiating ensemble has primarily involved recurrent extended ceasefires.[5] These have not resulted in a cessation of violence, but appear to be acquiring the character of ends in themselves. In the long run, peace can be built only on the basis of a compromise and consequently, mutually exclusive solutions will have to be abandoned. At present, however, a negative scenario which precludes the necessary space for the transformation of the dynamics of the Naga peace process, prevails. 'Windows of opportunity' do not exist, or they have not been seized to further the transformation.

The Union government has long fulfilled two of the NSCN-IM's conditions—talks at the highest level and outside India—but there were no reciprocal concessions. Unless there is a clear move beyond an exclusive focus on competitive bargaining, and towards a greater degree of cooperation, the process will remain bogged down. There was, however, little evidence of any dilution of the NSCN-IM's intransigence. Unless negotiating parties cooperate to a certain degree to redefine possible solutions, exploring the negotiating ensemble to take advantage of existing windows of opportunity to remove stalemates, progress is not a possibility.[6]

The negotiations could be utilized as a bargaining tool to terminate violence, but there existed an equal danger of resumption of open hostilities and an escalation of violence, with the NSCN-IM jettisoning the ceasefire and renewing its bush war, as it has threatened to do from time to time.[7] In many ways, the cynicism of the question, 'Is war *a* safer bet than peace?' hung like Damocles' sword over Nagaland.

After nearly 50 years of insurgency, peace in Nagaland would admittedly be a journey into the unknown. That, in some measure, is perhaps why bargaining, concessions and trade-offs have come constantly undone in the past. There has, evidently, been a substantial loss of political control and cohesion, and a process of political reconstruction, quite naturally, will have to precede any eventual resolution of this tenacious predicament. The highest price of peace, says Crick, is likely to be the giving up of hopes of victory, a realization of the limits of power.[8] How can inviolate sovereignty be kept and lost?[9] Bell argues that the 'dream, never denied, need not be achieved whole, at once, soon, without discussion—achieved at the point of a gun. The dream, itself may have evolved—undergone a sea change underground; but most important is the perception of the rebels.'[10] Thus, the dream must be receptive to adjustment and the dreamers' perception must shift in ways congenial to negotiation.[11] Is it so in the case of *Nagalim?*

Reward Structures

There was a discreet set of interactions which could facilitate negotiations, as freeing the negotiators and allowing them to move forward without serious harm to their perceived power bases. When parties have evidently been unable to arrive at a consensus vis-á-vis the modalities of an agreement in the existing paradigm, forward progress becomes contingent on agreements on an alternative range of options. However, who is to provide these alternate options and within what structure? Imperative in this context is the need to effectively assess the existing reward structures. The NSCN-IM had not, despite the threats, decided to back out of the ceasefire and 'return to the jungle' consequent upon the 27 July 2001, decision by the Union government to restrict the ceasefire to Nagaland.[12] Among other factors, this was primarily due to the fact that the IM realized that any jettisoning of the peace process would result in a loss or erosion of 'legitimacy' among certain significant sections of Naga civil society. Furthermore, the reward structure at the time was radically different from the pre-25 July 1997 scenario when there was no ceasefire.

There were in the situation at hand, a complex pattern of incentives and rewards for continuing violence in Nagaland, and neutralizing these was not merely a matter of principle. The process of negotiations to terminate violence was expectedly riddled with bottlenecks, and existing concessions to the NSCN-IM proved insufficient for a durable solution to the Naga crisis. Furthermore, within the backdrop of fragmented responses and a paradigm that was based on the fact that violence has an exponential reward structure, the negotiating dynamics were designed to fail. The process of negotiations was complicated by insurgent groups that appropriated attributes of crime and that circumvent the due process of law without any scruples. Substantive future enforcement action must be conceived in relation to an identification of the underlying and structurally deep aspects of the criminality of these groups, as also the force structures that are imperviously capable of countering domains of crime.

Any cost–benefit analysis undertaken by the Union government during the decision to revert back to *status quo ante* on the 'territorial extension of ceasefire' would plausibly have taken into account the fact that the NSCN-IM, pressurized by the Naga society's desire for peace, would be forced to continue with the peace process. Furthermore, there appeared to be a certain degree of battle fatigue among the IM cadres. Many IM cadres, including senior members of the 'Naga cabinet', had gradually returned to leading normal lives ever since the ceasefire saw the security forces and the Naga outfit terminating military operations against each other.[13] The Union government's calculation was that, since the cadres had come over ground, it may not be easy for them to go back to the hard life in the jungles and, consequently, if Muivah was to jettison the ceasefire at this stage, it would not be very easy for him to restore the original fighting strength and instinct among his cadres.[14] The ceasefire period has reportedly dented the fighting capability of insurgents who were more used to city life and less willing to go to the jungles.[15] With discipline among the cadres of Naga outfits having reportedly deteriorated along with a lack of commitment to the 'cause', intelligence officials revealed that most of the insurgent leaders had reportedly made 'big money during the ceasefire period and amassed huge properties both in Nagaland and abroad. . . None of these leaders will be willing for the ceasefire to break and thus lose everything.'[16] The reward structures, clearly, had not been engineered or created by the Union government, and could not consequently, be unilaterally altered by it. They could only be altered or transformed through negotiated settlements.

The pressures for such a settlement were growing within the NSCN-IM. Muivah and Isak Swu were ageing and their younger cadres had lost the elan and fervour of jungle-hardened guerillas, preferring creature comforts and easy money. There was evidence of several key figures in the NSCN-IM having acquired property in Meghalaya, particularly in Shillong, where many of its younger sympathizers were enrolled as students, which provided a cover for movement into Bangladesh.[17] In the situation under discussion, certain cadres had considerable freedom in maintaining their share of illegally acquired monies, so long as they did not deviate from the general parameters agreed upon. It is widely believed that there is a collusive relationship between underground elements, hankering after easy money and the comforts of over ground life, and politicians who wish to have their own hit-men and servitors around. [18]

Thus, despite the fact that the ceasefire agreement between the Union government and the NSCN-IM was in operation for the four years preceding 2001, extortion by the group continued unabated in every district of Nagaland under the guise of taxes for the 'Republic of Nagalim.'[19] In addition to the NSCN-IM, the National Socialist Council of Nagaland-Khaplang (NSCN-K) has also adopted the system of collection of 'taxes' from every government employee, as also the trading community. 25 per cent of the gross salary twice a year was been fixed by the IM group as 'tax,' while the Khaplang group has fixed 20 per cent as its share from each of the government employee and the business community depending upon their salary and income.[20] The collection of 'taxes' extended to the common citizens as well, and a very high level of compliance prevailed as a result of the fear that those who failed to cooperate would have to leave the state under threat of violence. Such collection of 'taxes' was a direct contravention of the Revised Ground Rules for Ceasefire, between the Government of India and the NSCN-IM.[21]

Phunthing Shimrang, a senior NSCN-IM leader, when asked about continuing tax collections by the group despite the ceasefire, said, 'It's our right, . . . Will the Government stop collection of taxes during the ceasefire?' In 1998, every village household paid Rs. 110 annually as "house tax". Before May 1998, the NSCN-IM also introduced a 'loyalty tax'; by paying Rs. 1 lakh, businessmen became 'taxpayers.'[22]

The inability and disinclination on the part of the state to curb the criminal operations of the militant groups adversely affected the peace process. As a senior officer of the intelligence organization of the Border Security Force (BSF-G) stated, 'There has not been any check on flow of money to factions during 'ceasefire' period. Insurgency has become a sprawling business where no qualification is required to earn money. Different Naga outfits have been openly collecting taxes from villages, businessmen, government officials, transporters, and government contractors in the name of national movement.'[23] While disclosing that the NSCN-IM had been passing an annual budget to the tune of Rs. 200 to Rs. 250 million each year, he added that, closely linked with insurgency and gun-running, was the serious problem of narcotics, emerging from the 'Golden Triangle'.[24] Most of the militant groups, including NSCN-IM, added the officer, utilize the money earned through the narcotics trade to purchase arms and also pay for training of their cadres in camps run by other outfits.[25] The cessation of operations during the ceasefire period has, according to him, made it easy for the NSCN-IM to indulge in the circulation of fake currency without being detected.[26]

The NSCN-IM in 1998 while issuing notices—in the name of self-styled principal secretary of the Government of the People's Republic of Nagaland (GPRN), L. B. Singh—to various banks, government departments, and traders, saying that it needs funds to carry on its dialogue with the Union government, asked both Nagas and non-Nagas to contribute their mite for the interest of peace.[27] In July 2000, when Naga insurgent groups increased their extortion drive in the 'B' and 'C' sectors of the Assam–Nagaland border within Golaghat district, the people of Natun Raja Pukhuri, Ranipukhuri, Chetiagaon, Chandalachung, and Dolipather within the Dhansiri sub-division alleged that the district administration was ineffective against the insurgents, who continued their campaign of killing, abduction, and looting of non-Naga people.[28] According to Assam government sources, the NSCN-IM had commenced issuing extortion notices to the people residing in Upper Assam districts, which were included in the *Nagalim* map, and this was consequent to the Union government's acceptance, on 14 June 2001, of the long-standing demand of the NSCN-IM to 'territorially extend' the ceasefire to the Naga-dominated areas of Assam, Arunachal Pradesh, and Manipur.[29] In July 2001, security had been put on maximum alert in the Pallel area in the Chandel district of Manipur in view of the extortion call issued by the NSCN-IM, and when the villagers of Kuraopokpi Tarung Louchan were threatened by the group to leave the place if they did not clear their 'tax dues'.[30]

Organizational longevity is largely a function of adaptability. The most durable insurgent groups are those that adjust to changing circumstances without jettisoning their support base. Such a reorientation occurs when large criminal revenues begin to accrue from secondary activities and operations of such groupings. There is growing cumulative evidence of increasing reluctance on the part of such groups to cooperate with peace initiatives, especially where these can lead to a complete termination of underground operations, when the rewards accruing to them as a result of criminal operations, and the intractability of the conflict appear to be much higher than the those that may be offered by any peace settlement. Clearly, the issue of criminality assumes more potent dimensions in the context of a political authority that is sufficiently inept.

Negotiating from Strength

Many of the broad steps that need to be laid out and negotiated over time are essential ingredients of any successful and enduring structure of peace in Nagaland. Details are, of course, subject to changes—large and small—along the long road to a greater tranquillity than has been known through several rounds of peace processes. The Union government has evidently, specifically in the context of the recent ceasefire extension and rollback—done an extremely poor job of scrutinizing the long-term solution to the Naga problem, and has settled on a strategy of making extreme demands on the short-term that the other constituents—detached from the negotiations, find completely unacceptable. Even as the 14 June 2001 agreement between the NSCN-IM and the Union government on the ceasefire extension 'without territorial limits' received approval among certain sections in Nagaland, including organizations such as the Naga Hoho, the apex tribal council, groups such as the Naga National Council-Federal (NNC-F) and the NSCN-K, the move was viewed as an intrusion upon the territorial integrity of the neighbouring states of Manipur, Assam, and Arunachal Pradesh, leading to frayed passions and large-scale violence in those states, especially in Manipur.[31] The Union government was forced to review the decision of extending the ceasefire without territorial limits and it eventually ordered a roll-back to status quo ante. Given the intractability of the Naga conflict, the imperative as far as the Union government was concerned was to have ensured that its decisions would not result in worse injustice than the condition the insurgents oppose.[32]

Widespread protests in Manipur and the resultant violence may also be construed to have occurred due to the absence of an institutional apparatus and appropriate processes of containment and adaptation in the dynamics of state politics.[33] The proclivity to adopt hyper vigilant decisions, while acting primarily on first information, and without considering appropriate alternatives or options, can have disastrous consequences, as was evident in the events in Manipur.[34] 14 persons lost their lives in large-scale violence in Manipur on 18 June 2001, four days after the decision to extend the ceasefire beyond territorial limits of Nagaland,[35] bringing to mind Martha Crenshaw's observation that 'terrorism may produce further violence in a context of fragmented power'.[36] Unimaginative response mechanisms of the Union government towards combating insurgencies, more often than not, have a tendency to degenerate into a 'destructive cycle of violence'.[37]

Among the most significant aspects of this dynamic is the detachment of 'implementers' (parties involved or the states in which the territorial extension was to have an impact) from the negotiations. Apart from the Union government and the NSCN-IM, all other concerned and affected parties are completely divorced from and ignored by the mediation process. This is crucial. Hypothetically, even if a 'final solution' is arrived at with the consensus of the state governments of Assam, Arunachal Pradesh, and Manipur, it would still be immensely difficult to implement, and to reconcile, the various insurgent groups operating in these areas. In the absence of such a consensus, any permanent resolution is manifestly impossible. Consequently, the inclusion of one or more additional concerned parties to the process of negotiation should be one of the early goals of the present process. Clearly, the affected state governments, or a commonly agreed upon representative, must be involved. The non-participation of the affected states cannot be justified merely on the fact that the NSCN-IM is demanding secession, something the Union government claims that it alone can handle.

In the context of the Union government's roll back to status quo ante on the 'without territorial limits' issue, the NSCN-IM's concept of *Nagalim* may still be in the realm of illusion. It was, however, perhaps for the first time, that the concept held centre stage in the discourse on the Naga insurgency. The immediate aftermath of the roll-back and the current positioning of the NSCN-IM evidently gives indications of a long-term strategy. Thus, however partial the movement towards *Nagalim* may have been as a result of the developments in June 2001 and the consequent ethnic polarization, the NSCN-IM has reason to regard this partial movement as a 'success'. Consequently, any increase—albeit limited—accruing to the outfit's influence over the negotiating process is 'meaningful' in the long run.[38] The NSCN-IM's acceptance of the roll-back decision may, of course, have reduced its bargaining capacity in the short run, but it did, at the same time, demonstrate its support base, a crucial long run element. Another factor that came to the fore through this episode was the manifestation of unanimity vis-á-vis the NSCM-IM's unchallenged writ within its support constituency. Despite its *volte face,* the NSCN-IM has succeeded in increasing its power base despite an apparent 'weakening' as a result of its failure to realize its threat to 'return to the jungle'. This was substantially facilitated by the Union government's inconsistent response mechanism, reinforcing the symbolic effectiveness of *Nagalim* in the NSCN-IM constituency.

State responses are complicated and compromised further by the fact that, even as it initiates myriad forms of peace processes, certain manifestations that appear less straightforward have also emerged on the canvas. These latent manifestations are as much a result of the proliferation of fragmented state responses as also a process of mutation of the insurgent groups' responses. Prior to entering negotiations, the Union government ought to clearly set maximum and minimum goals, where the minimum is the very least with which it would be satisfied. The state should never compromise on this predetermined minimum. Experience, however, indicates that this is far from the case, and this is critical in view of the NSCN-IM's consistency in holding on to its high demands and unwillingness to make concessions. The imbroglio over the ceasefire extension demonstrates, moreover, that *the*

Union government tends to compromise on its negotiating paradigm without any thought of future consequences. This appears to reflect a consistent tendency on the part of the government to think short range, presumably on the assumption that it is only the short range that is 'negotiable'. The long range, on the other hand, is regarded as being fraught with too many uncertainties, too many potential and unpredictable changes, to be properly considered.

The NSCN-IM, on the other hand, appears clearly to be visualizing the long range: What will *Nagalim* be like in the future? Indeed, they appear to confront what must be a distressing possibility: Will it even *be* in the future? In drawing out alternative responses to these fundamental questions, they have demonstrated a willingness to sacrifice certain short-term gains (witness the 'agreeable' line to the centre's decision to roll back to *status quo ante* in July 2001) on the basis of their long-term expectations, gradually pushing the idea of *Nagalim* closer to the centre stage.

This might put the Union government at a serious disadvantage in various ways, including the acceptance of the adversary's short range concessions or apparent concessions at face value, without a proper assessment of unintended transformations in the negotiating paradigm itself. The temptation, more often than not, has been to press forward without any focus on the outcome. The necessity and pressure to reach an agreement—any agreement—becomes paramount, marginalizing the qualitative elements of sustainability and durability. Long-term stability has often been sacrificed for short-term expediency, creating a tenuous ceasefire and a negotiating process that tends eventually to collapse in favour of actors who are steadfast in their goals.

Is there a 'threshold factor' that militates against the NSCN-IM's desire to hold on to its 'high ground' vis-á-vis the territoriality issue? A critical factor in this context is the *war of attrition* between the NSCN-IM and other insurgent groups operating in the so-called area of Greater Nagaland. Seven insurgent groups active in the area which oppose the 'Greater Nagaland' concept have constituted a platform called the United Liberation Front of Seven Sisters (ULFSS).[39] The seven groups, while opposing the NSCN-IM's demand of 'Greater Nagaland', also decided to mobilize other insurgent groups of the region against the NSCN-IM. The United

Liberation Front of Asom (ULFA), a front ranking insurgent outfit, has said that the NSCN-IM's claim of eight Assam districts as part of *Nagalim* has 'neither credibility nor any historical basis.'[40] Arabinda Rajkhowa, the ULFA's 'chairman', while calling upon the NSCN-IM to remove the eight Assam districts from its *Nagalim* map,[41] also claimed earlier that that the Naga insurgents were engaged in unauthorized entry into Assam territory, as also in the extortion of 'taxes' and the killing of people, 'which the ULFA cannot tolerate.'[42]

It is clear, consequently, that 'the decision by the Union government, and the resultant exultation exhibited by the Naga bodies 'including the NSCN-IM, has begun to be perceived as a threat by the other terrorist outfits operating within the ambit of the proposed Nagalim.'[43] Any 'land for peace' settlement will, therefore, perforce invite retaliation from other insurgent groups in the region. It was, in fact, the alignment of other such insurgent organizations, as also the severity of opposition in Assam, Arunachal Pradesh, and Manipur, that influenced the NSCN-IM to recognize that opposition to the roll-back decision, at this point of time, would be counter-productive.

Substantial misgivings persist regarding the Naga peace process, certainly among neighbouring states, despite the Union government's assurance that the territorial integrity of Manipur would be protected and preserved.[44] In Manipur, there is a strong feeling that the territorial interests of the state were compromised by the June 2001 agreement with the NSCN-IM, and that, despite the subsequent roll-back, future negotiations and concessions would tend to impinge upon the legal and administrative jurisdiction of the state.[45] This sentiment is strengthened by the complex character of interdependencies between the various states in the north-east, which creates a tendency for conflicts to overflow boundaries of particular states, and to rapidly diffuse and enmesh other states, or parts of states, in a spiral that often escalates well beyond the contours of the original intra-state conflict.

Broader Negotiating Structure

The NSCN-IM has consistently pursued a 'politics of exclusion' with regard to other insurgent groups and organizations, and this has, more often than not, led to increasing fratricidal warfare. This approach has clearly been one of the significant detrimental factors to the processes of conflict resolution in Nagaland. While the group has, on the one hand, persistently demanded a 'broadening of the structure of negotiations' in terms of what can be placed on the table by the Government of India (GOI), it has, on the other hand, insisted on a deliberate narrowing of options through its demand that it be recognized as the 'sole arbiter' of all Naga interests.

The primary target of this exclusionary demand is the NSCN's Khaplang faction. The NSCN-IM argues that the Khaplang faction cannot be included in the dialogue process by the GOI because S. S. Khaplang, a Konyak Naga, is Myanmarese by birth.[46] There is a curious contradiction here, since the *Nagalim* concept proposed by the NSCN-IM includes significant territories and populations in Myanmar. It is an inescapable fact, moreover, that the Khaplang group is quite active on Nagaland's violent landscape.

The inclusion of all interests and especially of the hitherto excluded insurgent groups is, in fact, key to a more durable framework of resolution, and the absence of other parties has, in the past, created an incompleteness that undermines the possibilities of success of the peace process.[47]

Among the excluded groups, the NSCN-K, with the power to wreck any projected solution, will eventually have to be included in joint negotiations at one level or another. With a ceasefire with the NSCN-K[48] in place, the next ideal step is naturally the definition of their status and circumstances of their inclusion in negotiations, irrespective of the IM group's opposition to such a development. The imperatives of such an inclusion are also linked to creating circumstances that will break through the existing stalemate and 'oil the wheels of negotiation'.[49]

The underlying rationale for broadening the negotiating structure is not just one among the myriad responses available to the liberal state. There are more practical justifications. As Liz Philipson expresses it in a general context, 'the wider the domestic base of those involved in and committed to the settlement the harder it is to overturn and the more viable it is to sustain. Furthermore, the narrower the base of participation, the greater the likelihood of any agreement requiring enforcement and intervention to coerce a settlement.'[50]

Creating this 'broader base' for the negotiation, however, is not a simple matter, given the deep animosities between the IM and Khaplang factions, and the fratricidal campaigns they have carried out against each other. Thus, Muivah has described his arch rival Khaplang as a 'man without discipline, involved in drug-trafficking and poppy cultivation, and willing to be utilised by the Indians'.[51] At the other end of the spectrum, Kitovi Zhimomi, the NSCN-K General Secretary, while accusing Muivah of being a 'power monger', has alleged that he is responsible for 'eliminating various frontline Naga leaders. . . Why is Muivah masterminding the elimination of prominent Naga leaders? We don't know what his ideology is. After all, it is easy to sit abroad and remote-control operations in Naga areas here. If we can lead our movement by remaining among our people, why can't Muivah?'[52]

The NSCN-K has clearly indicated that any solution to the Naga problem cannot be based on an agreement with the IM group alone. While pointing out that the Union government cannot ignore other groups, it has added that the Naga groups should hold talks with the GOI under a common banner. Holding forth on this aspect, Zhimomi stated that,

> the NSCN-I-M led by leaders like Thuingaleng Muivah does not have the mandate of the Naga people. . . . Unless the Naga revolutionary groups unite and hold talks with the Indian government together, there can be no political solution. And a piecemeal solution cannot restore lasting peace in the Naga areas. We have seen the cease-fire between New Delhi and the NSCN-IM for the past four years. The problems have continued.[53]

Criticizing the negating tactics of the IM group, he observed that

> in keeping with the people's desire, we have sent feelers to the NSCN-IM a number of times for a general ceasefire between our two groups. But, there has always been a negative response from Muivah. Our doors are, however, open for a broad-based truce as well as a possible unification by adopting the principle of forgive and forget as initiated by the Nagaland Baptist Church Council. [54]

By contrast, Muivah rejects all such moves by the Khaplang faction, claiming that the NSCN-K has betrayed the Naga cause and that 'they have accepted the Indian Constitution'.[55]

Evidently, the number of parties to be involved in the process of negotiations has been and remains a contentious issue. The NSCN-IM antipathy to participation by the Khaplang group is not only driven by a fratricidal history. The IM faction has long struggled to safeguard its status as the sole arbiter of the 'Naga destiny'. Indeed, the IM group regards the possibility of the involvement of the Khaplang faction as a potential move that could actually block the ongoing peace process. Any move to broaden the base of negotiations by involving other parties is similarly interpreted by the IM group as an attempt by the GOI to dilute the NSCN-IM's influence among the Naga people, and Muivah has made this clear on several occasions, arguing that 'if you say that you will talk to us, then you have to honour it. Apart from that, if you take initiative to talk with anyone else we will not be party to that.'[56]

Thus, there emerges a web of complexity. One of the negotiating parties is not considered (both by the Union government and even by certain sections of Naga civil society) as a single unified group, but as being comprised at least four groups[57] riven with mutual conflicts. This internal dissonance has particular significance for the demands for self-determination and secession. Clearly, the GOI's interest and intent would be to dilute or pre-empt the insurgents' stance on secession, and this is one possible motive for a broader negotiating structure in terms of the parties involved, since other parties may not subscribe, or may not be as committed, to the idea of self-determination. Here, while the fratricidal divisions between the groups may assist the government to the extent that they undermine the NSCN-IM's negotiating strengths, they also undermine the efforts and attempts to create the basis of a wider consensus between the various Naga interests. Feuds between the two principal Naga insurgent factions, consequently, continue to be a grey area for the negotiating process.

Is there a possible compromise formula that could unite the various groups? Or is it the case that the idea that is actually being tested is the isolation of the NSCN-IM by facilitating a measure of unity among all the groupings that oppose this faction? It is very clear that the NSCN-IM perceives the Khaplang group as a spoiler, and the GOI's game plan can be understood and explained in terms of the Khaplang group being positioned as an effective counterweight to the IM. This can also be construed as the initiation of a process of 'competitive negotiation', through which the existing polarization vis-á-vis the negotiations may gradually be dissolved.

None of these processes, however, appear to have strong probabilities of a forward movement unless the NSCN-IM shows some signs of diluting its consistently held position that questions the inclusion of Nagaland as part of the Indian Union, and rejects the framework of the Indian Constitution as an acceptable context of resolution. It is difficult, under these circumstances, to visualize how a semblance of unity can be induced within the other pole, or how a constructive dynamic can be evolved within the existing structures of negotiation.

Another aspect of the negotiating process that requires attention is the need to maintain a balance between certainty and uncertainty. Guarantees of post-conflict survival are necessary for the negotiating parties if later defection from the negotiated settlement are to be discouraged. For the NSCN-IM to maintain the allegiance of its cadres after a negotiated settlement, it must secure certain measurable rewards, including prisoner release and a dismantling of the existing security apparatus. These rewards are rarely immediate, and there is always a risk that the pendulum may swing back towards insurgent activities. There is, thus, a delicate problem of balance in the negotiating ensemble: How can cohesion among the various factions be increased without, at the same time, destabilizing levels of cohesion within the dominant groups—either through radical increase or decrease—to an extent that would undermine the objectives of a broadened negotiating framework. It is significant, within this context, that the incentive to cooperate is, more often than not, outweighed by the incentive to defect. Both the parties—and elements within each—have chosen at times to defect rather than cooperate.

The endeavour to involve other groups is construed by the NSCN-IM as the Union government's plan to split the Naga secessionist movement, and the IM group has consistently held that the Khaplang faction is a surrogate of, and is propped up by the S. C. Jamir regime in Nagaland. It is, however, also a truism that, after decades of incessant violence, it would be impractical to expect that an agreement with a single group could terminate the intractable Naga conflict.

One positive development in this context is the increasing popular support for a political settlement and a final end to the politics of violence which may prove to be a very critical input towards ending the insurgency. Indeed, juxtaposing the NSCN-IM's perception of a divisive GOI policy against the rising popular mandate for peace, Major-General R. N. Kapur notes that 'if you involve more people in the talks, you are uniting, not dividing . . . therefore the apprehension of some people that the Centre is trying to derail the peace process by inviting the Khaplang faction to the negotiating table is unfounded.'[58] This view is reinforced by Chief Minister S. C. Jamir's argument that a meaningful peace process would have to include a ceasefire, not only between the Union government and NSCN-IM and other outfits, but also between the insurgent groups themselves. Reflecting on a 'real ceasefire', Jamir opines that meaningful talks between the Union government and insurgent groups can be possible only if all parties are involved, and this must not only include the insurgent groups but other significant political players in the state. Indeed, the absence of the state government is one of the inexplicable elements of the current peace process. It is clear, however, that unity among the various insurgent groups is the minimum, though not sufficient, condition for the success of any proposed solution to the conflict. Jamir is emphatic on this, insisting that negotiations with one faction cannot lead to a lasting solution, as any single faction alone cannot determine the destiny of the Naga people. Officials involved in the negotiations have also claimed that if the two NSCN factions 'come together', a peace agreement would be easier to accept and implement.[59] One senior official is reported to have stated that 'we have a generous negotiating brief from the Prime Minister. Short of sovereignty and some key departments with the centre, everything else is on the negotiating table.'[60]

The involvement of all the parties in negotiations has, however, remained a theoretical exercise in Nagaland thus far. The NSCN-IM, on many occasions, has stated that it does not regard either the Khaplang faction or the NNC as 'freedom fighters'.[61] The IM has asked for an apology from Khaplang for 'the mistakes he committed' and also demanded that it must accept the leadership of Isak Swu and Muivah.[62] The NSCN-K, at the other end, has said that it did not recognise the word *Nagalim* as coined by the IM.[63] Kughalu Mulatonu, a senior leader of the Khaplang group, has indicated that Muivah's stance of withdrawing from the ongoing peace process if the Union government initiated talks with the NSCN-K was sufficient evidence that he was 'neither willing to unite the Nagas or represent the Nagas.'[64]

On the other hand, V. Horam, a senior leader of the IM faction, reflecting on the IM's antipathy towards Khaplang, stated, 'the Khaplang faction should sit on the Indian side during negotiations . . . Khaplang was expelled from the NSCN for anti-national activities. There is one Naga nation, one sovereignty and we represent the Nagas.'[65] On the NNC Federal, another of the Naga factions, Horam adds: 'Their representative unconditionally accepted the Indian Constitution through the Shillong Accord of 1975 . . . since then they have stopped resisting the Indian occupation of Nagalim.'[66]

Truce overtures made by the Khaplang group have not met with any effective response from the IM faction. In fact, the NSCN-K leadership has even expressed willingness to guarantee the safety of Muivah and Isaak Chisi Swu, IM leaders, 'should they wish to return to the Naga Hills and assess the wishes of the people with regard to a long-term settlement of the Naga problem.'[67]

In an attempt to further consolidate the Naga peace process, the NSCN-K, on 18 December 2001, while offering a month-long ceasefire to the IM, also announced suspension of military operations during this period.[68] NSCN-K General Secretary Kitovi Zhimomi said, 'with the fullest acknowledgement of prime aspirations of the Nagas and implementing the sacred code of unity and peace [we] hereby declare a cease-fire amongst warring Naga brothers for a period of 30 days effective from 19 December.'[69] However, the trajectory of Naga peace process thus far has been incompatible with the aspiration for unity among the various groups.[70] Ceasefires have not been able to terminate internecine killings, and these have contributed to a large extent in undoing peace agreements. The pattern reflects John Darby's observation that, 'even when political violence is ended by a ceasefire, it reappears in other forms to threaten the evolving peace process.'[71] Fratricidal or schismatic violence[72] is seen as being, more often than not, more avidly pursued than the 'struggle for Nagalim.' The NSCN cadres have been more determined to kill their own rather than encounter the 'avowed enemy', 'for their own can betray the dream while the enemy can only destroy the dreamer.'[73]

Past efforts towards uniting the two dominant factions on the Naga landscape have, consequently, failed. Appeals from the Naga Hoho, the Church, and other civil society groups have never been reciprocated by the two groups. Indeed, a unique aspect of the Naga insurgency since the ceasefires with the groups began has been that 'armed confrontation and clashes are not between the Indian army and the insurgents but among the different Naga groups . . . . Extortions of professionals, government officials and businessmen by all sides has left a very unpleasant taste in the mouths of many Nagas who want to live in peace, without harassment either from the security forces or the militants.'[74] Reflecting on the frozen nature of the peace process, Niketu Iralu, a leading Naga thinker, said,

> We are struck in a logjam, largely of our own making. No amount of complaining about Delhi will help . . . we have to deal with our logjam, that is, the inter-tribal or inter-factional rivalry or distrust, which has not been addressed. They were there originally even before the Naga struggle started. But that was just human frailty. However, with the complications of our political struggle, it became very destructive because, I believe, who'll control the struggle became the strongest issue . . . the so-called struggle for the Naga people and the talks with Delhi brought nothing. Because when you've frozen hearts against one another how can good politics come out? That's where the logjam is.[75]

Both parties, insistent on their stated positions, are currently boxed into a zero-sum definition of the problem. Within this paradigm, the demands of one can only be satisfied at the expense of the other,[76] and there is a distinct absence of options that hold the promise of mutual gain. The parties have been involved in negotiations for years now, and have become entrenched in their respective positions. Adding to the complexity is the high level of mistrust and the generation of emotional baggage, primarily due to historical reasons and the continuing incidence of violence. As one analyst expresses it, 'as long as the gunman is tolerated, has a role and a clearly defined mission, and emerges from history, there is prospect of violence; and for a generation the violence has continued.'[77]

The more hard-line 'take it or leave it' approach has more often than not blocked any consequential movement towards a durable solution to the Naga imbroglio. In response to the Prime Minister's invitation to the NSCN-IM leaders to hold the next round of confabulations in India, Muivah replied, '. . . if you want us to come to Delhi, we told them you have to pave the way. We told them there are so many obstacles like warrants of arrest and also NSCN continues to be a proscribed organisation. How could we go back to India?'[78] All past concessions by the GOI have secured only strategic manoeuvres on the part of the NSCN-IM, and this approach—bordering on adversarial tactics—has created little room for a compromise on the core issues at stake. Such an approach creates possibilities only of capitulation or a complete rejection of the available options.[79] The Union government has also, on many occasions, sought to entrench itself in such 'lock in' arenas, where the only possibilities of an eventual compromise involve a critical loss of credibility, leading ultimately to what Roy Lewicki referred to as a 'perpetual distortion in negotiation.'[80]

The peace process, in its current form, has been a game in which none of the parties can really win or lose, and the result is that the Nagas are caught in an unacceptable cycle of high levels of violence.[81] The pyrrhic war between the two factions and the unending process of negotiation without solution has created self-fulfilling expectations of persisting violence.

NOTES

* Kanchan L. is a Research Associate at the Institute for Conflict Management and Assistant Editor, *Faultlines: Writings on Conflict & Resolution.*

1. 'Solution to Naga impasse: PM, NSCN-IM set deadline in Osaka,' *The Assam Tribune.* Guwahati, 9 December 2001.
2. Bernard Crick said, 'My moral is not peace at any price but the terribly high price and unpredictability of victory if it comes to winner takes it all.' See Bernard Crick, 'The High Price of Peace,' in H. Gilliomee and J. Graziano, eds, *The Elusive Search for Peace: South Africa, Israel and Northern Ireland*, Cape Town: Oxford University Press, 1990, p. 269.

3. The purported objective of the National Socialist Council of Nagaland-Isak Muivah (NSCN-IM) is the establishment of a *Nagalim* (Greater Nagaland), consisting of all the Naga-inhabited areas of the neighbouring states of Assam, Manipur, Arunachal Pradesh, and some portions of Myanmar, which it considers to be the rightful homeland of the Nagas. Slated to be an independent state, the *Nagalim* lies in the Patkai range between the 930 and 970 East longitude and 23.50 and 28.30 North latitude at the trijunction of China, India, and Myanmar. The proposed *Nagalim* spreads over approximately 1.20,000 sq. km. in contrast to the present state of Nagaland that has an area of 16,527 sq. km. Source: www.satp.org/India/Nagalim.htm. Also see www.angelfire.cm/mi/Nagalim/Table.html.
4. J. Bowyer Bell, *The Dynamics of the Armed Struggle*, London: Frank Cass Publishers, 1998, p. 243.
5. The ceasefire agreement between the NSCN-IM and the Union government was first signed on 25 July 1997 and extended for a period of three months on 30 October 1997. It was extended for another year on 31 August 1998. Three extensions of a year each were announced on 4 August 1999, 31 July 2000, and 14 June 2001.
6. G. M. Srivastava, presentation at seminar 'Addressing Conflicts in India's North-east', pp. 25–7 June 2001, New Delhi.
7. 'Separatist group in India's northeast threatens to resume insurgency if truce is reviewed'. http//home.nycap.rr.com/Nagaland/nnews46.html. Also see 'NSCN(I-M) plans to resume war after talks with New Delhi fail', http://www.thenewspapertoday.com/india/insde.phtml?NEWS ID= 23467.
9. J. Bowyer Bell, 'Ireland: The Long End game', *Studies in Conflict and Terrorism*, vol. 21, no. 5, 1998, p. 7.
10. J. Bowyer Bell, *The Dynamics of the Armed Struggle*, p. 243.
11. Ibid., p. 244.
12. See 'Cloud lifts over North-East as Govt rolls back Naga ceasefire', *The Indian Express*, New Delhi, 28 July 2001; 'Centre's decision unacceptable: NSCN(I-M)', *The Hindu*, Chennai, 31 July 2001.
13. 'Govt banking on Naga pressure to prevent Muivah from shunning pact', *The Economic Times*, New Delhi, 22 July 2001.
14. Ibid.
15. 'Ceasefire' in Nagaland extended BSF(G) has highlighted ominous developments', *Daily Excelsior*, Jammu, 8 January 2001.
16. Ibid.
17. Balwally, Darshan, May 1995, cited in B. G. Varghese, *India's Northeast Resurgent: Ethnicity, Insurgency, Government, Development*, New Delhi: Konark Publishers, p. 100.
18. B. G. Varghese, *India's Northeast Resurgent Ethnicity, Insurgency, Govemment, Development*, p. 99.

19. 'No let-up in NSCN (I-M) extortions,' *Assam Tribune*, 10 December 2001.
20. Ibid.
21. According to the revised ground rules signed on 13 January 2001 between representatives of the Government of India and the NSCN-IM, 'the concern that forcible collection of money on essential supplies and intimidation of individuals including Government officials were taking place was denied by the NSCN. However, in the interest of promoting the peace process, the NSCN representatives agreed that the above activities would be prevented.' For the full text of the ground rules, see 'South Asia Terrorism Portal; Countries; India; States; Nagaland; Documents; Revised Ground Rules for Cease-fire between Government of India and NSCN-IM,' www.satp.org. The NSCN-K, in a separate agreement with the Union government signed on 28 May 2001, also agreed to 'refrain from extortions, forcible collection of money and supplies and intimidation of individuals including Government officials.' (see 'South Asia Terrorism Portal; Countries; India; States; Nagaland; Documents; Revised Ground Rules for Ceasefire between Government of India and the National Socialist Council of Nagaland-Kharlang (NSCN-K),' www.satp.org.
22. 'Nagas pin their hopes on talks to usher in normalcy,' *India Today*, New Delhi, 18 May 1998.
23. M. C. Mahapatra, Additional Deputy Inspector General (DIG) of BSF(G), in a paper in BSF publication, *Borderman*, cited in '"Cease-fire" in Nagaland extended: BSF(G) has highlighted ominous developments,' *Daily Excelsior*, Jammu, 8 January 2001.
24. Ibid. The Golden Triangle comprises 38 million hectares of rainforest-covered mountains in Laos, Thailand, and Myanmar (formerly Burma).
25. Ibid. The officer discloses that these outfits have established reliable contacts for arms procurement in Thailand and other South-East Asian nations. They also have well-established links for transportation to Bangladesh and Myanmar.
26. Ibid.
27. 'NSCN (IM) on fund raising spree: 94 cases of violation of ground rules reported,' *Nenanews*, vol. 1, no. 28–9, 7 December–21 December 1998. GPRN is the political wing of the NSCN-IM.
28. 'Naga ultras step up extortion drive in border areas,' *Assam Tribune*, 31 July 2000.
29. 'Centre restricts truce extension to Nagaland,' *The Deccan Herald*, Bangalore, 28 July 2001.
30. Each farmer was threatened to pay an annual tax of Rupees one thousand to the outfit. See 'Security Alert in Pallel,' *Hueiven Lanpao News Service*, 31 July 2001 at http://manipuronline.tripod.com/august news.htm.

31. See 'South Asia Terrorism Portal; Countries; India; States; Nagaland; Assessment 2001', www.satp.org.
32. See Martha Crenshaw, ed., *Terrorism, Legitimacy and Power*, Connecticut: Wesleyan University Press, 1983, p. 3.
33. The three-month-old Samara Party-led People's Front government was voted out on 21 May 2001 on the floor of the State Legislative Assembly, with 17 members voting in favour of the confidence motion moved by the then Chief Minister Radhabinod Koijam and 39 members opposing it. See 'Koijam voted out, Samata calls in BJP's final act of deceit', *The Hindustan Times*, New Delhi, 21 May 2001. Also see 'Manipur CM Koijam loses trust vote'. http://www.rediff.com/news/2001/may/21mani2.htm.
34. Brad McRae, *Negotiating and Influencing Skills: The Art of Creating and Claiming Value*, California: Sage Publications, 1998, p. 9.
35. Shantanu Nandan Sharma, 'The Naga Question: Violence and the Peace Process', *Faultlines: Writings on Conflict and Resolution*, vol. 10, New Delhi, January 2002, p. 99. Also see Pradip Phanjouham, 'Ethnicity, Identity and Conflict', *Faultlines: Writings on Conflict and Resolution*, vol. 10, New Delhi, January 2002, pp. 23–5.
36. Crenshaw, ed., *Terrorism. Legitimacy and Power*, p. 18.
37. Ibid.
38. Ibid., p. 25.
39. The seven ULFSS groups are United Liberation Front of Asom (ULFA) of Assam, Dima Halim Daugah (DHD) of Assam, United People's Democratic Solidarity (UPDS) of Assam, Arunachal Dragon Force (ADF) in Arunachal Pradesh. People's Liberation Army (PLA) of Manipur, and the Revolutionary Democratic Front (RDF). See 'Joint militant forum against "greater Nagaland"', *Nenanews*, vol. 4, no. 11–2, 22 August–6 September 2001, www.nenanews.com/OT%20Aug.%2022-%20Sept.6.01/ohl.htm.
40. See 'If referendum is required for peace in Assam, so be it', http://www.thenewspapertodav.com/india/inside.phtml ?NEWS ID=22399.
41. Ibid.
42. 'ULFA outrage over NSCN bid for Assam's Naga tracts', *Indian Express*, 19 May 1998.
43. Bibhu Prasad Routray, 'Naga-Cease-Fire Extension: Clash of Imagined Homelands', http://www.ipcs.org/issues/articles/531-ne-bibhu.html. According to him, 'the comparative compulsions and the common feeling of isolation, as a result of a perceived expansionist policy of the NSCN-IM, presents a scenario when these outfits find themselves in a common forum in opposing the cease-fire'.
44. 'Advani's assurance to North-Eastern States', The *Hindu*, 7 July 2001.
45. See Phanjoubam, 'Ethnicity, Identity and Conflict', pp. 23-35.

46. 'Alienating the NSCN (I-M) will be a blunder', *Hindustan Times*, 16 May 2001.
47. See 'Naga Peace Talks: Another Setback', *Economic and Political Weekly*, Mumbai, 31 July–6 August 1999. Also at www.epw.org.in/34-31/edit3.htm.
48. The Union government announced a ceasefire for the first time with the NSCN-K for two months from 15 November 1998 to 15 January 1999; NSCN-K declared a unilateral ceasefire for 20 days on 26 December 1998; NSCN-K offered unilateral ceasefire for three months with effect from 11 January 1999 till 11 April 1999. The security forces also suspended operations against NSCN-K for three months effective, from 15 January 1999. On 8 April 2000, the NSCN-K announced a six-month long ceasefire and in response, security forces unilaterally decided to suspend operations for six months, from 16 April 2000 to 16 October 2000. The NSCN-K called for a formalization of the ceasefire agreement with the Union government and in response, on 16 October 2000, ceasefire with NSCN-K was extended for another six months. On 28 April 2001, for the first time, a year-long ceasefire was announced with the NSCN-K.
49. Liz Philipson, 'Breaking Recurring Themes in the Cycles of War and Peace in Sri Lanka', Research Paper no. 3, Centre for the Study of Global Governance, The London School of Economics, London, December 1999, p. 35.
50. Liz Philipson, p. 37.
51. Muivah quoted in Varghese, *India's Northeast Reasurgent*, p. 100.
52. Wasbir Hussain, 'Deal with NSCN (I-M) alone is no solution: Khaplang faction', 13 September 2001, www.thenewspapertoday.com
53. Ibid.
54. Ibid.
55. 'Question of claiming territories doesn't arise: Muivah', www.rediff.com/news/2001/jun/25naga.htm.
56. 'Uncertainly looms large over Naga peace talks', www.axom.faithweb.com/news/oct1.html.
57. NSCN-IM, NSCN-K, the Naga National Council (Adino faction) and Naga National Council (Merupfu faction).
58. 'Fighting table: Muivah faction against involving Khaplang in talks', *The Week*, Kochi, 13 May 2001. Also see www.the-week.com/21may13/events3.htm.
59. 'After 33 years, Naga rebel bosses return', *Indian Express*,15 May 1999.
60. Ibid.
61. 'NSCN (IM)'s rigidity a spanner in peace process', *Nenanews*, vol. 2, no. 5–6, 7 June–21 June 1999.
62. Ibid.

63. 'NSCN(K) objects to Nagalim nomenclature', *Imphal Free Press*, Imphal, 20 October 2000.
64. Ibid.
65. 'Fighting table: Muivah faction against involving Khaplang in talks', *The Week*, 13 May 2001. Also see www.the-week.com/21may13/events3.htm.
66. Ibid.
67. Kitovi Zhimoni, general secretary of the NSCN-K, declared in November 2001 that Muivah and Swu 'should come to Nagaland. We will not harm the leaders, we will not commit the same crime as against Daly Mongro.' Mongro, a top Khaplang faction leader, was killed allegedly by the IM group in year 2000. See 'Khaplang's Nagas want to smoke peace pipe', *The Indian Express*, 5 November 2001.
68. 'NSCN(K) offers month-long truce to rivals', *Assam Tribune*, 19 December 2001.
69. See 'NSCN (K) offers truce to rivals', http://www.e-pao.net/GP.asp?src=9.9.191201.dec01
70. Clannish divisions among the Nagas (Konyaks and Tangkhuls) resulted in the split of the NSCN in 1988. The Konyaks formed the NSCN-K (Khaplang) under the leadership of Khole Konyak and S. S. Khaplang. The Tangkhul faction, the NSCN-IM (Isak Muivah), was led by Isak Swu and T. Muivah. The two groups are now violently opposed, and there have been a number of clashes, the worst of which occurred in April 1988, when NSCN-K cadres reportedly attacked the 'General Headquarters' of the IM faction and killed over a hundred cadres.
71. John Darby, 'The Effects of Violence on Peace Processes', http:// www.usip.org/pubs/catalog/violence.html.
72. As per the Nagaland police, during the period of ceasefire since 1 August 1997–22 March 2000, total number of persons killed in factional fights are 317. The break-up of 317 persons killed of various factions is: NSCN(IM)—61; NSCN(K)—133; NNC/NFG—22; civilian—65, government servant—1 2, police—3, SF/PMF—13, and unidentified—8. See Dinesh Kotwal, 'The Naga Insurgency: The Past And The Future', *Strategic Analysis*, New Delhi: Institute for Defence Studies & Analyses, vol. XXIV, no. 4, July 2000, p. 772. According to media reports, on 26 July 2000, during the three-year-long ceasefire till then, at least 536 deaths were reported and 165 persons were killed in clashes between various insurgent groups, primarily between the IM and Khaplang factions. The IM justified its action against members of other groups by saying that the ceasefire was only with security forces. See 'NSCN for extension of cease-fire', *The Statesman*, Kolkata, 26 July 2000.
73. J. Bowyer Bell, *The Dynamics of the Armed Struggle*, p. 52.
74. 'Suicidal fights', *The Indian Express*, 14 April 2000.

75. 'Frozen hearts produce dangerous politics', *The Pioneer*, New Delhi, 12 November 2000.
76. Herbert C. Kelman, 'Interactive Problem Solving: The Uses and Limits of a Therapeutic Model for the Resolution of International Conflicts' in Vamik Volkan, Demetrios A. Julius and Joseph V. Montville, eds, *The Psychodynamics of International Relationships: Vol. II: Tools of Unofficial Diplomacy*, Lexington, MA: Lexington Books, 1991, p. 157.
77. J. Bowyer Bell, 'Ireland: The Long End Game', *Studies in Conflict and Terrorism*, vol. 21, no. 5, 1998, p. 8.
78. See Deepak Dewan's Interview with Muivah, 'Vajpayee invites Isak-Muivah to Delhi', *North East Sun*, New Delhi, 15–31 January 2002, p. 6.
79. The incidents in June 2001 regarding the extension of ceasefire is an example of such capitulation or rejection.
80. See Roy J. Lewicki, et al., *Essentials of Negotiations*, Homewood, IL: Richard D. Irwin 1997, pp. 135–8.
81. J. Bowyer Bell, 'Ireland: The Long End Game', p. 22.

CHAPTER 22

Air Power in the Information Age

Squadron Leader P. M. Sinha

The weapon of superior reach or range should be looked upon as the fulcrum of combined tactics. Thus, should a group of fighters be armed with bows, spears and swords, it is around the arrow that tactics should be shaped; if with cannons, muskets, and pikes, then around the cannon; and if with aircraft, artillery, and rifles, then around the airplane.

—Major-General J. F. C. Fuller

Background

Armed forces and defence planners throughout history have always eagerly sought accurate and timely information. 2000 years ago, Kautilya, the military strategist, extensively articulated the salience of information management. Chengiz Khan, the Mongol conqueror, was the master of employing horse cavalry in outflanking forays against enemy dispositions for vital information gathering prior to the main offensive. Today, advances in technology have made vast amounts of information virtually available at the click of a mouse. The twenty-first century would be the information age, with global information transcending national boundaries. Networking would be the order of the day and a commander would be inundated with a plethora of information. Air power would be largely affected by this connectivity, due to its inherent characteristics of speed and reach. Dominance in the information environment possessing more and better information than the adversary and reacting to it more quickly has always provided strategic and tactical advantage to the force possessing it. Superiority in the processing and use of the vast quantities of available information is critical to military success.

For nearly a century since its inception, air power has played a dominant role in the generation and successful enforcement of favourable asymmetry. A look at the conflict paradigm of the future suggests that air power will make an even greater impact. The unique attributes of combat aircraft along with calibrated escalation and disengagement control makes air power an ideal weapon for achieving a resounding victory in war. The attributes of high speed, long reach, quick response and termination, technological intensity, precision fire power and shock effect—without regard to frontiers and coastlines—have made air power a formidable component of national military power.

The foremost lesson of the twentieth century is that no war can be prosecuted successfully without air power and that it would doubtless be lost without the befitting application of air power. Therefore, the employment of air power in modern war has become the most important and sometimes the most exclusive component. Aerial warfare has changed dramatically due to the introduction of precision weapons and more importantly the ability to accurately target these weapons onto the enemy's centre of gravity. This has been achieved by the setting up of the command, control, communications, computers, intelligence, surveillance, and reconnaissance network.

Development

Past Milestones: Airpower dawned at the beginning of the previous century. Some of the significant chronological milestones in military aerospace history point to a technology driven transformation, all the more remarkable because of its rapidity. These were as follows:

- 1908—First military airplane flies.
- 1911—Aircraft attack against surface forces.
- 1918—Aircraft carrier attack against land targets
- 1936—First militarily significant airlift of combat forces.
- 1939—First jet engine flown.
- 1940—First use of integrated air defence systems.
- 1943—Precision guided munition attacks against surface forces.

- 1944—Era of strategic cruise and ballistic missile attack begins.
- 1949—First air-refuelled around-the-world flight.
- 1960—Era of surface-to-air missile combat operations begins.
- 1960—First reconnaissance satellite orbited.
- 1983—First operational stealth aircraft.
- 1991—Aerospace Warfare in the Gulf.

Lethality: The offensive capability of air power has increased manifold over the years. During 1943, the entire US Eighth Air Force attacked no more than 50 strategic targets in the whole year. In 1991, during the first 24 hours of operation Desert Storm, the coalition air forces attacked 150 strategic targets. By 2020, precise attack forces may be capable of attacking up to 500 important strategic targets during the very first minutes of an air campaign. Flow of information and real time intelligence would dramatically change the way future air operations would be conducted. However, this new method of conducting campaigns would need large investment in technology-related systems and weapons, the cost of which may be prohibitive for a developing nation.

Information and Speed of OPS

Employment of air power in the future would be intrinsically linked to the availability of accurate information and networking. Platforms of destruction would only become a part of the entire gamut of operations and the mere possession of multi-role aircraft and PGMs would not suffice. What would need to be put in place, is an effective and viable C^4ISR set-up.

Decision Cycle: The basic element of military activity on the battlefield is the information–decision–action (IDA) cycle. The information part of the cycle is carried out by sensors and associated systems responsible for the generation of information. This activity is followed by decision and action in a cyclic fashion till the specific activity is completed. The smaller the cycle, the greater is the compression of time, or faster is the completion of the IDA cycle. Due to the increasing reach, speed, and lethality of airpower, the information–decision–action cycle in the future would assume greater importance for air commanders. The inflow and outflow of information would be very large, the systems would be more complicated, the chain of command more convoluted and there would be a requirement of faster decision-making. Air power is heavily dependent on technology and modern technology brings with it a deluge of information, which can overload the decision-making cycle. Thus, the IDA cycle would be a critical factor in future air operations. As one goes down from the strategic to the tactical level, the time available for making a decision decreases. At the tip of the spear, it is very short. A soldier engaged in close quarter combat would cycle through his OODA loop much faster than the HQ staff running the entire campaign. In an aerial combat, the victor would be the pilot who can cycle through his OODA loop the quickest. History is littered with examples of aces which had out cycled their opponents by making unexpected moves that the adversary had been unable to counter.

Information and Decision-Making: Modern information technology has had a dramatic effect on Command Headquarters. Modern sensors such as AWACS, JSTARS, UAVs and satellites can penetrate the fog of war and help to build up the commander's situational awareness. These aerial platforms will be able to look deep into enemy territory and provide the commander with data linked real time information. This capability of real time information would greatly speed up the OODA loop of the commander. This transparent battlefield can shorten the first 'O' of the OODA loop, while maintaining enough centralized command to optimize the employment of airpower. The data providers would have to filter out unnecessary information and provide an uncluttered picture to the commander to allow him to rapidly orientate and decide.

Information and Situational Awareness: Situational awareness has recently become a fashionable term among defence experts. Air warriors, however, have used it for years to describe the crucial difference between winning and losing in aerial combat. The aim of any commander is to attain a high level of situational awareness so that he can conduct the battle or a campaign in an effective manner. It is felt that the future battlefield will become transparent and the fog of war and friction would reduce, leading to a high situational awareness. However, if an asymmetry does not exist between the two adversaries and they are matched technologically, then they both can create an immense amount of confusion and fog, since the systems in use are highly vulnerable and prone to cyber attacks. This can lead to a rapid loss of situational awareness. Thus foresight, pre-planning, building up of enemy database and out thinking the adversary would lead to the penultimate victory. For a high level of situational awareness a commander should have the ability to be proactive in the planning process, to be prepared to react and exploit opportunities when direct confrontation must occur, and to shape expected actions to stay inside an enemy's decision cycle and keep him outside his own.

Command and Control

Organizational Changes: Presently, too much attention has been devoted to technological magic at the expense of the organizational, conceptual, and other human inputs needed to convert the magic from lifeless hardware into combat outcomes. The speed of future air battles will be swift and there may be no time to consult the higher echelons for instructions and decisions. The present-day military hierarchical structure in such an environment may not work. Decentralization and delegation are few imperatives which need to be addressed in such a scenario. Commanders and officers at lower levels would have to be fully aware of the rules of engagement so that they can take quick decisions. There will be the shift from platform-centric warfare to network-centric warfare, and this would need new concepts of command and control structure. Network-centric warfare allows new concepts of speed of command and self synchronization to be brought into play. The present hierarchical set-up can make decisions more quickly than networks because authority is centralized. They can implement their decisions more quickly and reliably. This means that they are better at managing risk in the short term than decentralized organizations, whose members are free to respond to local conditions and thus are hard to guide through difficulties. On the other hand, this freedom to respond makes decentralized networks more agile and adaptive than hierarchies. Such adaptation, in turn, means that networks would tend to manage long-term risk better than hierarchies. As this summary of strengths and weaknesses makes clear, hierarchies and networks are best suited for different activities. Thus, a combination of both these organizational characteristics should be maintained to suit the circumstances.

Information and Command: Commanders will have more information available than ever before, while having less time to use it. This suggests that the responsibility for comprehending what the information means and using it may have to be increasingly shared with lower and more junior command levels. An increase in the capacity of C^4ISR technologies, and an increase in the lethality, accuracy, and reach of weapons systems will allow units and formations to decrease in size. Communications technologies will allow the physical span of control of commanders to increase and this will assist in the coordination of widely dispersed units. The information superiority that these capabilities provide will significantly increase the speed of command, enabling forward deployed and initial forces to wrest the initiative away from the enemy forces and possibly set the conditions for early, favourable termination of the conflict.

Reconnaissance Surveillance and Target Acquisition (RSTA)

Knowledge of the Enemy: 'You can't fight what you can't see.' This is one of the golden rules in aerial combat. The 'see' does not only imply visual spotting, but it also means knowledge of the enemy's disposition and strength by means of electronic surveillance. Knowledge and information of the enemy is vital, and this can be achieved through reconnaissance, surveillance, and target acquisition systems. The employment of RSTA technologies is moving warfare further towards greater utilization of aerial, including space assets for gathering of information, greater range of striking power through long range offensive systems, and higher accuracy through availability of better target information. RSTA technologies gather information and this information requires filtering, analysing, and dissemination to the users through communications technologies. If viewed holistically, then RSTA with communications gives military forces the ability to locate targets with accuracy, carry out designation and cueing of weapon systems that significantly enhances combat power.

Battlefield Transparency: The use of RSTA systems like AWACS, Unmanned Aerial Vehicles (UAVs), strategic reconnaissance aircraft, satellites and their integration into a C^{4}ISR system enables the use of sophisticated weapons like the Precision Guided Munitions (PGMs). Long-range precision weapons are of no use if the location of targets is not known and only sophisticated electronic surveillance devices in a C^{4}ISR network can provide this. Forces able to harness these potential capabilities will gain dominant battle space awareness. The fusion of sensors, platforms, command organizations and logistic centres into a single system will allow more operational tasks to be completed faster. Thus the battlefield would be more transparent to a commander and it would be his ingenuity which would dictate the progress of the battle.

Fog of War: It would be incorrect to assume that there will be no fog of war and lapses in intelligence, even with the availability of a huge quantum of information. The gaps in knowledge about the enemy would exist due to intangibles like weather, deception techniques, and information overload. This will place great stress on the operators responsible for making sense of the information being received. As operators and their computer systems are overloaded, useful and indeed vital information may get lost in the ensuing clutter. Other information may take so long to be processed that it could end up being of little use to commanders. The fog of war is thus likely to remain. Unable to fully lift the fog of war, commanders will be forced to deliberately focus on battle space awareness.

Future OPS

This futuristic war fighting methodology would rely heavily upon air power due to its inherent characteristics of speed, lethality, and mobility. A template for the utilization of the air power cannot be laid out, since it can be used in different situations in various ways. For example, in the Kosovo operations, precision weapons were used effectively against non-hardened civil infrastructure targets from stand-off distances with minimum collateral damage, whilst the use against military forces was limited to a little more than interdiction purposes. Conversely, in the Gulf conflict, the military targets were attacked in large numbers due to the prevailing conditions and requirements. Future air operations would see some dramatic changes with the induction of certain capabilities like uninhabited combat air vehicles (UCAVs), increase and precise airlift, space-based systems, and more potent aircraft.

Uninhabited Combat Air Vehicles: These UCAVS would be flown potentially anywhere in the world through high-speed fibre-optic and satellite communication links. They will not be bound by the limits of human tolerance and can be designed to accelerate in any direction instantaneously. Also, UCAVs will be less costly than manned aircraft of similar capability.

Space: Space-based and ground deployed systems, in combination, already allow worldwide weather monitoring. Within a decade, an aircraft and mission planning system could include a map of the world of up to one metre accuracy. It will offer an on-board navigation database to fly anywhere in the world without the need for external data. Joint tactical information distribution system (JTIDS) will allow a real time exchange of digital information between aircraft on relative positions, weapons availability and fuel states, thus reducing the need for intra-flight voice communications. Because of the clear situational awareness picture it offers, JTIDS type of systems would also permit the use of data for tactics at night, such as an offensive fighter sweep. Other systems offering real time joint connectivity include advanced data fusion software, interlinked but physically dispersed databases, and high speed large capacity communications nets, all of which will enable the prompt and precise application of force. Once operational, such awareness nets would help greatly to ease the problem of real time intelligence fusion.

Path for India

For India, the threat is multifarious and the path towards building a powerful arm of air power is inescapable. In the coming years, India would require to build up a full spectrum capability. It may be engaged in low intensity conflict operations and the proxy war being waged from across the border, and also it will have to be prepared for a conventional war in a nuclear backdrop

Technological Changes: According to Air Marshal C. V. Gole, former Deputy Chief of Air Staff, 'Technology asymmetry in air war can be decisive, but technology for its own sake is dangerous. Technology as applicable, to a nation's military doctrine and requirements is what should be pursued.' This would imply that India should prioritize and aim to acquire the capability of precision stand-off tactical strike, digitization to tactical level C^4ISR, and suitable aerial platforms for weapon delivery and specialized roles.

Organizational Changes: In future wars in which air activity will be the precursor to any land operation, the overarching interests of mission effectiveness will require a breakdown of narrow and retrograde parochialism and have a greater professional cross communication as a routine matter of peacetime business. Organizational change is the greatest challenge of the emerging information age. However, in India it may be difficult to gain support for change in an institution that is as steeped in tradition as the services. Nonetheless, the future environment will demand organizational concepts different from those we know today. While it is too early to identify the design specifications of the future services organization with any precision, it is important to begin thinking about different alternatives, and perhaps, most importantly, to begin thinking about organizations that will be flexible and robust enough to be decisive in a variety of different potential situations. Fostering the technology revolution will also require embracing the need for cultural change within the services. It will demand more joint service cooperation, greater operational synergies, and, in particular, operations and intelligence must work more closely together. This change will require not merely paying due obeisance to so-called jointness, but for a true team spirit on a daily basis. Inter-service friction and petty jockeying for institutional position would need to be dispensed with. Creating such an outlook may be a more difficult challenge than building and integrating the new technologies.

Conclusion

The information age dawning upon us would greatly affect the employment of air power; due to the increased tempo of operations, air power is neither magic nor a panacea that can compensate for absence of clear, consistent, and determined policy goals. Air power now offers the promise of being the determinant factor in an ever-widening variety of circumstances if its future development and evolution are properly planned. The challenge to military leadership will be in finding ways of best employing these diverse assets in an integrated fashion with other force elements towards attaining declared national goals. Service interests must give place to national interest if effective exploitation of new technologies by doctrinal and organizational changes is to be realized.

During crises, the threat or the use of conventional air strike would equip the government with a flexible and responsive tool for crisis management. In a hot war, air interdiction against strategic targets such as power grids communication networks and their key nodal points would require multi-role aircraft with PGMS or ALCMS for long range precision strikes. India's air power cannot afford not to have such a capability in the future. However, most of the determinants of success in war, from courage and willpower to small unit initiative and cool decision-making under fire, have little to do with technology and the human aspects will always predominate. To win wars, it has to be an effective, suitable, and synergetic combination of all elements of national power which would achieve a decisive victory in the battle space of the future.

CHAPTER 23

Maoist Uprising in Nepal

*Fahmida Ashraf**

Introduction

In Nepal, the Maoists, under the Communist Party of Nepal (Maoists) (CPN-M), have been waging an insurgency since 1996, which has now become a threat to the security of the State. The Maoists are basically advocating the replacement of the constitutional monarchy in Nepal with a communist republic.

The political parties in Nepal view the Maoist insurgency differently. As Shom Prasad Luitel, an advocate in Kathmandu, writes: 'The Nepali Congress does not have a clear view on the Maoist People's War. Some of its leaders consider it to be a terrorist group and the problem one of law and order. That is the official line. However, other members consider the Maoist problem a political issue that should be solved politically. The Rastriya Parjatantra Party and Nepal Sadvawana Party do not have clear-cut views on, but consider the war a political problem. All Communist parties consider it a political problem, but sometimes condemn it for terrorist activities. There are slight differences in views between Communist parties on the Maoist People's War. The Nepal Communist Party (UML) and Nepal Communist Party (ML) want to change society by peaceful means. The other Communist parties consider armed struggle necessary for revolution, but argue that the situation is not ready to start armed struggle.'[1] The purpose of this article is to analyse the nature of the Maoist uprising in the light of the domestic debate in Nepal over the issue.

Nepal's Political System

For many decades, Nepal was ruled by a strong monarchy. Though the 1959 constitution provided a bicameral parliament, political parties were banned and the king had strong executive, legislative, and judicial powers. As the demand for democracy and constitutional reforms gained strength in Nepal, the 1962 constitutional amendment established a partyless panchayat system, which continued for 30 years. Ananta Raj Poudyal, a Nepali Professor of Political Science, wrote in one of his articles, 'Politically, the 30 years were characterized by inconsistencies and contradictions. Not only politics but also the economy of the country deteriorated under the Panchayat system. Its objectives like "exploitation-less society" became a fantasy, and the rhetoric "politics for development" had little impact on the life styles of the general public.'[2] Therefore, in view of the pressures from the pro-democracy movement and widespread unrest in the country, in 1990, King Birendra had to abolish the partyless panchayat system. He established a constitutional monarchy and an elected parliament based on a multi-party system. According to Bertil Lintner, a journalist, in an article he published in 1997, more than 500 demonstrators were killed in violent clashes with the police in Kathmandu before the king eventually gave in to popular demands for an end to the old system.[3] As a result of the constitutional changes there emerged several political parties, such as, the Nepal Communist Party-United Marxist Leninist (NCPUML), Nepali Congress (NC), Rastriya Prajatantra Party (RPP), Nepal Sadbhavana Party (NSP), Rastriya Jana Morcha, Nepal Workers & Peasants Party (NWPP), and Samyukta Janmorcha Nepal.[4]

As a result, the first general elections in three decades on a party basis were held in 1991. The Nepali Congress Party emerged as the major party. However, in about 10 years of parliamentary democracy in Nepal, there have been eight different prime ministers as one government after another was not able to perform successfully. As observed by Karl H. Kramer, a German scholar, 'in practice, the politicians have not been able to implement many aspects of the constitution. Even fundamental rights guaranteed by the constitution, like that of equality of all citizens, have not even legally been realized after ten years. Corruption and selfishness of the politicians and traditional ways of thinking must be regarded as the main reasons for such shortcomings. The poor state of affairs is reflected by the instability of governments. It opens room for the development of radical forces like that of the Maoists who reject the current constitution and fight a violent so-called "people's war" that has cost the life of more than 1,500 people since February 1996.'[5] Poudyal, in one of this articles written in 1997 concludes, 'A lot needs to be done to consolidate the democratic process of Nepal. The most urgent seem to be bringing about democratic behaviour among the political parties and raising of civic consciousness among the people.'[6]

As a result of the unconstitutional practices of political parties, the movement for constitutional reforms gained momentum in Nepal and three schools of thought emerged by the end of the year 2000. One school of thought supported a complete replacement of the political system; the second school advocated substantial amendments; and the third supported continuity with suitable reforms. As pointed out by the Nepali scholar Lok Raj Baral, 'The Maoist and the die-hard supporters of the dismantled partyless regime represented the replacement school. Demands for substantial constitutional amendments came from the left opposition parties. The view for continuity with minor changes came from the rest of the parties.'[7]

Communist Party of Nepal

The Communist party of Nepal (CPN) has been active in the state since 1949. 'Civil Liberty for all the classes; let us form Revolutionary Civil Liberty Committee' was the main slogan in the first pamphlet issued on the occasion of the establishment of the CPN.[8] However, by 1960, the growing debate on monarchy caused sharp divisions within the party resulting in the emergence of several factions. Seven left-wing parties and the Nepali Congress party supported the democratic movement.

The Communist Party of Nepal (Maoist) adheres to the ideals, aspirations and course of action based on Mao's style of dictatorship of the proletariat. As one of the extreme left organization, its main objective is to 'establish a "people's government" through a "people's war". The executive head of the CPN (Maoist) is its general secretary Pushpa Kamal Dahal (Prachanda). Baburam Bhattarai, considered a moderate, is the political face of the Maoists. The political party structure consists of a politburo central committee, regional bureaus, subregional bureaus, district committees, and cell committees. The party has emphasized its course of action on political and military strategies. For administrative convenience it has divided the country into three zones and 27 districts. On the military front it has a central military commission, regional military commissions, and district military commissions. The Maoists have maintained fraternal and ideological linkages with the People's War Group and Maoist Communist Centre in India who also provide them with arms and ammunition.'[9]

The Communist Party of Nepal (Maoist) is a member of the Revolutionary Internationalist Movement (RIM). It has links especially with the Maoists in Peru, India, Turkey, Philippines, Bangladesh, Sri Lanka, Iran, Italy, New Zealand and the United States. The CPN (Maoist) has support groups and solidarity forums outside the country in India, Hong Kong, Germany, and Belgium.[10]

In 1990, the two major communist factions united into the United Marxist-Leninist party UML. The Communist Party (UML) emerged as the second main party in the parliament during the first general elections, held in 1991.[11] The Nepali Congress, led by G. P. Koirala, emerged as the major party and formed the government. However, Koirala resigned in 1994, and during the ensuing mid-term elections the Communist Party (UML) won and formed the government under the leadership of Manmohan Adhikari. However, the communist government was not able to perform well and fell after nine months. According to Bertil Lintner, 'the CPN (UML) was not radical enough; it resembled a European social democrat party rather than a militant organisation that was going to introduce any radical political or economic changes'.[12] It was because of these reasons that differences arose within the party and the main factions, including Samyukta Jana Morcha (United People's Front) under the leadership of Baburam Bhattarai, left the Communist Party (UML). This faction had won nine seats during the 1991 elections. Baburam Bhattarai was dissatisfied with the working of the left parties who according to him, had digressed from the Marxist goal of creating a classless society.[13] The Samyukta Jana Morcha united with the Communist Party (Maoist) and launched the People's War in 1996.

CPN (Maoist)'s People's War

The Communist Party of Nepal (Maoist) launched the People's War on 13 February 1996, with the aim 'to smash the existing semi-feudal and semi-colonial state and build a people's New Democratic State.'[14] According to Baburam Bhattarai, Chairman United People's Front, 'An armed People's War has been initiated in Nepal from 13 February 1996 under the leadership of the Communist Party of Nepal (Maoist) with the proclaimed aim of establishing a New Democratic socio-economic system and state by overthrowing the present socio-economic structure and state. This should be understood against the background that Nepal has slid to the status of the second poorest country in the world in terms of physical and cultural developments.'[15]

Explaining the rationale behind the 'People's War', Bhattarai emphasized that 'the Nepalese Maoists' attempt to create a new democratic system through the People's War began only after all attempts to carry out reforms within the old semi-feudal and semi-colonial system had failed. The ruling classes want to continuously exploit the people through the present socio-economic system, and international forces also exploit the people through internal means. From this point of view, the People's War in Nepal is part of the world anti-imperialist national liberation movement.'[16] Li Onesto, a commentator for the Pacific News Service, in 1999 visited the Maoist-controlled areas in western, central and eastern Nepal. In her reports, she stated that the rural areas were underdeveloped, without electricity, running water, and basic sanitation.[17] The statistics of deprivation, according to Shom Prasad Luitel, that make Nepal the second poorest country in the world are: '71% of the population is below absolute poverty level; 46.5% of national income is in the hands of 10% of the richest people; more than 60% of its total population are illiterate, more than 90% of its total population live in rural areas and 81% of the labour force is engaged in backward agricultural occupations; 10% are totally unemployed and 60% are under-employed or in disguised employment.'[18]

As commented by Onesto, the rural population, including farmers and women, supported the Maoists as they were advocating land ownership rights, development and equality for women. According to other reports, the Maoists in these regions 'burned property-ownership records and redistributed land among farmers. Women, in these areas, were also given various rights.'[19] Thus, the Maoists gained support at the grassroots level by appealing to their sense of deprivation and grievances.

The CPN (Maoist) has two organizational structures—the political front and the military front. The political front's responsibility is to organize, create awareness and spread Maoist ideas. The military front organizes attacks on police and other targets. It has around 5,000 armed personnel, including the militia.[20] Various other organizations affiliated with the Maoist party are the All Nepal National Free Students Union (Revolutionary), All Nepal Women's Association (Revolutionary), All Nepal Trade Union Federation, and National People's Movement Coordination Committee.

When in 1994 the Samyukta Jana Morcha, led by Baburam Bhattarai, disassociated itself from the Communist Party (UML) and continued its armed rebellion in the rural areas, the State authorities intensified their campaign to crush the movement. The Nepali government launched 'Operation Romeo' in November 1995 against the extreme communists. It was in this backdrop that Samyukta Jana Morcha united with the Communist Party (Maoist) and launched the People's War. According to Bertil Lintner, this campaign is based on the Peru's Shining Path model. 'It has established strongholds in remote mountain regions, where police outposts are few and far between, enabling the guerrillas to move about freely.'[21] Their arms are primitive and generally collected in the villages from farmers or snatched from the police in encounters. However, some small arms, as pointed by Lintner, were bought in the black arms market in the Indian State of Bihar. During this period, there was anti-India feeling among the Nepalese because of the water and hydroelectric power issue (the Mahakali Treaty).[22] The Maoists also exploited these nationalist feelings and won support in the rural community. Bhattarai, in his article 'Politico-economic Rationale of People's War', states, 'the biggest direct manifestation of world imperialist oppression and exploitation in Nepal is Indian expansionist exploitation and oppression.'[23]

The CPN (Maoist)'s political front, as part of the People's War in 1996, put forward 40 demands to the government headed by the Nepali Congress Party.[24] These were within the following categories:

I. Demands Related to Nationalism

1. Regarding the 1950 Treaty between India and Nepal, all unequal stipulations and agreements should be removed.
2. The government (HMG) should admit that the anti-nationalist Tanakpur agreement[25] was wrong, and the Mahakali Treaty, incorporating the same, should be nullified.
3. The entire Nepal–India border should be controlled and systematized. Cars with Indian number plates, which are plying the roads of Nepal, should not be allowed.
4. Gorkha recruiting centres should be closed and decent jobs should be arranged for the recruits.
5. In several areas of Nepal, where foreign technicians are given precedence over Nepali technicians for certain local jobs, a system of work permits should be instituted for the foreigners.
6. Monopoly of foreign capital in Nepal's industry, trade, and economic sector should be stopped.
7. Sufficient income should be generated from customs duties for the country's economic development.
8. The cultural pollution of imperialists and expansionists should be stopped. Hindi video, cinema, and all kinds of such newspapers and magazines should be completely stopped. Inside Nepal, import and distribution of vulgar Hindi films, video cassettes and magazines should be stopped..
9. Regarding NGOs and INGOs: bribing by imperialists and expansionists in the name of NGOs and INGOs should be stopped.

II. Demands Related to the Public and its Well-being:

10. A new Constitution has to be drafted by the people's elected representatives.
11. All the special rights and privileges of the King and his family should be ended.
12. Army, police and administration should be under the peoples' control.
13. The Security Act and all other repressive acts should be abolished.
14. All the false charges against the people of Rukum, Rolpa, Jajarkot, Gorkha, Kavre, Sindhuphalchowk, Sindhuli, Dhanusha

and Ramechap should be withdrawn and all the people falsely charged should be released.

15. Armed police operations in the different districts should immediately be stopped.
16. Regarding Dilip Chaudhary, Bhuvan Thapa Magar, Prabhakar Subedi,[26] and other people who disappeared from police custody at different times, the govenment should constitute a special investigating committee to look into these crimes and the culprits should be punished and appropriate compensation given to their families.
17. People who died during the movement should be declared as martyrs and their families, and those who have been wounded and disabled, should be given proper compensation. Strong action should be taken against the killers.
18. Nepal should be declared a secular state.
19. Girls should be given equal property rights to those of their brothers.
20. All kinds of exploitation and prejudice based on caste should be ended. In areas having a majority of one ethnic group, that group should have autonomy over that area.
21. The status of dalits as untouchables should be ended and the system of untouchability should be ended once and for all.
22. All languages should be given equal status. Up to the middle high school level (uccha madyamic) arrangements should be made for education to be given in the children's mother tongue.
23. There should be guarantee of free speech and free press. The communications media should be completely autonomous.
24. Intellectuals, historians, artists and academicians engaged in other cultural activities should be guaranteed intellectual freedom.
25. In both the *terai* and hilly regions, there is prejudice and misunderstanding in backward areas. This should be ended and the backward areas should be assisted. Good relations should be established between the villages and the city.
26. Decentralization in real terms should be applied to local areas, which should have local rights, autonomy and control over their own resources.

III. Demands Related to the People's Living:

27. Those who cultivate the land should own it. (The tiller should have right to the soil he/she tills.) The land of rich landlords should be confiscated and distributed to the homeless and others who have no land.
28. Brokers and commission agents should have their property confiscated and that money should be invested in industry.
29. All should be guaranteed work and should be given a stipend until jobs are found for them.
30. The government (HMG) should pass strong laws ensuring that people involved in industry and agriculture should receive minimum wages.
31. The homeless should be given suitable accommodation. Until the government (HMG) can provide such accommodation, they should not be removed from where they are squatting.
32. Poor farmers should be completely freed from debt. Loans from the Agricultural Development Bank by poor farmers should be completely written off. Small industries should be given loans.
33. Fertilizer and seeds should be easily and cheaply available, and the farmers should be given a proper market price for their production.
34. Flood and drought victims should be given all necessary help.
35. All should be given free and scientific medical service and education and education for profit should be completely stopped.
36. Inflation should be controlled and salaries of labourers should be raised in direct ratio with the rise in prices. Daily essential goods should be made cheap and easily available.
37. Arrangements should be made for drinking water, good roads, and electricity in the villages.
38. Cottage and other small industries should be granted special facilities and protection.
39. Corruption, black marketing, smuggling, bribing, the taking of commissions, etc. should all be stopped.
40. Orphans, the disabled, the elderly and children should be given help and protection.

The government of the Nepali Congress Party rejected these demands and adopted repressive measures to suppress the Maoist activities. In reaction, the Maoists increased their guerrilla activity. According to official reports, since 1996 about 1,800 people have died, whereas unofficial reports claim about 4,000 deaths, mostly of Maoists, the police, and villagers.[27] The Maoists have influence in 68 of Nepal's 75 districts. According to government sources, 32 are regarded as 'hardest hit' areas. In five western districts, the Maoists have organized a parallel government. These are Rolpa, Rukum, Jararkot, Salyam, and Kalikot.[28]

In the Maoist related issues, human rights groups in Nepal have been active in two respects. First, they have supported an end to human rights violations. Second, they have stressed upon and mediated peace talks between the Maoists and the government. The Maoists have also shown a more accommodating attitude towards the human rights institutions and activists.[29]

International organizations have called for respect of human rights by the government of Nepal and by the Maoists. For example, Amnesty International, in one of its reports, says, 'Amnesty International joins human rights defenders in Nepal in demanding accountability from the authorities in upholding the fundamental human rights guaranteed in Nepal's Constitution. We also urge the leadership of the CPN (Maoist) to put an end to abuses and issue strict orders to its cadres not to attack civilians, take hostages, kill or torture prisoners or recruit children into their ranks.'[30]

Present Situation

After the royal massacre of 1 June 2001, the Maoists have intensified their military campaign. While dealing with the Maoists, King Birendra was not in favour of using the Nepalese army. As commented by commentator Li Onesto, 'One of the biggest disputes within the government over the last year has been whether or not to send the army against the Maoists. Some troops have been deployed to areas hardest hit. Birendra has been reluctant to unleash the army against the guerrillas.'[31] The Maoists, even though they regarded King Birendra as part of the feudal system, yet they considered him 'a nationalist.'[32] The reasons for that, according to senior Maoist leader Baburam Bhattarai, were, 'he introduced democracy and took a keen interest in the well being of our country, for which extremist reactionaries assassinated his whole family.'[33] Regarding the royal massacre as a conspiracy, the Chairman of the CPN (Maoist), Prachanda, said, 'terming it a family conflict, planned propaganda of both national and international reactionaries, and the drama seen while performing the last rites clearly prove that the massacre is a result of conspiracy. To think that King Birendra's patriotic stand and liberal political ideology were not the reasons for the royal deaths would be very misleading politics. The late King was not in favour of PM Koirala's plan to mobilise the army against the people's war.'[34] Prachanda also said, 'this pre-planned massacre designed in this political background will have a long term effect on the future of Nepal and Nepali history. This massacre portrays the end of the present political system.' He threatened that the Maoists would step up their activities.[35]

As a reaction to the royal massacre, the Maoists gathered in Kathmandu to plan their strategy for a revolution and stepped up their military activities in June 2001.[36] However, in July 2001, the Nepalese Prime Minister and the Maoists agreed on a ceasefire and held their first round of peace talks. During the second round of talks, held in September 2001, the Maoists put before the government their 31 demands.[37] These demands were based on the previous 40 demands given in 1996. The government rejected the three main demands by the Maoists. These were: 1. calling for a republic, 2. an interim government, and 3. a constitutional assembly. The government agreed to consider the other demands. The government's argument was that the Constitution does not allow the government to act on the three demands. 'There is no clause in the Constitution for an interim government or Constitutional assembly. The clause providing for a Constitutional monarchy is also unchangeable.'[38] The third round of talks concluded in November 2001, without any progress. Two human rights activists, Padma Ratna Tuladhar and Daman Nath Dhungana, were involved in the peace talks as facilitators.[39] On 21 November 2001, the Maoist leader, Chairman Prachanda, withdrew from the peace talks, saying: 'ceasefire had lost its justification because of the governments insincerity in finding a peaceful solution.'[40] The Maoists then formed the 'central people's government' called the Central Revolutionary People's Council Committee, headed by a top Maoist ideologue, Baburam Bhattarai. On 24 November 2001, the People's Council subsequently formed the People's Liberation Army (PLA). On the same night, the PLA launched an attack at the district headquarters of Dang and Syanjya and a military base camp and killed dozens of policemen and Royal Nepal Army (RNA) personnel, and injured many more. Similarly, the Maoists launched a daring attack in Solukhumbu district and killed the police personnel, including the Chief District Officer, on 25 November 2001.[41] King Gyanendra, on the recommendation of the Council of Ministers, announced a state of Emergency on 26 November 2001, and formally deployed the Royal Nepal Army and imposed the Terrorist and Disruptive Activities (Prevention and Control) Ordinance 2001 (TADO 2001).[42] The Emergency was extended in March 2002. However, on 4 April 2002, the government relaxed the state of Emergency.

During the Emergency period, the Maoists stepped up their activities of target attacks on police posts and also their calls for strike. As this study goes to print, the Maoists are demanding that Prime Minister Deuba should hold talks on the question of redrafting of the Constitution. The government has refused to hold talks until the Maoists lay down their arms. However, there is division within the ruling party and the opponents are supporting a political settlement of the Maoist uprising. The opponents in the party have already given proposals for constitutional amendments to Prime Minister Deuba.[43] Also, there is pressure on the government from other political parties for a political solution. For example, the Nepal Communist Party (UML), the main opposition party in Nepal, has said that the government should resume talks with the Maoists immediately without preconditions.[44]

Conclusion

The Maoist militant uprising in Nepal, which basically started as a political problem has now become an armed threat. The government regards it as a terrorist movement and is trying to suppress it militarily. The Maoist uprising has revealed that the Nepali police is ill-equipped to counter the Maoists, lacking sophisticated weapons and training.[45] Nepal is, therefore, seeking material support from India, the United States, Russia, and Britain. The Nepali Foreign Secretary, during his visit to United

States in April 2002, discussed the possibility of obtaining military hardware.[46] Meanwhile, during his visit to New Delhi in March 2002, the Nepali Prime Minister told the Indian Prime Minister that 'Indian Maoists are providing shelter to Nepal's Maoist rebels on Indian soil.'[47]

The Prime Minister of Nepal, Sher Bahadur Deuba, visited the US and UK in May 2002, seeking material help to combat the Maoist uprising. President Bush and Prime Minister Blair assured moral, material, and financial help to Nepal in this regard. The present government in Nepal is trying to tackle the issue militarily. Currently, the Maoist uprising has intensified its armed activity. The instances of attacks on police and army posts, bomb explosions at sensitive places like ministers' houses, etc., have increased. There is also a growing realization in Nepal that a military solution has not been successful. Therefore, various groups in Nepal are pressing for a political solution. Political observer Hari C. Shrestha observed, 'the main reason for the Maoist insurgency lies in the numerous problems faced by the poor people of far northwest and mid-western remote region.'[48] Advocate Shom Prasad Luitel, in his article, says, 'The Maoist problem is a political problem. The Maoists are engaging in armed struggle to establish their political system. Their aim is political and they are guided by a political philosophy, but their means are violent. Accordingly, we should search for a political solution rather than using the military and armed police.'[49] According to other reports, the Human Rights Organisation of Nepal (HURON) is working for a dialogue between the government and Maoists.[50] Moreover, there is concern in Nepal regarding Prime Minister Deuba's efforts to get external help for combating the Maoists. For example, the leader of the opposition in Nepal and the ruling Nepali Congress President, G. P. Koirala, have expressed fears that Nepal may not become 'a play field of foreign powers.'[51]

In Nepal, the 'People's War' launched by the Maoists in 1996 with the aim 'to smash the existing semi-fedual and semi-colonial state and build a people's New Democratic State' has transformed into an armed militant uprising and is being regarded as a terrorist movement by the Nepali government. The policy of the present government to tackle it militarily is not successful so far. It seems that the Nepalese government may have to make certain political concessions in order to control the uprising.

Notes

*Ms. Fahmida Ashraf is a Senior Research Fellow at the Institute of Strategic Studies, Islamabad.

1. Shom Prasad Luitel, 'The Maoist People's War and Human Rights in Nepal', 10 October 2001, www.nepalnews.com
2. Ananta Raj Poudyal, 'Fifty Years of Political Experience in Nepal', *Liberal Times*, vol. V, no. 2, February 1997.
3. Bertil Lintner, 'Nepal Struggles to cope with diehard Maoist violence', *Jane's Intelligence Review*, June 1999.
4. Ibid., 'Nepal', www.infoplease.com/ipa/A0107820.html
5. 'Nepal Index', www.uni-wuerzburg.de/law/np_indx.html
6. Ananta Raj Poudyal, op.cit.
7. Lok Raj Baral, 'Nepal in 2000: Discourse of Democratic Consolidation', *Asian Survey*, vol. XLI, no.1, January/February 2001.
8. 'History of Communist Party of Nepal', www.cpnuml.org/history.htm
9. Sangeeta Thapliyal, 'Maoist in Nepal are a burgeoning problem', *Strategic Affairs*, November 2000, www.newslookmag.com-topics-maoistwar
10. Shom Prasad Luitel, op. cit.
11. 'History of Communist Party of Nepal', op. cit.
12. Bertil Lintner, op. cit.
13. S. Thapliyal, op.cit; also see B. Lintner, op.cit.
14. Ibid.
15. Baburam Bhattarai, 'Politico-economic Rationale of People's War in Nepal', www.humanrights.de-n-nepal-politics-010298 pol eco.htm
16. Ibid.
17. Li Onesto, 'Nepal: Intrigue and Insurgency', 6–12 July 2001, www.rwor.org
18. Shom Prasad Luitel, op. cit.
19. Li Onesto, op. cit.
20. 'UML report on the Maoists', 2001, www.nepalnews.com
21. Bertil Lintner, op. cit.
22. The Mahakali Integrated Development Project Agreement was signed between Nepal and India in 1996 for the mutual exploitation of the Mahakali River, recognized as the boundary river between Nepal and India. However, it has not been implemented because of the differences between the two countries over interpretation of some of its clauses. For the text of the treaty, see www.humanrights.de/n/nepal/treaty/12021996
23. Baburam Bhattarai, op. cit.
24. Shom Prasad Luitel, op. cit.

25. The Tanakpur agreement was signed in 1992, when the Prime Minister of Nepal, G. P. Koirala, visited India. He agreed to the Indian request for allowing New Delhi to extend the left afflux bund of the Tanakpur Barrage 577 metres into the Nepalese territory. In return, India was to supply 10 million units of electricity free of cost and 1,000 cusecs of water to Nepal. The Communist Party of Nepal has opposed it and regarded it as against the interests of Nepal. For details, see 'What turn to Tanakpur' at www.lawsofnepal. com/generalindex/miscellaneous/what_turn_to _tanakpur: htm
26. The police arrested the communist activists during its campaign launched to crush the movement.
27. 'The People's War-Maoist Insurgency in Nepal,' March 2002, www.maoist.org
28. Ibid.
29. Shom Prasad Luitel, op. cit.
30. www.web.amnesty.org/ai.nst/1ndexlASA310132000
31. Li Onesto, op. cit.
32. Shom Prasad Luitel, op. cit.
33. Baburam Bhattarai, 'The Birth of a Republic,' www.humanrights.de-n nepal-politics
34. 'The Maoists strike with vengenence,' www.saag.org/notesz/note128.html
35. 'Nepal's Maoist call it a conspiracy,' www.rediff.com/news/2001/jun/04nep.4.htm
36. Melinda Liu and Patricia Roberts, 'The Maoist Threat,' *Newsweek*, 18 June 2001.
37. Shom Prasad Luitel, op. cit.
38. Ibid.
39. 'Nepal: State of Emergency and TADO,' www.ahrchk.net/ua/mainfile.php/2002/194/
40. Sushil Sharma, 'Analysis: Maoist threat to Nepal peace,' BBC News, 23 November 2001.
41. 'Nepal: State of Emergency and TADO,' op. cit.
42. Ibid.
43. 'Sher Bahadur Deuba mired in cumulative mess,' *The Telegraph*, March 2002.
44. 'Nepal assesses losses after brutal Maoist attack,' *The News*, 14 April 2002.
45. Lok Raj Baral, op. cit.
46. 'US agrees to supply military help to Nepal,' *The News*, 12 April 2002.
47. 'No joint operation against rebels: Nepal PM,' *The News*, 25 March 2002.
48. 'Civil war feared as Maoist rebellion escalates,' *The News*, 1 March 2002.

49. Shom Prasad Luitel, op. cit.
50. 'Lower Houses passes anti-terrorism Bill', *Kathmandu Post*, 5 April 2002.
51. *The Hindustan Times*, 3 May 2002.

CHAPTER 24

Insurgency

Lieutenant-General Depinder Singh

Tasks Before IPKF

Following the capture of Jaffna, as I had apprehended earlier, the LTTE escaped into the forests and, after a brief interlude in which camps were set up and regrouping was carried out, they started classic insurgent tactics. I was quite clear in my mind that no insurgency has ever been or can ever be settled militarily. Therefore, a political solution had to be found. To this end the battle had to be waged on two fronts, both equally vital. On the military plane, we had to mount unrelenting pressure against the insurgents to force them to negotiate at some point in the future. To achieve this, redeployment ordered earlier was quickly effected, so that operational domination could be extended to hitherto vacant areas. Simultaneously, we had to win the minds and hearts of the local populace so that reinforcements were denied to the insurgents and pressure was mounted on them to negotiate. This, obviously, is a long-term measure and success can only accrue after a considerable time has elapsed. In my report to Army Headquarters, I mentioned that if we wanted to fight a classic counter-insurgency operation and achieve success in a shorter time frame, we should do it properly by grouping villages so as to effectively isolate the insurgents. This course of action had its own disadvantages, political and financial, and I heard nothing more about it. However, there is no doubt that unless contact between the local population and the insurgents is broken (and as experience from Mizoram and Nagaland tells us, this is most effectively achieved by grouping villages), insurgency will drag on. Incidentally, insurgency in India first surfaced in 1956 in the Naga Hill Tracts (now known as Nagaland), and it spread to what is now the state of Mizoram a couple of years later. While an insurgency situation continues in Nagaland even today after three and a half decades, it ceased in Mizoram after a political settlement was reached. The point I wish to make is that insurgency can be a never-ending business unless a political solution can be arranged, and the sooner the better.

Civil Affairs

The IPKF now encountered a novel problem which officers discussed in various schools of instruction, but of which we had had no practical experience. This was in the matter of civil affairs generally, and specifically running the administration of a town.

On Brigadier R. I. S. Kahlon fell this onerous task; he was moved prematurely from the National Defence College where he was taking a course to assume the appointment of Town Commandant Jaffna (TCJ). Time, fortunately, was available to him as he arrived in Palaly before Jaffna fell, and so was attached to HQ 54 Infantry Division for about a fortnight prior to taking up his new assignment in order to get his bearings, and was not totally unfamiliar with the mission in hand.

With over 70,000 displaced persons and a population of about 10 lakh, Jaffna was a town without an administration, as the LTTE administrators, had either died in the fighting or fled to outlying areas to continue the fight from there. At this juncture, the IPKF was the only effective organization available to fill the breach. The TCJ with his small complement of officers, had to get an immediate 'feel' of the situation and ensure that improvement was effected as soon as possible. The bringing in of food supplies and their distribution, and the provision of medical facilities were obviously the number one priority. Whatever food supplies it had been possible to move into Jaffna under the arrangements of the IPKF during August and September 1987 had been exhausted and the Multi-Purpose Co-operative Societies were empty. Though food supplies arrived at the KKS Jetty promptly from India, the problem was to move the stocks to Jaffna as IPKF vehicles, the only transport readily available, ran the risk of ambush. Civil vehicles were pressed into service with a mixture of arm twisting and cajoling, and stocks soon started pouring into Jaffna where the IPKF and Red Cross commenced free distribution. Later on, Sri Lankan government supplies started reaching KKS by sea and, when the road and rail services resumed between Colombo and Jaffna, by these means. By this time, shops also started to fill up and, as banks opened and money became available, the public could purchase their requirements from the bazaar, though refugee camps continued to be dependant upon free supplies.

The medical resources of the 54 Infantry Division and Southern Command played a significant role in the reopening of existing hospitals and dispensaries, and the opening of additional ones, all manned by Indian doctors and nursing staff where locals were not available. Food to patients was provided from IPKF stocks. Gradually, the local medical staff started to return to their jobs, thus easing the burden on the AMC. Mention has already been made of the repairs to medical equipment by IPKF technicians. Conservancy staff had to be located, transported back to their jobs, and assured of security. Until their arrival, the public had to be motivated to do the scavenging.

Immediately after Jaffna was secured, radio intercepts of LTTE groups indicated critical shortage of ammunition, supplies and medicines. There were constant complaints of 'I have not eaten for the past four days, how do you expect me to live'; 'So and so is very ill, we have no medicines, so I am giving him (Code word for) cyanide'. Within a day or so of Red Cross supplies coming in, however, though complaints of ammunition and battery shortages persisted, complaints of food and medicines stopped. Obviously, supplies to refugee camps were making their way to the LTTE through their cadres sheltering in such camps.

Restoration of the electricity supply was another priority task, so that the running water supply could commence and essential lighting for hospitals could be provided. While Sappers of 51 Engineer Regiment worked around the clock to repair pylons, transformers and water supply pipes, generators were provided to hospitals to tide over the immediate problem. A 200 line telephone exchange was commissioned and lines provided to hospitals, officials and so on. This, of course, was a temporary arrangement and work was taken in hand, in conjunction with the local P&T

staff, to repair and bring into use the 4,000 line exchange damaged by the LTTE during fighting. Priority was also given, by employing troop labour, to repairing places of worship and educational institutions. In addition, there were a multitude of other tasks like carriage and delivery of mail, reopening of banks and educational institutions and persuading teachers and children to attend them, conduct of examinations including, where necessary, carriage of question papers from Colombo to ensure secrecy, provision of books, policing, recommencing bus services, encouraging displaced persons to return to their homes, re-establishing the credibility of the police and judiciary, and a myriad other jobs which an inhabitant in any city or town is dependant upon so completely that he takes it for granted.

The provision and distribution of petrol, diesel and kerosene oil was another function. It was particularly important to ensure that petrol and diesel did not fall into LTTE hands; so a rationing-cum-screening system was introduced. Until the situation clarified somewhat, a very strict curfew had to be imposed and this was gradually lifted as the situation improved. A major problem faced was that of allowing fishing boats to proceed to sea to enable the fishermen to carry out their vocation. The apprehension was that some of the boats, in the guise of fishing, may be utilized by the LTTE for their own purposes. However, the risk was accepted as I did not want to impose further hardships on a battered and hungry people.

With the passage of time, as the HQ TCJ was augmented by more staff (there were three IAS officers from the Tamil Nadu cadre and a battalion of CRPF including a women's wing), its functioning became further streamlined and, by the excellent relationship it maintained with the inhabitants of Jaffna, it won accolades for itself and the Indian Army. Two actions deserve particular mention. In the first, there was popular demand that the Class X examination be postponed from December 1987, when it was due, to July 1988. This was done through the High Commission in Colombo and saved the students a full year. In the second, gold pawned by the locals with the 'Peoples Bank' during the years 1983–6 and moved to Colombo for security had to be brought back, as the people concerned wanted their gold back having paid their dues, but were encountering red tape and stone-walling tactics. It was finally brought back through the intervention of the TCJ with the Sri Lankan government.

HQ TCJ was also entrusted with the task of public relations and psychological warfare: this involved beaming specially created TV and radio programmes, the printing of newspapers after necessary censorship and the printing of posters on an as required basis. In our anxiety for speed, we started the TV programmes and only then realized that, without electricity, no one in Jaffna could see those programmes! So, restoration of the electricity supply became an even more urgent task. I also assigned HQ TCJ the special task of maintaining a conduit to the LTTE for receipt and passage of messages. As far as intelligence resources were concerned, none was allotted to TCJ as far as I recollect which, on reflection, was a mistake. Despite this shortcoming, an excellent rapport was established with the local population. The measure of this was evident on at least two occasions: one, schools were opened and attendance was good in spite of a call by the LTTE to boycott the institutions. Two, the same thing happened in the courts, where first the court staff made their appearance, followed gradually by litigants. HQ TCJ was raised to carry out a near impossible mission; that it succeeded beyond measure in adapting to a novel task in the service of the people will remain a shining example of courage, dedication and innovation. Brigadier R. I. S. Kahlon was awarded the Uttam Yudh Seva Medal on 26 January 1988 for his magnificent performance.

While on the subject of relief and rehabilitation, it was now time to bring back the refugees who had sought shelter in Tamil Nadu. Great persuasive skill was required to get these people back, not only because of the mortal fear in their minds of Sinhala retribution, but also because some of the refugees had picked up jobs in India which they were loath to leave. The refugees were brought to Mannar in Indian Naval craft and the job of rehabilitating them then devolved on the International Red Cross and the United Nations Agency for Refugees which provided each returning family a fixed sum of money to construct a temporary shelter, basic utensils, some items of clothing, and free stocks of food. Interestingly, we learnt that when a head count was taken of Sri Lanka Tamil refugees in

India only about 60,000 could be located, whereas relief was being provided by the central and state governments to over one lakh. Where did the money go?

It was anticipated that after the fall of Jaffna, the LTTE survivors would melt into the jungles and the insurgency would switch from an urban bias to a rural one. The optimists thought that, being an urban animal, the terrorist would be unable to persevere in the rural environment he now found himself in. However, the IPKF was under no such illusions and girded itself for a long drawn out insurgency. Initially, there were numerous radio intercepts of LTTE transmissions indicating that there was no ammunition, no food, no medicines, and even no respite. There were even reports where the more seriously injured cases were given cyanide capsules to put them out of their misery. It never struck these heartless people that if the IPKF was informed of such cases, they would have been picked up and given proper medical treatment. But then, such chivalrous and humane feelings were totally alien to the LTTE.

Redeployment of IPKF

Coming now to the operational side: by this time the force level available to HQ OFC, IPKF had risen to about 10 infantry brigades. Whereas it would have been desirable to carry out regrouping so that units could rejoin original formation HQ and brigades could rejoin the original divisional HQ, the fact that unrelenting pressure had to be maintained against the LTTE to bring them to the negotiating table precluded this course of action immediately after the fall of Jaffna. However, this aspect was kept in mind and implemented whenever feasible.

Fighting the Insurgent

In the meanwhile, redeployment was ordered so that the areas that had been left vacant while all resources were employed against Jaffna could return to our domination. Fighting the insurgents, a job so familiar to the Indian Army as it has waged counter-insurgency operations in Nagaland and Mizoram since 1956, is a thankless, arduous and extremely hazardous task where constant patrolling is necessary and each patrol is the bait to draw the insurgent to show himself. Numerous days may pass without contact with an insurgent and the monotony can, inevitably, bring carelessness in its wake. And then, suddenly one day, contact is established; there is a brief fire fight and the careless pay heavily. Junior leadership plays a particularly important role in ensuring that complacency never sets in and men remain alert all the time. Equally important, the junior leader has to ensure that tiredness and frustration do not end up in indiscipline. Troops are human and it is easy, if effective control is not exercised, for cases of indiscipline to creep in, which is not only bad per se but also alienates the public when the need of the hour is to win them over by good discipline, upright and correct behaviour and complete fairness.

The LTTE, meanwhile, continued its hit and run tactics and, from the number of incidents that occurred, it was apparent that the majority had fled to the eastern provinces, though a few still remained in Jaffna. Aware of their proclivity towards suicide attacks and the existence of a 'Suicide Squad'(if memory serves me right I think this squad was called 'Black Tigers'), I ordered my MG EME to fabricate a steel road block that could be fixed at each vehicle entrance to our camps with a mechanism that could be easily activated to prevent LTTE suicide squads from driving into these camps. The SLAF (Sri Lankan Armed Force) had a taste of this on at least two occasions; the reader would also recall a similar incident that occurred in Lebanon in 1983 where over 300 US Marines were killed by a PLO terrorist. Belated intelligence indicated that the LTTE had received one shipment of arms, ammunition and explosives from Singapore in September 1987 (while they were professing brotherly feelings towards us) and another consignment which arrived in February 1988. A cache of .25 pistols from this latter consignment was recovered by 18 Infantry Brigade; the weapons and ammunition were brand new, apparently destined to be wielded by the fair sex. How this second consignment managed to be smuggled in despite the naval blockade imposed by the Indian and Sri Lankan Navies will remain a mystery.

There was a major incident in the Mullaittivu area (north of Trincomalee), where a large LTTE gang was located. In the ensuing fire fight both sides suffered some casualties and, by the time reinforcements reached the area, the LTTE disengaged and disappeared into the forested area. In another incident in the

Jaffna sector, a patrol of 8 Mahar under Major R. Parmeshwaran was ambushed. In the ensuing fire fight, Major Parmeshwaran made a most gallant charge into the LTTE, killing the firing group and, though he was fatally wounded, managing to overcome the opposition. He was posthumously awarded a well-deserved Param Vir Chakra, India's highest decoration for valour in the field.

As always, the LTTE communications continued to be excellent and the exact location of an IPKF patrol could be discovered by monitoring LTTE communication networks. Intercepting LTTE radio messages often provided excellent information because of the odd lapse a radio transmission can always contain. Units were encouraged to act aggressively on such intercepts and we had a few successes. However, we were still a long way from perfecting the art of distinguishing fact from fiction, wherein the broadcaster makes a deliberate attempt to mislead the interceptor. On one occasion an intercept indicated that Prabhakaran was located in Mulai, a village on the west coast of the Jaffna Peninsula. A raid was mounted by landing para commandos from the sea. They made rapid progress until they were fired at; thereafter, instead of containing that fire with a small element and proceeding posthaste to the target area with the remainder patrol to execute the given task, the whole patrol became involved in the desultory firing, giving Prabhakaran, who it was later confirmed was in the area, a chance to escape. Numerous questions were to be asked as to why the IPKF could not capture or kill Prabhakaran; another equally wild allegation was that the IPKF had orders not to kill Prabhakaran. Apart from the impossibility of singling out an individual target for destruction or protection in such an environment, we must remember that by virtue of the fact that the LTTE had an effective junior leadership, the loss of Prabhakaran could never have resulted in the disintegration of the LTTE.

It was gratifying to note that, after a few days, the civil population started reacting favourably. Starting with a trickle that soon became a torrent, the civil populace began coming to the IPKF through grievance cells that were created in most villages to record complaints. There were reports of indiscipline or some other excess, all of which would be promptly and fairly investigated and, where fault was established, equally promptly acted upon; there were requests for medical assistance, again promptly and efficiently met; requests for supplies which would be met, sometimes even by troops sharing their rations; and so on. All these humanitarian acts, allied with the civic action undertaken by TCJ, and the divisions on their own initiative employing their own medical and engineer resources, finally started paying off and provided us with a most unexpected and welcome bonanza. Reports started coming in of where LTTE weapons, ammunition and explosive were hidden and where LTTE militants were hiding. Of course, no informer was brave enough to guide our troops to the site, but verbal guidance was sufficiently explicit and, in almost all cases, the results were positive. One such tip led our patrol to a consignment of bulletproof vests. I ordered that these be distributed to the helicopter pilots as they had no protection against smallarms fire. I hope these vests proved to be of some use. On yet another occasion a battalion recovered, among other items, a complete rubber scuba diving suit. This was an alarming find as, if the LTTE had trained divers, there was the risk that our naval craft would be attacked. If one ship was sunk in Madras harbour, supply from this port would cease. That evening, I informed my opposite number in the Eastern Naval Command of the find and my apprehension, only to learn that the Eastern Naval Command knew about this as they had had a hand in the training!

Winning the Hearts and Minds of the Local Population

We were to discover in time that the change of heart on the part of the civil populace was motivated not so much by humanitarian aid and correct behaviour, important as these were, nor even by increasingly effective PR, important as this aspect is too, but by our treatment of prisoners. I had directed that the LTTE prisoners would be kept in places not known as prisons, but rehabilitation centres. They would be treated humanely though security would continue to be tight. Screening was required to be done as fast as possible and prisoners graded black and grey (implying hardcore and suspected hardcore respectively) would be retained while those graded white (innocent) would be released. All prisoners were to be accounted for and there were to be no 'shot while trying to escape' stories. Families were to be allowed to visit the reformatories and inmates were to be provided vocational training by inducting instructors from the Madras Engineering Group, Bangalore, and the Madras Regimental Centre, Wellington. The collective result of these verbal semantics and measures was that relatives started prevailing upon their kin serving with the LTTE to surrender, convinced that once he became a prisoner he would be safe.

Effect on the LTTE

Inevitably, the unrelenting military pressure on the militants and the gradually increasing alienation of the civil population from them started having an effect on the LTTE; this was evident from feelers we started to receive from at least two sources—the Jaffna Town Commissioner through TCJ, and Balakumar, the leader of EROS through 54 Infantry Division. EROS was always aligned with the LTTE and, I presume, to prove their bona fides had voluntarily foresworn possession or carriage of weapons. I met Balakumar in an abandoned hut outside Palaly Airfield and, during the ensuing conversation, I could detect a degree of flexibility never before reflected in the LTTE official pronouncements. The tone and tenor of the feelers emanating from Jaffna Town through the TCJ were basically the same.

The LTTE had made a conditional offer of ceasefire, the main condition being that the IPKF withdraw to pre-10 October 1987 positions. This, of course, was totally unacceptable; what Balakumar was trying to tell me was that even this condition was negotiable. Since I was not empowered to negotiate, I explained that the gist of our conversation would be conveyed to Delhi for a decision which, when received, would be conveyed to him. Regrettably, the view taken in Delhi was that these feelers indicated that the end was close and, therefore, the requirement was to stop talking *and turn the* screw some more. It was quite apparent that the Ministry of External Affairs and the R&AW were recommending a course of action contrary to what the Army thought; the tragedy was that their view was prevailing. I remember a telegram the High Commissioner sent from Colombo to Delhi stating inter alia that, according to information available to him, the LTTE collapse was imminent. On that I sent a message to Army Headquarters stating that while I prayed that the optimism was justified, the factual position was that the LTTE was far from finished.

The reason why the Army view did not or could not prevail, perhaps, can be ascribed to the lack of rapport between the COAS and the Prime Minister—undesirable in normal times, completely fatal in an emergency. I am not aware of why such a situation developed; perhaps it was fallout from the days preceding Exercise Brasstacks in early 1987 when we almost went to war with Pakistan. Be that as it may, what I do know is that, when I queried the COAS why our point of view was not being projected, his revealing reply was, '*Woh sunta nahi hai*' (he does not listen). A word about General Sundarji, as he has been a very high profile and flamboyant personality who has managed to remain in the public eye not only since his appointment as COAS, but even after his retirement, courtesy of Bofors and sundry perceptive articles he keeps writing. His intellectual brilliance cannot be denied nor his professionalism and forward thinking, particularly in the conceptual and technical fields. A wave maker, impatient with lesser mortals, he could overawe with his vastly articulate and persuasive skills combined with a constant quoting of facts and figures, the latter from an array of staff officers who would be in attendance whenever he conducted a briefing. Sadly, he lacked humility and it was, perhaps, this deficiency which led him to assume, erroneously, that, since everything was wrong with the army when he took over as COAS, he was going to set everything right.

Obstacles in the IPKF's Path

I have already referred to the massive doses of financial assistance with which the Tamil Nadu government had been providing the LTTE. Some estimates place the figure at over Rs. 5 crore, and this does not include other forms of assistance like training, hospitalization and so on. However, what we were facing was brought home to me by some incidents which, for some strange reason, never received the publicity they deserved.

In January 1988, IPKF signals intercepted a radio message between the LTTE HQ and a station in or around Madras seeking the latest information on the arrest of three LTTE personnel earlier that morning by a team of customs officials outside Madras.

This bit of information, naturally, made us prick up our ears and investigations were immediately launched to ascertain more details. What we learnt was truly amazing: early that morning a customs team, on a routine road check, intercepted a van in which they discovered three men who confessed to belong to the LTTE; inside the van were some arms, ammunition, explosives, and radio sets. The customs officials then sought directions from higher authorities, and were directed to impound the van and its contents, but to release the men!

On another occasion, a consignment of cordite (wire used between an explosive device and its trigger or firing mechanism) was recovered by an IPKF patrol based on information provided by a local. The manufacture date discovered from the packing material was October 1987 and the place of manufacture, hold your breath, a factory near Wellington in Tamil Nadu!

Yet another incident: there were any number of Tamil militant radio stations clandestinely functioning from the Tamil Nadu coastline and though we had repeatedly asked that these be closed, no action was taken by the state government. One day the CSO, Major-General Deva, sought my permission to raid one such station which, through his resources, he had been able to locate. I readily gave permission and a raid was mounted to recover not only a sophisticated radio and allied equipment, but also a box full of books on electronics and publications like *Amateur Radio*, *Electronics for You*, and the like. Another incident that illustrates the patronage Prabhakarn enjoyed from the government then in power. In 1982, Prabhakaran and his gang ambushed a former colleague (and later rival), Uma Maheshwaran, in a crowded Madras city street. The police arrested Prabhakaran, but released him on bail reportedly on orders of the Chief Minister. Prabhakaran jumped bail and, even today, the case remains registered and open. There were also rumours, which we could not confirm, that some LTTE casualties were being brought into Tamil Nadu for treatment. I hope this was not true, because if it was, I cannot imagine a more anti-national act.

These, then, were the odds against which the IPKF was fighting to implement a political decision. With this background, it was amusing to read of the criticism, the then Chief Minister, Mr

Karunanidhi's, absence evoked from the welcoming ceremony for the IPKF at Madras in 1990. I am certainly not condoning that absence and I consider it reprehensible that a Chief Minister should so display his displeasure towards the country's armed forces returning after successfully completing military tasks allotted to them by the political masters; the point is that anti-national acts were perpetrated earlier also and swept under the carpet to suit political exigencies.

Administration

With the sustained operations and concurrent civil action, administration continued apace. After the fall of Jaffna there was a need to carry up the heavy stores and vehicles of the newly inducted formations and units into Jaffna from Trincomalee where they were piling up as they came in by sea. This was successfully done by the 36 Infantry Division up to Elephant Pass and the 54 Infantry Division beyond that, no mean feat considering that every inch of the road the convoy traversed on this long journey had to be physically searched to ensure there were no mines. Until these stores fetched up, some men had been existing in clothes they carried on themselves. Would they ever complain? Never!

Though every effort was made to carry the dead to original peacetime locations for the last rites to be performed by their families, there were unfortunate exceptions where this was just not possible. In one particularly poignant case a young subaltern, 2/Lt Nagar of 16 Sikh, who died around mid October 1987, had to be buried in the same area, with the unit planning to recover the body when the situation permitted as, at that particular time, they were heavily engaged by the LTTE. A few days later the monsoons broke and the whole area became a lake, making recovery impossible. The young officer's father, a retired Colonel who had commanded the same battalion, wished to be taken to the site to see if some more effort could be made to recover the body. A fresh search was launched but unfortunately, the site could never be located.

Battle casualties, meanwhile, were being evacuated and treated promptly and efficiently. It is to the credit of the Army Medical Corps that, apart from the magnificent job they performed in providing expert medical attention to the local population, quite often at considerable risk to themselves, not a single battle casualty was allowed to succumb after he was brought alive to an aid post or dressing station.

The Prime Minister visited the casualties in the Military Hospital at Madras and the Command Hospital at Pune, and the Defence Minister visited the latter once. The former had combined his visit with some political meetings and, perhaps for this reason, never asked me for a briefing or my views; the Defence Minister did and I stressed the need to start a dialogue with the LTTE who were asking for that. He agreed that we should and accorded approval, only to call me up early next morning and state that I should await instructions, as he wanted to obtain the Prime Minister's clearance first. Needless to say, the call never came.

Apart from new weapons, what a soldier likes best is medals: honours and awards have always played an important motivatory role and, therefore, it is normal procedure for units and formation HQ to recommend names of personnel who had distinguished themselves in battle. Very strict and detailed screening is done on these recommendations at each stage, the underlying idea being that no genuine case should be missed out and no fake case included. It was gratifying that the Republic Day List 1988 included a very large number of awards of personnel involved in Operation Pawan. Perhaps this was what led Mr G. C. Katoch, a retired Financial Adviser to the Defence Ministry, to mention in an article he wrote about General Sundarji, 'The God who Failed', that most awards went to the Mahar Regiment (General Sundarji's) and Gorkhas (Lieutenant-General Depinder Singh's). To correct any misconception that may exist, the Mahar awards were my doing and I can vouch for the fact that each one was well deserved; the Gorkha awards, at least most of them, went to 3/4 GR for their performance in Siachen (Northern Command) which was, in any case, not under my command.

Worst Case Scenario

Contingency planning was, of course, a continuing process at HQ OFC, IPKF. We came to the conclusion that, since politics makes strange bedfellows, the worst case scenario at that point of time was a situation where the LTTE and the Sri Lankan government worked out some form of rapprochement and both demanded the ousting of the IPKF. To counter such an eventuality, it was essential that some Tamil voices be raised seeking the continued presence of the IPKF, even though it was appreciated that these could never be the stalwart allies our intelligence agencies thought they would be. This proposal was passed on to Army Headquarters and, I suppose, was the basis of what happened later.

In our efforts to develop confidence among the local population, we had to tread a wary path. They could repose confidence in us only if they knew that we would be staying on; however, any statement by the IPKF that it would, immediately drew flak from the Sri Lankan government and press. So the wording would be on the lines that we would stay till normality was established. The locals would also get very apprehensive if we tried to move a unit that had been located in a particular area. I recall one particular incident where the Muslim population of an area north of Trincomalee desperately wanted the Sikh battalion located there to continue to stay on, and made repeated requests until these were accepted.

Public Relations

For some unfortunate reason the IPKF continued to have a bad domestic press, though the Sri Lankan press after 10 October was generally most effusive in their praise, toeing the government line. There were, of course, exceptions, notably *The Hindu*, at that time published only from Madras. In one incident, *The Hindu*'s correspondent in Colombo reported an official in Jaffna alleging rape of some Tamil women by IPKF soldiers. A flurry of enquiries following the publication of the report indicated the that named official had made no such report and there were no cases of rape. I spoke to Mr N. Ram, the Associate Editor (I think I also mentioned that if one accepted every LTTE complaint of rape, there would be very few 'innocent' IPKF personnel!), and he published a prominent apology the following day. What he said (or did) to his correspondent, I never found out. Mr Ram was always a pillar of strength of the IPKF with his vast knowledge and complete dedication; a thorough professional who was (and remains) honest and impartial, giving praise where due and never hesitating to criticize if criticism was warranted. As far as the foreign press was concerned it was mostly impartial though, on occasion, it did pick up some of the LTTE handouts which were regularly issued.

Perhaps the reason for the antagonistic press was the strict censorship rules enforced, which forbade press persons from visiting the area where fighting was taking place. So the more intrepid among the community contacted the LTTE and had themselves smuggled into the Jaffna Peninsula and saw the fighting from the other side. I remember the *Calcutta Weekly*, and *The Sunday*, getting some stories like this, also *India Today*, and there must have been others. Location naturally effects perception; therefore, while the *Sunday* correspondent reported a barbaric rocket attack by an Indian armed helicopter on a petrol station in Chavakcheri. Had he been on our side, the story would have complimented the IPKF on getting confirmed information that the petrol pump was manned by the LTTE and then on the accuracy of the rocket attack that destroyed the target. Incidentally, I was to visit Chavakcheri a few days later to see the damage; the petrol pump was, of course, totally destroyed and, admittedly, the lives of those in or immediately around would have been lost. Opposite the petrol pump was the burnt out hulk of a huge U-shaped building which I learnt was a court building, torched by the LTTE in their heyday, with some innocent occupants inside burnt alive. I concede that two wrongs do not make a right but surely, this fact too could have been mentioned to lend objectivity to the reporting.

I have always been of the view that the press must be given the factual position and, in my capacity as OFC, I gave numerous press conferences and briefings, always endeavouring to ensure truthfulness as I saw the truth and frankness within the constraints of security. There is need for more openness with the press so that this powerful voice projects the factual position and dispels misconceptions and misapprehensions.

Staffing

HQ OFC was by now a full-fledged Corps Headquarters equivalent with an additional officer of the rank of brigadier to handle civil affairs. Lieutenant-General Khajuria, who had been an able deputy until now had to revert to his original assignment in Army Headquarters. I asked Major-General A. S. Kalkat, who was my

Major-General Staff in Headquarters Southern Command and due for promotion, if he was interested in taking up the deputy's assignment. He signified his willingness and I had him side-stepped on promotion. Later, after I left, the post of Deputy OFC was abolished and the General Officer was re-designated GOC, IPKF.

In January 1988, I had taken a few days leave to attend a marriage and it was in Chandigarh that I had news of Major-General Sardeshpande's reported arrival in Jaffna to take over the command of the 54 Infantry Division, *Vice* Major-General Harkirat Singh posted out. All I could do at that stage was to suggest to Harry that he could represent against the posting, as the change (and his transfer) were not at my instance. He did and, though I recommended his case, it was some months before he was posted from the staff assignment he was on to command Maharashtra and Gujarat area. Later, I was to question the COAS as to why we had been unjust to Harry; he agreed that we had been unfair but stated that redressal could only come from his successor (Sundarji was to retire on 30 April 1988 and General V. N. Sharma's name had been announced as the next COAS).

Farewells

February was drawing to a close and it was time for me to say my farewells as I was to retire on the last day of that month. I recall mentioning in some of my farewell speeches how grateful I was to a kindly fate that had given me so such, even in my retirement it did not forget to give me an extra day—1988 was a leap year and February contained 29 days. Southern Command, which it was my privilege to command, is a vast area covering almost half of the subcontinent. Farewells, therefore, had to be few and, since time was at a premium, they had to be fast. So it was breakfast at Wellington (DSSC), lunch at Palaly, Jaffna (54 Infantry Division), and dinner at Madras (HQ, OFC). The next day after breakfast in Madras, it was lunch at Trincomalee (36 Infantry Division) and dinner at Colombo (High Commissioner). The third day, after breakfast at Colombo, it was lunch at Bangalore and dinner at Pune. This continued for another two days, leading my very tired (and, since July 1987, neglected) wife to exclaim, when we reached

Panchkula, 'Thank God you've retired.' While at Colombo, I paid my farewell call on Sri Lankan President, Mr Jayewardene, 'Where are you going to settle?' he asked me and to my reply, 'Panchkula near Chandigarh,' he said, 'That's in Punjab, very dangerous.' 'Well my President,' I answered, 'firstly it is home; secondly, it is no more dangerous than Colombo.'

I had sought appointments to call on the President and Prime Minister but heard nothing and so can only assume that they were preoccupied. Instead, after much insistence I accepted a farewell dinner hosted by the COAS on 29 February 1988, explaining in my after-dinner speech that my reluctance had stemmed from the fact that at midnight that night the prince would turn into a frog and how could I get back to Panchkula? Very graciously the COAS gave me a choice—his personal staff car or a new Rover that was under trial. I chose the latter and my staff, who were accompanying me home, travelled in style while I travelled in my own car which had come in by air from Pune.

A postscript, before we go into the next chapter, to show the dark and fair sides of red tape. Since rules permitted allotment of government accommodation for two months after retirement, I had sought and obtained allotment of a house in Panchkula. Construction of my house, proposed to be started around mid-1987, had to be postponed thanks to the LTTE and so construction could start only in January 1988. Since the house could not possibly be ready by April 1988, I applied for two extra months, to be informed very promptly by Army Headquarters that the Defence Ministry had not approved the request. I wrote to Mr K. C. Pant, the Defence Minister, and within a month he replied, approving retention of accommodation for a period of not two, but four extra months.

CHAPTER 25

The Proposed Indian Nuclear Doctrine

Matin Zuberi

The study of nuclear strategy is . . . the study of the nonuse of these weapons.[1]

Weapons that do not have to fight their like do not become useless because of the advent of newer and superior types.[2]

I

One of the fateful ironies of the brutal twentieth century is that the crescendo of discovery in physics not only paralleled the rise of the Hitler in Germany but was significantly influenced by it. The successes of James Chadwick, Ernest Lawrence, John Cockcroft, and Ernest Walton made 1932 a miraculous year in the history of physics. Chadwick's discovery of the neutron in February 1932 was followed by the formal assumption by Hitler of the Chancellorship of Germany in January 1933. The Nazi persecution of the Jews disturbed the peace of German universities where a large number of distinguished physicists happened to be Jewish. Politics began the fateful collision with science, which characterized the later half of the twentieth century. The exodus of scientists had begun. Escaping from advancing fascism between 1933 and 1941, about a hundred eminent physicists, including eight of the Nobel prize-winning calibre, found refuge in the United States. The momentous discovery of atomic fission by Otto Hahn and Fritz Strassmann on Christmas Eve in 1938 came three months after the Munich agreement. By the end of 1939, more than a hundred research papers on fission were published. No other single discovery has had such dramatic consequences in peace and war in such a short time.

Niels Bohr, exemplar of the good citizen in the republic of science, tried to pre-empt a nuclear arms race even before the first weapon had been fabricated. His apocalyptic imagination made him uneasy about the terrifying potential of the new weapon. In a memorandum to President Roosevelt, he warned that any advantage which the United States might initially have would be outweighed by 'a perpetual menace to human security.' He tried to persuade Roosevelt and Prime Minister Winston Churchill to abandon their faith in nuclear secrecy and to inform the Soviet ally of the existence of the project without giving any technical details. This could facilitate post-war nuclear planning and ensure that atomic energy was 'used for the benefit of all humanity.' He urged them to make arrangements that offered 'safety against secret preparations.'[3] Bohr believed that the international contacts of scientists could moderate 'international rivalries in the nuclear arena.' To Roosevelt and Churchill, however, Bohr's campaign was a most unwelcome trespass into their political territory. In an unwarranted slur on Bohr's integrity, Roosevelt and Churchill directed in a secret document dated 8 September 1944 that 'Enquires should be made regarding the activities of Professor Bohr and steps taken to ensure that he is responsible for no leakage of information, particularly to the Russians.'[4] Bohr's failure to bring about an understanding among the major powers while they were still allies revealed the basic issue concerning the bomb: How did political leaders think about it? Was it a threat to human society forcing competing states to come together in the face of common danger? Or was it a 'winning weapon' and thus a valuable instrument of state policy?

While the Charter of the United Nations was being drafted at the San Francisco Conference, scientists in the Los Alamos laboratory were engaged in a frantic effort to fabricate the bomb for the first test. Some of them were worried about the impending military use of the bomb and its post-war consequences. At a meeting convened by these agitated scientists, the director of the laboratory Robert Oppenheimer presented an ingenious imaginary scenario. The United Nations was being organized, he said, and it was necessary for the destructive potential of the bomb to be demonstrated so that world statesmen would ban its use forever. But if the bomb did not become a reality, its existence would be kept secret to be used in the next war.[5] James Conant, President of Harvard University and one of the scientific overlords of the Manhattan Project, also believed that without a combat use of the bomb' 'there was no chance of convincing the American public and the world that it should be controlled by international agreement'.[6] Nobel laureate Arthur Compton believed that without its military use, 'the world will have no adequate warning as to what was to be expected if war should break out again'.[7] Thus, the bomb was already being hailed as an enforcer of peace. The technology of death would preside in a benevolent manner over human destiny. Atomic bombing would shock Japan into surrender and a sufficiently spectacular demonstration of its destructive power would have a salutary effect on the anticipated confrontation with the Soviet Union. The bomb was an instrument for peace as well as an instrument of diplomacy in the post-war world.

Another group of scientists in the Manhattan Project arrived at diametrically opposite conclusions. The famous Franck Report of June 1945 started with the basic assumption that the manner in which the new weapon was used would determine the future course of events. It suggested a demonstration of the power of the bomb 'before the eyes of the representatives of an the United Nations, on the desert or a barren island'. It might then be used after an ultimatum to Japan if the sanction of the United Nations and of American public opinion could be obtained. Pointing out the urgency of international control of atomic energy, the report warned that if it were not established, the race for nuclear armaments would be on in earnest not later than 'the morning after our first demonstration of the existence of nuclear weapons'. It also asserted that the US could not hope to avoid a nuclear arms race either by keeping secret the basic scientific facts or by cornering the raw materials required for such a race. The authors of the report did not know that the basic decisions regarding the bomb's combat use had already been taken.[8]

The post-war nuclear disarmament negotiations, however, were a 'souffle that never rose'. Scientific leaders like Robert Oppenheimer devoted apprehensive attention to the nuclear danger and warned that the American nuclear monopoly was 'like a cake of ice standing in the sun and melting every hour'.[9] Jawaharlal Nehru's appeal in 1954 for a nuclear test moratorium was designed as a disarmament measure.[10] There were only three nuclear weapon powers at that time—the US, the Soviet Union, and Britain— and the two superpowers had just conducted their first thermonuclear tests. In fact, there had been only four Soviet nuclear tests. France was in the early stages of its nuclear effort and China had not even started its programme. Simulation techniques had not yet developed and a total ban on testing would have considerably impeded development of thermo-nuclear armouries. A favourable response to Nehru's appeal would have avoided subsequent follies like MIRVs, Star Wars, and so on.

In June 1954, an Anglo-French plan for the abolition of nuclear weapons and drastic reductions in conventional forces was presented at the United Nations Subcommittee on Disarmament. The US also supported the plan. On 10 May 1955, the Soviet Union unexpectedly proposed a scheme which substantially accepted the Anglo-French plan. British disarmament expert Philip Baker called it the 'moment of hope'. The American delegate, however, announced the withdrawal of all previous American disarmament proposals submitted at the United Nations. He declared: 'It is our view that if armaments, armed forces and military expenditure are brought down to too low a level, then . . . instead of the prospects of peace being improved, real danger of war is increased.'[11] This bold assertion of the dangers of disarmament was an important landmark in the nuclear age. The American civilian nuclear strategists, who were exponents of the strategy of nuclear deterrence, evolved a concept of 'arms control' to supplement that strategy. The objective of arms control was stability in an armed world. It became a vehicle for the rational management of arms races and for reducing the risks of a nuclear war. It was claimed that there was safety in large stockpiles. Arms control negotiations themselves accelerated the arms race through incessant comparisons of relative numbers, yields, circular errors probable, and so forth. Many weapons systems were started as bargaining counters for the arms control negotiations; having gathered large scientific, industrial, and military constituencies in their support, they were incorporated in the arms build-up.[12]

Indian nuclear policy and disarmament diplomacy worked in tandem. India continued to push for nuclear disarmament and sponsored the General Assembly Resolution 1653 (XVI) of 24 November 1961 that declared the use of nuclear weapons 'a crime against mankind and civilization' and a direct violation of the Charter of the United Nations. The Rajiv Gandhi Action Plan, presented at the UN Special Session on Disarmament on 9 June 1988, contained a scheme for a phased elimination of nuclear weapons by the year 2010. It was one of the most comprehensive schemes for the elimination of the nuclear threat; its special feature was a time-bound series of steps to be taken by the two nuclear superpowers, the three secondary nuclear weapon powers, and the so-called threshold countries. But continued reliance on nuclear deterrence and the Cold War were driving nuclear weapon states to acquire more diversified nuclear arsenals.[13]

India's active involvement over the years in nuclear disarmament negotiations was based on a commitment to a nuclear weapon-free world. The unlimited extension of the NPT in 1995 perpetuated the monopoly of the 'official' nuclear weapon powers. Additional curbs on technology transactions were put through the London Club of Nuclear Suppliers, the Missile Technology Control Regime (MTCR), and the Wassenar Arrangement. The deterioration in India's security environment over the years, the Sino-Pakistani nuclear axis, and the CTBT negotiations, especially the entry-into-force clause of the proposed treaty, forced India to cross the nuclear Rubicon. The distinctive feature of the Indian nuclear weapons 'option', however, was that it emerged from the expansion of its civilian nuclear enterprise. Other nuclear powers produced fissile material in installations dedicated to military pursuits; their nuclear power stations came much later. China, for instance, started building nuclear power stations only in the 1980s. Moreover, while other nuclear weapon powers resolutely proceeded from their first atmospheric nuclear tests to weaponization, India conducted an underground peaceful nuclear explosion in 1974 and then paused for 24 years. These powers first accumulated nuclear weapons stockpiles and then built missiles, but the testing and development of missiles preceded the Shakti tests of 1998.

II

The first five nuclear weapon powers decided to manufacture nuclear weapons in complete secrecy. The American decision was that of a single individual—President Roosevelt. Even Vice-President Truman was kept in the dark and was briefed on the subject only when he succeeded Roosevelt as President in April 1945. Stalin alone took the fateful decision on behalf of the Soviet Union. The British, French and Chinese decisions were also wrapped in total secrecy. An ad hoc committee of the British Cabinet, from which even the Chancellor of the Exchequer was excluded, decided in January 1947 to produce the bomb; the House of Commons was initially kept in the dark about it. There was some public discussion in France, but it was mainly about peaceful uses of atomic energy. The French nuclear weapons programme moved secretly and incrementally without political direction until a date for the first nuclear test had to be fixed. The Chinese decision was taken in complete secrecy on 15 January 1955 at a meeting presided over by Chairman Mao. The Indian nuclear weapons 'option', however, was discussed in a protracted public debate from 1964 to 1998.[14]

Nuclear weapon powers in the past first developed an operational nuclear force before enunciating a nuclear doctrine. For about 30 years after China's first nuclear explosion, there was no coherent, publicly articulated Chinese nuclear doctrine.[15] There was no American policy guidance regarding employment of nuclear weapons until 1948, three years after the bombing of Hiroshima and Nagasaki. Emergency war plans 'Pincher', 'Broiler', and 'Frolic' provided for atomic bombs to be dropped on Soviet cities, but a nuclear doctrine had not been evolved. The 'Halfmoon' plan called for all the 50 atomic bombs then in the stockpile to be dropped on 20 Soviet cities. Truman was uneasy about it and ordered an alternate plan based only on conventional weapons; but the Berlin crisis of 1948 intervened and the alternate plan was abandoned. The secret National Security Council directive NSC-30 of 16 September 1948 simply stated that 'in the event of hostilities, the National Military Establishment must be ready to use promptly and effectively all appropriate means available, including atomic weapons in the interest of national security'. The decision to use these weapons 'must be made by the Chief Executive'. It did not address the objectives for which nuclear weapons were to be used. This cursory guidance, even without endorsement by Truman, remained the sole statement on American policy approved by the NSC until 1960. NSC-20/4 of 23 November 1948 declared that the goal in a general war would be to reduce or eliminate 'Bolshevik' control inside and outside the Soviet Union.[16] Rivalry among the services resulted in the US having three separate strategic doctrines: 'credible deterrence' of the army, 'finite deterrence' of the navy, and 'counterforce deterrence' of the air force.[17]

Instead of nuclear doctrine determining the contours of American force deployments, its military technological innovation process shaped the nuclear doctrine. Moreover, there was a wide gulf between the nuclear doctrine and what was in the Single Integrated Operational Plan (SIOP). The US toyed with the idea of preventive war until 1954; massive retaliation entailed massive pre-emption. The American nuclear doctrine has been extremely transitory, oscillating between simple notions of city busting to extremely complex and demanding notions of 'flexible response', 'limited nuclear options', 'escalation dominance', and 'countervailing strategy'.[18] Counterforce drove the nuclear arms race. The number of potential targets in the American war plan increased from 70 to 50,000 by the early 1980s, 60 out of which were within Moscow city. The incineration of a minimum of 200 Soviet cities remained the basic requirement of the SIOP.[19]

Both the US and the former Soviet Union invested billions of dollars and rubles in early warning installations, blast-proof bunkers, redundant communication networks, and air-borne command posts like the so-called Looking Glass aircraft and Take Charge And Move Out (TACAMO) planes. Intelligence systems merged with early warning systems and then, through a process of incremental additions, were vertically integrated with the military forces to a degree unprecedented in military history. A similar process took place in the Soviet command and control system. This eventually led to a tight coupling of American and Soviet nuclear forces, producing what an American expert called 'a single gigantic system'. He added: 'If the situation were not so potentially grave, we could dismiss this as science fiction.'[20]

III

Reversing the trend set by the earlier nuclear weapon powers, an Indian nuclear doctrine was publicly articulated before the development and deployment of an operational nuclear deterrent force. The draft nuclear doctrine, prepared by the nuclear doctrine group of the National Security Advisory Board, was unanimously approved by the whole Board.[21] This consensus document, released by National Security Adviser Brajesh Mishra on 17 August 1999, provides only a broad framework for the development, deployment, and employment of India's nuclear forces. As the document was designed for informed public debate, details regarding the configuration of nuclear forces and targeting schemes flowing from the broad framework have to be laid down separately.

What distinguishes the consensus document from all other nuclear doctrines is that it is anchored in India's continued commitment to global, verifiable, and non-discriminatory nuclear disarmament that is considered to be India's national security objective. The Preamble categorically states that any use of nuclear weapons would constitute 'the gravest threat to humanity and to peace and stability in the international system.' As nuclear disarmament has been discarded even as a distant possibility, it is incumbent on India to maintain its old links with the large global constituency that continues to struggle for the complete elimination of nuclear weapons.

Another distinctive feature of the proposed Indian nuclear doctrine is the rejection of nuclear war fighting. Nuclear deterrence rests on the paradox that while the utility of nuclear weapons lies in their non-use in combat, the ability and willingness to use them in combat if deterrence fails is essential for its effectiveness. The terrible apparatus of deterrence is set up precisely to deter the threat or use of weapons of mass destruction. Although often presented as complementary, there is a fundamental difference between strategies of nuclear deterrence and nuclear war fighting. For nuclear deterrence, it is necessary that warheads should be matched with warheads and missiles with missiles. A secure second strike capability is enough. For nuclear war fighting, however, there is always a quest for nuclear superiority; more accurate delivery systems are also needed to destroy a large number of military targets. Nuclear deterrence threatens only punishment, while the objective of nuclear war fighting is victory.[22] Professor Michael Howard of Oxford University observed: 'When I read the flood of scenarios in strategic journals, about first-strike capabilities, counterforce or countervailing strategies, flexible response, escalation dominance and the rest of the postulates of nuclear theology, I ask myself in bewilderment, this war they are describing, what is it about?'[23]

This basic difference is reflected in force requirements and deployment patterns. 'Intra-war deterrence', 'intra-war bargaining', and 'escalation dominance' are some of the requirements of a war fighting strategy. The open-ended nuclear arms race of the Cold War was driven by incessant search for nuclear advantage demanded not only by the dilemmas of extended deterrence, but also by the war fighting strategies of the major contenders. The declaratory policies of the US and the former Soviet Union were couched in the language of deterrence; but the deployment patterns of their nuclear forces were geared to fighting and 'prevailing' in a nuclear war. As former US Defence Secretary, Caspar Weinberger, once put it: 'You show me a Secretary of Defence who's planning not to prevail and I'll show you a Secretary of Defence who ought to be impeached.'[24] The proposed doctrine rejects such nuclear follies. The long tradition of non-use since the atomic bombing of Nagasaki on 9 August 1945 suggests that nuclear weapons are basically political instruments, not military tools for waging and winning nuclear wars. Their efficacy lies in their deterrent effect against nuclear blackmail and coercion. Weapons have military utility, says a former scientific adviser to the British government, if their effects can be predicted and their consequences can be controlled. 'As weapons of war, nuclear weapons comply with neither condition.' [25]

A categorical and unambiguous commitment to no first use of nuclear weapons in case of conflict determines the contours of India's nuclear posture. This commitment is not just a verbal assurance; it has to be reflected in the structure, deployment, and state of readiness of Indian nuclear forces.[26] China announced its unconditional commitment to no first use immediately after its first nuclear test in October 1964 and then repeated it on many occasions. This unconditional commitment was dropped in 1995 when it was officially stated that it was 'applicable to non-nuclear countries which are signatories of the Nuclear Nonproliferation Treaty or non-nuclear countries which have made a similar internationally binding pledge on the non-proliferarion and non-procurement of nuclear weapons.'[27] In 'the moment of truth,' however, 'when the possibility of major devastation occurs, one is likely to discover sudden changes in doctrine.'[28]

The consensus document proposes that India should work for an internationally binding and unqualified commitment by all nuclear weapon powers not to threaten or use nuclear weapons against non-nuclear weapon states. The so-called 'negative security assurances' given by the five permanent members of the UN Security Council to non-nuclear weapon states are being eroded; it is being claimed that nuclear weapons will be used to deter an attack with chemical or biological weapons by a non-nuclear weapon state. India should also campaign for an international treaty banning the first use of nuclear weapons. Such a treaty could be the first stage in the process of delegitimization of nuclear weapons. If all nuclear weapon powers subscribed to such a treaty, it would be tantamount to a complete ban on any use of nuclear weapons.[29]

A modest deterrent retaliatory capability would require a command and control system radically different from that needed for a first strike capability or for nuclear war fighting. A first strike posture would necessitate pre-delegation of authority to release nuclear weapons. No first use posture, however, facilitates tight civilian control. The dangers of unauthorized or accidental detonations are also reduced. Commitment to no first use, however, necessitates a robust command and control system that can survive a nuclear first strike and then deliver a devastating blow. This will be a demanding task. The survivability of the arsenal as well as of the command, control, communications, and intelligence systems will have to be ensured. Space-based assets will have to be created to provide early warning, communications, and damage assessment. A manifest capability and willingness to inflict unacceptable punishment on an adversary, in case it uses nuclear weapons against India, will demonstrate the credibility and effectiveness of the Indian nuclear deterrent. This manifest capability should not be confused with the bizarre calculations of Mutual Assured Destruction of the Cold War era. The proposed doctrine does not provide a calculus of unacceptable punishment because the stakes involved in a specific nuclear crisis would determine it. The US spent billions of dollars on a far-flung and technologically complex nuclear command and control system; it was, however, not adequate for a posture of first use of nuclear weapons.[30]

The consensus document proposes a credible, minimum, nuclear deterrent retaliatory capability, consisting of sufficient, survivable, and operationally prepared nuclear forces with the necessary support of an effective intelligence and early warning system. Credible minimum deterrence, however, is difficult to quantify; it will have to take into account the evolving capabilities of possible adversaries. Nuclear forces are to be based on a triad—bombers, land-based ballistic missiles, and ballistic missiles launched from submarines. Commitment to no first use necessitates reliance on an invulnerable sea-based deterrent. As the present Indian capabilities are limited, the triad will take many years to materialize.[31]

The proposed doctrine incorporates the cardinal principle of civilian control with the necessary military underpinning. Since it would be the responsibility of the armed forces to deliver nuclear weapons on target in case of failure of deterrence, they have to be an integral part of the decision-making loop. The final authority for the release of nuclear weapons, however, would have to be with the Prime Minister or his designated successor(s). This imposes major responsibilities on the Indian political leadership. In order to raise the threshold or outbreak of conventional military conflict and the threat or use of nuclear weapons, highly effective conventional military forces will have to be maintained. Nuclear arms control as well as confidence building measures with our nuclear neighbours can increase transparency and reduce the dangers of an open-ended nuclear arms race.[32]

The development and deployment of deterrent forces to cope with threats posed by two linked adversaries would be a novel and laborious task for India. It has to be done incrementally over the next few years, The delivery systems have to acquire a longer strategic reach, mobility, and flexibility. Operational Indian nuclear forces are going to be very modest for several reasons. The purpose for which they would be developed excludes extended deterrence and war fighting. Moreover, financial and technological constraints are major limiting factors.[33]

Notes

1. Lawrence Freedman, 'The First Two Generations of Nuclear Strategists' in Peter Paret, ed., *Makers of Modern Strategy*, Oxford: Clarendon Press, 1986, p. 735.
2. Bernard Brodie, *War and Politics*, London: Cassell, 1973, p. 321.
3. Memorandum submitted by Neils Bohr, 8 May 1945; and Neils Bohr to President Roosevelt, 24 March 1945 in *Private Papers of Robert Oppenheimer*, Box 34, Library of Congress, Washington D.C.
4. Martin J. Sherwin, *A World Destroyed*, New York: Alfred A. Knopf, 1975, p. 284.
5. Peter Wyden, *Day One*, New York: Simon and Schuster, 1984, p. 148.
6. Martin J. Sherwin, 'Scientists, Arms Control and National Security', in Norman A. Graebner, ed., *The National Security*, New York: Oxford University Press, 1986, pp. 114–8.
7. Arthur Holly Compton, *Atomic Quest*, New York: Oxford University Press, 1956, pp. 239–40.
8. For an analysis of the American decision to drop the bomb on Hiroshima and Nagasaki and the Japanese decision to surrender see Matin Zuberi, 'Atomic Bombing of Hiroshima and Nagasaki', *Strategic Analysis*, vol. XXXV, no. 5, August 2001, pp. 623–62. The Franck Committee report is reproduced as an appendix in Alice Kimbal Smith, *A Peril and a Hope*, Chicago: University of Chicago Press, Chicago, 1956.
9. J. Robert Oppenheimer, 'The Scientific Foundations of World Order', in Ernest Lleweyllen Wood et al., eds., *Foundations for a World Order*, Denver: Denver University Press, 1949, p. 43.
10. Jawaharlal Nehru, *India's Foreign Policy*, New Delhi: 1961, pp. 187–202; Robert A. Divine, *Blowing on the Wind*, Oxford University Press, 1978, p. 20.
11. Ramsdell Gurney, Jr., 'Arms and the man', *Bulletin of the Atomic Scientists*, December 1975, pp. 23–33; Philip Noel Baker, *The Arms Race*, New York: Oceana Publications, 1958, p. 23.
12. For a concise history of arms control negotiations see Michael J. Sheehan, *Arms Control*, Oxford: Blackwell Publications, 1988.
13. The Rajiv Gandhi Action Plan for Ushering in a Nuclear Weapon free and non-violent world is reproduced as Appendix 5 in Mani Shankar Iyer, *Pakistan Papers*, New Delhi: UBSPD, 1994, pp. 204–14.
14. For an analysis of the American, British, Chinese, French, Russian, Indian, and Pakistani decisions to produce the bomb see Matin Zuberi,

'Building the Bomb: Collaboration for Self-Reliance and the Counter-Example of India', *U.S.I. Journal*, vol. CXXIX, no. 535, January–March 1999, pp. 28–49.

15. Alastair Ian Johnson, 'Prospects for China's Nuclear Force Modernisation: Limited Deterrence Versus Multilateral Arms Control', *The China Quarterly*, no. 146, June 1996, p. 552.
16. David Alan Rosenberg, 'The Origins of Overkill', *International Security*, vol. 7, no. 4, Spring 1983, pp. 13–14.
17. Janne E. Nolan, *Guarding the Arsenal: The Politics of Nuclear Strategy*, New York: Basic Books, 1989, pp. 71–2.
18. Desmond Ball, *Can Nuclear War Be Controlled?*, Adelphi Papers no. 169, London: IISS, 1981, p. 6.
19. Bruce G. Blair, *Strategic Command and Control*, Washington, D.C., 1985, p. 26. Emphasis added.
20. Paul Bracken, *The Command and Control of Nuclear Forces*, New York: Yale University Press, 1983, p. 59.
21. See Appendix C for the full text in Gurmeet Kanwal, *Nuclear Defence: Shaping the Arsenal*, New Delhi: Knowledge World, 2001, pp. 235–8.
22. See Colin Gray, 'Nuclear Strategy and the Case for a Theory of Victory', *International Security*, vol. 4, no.1, Summer 1979, pp. 54–87.
23. Michael Howard, *The Causes of Wars*, London: Unwin, 1984, pp. 140–1. Emphasis in the original.
24. Cited by Admiral Gene LaRoueque (ret.), 'Introduction', in Paul Joseph and Simon Rosenblum, eds., *Search for Sanity: The Politics of Nuclear Weapons and Disarmament*, Boston: South End Press, 1984, p. xv.
25. Lord Zuckerman, *Star Wars in a Nuclear World*, London: William Kimber, 1986, p. 48.
26. See Li Bin, 'Visible Evidence of No-First-Use Nuclear Strategies', *Inescap Information Bulletin*, no. 17, August 1998, pp. 44–5.
27. Xinhua News Agency, 5 April 1995.
28. Colin S. Gray, 'Targeting Problems for Central War', in Desmond Ball and Jeffrey Nichelson, eds, *Strategic Nuclear Targeting*, Ithaca: Cornell University Press, 1986, p. 179.
29. For an Indian military perspective on the commitment to no first use see Gurmeet Kanwal, op, cit., pp. 64–70.
30. See Desmond Ball, op. cit., pp. 9–26.
31. See Rear Admiral Raja Menon, *A Nuclear Strategy for India*, New Delhi: Sage Publications, 2000, pp. 224–7.
32. For a comprehensive analysis of India's evolving nuclear capabilities see Ashley Tellis, *India's Emerging Nuclear Posture: Between Recessed Deterrence and Ready Arsenal*, Santa Monica: RAND, 2001.
33. Brahma Chellaney, 'Nuclear Deterrent Posture', in Brahma Chellaney, ed., *Securing India's Future in the New Millennium*, New Delhi: Orient Longman, 1999, pp. 141–222.

CHAPTER 26

The Role of Special Forces in the War in Afghanistan

Bhashyam Kasturi

The United States of America launched Operation Enduring Freedom aimed at ridding Afghanistan of the al-Qaida and Taliban. This military operation is six months old* and continues in the rugged mountains of Afghanistan. It is a conventional war, fought with conventional weapons against an unconventional and elusive enemy. But as experience has shown, the US-led forces have now innovated their capabilities to fight an unconventional war with conventional weapons.

The war so far has resulted in the killing of several hundred Taliban and al-Qaida cadres, and dismantling the authoritarian rule of the Taliban, under Mullah Mohammed Omar. But there is no sign that the top leadership of the terrorist groups, identified by the US as perpetrators of the 11 September 2001 attacks on the World Trade Center, is in the dock.

Thus, the application of military force against a terrorist network has yielded some results, but has not yet fulfilled the main task of establishing long-term stability in Afghanistan and destruction of terrorist capability to mount another World Trade Centre type of attack. In fact, political stability that was provided by the single Taliban rule has rapidly disappeared, leaving in its wake 'warlordism' and tribal in-fighting that threatens to break up Afghanistan.

This analysis focuses on the military confrontation between the coalition forces led by the US and the Taliban and the al-Qaida. Events show that US military power reinforced by the Special Forces, Northern Alliance, and a wide range of high-tech equipment went a long way in winning the military conflict.

Of specific interest in the present context is the deployment of Special Operation Forces (SOF) in Afghanistan. Having gained experience in the Gulf War and Bosnia, the US decided to utilize these forces fully. The SOF performed three major tasks: synchronized air power by designating targets; rallied Northern Alliance forces; and increased their striking capabilities.

The SOF presented a new window of opportunity for the war against terrorism and this holds important lessons for India in its war against Pakistan-sponsored terrorism.

The United States of America launched a global war against terrorist networks in the aftermath of the 11 September 2001 attacks on the World Trade Centre. It began with an economic, political, and legal operation to crack down on known terrorist networks and was then transformed into a military operation, whose main target was Afghanistan, home to the al-Qaida, the brainchild of Osama bin Laden and the Taliban, the Islamic students organization raised and funded by Pakistan's Inter-Services Intelligence.

Being involved in Afghanistan was not new to the US. The US Central Intelligence Agency (CIA) had, after all, trained and armed the Mujahideen who fought the Soviet Army in the 1980s. The US also knew the kind of support and training Pakistan had given to the Taliban. In engaging the al-Qaida and Taliban, the US knew the risks involved in committing ground troops in large numbers, as the experience of the former USSR showed. And to this end, they decided to follow their experience of the military operations undertaken in the Gulf War and Bosnia. While the terrain and other factors, such as availability of locally sponsored opposition forces, varied in each of these areas, using aerial bombing, high technology, and intelligence operations to create a conducive atmosphere for the political reconstruction of Afghanistan remained at the forefront of military operations.

The US aim was to remove the Taliban from power, and smash the al-Qaida networks and put in place a political administration that would be friendly to it. To this end, by April 2002 they appeared to have achieved some of their aims by military means. But as of today they have not captured either Osama bin Laden, the top leader of the al-Qaida or Mullah Mohammed Omar, Amir of the Taliban. They can claim to have several thousands of the al-Qaida cadres in their hold, but the main leadership is missing.

The swift US military action, in conjunction with the opposition Northern Alliance forces, has led to the setting up of an interim administration in Kabul. But the sudden disappearance of the single control of the Taliban in Afghanistan has meant a return to warlordism and tribal in-fighting, which threatens to disrupt peace. Therefore, the US will have to stay in Afghanistan for some time.

This suits the United States, for their forces are now stationed across Central Asia and Pakistan, giving them access to every part of this region. While the US will claim that it does not seek a permanent presence in the region, their actions in Pakistan and Afghanistan make it clear that 'forward presence' is what the US is looking at. This will help in their future battles against other terrorist networks and state sponsors of terror.

The military phase of the anti-terror campaign, code-named Operation Enduring Freedom, began on 7 October 2001. Since then, allied forces led by the US have succeeded in liberating those areas of Afghanistan which were under the control of the Taliban. The US-led 'war against terrorism' began with air and cruise missile strikes against targets in Afghanistan.

In announcing the attacks, US President George Bush stated: 'The United States military has begun strikes against al-Qaida terrorist training camps and military installations of the Taliban regime.' The operations, Bush said, 'are designed to disrupt the use of Afghanistan as a terrorist base of operations and to attack the military capabilities of the Taliban.'[1]

These attacks mark the second phase of the conflict over terrorism. The first phase included the application of economic, political, diplomatic, and psychological pressure on terrorists and their networks, and also included the extensive use of intelligence gathering systems.

Both US President Bush and Secretary of Defence Donald Rumsfeld have stated that this is a different kind of war against a different kind of enemy. The enemy is not a nation—the enemy is terrorist networks that threaten the way of life of all peaceful people. To that end, the sole superpower in the world is fighting against an amorphous entity. They tried to give this a more distinct shape, by identifying bin Laden and the Taliban as the main perpetrators of the World Trade Center attacks and thus it was logical that Afghanistan be made an example for others to see.

The goals and strategy of Operation Enduring Freedom in Afghanistan underwent several revisions during the course of the war—actually, during the first three weeks of the campaign itself. These shifts reflected the difficulty of finding a strategy that could reconcile the USA's immediate war aims with a set of broader, long-term strategic considerations relating to the establishment of political stability in Afghanistan. By the third week of the war, it became clear that there was no such grand strategy in place, and thus the Americans were posed with a choice. Either they would have to accept the prospect of a long war or set aside some of their broader stability concerns. Given the potential political risks associated with any long-war scenario, this was an easy choice to make; the broader concerns were set aside.

Since the time the military operations started, by a coalition of political and military forces, the US has achieved certain ends. While it has put in place an administration under the leadership of Hamid Karzai, the larger political task of stabilizing Afghanistan, controlling factionalism and tribalism, and above all, of getting rid of the remaining Taliban and al-Qaida elements who are still holed up in the vast cave complexes, remains. In fact, the possibility of these cadres having slipped into Pakistan or even Central Asia should keep the US forces in the region active for many months to come.

This war has several characteristics and pointers. For one, the US swung into action with remarkable speed and manoeuverability to employ its forces, on all three fronts, to launch devastating attacks on the Taliban and al-Qaida infrastructure and organization, with the singular aim of de-Talibanizing Afghanistan. Air power was at the forefront of this war; it assisted ground troops during special missions and attacks on Taliban forces, and also gave vital assistance to Northern Alliance forces in launching major assaults on the Taliban strongholds.

The War

In the first week of October 2001, warplanes of the USAF from several bases round the region struck at targets in Afghanistan. The cities of Kandahar, Kabul, Jalalabad, and Herat were confirmed struck, while other locations such as targets in Mazar-e-Sharif were also hit. The attacks involved 50 Tomahawk land attack cruise missiles (TLAMs) fired from US and UK ships and submarines in the Arabian Sea; 15 B-1 and B-2 stealth bombers flying out of the continental USA; B-52H bombers launched from Diego Garcia in the Indian Ocean; and 25 US strike aircraft based on aircraft carriers. The B-1 and B-2 bombers primarily used 'smart-bombs' such as Joint Direct Attack Munitions (JDAMs), while the B-52s were likely to have used Conventional Air Launched Cruise Missiles (CALCMs).[2]

By the second week of November, US aerial bombardment had paved the way for the opposition, United Front (UF), to capture Mazar-e-Sharif and then move on to Kabul. On 13 November, the UF forces took Kabul. Taliban lines north of Kabul broke on the afternoon of 12 November 2001, following repeated air strikes by USAF B-52H Stratofortress strategic bombers combined with a two hour-long artillery barrage from UF forces and small arms exchanges prior to the final advance on the city. By 1600h local time, armoured units of the UF Guards Brigade were advancing south along the Old Road leading to Kabul as lines of infantry units swept through Taliban positions on both sides of the highway. However, by that time Taliban forces appeared to be pulling back in something close to a rout, leaving behind their fatalities and large quantities of equipment.

By December 2001, the coalition forces, in conjunction with the opposition UF, had managed to get the Taliban out of power in most of Afghanistan. The UF was in power in Kabul and while bombing of select targets and occasional fire fights did take place, the region was less of a war zone.

Then in March 2002, the US forces fought their fiercest battle in Shah-e-Kot in the Paktia province. This battle resulted in eight American casualties and brought home to the US that the al-Qaida was yet to be routed fully.

The real long-term challenge before the US is to de-Talibanize Pakistan, and ensure that its roots as a state sponsor of terror are removed. This is so because it has nurtured and harboured terrorist groups and training centres, which form the core of a global terrorist jihad factory spreading outwards. That Pakistan played a double game with the US is a matter for separate study, but it suffices to say here that those extremist organizations, Islamists who operate out of Pakistan, played a prominent role in fighting the US-led coalition forces even as Operation Enduring Freedom was going on.

The Role of Special Operation Forces

Throughout the ongoing war in Afghanistan, the media has reported extensively on the role of Special Operation Forces (SOF) and their performance. Several major US SOF including the Green Berets, the UK Special Air Service (SAS), and others have been active even before the official start to the anti-terror campaign in October last.

Since the operations conducted by the SOF remain under a cloud of secrecy, it is difficult to perform an operational analysis, but, nevertheless, a preliminary assessment based on media reports is undertaken here.

While the conflict in Afghanistan has given the West the opportunity to employ its SOF in the war against terrorism, there is still some confusion over what constitutes Special Operation Forces. At the core of the problem lies the differing classifications that nations give to their Special Forces. In general terms, Special Forces today include the US Delta Force, Green Berets, and Navy SEALS, plus the UK SAS and SBS (Special Boat Service).

While the US and the UK have a small number of Special Forces, they have much larger forces, which can be classified as specialist forces capable of special area or functional missions. It is these forces, such as the US Rangers or Marines who are in Afghanistan conducting the core of the ground campaign against the Taliban. It appears that in operations, the smaller units have undertaken close reconnaissance of likely targets and larger forces—probably in company strength have then attacked the targets.[3]

The forces used by the US and their allies included several elements of SOF. On the ground US SEALS, the Delta Force, Green Berets, and other forces have been active. The main aim is to hunt for Osama bin Laden and his companions. The target is also the other Taliban and al-Qaida leaders. The main assault on the Tora Bora cave complex in November was aimed at flushing out bin Laden, but it appears that he slipped out well in advance.

According to Senator John McCain, the Afghan campaign has set a precedent and provides a model, 'the success of air power, combined with Special Operation Forces working together with indigenous opposition forces, in waging modern war'.[4]

The fact that Afghanistan provided a model is understandable, for the opposition in this case was not technology savvy and was not ready to withstand the aerial onslaught of the US forces. But this does not mean that future wars against terrorism will be fought along similar lines. As the Bush administration prepares for the next step in its war against terrorism, it will have to weigh the lessons learnt from Afghanistan.

The Induction of Special Forces

US Special Operation Forces from the Army and Air Force, and units of the 82nd and 101st Airborne Divisions, landed in Peshawar and Quetta in early September, and a command centre was set up in the region to coordinate activities. Among the earliest insertions of Special Forces into Afghanistan was Team 555 (from US Army Special Forces 5th Group based at Fort Campbell, Kentucky) that constituted the A-team into the region.

At the end of September 2001, reports emerged of British and US SOF operating on reconnaissance missions inside Afghanistan alongside the Northern Alliance forces. This was basically a twofold mission, path finding and identifying targets that could be designated for destruction by aerial power.[5]

Most of the US forces that were employed in Afghanistan operated out of Pakistan and the Central Asian Republics. The SOF worked mainly out of the Central Asian Republics of Uzbekistan and Tajikistan. Uzbekistan was the first former Soviet Central Asian Republic to signal its willingness to assist the US-led military operations in Afghanistan in the days immediately after the 11 September terrorist attacks against the US; American military transport had arrived in Uzbekistan as early as 22 September.

Both Uzbekistan and Tajikistan fall within the area of responsibility (AOR) of the US Central Command (CENTCOM), which directed Operation Enduring Freedom. The United States Army, Navy, and Air Force SOF played key roles in carrying out CENTCOM's primary peacetime strategy of working cooperatively with friendly nations in its AOR to strengthen ties with these potential coalition partners. The SOF deployed to CENTCOM's AOR are under the operational control of Special Operations Command Centre (SOCCENT), co-located with CENTCOM at MacDill Air Force Base, Florida. SOCCENT also maintains a forward headquarters in Bahrain.

While soldiers from various American SF groups were deployed for Operation Enduring Freedom, the primary unit was the 5th SF Group, which focuses on the Middle East and south-west Asia in support of CENTCOM, and has a forward operating location in Kuwait. The 5th SF Group conducted the periodic training sessions in the four Central Asian Republics that began in 1999. Some of its soldiers speak Uzbek, Tajik, and Afghan languages.

The military linkages forged by Army Special Forces A-Teams in Central Asia since 1999 were instrumental in securing the valuable political support that the US received from Uzbekistan and Tajikistan during Operation Enduring Freedom.[6]

By early October 2001, personnel of the 5th SF Group and a SOCCENT headquarters contingent were stationed at Khanabad airbase outside Karshi in southern Uzbekistan, 130 miles north of Afghanistan, along with helicopters of the army's 160th Special Operations Aviation Regiment and about 1,000 troops of the US Army's 10th Mountain Division. Uzbekistan authorized the use of Khanabad for all but offensive combat operations, and the air base provided a key early staging base for US SOF operations in northern Afghanistan, particularly the insertion of liaison teams that worked with anti-Taliban Northern Alliance forces.

US Defence Secretary Donald Rumsfeld met with government officials in Uzbekistan on 5 October and returned to the region on 3–4 November 2001 for successive meetings with officials in Tajikistan and Uzbekistan. During Rumsfeld's visit, Tajikistan offered the US the potential use of three former Soviet air bases within its borders. A week later, following inspections of the bases by American teams, the Pentagon said that one of the bases, which was not identified, was suitable for supporting fighter bombing operations.

Thus, Tajikistan was the first nation to provide an available inland base for launching US aircraft, particularly US Air Force fighters for offensive operations in Afghanistan. Previously, only a limited number of USAF F-15Es had flown occasional strike missions there from faraway bases in either Kuwait or Oman. Most of the attacks were conducted by Navy F/A-18 and F-14 fighters flying 1,000 mile round trips from aircraft carriers in the Arabian Sea and off the coast of Pakistan, supplemented by USAF B-52 bomber attacks launched from the Indian Ocean island of Diego Garcia.

The *New York Times* noted on 10 October, 'The five countries that emerged in Central Asia after the collapse of the Soviet Union a decade ago are unknown to most Americans but are now being urgently courted as the US seeks to destroy terrorist bases in nearby Afghanistan .... With the exception of the Pentagon, which early on recognised that the Central Asian states might some day prove a valuable security asset, American and many other diplomats viewed them as dangerous places, and best avoided .... The focus on military cooperation rather than promotion of democracy proved a success.'

Pakistan, the other country in the region which sought to ally itself with the USA in the war against terrorism, asserted that it had given America only logistics/emergency facilities. In fact, in the early October raid by US forces on Afghanistan, Islamabad claimed that the hit and run operation was not mounted from Pakistani territory.

The emergency facilities required by the US consist of emergency landing facilities for crippled aircraft/helicopters and communications/take-off/landing facilities for helicopters sent on rescue missions to pick up US personnel shot down in Afghan territory. Such helicopter-borne rescue missions also required fighter aircraft for escort and communications/radar infrastructure.

The US, therefore, stationed an unspecified number of helicopters and fighter planes at the PAF bases at Jacobabad in Sindh and at Pasni and Dalbandin in Baluchistan along with the rescue teams, medical personnel, and back-up logistics personnel, all numbering around 2,000. State-of-the-art communications and radar equipment was flown from the US Central Command and installed at these bases. US personnel took over complete responsibility for the security of these air bases, with the Pakistanis playing only a peripheral support role. US troops are still stationed in strength in Pakistan and these will continue to act as support for the SOF in the region.

But preceding the induction of regular SOF into Afghanistan were men from the CIA's Special Activity Division, who formed the links on the ground with the Northern Alliance. The CIA operatives had been inserted into Afghanistan beginning 27 September 2001 to designate landing zones, secure safe houses, vet anti-Taliban commanders, and supply their troops with weapons, communications gear, medical supplies and clothing.

It was only after the CIA personnel had accomplished their task that teams of three to five soldiers, backed by Blackhawk MH-60K helicopters deployed at airbases outside Afghanistan, began deploying into that nation's mountainous regions in an attempt to locate the elusive bin Laden. They have been concentrating their searches in caves and underground bunkers in south-west Afghanistan near the city of Kandahar. Osama bin Laden has long been known to operate in that region.

Several elite military units continue to be involved in the effort to find bin Laden, including the US Army's Green Berets, Navy SEALS and the British Army's Special Air Services. Among other countries, Turkey was the first to offer Special Forces that were sent in. Several European nations, including Germany and France, are also reported to have offered to send some of their special forces to search for bin Laden and others.

The SOF in Afghanistan performed reconnaissance and path finding missions. Intelligence gathering has been another area of operations given the lack of hard ground intelligence in the initial phase. A few select operations like capturing an airfield or providing intelligence for strikes were conducted. That they have done, but there seems to be no evidence that they played a role in capturing or killing any major Taliban leader, the main US aim.

The Special Forces teams executed three missions: synchronizing the unorganized forces of ethnic Uzbek and Tajik Afghan opposition groups in the north; building small armies out of Pashtun tribesmen in the south; and providing the targeting information that enabled navy and air force pilots to fire guided bombs at al-Qaida and Taliban fighters and equipment, most of the time with devastating precision.

These missions depended on a new relationship forged between the US military and intelligence personnel, and a highly improvisational partnership between US soldiers on the ground and their Afghan counterparts. But under the pressures of war, these relationships developed quickly.[7]

The SOF presence in Afghanistan is very small and that is their real strength; the special tasks they perform are often done quietly without too much visibility. Their training and operational skills make them exceptional for special tasks and that is why the selection of such soldiers is rigorous. In the SAS, for example, for every 100 soldiers that volunteer for selection, only about 15 are accepted for training; of these 15, probably 10 actually complete the training.

These soldiers are different: they have to be intelligent, lateral thinkers, superbly fit and have the mindset that keeps them going when others would give up. For all armies, their Special Forces are the 53rd card in the pack of cards, the 'ace up their sleeve'. They are a strategic strike element that are to be used sparingly and under special circumstances.

In fact, according to one source, there were just 316 US Special Forces soldiers in Afghanistan: 18 A-teams, four company level units and three battalion level commands, all reporting to a Joint Special Operations Task Force at the Khanabad Air base in Karshi, Uzbekistan, 100 miles north of the Afghan border. Nearly every team also included one or two CIA operatives and an Air Force Special Operations combat controller, expert at guiding high-flying aircraft to targets.[8]

Special Forces Operations

The US-SOF, which had been inserted into Afghanistan, had their mission clearly laid out right from the beginning. Their guidance from the ground was required to help US warplanes destroy the Taliban front line. They were also present to search for and destroy Taliban and al-Qaida targets in the 35 mile stretch south to Kabul. And finally, they were to help the Northern Alliance seize Kabul.

The 555 team, which had been dropped into northern Afghanistan, first was being tracked by Special Forces soldiers 1,500 miles away in a Combined Air Operations Center at the Prince Sultan Air base outside Riyadh, the capital of Saudi Arabia.

That group also analysed pictures and other intelligence on the A-teams' targets.

Thus by the end of October, Special Forces from the US and UK were already 'in place' to carry out reconnaissance and path finding operations. Team 555's work north of Kabul set a pattern for three more A-teams that infiltrated beginning in the second half of October: 553 in the central Bamiyan province, 585 around Kunduz and 595 in Dara-e-Suf, a remote mountain village and headquarters for their new partner, General Abdur Rashid Dostum.[9]

For 18 days those four teams, plus two 15-person battalion level units—only 78 soldiers in all—accounted for the entire Special Forces presence in Afghanistan, according to the US Army Special Forces Command. Yet, it was these forces that set the stage for the fall of the northern two-thirds of Afghanistan.

One of the earliest incidents reported was of the SAS fighting it out with the Taliban, while on a reconnaissance mission near Kabul in early September 2001. The British SAS was reportedly amongst the first SOF to be inducted into the battle zone.[10]

In the first openly admitted ground operation on the night of 19/20 October, over 100 specially equipped personnel, most of them from the army's 75th Rangers Regiment, were para dropped at two places in southern Afghanistan. They were airlifted from the US Aircraft Carrier, Kitty Hawk, off the Makran Coast of Baluchistan.

After they had been on the ground for a few hours, they were picked up by MH-60 Blackhawk helicopters. It is not clear whether these helicopters flew them direct to Kitty Hawk or they were first taken to Pakistan's Dalbandin air force base 20 miles from the Afghan border and then transported to the aircraft carrier from there. Two US soldiers died in a helicopter crash in Pakistan while backing up the military operation. The crash occurred as they prepared to perform search-and-rescue operations.

The targets of the first ground operation were reportedly the residential complex of Mullah Mohammad Omar and an airport. It is not clear whether the airport was that of Kandahar or Jalalabad, where the US had been trying to help the followers of Abdul Haq, a Pashtun leader, or Herat, where the US had been trying to help the men of Ismail Khan, the Shia leader.

The Amir of the Taliban, his family and staff had vacated the residential complex in the beginning of October. Similarly, the staff of the offices of the Taliban's intelligence agency and the religious police, which were located there, had also vacated at the same time. The purpose of the raid, therefore, seems to have been to look for tell-tale documents and equipment, mainly of intelligence value, which they might have abandoned while making the emergency evacuation.[11] The commandos' helicopters had been launched from the USS Kitty Hawk in the Arabian Sea, and close air support for the operations was lent by AC-130 gunships.[12]

US-SOF played a key role in the Northern Alliance offensives in Afghanistan, especially in the capture of Kabul. They also helped coordinate the Northern Alliance tactical victory at Mazar-e-Sharif on 9 November and coordinated air attacks that assisted in neutralizing Taliban capabilities.[13]

The basic SF task was to provide communications facilities to the Afghan opposition leaders and ensure coordination of the battle. They also helped to guide US artillery and aerial softening of targets. On 3 November, Lieutenant-Colonel Max Bowers, a 5th Group battalion commander, and seven others arrived at Dara-e Suf, joining Team 595. His mission was to coordinate the battles of three major Northern Alliance commanders for the fight for Mazar-e-Sharif. Dostum had the control of this city between 1992 and 1997 and it was strategically important because it could open a supply pipeline to allied forces elsewhere in the north of Afghanistan.[14]

Dostum had, in the meantime, allied himself with his former enemies Attah Mohammed and Mohammed Mohaqiq to take Mazar. All of the opposition commanders wanted to have American communications capability, with which they could link up and keep track of each other.

Bowers carried a 4 by 6-feet laminated map of Afghanistan that was marked with Xs and Os and arrows in preparation for the offensive on the city of Mazar-e-Sharif. Dostum would take the plans to his war council, where Bowers would sit silently with him. Dostum and Bowers' plan was to encircle Mazar-e-Sharif.

Each Northern Alliance commander was given an Inmarsat satellite phone to communicate with each other and the US force commanders. Colonel Bowers also had his own line of communication with the A-teams attached to each commander. The night before the battle, with Dostum and the other commanders' troops arrayed on the ridges overlooking Mazar-e-Sharif, they watched convoys of Taliban troops flee. Bowers' men called in fierce air strikes. Troops on the hilltops, he said, 'were simply ecstatic'.

'We saturated the battlefield with small close-air-support cells and we hit the Taliban if they were engaging us, if they were trying to maneuver in a favourable position', he said. 'We engaged them while they were moving and if they tried to retreat. They simply could not move.'

The Taliban front line collapsed nearly immediately on the night of 9 November. Taliban soldiers ran away, abandoning trenches, leaping from tanks, and scrambling into trucks and jeeps for a getaway. Hundreds fled to Samangan and Kunduz provinces. US forces used aircraft to attack some of the fleeing fighters, but did not ask the Afghans to intercept them on the ground, Bowers said.[15]

In mid-October, US aircraft began dropping leaflets over Afghanistan. They included pictures to influence those who could not read. They were designed by the US Army's 4th PSYOP Group at Fort Bragg with help from the 5th Group at Fort Campbell, which specialize in the Middle East and South West Asia. The leaflets were printed in Dari on one side and in Pushto on the other, the two main languages in the region.

Simultaneously, special operations EC-130 E Commando Solo II PSYOP aircraft began transmitting radio broadcasts into Afghanistan. These aircraft flew round the clock, broadcasting music, news and information in various languages. The message sent out was to the local Afghan population to warn them not to go near the Taliban and al-Qaida centres which were going to be bombed. They also stressed that the coalition campaign was not aimed at the Afghan people, but at the al-Qaida terrorists and their Taliban supporters.[16]

One of the secret aspects of SOF tasks in Afghanistan was their search for weapons of mass destruction (WMD) in the supposed possession of the al-Qaida. In many such operations, no journalists were allowed. All along, the US was concerned about the possibility of the al-Qaida possessing WMD weapons. Therefore, the SOF were tasked with searching and locating the presence of these caches, if any. To this end, they extensively scoured the Tora Bora mountain cave complex for the al-Qaida's WMD capability.

While there has been no official confirmation of these operations, one web-based source notes that SOF were involved in a major operation wherein some 3,000 troops were deployed and they operated in NBC protective clothing, according to this source.[17]

Even in south Afghanistan, US bombing directed by US-SOF and military action by opposition forces led to the capture of key cities and towns. But this was not so successful as in the north. Which is why, in the Pashtun south, the US landed a marine expeditionary force to an airhead near Kandahar to track down bin Laden and Mullah Omar and to conquer territory. Obviously, the US did not have enough faith in the local opposition forces to do the job.

These marines established an airhead at the disused Dalangi airfield some 100 km south-west of Kandahar in the Reg Desert. By the first week of November, Omar was ready to hand over Kandahar to Mullah Naquibulla, the surrender arrangement being negotiated by Hamid Karzai.

After the fall of Kandahar in December 2001, the Special Forces moved their focus on a valley east of the Tora Bora Mountains, where they found ammunition of various ordnances piled up in readiness. The members of the Python 36 Special Forces Team and US Army Ordnance set to diffuse a huge stack of ammunition and ordnance that had been left behind by Taliban fighters.[18] Throughout the winter months of January–February 2002, the US forces continued mopping up operations and aerial attacks on suspected al-Qaida targets.

Then in March 2002, US forces were forced to undertake an operation, code-named Anaconda, in the Shah-e-Kot area (Arma Mountains) near Gardez in the Paktia province of eastern Afghanistan. This involved a major confrontation between the allied forces led by the US and a mixed group of determined guerilla fighters, operating from inside a cave complex in the area.

US troops had traced a group of some 500 suspected bin Laden loyalists to a cave network in the Shah-e-Kot mountain range. Then 1,000 US troops, including those from the 10th Mountain Division and 101 Airborne Brigade together with 200 special forces troops from Australia, Canada, France, Germany, Denmark, and Norway took the lead role in the ground offensive.

Although US soldiers were accompanied by a similar number of anti-Taliban Afghan fighters, the assault on the Tora Bora cave complex at the end of 2001 showed that local militia men do not necessarily share the incentive of western troops to take the risks necessary to finish the job. At Shah-e-Kot, therefore, US forces were less reliant on proxies, making it the biggest battle the Americans have fought in Afghanistan and it is perhaps this that has led to the inevitable rise in casualties.

Those opposing the US-led forces in Shah-e-Kot were described as a mix of the remnants of the Taliban and Osama bin Laden's al-Qaida. However, other reports describe them as a moderate sized contingent of Pakistanis led by Arab instructors of the 055 Brigade of the al-Qaida. Operation Anaconda also revealed that Pakistan-based extremist organizations were still active in the fighting.

The Pakistanis involved were members of the Sunni extremist Sipah-e-Sahaba Pakistan (SSP), the Harkat-ul-Mujahideen (HUM), the Harkat-ulJihad-AI-lslami (HUJI), the Jaish-e-Mohammad (JEM), and the Lashkar-e-Taiba (LET). They had survived the US air strikes in Afghanistan and had managed to return to Pakistani territory. They had regrouped and after being retrained by a team of retired officers of the Pakistani military intelligence establishment, many of them were re-inducted into eastern Afghanistan (Gardez, Wardak, Ghazni and Khost) to resume the fight against the US troops.[19]

The Shah-e-Kot battle demonstrated both to the Afghan people as well as the rest of the world that contrary to the American claims of having vanquished the Taliban and damaged the al-Qaida-inspired terrorist infrastructure in Afghanistan, these forces were still alive and kicking.

Eight Americans were killed and 40 wounded in the assault in the Shah-e-Kot battle. The al-Qaida men were reportedly well armed, well-organized and highly motivated. That, and the altitude and icy conditions, made for a slow allied advance, although the Pentagon showed confidence that this time, there would be no escape.

The White House had long prepared the American people for US casualties in Afghanistan, and those occurring in Shah-e-Kot will only stiffen domestic resolve to complete the war. But the clashes are a sharp reminder of how much remains to be done, the perils that continue to face the US operations, and the limits of technology in making war safe for US personnel.

The Assessment

There is little doubt that the war against terrorism in Afghanistan is far from over and the US has still some distance to cover. But the military operations that began in October 2001 did achieve some results. While proper assessments will have to wait for the release of official US military analysis, a preliminary effort is made here and attention is focused on the role of the SOF.

Most observers in the West had marvelled at the relative absence of casualties in the war's first phase, as US forces appeared to destroy the Taliban with air power and a mix of Special Forces and opposition ground troops. But while the American B-52s and other air assets have driven the Taliban from the urban centres and put to flight the al-Qaida, the US still has on hand the task of rounding up the remaining al-Qaida members still at large in Afghanistan. This is an exceedingly difficult job and cannot be completed until the new government of Hamid Karzai is able to extend its authority beyond the capital of Kabul. The US speaks optimistically of Karzai building an Afghan national army, but power struggles between local warlords threaten to scuttle that plan and plunge the battered country into a new season of chaos.

The US initially claimed that it had fewer than 3,000 ground troops in Afghanistan, though the figures are probably more than double. What the Afghan experience does show is that the US military has the capability to react quickly to the challenges of counter-terrorism and can adapt itself to a 'distant, harsh and ever-changing battlefield'. The Pentagon has expressed the view that US troops have perfected the art of waging war with a combination of modern technology and last century tactics. The combination of medieval war fighting tactics with modern-day weapons and technology has proved useful. It may be added that given the topography of Afghanistan and the nature of the enemy, the US would have anyway adapted to fight its battles in an unconventional manner.

The first phase of operations from October to December 2001

saw the US-led coalition forces driving out the Taliban from its centres of power. Heavy bombing of rural and urban military infrastructure ensured that the al-Qaida deserted its command and control posts. Taliban leaders surrendered major cities to opposition forces, including Kandahar, Kabul, Kunduz, and Mazar-e-Sharif.

The US military claims to have destroyed at least 11 terrorist training camps and 39 Taliban command and control sites. The *Wall Street Journal* reported on 13 December that as many as 50,000 terrorists from more than 50 countries may have received training in al-Qaida camps in Afghanistan in recent years.

Both US political and military leaders have made clear, from the beginning, that they see the war against al-Qaida and the broader war on terror as a long-term effort, one which may well take many years; al-Qaida is a more specific target than the more amorphous, generic target of supporters of terrorism in general (since terrorism is a tactic used by many different movements at different times). Thus any discussion of 'who is next' involves a variety of judgements, including prioritization of targets and assessments of risks and costs involved. It is also clear that within the present US administration are those who want to focus, initially, on those directly involved in the 11 September attacks on the US, and not be diverted by other targets, however tempting; while others cry 'On to Baghdad' and want to deal with Iraq before dealing with smaller terrorist groups, even if the latter are directly linked to al-Qaida.

The US Pentagon is of the view that there are as many as 50 pockets of resistance similar to the one at Shah-e-Kot left in Afghanistan, and emphasize that the campaign to eliminate the remaining elements of al-Qaida will continue for some time to come. In effect, it will be a hard, cave-to-cave fight that will probably mean more US casualties. And at the same time, the longer US forces remain deployed in the region, the greater the pressure will be to take on more of the 'nation building' responsibility the Bush administration has tried so hard to avoid.

To recap the remarkable speed with which the Taliban collapsed; the US began its bombing campaign on 7 October, naturally enough concentrating on Taliban air defence and command-and-control capabilities. There appear to have been some initial problems involved in working with the Northern Alliance, and as a result there were few visible results in the first few weeks. As some critics were already accusing the administration of a Vietnam style 'quagmire' after less than a month of bombing, the US shifted its bombing campaign from the largely destroyed air defence and command infrastructure and began destroying Taliban military formations on the front lines.

At that point the Northern Alliance became actively involved, and everything happened quickly. The 'quagmire' of late October became a stunning victory in a matter of weeks in early November, as Mazar-e-Sharif, then Herat and Kabul itself, and finally Kunduz and Kandahar fell to the anti-Taliban forces. Though pockets of resistance remain, and the new government is somewhat fragile due to its internal fractures, the Taliban have been driven from all the Afghani cities and hold on only in a few remote outposts.[20]

Through the end of October, the air campaign failed to either compel Taliban cooperation or disintegrate the movement. During most of this period air attacks focused largely on air defence, command and control, political, and infrastructure targets as well as military bases and storage sites. What should have been clear from the experience of Operation Allied Force in Bosnia was that the 'lever' of air power requires a 'fulcrum' on the ground.

The available ground fulcrum in Afghanistan—the Northern Alliance—was regarded initially (and accurately) as unlikely to produce the desired political outcome, should it sweep to victory. Thus, support for the Alliance's war effort was minimally configured to sustain their front and pressure the Taliban without enabling a rapid Alliance sweep. Of course, the only completely reliable fulcrum would have been US troops on the ground in large numbers. But practical and diplomatic problems precluded this option, at least in the chosen time frame.[21] In the Northern Alliance's troops, US air power found its required ground fulcrum. But it was a devil's bargain that cost America leverage and control on the strategic level.

The bombing campaign had been intensified during the second week—daily sorties rose from about 25 to 90—after the Taliban had proved more resilient than initially expected and the Northern Alliance had failed in its initial effort to take Mazar-e-Sharif. But this was still consistent with hopes that the Taliban might be split and co-opted. The truly significant shift was the decision to cast America's lot with the Northern Alliance military effort.

This gained substance during the last week of October when B-52s began to carpet-bomb Taliban positions opposite the Northern Alliance and US Special Operations troops assumed a bigger role in guiding both the air attacks and the Alliance's efforts. Throughout the first 10 days of November, air support for the Alliance grew in tandem with criticism of the war's slow progress and its mounting civilian costs. Alliance air support was accentuated by bringing into play 15,000 pound slurry bombs (the BLU-82 'Big Blue' or 'daisy-cutters') and by increasing the expenditure of cluster bombs.

One authority on Afghanistan notes that this rapid military success was due to the low force-to-space ratio and US close air support. It is estimated that the Taliban overall strength was around 40,000. But the core group was only 25,000; the rest were recruited on an emergency basis. Thus, these troops were not in a position to withstand any deep penetration.[22]

These troops were also being constantly bombarded, as a result of which Taliban communication and command and control centres had been taken out right in the beginning by US airplanes. It may be pointed out that the Taliban, though equipped and armed by Pakistan was mainly a Toyota pick-up force. By the time the US had begun its attacks, Pakistan had withdrawn its 'advisers' and other back-up facilities.

Perhaps the most efficient strategy conducted by the US military in Afghanistan was the employment of Special Forces troops to train anti-Taliban forces, communicate ground information to bombers, and prepare the Kandahar base for the Marines. By deploying Special Forces teams, the military reduced risk to American soldiers, sharpened bombing precision, and established contact, with the local Afghan forces opposing the Taliban.

The combination of air power and Special Forces demonstrated the value of using small groups of men to perform a variety of tasks. These forces also had ultra lightweight, secure and reliable communications, which eased the mission profile. The new Target Designation Equipment (TAMBER Laser enhanced binoculars) in the hands of US and other SF had the capability to measure target coordinates and distance and subsequently paint the target for guiding laser-guided bombs delivered by attack aircraft.[23]

SF were already using these laser designation devices as far back as the Gulf War in 1991 and the war in Afghanistan proved that this technique was particularly useful in environments where the air force had to bomb from a height. In fact, in Bosnia the US forces lacked this combination of air power and SF teams working on the ground. Combining high technology with highly trained and motivated SF personnel proved to be an asset in Afghanistan, but only for specific tasks.

In February 2002, the US Department of Defense proposed a 21 per cent hike in the FY 2003 budget for USSOCOM that includes upgrades to helicopters and gunships that were used in Afghanistan. The USSOCOM found itself short in logistics, communications, and mobility assets to execute missions in 'Enduring Freedom'. The command had to borrow additional systems and resources from other commands. USSOCOM leaders are also seeking additional helicopters, aviators, and support infrastructure.[24]

The global war against terrorism and its specific military operations in Afghanistan, while not having universal applicability, does demonstrate the potent combination of Special Forces and air power. Responsive air effort can greatly multiply the force effect of small groups of Special Forces and this was demonstrated in no small measure in Afghanistan. US and other allied special forces, who were present in small numbers, were able to inflict damage far out of proportion to their numbers. A combination of US Special Forces, US-sponsored local opposition forces, and air strikes have proved that conventional weapons can be used effectively against unconventional enemies.

A most telling illustration of this is a US commando's description of training anti-Taliban fighters in the finer points of mounting a cavalry charge against artillery positions. These warriors riding straight out of the nineteenth century into the twenty-first century had something in their arsenal that their forebears from the Asian steppe lacked: F-15 Strike Eagles packing precision-guided bombs.[25]

Conclusion

A potent combination of high-tech weaponry and ancient forms of warfare have led to success for the US military in Afghanistan success that remains incomplete until Osama bin Laden is found.

The US used a wide array of weapons, some high technology munitions, and some primitive ones to fulfil their objectives. Unmanned spy planes, some carrying missiles that could be fired by an operator at a computer terminal in the US, have played an important role. So have horses and mules that carried US-backed Afghan fighters and even some US commandos over otherwise impassable terrain. It was this eclectic mix of man, machine and beast that provided the leverage for tactical success in Afghanistan. As the US military begins to examine the Afghan campaign for lessons they may apply later in the war on terrorism, some preliminary conclusions are already available.

It is realized that most engagements in Afghanistan were small-scale and thus the war against terror need not be waged with massed troops seeking to conquer territory. A combination of local allies, Special Forces, and precision-guided munitions delivered by air and sea can deliver the lethal punch. The key to the successful integration of these resources is: good, hard intelligence, help from knowledgeable locals, streamlined decision-making, and the quick strike power to make those decisions count.

It has to be kept in mind that the US fought the war in Afghanistan with existing capabilities and forces. But given the unconventional nature of the enemy, US forces did innovate their existing doctrines and capabilities and mould them to suit local circumstances.

The US forces have already begun to catalogue problems that came into clear view during the Afghan campaign. They include the challenges that arise when countries in the immediate area of a campaign deny basing rights to US combat planes, shortages in precision-guided munitions, the limits of air power operating from sea and flying long distances, and the compromises that must be made when relying on locals to carry out much of the ground war.

A key problem continuously facing the Bush administration even as it was seeking to retain sole control of the fight in Afghanistan globally—there was no avoiding the occasional struggles in the working relationship with the local fighters and tribal leaders.

Tribal leaders were fighting each other for virtually everything—from weapons to control of key cities—and the US forces had their hands full in keeping the alliance together.

In some cases, as the intensity of conflict wore down, US troops were besieged with requests for aerial strikes on so-called Taliban targets. On cross-checking, it was found that the opposition leaders were wanting to use US firepower to destroy their own rivals within the alliance.

In terms of the opposing forces of the al-Qaida and the Taliban, the US will have to work on the assumption that these forces will seek to strike at US and other allied physical and psychological targets across the region and perhaps even in continental US. The task of catching the top leadership of the al-Qaida and Taliban remains and until that is done, the US can expect some efforts by these terrorist groups to regroup, within and outside Afghanistan. But it is clear that these groups will not try to regroup in large formations again.

They tried that in the mountains of Tora Bora in end 2001 and were pulverized by US air power. The terrorist outfits tried it again in March 2002 in the mountains around the Shah-e-Kot Valley and were punished by Operation Anaconda, a 17 day assault by 2,000 US and allied troops backed by air power.

There were some who doubted US strategy in the Tora Bora assault and opined that it was flawed. Their contention was that it was better to use proxies to fight the battle—in this case anti-Taliban Afghans—rather than send US troops into the mountains in large numbers.

As per ongoing routine, US warplanes, guided to targets by American special operations troops, pounded the caves to which the Islamists had retreated and regrouped. But according to some analysts, the Afghan 'proxies' were less aggressive than necessary, allowing hundreds of enemy fighters to escape.

The lesson of Tora Bora was that there is a limitation with what militaries can do with local opposition forces, however hard one tries. This is especially so in a multi-tribal nation like Afghanistan. That is perhaps why US Army General, Tommy Franks, took that lesson to heart and used more than 1,000 American ground troops during Operation Anaconda. There are in all about 6,500 US troops in Afghanistan reinforced by 1,700 British soldiers according to General Franks.

There is a feeling amongst some that most of the 500 to 800 enemy fighters estimated to have been holed up in the Shah-e-Kot area escaped. Only a few dozen enemy corpses were found. General Franks claimed that 'hundreds' were killed. The US commander on the scene, Major-General Frank Hagenbeck, observed that few bodies were found because many enemy troops were blown to bits by US bombs.

Whatever the body count or numbers killed, the fact remains that the enemy fighters got away. And those who got away will continue the fight in the future, though probably by other means. While the battle at Shah-e-Kot showed the bunker busting power of the US forces, it also meant that the guerilla can always fight without directly confronting a superior military force.

Al-Qaida and Taliban forces can be expected to attempt hit and run attacks on American troops based at Kandahar and Bagram or on allied forces. And Islamic radicals in eastern Afghanistan have circulated leaflets offering $50,000 for a dead American and $100,000 for a live one.

Experts opine that officials of the Karzai government may be targeted. Mr Karzai faces internal opposition of another sort, as was demonstrated in early April by what his aides say was a foiled coup attempt.[26]

The Taliban and al-Qaida may try to avoid giving General Franks another big target, and that will make the US military task more difficult. There is no particular will in the Taliban or al-Qaida to defend any entity, because they know that it will be destroyed by US aerial bombing. Even otherwise, the Taliban collapsed under the weight of US pressure, demonstrating that for all their bluster, they are not infallible.

US military operations in Afghanistan demonstrate the importance of the SOF in counter-terrorist and counter-insurgency operations, a message that India has long understood. But the very nature of the Indian SOF, their command and control and lack of technology, makes them unsuitable for the kind of far-reaching, politico-military operations undertaken by the US.[27] This is a matter to be analysed by the Indian establishment both in the context of internal security and its relations with Pakistan and China.

Notes

*Editor's Note: This was the situation when the article was orginally published in April 2002.

1. Andrew Koch, 'Air and Missile Strikes herald new phase in the fight against terrorism', *Jane's Defence Weekly*, 7 October 2001.
2. Ibid.
3. Charles Heyman, 'Special Forces and the reality of Military Operations in Afghanistan', *Jane's Defence Weekly*, 5 November 2001.
4. Cited in Afsir Karim, 'War on Terrorism: A Variation of the Great Game', Editorial Perspective in *Aakrosh*, vol. 5, no. 14 January 2002, p. 16.
5. Sources: 'Reconnaissance ops underway in Afghanistan', <CNN.com>, 28 September 2001.
6. Glenn W. Goodman, Jr, 'Central Asian Partners: Low-Key Spadework by Green Berets Reaps Valuable Benefits for War in Afghanistan', *Armed Forces Journal International*, January 2002.
7. Dana Priest, ' "Team 555" Shaped a New Way of War: Special Forces and Smart Bombs Turned Tide and Routed Taliban', *Washington Post*, 3 April 2002.
8. Ibid.
9. Ibid.
10. Report: 'SAS in Gun Battle', <CNN.com>, 24 September 2001.
11. Jim Garamone, 'Northern Alliance, US Special Forces at the Gates of Kabul' US Department of Defence, American Forces Press Services, 13 November 2001.
12. B. Raman, 'USA Afghan Ops: A Critical Analysis', South Asia Analysis Group, Paper No. 345, 22 October 2001.
13. 'Two Soldiers Killed in Pakistan Crash', <CNN.com>, 19 October 2001.
14. Dana Priest, op. cit.
15. Ibid.
16. Glenn W. Goodman Jr, 'The power of the word: US Special Forces used leaflets and radio broadcasts to sway Afghans', *Armed Forces Journal International*, February 2002, p. 30.
17. 'Nuclear Chase in the Tora Bora Complex', Debkafile net weekly, *Intelligence Journal*, 2001.
18. Susan Sevareid, 'Forces Scour Afghan Ammo Valley', *Los Angeles Times*, 3 January 2002.
19. B. Raman, 'The Omens of Op Anaconda', SAAG Paper No. 425, 14 March 2002.
20. *The Last War and the Next One: Lessons to Learn and Not Learn, I. The Estimate. Political and Security Intelligence Analysis of the Islamic World and its Neighbours*, vol. xiii, no. 24, 28 December 2001.
21. Carl Conetta, 'Strange Victory: A Critical Appraisal of Operation Enduring Freedom and the Afghanistan War', Cambridge, MA: Commonwealth

Institute Project on Defence Alternatives, Research Monograph #6, 30 January 2002. http://www.comw.org/pda/0201strangevic.html

22. G. D. Bakshi, 'End Game in Afghanistan', *Indian Defence Review*, vol. 16, no. 4, p. 56.
23. John Barry, 'A new breed of soldiers', *Newsweek*, 10 December 2001, pp. 20–1.
24. *Jane's Defence Weekly*, 20 February 2002, p. 2.
25. John Diamond, 'Plumbing the lessons from war', *Chicago Tribune*, 14 January 2002.
26. Richard Whittle, '6 Months into war, no end in sight. With 2 goals long since achieved, US forces face protracted mission', *The Dallas Morning News*, 7 April 2002. www.dallasnews.com
27. Bhashyam Kasturi, 'Military Special Forces in the Indian Context', *Indian Defence Review*, vol. 16, 4, pp. 71–6.

Bibliography

Decisive Battles

Creasy, Edward, *The Fifteen Decisive Battles of the World* (n.d., reprint, London: Everyman's Library, 1963).

Malleson, Col. G.B., *The Decisive Battles of India from 1746 to 1849* (n.d., reprint, Jaipur: Aavishkar Publishers, 1986).

Roy, Kaushik, *India's Historic Battles: From Alexander the Great to Kargil* (New Delhi: Permanent Black, 2004).

Military Historiography

Deshpande, Anirudh, *The Stigma of Defeat: Indian Military History in Comparative Perspective* (New Delhi: Nehru Memorial Museum and Library, 2003).

France, John, 'Recent Writings on Medieval Warfare: From the Fall of Rome to c. 1300', *Journal of Military History*, vol. 65, no. 2 (2001).

Gommans, Jos J.L., and Dirk H.A. Kolff, 'Introduction: Warfare and Weaponry in South Asia: 1000-1800 AD', in Gommans and Kolff (eds.), *Warfare and Weaponry in South Asia: 1000-1800* (New Delhi: Oxford University Press, 2001).

Roy, Kaushik, 'The Historiography of the Colonial Indian Army', New Series, *Studies in History*, vol. 12, no. 2 (1996), pp. 255-73.

——, Mars in Indian History', *Studies in History*, New Series, vol. 16, no. 2 (2000), pp. 261-75.

——, 'Introduction: Armies, Warfare and Society in Colonial India', in Roy (ed.), *War and Society in Colonial India* (New Delhi: Oxford University Press, 2006).

——, 'Introduction', in Roy (ed.), *1857 Uprising: A Tale of an Indian Warrior* (New Delhi: Anthem, 2008).

Military Philosophy

Beyerchen, Alan, 'Clausewitz, Nonlinearity, and the Unpredictability of War', *International Security*, vol. 17, no. 3 (1992-3).

Brekke, Torkel, 'Wielding the Rod of Punishment--- War and Violence in the Political Science of Kautilya', *Journal of Military Ethics*, vol. 3, no. 1 (2004), pp. 40-52.

——, 'The Ethics of War and the Concept of War in India and Europe', *NUMEN*, vol. 52 (2005).

Karnad, Bharat, *Nuclear Weapons & Indian Security: The Realist Foundations of Strategy* (Delhi: Macmillan, 2002).

Roy, Kaushik, 'Just and Unjust War in Hindu Philosophy', *Journal of Military Ethics*, vol. 6, no. 3 (2007).

Smith, Hugh, *On Clausewitz: A Study of Military and Political Ideas* (Houndmills, Basingstoke: Palgrave, Macmillan, 2005).

Unconventional Warfare

Beckett, Ian. F.W., *Modern Insurgencies and Counter-Insurgencies: Guerrillas and their Opponents since 1750* (2001, reprint, London/New York: Routledge, 2005).

Das, Gautam and M.K. Gupta-Ray, *SriLanka Misadventure: India's Military Peace-Keeping Campaign, 1987-90* (New Delhi: Har-Anand, 2008).

Ibrahim, Azeem, 'Conceptualisation of Guerrilla Warfare', *Small Wars & Insurgencies*, vol. 15, no. 3 (2004).

Kaldor, Mary, *New & Old Wars: Organized Violence in a Global Era* (1999, reprint, DehraDun: Natraj, 2005).

Moreman, T.R., *The Army in India and the Development of Frontier Warfare, 1849-1947* (Houndmills, Basingstoke: Macmillan, 1998).

——, '"Passing it On": The Army in India and Frontier Warfare, 1914-39', in Kaushik Roy (ed.), *War and Society in Colonial India* (New Delhi: Oxford University Press, 2006).

Munkler, Herfried, 'What is Really New about the New Wars?—A Reply to the Critics', in John Andreas Olsen (ed.), *On New Wars* (Oslo: Norwegian Institute for Defence Studies, 2007).

Murshed, Mansoob S. and Scott Gates, 'Spatial-Horizontal Inequality and the Maoist Insurgency in Nepal', *Review of Development Economics*, vol. 9, no. 1 (2005).

Osinga, Frans, 'On Boyd, Bin Laden, and Fourth Generation Warfare as String Theory', in John Andreas Olsen (ed.), *On New Wars* (Oslo: Norwegian Institute for Defence Studies, 2007).

Rajagopalan, Rajesh, *Fighting like a Guerrilla: The Indian Army and Counterinsurgency* (New Delhi: Routledge, 2008).

Smith, Rupert, *The Utility of Force: The Art of War in the Modern World* (2005, reprint, London: Penguin, 2006).

Warren, Alan, '"Bullocks treading down Wasps"?: The British Indian Army in Waziristan in the 1930s', *South Asia*, vol. 19, no. 2 (1996).

——, *Waziristan: The Faqir of Ipi and the Indian Army, The North West Frontier Revolt of 1936-7* (Karachi: Oxford University Press, 2000).

War and Culture

Barkawi, Tarak, 'Peoples, Homelands, and Wars? Ethnicity, the Military, and Battle among British Imperial Forces in the War against Japan', *Comparative Studies in Society and History*, vol. 46, no. 1 (2004).

——, 'Culture and Combat in the Colonies: The Indian Army in the Second World War', *Journal of Contemporary History*, vol. 4, no. 2 (2006).

Caplan, Lionel, *Warrior Gentleman: "Gurkhas" in the Western Imagination* (Providence/Oxford: Berghahn Books, 1995).

Digby, Simon, 'Dreams and Reminiscences of Dattu Sarvani, A Sixteenth Century Indo-Afghan Soldier', *Indian Economic and Social History Review*, vol. 2, no. 1 (1965), no. 2 (1965).

——, *Sufis and Soldiers in Awrangzeb's Deccan* (New Delhi: Oxford University Press, 2001).

Duby, Georges, *The Legend of Bouvines: War, Religion and Culture in the Middle Ages* (1973, English translation by Catherine Tihanyi, Cambridge: Polity Press, 1990).

Greenhut, Jeffrey, 'The Imperial Reserve: The Indian Corps on the Western Front, 1914-15', *Journal of Imperial and Commonwealth History*, vol. 12, no. 1 (1983).

——, 'Sahib and Sepoy: An Inquiry into the Relationship between the British Officers and Native Soldiers of the British Indian Army', *Military Affairs*, vol. XLVIII, no. 1 (1984).

Johnston, Alastair Iain, 'Thinking about Strategic Culture', *International Security*, vol. 19, no. 4 (1995).

Keegan, John, *The Face of Battle: A Study of Agincourt, Waterloo and the Somme* (1976, reprint, Middlesex: Penguin, 1978).

Lynn, John A., 'Heart of the Sepoy: The Adoption and Adaptation of European Military Practice in South Asia, 1740-1805', in Emily Goldman and Leslie C. Eliason (eds.), *The Diffusion of Military Technology and Ideas* (Stanford: Stanford University Press, 2003).

Pinch, William R., *Warrior Ascetics and Indian Empires* (Cambridge: Cambridge University Press, 2006).

Stanley, Peter, '"Dear Comrades": Barrack Room Culture and the "White Mutiny" of 1859-60', *Indo-British Review*, vol. 21, no. 2 (1996).

Streets, Heather, *Martial races: The Military, Race and Masculinity in British Imperial Culture, 1857-1914* (Manchester/New York: Manchester University Press, 2004).

War and Ecology

Gommans, Jos, 'The Silent Frontier of South Asia, c. AD 1100-1800', *Journal of World History*, vol. 9, no. 1 (1998).

——, *Mughal Warfare: Indian Frontier and High Roads to Empire, 1500-1700* (London/New York: Routledge, 2002).

Kolff, Dirk H.A., *Naukar, Rajput & Sepoy: The Ethnohistory of the Military Labour Market in Hindustan, 1450-1850* (Cambridge: Cambridge University Press, 1990).

Lindner, Rudi Paul, 'Nomadism, Horses and Huns', *Past and Present*, no. 42 (Aug. 1981).

War and Economy

Barendse, J., 'The Feudal Mutation: Military and Economic Transformations of the Ethnosphere in the Tenth to Thirteenth Centuries', *Journal of World History*, vol. 14. no. 4 (2003).

Bayly, C.A., 'The British Military-Fiscal State and Indigenous Resistance: India 1750-1820', in Bayly, *Origins of Nationality in South Asia: Patriotism and Ethical Government in the making of Modern India* (New Delhi: Oxford University Press, 1998).

Chakravarti, Ranabir *Warfare for Wealth: Early Indian Perspective* (Calcutta: Firma KLM Pvt. Ltd., 1986).

Cooper, Randolf G.S., 'Beyond Beasts and Bullion: Economic Considerations in Bombay's Military Logistics, 1803', *Modern Asian Studies*, vol. 33, no. 1 (1999).

Dewey, Clive, 'Some Consequences of Military Expenditure in British India: The Case of the Upper Sind Sagar Doab, 1849-1947', in Dewey (ed.), *Arrested Development in India: The Historical Dimension* (New Delhi: Manohar, 1988).

Mazumder, Razit, 'Military Imperatives and the Expansion of Agriculture in Colonial Punjab', *International Journal of Punjab Studies*, vol. 8, no. 2 (2001).

Peers, Douglas M., 'War and Public Finance in Early Nineteenth-Century British India: The First Burma War', *International History Review*, vol. 11, no. 4 (1989).

WAR AND SOCIETY

Alavi, Seema, *The Sepoys and the Company: Tradition and Transition in Northern India, 1770-1830* (New Delhi: Oxford University Press, 1995).

Andreski, Stanislav, *Military Organization and Society* (1954, reprint, Berkeley/Los Angeles: University of California Press, 1968).

Danchev, Alex, 'The Army and the Home Front 1939-45', in David Chandler (General Editor) and Ian Beckett (Associate Editor), *The Oxford Illustrated History of the British Army* (Oxford: Oxford University Press, 1994).

Deshpande, Anirudh, *British Military Policy in India, 1900-45: Colonial Constraints and Declining Power* (New Delhi: Manohar, 2005).

Ellinwood, DeWitt C., 'The Indian Soldier, the Indian Army, and Change, 1914-18', in Ellinwood and S.D. Pradhan (eds.), *India and World War I* (New Delhi: Manohar, 1978).

Ellinwood, DeWitt C. and Cynthia H. Enloe (eds.), *Ethnicity and the Military in Asia* (New Brunswick/London: Transaction Books, 1981).

Gilbert, Arthur N., 'Recruitment and Reform in the East India Company Army, 1760-1800', *Journal of British Studies*, vol. 15 (1975).

Hanson, Victor Davis, *Warfare and Agriculture in Classical Greece* (Berkeley: University of California Press, 1998).

Hoover, James W., *Men without Hats: Dialogue, Discipline and Discontent in the Madras Army, 1806-1807* (New Delhi: Manohar, 2007).

Irvine, William, *The Army of the Indian Moghuls: Its Organization and Administration* (1903, reprint, Delhi: Low Price Publications, 1994).

Marston, Daniel P., and Chandar S. Sundaram (eds.), *A Military History of India and South Asia: From the East India Company to the Nuclear Era* (Westport, Connecticut: Praeger, 2007).

Mason, Philip, *A Matter of Honour: An Account of the Indian Army, Its Officers and Men* (n.d., reprint, DehraDun: EBD Educational Pvt. Ltd., 1988).

Omissi, David, '"Martial Races": Ethnicity and Security in Colonial India, 1858-1939', *War & Society*, vol. 9, no. 1 (1991).

——, *The Sepoy and the Raj: The Indian Army, 1860-1940* (Houndmills, Basingstoke: Macmillan, 1994).

Rosen, Stephen Peter, 'Military Effectiveness: Why Society Matters', *International Security*, vol. 19, no. 4 (1995).

——, *Societies and Military Power: India and its Armies* (Delhi: Oxford University Press, 1996).

Roy, Kaushik, *Brown Warriors of the Raj: Recruitment and the Mechanics of Command in the Sepoy Army, 1859-1913* (New Delhi: Manohar, 2008).

Stanley, Peter, *White Mutiny: British Military Culture in India, 1825-75* (London: C. Hurst, 1998).

Sundaram, Chandar S., 'Soldier Disaffection and the Creation of the Indian National Army', *Indo-British Review*, vol. 18, no. 1 (1990).

Watanabe-O'Kelly, Helen, 'Tournaments and their Relevance for Warfare in the Early Modern Period', *European History Quarterly*, vol. 20, no. 4 (1990).

WAR AND STATE

Bachrach, Bernard S., 'Military Organization in Aquitaine under the Early Carolingians', in Bachrach, *Armies and Politics in the Early Medieval West* (Brookfield: Variorum, 1993).

Barat, Amiya, *The Bengal Native Infantry: Its Organization and Discipline, 1796-1852* (Calcutta: Firma KLM, 1962).

Barua, Pradeep P., *The State at War in South Asia* (Lincoln/London: University of Nebraska Press, 2005).

Bhattacharya, Sanjoy, 'British Military Information Management Techniques and the South Asian Soldier: Eastern India during the Second World War', *Modern Asian Studies*, vol. 34, no. 2 (2000).

——, *Propaganda and Information in Eastern India, 1939-45: A Necessary Weapon of War* (Richmond, Surrey: Curzon, 2001).

Brewer, John *The Sinews of Power: War, Money and the English State, 1688-1783* (London: Unwin Hyman, 1989).

Bryant, G.J., 'The Cavalry Problem in the Early British Indian Army, 1750-1785', *War in History*, vol. 2, no. 1 (1995).

Callahan, Raymond, *The East India Company and Army Reform, 1783-98* (Cambridge, Massachusetts: Harvard University Press, 1972).

Cohen, Stephen P., *The Indian Army: Its Contribution to the Development of a Nation* (1990, reprint, Delhi: Oxford University Press, 1991).

——, *The Pakistan Army* (1984, reprint, Karachi: Oxford University Press, 1993).

Cooper, Randolf G.S., *The Anglo-Maratha Campaigns and the Contest for India: The Struggle for Control of the South Asian Military Economy* (Cambridge: Cambridge University Press, 2005).

Crowell, Lorenzo M., 'Military Professionalism in a Colonial Context: The Madras Army, circa 1832', *Modern Asian Studies*, vol. 24 (1990).

——, 'Logistics in the Madras Army circa 1830', *War & Society*, vol. 10, no. 2 (1992).

Gommans, Jos, 'Warhorse and post-nomadic empire in Asia, c. 1000-1800', *Journal of Global History*, vol. 2 (2007).

Kamtekar, Indivar, 'A Different War Dance: State and Class in India, 1939-45', *Past & Present*, no. 176 (Aug. 2002).

Kundu, Apurba, 'The Indian Armed Forces' Sikh and Non-Sikh Officers' Opinion of Operation Blue Star', *Pacific Affairs*, vol. 67, no. 1 (1994).

MacMillan, Margaret, 'The Indian Army since Independence', *South Asian Review*, vol. 3, no. 1 (1969).

Peers, Douglas M., 'Between Mars and Mammon; The East India Company and Efforts to Reform its Army, 1796-1832', *Historical Journal*, vol. 33, no. 2 (1990).

——, *Between Mars and Mammon: Colonial Armies and the Garrison State in India, 1819-1835* (London: I.B. Tauris, 1995).

Richards, John F., 'Warriors and the State in Early Modern India', *Journal of the Economic and Social History of the Orient*, vol. 47, no. 3 (2004).

Roy, Kaushik, *From Hydaspes to Kargil: A History of Warfare in India from 326 BC to AD 1999* (New Delhi: Manohar, 2004).

Saxena, R.K., 'The Mughal and Rajput Armies', in S.N. Prasad (ed.), *Historical Perspectives of Warfare in India: Some Morale and Material Determinants* (New Delhi: Motilal Banarasidas in association with the Centre for Studies in Civilizations, 2002).

Shyam-Babu, D., 'India's National Security Council: Stuck in the Cradle?', *Security Dialogue*, vol. 34, no. 2 (2003).

Sundaram, J., 'Chola and other Armies---Organization', in S.N. Prasad (ed.), *Historical Perspectives of Warfare in India: Some Morale and Material Determinants* (New Delhi:

Motilal Banarasidas in association with the Centre for Studies in Civilizations, 2002).

——, 'Chola and other Armies---Deployment', in S.N. Prasad (ed.), *Historical Perspectives of Warfare in India: Some Morale and Material Determinants* (New Delhi:

Motilal Banarasidas in association with the Centre for Studies in Civilizations, 2002).

Thapliyal, U.P., 'Military Organization in the Ancient Period', in S.N. Prasad (ed.), *Historical Perspectives of Warfare in India: Some Morale and Material Determinants* (New Delhi: Motilal

Banarasidas in association with the Centre for Studies in Civilizations, 2002).

Wink, Andre, 'Sovereignty and Universal Dominion in South Asia', in Jos J.L. Gommans and Dirk H.A. Kolff (eds.), *Warfare and Weaponry in South Asia: 1000-1800* (New Delhi: Oxford University Press, 2001).

Yong, Tan Tai, 'Maintaining the Military Districts: Civil-Military Integration and District Soldiers' Boards in the Punjab, 1919-39', *Modern Asian Studies*, vol. 28, no. 4 (1994).

——, *The Garrison State: The Military, Government and Society in Colonial Punjab, 1849-1947* (New Delhi: Sage, 2005).

WAR AND TECHNOLOGY

Athar, Ali, *Military Technology and Warfare in the Sultanate of Delhi: 1206-1398 CE* (New Delhi: Icon Publications Pvt. Ltd., 2006).

Bachrach, Bernard S., 'Charles Martel, Mounted Shock Combat, the Stirrup, and Feudalism', in Bachrach, *Armies and Politics in the Early Medieval West* (Brookfield: Variorum, 1993).

Balasubramaniam, R., 'Development of Cannon Technology in India', *Indian Journal of History of Science*, vol. 40, no. 4 (2005).

Barua, Pradeep, 'Military Developments in India, 1750-1850', *Journal of Military History*, vol. 58, no. 4 (1994).

Black, Jeremy, 'A Military Revolution? A 1660-1792 Perspective', in Clifford J. Rogers (ed.), *The Military Revolution Debate: Readings on the Military Transformation of Early Modern Europe* (Boulder: Westview, 1995).

Bryant, G.J., 'Asymmetric Warfare: The British Experience in Eighteenth-Century India', *Journal of Military History*, vol. 68 (2004).

Chattopadhyay, Pranab Kumar, 'Cannons of Eastern India', *Indian Journal of History of Science*, vol. 40, no. 4 (2005).

Creveld, Martin van, 'Technology and War II: Postmodern War?', in Charles Townshend (ed.), *The Oxford Illustrated History of Modern War* (Oxford: Oxford University Press, 1997).

Deloche, Jean, *Military Technology in Hoysala Sculpture (Twelfth and Thirteenth Century)* (New Delhi: Sitaram Bhartia Institute of Scientific Research, 1989).

——, *Studies on Fortification in India* (Pondichery: Pondichery Centre of the EFEO, 2007).

DeVries, Kelly, 'The Effectiveness of Fifteenth-Century Shipboard Artillery', in DeVries, *Guns and Men in Medieval Europe: 1200-1500: Studies in Military History and Technology* (Aldershot: Ashgate, 2002).

——, 'Catapults are not Atomic Bombs: Towards a Redefinition of "Effectiveness" in Premodern Military Technology', in DeVries, *Guns and Men in Medieval Europe: 1200-1500: Studies in Military History and Technology* (Aldershot: Ashgate, 2002).

Friel, Ian, 'Winds of Change? Ships and the Hundred Years War', in Anne Curry & Michael Hughes (eds.), *Arms, Armies and Fortifications in the Hundred Years War* (1994, reprint, Woodbridge, Boydell, 1999).

Gommans, Jos, 'Indian Warfare and Afghan Innovation during the Eighteenth Century', *Studies in History*, vol. 11, no. 2 (1995).

Gordon, Stewart N., 'Symbolic and Structural Constraints on the Adoption of European-Style Military Technologies in the Eighteenth Century', in Richard B. Barnett (ed.), *Rethinking Early Modern India* (New Delhi: Manohar, 2002).

Hook, Judith, 'Fortifications and the End of the Sienese State', *History*, vol. 62, no. 206 (1977).

Khan, Iqtidar Alam, *Gunpowder and Firearms: Warfare in Medieval India* (New Delhi: Oxford University Press, 2004).

Kingra, Mahinder S., 'The *Trace Italienne* and the Military Revolution during the Eighty Years' War, 1567-1648', *Journal of Military History*, vol. 57 (1993).

Knox, MacGregor and Williamson Murray (eds.), *The Dynamics of Military Revolution: 1300-2050* (2001, reprint, Cambridge: Cambridge University Press, 2003).

Kurup, K.K.N., 'Indigenous Navigation and Ship-building on the Malabar Coast', in K.S. Mathew (ed.), *Ship-building and Navigation in the Indian Ocean Region: AD 1400-1800* (New Delhi: Munshiram Manoharlal, 1997).

Lynn, John A., 'The *trace italienne* and the Growth of Armies: The French Case', in Clifford J. Rogers (ed.), *The Military Revolution Debate: Readings on the Military Transformation of Early Modern Europe* (Boulder: Westview, 1995).

Oman, C.W.C., *The Art of War in the Middle Ages: AD 375-1515* (Oxford: Oxford University Press, 1885).

Pant, G.N., 'The Saga of Indian Arms', *Journal of Indian History* (Golden Jubilee Volume, 1973).

Parker, Geoffrey, *The Military Revolution: Military Innovation and the Rise of the West, 1500-1800* (Cambridge: Cambridge University Press, 1988).

Qaisar, A. Jan, 'Horseshoeing in Mughal India', *Indian Journal of History of Science*, vol. 27, no. 2 (1992).

Rogers, Clifford J., 'The Military Revolutions of the Hundred Years War', in Rogers (ed.), *The Military Revolution Debate: Readings on the Military Transformation of Early Modern Europe* (Boulder: Westview, 1995).

Sarkar, Jadunath, *Military History of India* (1960, reprint, Bombay: Orient Longmans, 1970).

Saxena, R.K., 'Medieval Forts, Logistics and Heraldry', in S.N. Prasad (ed.), *Historical Perspectives of Warfare in India: Some Morale and Material Determinants* (New Delhi: Motilal Banarasidas in association with the Centre for Studies in Civilizations, 2002).

Smith, Robert Douglas, 'Monster Cannons: Wrought Iron Bombards of Europe', *Indian Journal of History of Science*, vol. 40, no. 4 (2005).

Stone, John, 'Technology, Society, and the Infantry Revolution of the Fourteenth Century', *Journal of Military History*, vol. 68, no. 2 (2004).

Toffler, Alvin and Heidi, *War and Anti-War: Survival at the Dawn of the 21st Century* (1993, reprint, London: Warner Books, 1994).

Index